Restless Giant

The Oxford History of the United States

David M. Kennedy, *General Editor*

RESTLESS GIANT

The United States from Watergate to *Bush v. Gore*

JAMES T. PATTERSON

OXFORD
UNIVERSITY PRESS

OXFORD
UNIVERSITY PRESS

Oxford University Press, Inc., publishes works that further
Oxford University's objective of excellence
in research, scholarship, and education.

Oxford   New York
Auckland   Cape Town   Dar es Salaam   Hong Kong   Karachi
Kuala Lumpur   Madrid   Melbourne   Mexico City   Nairobi
New Delhi   Shanghai   Taipei   Toronto

With offices in
Argentina   Austria   Brazil   Chile   Czech Republic   France   Greece
Guatemala   Hungary   Italy   Japan   Poland   Portugal   Singapore
South Korea   Switzerland   Thailand   Turkey   Ukraine   Vietnam

First published by Oxford University Press, Inc., 2005
198 Madison Avenue, New York, NY 10016
www.oup.com

First issued as an Oxford University Press paperback, 2007

Oxford is a registered trademark of Oxford University Press

Library of Congress Cataloging-in-Publication Data
Patterson, James T.
Restless giant : the United States from Watergate to
Bush v. Gore / James T. Patterson.
p. cm. — (The Oxford history of the United States ; v. 11)
Includes bibliographical references and index.
ISBN 978-0-19-512216-9
ISBN 978-0-19-530522-7 (pbk.)
1. United States—History—1969– I. Title. II. Series.
E839.P38 2005   973.92—dc22   2005016711

ISBN 978-0-19-512216-9

To Cynthia, with love

Acknowledgments

Many people offered helpful comments on earlier drafts of this book and in so doing enabled me to bring forth the final version. Among these are former and current graduate students at Brown University, where I taught United States history from 1972 until 2002. They include Richard Canedo, Robert Fleegler, and Daniel Williams. John Snyder, a long-ago undergraduate research assistant, had an important role in shaping my prologue. I also thank present and former history faculty colleagues at Brown who criticized various draft chapters: Philip Benedict, Howard Chudacoff, Carl Kaestle, Luther Spoehr, John Thomas, and Gordon Wood. Cherrie Guerzon of the history department offered expert assistance in editing and distributing a series of drafts. Other scholars whose advice improved substantial parts of drafts include William Berman, John Morton Blum, Gareth Davies, Michael Heale, Morton Keller, David Patterson, Tom Roberts, Daniel Rodgers, John Skrentny, Alan Wolfe, and Joshua Zeitz.

Tony Badger, Brian Balogh, Gareth Davies, Townsend Ludington, John Thompson, and Stephen Tuck invited me to present overviews of my book to informed audiences. My children, Stephen Patterson and Marnie Cochran, encouraged me to rethink some of my ideas. Susan Ferber of Oxford University Press commented constructively on some of my chapters. Others at the press who provided vital help in the production process include Joellyn Ausanka, India Cooper (who copyedited the manuscript), and Furaha Norton.

I am especially grateful to the following, all of whom carefully evaluated one or another draft of the entire manuscript: Steven Gillon, Michael

Klarman, and Bruce Schulman. Andrew Huebner commented thoughtfully and at length on an entire early draft. Trevor O'Driscoll, a former Brown student, joined me in going over every line of a near-final draft. His perceptive eye caught many errors of fact and interpretation. The extensive comments of David Kennedy, general editor of the Oxford History of the United States series, and of Peter Ginna, my editor at Oxford University Press, were invaluable.

My wife, Cynthia, was a constant source of encouragement and advice. Without her intelligent and patient help I would have needed far more time to write this book.

Providence, R.I.   James Patterson
May 2005

Contents

Illustrations appear following pages 144 and 304

Editor's Introduction

Grand Expectations: The United States, 1945–1974, James Patterson's earlier volume in *The Oxford History of the United States*, opened with a masterful evocation of the exuberant American mood in the post–World War II years — a time aptly characterized by the novelist Philip Roth as "the greatest moment of collective inebriation in American history . . . the clock of history reset and a whole people's aims limited no longer by the past" (*American Pastoral*, 40–41). *Grand Expectations* went on to chronicle the remorseless tempering of that extravagant mood in the cauldron of postwar history, as events like the hardening Cold War, the escalating nuclear arms race, the scourge of McCarthyism, the bloody American humiliation in Vietnam, the struggles to secure full citizenship for African Americans and women, the abortive war on poverty, and the assassinations of John and Robert Kennedy, Malcolm X, and Martin Luther King Jr. provided painful reminders that reality would not easily yield to the aspirations of history's most hopeful dreamers, even at the height of their national power and self-confidence. *Grand Expectations* concluded with the trauma of the Watergate scandal, which Patterson used to write a mordant epitaph for the inflated expectations of the post–World War II generation.

Restless Giant begins where *Grand Expectations* left off, in the sour atmosphere of disenchantment left in the wake of President Richard Nixon's disgrace and resignation. But if *Grand Expectations* told a story about chastised innocence, about a people reluctantly forced to disenthrall themselves from easy assumptions about the malleability of their world,

Restless Giant tells a tale of national resilience and even regeneration—until another enormous trauma, the terrorist attacks of September 11, 2001, once again threatened to transform the tenor and the very terms of American life.

Patterson, the only author to contribute two volumes to *The Oxford History of the United States*, begins his account of the post-Watergate era by imaginatively recapturing the odd blend of political disillusionment and pop-culture daffiness that gave the 1970s their distinctive flavor. Challenges abounded in that decade—from the oil shocks administered by the newly assertive Organization of Petroleum Exporting Countries, the "tax revolt" that spread from California in 1978 and helped to propel Ronald Reagan to the presidency, the agony of the Iranian hostage crisis, the Soviet invasion of Afghanistan, divisive Supreme Court decisions concerning abortion and affirmative action, the continuing sexual revolution, often wrenching redefinitions of women's role and the nature of the family, the emerging AIDS epidemic, and the stubborn persistence of "stagflation"—a devil's brew of faltering economic productivity and galloping price increases. All of these Patterson recounts with his customary crispness and color, enlivening his story with deft portraits of figures like Jimmy Carter and Ronald Reagan, George H. W. Bush and Bill Clinton, and a cast of supporting characters that includes Ayatollah Khomeini, Mikhail Gorbachev, O. J. Simpson, Bill Gates, and Steven Spielberg.

Patterson ranges broadly across the landscape of American life in the twentieth century's closing decades, weaving a rich narrative tapestry out of the incidents and anecdotes that he relates so artfully, including the advent of personal computers, the first Gulf War, the triumphs and foibles of televangelists, and the impeachment of President Bill Clinton. But larger patterns emerge as well. Patterson explains with admirable clarity the gathering economic recovery of the 1980s that culminated in the "dot-com" boom (or bubble) of the following decade; the halting efforts to redefine American foreign policy as the Cold War wound down and eventually ended with the astonishing implosion of the Soviet Union itself; the pervasive effects of the "information revolution"; the mixed implications of the commitment of successive administrations to free trade and the ongoing process of "globalization," as embodied in institutions like NAFTA (North American Free Trade Agreement) and the WTO (World Trade Organization); the impact of some 30 million immigrants on the nation's economy, politics, and culture; the "culture wars" of the 1980s and 1990s; and the vigorous growth of evangelical religion and its contribution to the powerful resurgence of political conservatism by the century's end.

Recounting the history of those several developments suggests that the last quarter of the twentieth century was a time of unusual stress for the American people—but, as Patterson emphasizes, a time of notable achievements as well. Despite all their travails, he concludes, "Most people of the affluent and enormously powerful United States, though restless, had more blessings to cherish in early 2001 than they had had in 1974."

It is often said that the history we know least well is the history of our own time, particularly the decades immediately surrounding our own birth. All readers will learn from this book, but James Patterson has done a special service to readers born during and after the Vietnam era. Here they will find a cogent and compelling account of how history has shaped the world they inherited—and the world they now inhabit. James Patterson has superbly delivered on the promise of the *Oxford History of the United States*—a series dedicated to bringing the very best of rigorous and imaginative historical scholarship to the widest possible audience.

David M. Kennedy

Restless Giant

Prologue, 1974

On the evening of Thursday, August 8, 1974, a wan and tired President Richard Nixon gave a televised address to the American people. Facing impeachment and removal from office, he finally fell on his sword: "I shall resign the presidency effective at noon tomorrow."

Most Americans welcomed the president's announcement, which ended two years of mounting public disillusion and anger about his attempted cover-up of a burglary in 1972 at Democratic National Committee headquarters in the Watergate complex in Washington.[1] Some of them joined a jubilant crowd of 3,000 in Lafayette Park across the street from the White House. One celebrator attached to the iron fence surrounding the White House a sign reading: DING DONG, THE WITCH IS DEAD. Others waved placards: SEE DICK RUN; RUN, DICK, RUN. Reflecting widespread opinion on Capitol Hill, Senator Edward Kennedy of Massachusetts exclaimed, "The nightmare of Watergate is over, the Constitution is safe, and America can become whole again."[2]

---

1. By the time of Nixon's resignation, the House Judiciary Committee had voted to impeach him on three counts: obstruction of justice; abuse of executive authority (involving among other things his illegal use of electronic surveillance and misuse of the CIA, FBI, and IRS); and violation of the Constitution stemming in part from his refusal to honor the committee's subpoenas. Recordings of conversations in the Oval Office of the White House had provided incriminating evidence, including a "smoking gun"—a tape of June 23, 1972, showing that Nixon had ordered the CIA to stop the FBI from investigating the break-in.
2. *New York Times*, Aug. 11, 1974; *Time*, Aug. 19, 1974, 9.

1

Many other Americans, while glad to see Nixon go, remained embittered — or fatigued — by the duration of the crisis. State Representative Julian Bond of Georgia, a civil rights activist, observed, "The prisons of Georgia are full of people who stole $5 or $10, and this man tried to steal the Constitution of the United States." A weary foe of the Nixon administration added, "This just doesn't feel as good as I thought it would."[3]

Onetime admirers of Nixon, too, solemnly accepted the resignation. Though a few die-hards insisted that he had been hounded from office, many seemed to agree with James J. Kilpatrick, a conservative commentator: "The lies, the lies, the lies! . . . What a pity, what a pity! Here was a President who got us out of Vietnam, ended the draft, restored a needed conservative balance to the Supreme Court, launched hopeful programs of new federalism, and by his bold overtures to Red China opened new avenues toward world peace. Now the good vanishes in the wreckage of the bad. The swearing-in of Gerald Ford can't come one hour too soon."[4]

That swearing-in took place in the East Room of the White House on the following day, August 9, 1974, when Ford reassured the nation, "Our long national nightmare is over." At that time, most Americans seemed to share at least one sentiment: relief that the nation's political institutions had managed to survive a constitutional crisis as grave as Watergate. After administering the oath of office to Ford, Chief Justice Warren Burger grabbed the hand of Senator Hugh Scott of Pennsylvania and said, "Hugh, it worked. Thank God it worked." Burger meant the constitutional system.[5]

The majority of Americans joined in support of their new president, who was widely praised as an open, straightforward man. George Reedy, former press secretary under Lyndon Johnson, spoke for many when he said, "Ford is one of the very few men in public life whose absolute honesty I do not question."[6] But Ford, having been thrust into office, had had little time to prepare an agenda or secure a staff. He lacked even the mandate of having been elected vice president — instead, he had been appointed to the office in 1973 after Spiro Agnew had resigned amid charges of tax evasion. Recognizing Ford's disadvantages, prominent Americans urged citizens to support him. Historian Henry Steele Commager, recalling Abraham Lincoln's famous words in 1865, wrote: "Now that Watergate and Mr. Nixon are behind us, President Ford has set himself to bind up

3. *Time*, Aug. 19, 1974, 9.
4. *National Review*, Aug. 30, 1974, 965.
5. *Time*, Aug. 19, 1974, 9. Luck — Nixon had kept the tapes — also helped the "system."
6. Ibid., Aug. 12, 1974, 9.

the wounds that they inflicted. With malice toward none, with charity for all, we must cooperate in this honorable task."[7]

THE UNITY OF MID-AUGUST 1974, however, proved to be short-lived. A host of obstacles blocked the road to reconciliation. The wounds that had opened as a result of America's bloody fighting in Vietnam, which ended in January 1973, remained raw—and continued to hurt for decades thereafter. When Ford sought to heal these wounds in September by offering draft evaders some sort of leniency, many people tore into him. Ford, one man wrote, "has proposed that draft dodgers and deserters be allowed to work their way back into American society. I agree. May I suggest 20 years' hard labor with time off for good behavior, and for the men responsible for their plight may I suggest burning in hell forever?"[8]

Tensions over issues of race and gender, sharp during the 1960s, also persisted at the time. Americans in 1974—and later—fought a host of "culture wars" over the legacies of that turbulent decade, one of the most divisive periods in modern American history. Earlier in the year, the black baseball star Henry "Hank" Aaron, beset by death threats as he approached Babe Ruth's career home run record, felt obliged to hire an armed guard. In September, court-ordered busing to advance racial balance in Boston's public schools ignited violent white resistance. Debate over gender issues, especially feminist activism, became equally clamorous. In 1972, Congress had sent the Equal Rights Amendment (ERA) to the states for possible ratification, and in 1973, the Supreme Court, in *Roe v. Wade*, had invalidated most state laws criminalizing a woman's access to abortion. The decision sparked super-heated debate in subsequent years.

These contentious developments indicated that many people of the United States, ever a restless, dynamic society, were prepared to challenge older ways. But the challenges encountered vigorous opposition. So did other legacies of the culturally subversive 1960s and early 1970s—long hair, beards, miniskirts, drug abuse, and sexual liberation—which suggested that many young people, especially people of the huge "boomer" generation, were rejecting hallowed American moral values. Escalating rates of violent crime evoked especially deep fears. Alarmed by these trends, religious conservatives and others were mobilizing their forces to march into politics.

International concerns also aroused large anxieties in 1974. In February, the Soviet Union had expelled its most famous dissident, the novelist

7. Ibid., Aug. 19, 1974, 88.
8. Ibid., Sept. 9, 1974, 9.

Aleksandr Solzhenitsyn, who later settled in the United States (where he deplored what he considered the grossness of American consumerism). His expulsion, inflaming other sources of friction between the USSR and the United States, threatened Nixon's much-vaunted policy of "détente" with the Soviet Union and showed that the Cold War remained frigid indeed. A month later, in March, heavy fighting broke out between Kurds and Iraqi Arabs near the Iraqi-Turkish border. In May, India successfully tested an atomic bomb, becoming the world's sixth nuclear power.[9] Throughout the year Jews and Muslims continued to kill each other in Israel and Lebanon. Shortly before Ford became president, Turkish forces, combating a pro-Greece coup, seized northern parts of the Mediterranean island of Cyprus, which remained rigidly divided for the next 30 years and more.[10]

An especially difficult question concerning international relations, for Ford and others in the decades to come, focused on how to manage foreign policy in the aftermath of the war in Vietnam. Then and later, many Americans—most of them liberals—believed that the United States had been not only foolish but also morally wrong to engage in that prolonged and bloody conflict. Others, however, insisted that America could have prevailed if it had summoned the will to do so, and that it must never again back down in fights for freedom. Ford, like his successors in the White House, had to decide whether and under what circumstances the United States should risk military action to promote freedom and democracy abroad—as LBJ and Nixon had claimed to be doing in Vietnam.

Ford faced a particularly delicate domestic problem: What should he do about his predecessor? Should Nixon stand trial for the crimes he was alleged to have committed in covering up the Watergate break-in of 1972? Some Americans demanded that he be prosecuted: No one, not even a president, should be above the law. Others disagreed, believing that Nixon had already paid a high price and that prosecution would prolong the "national nightmare." Braving predictable outrage, Ford sided with advocates of clemency. Barely a month after taking office—and before Nixon might have been indicted, tried, or convicted—he acted suddenly and decisively, giving Nixon a "full, free, and absolute pardon" for any crimes he might have committed.

9. The other five were the United States, Britain, the Soviet Union, France, and China. India did not test again until May 1998; in response, its bitter enemy, Pakistan, tested for the first time.
10. *New York Times*, July 20, 1974.

A storm of criticism erupted around this "thunderbolt," as some people called it. Ford's press secretary resigned in protest. Democratic senator Mike Mansfield of Montana, the majority leader, observed, "All men are created equal," and "that includes presidents and plumbers." Many Americans, inclined to believe in conspiracies since the assassinations of John F. Kennedy and the Reverend Martin Luther King Jr., were convinced that Ford had earlier struck a deal with Nixon in order to be selected as Vice President Agnew's successor in 1973: In the event that Nixon had to resign, Ford would pardon him. In any event, Ford's public approval rating plummeted after the pardon. As measured by a Gallup poll, it had been 71 percent in late August. It fell sixteen points overnight and plunged further, to 50 percent by the end of September.[11]

NOT EVERYONE, OF COURSE, was absorbed by these front-page events. Most Americans did not pay sustained attention to politics. Instead, they were normally concerned with day-to-day developments closer to home, some of which advanced personal comforts. Among the consumer goods that appeared for the first time in 1974 were microwave ovens, fully programmable pocket calculators, and automatic icemakers in refrigerators. The first bar codes greeted shoppers in stores. Automated teller machines, introduced a few years earlier, were slowly increasing in number and rendering obsolete the constraints of "bankers' hours." Touch tone phones, an innovation of the 1960s, were spreading rapidly and replacing dials.

There was more to please people in 1974. CAT scans for medical diagnoses were becoming widely available. Tobacco ads praised the blessings of "low tar" cigarettes that would supposedly be safer for the 45 million or so Americans—35 percent of the adult population—who still smoked.[12] Consumers in the mid-1970s could choose from a wide range of automobiles, many of which— Toyotas, Datsuns, Audis, Volvos—were manufactured abroad. In 1975, there were 106.7 million passenger cars registered in the United States, in a car-crazy country that had 129.8 million licensed

11. *Time*, Sept. 16, 1974, 13; Fred Greenstein, *The Presidential Difference: Leadership Style from FDR to Clinton* (New York, 2000), 113–18.
12. Though cigarette consumption had declined slowly since the surgeon general of the United States had warned in 1964 against the perils of smoking, roughly 40 percent of adult men and 30 percent of adult women still smoked in 1974. They averaged thirty cigarettes per day. The percentage of adults who smoked in 2000 had declined to 23.3 (24.4 percent of men and 21.2 percent of women). *Statistical Abstract of the U.S.*, 2002, 124. Henceforth cited as *Stat. Abst.*

drivers among the 156.7 million people who were sixteen years of age or older.[13]

The very wealthy, of course, had nearly infinite choices. The cover of *Time* during the week following Nixon's resignation featured the actor Jack Nicholson, who had recently starred in *Chinatown* and who was due in 1975 to appear in *One Flew over the Cuckoo's Nest*. His compensation for *Chinatown* was said to be $750,000, a huge sum for that time. Other luminaries of popular culture included Robert Redford and Paul Newman (both stars of *The Sting* in 1973), Barbra Streisand, and Clint Eastwood. They, too, reaped munificent rewards in a culture of celebrity that lavished near-worshipful attention on film stars, singers, and athletes. Muhammad Ali earned millions by taking the heavyweight title from George Foreman in Zaire in October 1974.[14]

The first issue of *People* magazine appeared earlier in the year, displaying on its cover the actress Mia Farrow (star of *The Great Gatsby*) nibbling on a string of pearls. *People*'s arrival as a hugely successful addition to American newsstands broadened the reach of tabloid-style journalism in the United States and ensured that millions of readers and consumers might know all—or almost all—about the beautiful, the rich, and the famous. Britain's Princess Diana was to grace fifty *People* covers in later years.

The explosive power of America's consumer culture, while liberating in many ways, was seductive and disorienting: The more people bought, the more they seemed to crave. Wants became needs. In the 1970s, as later in the century, the "lifestyles" of the rich and famous fostered a great deal of materialistic emulation. A miasma of cupidity, critics complained, was suffocating the culture and overwhelming traditional values that had made the nation strong.

Popular anxieties about the economy loomed especially large in 1974—larger, in fact, than Ford's political difficulties, racial divisions, or controversy over abortion, vexing though those issues were. The economy had been ailing since 1969, afflicted by inflation as well as rising unemployment. Nixon, struggling to cure these maladies, had astounded Americans by proclaiming, "I am now a Keynesian in economics," and by

---

13. *Stat. Abst.*, 1977, 4–5, 636, 638. In all, there were 132.9 million motor vehicles (including trucks, cabs, and buses) registered in the United States in 1975. The number of motor vehicles registered in 1960 had been only 73.9 million, of which 61.7 million were passenger cars.

14. Ali had been stripped of his title in 1967 after refusing to be drafted during the Vietnam War. His victory in 1974 helped make him *Sports Illustrated*'s Sportsman of the Year. Zaire became the Democratic Republic of Congo in 1998.

imposing controls on prices and wages. To increase the attractiveness of American exports, he had taken steps to devalue the dollar. Alas, after a brief upturn that helped him win reelection in 1972, the economy sickened again. Some contemporaries, badly affected by economic distress that worsened thereafter, referred to the next three years, between 1973 and 1975, as the Great Recession.

"Stagflation," as it came to be called, mystified a great many economists, who had educated people to be prepared for the ills of inflation or unemployment at any given time but not to anticipate suffering from both at once. In the aftermath of American support of Israel in the Yom Kippur War in October 1973, an oil embargo, followed by price hikes ordered by OPEC (Organization of Petroleum Exporting Countries), had led to dramatic jumps in America's energy prices. The cost of overseas oil rose from $1.77 per barrel in October 1973 to $10 by early 1974.[15] The spike in oil prices further favored Japanese automobile manufacturers, who far outdid Detroit in producing fuel-efficient cars.

Worse, the embargo intensified already widespread feelings of vulnerability in the United States. Rocked by losing a war in Vietnam, which President Johnson had called a "piss-ant country," Americans now fretted as their economy took a battering from Third World nations rich in oil. Politicians, economists, educators, and business leaders scrambled to reduce demand for oil and gasoline, supporting among other measures a national speed limit of fifty-five miles per hour.[16] Hoping to save on heating costs, a number of colleges and universities shortened their winter terms. Still, the stagflation persisted.

A host of other economic numbers at the time were equally disturbing. Between March and December 1974, the Dow Jones Industrial Average fell from 892 to 577, a loss of 37 percent.[17] As indicated by the growing appeal of foreign cars, some of America's leading heavy industries, notably steel and automobile manufacturing, suffered from sharply declining sales and a record number of work stoppages. A Rust Belt was encircling industrial parts of the Midwest. Unemployment, which had averaged 4.7 percent in 1973, rose to 7.5 percent by 1975. Inflation, at 6.2 percent in

15. James Reichley, *Conservatives in an Age of Change* (Washington, 1981), 361–62.
16. The national speed limit, initiated in 1974 as a temporary measure, lasted until repealed in 1995. It was credited with a major role in conserving energy and with producing a 16 percent decline in traffic fatalities, from 54,052 in 1973 to 45,196 in 1974. *New York Times*, Nov. 24, 2003.
17. Between December 1972 and December 1974, the stock market lost almost half its value.

1969, doubled to 12.4 percent for 1974, the worst peacetime inflation in American history. The gross national product (GNP) actually fell by 2.3 percent per capita in both 1973 and 1974.[18]

Facing discouraging numbers like these, George Shultz, a private citizen who had earlier served as secretary of labor, head of the Office of Management and Budget, and secretary of the treasury, exclaimed at a White House meeting in July 1974, "The country is in terrible shape, and I wish you guys in government would do something about it."[19] His comment exposed an often profound ambivalence that Americans—then and later—harbored about the proper role of the state: Again and again, people damned the federal government as bloated and bumbling, but they rarely stopped demanding that it act to help them and to expand their rights and entitlements.

THESE DEVELOPMENTS, NOTABLY WATERGATE, divisions over race and gender, and economic distress, caused many Americans in 1974 to fear the passing of what they had imagined as the golden age of American history that had followed World War II. The cherished American Dream of upward social mobility, sustained for many people in those prosperous years by vigorous economic growth, seemed endangered. Americans who fell prey to fears such as these were a bit too quick to dwell on the troubles of the country, which remained immensely powerful in international affairs and which—the economic doldrums notwithstanding—was still by far the world's most affluent society. America's per capita GNP in 1974 remained considerably higher than that of its closest rivals, West Germany and Japan.[20] The nation's official poverty rate, at 11.6 percent of the population in 1974, was slightly below what it had been (12.6 percent) in 1970, and roughly half as high as it had been (22.2 percent) in 1960.[21] And,

18. *Stat. Abst.*, 1977, 431.
19. Robert Collins, *More: The Politics of Growth in Postwar America* (New York, 2000), 153–55; Robert Samuelson, "The Age of Inflation," *New Republic*, May 13, 2002, 32–41.
20. Edward Luttwak, a pessimist, nonetheless later concluded that America's per capita GNP in 1974 (taking into account real purchasing power) was $4,022, as opposed to an equivalent in dollars of $3,380 in West Germany and $2,765 in Japan. Luttwak, *The Endangered American Dream: How to Stop the United States from Becoming a Third World Country and How to Win the Geo-Economic Struggle for Industrial Supremacy* (New York, 1993), 119–22.
21. *Stat. Abst*, 1977, 453. Disposable per capita income, in 1975 dollars, averaged $5,470 in 1975—approximately 8 percent higher in real dollars than in 1970. *Stat. Abst.*, 2002, 422. Legislation approved by Congress in 1972—which went into effect in 1974— indexed Social Security payments for inflation and established the Supplemental Security Income program (SSI), which for the first time placed a federal floor under payments for the indigent blind, disabled, and elderly. SSI, too, was indexed. Poverty among the elderly, before then very high, plummeted thereafter.

as the chief justice had exclaimed, the constitutional system had survived. With the soldiers home from Vietnam and the Watergate crisis resolved, Americans might well have looked forward to less tumultuous times and to celebrations of their nation's bicentennial in 1976. Young men, moreover, no longer had to worry about the draft, which had been ended in 1973. This was a significant freedom—one of many that endured in the future.

Yet many disgruntled Americans in 1974, and later, practiced a form of selective amnesia, which blotted from their consciousness some of the blights that had afflicted the nation in the 1950s—among them constitutionally protected racial segregation, a Red Scare that launched angry assaults on civil liberties, blatant religious intolerance, and systematic discrimination against women. Many of the people who yearned nostalgically for a return of the supposedly halcyon 1950s, and for a resurgence of the unity and patriotism that had seemed to motivate what would later be called the "greatest generation" (of the World War II era), assumed that progress had always graced America's historical development. Shaken by the problems of the 1970s, they appeared to believe that almost everything about the postwar years between 1945 and the assassination of President Kennedy had been better than the present.[22]

Nostalgic distortions aside, pessimists in 1974 were correct to remember that most years between 1945 and 1970 had featured vibrant economic growth. This had been especially true of the 1960s, when per capita GNP had risen by nearly 33 percent.[23] Growth of this magnitude had enabled rising percentages of people to earn higher real wages and salaries and move upward into middle-class occupations and "lifestyles." Young Americans in those years had seemed especially confident about the future. They had married early, produced a baby boom (of 75 million new arrivals between 1946 and 1964), bought houses in the suburbs, and acquired cars and many other consumer goods. They had sailed, or so it seemed, on a boundless sea of prosperity.[24]

In the process, these optimistic Americans had developed higher expectations—about the economy, government benefits, their marriages and friendships, their jobs, their health, and the futures of their children. Like Adam and Eve, they were restless in their new paradise, and they yearned

22. The popularity of Tom Brokaw's book *The Greatest Generation* (New York, 1998) and of an HBO miniseries, *Band of Brothers* (2001), later indicated the persistence of nostalgia about the "World War II generation."
23. *Stat. Abst.*, 2002, 422.
24. Steven Gillon, *Boomer Nation: The Largest and Richest Generation Ever, and How It Changed America* (New York, 2004), 1–16.

for more. They expected to enjoy greater personal freedom, choice, and self-fulfillment. Having witnessed the powerful civil rights movement, they had seen dramatic expansions of freedom in their own lifetimes, and they developed ever more hopeful visions both about their rights and entitlements and (before taking a beating in Vietnam) about the capacity of the country to do good in the world.

Numerous groups—women, blacks, the aged, the handicapped—had already organized to seek greater support from government. Backed by public interest lawyers—whose numbers and influence increased in coming decades—these groups engaged in battles on behalf of an ever larger cluster of rights, thereby advancing the role of government and of the courts in American life. Though they won many of these struggles—entitlements expanded in these and later years—they remained impatient to improve their own situations in life as well as to advance a "rights revolution," as it came to be called, that would benefit others. In America's open, rights-conscious, and future-oriented culture, it was possible to believe that one step forward would lead straightaway to another.[25]

The contentious mood of the mid-1970s prompted a spate of jeremiads, many of which echoed throughout the next thirty years in a culture that was to abound—even in better times—in complaints about cultural conflict and prophecies of national decline. As Commager remarked just before Nixon's resignation: "There is no consensus. There is less harmony in our society, to my mind, than at any time since, say, Reconstruction. Perhaps the '60s and '70s are a great divide—the divide of disillusionment."[26]

Americans who shared Commager's worries came to see the 1970s as the onset of a problematic new era, variously perceived as an "Age of Limits," a "Time of Conflict," or an "Era of Decline." Conditioned to expect progress, they were impatient, and they resisted leaders who asked them to sacrifice. Suspicious of authority figures, they were quick to direct their wrath at Ford, congressional leaders, big businessmen, lawyers—anyone in a position of power. No leaders—no institutions—seemed immune in the 1970s from criticism, a great deal of which flowed from the media, whose leaders had become considerably more skeptical and confrontational as a result of the travails of Vietnam and Watergate, and which

25. Key sources for the rise of a rights revolution—a major theme of this book—are Samuel Walker, *The Rights Revolution: Rights and Community in Modern America* (New York, 1998); Laura Kalman, *The Strange Career of Legal Liberalism* (New Haven, 1996); and Lawrence Friedman, *American Law in the Twentieth Century* (New Haven, 2002).
26. *Time*, July 15, 1974, 22–23.

questioned if any authorities could be trusted. As Harvard University president Derek Bok put it, "There is a very obvious dearth of people who seem able to supply convincing answers, or even to point to directions toward solutions."[27]

These were among the many developments that had worried Americans during the late 1960s, one of the most tempestuous times in modern United States history, and that still seemed to threaten national unity in 1974. Whether the country could surmount its problems and move ahead were questions that understandably chipped away at the confidence of many contemporary Americans.

THIS BOOK, PAYING SPECIAL ATTENTION to concerns such as these, also explores a wider range of trends and controversies over the next quarter of a century and more, from 1974 until early 2001. It looks at major developments both at home and abroad, and at social and cultural as well as political and economic events. It has a good deal to say about the many flaws that continued to trouble American society after 1974, notably racial injustice. An especially worrisome trend was rising income inequality, which became sharp during this period. Many public schools, especially in poverty-stricken areas of inner cities, remained wretched.

But this is not primarily a tale of Limits, Decline, or Conflict, for after the doldrums of the mid- and late 1970s, a number of more positive developments, many of which were driven by successive generations of aspiring young people, helped to raise popular hopes. Many social and cultural conflicts, loudly contested by partisan political antagonists and given exaggerated play in the media, turned out to be neither so profound nor so implacable as they seemed.

By 2001, Americans lived in an economy that had expanded to promote considerably greater affluence, convenience, and comfort for most people, and in a physical environment that had become cleaner and safer. Toleration — of various religions, styles of life, and sexual practices — had widened substantially. Discrimination against minorities and women had weakened. Important rights and entitlements had expanded. Well before 2001, the Cold War was history, positioning the United States as a giant on the world stage.

Flourishing in an open, competitive, and pluralistic society, popular complaints about decline and conflict — and about government — continued to

27. Ibid., 21. I am greatly indebted to John Snyder, a research assistant, for an early draft of this prologue.

proliferate after 1974. "Culture wars" appeared to splinter the country, especially in the 1990s. But the quality of life in the United States, bolstered by the bounteous resources and receptivity to change that had always been hallmarks of American history, improved in manifold ways between 1974 and 2001. Most people of the affluent and enormously powerful United States, though often dissatisfied, had more blessings to cherish in early 2001 than they had had in 1974.

AFTER WRITING A FINAL VERSION of this book, I labored over drafts of an epilogue that attempted to explore the impact of September 11, 2001. The horrors of that terrible day provoked widespread fear and anger among Americans, banishing complacency about terrorism and inciting calls for revenge. The killings led the *New York Times* to editorialize that 9/11 was "one of those moments in which history splits, and we define the world as before and after."[28]

As I write these words in 2005, it is obvious that this editorial was prescient: A great deal has changed since that world-shaking day, especially America's foreign and military policies, which have become far more interventionist—and divisive—than most people could have imagined in early 2001. Efforts to combat domestic terrorism have raised widespread fears about threats to civil liberties and personal privacy. Federal deficits have exploded in size. Still, it is also clear that many key developments of American life, having taken root between 1974 and 2001, have continued to flourish. Not even a disaster such as 9/11 completely "splits" history.

Following many rewrites of the epilogue, I decided to drop it. I believe that a span of four years is too short to provide a very reliable historical perspective on the legacies of dramatic events such as those of 9/11/2001. So, while my book tries to help readers understand why America was so poorly prepared for the attacks of September 11, it has little to say about the years since then. I ask readers to put themselves back a bit in time and to receive this book as an interpretive history of the United States during a fascinating era that helped to shape many characteristics of our own.

28. *New York Times*, Sept. 12, 2001.

1

The Troubled 1970s

In 1996, a popular comic strip, "The Buckets," offered a characteristically unflattering picture of American culture in the 1970s. Successive frames of the strip, which normally poked fun at the haplessness of the Bucket family, depict Mr. Bucket's recollections of the era: bell bottoms, disco, mood rings, "stupid hair," and a drawing of Nixon, Ford, and Carter. Nixon is jowly, dark-browed, and menacing; Ford looks determined though a little empty-headed; Carter wears a huge, moronic, buck-toothed smile. Mr. Bucket then appears and muses, "I can think of only one thing worse than the '70s." In the last frame, he stares at two long-haired young people clad in styles reminiscent of those from the 1970s and explains what that "one thing" is: "Doing them again!"[1]

Mr. Bucket's reflections capture a retrospective understanding of the 1970s: They were grim, tasteless years that are best put out of mind. A host of passions and fads that flourished in these years—heavy metal, punk rock, disco—bewildered and distressed traditionalists.[2] Major films of the decade, notably *Mean Streets*, *Taxi Driver*, and *Dog Day Afternoon*, offered dark visions that seemed to be appropriate portrayals of the era. Many of Bruce Springsteen's songs, in four highly popular albums of the late 1970s, expressed an apparently widespread sense of pessimism among

1. Cartoonist, Scott Stantis, Oct. 6, 1996.
2. Michael Willard, "Cutback: Skate and Punk at the Far End of the American Century," in Beth Bailey and David Farber, eds., *America in the Seventies* (Lawrence, Kans.), 181–207.

Americans who were struggling at the time to confront boredom and unsatisfying, low-paying work. In October 1975, Springsteen appeared on the covers of both *Time* and *Newsweek*.[3] In 1976, Tom Wolfe branded the 1970s as the "Me Decade," in which Americans—avid consumers all—looked out only for themselves. Six years later, one of the earliest books to survey the period carried the revealing title *It Seemed Like Nothing Happened*.[4]

A better history of the 1970s later emphasized that many seeds of change that had been planted during the stormy 1960s flourished in the 1970s. Rooting firmly, these strengthened in the years to come. But the history also concluded that much about the 1970s was "gaudy" and "depressing," especially the nation's "sometimes cheesy popular culture." When the author asked his students to name the one person who best embodied the decade, they chose John Travolta, who starred in the disco-centered movie *Saturday Night Fever* (1977). By contrast, they identified JFK, Robert Kennedy, and Martin Luther King Jr. as their models for the 1960s, and Ronald Reagan and Michael Milken as the men who are best remembered as symbols for the 1980s.[5]

These students, like Mr. Bucket, overlooked important developments of the 1970s, including lasting technological advances and substantial gains in the rights and entitlements of various groups—notably of women, the aged, and the disabled—that delighted many contemporaries. A rights revolution, having transformed American politics in the 1960s, continued to march forward in the 1970s and thereafter. The students also tended to focus on especially visible manifestations of popular culture, which are matters of ephemeral, personal taste. In this sense, as in others, the 1970s should not be set apart. Rather, those years witnessed the strengthening of many trends that were already in the making—especially from the culturally pivotal 1960s—and that continued in later years.

The students might also have emphasized that many Americans at the time were becoming profoundly uneasy about divisive social developments. Some of these—the flaring of racial tensions, troubled public schools,

---

3. William Graebner, "America's Poseidon Adventure: A Nation in Existential Despair," ibid., 157–80.
4. By Peter Carroll (New York, 1982). Its subtitle was *The Tragedy and Promise of America in the 1970s*.
5. Bruce Schulman, *The Seventies: The Great Shift in American Culture, Society, and Politics* (New York, 2001). Another useful survey of the 1970s is David Frum, *How We Got Here: The '70s, the Decade That Brought You Modern Life (For Better or Worse)* (New York, 2000). Milken was a notorious economic buccaneer who was convicted in the late 1980s of securities fraud.

alarm over crime and urban deterioration—accentuated the sense of national decline that had been evident during the pivotal year of 1974. The United States, many people thought, was teetering at the edge of an abyss. For these and other reasons, the mood of the late 1970s was in important ways the gloomiest in late twentieth-century American history.

IN 1903, THE EMINENT BLACK SCHOLAR W.E.B. DuBois had written that the "problem of the twentieth century is the problem of the color line."[6] In the 1970s, he would no doubt have agreed that racial issues stubbornly remained the nation's number one problem.

There are two dominant narratives about black-white relations in the United States during these and later years of the twentieth century. The first is optimistic because it looks at change over time, notably at the groundswell of progress lifted by the morally inspiring civil rights movement of the 1960s. This movement, the most powerful of the century, produced significant and lasting improvements in the lives of black people. Thanks to the historic Civil Rights Act of 1964 and the Voting Rights Act of 1965, America's black people finally broke free from all but a few of the chains of the racial segregation that had constitutionally shackled and isolated them since the late nineteenth century. Inasmuch as these chains had fastened them in a systematic, humiliating, dehumanizing, and often violently enforced form of subjugation, this was a long overdue and lasting deliverance. Most blacks, nearly 22.6 million in number in 1970 (11.1 percent of the population of 203.3 million people), knew that they had far more rights in the 1970s, especially legal rights, than they had had in the 1950s and early 1960s.

Liberals hailed other developments in race relations of the late 1960s and early 1970s. Supreme Court rulings between 1968 and 1971 finally gave teeth to civil rights laws and to the *Brown v. Board of Education* decision of 1954, thereby bringing about increasing desegregation of southern schools.[7] The 1970s were something of a golden age for long-discouraged advocates of school desegregation in the South. Assured of equal legal rights—most of which received diligent protection by federal officials—blacks slowly moved ahead in other ways during the 1970s. Affirmative action plans, "set-asides" (which guaranteed percentages of contracts to minority-owned businesses), and pressure from the federal government's Equal Employment Opportunity Commission (EEOC) to end discrimination in hiring—procedures

6. DuBois, *The Souls of Black Folk* (1903).
7. As late as 1964, only 1 percent of southern black children attended schools with white children.

and policies that had hardly been imagined in the mid-1960s—developed apace in those years.[8] Ever larger percentages of American blacks finished high school, entered colleges and universities, and found white-collar jobs. A black middle class, scarcely visible in the 1940s, rapidly enlarged after 1960.[9]

Black Americans advanced in other ways during the 1970s. Improved access to health care, mainly from the expansion of Medicaid, along with better nutrition, led to declines in previously high levels of black infant mortality and to increases in longevity. Growing numbers of African Americans won political office, especially mayoralties in black-dominated cities. Blacks who were elected as mayors in 1973 alone included Tom Bradley in Los Angeles, Coleman Young in Detroit, and Maynard Jackson in Atlanta—the first African American since Reconstruction to win such a post in the urban South. In 1974, the citizens of the District of Columbia gained limited home rule and were permitted for the first time in more than a hundred years to vote for their mayor, whereupon they chose a black aspirant, Walter Washington. America's first black Supreme Court justice, Thurgood Marshall, swore Washington into office in 1975. Even the world of popular culture seemed to be opening up to African Americans: In 1975, CBS offered *The Jeffersons*, a sitcom featuring a black couple as well as an interracial couple who went so far as to kiss on screen. The show lasted ten years on television, earning many high ratings.[10]

An astonishing cultural phenomenon of 1976–77 seemed to show how far blacks had come—and how far they might advance in the future. This was the excitement surrounding *Roots*, a book published in 1976 by the African American writer Alex Haley, who had earlier co-authored the best-

8. For the development of affirmative action, see Steven Gillon, *"That's Not What We Meant to Do": Reform and Its Unanticipated Consequences in Twentieth-Century America* (New York, 2000), 120–62; Hugh Davis Graham, "Legacies of the 1960s: The American 'Rights Revolution' in an Era of Divided Governance," *Journal of Policy History* 10, no. 3 (1998), 267–88; and Graham, "Unintended Consequences: The Convergence of Affirmative Action and Immigration Policy," *American Behavioral Scientist* 41 (April 1998), 898–912.

9. The percentage of black males employed in white-collar jobs rose from 12 in 1960 to 30 in 1990, compared to percentages of 36 and 47 for white males in those years. Percentages for black females rose during the same years from 18 to 58, compared to percentages for white females of 58 and 73. Andrew Hacker, *Two Nations: Black and White, Separate, Hostile, Unequal* (New York, ed. 1995), 259.

10. For an optimistic account of race relations in these years, see Stephan Thernstrom and Abigail Thernstrom, *America in Black and White: One Nation, Indivisible* (New York, 1997). A mixed interpretation concerning schools is James Patterson, *Brown v. Board of Education: A Civil Rights Milestone and Its Troubled Legacy* (New York, 2001).

selling *Autobiography of Malcolm X* (1965). *Roots* began by describing the world of a young African, Kunta Kinte, who was enslaved and shipped in chains to America in the 1700s. Haley, claiming to rely on oral accounts collected in Africa and on research in genealogical sources, identified Kinte as his own ancestor from seven generations back. With vivid characterizations of Kinte's descendants over these generations, *Roots* rejected the notion that American slaves had been docile. As scholars were also doing at the time, it portrayed Haley's ancestors as brave, resourceful human beings who had been proud of their African heritage and determined to shake off their shackles. Kunta Kinte had a leg amputated for daring to escape.

Roots topped the non-fiction best-seller list for six months after publication and garnered sales of 1.5 million hardbacks within a year and a half. It won a National Book Award and a special Pulitzer Prize in 1977. In January of that year it was also featured as a seven-part, twelve-hour television miniseries. Approximately 130 million Americans—or more than half of the nation's total population of 220 million—were estimated to have watched a part of the series. Some 100 million people tuned in for the final episode.

It is never easy to pinpoint why a commodity of popular culture—whether a book, a television show, or a movie—captures a large audience. In the case of *Roots*, it has been argued that its popularity reflected an earnest search by Americans, whites as well as blacks, for their own "roots," as a way of better anchoring themselves amid the social and economic turbulence of the times. Interest in genealogy and local history boomed in the next few years.[11] The stunning popularity of *Roots* may also indicate that millions of Americans were ready and willing by the mid-1970s to reconsider negative stereotypes of African Americans that had long flourished in textbooks, film, and television, and to react positively to Haley's inspirational account. Like moths to a flame, they were drawn to his seductive history. So it was that *Roots* struck many observers as a milestone of African American progress. Vernon Jordan, a leading black activist, called *Roots* "the single most spectacular experience in race relations in America."[12]

11. Christopher Capozzola, "'It Makes You Want to Believe in the Country': Celebrating the Bicentennial in an Age of Limits," in Bailey and Farber, eds., *America in the Seventies*, 29–49.
12. Cited in Myron Marty, *Daily Life in the United States, 1960–1990: Decades of Discord* (Westport, Conn., 1997), 207. Haley, it turned out, relied more on his imagination—and on a novel, *The African* (1967), by Harold Courlander, a white author—than on solid historical research. Charged with wholesale plagiarism by Courlander, he later settled out of court by paying him $650,000. See Stanley Crouch, *Jewish World Review*, Jan. 18, 2002; *Washington Post*, Feb. 11, 1992.

The second narrative of race relations in the 1970s is more doleful. Though it concedes that some progress occurred, its standard of measurement looks at where a truly egalitarian nation ought to be, in the present and in the foreseeable future. Its more pessimistic conclusions reflect the gap that exists between the reality of black–white relations and of the higher expectations that liberals and many black people had developed in the 1960s. Since the 1960s, this narrative—in many ways the more compelling one—has been the one that liberals and the majority of African American leaders have repeated.[13]

Advocates of this narrative concur that laws such as the Civil Rights Act of 1964 and the Voting Rights Act of 1965 destroyed most vestiges of legally mandated segregation and discrimination. These historic statutes went far toward guaranteeing a hallowed American value: equal opportunity under the law. But they point out that the laws did not greatly promote the still elusive, cardinal goal of African Americans: social and economic equality.

Statistics support this case, indicating that most of the gaps that had long separated blacks from whites shrank little if at all in the 1970s. Between 1970 and 1980, for instance, the median household income of African Americans did not rise (in inflation-adjusted dollars), whereas the median household income of whites slightly increased. Median black household income in 1980 stood at a little less than 60 percent of income for whites, a number that had hardly changed since 1965.[14] The net worth of black families—a measure not only of income but also of houses and other assets (many of them inherited)—was tiny compared to that of whites. The proportion of blacks in poverty in 1980, at around 33 percent, had decreased only slightly from 1970, when it had been 34 percent, thereby remaining—as it was to continue to do until it fell in the mid-1990s—at approximately three times the rate for whites.[15] Social conditions in many black areas of America's crowded, crime-ridden central cities were grim.

As in earlier decades of the century, the rate of black infant mortality declined encouragingly during the 1970s, from 33 deaths per 1,000 live births in 1970 to 22 in 1980. But because the rate of decline for whites fell a little more rapidly (from 18 per 1,000 in 1970 to 11 in 1980), the relative picture was a little gloomier for blacks than it had been ten years earlier. The rates for blacks were responsible for one of the most depressing facts about life in the United States: The rate of American infant mortality

13. For example, see Godfrey Hodgson, *More Equal than Others: America from Nixon to the New Century* (Princeton, 2004), 173.
14. *Stat. Abst.*, 2002, 433.
15. Ibid., 441.

remained high compared to other nations in the developed world. Black life expectancy at birth, at 68.1 years in 1980, compared poorly to the life expectancy of 74.4 for whites, a gap that had shrunk only a little from 1970—when it had been 64.1 for blacks and 71.7 for whites.[16]

Statistics concerning educational background were among the few that seemed fairly promising for blacks. As late as 1970, only 31 percent of blacks over the age of twenty-five had completed four years of high school or more, and only 4 percent had completed four or more years of college. The percentages for whites at the time were 55 and 11, respectively. By 1980, 51 percent of black people aged twenty-five or more had finished four years of high school, and 8 percent had completed four or more years of college. White percentages had risen by then to 69 and 17. Many of these trends, featuring relative as well as absolute advances for blacks, were to continue later in the century, to the point that high school graduation rates of blacks approached those of whites by 2000. But it was very clear to blacks in the 1970s, and later, that they were making relative gains only because they had begun at such a dismally low level. Blacks did not exult over statistics such as these.[17]

They had good reason to be somber, for conflicts over racial issues in the public schools rocked many American communities in the 1970s. Some of these controversies featured the efforts of public schools in the South, which were finally forced to desegregate following federal pressure and court rulings between 1968 and 1971, to delay or evade the law. Nixon, while sympathetic to such delays and evasions, counseled southern whites to obey the federal courts, most of which in the 1970s remained firm in their opposition to state-sponsored segregation. As a result, most southern schools capitulated: As of the late 1970s, public schools in the South had become the least segregated in the nation. They remained so, along with schools in the West, for the remainder of the century.[18] Given the potential in the early

16. Ibid., 71, 78.
17. Ibid., 139. By 2000, 85 percent of whites and 79 percent of blacks aged twenty-five or older had graduated from high school. In the same year, 26 percent of whites and 17 percent of blacks aged twenty-five or older had graduated from four-year colleges or universities. Ibid. See also Thernstrom and Thernstrom, *America in Black and White*, 179–80; Hacker, *Two Nations*, 73–80, 257.
18. Patterson, *Brown v. Board of Education*, tables, 228–33. The percentage of black students who attended majority-white schools increased in the eleven states of the Confederate South from around 1 in 1964 to 37 in 1980 and to a high of approximately 43 in the mid- and late 1980s, whereupon a process of re-segregation began that reduced this percentage to around 30 by 2001. This was still a higher percentage than those in the Northeast and Midwest. See chapter 9.

1970s for the resumption of the angry massive resistance that had stymied implementation of the *Brown* decision between 1954 and 1968, this was a welcome change.

No such movement toward more racially balanced schools (or toward inclusive racial relations of any kind) took place in many areas of the North, where de facto residential and school segregation, sometimes enforced in intimidating and violent ways, had long flourished. Though private decisions (parents moving their families to predominantly white neighborhoods) generated a good deal of this segregation, public actions (zoning ordinances, the placement of new schools, decisions about bus routes) solidified it.[19] *Brown v. Board of Education* had not challenged such practices; it targeted only state-mandated (de jure) segregation where it existed, in the South, the border states, and portions of other states. Foes of court-ordered directives for greater integration in other areas cheered a bitterly contested Supreme Court ruling of 1974, *Milliken v. Bradley*, which determined, five to four, that mostly white suburbs had no constitutional obligation to merge with predominantly black cities (such as Detroit, focus of the case) in order to create metropolitan school districts within which white and black students might be bused to achieve better racial balance. Justice Marshall dissented, observing, "Unless our children begin to learn together, there is little hope that our people will ever learn to live together." He added prophetically, "In the short run, it may seem to be the easier course to allow our great metropolitan areas to be divided up each into two cities—one white and one black—but it is a course, I predict, our people will ultimately regret."[20]

Strife in Boston, where court-ordered busing to overcome deliberate racial segregation in the public schools started in 1974, stunned liberals who had hoped for peaceful accommodation in America's "cradle of liberty." Three days before the schools were scheduled to open, a crowd of white activists belonging to ROAR (Restore Our Alienated Schools) marched on the Federal Building in Boston. When Senator Edward "Ted" Kennedy, a liberal backer of the court order whose own children attended private schools, appeared at the scene, the crowd set after him, chased him inside, and banged on barricaded glass doors until they shattered.

19. For racist activities of whites in northern and western cities in mid-twentieth-century America, see Thomas Sugrue, *The Origins of the Urban Crisis: Race and Inequality in Postwar Detroit* (Princeton, 1996); and Robert Self, *American Babylon: Race and the Struggle for Postwar Oakland* (Princeton, 2003).
20. *Milliken v. Bradley*, 418 U.S. 717 (1974). The vote was five to four, with four of the five in the majority having been appointed by Nixon.

On the first day of school in September, only 13 of some 550 white students from South Boston, a heavily Irish American, economically troubled, blue-collar area, showed up in Roxbury, a predominantly black neighborhood to which they had been assigned. Only 100 or so of the 1,300 blacks from the Roxbury area who had been directed to attend South Boston High, a previously white school, dared appear. Whites jeered and pelted them with rocks and bottles, injuring nine black students and damaging eighteen buses. Scattered violence continued: In December, a black student at South Boston was stabbed, forcing the school to shut down for a month. Police had to guard many schools. Shots zinged into the lobby of the *Boston Globe*, which supported the busing, whereupon newspaper managers felt obliged to station sharpshooters on its roof. Large numbers of white students boycotted these schools throughout the year.[21]

Though the violence in Boston, long a cauldron of racial, class, and ethnic furies, dominated the headlines, interracial hostilities gripped hundreds of other towns and cities in the late 1970s, the peak years of angry standoffs over court-ordered busing. By 1979, it was estimated that 1,505 American school districts educating more than 12 million students were operating under orders to achieve better racial balance. These orders affected nearly 30 percent of all public school children.[22] Many other districts hurried "voluntary" busing plans into service in order to avert litigation. While a few cities managed to cope fairly well with busing orders—Charlotte, Seattle, and Austin were often mentioned in this respect—most did not. Emboldened by the *Milliken* decision, many white parents seized the first opportunity they could to move to white suburbs. Though widespread out-of-the-city migration had long preceded the advent of court-ordered busing—suburbanization has a long history—the racial controversies surrounding schools in the 1970s clearly accelerated the process. In Boston, the number of white students in the public schools dropped from 45,000 in 1974 to roughly 16,000 by 1987.[23] "White flight" vividly demonstrated the enduring power of racist fears and misunderstandings.

These controversies quickly clouded the political arena, provoking widespread unease about court-ordered busing among blacks and whites alike.

21. See Schulman, *The Seventies*, 55–62, and Frum, *How We Got Here*, 256–63, for accounts of busing issues, including Boston. A gripping narrative of Boston's struggles is J. Anthony Lukas, *Common Ground: A Turbulent Decade in the Lives of Three American Families* (New York, 1986). See also Ronald Formisano, *Boston Against Busing: Race, Class, and Ethnicity in the 1960s and 1970s* (Chapel Hill, 1991).
22. *U.S. News and World Report*, May 14, 1979, 51.
23. *New Yorker*, July 26, 2004, 47.

A considerable minority of black parents, questioning the supposed virtues of greater racial balance in schools—who could say that blacks achieved better just because they went to the same school building with whites?—resisted sending their children off on buses to distant schools, the more so because it often seemed that the bus routes for blacks were longer. Neighborhood schools, they added, enabled their children to participate in afternoon activities, such as sports, and parents to take part in PTAs and other school-related organizations. Because of white flight, they said, bus routes and school assignments kept changing, weakening the identification of parents and children with particular schools. School administrators who echoed these complaints grumbled that this never-ending process of remapping bloated transportation budgets.

A substantial majority of white parents, many of them working-class people whose children were the most affected by busing, loudly backed these arguments. They emphasized that the Civil Rights Act of 1964 had been color-blind. Its key clause regarding schools, Title IV, stated that desegregation "shall not mean the assignment of students to public schools in order to overcome racial imbalance." Whites of this persuasion demanded to know how and why officials in non-elected, "elite" institutions—notably the ever more intrusive courts—had been allowed to "hijack" the statute and to run away with public policy. This, they said, was "liberal social engineering" of the worst sort. It turned innocent children into "guinea pigs," subjecting them to the travails of long bus rides, schooling in faraway neighborhoods, and frightening interracial tensions.

More generally, policies such as busing convinced many Americans that "big government" and "liberalism" had to be challenged. Backlash such as this was hardly new at the time; during the supposedly liberal 1960s, conservative complaints such as these had become attractive to millions of people, thereby helping Nixon to become president. But controversies over busing surely sharpened such antagonisms in the 1970s. Then and in the future, Americans continued to have profoundly ambivalent feelings about policy-making in Washington. On the one hand, they demanded a range of rights and entitlements. On the other, they denounced the evils of big government.

Mobilizing politically, white voters sparked near unanimous opposition by white officeholders to court-ordered busing. In 1974, the Democratic Congress passed, and Nixon signed, a law that among other things prohibited the use of federal aid to pay for court-ordered busing. In 1975, reinforcing *Milliken*, Congress approved legislation that prohibited the Department of Health, Education, and Welfare from requiring school systems to transport students beyond their neighborhood schools for purposes of racial balance. President Ford signed it.[24] In 1976, Jimmy Carter of Georgia, the Democratic presidential nominee, and Ford, his opponent, addressed the controversies caused by court-ordered busing. Ford said in July 1976: "It is a tragic reality that . . . busing under court order has brought fear to both black students and white students—and to their parents. No child can learn in an atmosphere of fear. Better remedies to right constitutional wrongs must be found."[25]

By the late 1970s, some of the popular anger aroused by court-ordered busing was subsiding, in part because many urban leaders were seeking other ways, such as magnet schools, of attacking racial discrimination, and in part because many white parents who stayed put—mostly working-class and poor people who could not afford to move—decided that busing was not always so horrible as they had first imagined. Resenting middle-class suburbanites who called them racists, they learned to live with it. But a key reason for the slow easing of tensions over busing was that a great many white parents had sent their children to private schools or had moved to predominantly white suburbs, where they no longer had to confront the issue.

By then, Marshall's prophecy that a chasm would divide large metropolitan areas (many of them growing blacker) from suburbs (many of them heavily white) had come to pass in a number of places. Blacks talked about a "white noose" that was choking the life out of the cities, and about "chocolate" cities and "vanilla" suburbs. In 1978, twenty-one of the nation's twenty-nine largest school districts had a black majority of students, and three more were about to join them. Eight of these twenty-one majority-black districts had gone that way between 1968, when the threat of court-ordered busing had become real, and 1976.[26] Thanks to demographic changes like these, and to overall population growth, the *number* (as opposed to the percentage) of black public school students who attended predominantly black schools was higher in 1980 than it had been in 1954.[27] Meanwhile, white flight continued: By 2003, minorities were 86 percent of Boston's public school students.

24. Hugh Davis Graham, "Civil Rights Policy in the Carter Presidency," in Gary Fink and Graham, eds., *The Carter Presidency: Policy Choices in the Post–New Deal Era* (Lawrence, Kans., 1998), 202–23.
25. *U.S. News and World Report*, July 5, 1976, 18.
26. Diane Ravitch, "The 'White Flight' Controversy," *Public Interest* (Spring 1978), 135–49.
27. Robert Carter, "A Reassessment of *Brown v. Board*," in Derrick Bell, ed., *Shades of Brown* (New York, 1980), 25.

So it was that on the twenty-fifth anniversary of *Brown v. Board of Education* in 1979, the *New York Times* deplored the "glacial pace at which school integration is taking place in big-city school systems." It added, "Those supporting integration are becoming increasingly lonely as black and Hispanic parents and leaders express mounting doubt about whether the little desegregation that can be achieved in the big cities is worth the cost and the effort."[28] This loneliness was to intensify in later years, when increasing numbers of blacks, like many whites, came to wonder if achieving "racial balance" in schools was worth all the fighting, or if such balance was effective in promoting educational progress or interracial toleration.

As battles over court-ordered busing began to subside, fights over affirmative action and minority "set-asides" rushed to the center of the political arena. Most of the framers of the Civil Rights Act of 1964 had not anticipated such issues. Seeking to eliminate intentional discrimination, they had assumed that the law, notably Title VII concerning employment, would advance color-blind (and gender-blind) hiring and contracting. Democratic senator Hubert Humphrey of Minnesota, the ardently liberal floor leader for the bill, had stood up in the Senate at the time to denounce the accusation by opponents that the legislation might sanction racial quotas. If that happened, he said, he would eat the pages of the bill "one page after another."[29]

Humphrey, like others in the early 1960s, failed to perceive the extraordinary force of rights-consciousness, which was to produce a host of unintended consequences. Beginning in the late 1960s, liberal activists—many of them officials in new federal agencies such as the EEOC—broadened the reach of civil rights laws: to advance the rights of elderly workers in 1967, of non-English-speaking students in 1970, of women in 1972, of the physically and mentally handicapped in 1973, and of handicapped schoolchildren in 1975. Moving beyond the color-blind principle—and gliding over the fact that the historical experience of African Americans (and Native Americans) had been uniquely brutal—they gradually expanded affirmative action and other anti-discrimination efforts so that in various ways these might include other minority groups of color.

The enforcement of affirmative action for women was relatively noncontroversial—and of considerable import for women in some areas of life, especially higher education. But the expansion of such programs to cover a range of minorities alarmed many observers at the time. Meg

---

28. *New York Times*, May 17, 1979.
29. Gillon, *"That's Not What We Meant to Do,"* 137.

Greenfield, a columnist for *Newsweek*, wrote that America was creating an "ethnic bath, an affirmative-action program gone mad."[30] A host of voices seconded her, charging that such expansion promoted "reverse discrimination," "Balkanization," and "retribalization," all of which endangered universalistic American values of equal treatment for all.[31] White ethnics, a leading scholar later wrote, were getting a "raw deal."[32]

Though conservatives led most fights against affirmative action, otherwise liberal blue-collar workers often backed them. Labor union members complained bitterly that affirmative action procedures violated hard-won contractual principles that guided hiring, promotions, and termination procedures. When a federal judge ruled in 1975 against the Detroit police department's "last hired, first fired" seniority principle, thereby protecting recently hired black officers, many white policemen were enraged. Hearing the decision, some of them (facing the loss of their jobs) moved to block the streets. "Talk about rights; we've got no rights," they shouted. "We're gonna kill you . . . niggers," one man shouted. Fighting broke out between several off-duty white policemen and one black off-duty policeman. Guns were drawn. The black officer suffered a broken nose and was taken to the hospital. Some Detroiters called the fracas a "police riot."[33]

The brawling in Detroit exposed the extraordinary contentiousness that exploded in the 1970s over programs aimed at countering racial discrimination. As in Detroit, this wrangling sometimes cut across party or "liberal"/"conservative" lines. It also revealed the growing power of rights-consciousness in America. Detroit's white police officers, angry that the courts were expanding the entitlement of blacks, countered with a rights-conscious language of their own. Struggles over affirmative action, as over abortion and many other contentious issues in late twentieth-century America, increasingly featured protagonists who talked the talk of rights.

Few people in the mid-1970s, however, anticipated that affirmative action for minority groups other than African Americans would become significant in numerical terms. Because immigration had been low since the 1910s, by the time of the 1970s ethnicity had come to play a relatively small role in American political life. In 1970, only 9.6 million Americans —4.7

---

30. Schulman, *The Seventies*, 75.
31. David Hollinger, *Postethnic America: Beyond Multiculturalism* (New York, 1995).
32. John Skrentny, *The Minority Rights Revolution* (Cambridge, Mass., 2002), vi.
33. Dennis Deslippe, "'Do Whites Have Rights?': Detroit Policemen and 'Reverse Discrimination' Protests in the 1970s," *Journal of American History* 91 (Dec. 2004), 932-60.

percent of the population—were foreign-born, the smallest percentage in more than 100 years.[34] People hailing from Europe, led by Italians, Germans, and Poles, numbered 5.7 million, or roughly 58 percent of the foreign-born. The number who had come from Latin America was only 1.8 million; from Asia, around 800,000. Words and phrases that later dominated discourse about race and ethnicity—"diversity," "multiculturalism," "minority groups" (in the plural)—were only beginning to find their way into everyday use.

Thanks to an immigration reform act in 1965, however, the number of legally admitted newcomers was far larger in the years to come, totaling some 28 million people between 1970 and 2000. Affirmative action procedures, gradually extended to cover many of the non-white foreign-born (and their descendants), came to have a broad reach.[35] Federal policies providing affirmative procedures of various sorts to minorities in 2000 potentially covered more than 80 million people—not only the 35 million (12.3 percent of the population) who were African American at that time but also the slightly larger number of 35.3 million (12.5 percent) who were of Latino origin, the 10.1 million (3.6 percent) who were Asian American, and the nearly 2.5 million (1.2 percent) who identified themselves as Native American, Eskimos, or Aleuts. This was more than 29 percent of the overall population of 281 million in 2000.[36]

34. In 1910, 14.7 percent of Americans were foreign-born. This percentage had never been below 11.6 between 1860 and 1930.
35. See chapter 9 for the long-range consequences—most of them unintended—of the immigration law of 1965 (and of later immigration acts).
36. Hugh Davis Graham, *Collision Course: The Strange Convergence of Affirmative Action and Immigration Policy in America* (New York, 2002); David Hollinger, "Amalgamation and Hypodescent: The Question of Ethnoracial Mixture in the History of the United States," *American Historical Review* 108 (Dec. 2003), 1363–90. The number of Americans in 2000 who had been born in Europe was 4.4 million, slightly below the number in 1970. The number in 2000 who had been born in Latin America was 14.4 million; the number born in Asia was 5 million. The figure of 80 million includes American-born descendants of Asians, Hispanics, and other minority groups (such as Aleuts and Pacific Islanders), some of which have benefited from affirmative action or minority set-aside procedures. In 1970, only 792,000 people told the Census that they were American Indians; rising ethnic consciousness, not substantial growth in the Indian population (Indian birth rates were very low), was primarily responsible for large increases (to 2,476,000 in 2000) of those who identified themselves as American Indians or Native Americans in later years. Andrew Hacker, ed., *U/S: A Statistical Portrait of the American People* (New York, 1983), 34; *Stat. Abst.*, 2002, 26.

The Supreme Court, too, advanced the trend toward protection of minority interests, ruling unanimously in 1971 that employers could be found guilty of racial discrimination in hiring even if there was no evidence that they had intended it. The Court, then headed by Nixon appointee Warren Burger, explained that the *consequences* of hiring criteria—that is, whether such criteria (in this case, requirements that employees have a high school diploma or pass a generalized intelligence test) resulted in the disqualification or exclusion of minority applicants—must be considered in determining whether an employer had violated Title VII.[37] In 1977, the Office of Management and Budget (OMB) affirmed already existing EEOC practices by issuing Directive 15, which identified not only African Americans but also Spanish speakers, American Indians, Asians, and Eskimos and Aleuts as groups that might be deserving of certain kinds of affirmative action.

This "ethno-racial pentagon," as it was later called, showed how far toward sanctioning group preferences and entitlements the tide of liberal opinion had surged by the late 1970s. It was a tide that rose in part from the actions of members of Congress, state legislators, and city leaders, who approved set-aside programs assisting minority contractors, and in part from non-elected public officials in federal agencies like the EEOC, from liberal public interest activists and lawyers, and from judges who favored rights-based policies. By 1980, the so-called Leadership Conference on Civil Rights, which represented more than 165 rights-conscious organizations, was developing considerable influence in Washington.[38]

Affirmative action programs, designed to facilitate upward social and economic mobility, did not much aid the masses of low-income minorities, most of whom were ill-educated and worked (if employed at all) in blue-collar or service sector jobs that offered little in the way of social mobility. Affirmative action did, however, give a substantial boost to the educational opportunity and advancement of middle class women, and to relatively small numbers of upwardly mobile minorities who were therefore admitted to universities and who moved ahead in the world. By the late 1980s, most large American corporations had adopted affirmative action

37. *Griggs v. Duke Power Co.*, 401 U.S. 424 (1971). The Court returned again and again in later years to complicated, racially charged employment issues, beginning most notably in *United Steelworkers of America v. Weber*, 443 U.S. 193 (1979), when it ruled that employers could voluntarily adopt affirmative action procedures in hiring plans. See chapter 7 for some of these decisions.
38. Graham, "Unintended Consequences." For a history of affirmative action, see Terry Anderson, *The Pursuit of Fairness: A History of Affirmative Action* (New York, 2004).

procedures in order to diversify their workforces and/or to avoid costly litigation alleging racial or gender discrimination concerning their hiring and promotion practices.[39] The military services, meanwhile, worked harder to promote racial integration.

Still, affirmative action distressed many contemporaries, who argued that it created overblown and unrealistic expectations about entitlements and that it encouraged minorities to revel in feelings of victimization, some of which led to costly and highly divisive litigation. They further complained that democratically elected national and state legislators had not enacted many of these procedures: Affirmative action, like court-ordered busing, was often damned as elitist and undemocratic, pressed into existence primarily by non-elected "limousine liberals" and the like. For all these reasons, many conservatives were appalled. Ronald Reagan, informed of Humphrey's statement, later said that if the senator had lived to see what the tide of rights-consciousness had done to the Civil Rights Act, he would have had a "severe case of indigestion."

University officials, too, supported policies advancing affirmative action. By the mid-1970s, most of the nation's selective universities had written anti-discrimination procedures and principles into their admissions practices. A few seemed to be going beyond affirmative action, which normally entailed special efforts at outreach and recruitment of women and minorities, in order to embrace admissions quotas for various minority groups. Advocates of these varying procedures sometimes defended them by pointing out that universities had long given preferential treatment to various applicants, notably "legacies"—sons and daughters of alumni, most of whom were white and middle-class. Advocates further stressed that minorities, who on the average scored poorly on various tests used for university admission, had suffered from historic discrimination—or from racially biased tests—and deserved compensatory justice in the present.

These university officials, like other supporters of policies such as these, often emphasized that deserving minorities had a *right* to them. By increasing the number of blacks and other minorities who might study at leading universities, they said, such efforts facilitated racial integration and "diversity" on campus, as well as all-important access to the networks of association that enabled students to advance in later life. Racially liberal admissions criteria, they insisted, boosted a Talented Tenth, or more,

39. Nelson Lichtenstein, *State of the Union: A Century of American Labor* (Princeton, 2002), 204–6.

into the middle classes. Minority graduates, serving as role models, would help to open doors throughout the wider society.[40]

These procedures at universities actually affected relatively few applicants, either whites or minorities. Most of those who succeeded in gaining admission were especially qualified students who competed with one another for a limited number of available places at America's most select colleges and universities—a small fraction of higher education overall.[41] Most other institutions outside the South, as in the past, took in high school graduates, whether white or non-white, who could pay tuition. Some colleges, desperate for students, continued to accept applicants who were semi-literate. Thus affirmative action procedures in higher education were numerically far less significant than the issue decided by *Milliken v. Bradley*, which affected millions of children in the public schools. Some observers saw affirmative action policies as mainly a symbolic cause—a kind of tokenism to ease white consciences about the socio-economic plight of minorities and the failings of inner-city public schools. Others viewed these policies as evidence of yet another selfish struggle for interest group advantage. Yet tempers about university affirmative action grew hot in the 1970s, in part because such programs could make a difference in the life chances of aspiring minorities and of the sons and daughters of articulate, politically engaged, middle-class white parents.

White parents who denounced the practice asked why their blameless, racially tolerant children should lose a place at Stanford or Brown because of the discriminatory sins of Americans in the past. They insisted that minority students admitted via preferential admissions policies would drag down academic standards. Students of color who were let in, perceived to be "undeserving" of admission, would therefore be stigmatized. Pointing to continuing interracial tensions on many campuses, critics further maintained that racial diversity in higher education did little to advance black–white friendships or understanding. If universities really hoped to attack discrimination in admissions, they said, they should consider programs that would counter policies that favored wealthy students over poorer applicants who could not afford tuition. If they expected to remedy

40. Orlando Patterson, *The Ordeal of Integration: Progress and Resentment in America's "Racial" Crisis* (Washington, 1997), 9–11.
41. Orlando Patterson, in *New York Times*, June 22, 2003, later estimated that affirmative action reduced the chances of white applicants getting into top colleges by only 1.5 percent. Polls, he added, indicated that only 7 percent of Americans with a European heritage ever complained that they had lost out from the programs. See also Anderson, *In Pursuit of Fairness*, 280–81.

the ills of education for minorities, they should seek to cure the ailments of inner-city elementary and secondary schools, not use universities as a Band-Aid or a crutch.

Above all, critics of affirmative action programs complained, as in the later words of one scholar, that they "cast even the lowliest Euro-American as a privileged oppressor."[42] They created "reverse discrimination" that violated ideals of fairness and constitutional guarantees of equal protection under the law. Some of these critics agreed, often grudgingly, that affirmative action might be justified as a way of countering the uniquely barbarous historic discrimination that had afflicted blacks and American Indians, but that it should not be extended to other minorities of color: These minorities, like white ethnics in the past, could and should make it on their own. Critics added that many young Americans of color—as from Cuban, African, and Asian families—had middle-class backgrounds. Why offer the entitlement of affirmative action to them? Deploying a principle that resonated with many Americans, foes of affirmative action demanded that universities—and employers—seek to identify only those applicants who had demonstrated merit, not reward categories of people with non-white skin colors.

As so often with controversies in late twentieth-century America, fighting over affirmative action moved into the ever expanding realm of the courts, where a host of interest groups entered briefs concerning admissions criteria employed by the University of California at Davis medical school. These established quotas for various minority applicants and were challenged by Allan Bakke, a white man who had twice been denied admission though he had higher test scores than most minority applicants who had been accepted. The university, he charged, had denied him equal protection under the laws. Most leading Jewish organizations, pointing out that American universities had long used quotas to limit the number of Jewish students, also joined the interest groups that opposed the university. So did the American Federation of Teachers, the Order of the Sons of Italy in America, and the Polish-American Congress. In October 1977, when the Court heard the *Bakke* case, it had a record number of briefs (fifty-eight) to consider. For the next eight months, Americans eagerly awaited the Court's decision.[43]

In June 1978, the Court finally decided, ordering the university to admit Bakke next semester. It did so, however, with a resounding lack of

42. Skrentny, *Minority Rights Revolution*, 353.
43. Anderson, *In Pursuit of Fairness*, 150–55.

consensus that reflected divisions in popular opinion. By a margin of five to four, with "swing man" Justice Lewis Powell casting a decisive vote, it ruled that the medical school's quota system reserving places for minorities violated both the equal protection clause of the Fourteenth Amendment and Title VI of the Civil Rights Act of 1964, which barred racial discrimination by any institution receiving federal funds. As Justice John Paul Stevens wrote, "Race cannot be the basis of excluding anyone from participation in a federally funded program." Justice Marshall, dissenting, lamented, "After several hundred years of class-based discrimination against Negroes, the Court is unwilling to hold that a class-based remedy for that discrimination is permissible."[44]

But all was not lost for advocates of anti-discriminatory admissions programs. The Court went on to say that flexible plans (such as one then in place at Harvard) that considered race or ethnic background among other qualifications for university admission were permissible. Powell, a conservative Virginian who had been named to the Court by Nixon, cited the virtues of campus "diversity" as the basis for his ruling. In so doing he hoped to skirt a troubling question—one that nonetheless aroused great debate in later years: *Which* groups should be compensated for past discrimination, how much, and for how long?

Perhaps the most poignant statement came from Justice Harry Blackmun, another Nixon appointee. Blackmun backed Powell's position, but he also made it clear that the need for such programs troubled him. "I yield to no one," he said, "in my earnest hope that the time will come when an 'affirmative action' program is unnecessary and is, in truth, only a relic of the past." "Within a decade at the most," he added, American society "must and will reach a stage of maturity where action along this line is no longer necessary." He concluded: "In order to get beyond racism, we must first take account of race. There is no other way. . . . In order to treat persons equally, we must treat them differently."[45]

The *Bakke* rulings temporarily quieted some of the controversy over affirmative action. Many people, though uneasy about the divisions within the Court, seemed to consider the outcome to be a commonsense compromise. *Time*, featuring the decision, summed up the result on its cover: "QUOTAS: NO / RACE: YES."[46] So not much changed. Most university

44. *University of California Regents v. Bakke*, 438 U.S. 265 (1978).
45. Ibid. See also Howard Ball, *The Bakke Case: Race, Education, and Affirmative Action* (Lawrence, Kans., 2000); and J. Harvie Wilkinson, *From Brown to Bakke: The Supreme Court and School Integration: 1954–1978* (New York, 1979), 298–306.
46. *Time*, July 10, 1978, 8.

plans, which did not specify quotas for minorities, survived. But the issue did not go away, in large part because blacks (and to a lesser extent other minorities) continued on the average to score far below whites on standardized tests used by many university admissions offices. Depressingly, the gaps in these test scores (branded as racially biased by many black people) increased in the 1990s.

Eager to promote diversity—and not to appear racist—leading universities continued to give preferential treatment to some minority applicants, thereby exciting endless debate over the next twenty-five years. In 2003, the Court again felt a need to enter the fray, this time in essence to reaffirm what it had said in *Bakke*.[47] In so doing, it revealed a significant fact about race relations and entitlements in the years since 1978: The principle of "diversity," supported by 2003 by a host of corporate leaders, university presidents, and military spokesmen, had by then taken considerably deeper root in American society. But the trying history of affirmative action also exposed the enduring educational and economic chasms that separated black and white Americans during these many years. Notwithstanding the Court's position, the issue, continuing to feature highly rights-conscious arguments and counter-arguments, remained an abrasive source of intergroup tensions in the United States.

These debates, along with other racial concerns, dispirited many black people in the 1970s, particularly, it seemed, those who were moving into the middle classes. More than lower-class blacks, who struggled just to make ends meet, those who were upwardly mobile had been especially energized by the great civil rights triumphs of the 1960s. Many had developed high expectations about their rights—affirmative action among them—and their futures. By the late 1970s, however, they had grown increasingly pessimistic about a number of things, including the intentions of the majority of white people. Some seemed to be doubting the American Dream. This was one of the sadder legacies of the troubled 1970s.[48]

47. In 2003, the Court rejected an admissions program for University of Michigan undergraduates that employed a point system favoring minorities but approved a more flexible University of Michigan Law School plan. These cases were decided by margins of six to three and five to four. Like Justice Blackmun in 1978, Justice Sandra Day O'Connor, who came around to support flexible versions of affirmative action, made it clear that she hoped such measures would become unnecessary over time—perhaps in twenty-five years. *New York Times*, June 24, 2003.

48. This is the conclusion of Jennifer Hochschild, *Facing Up to the American Dream: Race, Class, and the Soul of the Nation* (Princeton, 1995), 94–98. A more optimistic view is Paul Sniderman and Thomas Piazza, *Black Pride and Black Prejudice* (Princeton, 2002), 124–32.

CLAMOR OVER RACE, OF COURSE, had long created disharmony in America, so that arguments over busing and affirmative action merely added harsh new notes to old scores. Also disturbing to many Americans in the late 1970s were a number of related social trends that seemed to be provoking ever greater dissonance. Schools, cities, morals, family life, the economy—all appeared to be collapsing. It was no wonder that many people during these unusually restless times fretted that the nation was entering a state of disarray and decline.

Alarm about schools extended beyond the friction sparked by desegregation and busing. Increasingly, it rested on the sense that schools were failing in general. By the late 1970s, a host of complaints homed in on these supposed failings—notably lower standardized test scores and the dumbing down of curricula. Many of these criticisms, emanating from the business community, evaluated schools according to their potential for promoting the economy. They called on the United States to upgrade its educational standards so that it could prevail in the ever more technologically complex and competitive global economy that was emerging. Mounting in the early 1980s, laments of this sort reached an apogee in 1983, when the secretary of education, Terrel Bell, issued a gloomy report card on American education. Titled *A Nation at Risk: The Imperative for Educational Reform*, it declared that schools were swamped in a "rising tide of mediocrity" and concluded that Americans, in danger of being surpassed by nations such as Japan and South Korea, had been "committing an act of unthinking, unilateral educational disarmament."[49] Though this much-discussed report had little substantive effect at the time, it ushered in a growing movement for "standards" and higher "achievement"—and for greater federal enforcement of such standards—that was to gather considerable political strength in the 1990s.[50]

Exhibit A of this case for educational collapse was a decline in scores on the Scholastic Aptitude Test (SAT), which was said to measure the aptitudes of high school students. These scores had begun to drop in the mid-1960s and fell to all-time lows by 1980. Between 1967 and 1980, the average verbal score dipped from 543 to 502 and the math score from 516 to 492.[51] Exhibit B was grade inflation, at both the secondary and university levels. Some pessimists asserted that educational "failures" such as these reflected

49. Diane Ravitch, *Left Back: A Century of Failed School Reforms* (New York, 2000), 408–15. The report (Washington, 1983) was prepared by the revealingly named National Commission on Excellence in Education.

50. See chapter 7.

51. *Stat. Abst.*, 2002, 159.

a more general decline in American culture, owing mainly to "permissiveness" that had supposedly run rampant beginning in the 1960s. As an advocate of "back to basics" later wrote, the public schools suffered their worst days in the 1970s: "When the 1960s animus against elitism entered American education, it brought in its train an enormous cynical tolerance of student ignorance, rationalized as a regard for 'personal expression' and 'self-esteem.'"[52]

Many of these complaints rested on faulty premises. Most experts considered the SAT, which evaluated aptitude, to be a less reliable guide to student accomplishment than other measures, notably tests given by the National Assessment of Educational Progress (NAEP). These tests tracked academic achievement and showed little change in average scores between 1970 and 1990. The main reason why SAT scores fell in the late 1960s and 1970s was that higher percentages of America's young people, including many from the lower-middle and lower classes, were eager to go to college. For this and other reasons, they were staying in school and taking the tests. Under these circumstances it was hardly surprising that the average scores would dip.[53]

Educational policies did not seem to improve matters. Thanks to passage in 1965 of the Elementary and Secondary Education Act (ESEA), federal government money—most of it provided by Title I of the law for "compensatory education" to help the poor—had finally augmented state and local spending for schools, mostly for instruction in elementary grades. In the 1970s, as later, real per pupil spending for public schools increased steadily in the United States. Student-teacher ratios got better, not worse.[54] These developments reflected a major trend of the late twentieth century: Popular expectations about what schools ought to accomplish—notably better academic achievement—were rising. Yet the quality of public education did not seem to be improving. High percentages of students who graduated from high school were sadly deficient in basic academic skills, including reading.

Schooling for poor and minority children continued to be weakly supported in relative terms. To ensure congressional backing for ESEA, the law dispensed money to virtually all school districts, whether predomi-

52. Robert Hughes, *Culture of Complaint: The Fraying of America* (New York, 1993), 66.
53. Lawrence Stedman and Carl Kaestle, "The Test Score Decline Is Over: Now What?" *Phi Delta Kappa*, Nov. 1985, 204–10; David Tyack and Larry Cuban, *Tinkering Toward Utopia: A Century of Public School Reform* (Cambridge, Mass., 1995), 34–36.
54. From 1 teacher per 22.3 public school students in 1970 to 1 per 18.7 in 1980 to 1 per 17.2 in 1990 to 1 per 16 in 2000. *Stat. Abst.*, 2002, 150.

nantly rich or poor. Especially in the late 1960s and early 1970s, Title I money was not well targeted at the poor. Moreover, federal money was relatively small, never more than 10 percent of overall spending on public schools. Because schools continued to depend above all on state and local government support—that is, predominantly on property and sales taxes— per pupil spending varied enormously across school districts and across states. The inequality across districts and states that had always character- ized America's decentralized public education system endured. No won- der that social engineers fell back on Band-Aids such as affirmative action at the level of university admissions in order to compensate for economic inequities in the public schools.

Rights-conscious interest groups began to change public schools in two significant ways in the 1970s. Both of these changes exposed the unantici- pated consequences of public policies. The first, as often happened after the 1960s, owed much to a ruling by the Supreme Court. In *Lau v. Nichols* (1974), a case brought by Chinese Americans in San Francisco, the Court held unanimously that the promise of non-discrimination in the Civil Rights Act of 1964 required public schools to make special provision, in- cluding separate programs (often in separate classrooms) for students who had limited command of English. This provision must be offered, the Court said, even when there was no evidence of disparate treatment or of intentional discrimination: If there were disparate *outcomes* of academic *achievement*, students had a right to such assistance.[55] Congressional reau- thorization in 1974 of earlier legislation calling for bilingual education escalated this kind of special provision. By 1982, 500 school districts in the country, including every large urban district, were teaching 800,000 stu- dents in bilingual-bicultural education programs.[56]

In November 1975, Congress passed the Education for All Handicapped Children Act. This law, another far-reaching civil rights initiative, did not stem from grass-roots activism by disabled Americans; in the early 1970s, the handicapped had not yet become an effective pressure group. Instead, the act—like many other governmental measures in the rights-conscious

---

55. As the Court recognized, the requirement of provision for bilingual education might result in classes segregated by race or ethnicity. This often happened: The right of bilingual education could—and did—clash with the goal of racially integrated pub- lic education.

56. Gareth Davies, "The Great Society After Johnson: The Case of Bilingual Educa- tion," *Journal of American History* 88 (March 2002), 1405–29; Skrentny, *Minority Rights Revolution*, 337–39. In all, there were 3.6 million students with limited ability in English at that time.

1970s—owed its success mainly to the efforts of public interest lawyers, and to activist federal judges who ruled that children with disabilities had a constitutional right to an education. That fundamental principle having been established, congressional staffers and lobbyists for the disabled pressed for legislation. The act, which had bipartisan backing, entitled all children with disabilities to a "free, appropriate public education."

President Ford, worried among other things that the bill might commit public officials to raise large sums in the future for costly "special education," wavered before signing it. His concerns proved prescient: Within the next ten years, the number of special education teachers increased from 179,000 to 275,000. By 2000, the number of children with disabilities served by schools had risen to 5.7 million, or to approximately 11 percent of total enrollments. Though federal spending for special education increased, Congress, concerned about rising federal budget deficits, more and more called upon state and local governments to pay for it. Faced with an unreliably funded mandate from Washington, states and school districts were obliged to spend steadily larger sums for special education (and for bilingual education), thereby cutting into budget lines for mainstreamed academic programs and provoking fights over spending in local communities.[57]

The growth of specialized mandates such as these—of rights—sparked controversy.[58] Critics charged that bilingual education programs isolated non-English-speakers from the mainstream and deterred the acculturation of the students that they were designed to help. Special education programs, expensive to maintain, led observers to charge that school administrators widened the definition of "handicapped" so as to secure greater federal funding. Both programs added substantially to the costs incurred by school districts, especially in metropolitan areas populated by masses of minority children. Many of these schools were already struggling to operate with less money per pupil than did predominantly white schools. Because the Supreme Court had ruled in 1973 that local officials did not have to remedy inequality of resources across school districts, these disparities persisted.[59]

For all these reasons, American schools fell short of providing equality of educational opportunity. In the 1970s, as later, popular expectations

57. For special education legislation, see Gareth Davies, "Education for All Handicapped Children," chapter 6 of his forthcoming book concerning federal educational policy between 1965 and 1984. For statistics concerning special education in 2000, see *Stat. Abst.*, 2002, 133, 157. For local fights, see *New York Times*, April 24, 2005.
58. In 1986 Congress enacted a law that called on school districts to provide for handicapped children attending pre-schools.
59. *San Antonio Independent School District v. Rodriguez*, 411 U.S. 1 (1973).

about education increased, as did the percentage of students who completed high school and went on to colleges and universities. Having access to a college education came to be regarded as a right—one of many in an ever longer list of rights—that millions of young Americans and their parents began to demand. By 2000, 63 percent of sixteen- to twenty-four-year-old students who had graduated from high school within the previous twelve months (64 percent of whites and 56 percent of blacks) were enrolled at colleges or universities—up from 45 percent in 1960 and 51 percent in 1975.[60] Real per student spending for public schools also advanced, doubling between 1970 and 2000. But serious racial inequities in educational opportunity and achievement, reflecting socio-economic differences in the culture at large, persisted—especially in inner-city schools—long after the 1970s.

THE ILLS OF URBAN SCHOOLS joined a long list of ailments afflicting cities in the United States. The phrase "urban crisis" constantly confronted readers of magazines and daily newspapers in the 1970s. There was good reason to feature such a phrase, because America's cities, particularly those with large populations of minority groups, faced a host of serious problems at the time.

One of these ailments, as school administrators well knew, was fiscal. Although the percentage of Americans residing in central cities did not change greatly in the 1970s or later (it was 32 in 1975, 31 in 1995), one of the strongest demographic trends of late twentieth-century America featured the flight—much of it white flight from the cities—of middle-class, taxpaying people to suburbs (which housed 35 percent of the population in 1970, 40 percent in 1975, and 50 percent in 1995).[61] In the 1970s alone, some 13 million people (more than 6 percent of the total population in 1970) joined this exodus to the greener subdivisions of suburbia.[62] Many who replaced them in the central cities migrated from areas where large-scale

60. *Stat. Abst.*, 2002, 164. Many students at four-year colleges and universities dropped out or took more than four years to graduate. In 2002, 18 percent of blacks and 36 percent of Americans between the ages of twenty-five and twenty-nine were graduates of four-year colleges or universities. *New York Times*, May 16, 2004.
61. Theodore Caplow et al., *The First Measured Century: An Illustrated Guide to Trends in America, 1900–2000* (Washington, 2001), 12; and Benjamin Kleinberg, *Urban America in Transformation: Perspectives on Urban Policy and Development* (Thousand Oaks, Calif., 1995), 122–23.
62. Paul Fishman, *Bourgeois Utopias: The Rise and Fall of Suburbia* (New York, 1987), 180–82; Kenneth Jackson, *Crabgrass Frontier: The Suburbanization of the United States* (New York, 1985), 272–80.

commercial agriculture was throwing small farmers and farm laborers out of work. Other people fled economically depressed rural regions and small towns.[63] The stream of migrants to northern cities from the South—of poor whites as well as blacks—had been huge in the 1950s and 1960s and by the 1970s had created extraordinary crowding in central-city areas. As time went on, millions of very poor people from Mexico, the Caribbean, and Central America added to the numbers that helped overwhelm the resources of these urban centers.

These demographic shifts owed a good deal to technological changes, notably the mechanization of agriculture, which dramatically reduced the need for farm workers, especially cotton pickers in the South. The changes also stemmed from federal policies, especially farm subsidies promoting the growth of agribusiness that helped to drive small farmers off the land. Other federal policies promoted suburban development: low interest rates for home mortgages facilitated by agencies such as the Veterans Administration and Federal Housing Administration, and generous appropriations for interstate highway construction. The number of motor vehicle registrations (cars, trucks, and buses) in America exploded from 156 million in 1980 to 221 million in 2000, by which time there were 190.6 million licensed drivers among the 217 million Americans who were sixteen years of age or older.[64]

The dominance of car culture hastened suburban "sprawl," or "slurbs," which appalled a host of urban planners and architects. A great many suburbs, they lamented, were all-white, socially homogenous havens that served to shelter people from the lower classes. Other suburbs featured rapid in- and out-migration, which damaged volunteerism and community spirit. Environmentalists, among others, assailed politically connected developers who struck deals allowing suburbanites to encroach on wetlands, destroy flood plains, and cut down trees.[65] Critics of suburbs, then and later, denounced them as "cultural wastelands" and as enclaves of tastelessness and banality. With characteristically cosmopolitan asperity, Ada Louise Huxtable of the *New York Times* complained in 1974, "There is [in these suburbs] no voyage of discovery or private exploration of the world's wonders, natural and man-made; it is cliché conformity as far as the eye can see, with no stimulation of the spirit through quality of the environment."[66]

---

63. For a bittersweet history of one such town, Camden, Ohio, see Richard Davies, *Main Street Blues: The Decline of Small-Town America* (Columbus, Ohio, 1998).
64. *Stat. Abst.*, 2002, 13, 674, 675. Of the 221 million motor vehicle registrations in 2000, 134 millions were passenger cars. Most of the rest (87 million) were trucks.
65. Adam Rome, *The Bulldozer in the Countryside: Suburban Sprawl and the Rise of American Environmentalism* (New York, 2001).
66. Fishman, *Bourgeois Utopias*, 203.

Most city leaders did not worry a great deal about suburban aesthetics. Rather, they had to cope with deteriorating tax bases caused not only by the exodus of the middle classes but also by the flight to suburbs—and to the South and West—of many businesses. Other industries, notably in manufacturing, were laboring to stay afloat. All such companies had been key sources of property tax revenue and of jobs. Deprived of these resources, many cities struggled to support basic services, not only schools but also mass transit and police and fire protection. In 1975–76, New York City suffered a traumatic fiscal crisis that caused the discharge of some 3,400 police officers, 1,000 firefighters, and 4,000 hospital workers. Nationally aired, the city's desperate straits symbolized the larger plight of urban America in the economically troubled late 1970s. Three years later, Cleveland, widely ridiculed as the "mistake by the lake," defaulted on its debt.

In New York City, as in many other metropolises, the "urban crisis" particularly afflicted low-income workers and the "underclasses," as contemporaries came to brand the residents, most of them black, of poverty-stricken central cores. By the late 1970s, investigative reporters, politicians, and others were graphically exposing the social ills of these "miserable," "disorganized," "dysfunctional," and often "dangerous" "ghetto dwellers." Some of these accounts were sensationalized, ignoring viable inner-city connections of extended families, churches, and civic groups that combated social disorganization. These accounts followed in a long tradition of scare-mongering exposés of the "dangerous classes" and of the "other Americans." But there was no doubting that many people living in these areas confronted extraordinarily serious hardships, which stemmed from white racism as well as from structural flaws in the economy, notably the exodus of jobs from the cities.[67] In 1978, Senator Kennedy warned of "the great unmentioned problem of America today—the growth, rapid and insidious, of a group in our midst, perhaps more dangerous, more bereft of hope, more difficult to confront, than any for which our history has prepared us. It is a group that threatens to become what America has never known—a permanent underclass in our society."[68]

Kennedy, a liberal, sought to direct more federal resources to the underclasses. But many other Americans were frightened by the specter

67. William J. Wilson, *When Work Disappears: The World of the New Urban Poor* (New York, 1996).
68. Cited in a widely noted journalistic account, Ken Auletta, *The Underclass* (New York, 1982), 30. See also James Patterson, *America's Struggle Against Poverty in the Twentieth Century* (Cambridge, Mass., 2000), 209–16.

of disorder, crime, and violence that seemed to be threatening central cities. In 1977, a massive power blackout in New York City unleashed a terrifying spate of looting and burning. Within minutes of the blackout at 9:30 P.M. on July 13, a hot and sticky evening, looters—most of them black, many of them teenagers—poured into streets, especially in parts of Brooklyn and the Bronx. Armed with crowbars to pry loose steel shutters and saws to cut through padlocks, they smashed windows and brazenly carried off merchandise. Police, their numbers seriously depleted since the fiscal crisis of 1975, tried to stop them but were hit by barrages of bricks and bottles. Soon the looters, gleeful and defiant, began burning buildings and pelting firefighters who intervened. The mobs seemed indiscriminate. A priest in the Bronx discovered that his altar had been stolen. "Soul Brother" signs erected as safeguards by black storeowners did little to deter the rampaging crowds.[69]

By the time the rioting subsided some five hours later, more than 1,600 stores had been looted, and more than 1,030 fires—50 of them serious—had been set. Damage was estimated at $1 billion. Police arrested some 3,800 people—compared to 373 who had been charged following disturbances in Harlem in 1964, and 465 who had been arrested in the city as a result of unrest that broke out after the assassination of the Reverend Martin Luther King Jr. in 1968. For many New Yorkers, the blackout of 1977 deepened a culture of despair that lasted for many years.[70]

Frightening though this rampage was, it was for many Americans but one grim sign of a much larger breakdown of "law and order" that had seemed to spread in the late 1960s and to peak in the 1970s. Murder rates, which had hovered at around 4.5 to 5 per 100,000 people per year in the 1940s and 1950s, swelled after 1963, doubling to 9.6 per 100,000 by 1975. They climbed to an all-time high in the late 1970s and early 1980s of around 10 per 100,000. By then it was estimated that the murder rate in the United States was eight times that of Italy, the next most afflicted industrial nation.

Record rates of other violent crimes in America—rape, aggravated assault, robbery—accompanied these increases in murder. The rate of property crimes such as burglary, larceny, and theft rose almost as rapidly—up

69. *New York Times*, July 14, 1977.
70. Jonathan Mahler, "The Darkest Night," *New York Times Magazine*, Oct. 5, 2003, 76–82; James Goodman, *Blackout* (New York, 2003). An outage in New York in 1965 had caused no such scenes. Nor did a wider blackout that darkened not only New York City but also other parts of the East and Midwest (including Detroit) in 2003.

76 percent between 1967 and 1976—and also peaked by 1980.[71] As early as 1971, many Americans were applauding the film *Dirty Harry*, in which Clint Eastwood, playing a rock-hard cop who abuses the civil liberties of a psychopathic killer, welcomes the chance to blow him away. By the mid-1970s, millions of Americans, though beset by stubborn economic problems, were telling pollsters that crime was the nation's most serious problem. They were also denouncing the Supreme Court's decision in *Miranda v. Arizona* (1966), which had enlarged the rights of criminal defendants, and its ruling in *Furman v. Georgia* (1972), which had struck down all existing capital punishment laws.[72]

Why these dramatic increases in crime? Then and later, criminologists and others struggled to find the answer. Many correctly blamed an upsurge in drug abuse, which peaked in the early 1970s and incited violent gang warfare over control of the trade. Others blamed poverty, which played a role. But they had to concede that hard times in the past—as in the 1930s—had not provoked a rise in crime. Officially measured poverty rates in the 1970s, though serious (hovering throughout the decade at around 12 percent of the population), were a little more than half what they had been in the early 1960s, before the surge in crimes began. An increase in economic inequality that began in the 1970s, thereby sharpening feelings of relative deprivation, may have played a role in the rise of crime. But this inequality also intensified in the late 1980s and in the 1990s, when crime rates at last began to fall off. It was therefore difficult to establish a strong and clear causal connection between economic forces and crime rates.

Some Americans who joined the acrimonious debates about crime that persisted after the 1970s urged fellow citizens to work together in order to advance community cohesion and cooperation. Parents, ministers, and youth leaders, the argument went, should get together with the police to restore communication and order to their neighborhoods. Others came to rely on a "broken window" theory of crime. This held that city leaders and police must act quickly to curb relatively minor acts of vandalism in order

---

71. *New York Times Almanac, 2000*, 303; *Stat. Abst.*,1977, 168. Many statistics on crime derive from the FBI, which relies on reports from police departments. Critics warn that these numbers may be flawed, inasmuch as police departments may downplay the extent of crime or (seeking more manpower) may wish to exaggerate it. Increases in crime between the mid-1960s and late 1980s, however, were clearly high.

72. *Miranda v. Arizona*, 384 U.S. 436 (1966); and *Furman v. Georgia*, 418 U.S. 238 (1972).

to avert the proliferation of more serious crime. In the 1990s, many cities credited this approach with helping to reduce crime.[73]

Most Americans in the 1970s, however, were inclined to blame "softness" for the rise in crime. They demanded better patrolling of neighborhoods, larger and better-trained police forces, and tougher laws and sentences. The Supreme Court, having ruled in 1972 against death penalties as then applied, backed off and in 1976 allowed executions for certain types of murders, thereby setting the stage for the return of the death penalty in most American states. Utah executed Gary Gilmore, a convicted murderer, by firing squad in January 1977. The execution of Gilmore, the first in the United States in ten years, was followed over the ensuing twenty-seven years by 943 more, most of them in southern and western states.[74] But neither the reinstatement of the death penalty nor a decided trend in subsequent years toward tougher prosecution and sentences brought crime rates anywhere near to pre-1963 levels.

Still other Americans pointed their fingers at their country's "gun culture" or, more broadly, at a "culture of violence" exacerbated by bloodletting in Vietnam and by a virtual choreography of mayhem, as they saw it, on television and in films. Would-be assassins, they emphasized, twice tried to kill President Ford in 1975. Films of the early and mid-1970s such as *The Godfather* (1972), *The Godfather Part 2* (1974), *The Texas Chain Saw Massacre* (1974), *Death Wish* (1974) and its four sequels, which made the brooding Charles Bronson into a star, and *Taxi Driver* (1976) appeared to revel in depicting blood and gore and to highlight the helplessness of authorized law enforcers.

Violence on television, often viewed by children, caused special outrage among contemporary parents and media critics, who charged that it helped to unleash all sorts of evil instincts into the real world. The nation's best-known historian of the broadcast industry, Erik Barnouw, agreed that TV was a major villain of the piece: "I can't imagine that this constant display of violence would not affect [people] in some way. . . . We are actually merchandising violence."[75]

73. Most famously advanced as a theory by James Wilson and George Kelling, "Broken Windows: The Police and Neighborhood Safety," *Atlantic Monthly* 249 (March 1982), 29–38. Mayor Rudy Giuliani of New York City became a visible advocate of this idea in the 1990s.
74. From 1977 through the end of 2004. A disproportionate number of those executed were blacks. Texas led the way in executions. New York, New Jersey, and the six New England states executed no people between 1964 and the end of 2004. *Christian Science Monitor*, Nov. 22, 2004. See also chapter 8.
75. Cited in Mary Ann Watson, *Defining Visions: Television and the American Experience Since 1945* (Fort Worth, 1998), 94.

Many years later, there existed no solid consensus on the causes of rising crime in America. Blaming guns, notably semi-automatics, did draw attention to a major source of violent crime (some 70 percent of murders in the United States in these and later years were caused by guns) but slighted the fact that the non-gun homicide rate in New York City, for example, had long been considerably higher than the rate in London. Those who pointed fingers at TV and film failed to recognize that America had always had considerably higher rates of violent crime (though not of property crime) than other industrialized nations. They added that just as much violence seemed to suffuse television shows (many of them originating in the United States) in other Western nations that had far lower rates of crime, and that the increases in crime that so distressed Americans in the 1970s had started in the mid-1960s, when such depictions in film and on television had been less graphic or commonplace.[76]

The historian, confronted with so many uncertainties, often falls back on a favorite tool, multiple causation, to fashion explanations for the scourge of crime that frightened Americans in the 1970s and later. One important cause, it seems clear, was demographic: the coming of age of millions of males who were among the 75 million people who had been born in the baby boom years between 1946 and 1964. In 1950, there had been 24 million people in America who were aged fourteen to twenty-four; by the mid-1970s, there were 44 million.[77] Men in their teens and twenties are far more likely to engage in crime than are women or older men. Similarly high rates of increase in violent crime occurred in some other industrialized nations, notably Japan and Britain, in these years — in part, it was believed, for similar demographic reasons.

A related cause was racial in nature. Millions of African Americans in the 1960s and 1970s were growing up in unstable families and in crowded, poverty-stricken, central-city neighborhoods. Angry about white privilege and discrimination, and anticipating futures of futility, thousands of these young people — mostly young black men — found a niche in gangs or turned to crime. The rates of arrests and incarcerations of black males far exceeded those of white males and continued to be higher throughout the century. Black males were six times more likely than white males to commit murder. Most of these murders were black-on-black, indicating that interracial hostility was not normally or directly involved. These caused

76. James Wilson, "Hostility in America," *New Republic*, Aug. 25, 1997, 38–41.
77. Steven Gillon, *Boomer Nation: The Largest and Richest Generation Ever, and How It Changed America* (New York, 2004), 98.

homicide to become the leading cause of death of black men. (Among Americans overall, it was the tenth leading cause.)[78]

Numbers such as these, highlighted in the media, made it very clear that racial issues were linked to violent crime in the United States. Widespread popular awareness of this connection contributed to a sense among millions of Americans in the troubled late 1970s that the country was badly divided along lines of race and social class and that it was plunging into decline.

78. Wilson, "Hostility in America."

2

Sex, Families, Stagflation

Though racial tensions and rising crime rates especially agitated Americans in the 1970s, related anxieties about "moral decline" — and about the "younger generation" — were almost as unsettling. Many older Americans complained that standards of behavior among young people in the huge baby boom cohort had been slipping since the subversive '60s.[1] A number of public school students seemed out of control. Many pupils apparently thought nothing of swearing in the classroom or within earshot of people on the street. Other young people sprayed graffiti on buildings, sidewalks, subway trains, and buses. Per capita consumption of wine and beer and use of cocaine and marijuana, much of it by young adults, soared to frightening highs in the 1970s.[2]

Then there was sex. Some manifestations of this eternally hot topic did not change appreciably in the 1970s. Informed discussion about a number of sexually related health matters, such as menopause, impotence, and venereal disease, was still difficult to discover in newspapers or on TV. It was even harder to find authoritative articles about homosexuality (which most Americans considered an abomination). Sex education ("health education") in schools sparked inflammatory debates. Reporters were told not to use "vagina" or "penis" in their stories. It took the AIDS pandemic in the 1980s to push concerns like these a little more into the open.

1. Daniel Patrick Moynihan, "Defining Deviancy Down," *American Scholar* (Winter 1993), 17–30.
2. Theodore Caplow et al., *The First Measured Century: An Illustrated Guide to Trends in America, 1900–2000* (Washington, 2001), 142–43, 146–47; *Stat. Abst.*, 2002, 197.

But sex of a more titillating sort seemed to be advancing in the culture almost as rapidly as violence. Some central-city areas in the 1970s, notably New York City's Times Square, became virtual Sodoms where massage parlors, live sex shows, porn theaters, and street prostitution literally confronted passersby.[3] Commercialized, erotica sold briskly. Sexually graphic movies such as *Last Tango in Paris* (1973), starring Marlon Brando, left little to the imagination.[4] Erica Jong's *Fear of Flying: A Novel* (1973) celebrated the "zipless fuck" and dwelt on scenes of meaningless sex between strangers. It sold 6 million copies in the United States alone.[5]

Sexual themes on TV, reaching families in the supposed sanctity of the home, became more explicit and widespread, in advertisements as well as in programs. In 1967, Ed Sullivan, emcee of the nation's leading variety program, had told the Rolling Stones that they could not appear on his show unless they agreed to change the lyric, "Let's spend the night together" to "Let's spend some time together." Thereafter, standards changed with startling speed. In a scene on the popular *Mary Tyler Moore Show*, which started in 1970, Mary's mother reminds her father, "Don't forget to take your pill." Mary, thinking that her mother is talking to her, replies, "I won't." At that time, this was thought to be a daring conversation. By 1976, the widely watched show *Charlie's Angels*, which featured sexy young women chasing bouncily after villains, struck one critic as "an excuse to show sixty minutes of suggestive poses by walking, talking pinup girls." Another critic quipped that the show was a "massage parlor in the living room." *Three's Company*, a sitcom that began a long and successful run in 1977, followed the romantic adventures of a young man and his two often scantily clad female roommates. Critics labeled it "Jigglevision."[6]

Television hits like these reflected a sexualizing of the culture at large in the 1970s—the decade when the long-emerging sexual revolution that had surged speedily ahead in the 1960s shot still farther forward to become a mainstream phenomenon in the United States. This was in many ways a generational phenomenon that especially affected young people; many older Americans were appalled by the goings-on. Wider availability

3. Peter Braunstein, "'Adults Only': The Construction of an Erotic City in New York During the 1970s," in Beth Bailey and David Farber, eds., *America in the Seventies* (Lawrence, Kans., 2004), 129–56.
4. David Allyn, *Make Love Not War: The Sexual Revolution, An Unfettered History* (Boston, 2000), 295–97.
5. Ibid., 266-68.
6. Mary Ann Watson, *Defining Visions: Television and the American Experience Since 1945* (Fort Worth, 1998), 112–13.

(by prescription) of birth control pills, which had been legalized in 1960, and of other methods of contraception helped to drive the changes. So did the rise of women's liberation, which advanced in the late 1960s and 1970s. An especially powerful force propelling these trends, as it did so many of the cultural changes that affected the United States in these and later years, was the greater emphasis that millions of people—especially young people—were placing on personal choice and freedom.

Mainly affecting the behavior of young women, whose sexual experiences until the late 1960s had generally been less extensive than those of men, the revolution offered a bonanza for males, who discovered that it was considerably easier than in the past to find willing sexual partners.[7] For instance, the percentage of unmarried white girls aged nineteen who had engaged in sexual intercourse had been around 20 to 25 in the mid-1950s; by the mid-1970s, it was still lower than that of white men, but it was racing upward, reaching nearly 75 percent by 1990.[8] The age-old double standard, which had restrained the sexual freedom of women, was collapsing. As the critic Tom Wolfe put it, the "uproars" of sexual experimentation that had created anxiety in the 1960s became by the 1970s "part of the background noise, like a new link of I-95 opening up."[9] The journalist David Frum later added, "The 1970s blew to smithereens an entire structure of sexual morality."[10]

Reflecting these trends, the Supreme Court in 1972 voted, six to one, to advance the right of privacy, by branding a Massachusetts law that had barred the sale of contraceptives to single people an "unwarranted governmental intrusion." "Everyone," the Court added, "including unmarried minors, had a right to use contraception."[11] Millions of unmarried Americans, relying on condoms already, scarcely noticed. On a more exotic sexual front, the porn movie *Deep Throat* (1972) became a hit. (With later videocassette and DVD sales and rentals, it ultimately made more than $600 million, thereby becoming one of the most profitable films in

---

7. John D'Emilio and Estelle Freedman, *Intimate Matters: A History of Sexuality in America* (Chicago, 1997), 370–71.
8. Ibid., 334–35; Caplow et al., *The First Measured Century*, 71. Statistics on sexual behavior rely on interviews and polls and are understandably inexact. There is no mistaking the general trend, however.
9. Tom Wolfe, *In Our Time* (New York, 1976), 4.
10. Ibid.; David Frum, *How We Got Here: The '70s, the Decade That Brought You Modern Life (For Better or Worse)* (New York, 2000), 173.
11. *Eisenstadt v. Baird*, 405 U.S. 438 (1972); Allyn, *Make Love Not War*, 265–66.

history.)[12] Linda Lovelace, the star of the film, was featured as a guest on the *Tonight Show* with Johnny Carson. Even more successful was Dr. Alex Comfort's illustrated *The Joy of Sex*, which also appeared in 1972. Appropriately subtitled *A Gourmet Guide to Lovemaking*, the book was organized like a cookbook, with chapters such as "Starting," "Main Courses," and "Sauces and Pickles." By the early 2000s, it had sold an estimated eight million copies.

The shift toward a freer, more open sexuality in the United States was part of a larger trend that affected the Western world. *Last Tango in Paris* was made in Paris and had an Italian director. Comfort was a British author, and his book was first published in Britain. Still, the changes in America were sharp and significant, indicating that sexually explicit material was attracting a large and mainstream audience that no longer worried about being seen as sexually venturesome. As Gay Talese, whose book *Thy Neighbor's Wife* (1980) explored sexual behavior in the United States, later pointed out: "What was special about *Deep Throat* was that it required people to expose themselves, to go into a theater, to be seen walking in or walking out. That was a revolutionary act in the 1970s."[13]

In the late 1970s, resurgent conservatives, allying with women's groups opposed to pornography, struggled to stem the tide of sexual material in mass culture. But the onrush of more liberal sexual behavior in the 1970s, the last pre-AIDS era, seemed unstoppable. Even in the 1980s, a decade of growing conservative presence in politics, liberals gained ground in "culture wars" concerning sex. Some of the old ways seemed to weaken without a serious struggle. In 1970, 523,000 unmarried couples cohabited; in 1978, more than twice as many, 1,137,000, did. In 1979, a *New York Times* poll revealed that 55 percent of Americans—twice the percentage in 1969—saw nothing wrong with premarital sex. In the same year, 75 percent of people said that it was "morally acceptable" to be unmarried and to give birth to children. As Wolfe wrote, "The ancient wall about sexual promiscuity declined. And it fell like the walls of Jericho; it didn't require a shove."[14]

Increases in out-of-wedlock pregnancy—or illegitimacy, as it was generally called at the time—were striking. Between 1970 and 1980 the percentage of births delivered by unmarried mothers rose from 11 to 18—and to 28 by 1990. The statistics by race were shocking: In 1970, 38 percent of

---

12. *International Herald Tribune*, Sept. 4, 2004; Anthony Lane, "Oral Values," *New Yorker*, Feb. 28, 2005, 96–97. The budget of the film was said to be around $25,000.

13. *International Herald Tribune*, Sept. 4, 2004.

14. Allyn, *Make Love Not War*, 271–80; Wolfe, *In Our Time*, 4.

black babies were illegitimate, compared to 6 percent for whites. By 1990, 67 percent of black babies were illegitimate, as opposed to 17 percent for whites.[15] African American families tended to be fragile: By 2000, 50 percent of black families with children under eighteen were headed by women—compared to a percentage for white families of this sort of 21.[16]

Developments such as these helped swell reliance on public assistance—or "welfare." The number of recipients of Aid to Families with Dependent Children (AFDC), the means-tested, federal-state program that assisted such families, rose from 7.4 million in 1970 to 11.1 million in 1975, before leveling off at 10.6 million in 1980.[17] Funding for the program increased in current dollars from $4.1 billion in 1970 to $8.4 billion in 1975 and to $12 billion in 1980. These increases did not occur because the incidence of poverty rose rapidly among single mothers; as measured by the government, this incidence—always very high—went up only slowly. Rather, AFDC expanded because the number of single mothers, driven up by increases in out-of-wedlock pregnancies and in divorces, kept rising, and because activists—some of them welfare mothers, some of them liberals who staffed legal aid and legal services programs—at last enabled poor single mothers to become aware of their eligibility. By the late 1960s, many more of these mothers were asserting their rights to aid, and receiving it.

Americans who complained about the "explosion" of welfare claimed that the costs were becoming outrageous. Some critics of AFDC also emphasized that blacks, though a minority of the population (11.8 percent in 1980), outnumbered non-Hispanic whites who received benefits under the program.[18] Mothers such as these, racists said, were lazy and irresponsible "brood mares." These were exaggerated laments: Means-tested social benefits in the United States continued to be considerably less generous (as a percentage of GNP) than in most developed nations and remained far smaller than American social insurance programs (notably Social Security and

15. *Stat. Abst.*, 2002, 59.
16. Ibid., 51.
17. House Committee on Ways and Means, "Overview of Entitlement Programs," 1992 *Green Book*, 102d Congress, 2d Session (Washington, 1992), 654, 660; James Patterson, *America's Struggle Against Poverty in the Twentieth Century* (Cambridge, Mass., 2000), 156, 166.
18. In the 1970s, between 43 and 46 percent of parents receiving AFDC were blacks, and between 38 and 40 percent were non-Hispanic whites. Most of the rest were categorized as Hispanic. In the 1980s, the percentage of AFDC parents that was categorized as Hispanic crept up, from 13 in 1969 to 17 in 1990. The number of black parents in the program continued in those years to be slightly larger than the number of white parents. *Green Book*, 670.

Medicare) that benefited millions of middle-class people along with the poor. In the 1980s, moreover, conservatives fought against higher appropriations for AFDC, whose outlays per recipient failed to keep pace with inflation.[19] But until 1996, when AFDC was dismantled, three forces prevented opponents from scuttling the program: the belief that the poor could not simply be abandoned; the power of rights consciousness, which was energizing the poor as well as the middle classes; and a gradual decline in the age-old stigma attached to bearing babies out of wedlock.

Whether the rise in illegitimacy was "bad" provoked rancorous debate. Many liberals, avoiding moralistic judgments, refused to agree that any one family form was necessarily preferable to another. Many single mothers, they pointed out, were better off without irresponsible or abusive mates. Struggling single women obviously faced obstacles in raising their children, however, and female-headed families suffered economically. The "feminization" of poverty, as scholars came to call it, was an abstract way of saying that families headed by women were three times as likely to be poor as those headed by married couples.[20] Largely for this reason, the United States, where public assistance was relatively meager, had the highest child poverty rates in the developed world.[21]

A huge rise in divorce also affected family life in America. Divorce rates per 1,000 of population doubled—from 2.5 per 1,000 people in 1965 to a peak of between 5 and 5.3 per 1,000 between 1976 and 1985.[22] During these years the number of divorces per marriage increased from one in four to one in two. Tom Wolfe called this the "Great Divorce Epidemic." It was estimated at the time that 40 percent of children born in the 1970s would spend some of their youth in a single-parent household. After 1985, the divorce rate declined slightly, but in large part because cohabitation between never-married couples had increased. These couples, never having married, could separate without having to divorce.[23]

19. Patterson, *America's Struggle Against Poverty*, 157–60.
20. *World Almanac, 2001*, 873; Andrew Hacker, *Two Nations: Black and White, Separate, Hostile, Unequal* (New York, 1995), 73–74.
21. *Stat. Abst.*, 2002, 441. These rates, for children under the age of eighteen, rose from 15 percent in 1970 to 18 percent in 1980. The rates for black children were fairly stable during these years, at around 42 percent, or three to four times the rates for white children alone.
22. Ibid., 59.
23. Ibid. See also William Strauss and Neil Howe, *Generations: The History of America's Future, 1584 to 2069* (New York, 1991), 324–26; Francis Fukuyama, *The Great Disruption: Human Nature and the Reconstitution of Social Order* (New York, 1999), 40–42; Frum, *How We Got Here*, 80; *New York Times Almanac, 2003*, 277; and Wolfe, *In Our Time*, 5.

Why the rise in divorce? It was not because Americans disdained marriage. On the contrary, the ideal of marriage remained strong. Though people married later and had smaller families after the end of the baby boom, the vast majority of adults—90 percent—continued to say "I do" at some point in their lives.[24] Most divorced people remarried and cherished hopes of a happy family life. A better explanation for the rise in divorce emphasized the implementation of more liberal "no-fault" state laws, which spread to virtually all states between 1969 and 1985, but these were less the cause of surging divorce rates than the result of larger trends in the culture. One of these trends, of course, was steady growth in female employment: Wives who worked often had greater economic autonomy than those who did not. As with rising rates of out-of-wedlock pregnancy, escalating divorce rates also reflected powerful cultural trends, notably the ever stronger attachment of Americans to personal freedom and to individual rights and entitlements. More and more, Americans came to believe that the right to divorce, like other rights that were becoming cherished in these and later years, could promote the acquisition of greater "self-realization" and liberating personal growth.[25]

Popular reactions to these sweeping social trends—greater sexual freedom, increasing out-of-wedlock pregnancy, soaring divorce rates—differed sharply, but a generational gulf was obvious: Younger people were much more likely to defend the new ways. Older Americans were more frightened by what was happening to family life. Nostalgic for what they saw as the golden age of the 1950s, they deplored the "plagues" of "fatherless families," "permissive" child rearing, and "latchkey" children. Hoping to save the "traditional family," they were shortly to mobilize behind conservative spokespeople who waged "culture wars" on behalf of an earlier, better America.[26]

In looking for villains, some of these Americans blamed the rise of the feminist movement, which in their view diminished paternal authority and threatened the family. This movement, which had expanded rapidly in the late 1960s, championed varied goals that included sexual liberation as well as equal rights under the law. Fissures along class and racial lines

24. During the 1970s, America's population increased by only 11.4 percent (from 203.3 million to 226.5 million)—the smallest rate of growth since the Great Depression years of the 1930s.
25. Because Americans lived longer, married couples faced a longer road than in the past. This demographic reality also helped increase divorce rates.
26. See chapter 4 for the rise of social conservatism in American political life in the late 1970s.

consistently hampered unity among women in the movement. But agitation for rights was nonetheless vibrant in the "She Decade" of the 1970s, when feminists, led by the National Organization for Women (NOW), became far more visible than in the past. Aided by the extension of affirmative action policies, they battled to move from "the bedroom to the boardroom."

In so doing, feminists for the first time forced Washington to listen. In 1972, Congress sent the Equal Rights Amendment, which had been stalled on Capitol Hill since the 1920s, to the states for possible ratification. It stated, "Equality of rights under the law shall not be denied or abridged by the United States, or by any State, on account of sex." By 1977, thirty-five of the thirty-eight states needed for ratification had approved it. In 1972, Congress also added Title IX to existing civil rights law. Title IX barred sex discrimination in any educational institution receiving federal aid, thereby in time promoting changes in university procedures. The law later did a good deal to advance women's athletics in schools and colleges. In 1975, the major service academies admitted women for the first time.

The year 1973 proved to be another banner year for feminism. In *Roe v. Wade* the Supreme Court invalidated most state laws that criminalized a women's access to abortion, enhancing privacy as a constitutional right. Between 1974 and 1977, 3.5 million legal abortions were performed in the United States—or nearly four for every ten live births. The number of abortions further increased in the early 1980s and remained high until the early 1990s, averaging over 1.5 million a year between 1980 and 1990. Starting in the mid-1990s, decreases in teen pregnancy and slight increases in use of contraceptives slowly lowered the number of abortions from their peak in 1990 of 1.6 million, but large numbers persisted, among both married and unmarried women.[27] It was hardly surprising that feminists and others who cherished the right to privacy and choice continued to place preservation of *Roe*, which was greatly embattled, at the top of their rights-conscious agendas.[28]

27. *Stat. Abst.*, 2002, 70; *New York Times*, Jan. 16, 20, 2003. The abortion ratio (which measures the number per 1,000 live births) peaked in 1983 at 436 per 1,000 births, after which it slowly but steadily declined to 340 per 1,000 by 1997. This was roughly the ratio that had existed in 1975, shortly after *Roe v. Wade*. Abortions per 1,000 women aged fifteen to forty-four declined from a peak of 29.3 in 1980 and 1981 to 21.3 in 2000. *Stat. Abst.*, 2002, 70.
28. Andrew Hacker, "How Are Women Doing?" *New York Review of Books*, April 11, 2002, 63–66; *New York Times*, Jan. 17, 1998.

A less serious but widely noted gain for women in 1973 took place on the tennis court. Billie Jean King, twenty-nine, a top female tennis player, whipped Bobby Riggs, who had been a men's tennis champ in the 1930s, in three straight sets. The fifty-five-year-old Riggs, having bragged that he would clean up the court with her, was humbled before 30,000 people — the largest crowd ever to see a tennis match — at the Houston Astrodome. Of this widely touted "Battle of the Sexes" the *Los Angeles Herald American* crowed, "Pigs Are Dead . . . Long Live the King." King's triumph greatly strengthened the Women's Tennis Association and advanced the growth of a women's professional tennis circuit.

The forward strides continued. In 1974, Ella Grasso won a gubernatorial race in Connecticut, thereby becoming the first woman governor in American history who was not the wife or widow of a former governor. In 1976, a woman was selected as a Rhodes scholar, a first. In the same year, the Episcopal Church decided to ordain women as ministers. Dr. Benjamin Spock, author of a phenomenally popular guide to baby and child care, announced in 1976 that the next (fourth) edition would be the first one to "eliminate sexist biases." The new edition would refer to babies as "she" as well as "he." Spock, who had come under fire from feminists, now stressed that fathers, too, had major roles to play in raising children.[29]

Women, having long been demeaned in stereotyped images, either as airheads or as sex objects, also began to be portrayed in less predictable ways in movies and television. Films that broke with the old ways included *An Unmarried Woman* (1977), *Annie Hall* (1977), and *Norma Rae* (1979). The chief character of television's *Mary Tyler Moore Show*, Mary Richards, was an intelligent, independent, working woman who showed no real interest in securing the matrimonial knot and who confronted blundering, sexist men on the job. The show, which ran from 1970 through 1977, won top ratings and twenty-five Emmys.

Changes in the area of higher education, which had a long history of gender discrimination, were especially encouraging to women in the 1970s. Though affirmative action procedures helped these changes along, the advances mainly owed their force to the rising expectations of young American women.[30] These changes steadily gathered strength over time. Between 1970 and 1996, the percentage of PhDs granted to women rose

29. For feminism in these years, see Ruth Rosen, *The World Split Open: How the Modern Women's Movement Changed America* (New York, 2000).
30. Nathan Glazer, "The Future of Preferential Affirmative Action," in Phyllis Katz and Dalmas Taylor, eds., *Eliminating Racism: Profiles in Controversy* (New York, 1987), 329–40.

from 13 to 45; of MBAs, from 4 to 38; of MDs, from 8 to 41, and of law degrees, from 5 to 44. Virtually all the formerly male colleges and universities in America turned coeducational in the 1970s and 1980s, helping to lift the percentage of female BAs from 43 in 1970 to 55 by 1996. By that time, many colleges were anxiously looking for ways to attract male applicants so as to offer female students a better social situation on campus.[31]

In all these ways, agitation for women's rights in the early and mid-1970s mounted as never before. A counter-reaction then arose in 1976, at which point Congress approved an amendment limiting federal funds for abortions.[32] Foes of the ERA, predicting that it would lead to unisex toilets and to women in combat, helped prevent states from ratifying the measure after 1977. Congress extended to mid-1982 the time during which ratification might be accomplished, but to no avail. On June 30, 1982, the ERA died.[33] By that time, however, statutes such as the Civil Rights Act of 1964 and Title IX in 1972, along with a number of court decisions and bureaucratic decrees, had guaranteed women virtually all the rights that the ERA would have conveyed constitutionally.

The greatest change in the status of many women in these years — one that especially distressed many defenders of traditional family life — owed relatively little to the rise of feminism. That was the long-standing, inexorable increase in the employment of women outside the home. This advance had first appeared in a major way during World War II, when women had been in demand as defense workers. Though many of these workers lost or left their jobs during postwar demobilization, the percentage of women, including married women, who entered the labor market rose rapidly during the late 1940s and 1950s, even though feminism was weak at the time. What many of these women cherished was work for pay in order to help their families, not large feminist visions of equality. By 1960, 38 percent of American women (aged sixteen or older) were in the civil-

---

31. *New York Times*, March 26, 2001.
32. This was the Hyde Amendment. It restricted the use of federal funds under the federal-state Medicaid program, except in cases where an abortion was necessary to save a woman's life or where pregnancy had been caused by promptly reported rape or incest. These stipulations were upheld by a five-to-four vote of the Supreme Court in 1980 (*Harris v. McRae*, 448 U.S. 297).
33. Jane Mansbridge, *Why We Lost the ERA* (Chicago, 1986); Barbara Ehrenreich, *The Worst Years of Our Lives: Irreverent Notes from a Decade of Greed* (New York, 1990), 150–53. Many women, too, opposed the ERA, worrying that feminist causes posed a danger to family life. Opponents of the ERA were strongest in the South: Ten of the fifteen states that never ratified the amendment were southern.

ian labor force. Ten years later, 43 percent were, and by 1980, 52 percent, or 45 million women, were working outside the home. The trend continued in later years of the century, bringing the number of women in the labor force to slightly more than 60 percent of women — 66 million — by 2001.[34]

As these numbers mounted, activists for female equality mobilized to fight against sex discrimination in the work force. This called for waging an uphill battle, because sex segregation in employment stubbornly persisted, all but excluding women from a number of traditionally male occupations. Even liberals could be slow to come around. In 1960, Supreme Court Justice Felix Frankfurter, who during his long career in public life had backed a number of black and female causes, rejected on the grounds of gender the application of Ruth Bader Ginsburg to be his clerk, even though Ginsburg (later appointed by President Bill Clinton to the Court) had graduated number one in her class at Columbia Law School.[35]

Experiences such as Ginsburg's remained common in the 1970s and 1980s, thereby greatly swelling litigation alleging discrimination in hiring and wages. The gap between the wages of full-time male and female workers narrowed only slightly between 1960 and 1985, during which time the wages of women crept upward from 61 percent of men's wages to 65 percent. Later, women's wages improved more rapidly than men's, to an average of 77 percent of men's by 2001.[36] Even in the 1990s, however, many small businessmen, anxious to cut costs, still resisted provision of flex time or parental leave. Then, as in the 1970s and 1980s, few women managed to climb above the "glass ceiling" that kept them below top management. Legal battles against sexism in the workplace, though aided by the new legions of female professionals coming out of law and business schools, were long and frustrating.

While discrimination by employers was a considerable problem, it was not the only source of economic inequality facing women in the United States. For the most part, young, white, well-educated, and childless women did not face overt discrimination on the job. They tended to fare as well in workplaces as did men of comparable background.[37] But large numbers of women with children were also entering the workforce. By the mid-1980s,

---

34. *New York Times Almanac*, 2003, 332–33; *Stat. Abst.*, 2002, 368, 370. In 2001, 74.4 percent of men were in the American labor force.
35. In 1948, he had picked William Coleman to be his clerk at the Court. Coleman was the first African American to hold such a position.
36. Victor Fuchs, *Women's Quest for Economic Equality* (Cambridge, Mass., 1988), 1–4, 141; *New York Times*, Feb. 17, 2003.
37. Fuchs, *Women's Quest for Economic Equality*, 140–41.

some 55 percent of all mothers, a majority of them full-time employees, worked outside the home.[38] Most of them were not climbing career ladders, and they did not consider themselves to be feminists. Rather, they entered the labor market, often in relatively low-paying jobs, in order to add to household income, at least until such time as their children had grown up and left the home.

Still, increasing numbers and percentages of young women did start out on a career track, only to confront difficult dilemmas when they had children. More so than many men, they were likely to develop powerful commitments to parenting, but the United States—unlike some European nations—had no system of state-supported children's allowances that were allotted to mothers whether or not they worked outside the home. Generous children's allowances would have enabled some American mothers to consider staying at home instead of working for wages, or to use the allowances to pay for day care while on the job. Caught between monetary needs and strongly felt parenting obligations, many American mothers opted for part-time work or moved in and out of the labor force. If in time they decided to resume a career, they normally had to settle for positions that were several rungs down the ladder from men of comparable age.[39]

Many of the mothers who continued to be employed outside the home struggled hard to combine both family and work. Though their husbands generally helped a little more around the house than they had in earlier eras, most of the men had trouble coming to grips with this "revolution at home," as one scholar called it.[40] Men remembered, or thought they did, the golden age of their own childhoods, when *their* mothers had stayed at home, at least until their children had been old enough to go to school. *Their* fathers had not been expected to do a great deal of domestic work. The pull of sweet reminiscence aroused a sharp sense of loss.

Having put in long hours at the factory or the office, these husbands expected to rest when they came home. When their working wives, equally tired, asked for help, husbands often objected or procrastinated. When their wives complained, many husbands distanced themselves emotionally. Trying to keep the peace, most wives continued to do the cooking and cleaning, including virtually all of the dirty work, such as scrubbing

38. *Stat. Abst.*, 2002, 373.
39. Fuchs, *Women's Quest for Economic Equality*, 120–21, 130–38.
40. Arlie Hochschild with Anne Machung, *The Second Shift: Working Parents and the Revolution at Home* (New York, 1989).

toilets. They handled the shopping and the hassles involved with getting appliances repaired. And they were normally the first to attend to the needs and demands of their children. Though new labor-saving appliances eased their tasks a little, the double shift remained burdensome. It exposed the simple fact that women had not achieved parity at home. By the 1970s, one careful study concluded, wives who were also in the labor force worked (at home and outside the home) fifteen more hours per week than their husbands did. Over the course of a year this was an extra twenty-four days.[41]

Many wives necessarily settled for compromises. Some lacked the time to prepare home-cooked meals, relying instead on one of the most significant domestic additions of the era, the microwave oven. First introduced in 1974, microwaves enabled people to nuke leftovers and to eat on the run, thereby threatening the family supper hour. Still other family members regularly picked up fast food and ate it away from home, and in doing so helped to promote the fantastic growth of chains such as McDonald's. By the 1990s, physicians and nutritionists were insisting that fast food, along with a sedentary life featuring television and automobiles, was creating an "epidemic" of obesity, especially among children.[42]

It is possible, as some observers have argued, that stress in the family since the 1950s—not new in any event—has been exaggerated. After all, most late twentieth-century parents had fewer children.[43] Families in which both parents have jobs outside the home normally earn much more income in real dollars than families with one earner. Though these parents often lead hectic lives, they are far less likely to be poor. And because jobs were becoming increasingly white-collar in nature, parents were not so apt to be physically exhausted when they got home. Nostalgia for the Good Old Days dimmed memories of harsh realities of earlier years and obscured gains in the new era.

Still, there was no doubting the magnitude of the seismic shift in America's work and gender relationships, a shift that had become especially powerful by the 1970s. However working wives coped, they were weary from their "double day," which exacerbated domestic strife. "You're on duty at work," one wife complained. "You come home, and you're on duty. Then

41. Hochschild, *The Second Shift*, 2–3, 25–26, 214–15. Not much appeared to change in later years. A Labor Department survey of full-time workers (aged twenty-five to fifty-four) in 2004 concluded that women employed outside the home spent twice as much time (three hours a day) as men doing household chores and taking care of children. *New York Times*, Sept. 15, 2004.

42. Eric Schlosser, *Fast Food Nation: The Dark Side of the American Meal* (Boston, 2001).

43. *New York Times*, Aug. 25, 1999.

you go back to work, and you're on duty." Some women observed mordantly, "What I really need is a wife." Arguments between husbands and wives erupted again and again over domestic rights and responsibilities. They were the most frequently cited source of divorce during these years.[44]

ALL THESE CONTROVERSIES over sex and family life would have been cause enough for concern even in sunny economic times. But the late 1970s and early 1980s were not so sunny. Though ongoing advances in science and technology brightened a few future possibilities, discouraging developments, while often exaggerated in the media, darkened the mood of Americans and cast an especially deep shadow on those difficult years, which were in many ways the gloomiest of the late twentieth century.

First, the good economic news. A minority of Americans had reason to be relatively happy about rewards from the economy at the time. Among them, as always in the celebrity-conscious world of the late twentieth century, were popular performers and professional athletes. In 1975, Stevie Wonder signed a recording contract for $13 million. James "Catfish" Hunter, a top Major League Baseball pitcher, broke with the Oakland A's following the 1974 season, when he had earned $100,000. After winning an arbitration battle that freed him from the A's, he auctioned himself off to the New York Yankees, who signed him to a five-year contract for $3.25 million plus extras. It was by far the largest amount ever paid to a player before that time. Pressure from the Major League Baseball Players Union—the most successful labor union of the 1970s—then helped to end the "reserve clause" that had bound players to their owners. "Free agency" in Major League Baseball took hold. Average Major League Baseball salaries jumped from $52,300 in 1976 to $146,500 in 1980.[45]

Among other Americans whose economic prospects improved at the time, many lived in the South and West, which witnessed unprecedented economic and population growth in the 1970s. These years were pivotal in the late twentieth-century transformation of the Sunbelt, which, though remaining the poorest region of the nation, gained increasing cultural, economic, and political influence over time. Some of its cultural manifestations—country music, auto racing—later spread nationwide.[46]

44. Hochschild, *Second Shift*, x, 204–7.
45. And to $2.49 million by opening day of 2004. *Providence Journal*, April 4, 2004. See also Charles Korr, *The End of Baseball as We Knew It: The Players Union, 1960–1981* (Urbana, 2002).
46. Bruce Schulman, *From Cotton Belt to Sun Belt: Federal Policy, Economic Development, and the Transformation of the South, 1938–1980* (New York, 1991); Joshua Zeitz, "Dixie's Victory," *American Heritage*, Aug./Sept. 2002, 46–55.

The rapid expansion of air-conditioning to the region did a great deal to drive this growth. Though one southern homeowner grumbled that AC was a "damn-fool invention of the Yankees," most people were eager to install it. By 1980, 73 percent of southern homes had air-conditioning, as opposed to only 18 percent in 1960. "General Electric," one wit observed, "has proved a more devastating invader than General Sherman."[47]

The federal government, too, had already been promoting economic growth in the South and West, both by financing a vast expansion of the interstate highway system and by awarding a host of defense and space contracts to these regions. It also underwrote farm programs that advanced agribusiness interests. Observing the growing army of lobbyists for such programs, William Faulkner had commented:"We no longer farm in Mississippi cotton fields. We farm now in Washington corridors and Congressional committee rooms."[48] As economic stagnation hit the Northeast and the Midwest—the Rust Belt of the 1970s—many employers relocated to the South, a land of lower labor costs. Cities like Houston, Phoenix, Dallas, and San Diego boomed as never before. Overall per capita income in the South rose from 60 percent of the national average in 1960 to 80 percent in 1980.[49] Frances FitzGerald, who visited varied American communities in the 1970s, was one of many contemporaries fascinated by the rise of the "New" South. This was an area, she wrote, of "sleek, landscaped manufacturing plants and men in polyester suits riding local commuter airlines."[50]

The explosive growth of a new realm of business—personal computers—helped other areas, such as Seattle and "Silicon Valley," California, to flourish in the late 1970s and 1980s. In 1975, Bill Gates dropped out of Harvard to join his friend Paul Allen in founding Microsoft (originally Micro-soft), a software company that was booming by the 1980s. Their motto was "A personal computer on every desk and in every home." In early 1977, Steven Jobs and Stephen Wozniak, who in 1976 had founded Apple Computer, brought out the Apple II, which soon dominated a great new market for home computers.[51] The Apple II cost $1,298. As the price

47. Raymond Arsenault, "The End of a Long Hot Summer: The Air Conditioner and Southern Culture," *Journal of Southern History* 50 (Nov. 1984), 597–628.
48. Cited in Bruce Schulman, *The Seventies: The Great Shift in American Culture, Society, and Politics* (New York, 2001), 112.
49. Robert Samuelson, *The Good Life and Its Discontents: The American Dream in the Age of Entitlement, 1945–1995* (New York, 1995), 37.
50. Frances FitzGerald, *Cities on a Hill: A Journey Through Contemporary American Cultures* (New York, 1986), 17.
51. $1,298 was equivalent to $4,500 or more in the early 2000s.

fell and computer memory increased, sales climbed rapidly. By the end of 1980, Apple Computer was valued at $1.8 billion, more than the Ford Motor Company or the Chase Manhattan Bank.[52] In 1982, *Time* named the computer its Man of the Year, and by 1983, as ownership of personal computers grew explosively, Microsoft's motto seemed prophetic.

It was not widely noted at the time, but computer technology owed a great deal of its early development to the Cold War, which stimulated basic and applied research in the field, especially after the enormous promise of silicon chips had become recognized in the late 1950s. The Pentagon was a key supporter of research, especially at universities, which advanced other technological changes. One of these was the Global Positioning System (GPS), a network of twenty-four satellites that could pinpoint locations on earth. The Defense Department started an experimental GPS system in 1978. The government also advanced exploration in space, dispatching the first Shuttle test flight in 1977. More significant scientifically was the launching of probes into space, notably the spectacular Viking I and Viking II in 1976 and Voyager I and Voyager II in 1977. The Vikings soft-landed on Mars, sending back color photos of the planet's surface along with scientific data.[53] The Voyagers journeyed far into space to provide additional data on the planets. Still out there in the early 2000s, these left the solar system and are expected to send back information until their electricity runs out in 2020.

In time, an especially influential governmental research effort in these years was the development, also overseen by the Pentagon, of an interlocking network of giant computers working to advance America's military preparedness. This effort, fairly well advanced by the mid-1970s, was largely unknown to the public, but with the further aid of research that was under way in Europe, it was a fundamental scientific and technological basis for the network of computers—the Internet—that began to affect many aspects of life in the 1990s.[54]

Other scientific, engineering, and technological developments captured the imagination of many Americans in the late 1970s and 1980s. One was the federally aided completion in 1977—over the opposition of environmentalists—of an 800-mile Trans-Alaska Pipeline, which enabled oil to

---

52. Thomas McCraw, *American Business, 1920–2000: How It Worked* (Wheeling, Ill., 2000), 194–95; Timothy Moy, "Culture, Technology, and the Cult of Tech in the 1970s," in Bailey and Farber, eds., *America in the Seventies*, 208–27; Frum, *How We Got Here*, 70.

53. For Viking I, see *New York Times*, July 21, 1976.

54. See chapter 11.

flow from Arctic regions of Alaska to the northern Pacific.[55] Consumers welcomed a host of developments, among them the growth of cable TV. ESPN, appearing in 1979, ultimately soon brought sports to millions of fans, and C-SPAN, starting in the same year, began to offer coverage of the House of Representatives. Also pleasing consumers at the time were a host of new cordless household appliances using rechargeable battery packs—hand-held vacuums, hedge-trimmers, and screwdrivers—that had been developed to serve space exploration. Other advances of the era led to the first human magnetic resonance imaging scans (MRIs), color photocopiers, and the beginnings—with the arrival of synthetic insulin and growth hormone in 1979—of what was soon to become a growth industry: biotechnology. In 1975, videocassette recorders hit the market, as did Miller Lite, the first light beer. In 1978, Tamoxifen, a new weapon in the war against breast cancer, was marketed, and the first "test tube" (in vitro) baby was born. In 1979, the Sony Walkman went on sale in stores.

These scientific and technological developments, including the surge in computerization, did not contribute a great deal to economic growth in the late 1970s. Nevertheless, the economy did move slowly ahead following the doldrums of 1973–74, especially between 1977 and early 1979. Average per capita disposable personal income rose from $5,470 in 1975 to $8,869 in 1980.[56] In real dollars this was a growth rate of approximately 2 percent per year. Though other economies, notably those of West Germany and Japan, continued to expand at faster rates, and though some key domestic industries, such as automobile production and steel, remained depressed, many other American industries coped all right during these difficult times. Production in manufacturing held its share (around 25 percent) of the world market in the 1970s.

The United States, having pressed in the 1940s to lower trade barriers and to promote global economic interdependence that would advance national prosperity, continued in the 1970s to dominate such key institutions as the International Monetary Fund and the World Bank, which exerted wide influence abroad. America remained number one in the world in the manufacture and sale of aircraft, industrial and agricultural chemicals, engines, turbines, and office computing machines, and number two in the fields of plastics, drugs, and various forms of electrical machinery.[57] The American standard of living—characterized among other

55. Mike Coppock, "Oil from the Land of the Midnight Sun," *American History* 39 (Oct. 1994), 40–48.
56. *Stat. Abst.*, 2002, 422.
57. Joseph Nye, *Bound to Lead: The Changing Nature of American Power* (New York, 1990), 74–78; Robert Collins, *More: The Politics of Economic Growth in Postwar America* (New York, 2000), 130–31.

things by bigger houses, cheaper food, enlarging consumer choice, and improving quality of many goods and services—was still the highest in the world. Facts like these confirm two key points about economic life in the late 1970s: Most Americans were not suffering as calamitously from "de-industrialization" as some pessimists claimed, and the nation was not in long-range economic "decline." Titles of contemporary jeremiads, such as Andrew Hacker's *Decline of the American Era*, exaggerated the economic dangers facing the United States in the 1970s.[58] What these pessimistic accounts should have emphasized was that many Americans, benefiting from living in a still dynamic, risk-taking, and resource-rich country, were doing a little better but often felt a little worse.

BUT FOREBODINGS SUCH AS HACKER'S did rest on a good deal of bad economic news in the late 1970s. A number of worrisome developments in those years indicated that the American economy, while strong in many ways, was not so vibrant as it had been in the Good Old Days. These developments, in turn, threatened yet another right that many Americans had always cherished: the right to advance their material well-being in life.

The stagflation that had descended in the early 1970s persisted into the early 1980s. A key source of this misery was long-range and structural: the movement of the American economy (like other industrialized economies) from a base in manufacturing toward a "post-industrial" society that depended more heavily on services, where technological advances were normally small, where gains in productivity were modest, and where (in many cases) wages or salaries were relatively low. In retrospect, it appears that this transition was especially sharp and painful in the 1970s. It was estimated that service jobs, already 60 percent of the total in 1970, increased to 70 percent by 1980.[59] Increases in American productivity, which had averaged more than 3 percent per year between 1947 and 1965, fell to 2.4 percent per year between 1965 and 1970, and to 1.2 percent between 1973 and 1979.[60]

---

58. (New York, 1970). A later, best-selling lament about American decline was Paul Kennedy's *The Rise and Fall of the Great Powers: Economic Change and Military Conflict from 1500 to 2000* (New York, 1987). See chapter 6.
59. Service sector jobs rose to become an estimated 80 percent of all jobs in America's private sector by 2000. *New York Times*, Nov. 30, 2003.
60. Robert Samuelson, "The Age of Inflation," *New Republic*, May 13, 2002, 32–41; Frank Levy, *The New Dollars and Dreams: American Incomes and Economic Change* (New York, 1998), 59.

Other troubling trends, notably greater economic competition from abroad, compounded these problems. West Germany and Japan, energetically emphasizing research and development, offered sharp challenges. Japanese cars captured 23 percent of the American market by 1979, at which time Susan Ford, daughter of the former president, announced in a TV ad, "Take it from a Ford, drive Subaru."[61] Chrysler, battered by Japanese car imports, lost billions and was rescued in 1980 only when President Jimmy Carter signed into law a highly controversial $1.5 billion federal bailout.[62]

Finding jobs for the many millions of women and baby boomers who were looking for employment posed special difficulties. Mechanization in struggling sectors of the economy, notably coal mining and cotton textiles, cut back on employment in these areas. As earlier, small farmers and farm workers found it hard to make a living.[63] Residents in pockets of rural poverty, such as the Mississippi Delta area and Appalachia, suffered badly. Native Americans on reservations continued to face a wide range of economic ills, notably poverty. Many jobs, as in radio and television manufacturing, moved abroad. Thanks to these and other problems, unemployment rates, which had averaged 4.7 percent per year between the late 1960s and 1973, rose to an average of 7.4 percent between 1973 and 1986. Though the government's official poverty rate remained fairly stable (generally between 12 and 13 percent of the population in the 1970s), the overall population of the United States, thanks to increasing immigration, rose gradually, and the number of poor people increased between 1970 and 1980 from 25 to 29 million.[64]

Meanwhile, the federal minimum wage, at $2.10 an hour in 1975, was hiked in stages to $3.35 an hour by 1981, but the increases failed to keep pace with rapidly rising prices. The real wages of full-time male production workers stagnated, not only in the late 1970s but also for the next twenty-five-odd years.[65] Household debt shot up. These were key reasons,

61. Alfred Eckes Jr. and Thomas Zeiler, *Globalization in the American Century* (New York, 2003), 199.
62. In 2000, Chrysler, in trouble again, was bought by Daimler Benz, a German company, and then became DaimlerChrysler.
63. Godfrey Hodgson, *More Equal than Others: America from Nixon to the New Century* (Princeton, 2004), 207–9.
64. *Stat. Abst.*, 2002, 441.
65. McCraw, *American Business*, 163–64; *New York Times*, Feb. 17, 2003. Better benefits offset some of this stagnation, but not enough to enable many of these workers to move ahead.

of course, why so many wives looked for employment. When income in-equality in America increased, as it did with greater force in the 1980s and 1990s, the households that managed the best were those with more than one adult wage earner.

Workers complained bitterly that corporations were holding down wages, demanding faster output, and "outsourcing" jobs to the "cheap labor South" and to overseas locations. Some workers embraced protectionism, attach-ing bumper stickers to their cars that read: "BUY AMERICAN; THE JOB YOU SAVE MAY BE YOUR OWN." A few even took sledgehammers to Toyotas.[66] A wave of governmental deregulation in the late 1970s—of airlines, trucking, and communications—expanded the decision-making power of corporate lead-ers and further alarmed workers. Many employees worried above all about job security. This was probably no more endangered than in the past—blue-collar jobs had never been very secure, and they declined in number over time as a percentage of all jobs—but scare stories in the media publi-cized the issue, which was real for many people (including a considerable number holding white-collar positions). The stories added to a general perception that the American economy was heading for catastrophe, and described a real and disturbing trend: rising inequality of income.

The anger of American workers became especially hot in 1974, when strikes and lockouts affected 1.8 million employees, resulting in the loss of 31.8 million working days, a number that had been surpassed only twice in American history (1970 and 1971).[67] Later in the 1970s, losses in working days caused by strikes and lockouts ebbed a little but still averaged more than 20 million a year. This was considerably higher than the number of idle days in the 1960s and than were to be lost in most years of the 1980s, when union power dramatically decreased.[68] The most bitter controversy of the 1970s, a strike of coal miners that erupted in December 1977 and lasted more than three months, featured violence in Utah and Ohio.

Labor unions backed many of these stoppages, but except among teach-ers and other public service workers, their power, slipping since the mid-1950s, weakened considerably in the 1970s. In 1953, an all-time high of 35 percent of American non-farm workers had belonged to unions. This per-centage fell to 29 by 1973 and to 20 by 1983 (and to 13.5 by 2001).[69] These

66. Nelson Lichtenstein, *State of the Union: A Century of American Labor* (Princeton, 2002), 80–84, 202.
67. *Stat. Abst.*, 2002, 410. These numbers exclude stoppages involving fewer than 1,000 workers and lasting less than one day.
68. These numbers plummeted in the 1990s, to between 4 and 5 million days idle be-tween 1990 and 1998 and to 2 million in the prosperous year of 1999. Ibid.
69. Lichtenstein, *State of the Union*, 186; *Stat. Abst.*, 2002, 412.

dramatic declines stemmed in part from the complacent leadership of George Meany, head of the AFL-CIO from 1955 to 1979, and his aides. Meany asked, "Why should we worry about organizing people who do not want to be organized?"[70] More generally, the decline of unions reflected larger structural developments, such as generally tough corporate attitudes toward unions; the movement of jobs to the South and West, where organized labor had historically been weak; and increases in the numbers of women, part-time, and service employees, who were harder to organize. The traditional core of union power in America, manufacturing workers, shrank as a percentage of the national labor force.

For millions of Americans in the late 1970s, especially production workers, whose pay stagnated in real dollars, inflation was the archvillain of the age.[71] The cost of living rose between 1973 and 1983 at an average annual rate of 8.2 percent, more than double the rate between 1963 and 1973. This was the highest such increase for any ten-year period in the history of the United States.[72] The cost of a first class postage stamp, 8 cents in 1974, jumped to 20 cents by 1981 (and to 37 cents in 2002). A McDonald's hamburger cost 15 cents in 1967 and 50 cents by the early 1980s.

Various forces propelled this inflationary spiral in the mid-1970s, including large government deficits that had mounted to pay for the Vietnam War, and consumer demands that exceeded supplies. Huge hikes in oil prices, which leapt from $3 to $34 a barrel between the end of 1973 and the summer of 1979, spiked the already strong inflationary surge.[73] On June 13, 1979, 58 percent of American service stations, out of gasoline, turned off their pumps. Long lines of cars snaked around corners and awaited gasoline from stations that had not closed. Fights broke out among motorists. The oil crisis of 1979, like the embargo of 1973–74, heightened popular perceptions that America was vulnerable—nearly helpless—before economic onslaughts such as these.

The impact of rising taxes, which had already provoked sharp protests in the 1960s, further inflamed tempers and led to widespread grass-roots protests by the late 1970s. Workers who received pay raises—as from cost-of-living clauses in union contracts—often entered into higher income

70. Lichtenstein, State of the Union, 197.

71. Samuelson, "The Age of Inflation."

72. McCraw, American Business, 156–57; Michael Bernstein, "Understanding American Economic Decline: The Contours of the Late Twentieth Century Experience," in Bernstein and David Adler, eds., Understanding American Economic Decline (New York, 1994), 3–33.

73. New York Times, April 4, 2004.

tax brackets. This was "bracket creep," which left these taxpayers even further behind in the struggle to cope with the rapidly upward surge of prices. Totals paid in Social Security payroll taxes also increased significantly between 1964 and 1980. Capital gains taxes, which went up in the late 1970s, alienated many stockholders, helping to drive some of them out of the market altogether.[74]

Then there were property taxes, some of which hit middle-class homeowners especially hard and incited a range of protests in the 1960s and early 1970s. In 1978, a staunchly anti–New Deal Republican and activist, Howard Jarvis, helped to lead a powerful popular revolt in California against such taxes, which (because of new assessments and rising land values) had become considerably higher than those in most other states. This protest, leading to a popular referendum on so-called Proposition 13, aroused enormous enthusiasm in California and captured the attention of people throughout the nation. In June, Prop 13 carried, two to one, thereby reducing these taxes by 57 percent and seriously threatening public education and other government services. It especially benefited large corporations and wealthy homeowners. Prop 13 also amended the state constitution, by requiring a two-thirds vote in the legislature to increase state taxes and two-thirds of voters to approve any new local levies.[75]

The New York Times, which closely observed the fight for Proposition 13, lamented that the outcome signified a "primal scream by the People against Big Government."[76] This was hardly an exaggeration, for the mission of Jarvis and his many allies had tapped into—and further excited—widespread popular rage throughout the United States against high public spending as well as taxes. Prop 13 quickly inspired successful crusades against property taxes in thirty-seven states and against income taxes in twenty-eight states.[77] By 1980, millions of aroused taxpayers (though calling for better schools, roads, and other public services) were demanding a rollback of big government. They brought formidable strength to a surge of conservative activism that was beginning to challenge American liberalism and to reshape national politics.

74. Samuelson, "Age of Inflation," noted that the percentage of Americans in the stock market decreased during the 1970s from 15 to 13.
75. Robert Self, American Babylon: Race and the Struggle for Postwar Oakland (Princeton, 2003), 319–27.
76. Haynes Johnson, Sleepwalking Through History: America in the Reagan Years (New York, 1991), 68.
77. Schulman, The Seventies, 210–12.

NOTWITHSTANDING THESE MANY WORRISOME DEVELOPMENTS, it was possible to look back on the 1970s with some satisfaction. Most social programs that had developed or been liberalized in the 1960s and early 1970s—the historic civil rights laws for blacks; Medicare for the elderly; Medicaid for many of the poor; Supplementary Security Income that allotted federal aid to the indigent aged, blind, and disabled; various environmental statutes, such as the Clean Air Act of 1970—enjoyed fairly broad consensus by the 1980s and were bettering the lives of millions of people. Some older programs, like Social Security and SSI, were indexed in the early 1970s so as to keep pace with inflation, thereby markedly reducing the incidence of poverty among the elderly. Significant Supreme Court decisions of the 1960s that had guaranteed greater legal protection to the welfare poor, the mentally ill, and criminal defendants remained the law of the land.[78]

The advance of rights-consciousness in the 1970s added to these protections. Yielding to governmental pressure, southern public schools were desegregating at last; affirmative action procedures remained in place for blacks and other minorities; activists for women's rights, though embattled, were stronger than ever before; and other groups—the handicapped, school children with limited English—were securing entitlements that would have been unimaginable in the early 1960s. In 1973, Congress approved the Rehabilitation Act, which prohibited federal agencies and programs receiving federal funds from discriminating against individuals with disabilities.[79] Delighted advocates hailed it as the "Civil Rights for the Handicapped Act." Congress also enacted the Age Discrimination in Employment Act, which toughened existing laws protecting workers from such biases, and (in 1975) the Education for All Handicapped Children Act, which greatly advanced the civil rights of disabled schoolchildren. A few activists welcomed a ruling in 1976 that they hoped would promote yet another right: to die. In that year New Jersey's Supreme Court said that the family of twenty-two-year-old Karen Ann Quinlan, who had been in a vegetative state since 1975, might have her detached from a respirator.[80]

Scattered signs in the 1970s also suggested that Americans, for all their divisions, were becoming more cooperative and less judgmental than earlier.

78. Samuel Walker, *The Rights Revolution: Rights and Community in Modern America* (New York, 1998), 180–83.
79. See Edward Berkowitz, *Disabled Policy: America's Programs for the Handicapped* (New York, 1987).
80. This was done, but Quinlan was able to breathe on her own. She remained in a coma for almost ten years before dying from pneumonia at the age of thirty-one in 1985.

Thanks in part to the rise over time in educational levels, people were becoming more tolerant. Anti-Semitism and anti-Catholicism, for instance, were becoming less visible than they used to be. Ethnic and religious divisions, which had remained sharp in the 1950s, were slowly softening, especially among the young. Though some Americans lashed out at the greed, as they saw it, of big businessmen and the very rich, class resentments, such as existed in some European societies, continued to be muted. On the contrary, popular faith in the possibility of socio-economic advancement, perhaps enhanced by slowly rising access to higher education, seemed to remain strong, at least among white people.[81]

Landmarks of popular culture in the late 1970s offered signs that many Americans still cherished optimistic visions of the future. Just as the phenomenal success of *Roots* may have indicated a willingness on the part of millions of people to respect the courage of blacks, so did another blockbuster of 1977, the movie *Star Wars*, suggest the continuing salience of a historically durable American dream: the power of faith and struggle to achieve victory against high odds. The most commercially successful movie of all time, *Star Wars* was a religious and futuristic tale that conveyed a simple moral: Good (heroic Jedi knights) wins over evil, in this case an empire. Inspirational in difficult times, *Star Wars* appealed in part because its special effects were marvelous, and in part because its optimistic message was so characteristically American.

Rocky, a very different hit movie of the previous year, delivered a similar message. Sylvester Stallone, a rags-to-riches story in his own life, played Rocky Balboa, a bloodied boxer who at the end lost the big fight, but who showed great courage and rugged individualism and therefore prevailed (implausibly but in a heart-warming way) against almost everything else. Rocky won self-respect and the girl. Events that patriotically recognized the nation's bicentennial in that year also featured upbeat themes. These commemorations, highlighting the spirit of hardworking colonial housewives, entrepreneurial rural artisans, and self-reliant yeoman farmers, celebrated the stalwart virtues that had supposedly made the nation great. Supreme Court Chief Justice Warren Burger, a conservative, performed as a highly visible orchestrator of these hymns of praise to self-reliance and can-do values.

81. David Whitman, *The Optimism Gap: The I'm OK—They're Not Syndrome and the Myth of American Decline* (New York, 1998), 55–58; Daniel McMurrer and Isabel Sawhill, "The Declining Importance of Class," Urban Institute Report no. 4 (April 1997).

AMERICANS WHO SAVORED UPLIFTING MOVIES and celebrations such as these were in various ways contesting four interrelated social developments that prompted widely resonating laments in the late 1970s. The first lament—initially voiced by Tom Wolfe in 1976—was that the 1970s were the "Me Decade."[82] Three years later, Christopher Lasch, a historian, pursued similar themes in a popular book, *The Culture of Narcissism*.[83] Wolfe mainly damned what he considered to be the hedonism of American culture. He also satirized the surge in popularity of religious fads, obsessions, and enthusiasms, ranging from jogging and health foods to encounter groups and transactional psychology. All of these, Wolfe wrote, exposed a foolishly self-absorbed quest to find the "divine spark which is me." His full title was "The Me Decade and the Third Great Awakening."

Lasch, deadly serious, focused less on ridiculing hedonism than on documenting the anxiety that he thought was affecting family life and driving up divorce rates. He complained that Americans were becoming wrapped up in a "therapeutic culture" manipulated by self-appointed experts adept at psychobabble. Like Wolfe, though, he thought that obsessive self-concern aimed at promoting self-realization and personal fulfillment—that is, narcissism—was unraveling the fabric of American life. He asserted that a "lust for immediate gratification pervades American society from top to bottom. There is a universal concern with the self."[84]

Whether these Jeremiahs were accurate is hard to say. Many foreign observers, including Pope John Paul II, who in 1979 lambasted what he regarded as America's callousness toward its poor people, emphatically seconded them. Wolfe and Lasch, moreover, belonged to a long American line of critics, beginning with the Puritans, who had railed against materialism and shallow self-absorption. They offered large generalizations that might equally have been deployed (and later were) to characterize other decades. Still, they received a wide hearing in the late 1970s. Wolfe, a colorful journalist and speaker who had earned a doctoral degree in American studies from Yale, was hailed as a smart social critic. Lasch, to his surprise, found that his book became a best-seller. In 1979, President Carter invited him to the White House. Granted only a short visit with the president, Lasch was not sure if Carter, who prided himself on his ability as a speed-reader, had seriously perused his book. But Carter

82. "The Me Decade and the Third Great Awakening" (1976), rpt. in Wolfe, *The Purple Decades* (New York, 1983), 265–96.
83. Subtitled *American Life in an Age of Diminishing Expectations* (New York, 1979).
84. Ibid., 213.

soon echoed the professor, telling the nation that a vast "emptiness" had gripped Americans, who were slaves to the "worship of self-indulgence and consumption."

A second lament that swelled in the late 1970s—and later—was similar: that Americans were losing the sense of civic-mindedness, or "community," that had made the nation strong. Pessimists of this persuasion, who also inherited a long American tradition, identified a number of trends to make their case. One, they said, was the rise of narrow group-consciousness, notably as expressed by "selfish interests" that were demanding larger rights and entitlements: A rights revolution, though benefiting the nation in some ways, was also fragmenting America.[85] Community-conscious critics highlighted many manifestations of decline: a falling-off in voting and political participation; the growing power of mega-retailers, which were driving mom-and-pop stores out of business; the rising commercialization of public space, notably via the expansion of vast, privately owned malls; the spread of "niche" advertising—such as appeals to the "Pepsi Generation"— and of political campaign tactics catering to specific constituencies, thereby further segmenting the nation; and, more generally, the insatiable appetite that Americans seemed to be developing for private, personal pleasure and for the consumption of goods.

Critics such as these had still other grievances with social changes in the 1970s: the sprouting of gated or demographically homogeneous housing developments, such as Sun City, Florida, which by the early 1970s had 8,500 residents, virtually all of them middle-class people over the age of sixty; the decline of newspaper circulation (only 51 percent of adults read the papers by 1990, down from 73 percent in 1970); and the collapse of highly regarded newspapers such as the *Chicago Daily News* in 1978. A *bête noire* of many critics was television, which had become the most popular source of news and of entertainment. Americans on the average watched for four hours a day in 1975. Critics of TV were certain that it coarsened taste, isolated people, and damaged community activity. Television, they sniped, was truly a medium: because it was neither rare nor well done.[86]

---

85. For discussion of these complaints see Mary Ann Glendon, *Rights Talk: The Impoverishment of Political Discourse* (New York, 1991).
86. For material relating to newspapers, see Glendon, *Rights Talk*, x; for television, Putnam, *Bowling Alone: The Collapse and Revival of American Community* (New York, 2000), 221–22; for Sun City, FitzGerald, *Cities on a Hill*, 203–45. For discussion of the uses of public space, niche advertising, and consumerism, see Lizabeth Cohen, *A Consumer's Republic: The Politics of Mass Consumption in Postwar America* (New York, 2002), 288–309.

A third lament that gained force in the late 1970s targeted what many worried contemporaries considered the spread of disrespect for authority. "Punk rock" groups such as Britain's Sex Pistols, which attracted many American young people in the mid-1970s, struck critics as contemptuous of all civilized values. Public opinion polls revealed that ever increasing percentages of Americans distrusted public officials. Cool and often cynical television shows that flourished in the late 1970s, such as 60 *Minutes* and *Saturday Night Live*, were said to encourage such attitudes. So were popular books, such as Carl Bernstein and Bob Woodward's *All the President's Men* (1974), a best-seller that highlighted the lying of politicians during the Watergate scandal. A film version of the book did well at the box office in 1976.

Politicians were by no means the only group of people whose prestige dimmed in the 1970s. Once-powerful hierarchies—the army, the Catholic Church—were struggling to cope with internal dissension, much of which had broken out as a result of the social and cultural turmoil of the 1960s, and more specifically as a result of the Vietnam War and the Second Vatican Council ("Vatican II"), which between 1962 and 1965 had introduced a series of progressive reforms that divided Catholics throughout the world. Universities, while far more peaceful than they had been at the peak of anti-war demonstrations in the late 1960s and early 1970s, continued to face challenges from students, many of whom no longer bowed as readily as they had in the past to the dicta of deans. Corporate leaders and lawyers, frequently stereotyped as cold and avaricious, were if anything more widely targeted than they had been in earlier years. Public opinion polls revealed that the percentage of Americans who believed that "most people can be trusted" dropped from 55 in 1960 to 45 in 1975—and to 38 by 1985.[87]

Even physicians, a prestigious group that had been idolized in earlier TV shows like *Marcus Welby, M.D.* and *Dr. Kildare*, lost some of their luster. By the mid-1970s, it was obvious that a governmentally initiated "war on cancer" initiated in the late 1960s had been wildly oversold. Feminists and others insisted that the (male) "establishment" treatment for breast cancer, radical mastectomy, was often unnecessary. Many of these anti-authoritarian dissidents bemoaned a troubling contradiction that then and later seemed to be afflicting American medicine: Highly touted (and real) advances in costly medical technology coexisted with apparent declines in the quality of personal care from physicians.

87. Putnam, *Bowling Alone*, 140.

Paralleling doubts about authority figures was a widespread sense that the government had engaged in conspiracies and cover-ups. One of these supposed cover-ups, that authorities had suppressed evidence of aliens landing in Roswell, New Mexico, in 1947, was of long standing—and of no demonstrable veracity. Another, the belief that a conspiracy of people, perhaps involving the Mafia, perhaps involving the CIA, had been involved in killing President Kennedy, had a large following. Roughly 50 percent of Americans had always doubted the Warren Commission Report of 1964, which had named Lee Harvey Oswald as the lone gunman. Though doubters such as these never produced convincing evidence to support the ideas that lurked in the dark and feverish corners of their imaginations, they nonetheless engaged the attention of millions of people. By the early 1980s, 80 percent of Americans appeared to credit various conspiratorial theories surrounding the assassination of the president.[88]

Some conspiracies of the era were real. Americans had only to recall the dissembling of Lyndon Johnson and his advisers about the Gulf of Tonkin incident off Vietnam in 1964, or the cover-up by Nixon of events surrounding the Watergate break-in. In 1974, the *New York Times* reported that covert CIA activity between 1970 and 1973 had helped to overthrow the democratically elected government of Salvador Allende of Chile, a Marxist who died during the coup on September 11, 1973. General Augusto Pinochet, who ousted him, established a brutal dictatorship lasting sixteen years. In June 1975, a commission headed by Vice President Nelson Rockefeller disclosed that officials working for the CIA and the FBI had engaged in illegal wiretapping, opened people's mail, and assembled files on 300,000 citizens. A few months later, a Senate select committee chaired by Senator Frank Church of Idaho reported that the CIA, sometimes working with organized crime, had plotted to kill world leaders such as Fidel Castro of Cuba, Rafael Trujillo of the Dominican Republic, and Patrice Lumumba of the Congo. The CIA, Church had said earlier, was a "rogue elephant," but his committee's subsequent report left open the possibility that agency officials trying to kill Castro had been doing the bidding of higher-ups, that is, of President Kennedy, Attorney General Robert Kennedy, and others.[89]

88. *Providence Journal*, Nov. 22, 2003. For Kennedy's assassination, see Gerald Posner, *Case Closed: Lee Harvey Oswald and the Assassination of JFK* (New York, 1993); and Max Holland, *The Kennedy Assassination Tapes: The White House Conversations of Lyndon B. Johnson Regarding the Assassination, the Warren Commission, and the Aftermath* (New York, 2004).
89. Richard Powers, "The Failure," *New York Review of Books*, April 29, 2004, 4–6.

The sensational activities of the Church Committee led to the establishment for the first time of formal congressional oversight of American intelligence affairs: permanent select committees on intelligence in both houses. They also moved President Ford to act. In February 1976, he issued an order that expanded executive control over intelligence operations and that declared, "No employee of the U.S. government shall engage in, or conspire to engage in, political assassination."[90] A month later his attorney general, Edward Levi, slapped sharp restrictions on the FBI's authority to conduct investigations of domestic political groups, such as left- or right-wing extremists. Actions such as these indicated that Congress, the bit in its teeth, was charging ahead to challenge the power of the presidency. Much later, after terrorists succeeded in killing thousands of Americans on September 11, 2001, these restrictions, which remained in force, were said to have had a role in preventing the FBI from moving proactively against potentially violent extremists in the United States.[91]

Other rumors of plots persisted. In 1978–79 a select House committee, relying on a police recording, concluded that more than one assassin — one of them probably shooting from a grassy knoll near the motorcade route — had fired at Kennedy in 1963.[92] A conspiracy, the committee added, had also been behind the slaying of the Reverend Martin Luther King Jr. With claims of conspiracy emanating from so many official sources, who needed to fall back on paranoid suspicions?

Many critics in the mid-1970s raised a fourth lament: that the nation had to pare back its ambitions. This cry for restraint, rooted in the belief that Americans must shake off their lust for consumption, was perhaps the most widespread lament of all at the time. As California governor Jerry Brown put it, the United States had to realize that it had entered an "Age of Limits." The British author E. E. Schumacher's *Small Is Beautiful* (1973), a best seller on both sides of the Atlantic in the mid-1970s, called for a "maximum of well-being with the minimum of consumption." In 1977, Schumacher enjoyed a triumphal tour of the United States, during which Brown, Ralph Nader, and many others lionized him. President Carter

90. John Greene, *The Presidency of Gerald R. Ford* (Lawrence, Kans., 1995), 107–15.

91. Richard Powers, "A Bomb with a Long Fuse: 9/11 and the FBI 'Reforms' of the 1970s," *American History* 39 (Dec. 2004), 43–47.

92. Robert Goldberg, *Enemies Within: The Cult of Conspiracy in Modern America* (New Haven, 2001), 253–60. In 1982, a review by the National Academy of Sciences of the evidence cited by the House committee concerning Kennedy's assassination concluded that static or other noise, not gunshots, accounted for the sounds on the tape. *New York Times*, Aug. 3, 2004.

invited him to the White House.[93] When oil prices ballooned in 1979, denunciations of America's gluttonous appetite for material things—and consequent dependence on other countries—became stronger than ever. The nation, critics exclaimed, must consume less and conserve more. It must recognize and accept limits to its growth in the future. In 1980, Vice President Walter Mondale urged progressives to "adjust the liberal values of social justice and compassion to a new age of limited resources."[94]

THERE WAS SURELY NO DOUBTING that Americans (like other people) cherished material things. Later events, however, were to demonstrate that most American people continued to embrace ideals and visions that went well beyond dollars and cents. The United States in the late 1970s, moreover, had by no means entered a permanent "Age of Limits." Instead, between the mid-1970s and early 1980s, the nation was caught in shorter-term economic stagnation. It also continued to struggle against an array of social problems, most of which, like race, were long-standing. And it wrestled, then and later, with cultural and generational conflicts that had sharpened in the 1960s, and with the divisive legacy of the Vietnam War. All these developments advanced a sense in the late 1970s that conflict was destroying a consensus that was supposed to have blessed the nation since 1945. Cultural pessimists—hardly new in American or Western history—received lavish coverage from media that had become more critical and confrontational following American escalation in Vietnam and Watergate.[95]

Instead of prophesying a future of economic stagnation or decline, cultural pessimists might have attended more closely to other powerful forces of the 1970s. In these years, as throughout most of United States history, abundant resources and a hard-working, resilient, and innovative population combined to advance real economic growth over time. Though rising inequality accompanied this progress, most people, blacks included, fared a little better absolutely. The years of the late 1970s were hardly a great Age of Decline.

Yet nostalgia about the post–World War II golden age—particularly about family life—helped to induce many people in the late 1970s to feel

93. Collins, More, 133–34.
94. Ibid., 162.
95. Arthur Herman, The Idea of Decline in Western History (New York, 1997), 441–46. The economist John Kenneth Galbraith, musing on popular notions of decline, liked to tell people that every editor he knew wanted books to be titled "The Crisis of American Democracy."

a sense of loss. Moreover, most American adults, having lived through the economically vibrant years that preceded the 1970s, had developed ever larger expectations about life—expectations that the sociologist Daniel Bell in 1976 aptly linked to a "revolution of rising entitlements." In part for these reasons, and in part because of the economic trials and cultural controversies of the age, many people concluded in the late 1970s that the nation was in deep trouble. Even Americans who were doing a little better at the time often talked as if they were doing worse. As if caught on a treadmill, they were anxious about the present and wary about the future.[96]

96. Bell, *The Cultural Contradictions of Capitalism* (New York, 1976). The argument that virtually all human beings—not just Americans—are often caught on a "hedonic treadmill," is a key to the thesis of Richard Easterlin, *Growth Triumphant: The Twenty-first Century in Historical Perspective* (Ann Arbor, 1996), 52–53, 131–44.

3

The Political World of the Mid-1970s

Shortly before the 1976 election, which pitted President Ford against James Earl "Jimmy" Carter Jr., of Georgia, a middle-aged businessman bragged that he did not intend to vote. "I'm a three-time loser," he explained. "In 1964 I voted for the peace candidate—Johnson—and got war. In '68 I voted for the law-and-order candidate—Nixon—and got crime. In '72 I voted for Nixon again, and we got Watergate. I'm not going to vote this time."[1]

This was a characteristically sour opinion of American politics in 1976. Another citizen growled, "I'm not apathetic about non-voting, I'm emphatic about it."[2] Others heeded the advice of Mae West, who had quipped, "If you have to choose between two evils, pick the one you haven't tried." Many people who did go to the polls grumbled that they were casting a "clothes-pin vote"—holding their noses while voting for one poor candidate or the other. The turnout in 1976, 54.8 percent of eligible voters, was the lowest since 1948. Carter squeaked into office with 50.1 percent of the ballots, to 48 percent for Ford. He won the electoral college by 297 to 240, the narrowest margin since 1916.[3]

1. *Time*, Nov. 15, 1976, 20.
2. Ibid.
3. Turnouts of eligible voters had hovered around 60 percent between 1952 and 1968, before dropping to 55 percent in 1972. The low, in 1948, had been 51 percent. *Stat. Abst.*, 2002, 236, 254. Declining percentages such as these, however, did not mean that Americans were becoming more apathetic. See note 105, chapter 4, for a less gloomy explanation of American electoral turnouts since 1972.

THE POLITICAL WORLD inhabited by Ford and Carter reflected larger trends that had developed since the 1960s and that were to persist long after 1980. One of these was the virtual disappearance of the radical Left as an organized political force. In 1970, the Students for a Democratic Society (SDS), which in the late 1960s had been the largest left-of-center student group in American history, had imploded. After Nixon pulled American troops out of Vietnam and ended the military draft, only a few very small radical groups remained in the news. One, the far-left Weather Underground, took credit for some twenty bombings between 1970 and 1975. Another group, the American Indian Movement (AIM), agitated militantly for Indian self-governance and a return to tribal ways. In 1973, some 200 AIM adherents seized the Sioux village of Wounded Knee in South Dakota, forcing a seventy-one-day standoff with federal agents. The Symbionese Liberation Army (SLA), which included idealistic anti-war young people among its founders, evolved into a California gang of killers, robbers, and self-styled revolutionaries who captured nationwide headlines in early 1974 when it kidnapped nineteen-year-old newspaper heiress Patricia Hearst. Its slogan was "Death to the fascist insect that preys upon the people." Hearst, after having been held in a closet for two months, joined her captors and dubbed herself Tania, the name of the girlfriend of former Cuban revolutionary Che Guevara. Toting a carbine, she was photographed helping her former captors carry out an armed robbery of a San Francisco bank.

The confrontation at Wounded Knee, however, ended in a stalemate that did not improve the plight of American Indians, many of whom continued to confront extraordinarily high rates of poverty and disease on their reservations. AIM splintered badly in later years.[4] All the members of the small delusional "army" that kidnapped Hearst could have fit into a Humvee with room left over for hostages. Six heavily armed members of the gang, including its leader, died in a fire and televised shootout with Los Angeles police in 1975. Others, including Hearst, were captured, convicted, and jailed.[5] The pipe dreams of the SLA, like those of the Weathermen,

---

4. In June 1975, a shootout at the Pine Ridge reservation in South Dakota resulted in the deaths of one Indian and two federal agents. An AIM member, Leonard Peltier, was convicted in 1977 of the murders and sentenced to two life terms in prison. Believing that Peltier had been unjustly accused and sentenced, advocates helped to make him a human rights celebrity. As of mid-2005, however, Peltier remained behind bars.

5. Hearst was sentenced in 1976 to seven years in prison for her part in the bank robbery. She served twenty-one months, going free after President Carter commuted her sentence in January 1979. In one of the last acts of his administration, President Bill Clinton pardoned her in January 2001.

exposed the dying gasps in the mid-1970s of '60s-style radical activism in the United States.[6]

Liberals, a far more potent political force, also faced worrisome trends in the 1970s and thereafter. Persistent demographic and economic forces, notably the movement since World War II of millions of people into the middle classes and the suburbs, helped to drive these trends. As Americans headed upward and outward, they loosened their ties to the Democratic electoral coalition of blue-collar groups and urban political machines that had helped to elect FDR and Harry Truman in the 1930s and 1940s, and JFK and LBJ in the 1960s. Labor unions, which had been powerful allies of the Democratic Party, lost strength. For these reasons, class-related issues, which had been strong in American politics in the 1930s and 1940s, had lost some of their salience by the 1970s.

Compared to some nations of Western Europe, where social-democratic, labor-based political parties continued to command varying levels of popular support, the United States was a nation of relatively conservative people who valued individualism and were ambivalent about a wide-reaching central state. In the 1970s and later, the fervor and political strength of Americans who opposed gun control, abortion, and the teaching of Darwinian theories of evolution stunned and outraged a great many observers in Western Europe. Many of these observers equated the death penalty, which their societies had abolished, with barbarism, and regarded governmentally guaranteed health insurance coverage—also widespread on the Continent—as a sine qua non of advanced civilization.

Changes in racial allegiances especially threatened to hurt the Democrats. When LBJ championed civil rights in the 1960s, southern white voters, until then reliably Democratic, left the party in droves and began to vote Republican. Very high percentages of African Americans, who had already abandoned the GOP in the 1930s and 1940s, backed Democratic candidates after 1964. Though blacks helped elect liberal Democrats in northern cities, the surge to the right of white voters, especially male voters, in the South was a boon to the Republican Party. Democrats remained competitive in many parts of the South—especially in state and local elections—but the rise of the GOP in Dixie was inexorable over time. As much as any single force, racial concerns transformed the partisan preferences of Americans in the 1970s and thereafter, making the core

6. Most articulate scholars and writers on the left, including socialists, rejected violent approaches in the 1970s and thereafter, but these intellectuals and non-violent advocates of far-reaching social programs had no significant impact on politics or policy.

of the Republican Party more conservative and the Democrats more liberal than they had been.

Ever larger numbers of people in the Plains and Mountain states, meanwhile, came to perceive liberals in the Democratic Party as champions of
eastern, urban interests that catered to blacks, welfare recipients, and labor
unions. Though these westerners benefited greatly from federal largesse—
dams, irrigation projects, defense contracts, and the like—they increasingly
embraced conservative criticisms of big government. They blasted environmentalists, "elitists," and "faraway bureaucrats" who owned vast tracts of
their land and regulated their lives. Like white southerners, they were more
conservative concerning a number of hot-button issues of late twentieth-
century politics—such as gun control, the death sentence, and abortion.
Feelings such as these, like the racial divisions that were transforming politics in the South, shifted the core of the Democratic Party's base more strongly
to urban areas in the northeastern, mid-Atlantic, and midwestern regions.
They revealed that passionate regional loyalties, which had been expected
to decline as TV and other mass communications tied the nation more
closely together, more than held their own as the years passed.

Developments such as these by no means destroyed either the Democratic Party or American liberalism. It was already clear that the tumultuous cultural warfare of the 1960s had left a political mark on many young
people who had come of age during those years. Millions of baby boomers,
having grown up amid the excitement of the civil rights and women's
rights movements, had developed—and maintained—liberal views on a
range of social and cultural issues, such as abortion, affirmative action,
and federal governmental responsibility for health and welfare. In part
because of the spread of higher education, they were more tolerant than
their elders had been of the religions of other people. Affected by the
sexual revolution, they were more broad-minded than Americans in the
past had been about the private behavior of their friends and neighbors.
The beliefs and behavior of Americans such as these portended a central
trend of late twentieth-century life in the United States: Liberals, benefiting from the support of younger generations, were to prevail in many hotly
contested cultural struggles in the future.[7]

Liberals enjoyed special political blessings in the mid-1970s. Watergate
temporarily shattered the Republican Party. Already in solid command of

7. Steven Gillon, *Boomer Nation: The Largest and Richest Generation Ever and How It
Changed America* (New York, 2004); Peter Keating, "Wake-up Call," *AARP: The Magazine*, Sept./Oct. 2004, 55ff. For culture wars, see chapter 8.

Congress, Democrats gained fifty-two members in the House and four in the Senate in 1974, thereby commanding huge margins of 291 to 144 and 60 to 37.[8] The election gave the Democrats control of thirty-six governorships and thirty-seven state legislatures. Though this surge abated a little after 1976, liberal Democrats remained especially strong in the House. Thanks in part to gerrymandered or heavily one-party districts (which enabled most incumbents to enjoy near lifelong tenure), Democrats controlled the House without interruption from 1955 to 1995.[9]

In the 1970s, liberal Democrats in the North, having backed civil rights, civil liberties, entitlement programs such as Medicare and Medicaid, and other federal government social policies, solidified their strength among intellectuals, graduate students, teachers, artists, musicians, actors, and writers. A great many professionals and professors, including increasingly large majorities of those who taught at prestigious colleges and universities, joined them. While these liberal elites were relatively insignificant numerically, many were articulate and politically active, and they received considerable attention in the media. A clear omen was visible in 1972, when thirty-four of thirty-eight Harvard Law School professors voted for Democratic presidential candidate George McGovern, an ardent liberal, and thirty gave him campaign contributions.[10] Fighting back, conservatives were to fight a host of "culture wars" against liberal academics and other "elitists" on the left.[11]

Still, Republicans fared all right in presidential elections. Starting in 1968, when Nixon triumphed, they won five of eight presidential races through 1996, losing only to Carter in 1976 and to Bill Clinton in 1992 and 1996. Moreover, the GOP became more conservative after 1974, because the party gained a great deal of strength in the South, because religious conservatives entered politics as never before, and because centrist elements in the GOP, led by Nixon, had been discredited by Watergate.[12] Assailing liberals, Republican candidates and officeholders moved toward the right at the same time that Democrats, shorn of many conservative southerners, were turning toward the left.

Beginning in 1968, when Nixon crafted a "Southern Strategy" to lure white southern voters to the GOP, Republicans focused less on the bread-and-butter economic issues that had helped Democrats since the 1930s to

8. *Stat. Abst.*, 2002, 245. Both chambers had small numbers of third-party members.
9. Democrats also controlled the Senate most of the time in these years.
10. Laura Kalman, *The Strange Career of Legal Liberalism* (New Haven, 1996), 77.
11. See chapter 8.
12. For the rise of the Religious Right, see chapter 4.

muster working-class support. Instead, they emphasized social and cultural concerns—abortion, busing, affirmative action, school prayer, "law and order"—so as to attract white people, notably Catholics and blue-collar workers. By 1980, as Republicans began to shed a country-club image that had hurt them with many voters, it was clear that the political power of clear-cut, class-based divisions was abating, and that Democrats could no longer take the loyalty of white blue-collar workers for granted.

Changes such as these propelled two widely deplored trends that appeared to advance over the next three decades. Both trends, convincing millions of Americans that politics was a nasty business, threatened grass-roots political activism and may have depressed turnout at the polls. One was the growing ferocity of partisan rhetoric, which seemed on occasion to threaten elementary civility between Democrats and Republicans. Encouraged by a more strident media culture, many candidates and of-ficeholders plunged into a political culture of clamorous sound-bite communications and became increasingly uncompromising, ultimately descending into what one later study called a politics of "R.I.P."—"Revelation, Investigation, Prosecution."[13] Partisan polarization seemed at times to overwhelm the conduct of congressional business.[14]

The second trend was the phenomenon of "divided government" pitting Congresses that prior to 1995 were normally Democratic against Republican presidents.[15] Liberals on the Hill, moreover, became more assertive in their post-Watergate quest to enact reforms and to diminish the "imperial presidency," as critics called it in the 1970s. Retaliating against the zeal of Democrats, Ford vetoed sixty-six bills during his twenty-nine months in office, a number previously exceeded only during the administrations of Grover Cleveland, Franklin Roosevelt, and Harry Truman.[16] Divided government, then and later, intensified a popular sense that politicians could get nothing done. Sometimes, in fact, they were too divided to act, thereby shunting resolution of issues to non-elected officials in the bureaucracy and to the courts.

13. Benjamin Ginsberg and Martin Shefter, *Politics by Other Means: Politicians, Prosecutors, and the Press from Watergate to Whitewater* (New York, 2002).
14. At times, friendships across party lines in Congress—as between Democratic House Speaker Thomas "Tip" O'Neill of Massachusetts and Republican minority leader Robert Michel of Illinois in the early 1980s—moderated this incivility. Most of the time, however, partisan warfare was sharp and unforgiving on Capitol Hill.
15. Hugh Davis Graham, "Legacies of the 1960s: The American 'Rights Revolution' in an Era of Divided Governance," *Journal of Policy History* 10, no. 3 (1998), 267–88.
16. Most of Cleveland's vetoes were of private pension bills. FDR served a little more than three terms, Truman slightly less than two.

Though partisan warfare was often intense after 1970, it coexisted most of the time with a general decline in identification by voters with the major parties—or with electoral "de-alignment," as it was often called. Citizens were often turned off by the partisan vilification, as they saw it, practiced by their elected representatives.[17] In part for this reason, the percentage of voters who considered themselves "independents" rose from 23 or so in 1952 to 40 or so at the end of the century.[18] Increasing percentages of voters, as if eager to prevent either major party from taking charge of government, resorted to splitting their tickets.[19] Losing partisan voters, party leaders in the years ahead struggled to build dependable majority coalitions. As of the early 2000s, however, neither party had succeeded in clearly effecting such a realignment of politics in the United States.

The parties also lost some of their coherence and internal discipline. Especially after 1968, primaries proliferated, thereby undermining the power that party leaders had once enjoyed over nominations. No longer relying primarily on party endorsements or party funding, candidates for major offices—the presidency, the Senate, and governorships—tended instead to depend ever more heavily on new cadres of professionals, notably managers and pollsters who specialized in image-making and political maneuvering, and to reach voters through the expensive media of radio and television. Grass-roots efforts to register and mobilize voters declined. A more candidate-centered, television-driven, and entrepreneurial politics was taking center stage.[20]

So was a politics of bigger and bigger money. This had incensed many Americans in the 1972 election, when Nixon had raised large sums from lobbies and pressure groups doing business with the government. Determined to curb these practices, good-government groups such as Com-

17. James Fallows, *Breaking the News: How the Media Undermine American Democracy* (New York, 1996), 246; E. J. Dionne, *Why Americans Hate Politics* (New York, 1991).
18. John Judis and Ruy Teixeira, *The Emerging Democratic Majority* (New York, 2002), 32.
19. John Kenneth White, *The New Politics of Old Values* (Hanover, N.H., 1989), 96–99.
20. For trends in American political patterns during these years, see Sidney Milkis, *The President and the Parties: The Transformation of the American Party System Since the New Deal* (New York, 1999); Lisa McGerr, *Suburban Warriors: The Origins of the New American Right* (Princeton, 2001); Steven Schier, *By Invitation Only: The Rise of Exclusive Politics in the United States* (Pittsburgh, 2000); Byron Shafer, *The Two Majorities and the Puzzle of Modern American Politics* (Lawrence, Kans., 2003); Ginsberg and Shefter, *Politics by Other Means*; Dionne, *Why Americans Hate Politics*; and Shep Melnick, "Governing More but Enjoying It Less," in Morton Keller and Melnick, eds., *Taking Stock: American Government in the Twentieth Century* (New York, 1999), 280–306.

mon Cause pressured Congress to act, and in late 1974 the lawmakers approved amendments to existing campaign finance law concerned with federal elections. These set up a Federal Election Commission (FEC) as a watchdog group, established a system of public financing for presidential elections, and placed limits on the size of campaign contributions that individuals and political committees might give to presidential candidates who wished to qualify for federal funds in primaries and general elections.[21] Candidates for president and vice president were barred from spending more than $50,000 of their own money on campaigns. Federal officeseekers were required to disclose virtually all their campaign contributions. Ford reluctantly signed the bill in mid-October.

Almost immediately, however, opponents of the law challenged its constitutionality, and in January 1976 the Supreme Court partly agreed with them. In a complicated, controversial ruling of 137 pages, the Court upheld most of the law's public financing provisions, its requirements for disclosure of contributions, and its caps on contributions but ruled that the placing of limits on how much of their own money candidates might spend (except candidates who accepted federal matching funds under the public financing provisions) violated First Amendment rights of free expression. The decision upset advocates, who charged that money was corrupting American politics. Justice Marshall, dissenting, observed dryly, "It would appear . . . that the candidate with a substantial personal fortune at his disposal is off to a significant 'head start.'"[22]

As later events were to demonstrate, Marshall and others had a point: Rich people continued to enjoy great advantages in politics. In 1992, H. Ross Perot, a billionaire businessman, rejected federal funding and used his personal fortune to run for the presidency. John Kerry, the Democratic presidential nominee in 2004, had millions in family money at his disposal and (like his opponent, President George W. Bush) dispensed with public financing during the primary season. Thanks to the Court's decision, which remained the law of the land, it continued to be an unconstitutional infringement of free expression to limit what presidential candidates might spend of their own money.

Curbing excesses in campaign spending was but one of many efforts that reformers undertook in the somewhat frenzied political aftermath of American involvement in Vietnam and of the Watergate scandal. Indeed,

21. For much that follows about this law, see Steven Gillon, *"That's Not What We Meant to Do": Reform and Its Unintended Consequences in Twentieth-Century America* (New York, 2000), 200–234.
22. *Buckley v. Valeo*, 424 U.S. 1 (1976).

House liberals had already been scoring minor victories during the early 1970s in their struggles to advance openness in the conduct of House business and to weaken the power of autocratic committee chairmen. In 1973, Congress passed the War Powers Resolution, which sought to curtail the president's authority to send troops into battle without congressional approval. A Budget and Impoundment Control Act established the Congressional Budget Office to provide independent advice on government finance, created two budget committees on the Hill, and restricted the imperiousness of presidents who (as Nixon had done earlier) impounded congressional appropriations. The Freedom of Information Act, passed over Ford's veto in September 1974, offered citizens, scholars, and journalists greater access to federal documents.

Congressional reformers, buoyed by the outcome of the post-Watergate elections of 1974, became especially boisterous thereafter. A huge influx of freshmen Democrats—seventy-five in all—arrived on Capitol Hill in January 1975. In the Senate the newcomers included such figures as Gary Hart of Colorado, an avid environmentalist who had managed George McGovern's presidential bid in 1972, and Patrick Leahy, the first Democrat from Vermont to be sent to the Senate since the 1850s. Hart was then thrity-six years old; Leahy, thirty-five. Freshman House Democrats in 1975 included Tom Harkin, a legal aid lawyer from Iowa; Paul Tsongas of Massachusetts, who had served as a Peace Corps volunteer; and Harold Ford, the first black congressman ever to hail from Tennessee. In the late 1970s, and later, liberal Democrats remained strong in the House.

Many of the "Watergate babies" of 1975 represented a new breed of national legislator. Products of the civil rights revolution and of protests against the war in Vietnam, they were highly rights-conscious, reform-minded, and comfortable with the medium of television. Liberal staffers on the Hill, having increased in number and assertiveness during the 1960s, egged them on. As one such staffer explained,

> I'll tell you the frame of mind we all had. We had lived for three years under Richard Nixon, and under being told no, no, no, no, no by an executive branch which was totally unresponsive to the programs of the sixties. . . . We were angry at the Nixon administration. . . . It was an important thread running through everything that was done at those times. It was: I'll get those sons of bitches, they don't want to show any positive inclination toward doing things at all, then we're going to really stick it to them. And in the process, help people.[23]

23. Reminiscences of Nik Edes, an aide to Democratic senator Harrison Williams of Delaware, cited in Richard Scotch, *From Good Will to Civil Rights: Transforming Federal Disability Policy* (Philadelphia, 1984), 48.

Especially in 1975–76, when the Ford administration was finding its way, Congress seized the initiative. Perceiving the states as unimaginative and conservative, and states' rights ideology as anachronistic, members of Congress took the lead in passing legislation, such as aid to handicapped children and bilingual education, that enhanced federal power via-à-vis the states. Congress, they believed, must carefully define the ways in which federal money would be spent, set national standards, and closely scrutinize the activities of state officials who were charged with administering federal laws. The vigor of congressional activists, most of them liberals, in the mid- and late 1970s helped to ensure that a great many reforms of Lyndon Johnson's Great Society were retained and that new entitlements were passed.

Liberal Democrats were especially feisty in the House. In January 1975, they abolished the House Un-American Activities Committee, long the bane of civil libertarians. Because most of the new Democrats had been elected in traditionally Republican districts, they felt the need to display their independence from party leaders. They showed notably little deference to committee chairmen, many of them conservative southerners, who had traditionally ruled on the Hill. Taking charge, they succeeded in revamping rules that had previously awarded chairmanships to the most senior members. Henceforth, the chairs were to be chosen by secret ballot of the Democratic caucus at the start of congressional sessions—a change that led to the removal of three unregenerate committee chairs in 1975.[24]

In March 1975, reformers in the Senate also scored a victory, changing the rules governing filibusters: Only 60 percent of the Senate, not two-thirds as in the past, would be needed to cut off debate. A common denominator of these reforms, in the House as well as in the Senate, was the sense that concentration of authority was dangerous. The reformers sought to disperse power, both away from the executive branch and from the congressional barons who had dominated Capitol Hill.[25]

Three years later, in 1978, reformers embedded a final stone in the edifice that they were erecting against abuse of power: the Ethics in Government Act. The measure toughened restrictions on lobbying by former government officials and tightened financial disclosure regulations. It included a little-discussed provision that authorized the attorney general to

24. David Price, "House Democrats Under Republican Rule: Reflections on the Limits of Bipartisanship," *Miller Center Report* (University of Virginia) 20 (Spring/Summer 2004), 21–28.

25. For political reforms in the 1970s, see Julian Zelizer, *On Capitol Hill: The Struggle to Reform Congress and Its Consequences* (Cambridge, Eng., 2004), 157–76.

take steps for the naming of special prosecutors who would have the power to investigate allegations of misbehavior by high-ranking federal officials. A Carter administration spokesman, pressing for the bill, explained that its purpose "was to remove all sense of politics and therefore restore confidence in government."[26]

None of these measures accomplished as much as reformers had expected, and most of them had unintended consequences. Ford and his successors, arguing that the War Powers Resolution was unconstitutional, refused to abide by it, and presidents remained dominant in foreign affairs. Though changes in congressional procedures helped topple a few titans on Capitol Hill, their primary effect was to increase the number of committees and the resources and power of subcommittee chairs, whose numbers, both in the House and the Senate, escalated in the next few years. In 1975, the House had 154 committees and subcommittees. The number of congressional staffers exploded thereafter—from a total of 10,739 in 1970 to approximately 20,000 by 1990.[27]

With power decentralized, "subcommittee government" often took over on the Hill, and Congress became if anything more susceptible than in the past to the influence of interest groups that formed political alliances with long-term staffers and subcommittee chairmen. The provision for independent prosecutors, developing a political strength that no one had anticipated at the time, became an often used and sometimes abused partisan weapon over the years. Before Congress allowed the law to lapse in 1999, twenty such special prosecutors had been appointed, including Kenneth Starr, whose probes over the course of four and a half years led to the impeachment of President Bill Clinton in 1998. These twenty prosecutions cost taxpayers a total of $149 million.

The reforms did not stem a dominant trend of post-Watergate political life: expansion in the number and power of interest groups.[28] Given the growth of government—and of bureaucratic organizations of all sorts in the modern world—this was an understandable development. Moreover, some of the new groups, such as Common Cause and the Children's Defense Fund, sprang from the egalitarian social movements of the 1960s. Then and later, these public interest groups supported a range of liberal causes, including environmentalism, social welfare, civil rights, and good

26. Gillon, "That's Not What We Meant to Do," 38–40.
27. Theda Skocpol, Diminished Democracy: From Membership to Management in American Civic Life (Norman, Okla., 2003), 201.
28. Jack Walker, Mobilizing Interest Groups in America: Patrons, Professionals, and Social Movements (Ann Arbor, 1991), 23–27, 72.

government. Some contemporary pundits believed that the rise of groups such as these was a sign that political power in the United States was becoming more democratic.

Like most other lobbies in these and subsequent years, the majority of these public interest groups were not cross-class in membership; they did not have very deep local roots; and they rarely convened large-scale, face-to-face meetings where people could talk things through. Instead, these groups tended to operate from the top down, relying heavily for support on wealthy contributors and on tax-exempt foundations, which proliferated in these years. They became adept at gaining publicity in the media, purchasing mailing lists, and collecting checks from distant members. Their well-educated, upper-middle-class, and professional managers fashioned sturdy careers as activists and lobbyists who roamed the halls of Congress, state legislatures, and regulatory agencies.[29]

Unanticipated consequences of the new campaign finance reforms further advanced this rise of interest groups, especially private groups.[30] What well-meaning reformers did not fully understand was that candidates for political office would willy-nilly find financial support. As House Speaker Thomas "Tip" O'Neill of Massachusetts noted, money was "the mother's milk of politics." Like water, it always flowed down into the coffers of parties and political candidates. Officeseekers, barred from accepting sizeable contributions from individuals, turned to political action committees, or PACs, which were permitted to give out larger sums. PACs generally represented private interest groups. In 1974, when the campaign reforms were passed, the most important of these PACs were linked to the AFL-CIO—which is one reason why many Democrats, who had ties with organized labor, had supported the changes and many Republicans had resisted them. (Behind most "reforms" are partisan interests.) After 1974, corporate leaders retaliated by forming a host of new PACs, most of which tended to favor Republican candidates. Many Democrats later rued the day that the campaign finance law had passed in 1974.

Advocates of campaign finance reform underestimated the ingenuity that candidates soon demonstrated in raising so-called soft money. This was money that individuals, corporations, labor unions, and other interest groups were allowed to give in unlimited amounts to state and local party committees under more lenient state laws. When the FEC ruled in 1978 that soft money could legally be redirected to party leaders of federal campaigns, it

29. Skocpol, *Diminished Democracy*, 127–74, 199–228.
30. Jeffrey Berry, *The Interest Group Society* (New York, 1997), 220.

opened up another large loophole, through which presidential candidates began to race in the late 1980s. Thereafter the growth in soft money, reaching some $500 million by 2002, excited all manner of outrage among reformers. So did the upward surge in general of contributions to campaigns, which relied ever more heavily on paid professional advisers and pollsters, expensive computer technology, and highly expensive radio and television advertising. Democrats and Republicans thereafter engaged in periodic efforts to curb the evils, as reformers saw them, of Big Money in politics. But incumbents, coping under existing laws, did not fight hard for reforms that might level the playing field for challengers, and when apparently substantial reforms were enacted in 2002, they, too, failed to curb the cost of campaigns.[31]

Corporate and labor PACs had a great deal of company in Washington during the 1970s and beyond. Lobbyists representing minority groups, women, the handicapped, and gay people joined a swarm of corporate and agribusiness claimants that patrolled the hallways of federal office buildings and Congress. In 1970, some 250 corporations and 1,200 trade associations had offices in Washington; by 1980, these numbers had risen to 500 and 1,739, respectively. "It's like medieval Italy," one beleaguered government official complained. "Everyone has his own duchy or kingdom."[32] The area around K Street in Washington, the home of many politically connected law firms and of national headquarters for trade associations, came to be known as "Gucci Gulch." Membership in the American Association of Retired Persons (AARP), the nation's biggest lobby, increased from 1.5 million in 1969 to 12 million in 1980.[33]

Many of these lobbyists talked the compelling language of group "rights" and entitlements. Forming solid relationships with congressmen, congres-

---

31. In 2002, Congress passed the Bipartisan Campaign Reform Act, also known (after the names of its sponsors) as the McCain-Feingold Act. Among other things, this law placed a ban (after the election of 2002) on unlimited soft-money contributions to national political parties. A bitterly divided Supreme Court upheld by a five-to-four vote most of this law's provisions in December 2003. *New York Times*, Dec. 11, 2003. As many skeptics had predicted in 2002, party fund-raisers in the 2004 election managed to find large loopholes in the clauses limiting soft-money contributions. By mid-October 2004, the major parties had already raised more than $1 billion, a record amount that they used mainly for ads and get-out-the-vote efforts. Ibid., Dec. 3, 2004.

32. Kevin Phillips, *Arrogant Capital: Washington, Wall Street, and the Frustration of American Politics* (Boston, 1994), 32; Gillon, *Boomer Nation*, 190.

33. Bruce Schulman, *The Seventies: The Great Shift in American Culture, Society, and Politics* (New York, 2001), 84–87. In 2005, AARP claimed a membership of more than 35 million.

sional aides, and other federal officials, they also established wider "issue networks" that included reform groups, think tanks, foundations, and other specialists in particular areas of policy.[34] In doing so, they advanced a more pluralist—some said more sophisticated—world of policy development. Some of the lobbies, however, aroused widespread criticism. Popular disgust at the perceived expansion in these years of "special interests" and of "identity politics" lay at the heart of rising revulsion toward politicians in general. The percentage of citizens who said they could "trust the federal government" declined from roughly 75 percent in 1964–65 to a low of 25 percent in the late 1970s—and never exceeded 44 percent for the remainder of the century.[35] Disgust with politicians was an especially notable characteristic of American popular attitudes from the late 1960s forward.

Seeking to capitalize on such attitudes, a great many candidates for the presidency and other national offices hammered home a central message in their campaigns in the 1970s and thereafter: Politicians in Washington were responsible for a "mess" that was confronting the nation. Riding in as crusading outsiders, these noble knights of reform promised to scatter to the four winds the evil individuals who were endangering the republic. A notable champion of this message, which slighted the formidable structural obstacles to change, and which thereby excited unrealistic popular expectations, was Jimmy Carter in 1976.

BEHIND THIS RISING POPULAR REVULSION with national politicians were some questionable assumptions. One was that politics had been more gentlemanly in the Good Old Days. It was true that partisanship in the ugly aftermath of Watergate, an age of apparently endless investigations by partisan congressional committees and of "revelations" highlighted in the ever more voyeuristic media, was often sharper than it had been in the relatively serene mid-1950s.[36] But bipartisan harmony could hardly be said to have characterized politics throughout American history, in the FDR and Truman years, or in the heyday of Senator Joseph McCarthy and other anti-Communist Red-baiters who trampled the civil liberties of innocent people. At that time, too, incivility often dominated congressional

34. Hugh Heclo, "Issue Networks and the Executive Establishment," in Anthony King, ed., *The New American Political System* (Washington, 1978), 87–124.
35. David King and Zachary Karabell, *The Generation of Trust: Public Confidence in the U.S. Military Since Vietnam* (Washington, 2003), 2.
36. Ginsberg and Shefter, *Politics by Other Means*, 13–169. The media, while eager to poke into the personal behavior of candidates, were less aggressive when it came to examining large issues, such as sensitive decisions concerning war and peace.

debate. And partisan warfare had hardly ebbed in the 1960s: The 1964 presidential campaign between LBJ and Barry Goldwater featured an all-time high in attack advertising.

A good deal of the partisan fighting in the 1970s and thereafter amounted to blood sport, often waged clamorously for narrow interests, but some of it, as in the past, was healthy and to be expected. It reflected strongly held ideological points of view that are expressed in any democratic system that features competitive political parties. The United States, an open, pluralistic, and dynamic society receptive to change, then and later had such a system. Moderates, independents, and centrists—sometimes more effective than the partisans who captured many of the headlines—helped to fashion compromises that enabled America's democratic system to remain one of the most stable in the world.

Some of the complaints about the power of "interests" and of money in politics also tended to be overwrought. In a large, heterogeneous nation such as the United States, a host of groups seeking to influence the political process will organize and demand to be heard, especially in an era when the inclination of government to provide benefits expands dramatically, as it did in the 1960s and thereafter. Moreover, most of the public interest groups that arose in the 1960s and thereafter fought to preserve and to expand liberal policies, such as affirmative action, civil liberties, Social Security, Medicare, Medicaid, and other social and environmental programs. Aided by courts and liberal officials who dominated many federal agencies, they had a number of successes and advanced many rights. Conservative presidents and members of Congress after 1974 learned to their dismay that while people might claim to despise government, they also developed ever higher expectations from it. Many New Deal and Great Society programs expanded slowly over time.

It was also unclear whether politics had been better or purer in the Good Old Days, when fewer groups had possessed the resources to lobby effectively in Washington or in state capitals. Was it accurate to say, as many people did after 1970, that politics in general was "dirty"? Were all the newer groups and PACs simply "selfish," or did they have good reason to insist on the rights and entitlements that others had already enjoyed? Had Congress been a more democratically managed institution when it had bowed to the will of a boss like Lyndon Johnson, whose allies dominated the Senate in the late 1950s, than it later became, when power was more dispersed? Was the steadily increasing power of television in politics necessarily a bad thing? Prior to the TV age, the vast majority of voters had never even seen their candidates. Answers to these questions still provoke sharp debates. In any event, lobbies representing minorities and other once politically marginal groups, working with coalitions in Congress, managed from time to time to score victories in the partisan political arena of Washington.

Why fret so deeply about the role of money in politics? It was true that the system greatly advantaged wealthy candidates and discouraged able aspirants from running. Incumbents who anticipated having to compete against well-heeled challengers felt obliged to devote huge amounts of time to fund-raising efforts, thereby struggling to handle their official responsibilities. Representatives and senators, busy raising money, often did little real legislative work between Friday and Tuesday. Wealthy contributors obviously expected to influence the candidates they supported. And the cost of campaigning escalated: One later calculation estimated that the average cost of winning a seat in the Senate jumped from $600,000 in 1976 to $4 million in 1990.[37] For these reasons, reformers understandably struggled to level the playing field so as to wipe out these potential sources of corruption and to encourage people of moderate means to enter politics.

Whether the caps on contributions offered a significant solution to such problems, however, was doubtful. In many cases, the caps, which were low, had the effect of discouraging citizen involvement in political activity.[38] Whether money being spent by candidates was "excessive," moreover, depended on one's point of view. A careful study in 1978 of the effects of the campaign finance amendments of 1974 pointed out that federal candidates spent roughly $212 million in 1976. In the same year, corporations spent $33.6 billion advertising their wares. The report concluded: "Electoral politics is in competition with corporate advertising for the attention of American citizens. . . . Limited campaign funds often mean limited campaign activity, which, in turn, means a poorly informed and apathetic electorate."[39]

Most Americans, including representatives of the media, did not have much use for arguments such as these. Polls consistently indicated that people were disgusted with politicians and with politics in general. After all, the lies and deceptions of Vietnam and Watergate were fresh in people's minds. In the mid-1970s, when Ford had the task of combating such perceptions, Americans were quick to blame villains "inside the Beltway" for

---

37. Haynes Johnson, *Divided We Fall: Gambling with History in the Nineties* (New York, 1994), 324.
38. Skocpol, *Diminished Democracy*, 280–88.
39. Gillon, *"That's Not What We Meant to Do,"* 212.

the tarnishing of politics in the United States over time. It was the misfortune of this well-meaning man—and of Carter over the next four years—to lead the nation at a time when many angry Americans thundered against the evils of politics and of government.[40]

GERALD FORD INDEED MEANT WELL. Born in Omaha in 1913 as Leslie Lynch King, he was sixty-one years old when he replaced Nixon in August 1974. In 1914, his parents having separated, young Leslie moved with his mother, Dorothy, to her parents' hometown of Grand Rapids, Michigan. In 1916, she married Gerald R. Ford Sr., who owned and operated a paint and varnish company. Young Leslie later took his stepfather's name, becoming Gerald R. Ford Jr. Jerry was a hardworking and dutiful son who became an Eagle Scout and who starred in football. Earning an athletic scholarship at the University of Michigan, he waited on tables to help support himself. He served briefly as an assistant football coach at Yale, where he then attended law school, graduating in 1941 in the top one-fourth of his class and returning to Grand Rapids as an attorney. During World War II he saw combat as a naval officer in the Pacific. The war convinced him that the United States must play a major role in world affairs.[41]

Back in Grand Rapids after the war, Ford soon entered politics, in 1948 beating a Republican incumbent, an isolationist, in a primary and then winning a House seat representing his heavily Republican district. A conservative on most issues, he battled vigorously against liberal Democrats over the years. But most of his colleagues liked Jerry Ford, who worked hard and kept his word. President Johnson named him to the Warren Commission, which investigated Kennedy's assassination. His Republican colleagues entrusted him with growing responsibilities, including the post of House minority leader in 1965. He held this position until late 1973, when Spiro Agnew was forced to resign as vice president. Nixon seems privately to have favored John Connally, a Democrat who had been governor of Texas and had become his secretary of the treasury, as Agnew's replacement. Still, Nixon liked Ford, with whom he had been friendly as a House colleague in 1949–50. He realized that Ford, popular on the Hill, would have relatively little trouble getting confirmed as vice president. His judgment was accurate, and Ford was sworn into the vice presidency in December 1973.[42]

40. David Farber, "The Torch Had Fallen," in Beth Bailey and David Farber, eds., *America in the Seventies* (Lawrence, Kans., 2004), 11–13.
41. John Greene, *The Presidency of Gerald R. Ford* (Lawrence, Kans., 1995), 1–3.
42. Ibid., 1–6, 113–15.

Nixon, however, did not have great respect for Ford's intelligence. Believing that Congress shared this view, he anticipated that it would shy away from initiating impeachment proceedings, which if successful would elevate Ford to the White House. In this political calculation Nixon was of course mistaken, but he was correct in thinking that many politicians considered Ford to be a ponderous public speaker and a somewhat plodding, unimaginative party regular. "Good old Jerry," they said patronizingly. President Johnson had famously declared that Ford had played football once too often without a helmet. Richard Reeves, a decidedly antagonistic journalist, popularized Ford's image as inept in an article that he wrote for *New York* magazine in November 1974. Titled "Jerry Ford and His Flying Circus: A Presidential Diary," it chronicled the new president's blunders and speech errors during the congressional campaigns. Reeves punctuated his account with commentary such as "It is not a question of saying the emperor has no clothes—there is question of whether there is an emperor." The cover portrayed Ford as Bozo the Clown.[43]

Attacks such as these irritated Ford, but he had no choice but to accept them as part of the political game. As a graduate of the Yale Law School, he had confidence in his abilities. He was genuinely modest and unpretentious, memorably declaring on becoming vice president, "I am a Ford, not a Lincoln." On assuming the presidency, he told Americans that his watchwords would be "communication, conciliation, compromise, and cooperation."[44] As president he rejected the imperial trappings that Nixon had relished and directed that the Michigan fight song be played in place of "Hail to the Chief" on ceremonial occasions. Despite two attempts on his life in September 1975, he was unusually accessible for a president, traveling widely and holding thirty-nine press conferences in his 875 days in office. This was eleven more than Nixon had held during his more than five and a half years in the White House.[45]

Ford, an experienced, knowledgeable politician, chafed at the widespread view in late 1974 that he was merely a "caretaker president," but he also recognized the obvious: Americans were looking to him to put out the fires that had seared national life during the tumultuous years of the Vietnam War and Watergate. In his autobiography, revealingly entitled *A*

43. Reeves, "Jerry Ford and His Flying Circus: A Presidential Diary," *New York*, Nov. 25, 1974, 42–46; Greene, *The Presidency of Gerald R. Ford*, 62.
44. Fred Greenstein, *The Presidential Difference: Leadership Style from FDR to Clinton* (New York, 2000), 113–16.
45. President Jimmy Carter was to hold fifty press conferences in four years, and Ronald Reagan thirty-two in eight years.

Time to Heal (1979), he wrote, "If I'm remembered, it will probably be for healing the land."[46] This is what he tried to do in 1974.

In time, Ford had some success in these endeavors. As the columnist Hugh Sidey said in late 1976, "Ford's stewardship was a welcome change from the decade of disarray that began with the bullet that killed Kennedy."[47] But the scars that disfigured American society were deep, and some of Ford's early moves added to the pain. Many people opposed his offer of clemency to draft dodgers who undertook alternative service. Others, especially liberal Democrats, rejected his primary medicine against stagflation—lower federal spending. A relaxed and open administrator who gave subordinates fairly free rein, the president was slow to alleviate interpersonal tensions within the White House, many of which pitted Nixon-era holdovers against new appointees. A group of ranking Republican senators publicly complained in mid-October, "Some people feel that if Jerry Ford is not over his head in the Presidency, he's in very deep. He hasn't demonstrated, 'I am in charge.'"[48]

Ford's decision in early September to pardon Nixon especially damaged his standing. Critics, including Republicans who were worried about the upcoming fall election, were shocked and surprised at the move, for which Ford, secretive on the subject, had not prepared the nation. Opponents charged that he had made a deal, either at the time of being nominated for the vice presidency or in the last, dismal days of Nixon's presidency. General Alexander Haig, Nixon's chief of staff, had mentioned the possibility of such a deal to Ford prior to Nixon's resignation. There is no evidence, however, that Ford and Nixon ever discussed such a deal. Rather, Ford pardoned Nixon because he wanted the nation to move on. Later, many Americans agreed—Reeves included—that if he had not done so, endless investigations and trials would have ensued, reopening the wounds of Watergate.[49] Still, the blow to Ford's presidency was severe, and his party took an electoral drubbing in November. In January 1975, his personal popularity hit an all-time low of 37 percent.[50]

By then Ford had begun to bring greater discipline to his administration. In September he had replaced Haig, who had temporarily served as his staff coordinator, with Donald "Rummy" Rumsfeld, a political ally

46. *A Time to Heal: The Autobiography of Gerald R. Ford* (New York, 1979), 87.
47. *Time*, Nov. 15, 1976, 20.
48. *Newsweek*, Oct. 14, 1974, 37.
49. Greene, *The Presidency of Gerald R. Ford*, 42–52.
50. Greenstein, *The Presidential Difference*, 235. Ford's average popularity was only 47 percent.

who as a "Young Turk" congressman from Illinois had backed him for minority leader of the House in 1965. During the Nixon years, Rumsfeld had headed the Office of Economic Opportunity, which oversaw the War on Poverty, and then become American ambassador to NATO. It was evident to people who encountered Rumsfeld that he was a smart, combative, and tough administrator with considerable political talent. Some of his rivals in the Ford years thought he was imperious, self-promoting, and restlessly ambitious. Henry Kissinger, Ford's secretary of state, observed that Rumsfeld was a "skilled, full-time politician-bureaucrat in whom ambition, ability and substance fuse seamlessly."[51]

Though Rumsfeld only slowly moderated dissension within Ford's inner circle, he greatly centralized operations during his time as chief of White House operations, cutting 60 of 540 people from the staff by January 1975. In a Cabinet shake-up in late October that the media dubbed the "Halloween Massacre," Ford selected him as secretary of defense. Rumsfeld, only forty-three years old at the time, was the youngest man in American history to take over that key post. At the same time, George H. W. Bush, until then America's top envoy to the People's Republic of China, was named head of the CIA, and Brent Scowcroft, an air force general, replaced Kissinger (who continued to be secretary of state) as national security adviser. All three men were to play important roles in later years: Bush as president, Scowcroft as Bush's national security adviser, and Rumsfeld as George W. Bush's controversial, highly visible defense secretary.[52]

Both as Ford's staff coordinator and as defense secretary, Rumsfeld solidified his standing in the administration. In the process, he helped conservatives to marginalize more liberal Republicans who were close to Vice President Nelson Rockefeller. Recognizing his political weakness, Rockefeller announced in November 1975 that he would not run on the Republican ticket in 1976. Thirty-four-year-old Richard Cheney, who had worked under Rumsfeld both at OEO and in Ford's White House, replaced his patron as top White House aide to the president. Cheney's Secret Service code name, "Backseat," epitomized his manner, which was low-key and faceless. He had little time for small talk or for pomp and circumstance. Cheney was discreet, tough-minded, and efficient. Anxious to restore presidential authority that had been whittled away after

51. Lewis Gould, *The Modern American Presidency* (Lawrence, Kans., 2003), 135; A. James Reichley, *Conservatives in an Age of Change: The Nixon and Ford Administrations* (Washington, 1981), 274–75; James Mann, *Rise of the Vulcans: The History of Bush's War Cabinet* (New York, 2004), 9–20.
52. The theme of Mann, *Rise of the Vulcans*.

Watergate, he labored to ward off further congressional incursions on executive power. The youngest presidential chief of staff in history, he proved to be a skilled political operative. During Ford's campaign for election in 1976, he became a highly trusted adviser and strategist.[53]

Changes in personnel, however, could not solve problems that plagued Ford's efforts to cure the ills of the American economy. More of a traditional free-market conservative than Nixon, he hoped to reduce the role of government in the affairs of the nation. Like the chairman of his Council of Economic Advisers, the serious and influential Alan Greenspan, he yearned to cut discretionary spending on social services, notably in health and education, so as to reduce the growing federal deficit and to curb the rate of inflation, which had mounted to double-digit size in early 1974. In October, he called for a 5 percent surcharge on corporate and personal income taxes (for families earning more than $15,000 a year). After proclaiming that his administration would Whip Inflation Now (WIN), he and his aides pinned WIN buttons to their lapels.[54]

It was Ford's misfortune, however, that a sharp recession descended in late 1974. Seeking to counter it, Ford announced his support in January 1975 for sizeable income tax cuts and rebates. Congressional Democrats attacked this "flip-flop" and seized the political initiative. In March 1975, they approved an even larger tax cut, of $22.8 billion. Ford, overruling aides who worried that such reductions would increase an already rising federal deficit, concluded that it would be politically suicidal to veto the cuts (which are almost always popular with voters) and reluctantly signed the tax reduction bill into law. But he also used many of his sixty-six vetoes to curb governmental spending in the next few months. Though Democrats succeeded in overriding him on several occasions—twelve times during his twenty-nine months in office—they raged at his assertiveness and at the conservative Republicans who sustained his vetoes. "This has been a government by veto," Democratic senator John Pastore of Rhode Island complained in 1975. "We've got the minority dragging the majority by the nose."[55]

Still later, in October 1975, the president further surprised conservative foes of deficits by calling for a permanent tax cut of $28 billion, to be offset by reductions in federal spending. Though the Democratic Congress ap-

53. David Halberstam, *War in a Time of Peace: Bush, Clinton, and the Generals* (New York, 2001), 66–68; Reichley, *Conservatives in an Age of Change*, 305–15; Mann, *Rise of the Vulcans*, 10–12, 59–61, 64–65.
54. Mann, *Rise of the Vulcans*, 382–91.
55. *New York Times*, Sept. 11, 1975.

proved a bill in December that extended the earlier tax cuts for an additional six months, it refused to reduce spending, and Ford vetoed the bill. A year of partisan wrangling over taxes finally closed in late December, when Congress approved—and Ford signed—a tax cut like the one that he had earlier vetoed, in return for a vaguely worded promise from Congress that it would seek a reduction in government spending if tax revenues declined.

Battles over energy policy provoked further partisan warfare. These had already become contentious following the jacking up by OPEC of overseas oil prices after the Yom Kippur War between Israel and Arab foes in late 1973. Ford, consistent in his market-oriented approach to economic problems, believed that the answer to higher energy costs was a phased-in decontrol of domestic oil prices. Decontrol, he conceded, would lead to higher prices for consumers, but it would therefore discourage consumption and promote conservation. Higher oil prices, moreover, would act as an incentive for domestic producers to increase production. The law of supply and demand—more supply, less demand—would bring prices back down in the longer run.

When Ford outlined his plan in January 1975, however, Democrats (save some of those who represented oil-producing states and districts) were quick to oppose it. Decontrol, they charged, was a boon to energy producers and a burden on low-income Americans, who would have to pay more for heating fuel and gasoline. They called instead for the maintenance of controls and for a politically popular rollback of prices for newly produced domestic oil. Frustrated, Ford finally gave way and signed a compromise bill in December 1975. Though it rolled back prices, it also authorized gradual decontrol over a forty-month period. His decision, damned as yet another flip-flop, angered some of his advisers, including his conservative treasury secretary, William Simon, who insisted that the market should have been allowed to work its magical ways.[56]

Whether these governmental measures helped the American economy is difficult to say. This is because market forces do a great deal to determine the course of economic life. Pretending otherwise, politicians in charge of the economy claim credit when things get better, and blame opponents when they do not. In late 1975 and early 1976, the American economy did improve a little. Inflation, which had soared in 1974, fell, and unemployment dipped. On the other hand, the economy remained

56. Greene, *The Presidency of Gerald R. Ford*, 77–81; Reichley, *Conservatives in an Age of Change*, 358–71.

unsettled, worsening slightly as the 1976 election approached, and Ford, having been whipsawed between Democrats and conservative Republicans, did not seem in control of the situation. His administration had a huge $74 billion deficit in 1976 and received generally unflattering marks for its management of the economy.

Critics of the president, meanwhile, continued to depict him as a bumbler. After he stumbled while descending from Air Force One, comedians, notably Chevy Chase on television's new program *Saturday Night Live,* had great sport mimicking him. They poked fun at his golf game, which was erratic enough to place spectators at risk. Other critics cried that Ford was unfeeling, especially after he refused to support a federal bailout of New York City in October 1975. The *New York Daily News* ran a widely noted headline: "Ford to City: Drop Dead." Ford eventually relented by agreeing to support a federal loan to the city. This may have been too little too late. Many people complained that the president had flip-flopped yet again.

MANAGING FOREIGN AFFAIRS, with which Ford had had little experience prior to 1974, proved to be almost as frustrating over the next two years. Relying at first on key holdovers from Nixon's foreign policy team, he struggled to reconcile personal and bureaucratic struggles between Defense Secretary James Schlesinger and Secretary of State Henry Kissinger, an advocate of détente with the Soviets. Each was strong-willed and highly egotistical. Leo Cherne, a foreign policy adviser, observed that Kissinger was "one of the most gifted men ever to serve his government, and not altogether eager to deny it."[57] Until November 1975, when Rumsfeld replaced Schlesinger, bureaucratic infighting hampered foreign policy making.

At first the most troubling issues concerned Southeast Asia. Although the United States had pulled its soldiers from Vietnam in January 1973, bitter recriminations about the war continued to roil American society and politics. Later that year, after Congress passed the War Powers Resolution, aimed at curbing presidential authority to involve the nation in war. Ford made it clear that he considered the measure unconstitutional, thereby angering foes on the Hill. Throughout Ford's tenure (and for years thereafter) many conservative Americans complained that anti-war liberals had "tied the hands" of the military in Vietnam, thereby losing a struggle that could have been won. In 1974–75 they demanded that the United States give military

57. Greene, *The Presidency of Gerald R. Ford,* 119.

aid to South Vietnam. Returning veterans chafed at what they perceived to be the ingratitude of Americans who had stayed home. Other activists insisted that the government do something to help POWs and to locate the many fighting men who were MIA, or missing in action.[58]

Efforts to aid South Vietnam fell on deaf ears in Congress, which from 1973 on adamantly opposed efforts to supply increased military assistance to the beleaguered pro-American governments of South Vietnam, Cambodia, and Laos. Frustrated, Ford in mid-March of 1975 considered Kissinger's suggestion that the United States send B-52 bombers on a strike against enemy forces that were assailing South Vietnam. At this point David Hume Kennerly, Ford's irreverent, jeans-clad White House photographer, helped to nix this notion, telling him, "Mr. President, Vietnam has no more than a month left, and anyone who tells you different is bullshitting."[59] The B-52s stayed home.

As North Vietnamese invaders smashed through impotent South Vietnamese resistance in early April, Ford asked Congress to provide an additional $722 million in emergency military assistance and $250 million for humanitarian and economic aid. Congress refused, causing the normally even-tempered president to exclaim, "Those bastards!"[60] Anti-aid legislators retorted, as earlier, that the United States had blundered arrogantly and disastrously into the Vietnam War, in which more than 58,000 Americans and as many as 2 million Vietnamese had died. Use of napalm and Agent Orange had incinerated villages and devastated the countryside. American bombing and warfare in Laos and Cambodia had helped to intensify armed rebellions in both nations, which, like South Vietnam, were in danger of imploding in early 1975. Reciting these and other tragedies, opponents of military assistance gave Ford no quarter.

The foes of aid insisted that America learn a larger lesson from its blunders: It must never again send its soldiers into quagmires such as those that had swallowed so many young men in Vietnam. This insistence did not lead the United States to retreat into some sort of isolationist shell; in the 1970s, as later, Americans supported far-reaching military commitments, notably to NATO. Consistently resolute in containing communism, the United States stayed the course as the leader of the many nations that waged the Cold War against the Soviet Union and its allies. This was a

58. Some thirty years later there were still 1,875 American MIAs from the Vietnam War, along with some 78,000 from World War II, 8,100 from Korea, and 3 from the Gulf War of 1991. *New York Times*, Nov. 19, 2003.
59. Greene, *The Presidency of Gerald R. Ford*, 137.
60. Reported later in *Time*, April 24, 2000, 52–53.

perilous struggle that would last until 1990 and that had already helped to kill millions of people, most of them civilians, in Korea and Vietnam. The United States, continuing to dominate the International Monetary Fund and the World Bank, also protected, and whenever possible expanded, its economic interests throughout the world. Popular support by Americans for the diplomatic, economic, and political engagement of the United States on a large number of overseas fronts continued after 1974.[61]

Still, conflict over the lessons to be learned from the war in Vietnam persisted as a potent force in American life, affecting not only popular opinion about foreign policy initiatives but also military planners and diplomats for years to come. It also sharpened partisan divisions. Thanks to the Vietnam War, Democrats, who in the Truman years had been members of the more internationalist party, became more cautious than Republicans about calling for significant military commitments abroad. As the columnist Charles Krauthammer later observed, they came to see the term "Cold Warrior" as pejorative.[62] But it was not just liberals who looked at foreign policy through the lens of Vietnam. In the Ford years, as in later decades, wrangling over the "lessons of Vietnam" lay at the root of almost every significant foreign policy and military debate in the United States.

Controlling Congress, Democrats led the way in reducing defense spending, which declined between 1972 and 1975 both in constant dollars and as a percentage of gross national product. In 1980, Army Chief of Staff Edward Mayer lamented, "What we have is a hollow Army."[63] Critics of these cuts complained that the United States would now be able to fight only "Gilbert and Sullivan wars." America would no longer have the muscle to lead the Free World. But popular fears of another Vietnam remained powerful. In the late 1970s, a number of films concerned with the war—*The Deer Hunter* (1978), *Coming Home* (1978), and *Apocalypse Now* (1979)—revived many of the horrible memories, which continued to foment harsh domestic divisions.[64]

It is highly doubtful that even massive amounts of United States aid would have saved the pro-American governments of Southeast Asia. Un-

---

61. Alan Wolfe, *One Nation, After All: What Middle-Class Americans Really Think About God, Country, Family, Racism, Welfare, Immigration, Homosexuality, Work, the Right, the Left, and Each Other* (New York, 1998), 170.
62. As reported by David Brooks, *New York Times*, Feb. 17, 2004.
63. King and Karabell, *The Generation of Trust*, 21–24.
64. Tom Engelhardt, *The End of Victory Culture: Cold War America and the Disillusioning of a Generation* (New York, 1995); Michael Sherry, *In the Shadow of War: The United States Since the 1930s* (New Haven, 1995), 336–40.

der military siege in 1975, they were riddled with corruption and had little popular following. Communists took control of Laos, remaining in command into the twenty-first century. In Cambodia, an especially brutal Khmer Rouge regime quickly began slaughtering people. Within the next three years an estimated 1.5 million people, close to one-fourth of the nation's population, were murdered or died of disease or overwork in the infamous "killing fields" of that unfortunate country.

In Saigon, where the South Vietnamese government surrendered on April 29, thousands of panicked supporters of the old regime clamored to flee from their enemies. Communist forces threatened to overrun the American Embassy, leading to desperate scrambles of would-be refugees up a ladder to helicopters perched on a high part of the embassy roof. In order to enable already dangerously overloaded helicopters to leave, American Embassy personnel used clubs and their fists to beat away desperate Vietnamese seeking to climb aboard. Though the operation eventually managed to evacuate more than 1,000 Americans and 5,500 Vietnamese, it took nineteen highly tense hours to complete. It was a mad, miserable, and, for many Americans, humiliating melee that television captured and relayed to viewers around the world.[65] The next day, Saigon was renamed Ho Chi Minh City. Within the next few years, a million or so Vietnamese fled their homeland, many of them arriving eventually in the United States.

Only two weeks after the fall of Saigon, Ford and Kissinger sought a measure of revenge. When Khmer Rouge forces seized an American merchant ship, the *Mayaguez*, in the Gulf of Siam, Ford dispensed with diplomacy. Without consulting Congress, he called the seizure an "act of piracy" and dispatched warplanes, air police, and marines to the rescue. American forces that assaulted the island where the ship was anchored lost thirty-eight men and eight helicopters. Ford also authorized air strikes on the Cambodian mainland. When United States forces finally boarded the *Mayaguez*, they learned that the crew of thirty-odd had already been taken away and placed on a fishing vessel. The Cambodians eventually turned them over.

At other times such a venture, which had a comic opera quality to it, might have whipped up a storm of criticism. *Time* noted that the incident "had many of the gung-ho elements of a John Wayne movie." Critics

65. *New York Times*, April 30, 1975; Laura Kalman, "Gerald R. Ford," in James McPherson, ed., *"To the Best of My Ability": The American Presidents* (New York, 2000), 274–81; Greene, *The Presidency of Gerald R. Ford*, 141.

pointed out that Ford had acted imperiously and had launched attacks that hit the wrong targets and freed no one. More Americans died in the effort than would have been lost if the entire crew of the *Mayaguez* had been killed. Yet most Americans seemed thrilled by Ford's show of steel. Public opinion polls revealed a surge in his popularity. Senator Barry Goldwater of Arizona, a frequent advocate of strong American military action, proclaimed, "It shows we've still got balls in this country."[66] No comment better exposed the anger and frustration that gripped many Americans in the aftermath of the Vietnam War.

Ford encountered special difficulties in trying to manage the Cold War, which remained the central issue of American foreign policy. Massive stockpiles of nuclear weapons had the potential to incinerate much of the world. Following Kissinger's lead, Ford at first hoped that Nixon's policy of détente would alleviate tensions. Thus he joined Soviet leader Leonid Brezhnev in observing the terms of a Strategic Arms Limitation Treaty (SALT I, 1972) that called for a five-year freeze on the testing and deployment of intercontinental ballistic missiles (ICBMs). In mid-1975, he signed, as did the leaders of the Soviet Union and of thirty-one other nations, the so-called Helsinki Accords. Calling on signatories to seek peaceful solutions to disputes, to cooperate on scientific and economic matters, and to promote the free movement of people and ideas, the accords later encouraged anti-Soviet dissidents in Eastern Europe. They also confirmed the existing boundaries of Europe, thereby recognizing the Iron Curtain and infuriating Ronald Reagan and others on the Republican Right.

But détente had not succeeded in promoting warmer relations between the United States and the Soviet Union. Moreover, it faced determined enemies at home. One of these was Defense Secretary Schlesinger, who thoroughly distrusted the Soviets. Another was Democratic senator Henry Jackson of Washington, who had presidential aspirations. In late 1974 Jackson steered through Congress the Jackson-Vanik Amendment, which denied most-favored-nation trading status to the Soviet Union unless it permitted unlimited Jewish emigration. Brezhnev and others in the Kremlin hotly resented this intrusion into their domestic doings. By the time of the Helsinki conference, at which Brezhnev was icy toward Ford, support

66. George Lipsitz, "Dilemmas of Beset Nationhood: Patriotism, the Family, and Economic Change in the 1970s and 1980s," in John Bodnar, ed., *Bonds of Affection: Americans Define Their Patriotism* (Princeton, 1996), 251–72. Useful accounts of the *Mayaguez* incident include Greene, *The Presidency of Gerald R. Ford*, 143–50; and Sherry, *In the Shadow of War*, 337–38.

for détente was collapsing within the White House.[67] Ford, heeding the hawkish advice of Defense Secretary Rumsfeld, kept his distance from advocates such as Kissinger and avoided public use of the word during the campaign of 1976.[68]

Under Brezhnev, moreover, the Soviets added greatly to their arsenal of long-range weapons. By 1975, they were believed to lag behind America in numbers of nuclear warheads and manned bombers but to have 50 percent more intercontinental ballistic missiles than the United States.[69] Ford, like his predecessors, felt obliged to step up defense spending, thereby enlarging what critics called the potential for mutual assured destruction, or MAD. Critics of the buildup complained that America was indulging in overkill, and in so doing warping its economic priorities, but they were powerless to stop the arms race or to prevent the United States from selling weapons to anti-communist allies. Fears of nuclear catastrophe continued to loom over the world.[70]

Liberal critics of the president were equally ineffectual in getting the United States to shy away from authoritarian regimes that supported the American side in the Cold War or to show great interest in an international human rights movement that had gathered force during and after the Vietnam War. When Kissinger had served as Nixon's national security adviser, he had played a key role, along with the CIA, in abetting efforts to undermine Salvador Allende's left-leaning democratic regime in Chile. On September 11, 1973, a military coup overthrew Allende. During Ford's presidency Kissinger resisted congressional efforts to cut off arms sales to Allende's brutal successor, General Augusto Pinochet. Kissinger, an advocate of *Realpolitik* in the conduct of foreign relations, also backed the murderous military junta that seized control of Argentina in 1976.[71]

67. See Raymond Garthoff, *Détente and Confrontation: American-Soviet Relations from Nixon to Reagan* (Washington, 1985), 409–37.
68. Mann, *Rise of the Vulcans*, 56–78.
69. Reichley, *Conservatives in an Age of Change*, 347–48.
70. Gaddis Smith, *Morality, Reason, and Power: American Diplomacy in the Carter Years* (New York, 1986), 234–37; H. W. Brands, *The Devil We Knew: Americans and the Cold War* (New York, 1993), 161–63, 217. Joseph Nye, *Bound to Lead: The Changing Nature of American Power* (New York, 1990), 79–87, 107–12, argues that America and its allies maintained a strategic edge in nuclear weapons in the 1970s.
71. It was estimated that some 2,700 Chileans died in the bloody coup that overthrew Allende, and that some 30,000 people disappeared or died in the "dirty war" that the Argentinian military junta launched between 1976 and the late 1980s. *New York Times*, Dec. 28, 2003.

Cold War rivalries also continued to afflict the Third World, including the many African nations that were finally establishing their independence from colonial powers. One of these was Angola, which was scheduled to become independent from Portugal in November 1975. By then, however, both Ford and Brezhnev had intervened. The United States, allied with the racially discriminatory regime of South Africa, covertly aided one side in a civil war, and the Soviets the other, with the help of 40,000 troops from Fidel Castro's Cuba. By 1976, at which point pro-Soviet factions had gained control in Angola, Mozambique, and Ethiopia (where Cuban troops also were operating), many Americans worried that Brezhnev was right when he claimed that the USSR was winning the Cold War.

ALL THESE DOMESTIC AND FOREIGN PROBLEMS placed Ford on the defensive as he prepared for the election of 1976. As an incumbent he might have expected an easy run for the nomination, but that was not to be, thanks to the entry of Ronald Reagan into the race in late 1975. An affable man and a formidable campaigner, Reagan had been a popular two-term governor of California between 1967 and 1975. When he challenged Ford, he excited great enthusiasm among the party's politically engaged right wing, which celebrated his call for school prayer and his emergence (though belated) as an opponent of abortion.[72] Polls indicated that Republicans favored him over the president for the GOP nomination. In February, he almost triumphed in the key New Hampshire primary. A staunch anti-Communist, he attacked Ford and Kissinger for advocating détente with the Soviet Union and for contemplating a renegotiation of America's 1903 treaty concerning the Panama Canal. "We bought it, we paid for it, it's ours, and we're going to keep it," he proclaimed.[73] Rhetoric like this apparently helped him win big victories in primaries in North Carolina and Texas.

As late as May 1976, it seemed that Reagan might maintain what seemed to be a narrow lead in delegates to the party convention, but Ford fought hard, using presidential patronage to rally people to his side. He won the GOP nomination on the first ballot, but only by the narrow margin of 1,187 to 1,070. He then named Kansas senator Robert Dole, a conservative whom Reagan liked, as his vice-presidential running mate.[74]

The race for the Democratic nomination ultimately featured eleven contenders, one of whom, former Georgia governor Jimmy Carter, seemed

72. Reagan as governor of California had signed a liberal abortion bill in 1967.
73. Smith, *Morality, Reason, and Power*, 109–15.
74. Greene, *The Presidency of Gerald R. Ford*, 157–88.

to be the longest of long shots. When he told his mother that he was going to run for president, she asked, "President of what?" Undeterred, he had jumped into the race as early as 1975. Though only 2 percent of Americans in January 1976 had ever heard of him, he was an intensely ambitious and competitive super-achiever who was determined to win. He recognized shrewdly that the key to victory under Democratic Party procedures that had been developed since 1968 was to make a strong showing in early primaries, the number of which had swelled by then to thirty. He focused especially on the first two contests, party precinct caucuses in Iowa and the primary in New Hampshire.

Carter spoke in a soft drawl and wore a big, toothy smile. Identifying himself as a "born-again" Christian, he emphasized his commitment to family life and to high standards of personal morality. People seemed attracted to his down-home manner, which he played up as a way of identifying himself as an outsider to the wicked ways of Washington. Competing effectively in both early contests, Carter was anointed as a probable winner of the presidential nomination by the national media and rocketed ahead from long shot to front-runner. Soon he built up a formidable advantage in campaign contributions, which helped him best challengers such as Senator Jackson of Washington and Representative Morris Udall of Arizona and to win eighteen primaries. He took the nomination on the first ballot and selected Walter Mondale, a liberal senator from Minnesota, as his running mate. When the campaign against Ford opened in earnest, polls indicated that Carter had a lead of twenty percentage points.

Neither candidate seemed to excite voters during the campaign, which featured the first televised debates between major contenders since 1960. (In one of these, an audio failure left the two candidates frozen in silence at their positions for more than twenty minutes.) Carter, like Ford, was an uninspiring speaker. Eugene McCarthy, running in 1976 as an independent presidential candidate, called him an "oratorical mortician" who "inters his words and ideas behind piles of syntactical mush." A historian of his presidency later quipped that Carter was "allergic to all efforts at eloquence."[75] Though proud to identify himself as a born-again Christian and as a teacher of Sunday school, Carter agreed to an interview with *Playboy*, in which he was quoted as saying: "I have looked upon a lot of women with lust. I've committed adultery in my heart many times."

75. William Leuchtenburg, "Jimmy Carter and the Post-New Deal Presidency," in Gary Fink and Hugh Davis Graham, eds., *The Carter Presidency: Policy Choices in the Post-New Deal Era* (Lawrence, Kans., 1998), 7–28; Burton Kaufman, *The Presidency of James Earl Carter, Jr.* (Lawrence, Kans., 1993), 16.

Bumper stickers, recalling the 1964 campaign when a Republican slogan said of GOP presidential candidate Barry Goldwater, "In your heart, you know he's right," soon appeared with the message to Carter: "In his heart, he knows your wife."[76]

The interview may have cost Carter the affection—and perhaps the political support—of a number of evangelical Protestants, who were to become increasingly active in politics over the next few years.[77] But Ford also blundered, commenting in a televised debate, "There is no Soviet domination of Eastern Europe." What he seems to have meant is that Eastern Europeans, hating the Soviet presence, were eager to rebel. Indeed, he had said in the debate that there never would be Soviet domination of Eastern Europe in a Ford administration. But for five days he stubbornly resisted Cheney's pleas that he clarify his remarks, which especially alienated voters of East European descent and made him sound both ill informed and insensitive.

Carter, while highlighting Ford's gaffe, concentrated his fire on three other issues. The first was the unsettled economy, which he blamed on the incumbent administration. In doing so he deployed a "misery index" that focused on the nation's high inflation and unemployment rates. The second was the responsibility of Republicans for the Watergate conspiracy. The third zeroed in on the Beltway. Positioning himself as an honest and forthright crusader who would have nothing to do with the political establishment, Carter posed like Jimmy Stewart in the old movie *Mr. Smith Goes to Washington* (1939). He repeatedly proclaimed, "I'm Jimmy Carter, and I'm running for President. I will never lie to you."[78]

Whether this anti-Beltway image assisted Carter in November is hard to say. Ford and Dole waged vigorous campaigns. Carter lost almost all of the lead that he had enjoyed in late summer, and he barely won an extraordinarily close election, squeaking by with 50.1 percent of the votes to Ford's 48 percent.[79] Ford triumphed in the important states of California and Illinois. He was also fairly strong in the Northeast, winning four of six states in New England. Had the president not pardoned Nixon, he might have won in Ohio and Hawaii, where the margins were razor thin. Carter

76. Democrats had sniped at the GOP slogan in 1964, "In your guts you know he's nuts."
77. Garry Wills, *Under God: Religion and American Politics* (New York, 1990), 119; Daniel Williams, "From the Pews to the Polls: The Political Mobilization of Southern Conservative Protestants" (PhD diss., Brown University, 2005), chap. 3.
78. Greenstein, *The Presidential Difference*, 127–29.
79. Eugene McCarthy, running as the candidate of the Independent Party, won most of the rest of the votes.

displayed strength among black voters in the South, which he swept, except for Virginia. He also managed to retain the backing of economically hard-pressed Democratic loyalists, including labor union members and blacks, in key urban states such as Ohio, Pennsylvania, and New York. The New Deal coalition, while trembling, held firm in enough places to help make Carter president.[80]

Ford, a good loser, consoled himself with the thought that he had been an honorable, straightforward, and approachable chief executive. When he was asked how he wished to be remembered, he replied, "I want to be remembered as . . . a nice person, who worked at the job, and who left the White House in better shape than when I took it over."[81] This was a fair evaluation of Ford's brief, often troubled stint as president during politically polarized times.

80. Carter received 40,831,000 votes, and Ford, 39,148,000. McCarthy received 757,000. See note 3 and the start of this chapter for other statistics concerning the election.
81. Greene, *The Presidency of Gerald R. Ford*, 193.

4

Carter, Reagan, and the
Rise of the Right

Most people who became friendly with Jimmy Carter agreed that he was a decent, gracious, and compassionate man. One of these acquaintances was James Fallows, a top presidential speechwriter, who wrote in 1979 that Carter had a fair amount of personal charm and was "probably smarter than anyone." Carter was "patient" and would never push the wrong buttons. A "stable, confident man whose quirks are few," he was "perhaps as admirable a human being as has ever held the job."[1]

Like others, Fallows was impressed by the president's progress in life. Born in 1924 in Plains, Georgia, Carter was the eldest child of James Earl Carter Sr., a successful farmer and businessman, and of Lillian, a strong-minded, outspoken woman who later joined the Peace Corps at the age of sixty-six. Plains was a small place, with a population of around 500, and Jimmy left it after high school to attend the U.S. Naval Academy. There he excelled academically, moving on to submarine service between 1946 and 1953. A mentor, then and later, was Hyman Rickover, a controversial, perfectionist naval officer who headed America's nuclear submarine program.

When his father grew ill, Carter resigned from the navy and returned to Plains to take over the family business. He soon moved into politics, winning a seat in the state legislature in 1962 and 1964 and running unsuccessfully for governor in 1966. Trying again in 1970, he triumphed, and though he had courted white racist support in his campaign, he announced

---

1. James Fallows, "The Passionless Presidency: The Trouble with Jimmy Carter's Administration," *Atlantic Monthly* 243 (May 1979), 33–48.

in his inaugural address, "The time for racial discrimination is over." National publications hailed him as a progressive son of the "New South." *Time* placed him on its cover in May 1971.[2]

In 1977, when Carter entered the White House, it seemed that he had qualities that would bring him success as president. He started off all right. After being sworn in at the Capitol, he strolled down Pennsylvania Avenue to the White House. His wife, Rosalynn, their three sons and daughters-in-law, and nine-year-old daughter Amy walked with him as enthusiastic crowds roared their approval. Not long after taking office, he donned a cardigan sweater—a symbol of how Americans might conserve energy—to give a televised fireside chat to the nation. Seeming to spurn the trappings of office, he announced that he was selling the presidential yacht.

In those early days Carter reiterated the mantra of his campaign: He would bring fresh approaches to government and keep his distance from Washington insiders. He also would move quickly to tackle big, unresolved issues, including energy, welfare, health care, and urban problems. Talking like a Keynesian, he indicated that he would advance a tax rebate plan and increase public works employment in order to invigorate the economy. By March his popular approval rating had leapt to 75 percent.

Even then, however, many who came into contact with Carter were developing doubts about his manner, especially in dealing with Congress. By midsummer of 1977 his glow had dimmed, and Fallows, among others, grew disenchanted. The rest of his widely read two-part essay on Carter, published two years later, was decidedly uncomplimentary. Carter, he wrote, had proved to be complacent, arrogant, and lacking in sophistication. Like his overconfident Georgia aides, the new president had entered the White House with a "blissful ignorance" about how to get things done. Fallows complained especially that Carter was "passionless." His administration had the "spirit of a bureaucracy, drained of zeal, obsessed with form." His aides, taking their cue from their leader, had an "in-box mentality, of just pushing the paper."[3]

A year and a half after these words appeared, on the morning of the day his term was to end, Carter had large circles under his eyes. He had been up for most of the two previous nights trying desperately to free fifty-two Americans who had been held hostage for 444 days by Iranian revolutionaries.

2. Fred Greenstein, *The Presidential Difference: Leadership Style from FDR to Clinton* (New York, 2000), 127–32; Lewis Gould, *The Modern American Presidency* (Lawrence, Kans., 2003), 179–80.
3. Fallows, "The Passionless Presidency II," *Atlantic Monthly* 243 (June 1979), 75–81.

During these anxious months, the Soviets had invaded Afghanistan, and the Cold War had become icier than at any time since the early 1960s. Thanks partly to OPEC decisions that jacked up the cost of oil, America's inflation rate had soared into double digits. The president left office with a public approval rating of 33 percent, a number that was dismal by any standard.

SOME OF CARTER'S DIFFICULTIES, notably with economic problems, stemmed from events that were hard for the United States to control. Like Ford, Carter had the misfortune of taking office in the post-Watergate era of growing popular disenchantment with politicians in general and with the imperial presidency in particular. Recognizing the popular mood, he had relied heavily on this theme in his campaign. Many Democrats in Congress, including the Watergate babies elected in 1974, shared this distrust of executive power. Though they still enjoyed large majorities on the Hill, they were badly split along regional lines on racial matters and on a range of other issues. On many key questions, such as energy policy, Carter had to confront determined interest groups, some of them led by liberals who saw his election as a long-awaited opportunity to advance causes that Nixon and Ford had resisted.[4]

Having won barely 50 percent of the vote, Carter obviously lacked a strong popular mandate. Many commentators regarded him as a fluke; others, as a rube who was out of his depth in Washington. Tom Wolfe, reflecting this animus against rural southerners, sniped during the campaign that Carter was an "unknown down-home matronly-voiced Sunday-school soft-shelled watery-eyed sponge-backed Millennial lulu."[5] Many influential liberals, led by Ted Kennedy, who had set his sights on running for president in 1980, considered Carter to be a hick from Plains who had been lucky to reach the highest office in the land.

Still, Carter could be his own worst enemy. Supremely self-confident, he truly believed the rhetoric of his campaign: that he and his team of advisers from Georgia did not need help from the Washington establishment. Early in 1977, House Speaker Tip O'Neill, a skilled political insider, offered to help the new president develop productive relationships with his colleagues on Capitol Hill. Carter replied that he had been a

4. Bruce Schulman, "Slouching Toward the Supply Side: Jimmy Carter and the New American Political Economy," in Gary Fink and Hugh Davis Graham, eds., *The Carter Presidency: Policy Choices in the Post–New Deal Era* (Lawrence, Kans., 1998), 51–71.

5. William Leuchtenburg, "Jimmy Carter and the Post–New Deal Presidency," in Fink and Graham, eds., *The Carter Presidency*, 7–28; Tom Wolfe, "Entr'actes and Canapes," in Wolfe, *In Our Time* (New York, 1980), 22.

governor and knew how to deal with legislators. O'Neill, troubled, pointed out that most members of Congress enjoyed firm political bases in their districts and had minds of their own. When he asked Carter how he would respond if legislators resisted him, the president answered that he would react as he had done as governor: go over their heads to the people. O'Neill was astounded, commenting later that Ronald Reagan (whose policies he deplored) was far more skillful in dealing with Congress than Carter.[6]

O'Neill and others found it especially hard to warm to Carter's aloof, largely humorless manner. The president, surrounded by a team of young aides, many of them campaign workers from Georgia, ran a tight ship. The chief of his crew, which detractors dubbed the "Georgia Mafia," was Hamilton Jordan, who bragged that he did not bother to answer telephone calls from the Hill. Carter, a loner, a workaholic, and a micromanager, arose early and labored late. He pored over hundreds of memoranda, scribbling comments in the margins and replying with memoranda of his own, and he did not encourage Jordan or anyone else on his staff to make decisions.[7] For the first six months of his administration, he personally reviewed all requests for use of the White House tennis court. Only in the summer of 1979, after asking all top aides and Cabinet secretaries to offer their resignations, did he establish the post of chief of staff and give it to Jordan. Long before then, critics had likened him to Herbert Hoover. "Jimmy Hoover," like Herbert, was a hardworking but uninspiring technocrat and numbers cruncher who was fixated on detail.[8]

At times Carter seemed to understand that he could not do everything himself. In January 1977, he reflected in his diary, "Everybody has warned me not to take on too many problems so early in the administration, but it's almost impossible for me to delay something that I see needs to be done."[9] He then proceeded to ignore his own insights. In 1977, he oversaw the development of large-scale plans, some of them concocted in secrecy, concerning the economy, energy, and welfare. He then announced them to Congress, which had had little real say in their design. Carter did not understand that successful leaders must normally establish clear priorities and that members of Congress resent being snowed under by an avalanche of large legislative packages.

6. Greenstein, *The Presidential Difference*, 135–37.
7. Carter's personal papers at the Carter presidential library in Atlanta, which I have perused, amply reveal the president's great attention to detail.
8. A point made by the historian Robert Dallek, in Leuchtenburg, "Jimmy Carter," 10.
9. William Stueck, "Placing Jimmy Carter's Foreign Policy," in Fink and Graham, *The Carter Presidency*, 244–66. Quote on 249-50.

Like many others, they especially resented what they perceived as the president's pious and pedantic approach to politics. Carter could be politically hardheaded, especially when it came to campaigning for himself, but as a born-again Christian and Sunday school teacher, he struck many senators and representatives as a self-righteous prig who proclaimed that the "right" should prevail over the "political."[10] Vice President Mondale, though loyal, was one of many who made note of his boss's moralistic streak. "Carter," he said, "thought politics was sinful. The worst thing you could say to Carter if you wanted to do something was that it was politically the best thing to do."[11]

Early in 1977, Carter confirmed the worst fears of O'Neill and other Democrats on the Hill. Seeking support for his economic revitalization plan, he lined up Democratic congressional leaders behind it. In April 1977, however, he grew increasingly alarmed by the size of the deficit that he had inherited from the Nixon-Ford years. Abandoning the legislators who had stood by his side, he changed his mind and scuttled a tax rebate that he had earlier promised to support. His decision revealed a key aspect of Carter's economic thinking: He was a confirmed fiscal conservative. Like many other Americans in those economically unstable years, he also believed that there were "limits"–in this case, budgetary limits—to what the federal government should attempt. Again and again, however, his refusal to pursue a big-spending, Keynesian agenda touched off bitter rows with Kennedy and other liberals in his own party. Some never forgave Carter's abrupt reversal on tax rebates.

Many legislators of both parties reacted with equal fury against Carter's handling in February 1977 of a package of nineteen dams and water projects dear to the interests of many on the Hill, especially those from the West. At that time his secretary of the interior was on his way to a conference of western governors who were greatly concerned about drought. Carter, however, loved wild rivers and was cool to expensive pork barrel projects. Believing that as president he should do the right thing—that is, not capitulate to special interests—he rescinded funding for the projects for the 1978 fiscal year. Whatever the merits of his position, his actions were politically stunning. As one historian later observed, Carter's move revealed his "typical capacity for mind-boggling political naivete." Congress fought back by presenting him in August 1977 with an important appropriations

10. Burton Kaufman, *The Presidency of James Earl Carter, Jr.* (Lawrence, Kans., 1993), 210.
11. Gould, *The Modern American Presidency*, 182.

bill that also called for the projects to be funded. Recognizing that Congress had the votes to override a veto, he reluctantly signed it. Environmentalists, who had previously cheered the president, were demoralized.[12]

LIBERAL INTEREST GROUPS evaluating Carter's domestic policies had mixed feelings about his performance. Blacks, who had been strong allies during the 1976 campaign, were pleased by his appointment of thirty-eight African American federal judges, by the vigor with which the Equal Employment Opportunity Commission worked to curb discrimination in the labor force, and by the Justice Department's backing of the University of California at Davis's controversial affirmative action plan.[13] They welcomed passage in 1977 of the Public Works Act, which included a provision stipulating that minority contractors (if available in a local area) receive "set-asides" of 10 percent per year of federal grants for public works. "Minority" groups covered by this provision were "Negroes, Spanish-speaking, Orientals, Indians, Eskimos, and Aleuts." Though the act attracted relatively little attention at the time—like affirmative action affecting university admissions, it conferred a right that some observers expected to become unnecessary in the future—it was to remain entrenched in federal public policy. Its endorsement of quotas was to become increasingly controversial over the years and to enmesh the courts, including the Supreme Court, in a considerable amount of complicated litigation.[14]

Advocates of more generous social policy welcomed a number of presidential efforts, notably a "stimulus" package in 1977 that included $4 billion for public works programs. Liberals, still especially strong in the House, pressed successfully for enlargement of other social policies, such as the Earned Income Tax Credit (EITC), a program of tax credits for low-income working families with children that Congress had initiated in 1975. In the late 1970s, Congress also expanded the means-tested food stamp program. By 1980, food stamps were helping to support 21 million people (as opposed to 18.5 million in 1976).[15] These programs, like SSI for the indigent blind, aged, and disabled, Social Security and Medicare for the elderly,

12. Marc Reisner, *Cadillac Desert: The American West and Its Disappearing Water* (New York, 1993), 314; Jeffrey Stine, "Environmental Policy During the Carter Presidency," in Fink and Graham, *The Carter Presidency*, 179–201.
13. Culminating in the *Bakke* decision by the Supreme Court in 1978. See chapter 1.
14. Terry Anderson, *In Pursuit of Fairness: A History of Affirmative Action* (New York, 2004), 147, 155–57.
15. House Committee on Ways and Means, "Overview of Entitlement Programs," 1992 *Green Book*, 102d Congress, 2d Session (Washington, 1992), 1013–19, 1613–39.

and Medicaid for poor people who were disabled or elderly, continued to expand slowly in real dollars in many later years of the century, partially patching up holes in the nation's social safety net.

Blacks grumbled, however, that Carter seemed to be cool to court-ordered busing to advance racial integration in the schools and that he gave only lukewarm support to a fair housing bill, which failed to pass in 1978.[16] African American congressional leaders, banding together as the Black Caucus, chafed especially at his fiscal conservatism, which helped to spike liberal expectations for significant expansion of social welfare programs.[17] The United States Conference of Mayors, another of the many interest groups promoting social spending for inner-city needs, was unhappy that public service employment did not rise faster than it did. The Reverend Jesse Jackson, emerging as a presidential aspirant, exclaimed that Carter's economic policy was like a "domestic neutron bomb": "It doesn't destroy bridges—only people who are less organized and therefore less able to defend themselves from such an attack."[18]

A few labor leaders, notably of the National Education Association, had reason to applaud the Carter administration, which established a Cabinet-level Department of Education. Then and later, public employee unions such as the NEA, growing in size amid the overall decline of organized labor, offered significant support for liberal candidates and public policies. Many other labor leaders, however, were unhappy with Carter, who was generally skeptical of unions. They complained that Carter refused to back an expensive national health insurance bill and a large hike in the federal minimum wage. They were especially angry that he did little to promote the Humphrey-Hawkins bill. This measure, a longtime goal of AFL-CIO chief George Meany, had stated in its original form that the federal government, protecting workers from recessions, should be the employer of last resort. By the time the bill finally passed in October 1978, it had become so watered down as to be of only symbolic significance. Put off by Meany's criticisms, Carter refused to meet with him in 1978.[19]

Advocates of women's rights, too, had mixed opinions about Carter. They were pleased that he appointed many women to government positions. On the other hands, some activists thought he might have done

16. Hugh Davis Graham, "Civil Rights Policy in the Carter Presidency," in Fink and Graham, *The Carter Presidency*, 202–23.
17. James Patterson, "Jimmy Carter and Welfare Reform," ibid., 117–36.
18. Kaufman, *The Presidency of James Earl Carter, Jr.*, 134.
19. Ibid., 114.

more to promote the ERA, which no states ratified after 1977. Still others urged him to do more to enforce Title IX (1972), which was aimed at gender discrimination in American education.[20] Their disappointments reflected the high expectations from government that America's liberal interest groups, working as earlier with supportive staffers and subcommittee chairmen on the Hill, had developed by the late 1970s.

Liberals, who had long led the fight for greater governmental management of the economy, nonetheless acquiesced in a surge of deregulatory legislation that passed in the late 1970s. Carter signed a number of important measures into law. The Airline Deregulation Act of 1978 abolished the Civil Aeronautics Board and permitted airlines greater leeway in scheduling and related matters. Other laws cut back federal oversight of trucking and communications. The deregulatory wave of the era exposed a widespread feeling that the still sluggish American economy needed to be "unshackled" from strict public restraints so that the "liberating forces of market competition" could come into play.

The results of this wave seemed unclear at the time. Deregulation of the airlines stimulated sharp (and in many ways brutal) competition and brought about lower fares on many routes. In subsequent decades it benefited a great many cost-conscious travelers. Supporters of deregulation, led by market-oriented business leaders, emphasized that it loosened the "dead hand" of governmental oversight, aroused entrepreneurial energies, rewarded lean and competitive corporations, and stimulated economic growth.[21] Later, they asserted that deregulation spurred a resurgence of the economy and positioned American corporations to thrive in the globalizing world of the 1980s and 1990s.

Some liberals, however, remained skeptical about deregulation, which they said gave far too much freedom to big corporations. They also continued to chafe in the late 1970s at other presidential decisions, particularly where appropriations for social welfare were concerned. They especially deplored a widely noted statement—one that prefigured Republican rhetoric in the Reagan years—in Carter's second state of the union address: "Government cannot solve our problems. . . . It cannot eliminate poverty, or provide a bountiful economy, or reduce inflation, or save our cities, or cure

20. Susan Hartman, "Feminism, Public Policy, and the Carter Administration," in Fink and Graham, eds., *The Carter Presidency*, 224–43.
21. And led to a loss in jobs, many of them unionized. Nelson Lichtenstein, *State of the Union: A Century of American Labor* (Princeton, 2002), 236, estimated that union representation in these industries declined by one-third.

illiteracy, or provide energy." The progressive historian Arthur Schlesinger Jr., who had served under JFK as an adviser and had written laudatory accounts of the New Deal, was one of many critics who would have none of this. If FDR had believed these things, Schlesinger (a supporter of Ted Kennedy) snapped, "we would still be in the Great Depression."[22]

Liberals had slightly more favorable things to say about the Carter administration's environmental policies. The environmental movement, indeed, had come into its own during the early 1970s, when Congress had approved landmark legislation leading to creation of the Environmental Protection Agency (EPA) and the Occupational Safety and Health Administration (OSHA). Congress had also passed a Clean Air Act (1970), an Endangered Species Act (1973), and a Toxic Substances Control Act (1976). Thanks in considerable part to the indefatigable efforts of Ralph Nader, a Consumer Product Safety Commission had been established. By the time Carter entered the White House, environmentalism had become a strong and vibrant, if not always purposefully united, political movement that embraced a host of causes. Activists lobbied not only to preserve wilderness and endangered species but also to fight against suburban over-development, nuclear power, occupational diseases, acid rain, depletion of the ozone, wasteful use of energy, and dams and other huge reclamation projects. Advocates of population control, worried about the environmental consequences of immigration, which grew rapidly in the 1970s, established the Federation of American Immigration Reform (FAIR) in 1978.

A small number of environmental militants, embracing tactics described in Edward Abbey's *The Monkey Wrench Gang* (1975), chained themselves to trees and blocked bulldozers. A few of these activists spiked trees with long nails, which wrecked chain saws. In so doing, they invited widespread criticism. The environmental movement also received mixed reactions from blue-collar workers, blacks, and Native Americans, some of whom charged that it was elitist and that it threatened industrial jobs. A popular labor union bumper sticker read: IF YOU'RE HUNGRY AND OUT OF WORK, EAT AN ENVIRONMENTALIST. But environmental causes appealed especially to growing numbers of young, middle-class liberals. Suspicious of government ties to industry, they brought an almost religious intensity to their crusades.[23] It was estimated that the number of Americans enrolled in envi-

22. Leuchtenburg, "Jimmy Carter," 16.
23. Robert Gottlieb, *Forcing the Spring: The Transformation of the American Environmental Movement* (Washington, 1993), 292–96.

ronmental organizations swelled from 125,000 in 1960 to 1 million in 1970 to 2 million in 1980 and to 6.3 million in 1990.[24]

Growth such as this, along with technological developments, promoted environmental gains in the late 1970s. Catalytic converters, first introduced along with unleaded gasoline in the mid-1970s, helped to cut pollution from cars by some 75 percent over the next few decades. Clean air and water laws did not work wonders—alarm about acid rain intensified in the late 1970s—but they were important. Drinking water became purer, and putrid rivers and lakes regenerated. Workplace safety and health received better protection. Though California continued to suck water out of the West, many Americans became more conscious of the need to save rivers, wetlands, wilderness areas, and endangered species. Industrial polluters had to cope with tougher public restrictions. Gregg Easterbrook, who carefully evaluated these developments, did not exaggerate when he concluded later that "environmental protection is arguably the most impressive achievement of progressive government since the establishment of the Social Security system."[25]

Two troubling, highly publicized events in the Carter years further hastened environmental consciousness. The first took place in 1978 at Love Canal, near Niagara Falls in upstate New York. For some time, local residents living near the canal had complained that foul-smelling industrial waste had polluted the canal and the atmosphere, oozed into the ground, and caused serious health problems, including high rates of miscarriage and birth defects among children. Public officials, they charged, had deliberately deceived them about the seriousness of the situation. Taken to heart at last in July 1978, the complaints caused the state health commission to brand the canal as a "great and imminent peril to the health of the general public." The state then spent $30 million to buy nearby homes and to relocate hundreds of families. Intensive media coverage of the troubles at Love Canal caused a national outcry, especially when it

24. Estimate by Robert Putnam, *Bowling Alone: The Collapse and Revival of American Community* (New York, 2000), 115–16. Many of these people were active mainly or only to the extent of paying dues. For sources concerning environmentalism, see also Hal Rothman, *The Greening of a Nation? Environmentalism in the United States Since 1945* (Orlando, 1998); Ted Steinberg, *Down to Earth: Nature's Role in American History* (New York, 2002); Barbara Freese, *Coal: A Human History* (Cambridge, Mass., 2003), 167–72; and Stine, "Environmental Policy During the Carter Presidency."
25. Gregg Easterbrook, "America the O.K.," *New Republic*, Jan. 4/11, 1999, 25. See also Easterbrook, *A Moment on the Earth: The Coming Age of Environmental Optimism* (New York, 1995).

became clear that some of the people who lived near the canal had suffered chromosomal damage.[26]

Less than a year later, in March 1979, a frightening event created even greater alarm. At Three Mile Island, near Middletown, Pennsylvania, the radioactive core of a nuclear reactor overheated and partially melted down. The top half of the reactor broke up and caused leakage of radioactive steam. Terrified, more than 100,000 nearby residents fled their homes. It turned out that the steam had been confined to the interior of the reactor. No one was killed or injured. Fears that the near disaster had caused cancer were later shown to be unwarranted, and 2,100 lawsuits were dismissed. But the events at Three Mile Island shattered popular faith in nuclear power. Though many existing nuclear plants continued to operate (including one reactor at Three Mile Island), no new ones were built in the United States, thereby helping to make the nation more dependent on oil, especially overseas oil, as a major source of energy in the future.[27]

Carter, an outdoorsman himself, sympathized strongly with most environmental goals. During his term of office he signed clean air and water bills, as well as contested legislation regulating strip-mining. He also strengthened the Environmental Protection Agency. But it was not easy to satisfy contending forces within his party, some of which pressed for environmental causes, while some others, including local interest groups, stoutly resisted.

Political fighting over the Tellico Dam, which was then being constructed on the Little Tennessee River south of Knoxville, exposed these divisions. Advocates of the dam, including the Tennessee Valley Authority (TVA), were already building it when environmentalists discovered that the project would eliminate snail darters, a species of small fish that existed nowhere else. Relying on the Endangered Species Act, they resorted to legal action, which ultimately reached the Supreme Court in 1978. The Court upheld a lower court injunction against the dam. Infuriated congressional proponents of the project, which promised to promote employment and economic benefits in the area, retaliated by attaching to an appropriations bill a rider that mandated completion of the dam. Carter sympathized with the environmentalists, but he recognized that Congress was up in arms over the issue. Reluctantly, he signed the bill.[28]

26. Rothman, *The Greening of a Nation*, 148–55.
27. Ibid., 144–47. Starting in 1981, use of nuclear power slowly increased in the United States, from around 3 percent of total energy use in 1981 to nearly 8 percent by 2000. *Stat. Abst.*, 2002, 563. But nuclear power remained less important in the United States than in many other industrialized nations.
28. Stine, "Environmental Policy," 188–91.

In 1980, environmentalists finally scored two victories. One, the Alaska Lands Law, more than doubled the acreage of American land set aside as national parks and wildlife refuges. The other created a Superfund, which was expected to spend more than $1 billion a year to clean up toxic waste sites. Some of this money was to come from taxes on polluters, notably oil and chemical companies. The progress of Superfund was uphill over the years, in part because there were ever more numerous hazardous sites that had to be cleaned up. Restoring Love Canal (number one on the Superfund's list) took twenty-one years and cost nearly $400 million.[29] Still, the law was a significant environmental accomplishment of the Carter years.[30]

As the fight over the Tellico Dam made clear, energy policy issues complicated efforts for environmental protection. These issues gave Carter, who established a Cabinet-level Energy Department in 1977, no end of trouble, but he was determined to fashion a comprehensive energy policy, for he understood that energy use was intimately connected with economic and foreign policies. He hoped especially to promote conservation and to lessen American dependence on overseas oil, use of which was increasing. He therefore called for development of alternative (and clean) sources of energy, including solar power, and for a range of tax credits and regulations that would improve energy efficiency in buildings, cars, and home appliances.[31]

During these anxious years, a number of useful steps did lead to energy conservation in the United States, notably the enforcement of federal regulations (first established in the Ford years) that required auto manufacturers to produce cars that were more fuel-efficient. Until the mid- and late 1980s — by which point the cost of overseas oil had fallen considerably and Americans once again began buying large numbers of gas-guzzling cars — this reform, along with the lower speed limits imposed in 1974, had salutary effects. Major improvements in home appliances, especially refrigerators, and the spread of better home insulation, further curbed wastefulness. America's per capita energy consumption decreased by 10 percent from

29. New York Times, March 18, July 28, 2004.
30. Steinberg, Down to Earth, 261; Gottlieb, Forcing the Spring, 308-10. After 1995, money for Superfund, at a steady-state $450 million per year, came solely from the federal budget. In early 2004, Superfund had more than 1,200 sites on its list of places to be cleaned up. New York Times, March 9, Dec. 5, 2004.
31. Gaddis Smith, Morality, Reason, and Power: American Diplomacy in the Carter Years (New York, 1986), 56–58; John Barrow, "An Age of Limits: Jimmy Carter and the Quest for a National Energy Policy," in Fink and Graham, The Carter Presidency, 158–78.

1979 to 1983—during which time growth in the economy enabled the real per capita gross domestic product (GDP) to rise slightly.[32] Changes such as these had positive long-term consequences: America's total energy consumption, at approximately 18 percent of GDP in the mid-1970s, dropped over time, to roughly 9 percent in the early 2000s.[33]

Congress and state legislators, however, consistently refused to consider what European nations long had done to cut gasoline consumption: place high taxes on sales. These taxes, which helped to make gasoline in Europe some four times as expensive as it was in the United States, encouraged overseas car manufacturers to produce fuel-efficient motor vehicles and drivers to watch what they spent on gasoline. High taxes on gasoline seemed politically impossible in America, where oil and gas interests were strong, mass transit was ill supported, and people drove vast distances, especially in the West. For these and other reasons, the United States continued to consume large amounts of the world's sources of energy.

Carter's comprehensive energy program, moreover, did not succeed. He started off poorly by encouraging his secretary of energy, James Schlesinger, to develop the plan in secret. When the National Energy Plan (NEP) was unveiled in April 1977, its daunting complexity antagonized Congress. Once interest groups managed to comprehend it, they attacked it from all directions. Oil and gas interests demanded to be unshackled from government controls, without which, they said, they would be encouraged to explore and develop new resources. Environmentalists, fearing the exploitation of new fields, opposed these interests. Consumers balked (as they had in the Ford years) at paying more for gasoline or heating oil. As Speaker O'Neill observed sadly, energy policy was "perhaps . . . the most parochial issue that could ever have hit the floor."[34] In October 1978, a year and a half after NEP was introduced, Congress finally approved a bill that decontrolled natural gas prices and established tax credits for energy conservation measures. In general, however, the act fell far short of Carter's grandiose plans of 1977.

These struggles exposed an especially large obstacle to energy conservation in the United States: Americans, the most affluent people in the world, had historically used their ample resources as if there were no tomorrow, and they did not focus very much on long-term problems. Notwithstanding the oil crisis of 1973–74, they continued to resist serious

32. *Stat. Abst.*, 2002, 422, 563.
33. *New York Times*, Oct. 25, 2004.
34. Barrow, "An Age of Limits," 160.

restraints on their ability to consume. When Carter called on Americans to sacrifice — rarely a wise or successful political move — people resisted. When good times later returned, they became even less enthusiastic about conservation: Per capita energy use began to rise again in 1983. The reluctance of Americans to sacrifice exposed an equally durable aspect of popular attitudes in the 1970s and thereafter: While Americans regularly denounced their government, they expected it to assure and to expand their rights and comforts. Nothing must be allowed to dampen popular expectations about living standards that had ascended during the heady, upbeat years of the 1950s and 1960s.

THOUGH WHIPSAWED BY THESE PRESSURES, Carter soldiered on, but his last two years in office were in many ways grimmer than any in the recent history of the country. At the root of this grimness were two interrelated developments, one involving foreign policies, the other the economy. Together they unleashed an avalanche of conservative opposition that was to bury him and his party in the election of 1980.

Carter was a Wilsonian internationalist and idealist in his approach to foreign affairs. He took office believing strongly that the United States should speak out against nations that violated basic rights. In February he indicated that he would cut foreign aid to nations with poor human rights records. He and Cyrus Vance, his judicious secretary of state, seriously yearned to promote better relations with the Soviet Union and lessen the threat of nuclear war. In his inaugural address, he proclaimed, "We will move this year a step toward our ultimate goal — the elimination of all nuclear weapons from this earth."[35] Hoping to heal old wounds, the president quickly pardoned some 10,000 Vietnam War draft evaders. In 1977, he halted production of the B-1 bomber, which had been developed to replace the B-52 in America's defense arsenal. In 1978, he canceled development of the neutron bomb, which had been intended as a battlefield weapon in Europe. On January 1, 1979, the United States established diplomatic relations with the People's Republic of China, thereby infuriating conservatives who supported Taiwan.

In 1978, Carter scored two heartening diplomatic victories, winning Senate ratification of two treaties that promised to cede the Panama Canal to Panama at the end of 1999 and brokering a widely hailed treaty — the so-called Camp David Accord — in which Egypt recognized the state

35. Jimmy Carter, *Keeping Faith: Memoirs of a President, Jimmy Carter* (New York, 1982), 20.

of Israel and Israel agreed to return the Sinai Peninsula to Egypt.[36] Carter displayed considerable skill in waging the Panama fight, which aroused sharp conservative opposition. In the end, the two treaties barely received the votes of the necessary two-thirds of senators, many of whom worried about popular backlash at the polls.[37] (As it happened, twenty senators who voted for the treaties were defeated for reelection in 1978 or 1980.) The president was equally resolute in getting Menachem Begin of Israel and Anwar Sadat of Egypt to come to terms in September 1978. Before the agreement was reached, he held them together for thirteen days at Camp David. In the glow thereafter his popular approval ratings, which had tumbled to 38 percent in midsummer, rose to 50 percent.[38]

In dealing with the Soviet Union, however, Carter encountered difficulties from the start. By 1977, Soviet president Leonid Brezhnev was seventy-one years old and ailing. Requiring a hearing aid and a pacemaker, he seemed at times almost robotic in his movements and wore a glazed look that may have been caused by medication. Brezhnev had never been a serious supporter of détente, and he deeply resented Carter's complaints about Soviet abuses of human rights. The United States, he complained, did not seem nearly so critical of China, Iran, Nicaragua, the Philippines, or other nations that were widely believed to be guilty of such violations. In 1977, Brezhnev began deploying a new generation of SS-20 missiles that could hit targets anywhere in Western Europe. Cuban troops, serving as proxies for the USSR, remained active in Ethiopia and Angola.[39]

In June 1979, Carter and Brezhnev held a summit meeting in Vienna and announced agreement on SALT II, which called for limits on the numbers of missiles and bombers that each side might have. But anti-détente hawks in the Senate, led by Henry Jackson of Washington, retorted that the treaty undermined American security. Carter's national security adviser, Zbigniew Brzezinski, said he favored the agreement, but he, too, was known to be deeply distrustful of the Soviets and anxious to bolster American defense spending. Brzezinski, who had waged bureaucratic warfare with Vance since 1977, had an office near Carter's in the White House and often had the president's ear. Prominent Cold Warriors active in an increasingly vocal pressure group founded in 1976, the Com-

36. In 1981, however, angry Egyptians assassinated Sadat, and tensions mounted again in the Middle East.
37. The Senate vote on both treaties was 68 to 32. *New York Times*, April 19, 1978.
38. Kaufman, *The Presidency of James Earl Carter, Jr.*, 117–23; Greenstein, *The Presidential Difference*, 135–37. The treaty was signed in March 1979.
39. Smith, *Morality, Reason, and Power*, 211–13; Stueck, "Placing Carter's Foreign Policy."

mittee on the Present Danger, also intensified their criticisms of America's "cult of appeasement."[40] Amid rising anti-Soviet feelings, SALT II encountered tough sledding in the Senate, which failed to act on it in 1979.

As Carter confronted these pressures, he felt obliged to stiffen America's Cold War posture, first by agreeing in June to back full development of intercontinental MX missiles, which were to be shuttled about on underground rails in order to be mobile in the event of an attack. In mid-December 1979, he joined NATO ministers in stating that unless the Soviets removed most of their nuclear arsenal in the European theater, NATO would retaliate by deploying a limited number of cruise and Pershing II missiles there, beginning in 1983. The cruise missiles were small, intermediate-range, land-based, radar-guided weapons useful in theater actions. The powerful Pershing II missiles had a range of 800 miles, twice that of the Pershing I missiles already there, and could hit targets in the USSR.

This was the deteriorating state of Soviet-American relations on December 27, 1979, when the USSR launched an invasion of Afghanistan. Why it did so was unclear. Some experts said that the Kremlin sought mainly to preserve a pro-Soviet government threatened by rebels. Others speculated darkly that the USSR had designs on the oil-rich Persian Gulf region. Whatever the motivation, the invasion dashed any hopes that Carter, Vance, and others of their persuasion still held for moderating the Cold War. Carter quickly became a hawk, denouncing the invasion as "the most serious threat to peace since the Second World War." He also proclaimed what some observers called the Carter Doctrine, which warned that the United States would use armed force if necessary in order to prevent outside powers from gaining control of the Persian Gulf region. To show his seriousness he imposed an embargo of American grain exports to the Soviet Union, withdrew SALT II from Senate consideration, and called for a resumption of Selective Service registration for men who reached the age of eighteen. He announced that the United States would boycott the summer Olympic Games, which were scheduled to take place in Moscow in 1980. A total of sixty-four nations ultimately joined the boycott.[41]

40. Michael Sherry, *In the Shadow of War: The United States Since the 1930s* (New Haven, 1995), 352–53.

41. America did participate in the winter Olympic Games at Lake Placid in early 1980. When the United States men's ice hockey team upset the Soviets—and later won the gold medal—Americans were rhapsodic. *Newsweek* noted, "This was not just a sports story. It was a morality play on ice." Sherry, *In the Shadow of War*, 375. In 1984, the Soviets boycotted the summer Olympics in Los Angeles.

Carter also called in 1980 for 5 percent increases over each of the next five years in America's defense budgets. These increases were 2 percent higher than he had earlier requested. Congress readily complied with regard to fiscal 1981. When Ronald Reagan took the reins of power from Carter in 1981, he needed only to carry on—and to escalate—a defense buildup that his predecessor had started. The Cold War had hardened into a deeper freeze.[42]

While countering the Soviets, Carter had to deal with especially volatile developments in Iran. These had a considerable history, dating at least to 1953, when the CIA had helped to mastermind a coup that placed the pro-Western Mohammed Reza Shah Pahlavi in power in Tehran. In return for generous American aid, the shah guaranteed United States and Great Britain valuable oil rights in Iran. He also sided with the West in the Cold War, becoming the primary bulwark against the spread of Soviet influence in the Persian Gulf region. Though the shah ventured a few reforms—trying to advance secularization in education—these infuriated many leaders of the Shiite clergy. Over time he ran an increasingly brutal police state, but all American administrations after 1953 gave him strong support and sold him huge quantities of arms. In 1973–74, Secretary of State Kissinger had refused to cut off these sales, even though the shah had played a key role in the quadrupling of OPEC prices for oil.[43] Carter continued this backing. In December 1977, the president visited Tehran, where at a state dinner he lauded the Shah as "an island of stability in one of the more troubled areas of the world."[44]

What American leaders did not sufficiently appreciate was the hostility that their support of tyrants such as the shah had helped to foment in the Middle East. By the 1970s, many Iranians, including democrats and leftists in the middle classes, had become furious at America's hypocritical posture—proclaiming the virtues of democracy while backing an oppressor. American officials, including analysts at the CIA, were also unaware of the surging power of radical religious feelings in the Muslim world. In January 1979, followers of the exiled Ayatollah Ruhollah Khomeini, the dark-eyed, snowy-bearded, white-robed leader of these radicals, overthrew

42. Smith, *Morality, Reason, and Power*, 218–23; Chester Pach Jr., "Reagan and National Security," in W. Elliot Brownlee and Hugh Davis Graham, eds., *The Reagan Presidency: Pragmatic Conservatism and Its Legacies* (Lawrence, Kans., 2003), 85–112.

43. James Mann, *Rise of the Vulcans: The History of Bush's War Cabinet* (New York, 2004), 81–85.

44. Kaufman, *The Presidency of James Earl Carter, Jr.*, 86. For coverage of these events, see Smith, *Morality, Reason, and Power*, 180–207.

the shah. The shah moved about before settling in Mexico but was eager to come to New York City in order to undergo surgery for cancer. By October, with the shah's cancer at a life-threatening stage, Carter acceded to pressure and let him come.

Less than two weeks later, on November 4, 1979, a mob of youths over-ran the United States Embassy in Tehran and took sixty-six Americans hostage.[45] Khomeini refused to intervene or even to talk to American emissaries. Though the precise nature of the revolutionaries' demands was vague, three stood out: America, the "Great Satan," must return the shah to Iran, give back the huge wealth that he had supposedly stashed away in the United States, and apologize. In making such demands, the radicals were dramatically altering the way that international relations were to be conducted in the future.

Carter was trapped. To return the shah or to apologize was politically suicidal. No one seemed to have a good idea of the size of the shah's assets or how these might be legally turned over. After prohibiting the import of Iranian oil, freezing Iranian assets in the United States, and expelling ille-gal Iranian students, the president encouraged Vance to explore a range of options that might lead to negotiation. Meanwhile, Brzezinski and oth-ers quietly worked on plans for an American military rescue—an opera-tion that at first had seemed impossible inasmuch as Tehran was hundreds of miles from the nearest likely staging area for an American attack.

Weeks, then months, elapsed, during which the "Hostage Crisis," hav-ing at first helped to rally Americans around the president, gradually un-dermined his stature as a leader. The president claimed that he was too absorbed in the effort to free the hostages to engage actively in political matters and stayed close to the White House. His near-isolation became known as the "Rose Garden Strategy." The media seemed to report on nothing else. ABC ran nightly broadcasts called "America Held Hostage." On CBS, anchor Walter Cronkite adopted a nightly sign-off, as for ex-ample, "And this is the way it is, Thursday, [whatever date], 1979, the [numbered] day of captivity for the American hostages in Iran."[46]

In early April, by which time the shah had moved to Egypt, Brzezinski and his circle were ready for action. Choosing a weekend when Vance was out of town, they convinced the president to approve a rescue mission. When

45. The captors released thirteen hostages—all black or female—later that month, and one more later, keeping 52.
46. Mary Ann Watson, *Defining Visions: Television and the American Experience Since 1945* (Fort Worth, 1998), 254.

Vance returned, the president told him of this decision, at which point the secretary of state said he would resign whether the mission succeeded or not. The plan featured sending eight helicopters carrying a rescue team to a remote desert site in central Iran, where cargo planes would refuel them, so that the copters could transport the team several hundred more miles to a staging area some 100 miles southeast of Tehran. The rescue team would then climb onto trucks that had been bought by American agents, motor to Tehran, attack the building where the hostages were being held, overpower the captors, and save the captives. Taken to a nearby abandoned airstrip, the hostages would be flown by waiting transport planes to safety in Saudi Arabia.

It was a complicated scheme, and it failed. Swirling dust and hydraulic problems at the first site disabled three of the helicopters, whereupon the American commander recommended aborting the mission. Carter agreed, but before the rescuers could fly off, a helicopter crashed into a cargo plane. Ammunition blew up, lighting up the sky. The explosion and fire killed eight American soldiers and severely burned others. Seven aircraft were destroyed. Television later showed pictures of the wreckage and the bodies. Vance resigned, and the captors dispersed the hostages to a number of undisclosed locations. In September, Iraq, which had been ruled by Saddam Hussein since July 1979, invaded Iran, setting off a ten-year war (during which the United States gave support to Iraq). At this point Khomeini let it be known that he would negotiate. With Algeria as intermediary, talks finally got under way.[47]

But the captors were slow to budge. The fifty-two hostages, many of them badly treated, remained in Iran until America's inauguration day in January 1981. At that time the captors finally dropped their demand for an apology and accepted $7.955 billion and the unfreezing of Iranian assets. The settlement, though leading to the release of the hostages, was a victory for the radicals in Iran—and in the long run for anti-American and terrorist activities that were to multiply in the Middle East in the future. In a final insult to Carter, Iran waited until his successor, Ronald Reagan, had been sworn in before sending the hostages home. It was Reagan, not Carter, who then delivered the long-awaited news to the nation.

47. Carter, *Keeping Faith*, 510–18; Haynes Johnson, *Sleepwalking Through History: America in the Reagan Years* (New York, 1991), 36; Smith, *Morality, Reason, and Power*, 203–5; Douglas Brinkley, "Out of the Loop," *New York Times Magazine*, Dec. 29, 2002, 43–44. The shah had died in Egypt in July, removing as a stumbling block to the talks demands that he return to Iran.

THESE DRAWN-OUT, DEMORALIZING DEVELOPMENTS contributed to worsening economic conditions in the United States. Galloping inflation became an especially frightening specter in the late 1970s—and lasted until 1982. The roots of this inflation were deep, stemming in part from federal deficits that dated to spending on the Vietnam War in the late 1960s. Rising prices and unemployment afflicted many nations at the time and helped to drive a number of European leaders from office. In the United States, where Carter's "stimulus" package of 1977 had encouraged consumer spending, the president was slow to take steps against inflation. American prices, increasing alarmingly even before the ousting of the Shah, had already climbed to a rate that averaged 9 percent in 1978.[48]

As later events were to demonstrate, the staggering inflation of these years helped to transform American attitudes toward money. To let savings sit during inflationary times in a bank, where interest rates were relatively low, was to risk losing money. Thereafter, Americans were even more likely than earlier to borrow and to buy consumer goods—and to demand higher returns from investments than bank deposits could normally provide. A brave new world of credit cards and high-risk personal finance was at hand.[49]

After the Iranian revolution, the inflationary spiral began to spin out of control. OPEC hiked oil prices four times in five months, most sharply in June 1979. The war between Iran and Iraq then made oil shortages worse. Shortages of gasoline became serious in the United States. In 1979, fights broke out among angry American motorists desperate to find gasoline. Spurred in part by the rise in oil prices, the rate of inflation for 1979 ultimately averaged 11.3 percent. This was an extraordinarily high rate that more than any other single development unnerved the American people and damaged the president's political standing.

The restive mood of Americans in mid-1979 knocked down Carter's approval ratings to 29 percent and prompted him to reassess the course of his administration. In July 1979, he called Cabinet secretaries, top aides, and a host of thinkers and experts to an extended retreat at Camp David. Reporters, speculating madly, had no good information on what was happening. Finally, Carter emerged to deliver a televised talk to the nation. America, he said, was caught in a "crisis of confidence" and a "crisis of the spirit." At a press briefing later, an aide spoke about the "malaise" that had descended on American society. Then and later the word "malaise," which

48. Schulman, "Slouching Toward the Supply Side," 54–61.
49. Ibid., 67.

the president had not used, was what Americans remembered about Carter's message.[50]

Many people seemed to believe that Carter had spoken effectively. But they also sensed that he was blaming them for the nation's problems, and the pessimistic message was neither inspiring nor politically helpful. Carter then stunned the nation by announcing that he had asked for the resignations of all Cabinet secretaries and top aides. Four Cabinet resignations were quickly accepted, including Health, Education, and Welfare chief Joseph Califano, who was close to leading liberals in the party. It appeared to many Americans that Carter, shaken by the inflationary economy, had panicked and was losing control of his administration.

THE PRESIDENT HAD NO INTENTION OF GIVING UP. In these difficult days—as in the even more troubled days that followed the capture of the hostages in November—he was determined to rally his forces and win a second term. In waging his campaign, he encountered liberal revolts from within his own party. But the major story of the election—and of politics in the future—was a coming of age of political conservatism in the United States.

Liberals, having stewed since 1977 over Carter's fiscal conservatism, rallied during the campaign behind Ted Kennedy. Carter professed to be unafraid of him, reportedly commenting, "I'll whip his ass."[51] But when Kennedy announced his candidacy in the fall of 1979, polls indicated that he had a two-to-one lead over the president. The seizure of hostages, however, unleashed patriotic feelings that during the primary season benefited the commander-in-chief. Kennedy, moreover, could not shake people's memories of Chappaquiddick, on Martha's Vineyard, where in 1969 he had driven off a bridge, swum to shore, and gone home to bed at his hotel. The next morning it was learned that a twenty-eight-year-old passenger, Mary Jo Kopechne, had drowned in the accident. His irresponsible behavior did not hurt him with voters in Massachusetts, who seemed to accept an apology that he made over television, but it left him politically vulnerable as he sought the nation's highest office. Enjoying the advantages of presidential incumbency and of patronage, Carter outlasted Kennedy and won renomination on the first ballot. Mondale ran again as the Democrats' vice-presidential nominee.

The contest for the GOP nomination quickly turned into a two-person race between Ronald Reagan and George H. W. Bush, who had served

50. Greenstein, *The Presidential Difference*, 135–37.
51. Paul Boller, *Presidential Campaigns* (New York, 1996), 355.

two terms in the House, as Nixon's ambassador to the United Nations, as chairman of the GOP National Committee, and as Ford's last CIA director. Bush gave Reagan a scare early in the race by winning the Iowa caucuses and by ridiculing his opponent's call for a 30 percent tax cut as "voodoo economics." Reagan regrouped, campaigned vigorously, captured a string of primaries, and won the nomination on the first ballot. To secure party unity, Reagan selected Bush as his running mate.

Reagan had a varied background. Born in the small town of Tampico, Illinois, in 1911, he was the son of a pious mother and an alcoholic father who moved his wife and two sons to various towns in Illinois while trying to make a living as a shoe salesman. Eventually the family settled in Dixon, Illinois, where Reagan went to high school and which he considered to be his hometown. In the 1930s, his father landed a job with the WPA, a key public works program of Roosevelt's New Deal, thereby helping to steer the family through hard times. His mother, working as a seamstress, was also a breadwinner. Reagan later quipped, "We didn't live on the wrong side of the tracks, but we lived so close we could hear the whistle real loud." A handsome, athletic young man, Reagan was football captain and president of his class in high school and student body president at Eureka College in Illinois. All his life he made concerted efforts to please people, and he developed a special gift (which his father also had) as a teller of jokes and raconteur of humorous stories.

After graduating from college, Reagan worked as a radio sportscaster in Iowa before striking out for Hollywood. There he succeeded quickly as an actor, ultimately appearing in fifty-three films between 1937 and 1953. Though he was leading man in some of them, he joked later that he was the "Errol Flynn of the B's." Highly regarded by fellow actors, he headed the Screen Actors Guild, a union, between 1947 and 1952 (and again in 1959–60).[52] During the late 1940s—years of growing Cold War fears—Reagan came to believe that Communists were trying to take over Hollywood. Retaliating, he secretly provided the FBI with names of suspected Communists. Though these experiences turned him toward the right politically, Reagan was slow to abandon the Democratic Party. Having earlier voted for FDR, he remained an active member of Americans for Democratic Action, an anti-Communist, liberal political organization, in the late 1940s. He voted for Truman in 1948 and for Helen Gahagan Douglas, an ardently liberal Democrat who lost to Richard Nixon in his

52. Anthony Lane, "The Method President: Ronald Reagan and the Movies," *New Yorker*, Oct. 18, 2004, 190–202.

scurrilous race for the U.S. Senate, in 1950. Later, Reagan spoke of the "hemophiliac liberalism" that he had endorsed in his youth and early middle age.

Thereafter a series of developments—Reagan's anger at high income taxes, his marriage in 1952 to Nancy Davis, who came from a conservative family, and his work as a traveling spokesman for the General Electric Company from 1952 to 1962—moved Reagan solidly to the right of the political spectrum. Millions of Americans soon came to know him as the handsome, genial host between 1954 and 1962 of television's highly rated Sunday night program *General Electric Theater*. Then and later, he was an extraordinarily relaxed and effective performer on TV. In 1962, he formally became a Republican, and in 1964 he gave a widely noticed speech for GOP presidential candidate Barry Goldwater, an ardent conservative.

"The Speech," as admirers called it, earned Reagan great praise among conservatives throughout the nation. Financing his entry into statewide politics, these conservatives helped him to score an impressive victory as the GOP candidate for governor of California in 1966. In 1970, he won a second four-year term. Conservatives did not always like what he did—Reagan, a politically astute compromiser, raised taxes to cover a budgetary shortfall left by his predecessor and signed a liberal abortion bill into law—but they recognized that he was solidly in their camp on most issues and that he had outstanding skills as a speaker and campaigner.[53] For these reasons, he had nearly taken the 1976 presidential nomination from President Ford. Though he turned sixty-nine years of age in February 1980, he remained a fit and vigorous man.[54]

IT WAS REAGAN'S GOOD FORTUNE to ride on a large new wave that swelled in the late 1970s and that was to leave its considerable traces on American politics for the rest of the century and beyond: political conservatism. This wave, which greatly invigorated the Right, rushed ahead from a great many sources, for conservatives, famously disputatious, hardly saw eye to eye on all matters. Isolationists on the right challenged Cold War-

53. The abortion bill, signed in 1967, allowed abortion in cases of rape, incest, or fetal defect. It led to a large increase in legal abortions in California, from 5,000 in 1968 to 100,000 in 1972. Daniel Williams, "From the Pews to the Polls: The Formation of a Southern Christian Right"(PhD diss., Brown University, 2005), chapter 5.
54. For Reagan, see Lou Cannon, *President Reagan: The Role of a Lifetime* (New York, 2000), 1–77; William Pemberton, *Exit with Honor: The Life and Presidency of Ronald Reagan* (New York, 1998), 3–20; and James Patterson, "Afterword: Legacies of the Reagan Years," in Brownlee and Graham, *The Reagan Presidency*, 355–75.

riors and internationalists, fiscal conservatives battled against tax-cutters, and libertarians and foes of big government argued with advocates—some of them branded as "theo-cons"—of federal programs to promote socially conservative values. By 1980, however, several previously unconnected groups—white blue-collar workers, southern white foes of civil rights, Republicans who opposed big government, and socially conservative Catholics and evangelical Protestants—were converging to crusade for a range of causes and to fight on behalf of candidates who would promote them. This conservative coalition, adeptly exploited by Reagan, dramatically altered the landscape of politics in the United States.

Many of the new conservatives, so-called Reagan Democrats, were white working-class people in the North who still supported a range of liberal bread-and-butter economic programs. But like white Democrats in the Sunbelt who had earlier been turning to the GOP, these blue-collar Americans resented the "reverse discrimination," as they saw it, of social policies such as busing and affirmative action. They raged at the growth of crime, which they blamed on violent and lawless blacks. Some of these white Americans, having backed the presidential candidacies of Richard Nixon or Alabama governor George Wallace in the 1960s and the 1970s, seethed at the derisive and supercilious "elitism," as they perceived it, of well-educated, upper-middle-class liberal intellectuals and prominent figures in the media and Hollywood. Defending their ways of life, they were gathering together to fight against what they damned as the culturally permissive legacies of the 1960s.

Other conservatives, such as those who advanced the agenda of the Committee on the Present Danger, were aroused by what they regarded as the softness of Carter's military and foreign policies. Many of them were Republicans who had supported GOP presidential candidate Barry Goldwater's hawkish stance in 1964. Among them were a number of the thirty-six freshmen Republican congressmen elected in 1978. Two of these newcomers, Richard Cheney of Wyoming and Newt Gingrich of Georgia, moved rapidly up in the ranks of the GOP House leadership during the 1980s.[55] Deeply anti-Communist, these conservatives called for considerably greater spending on the military and for uncompromising opposition to Communism abroad. Though other conservatives—considerably more isolationist in their views—differed sharply with them, officeholders like Cheney and Gingrich helped to strengthen the already hawkish stance of the GOP in the 1980s.

55. Mann, *Rise of the Vulcans*, 96–97.

Other Americans who joined the loose but growing coalition behind conservatism in the 1970s included once-liberal intellectuals and public policy experts who concluded that the Great Society programs of Lyndon Johnson—notably the War on Poverty—had been oversold and had led to unintended and unhappy consequences. Some of these "neo-conservatives," or neo-cons as they were often called, contributed to journals such as *The Public Interest*, which developed a considerable readership among influential policy-makers. In the 1970s, they sought common ground with Republicans and conservative Democrats who had always been leery about liberal social welfare policies, high taxes, and Keynesian economic ideas. (Some of them, however, demanded that government expand its reach in certain policy areas—so as to build up the military, outlaw abortion, or restore "law and order.")[56] Editorialists for the *Wall Street Journal*, normally libertarian in their emphasis on the preservation of individual freedom and the virtues of the market, were generally consistent foes of the intrusiveness of the federal government.

The rise of the New Right, as many observers called it in the late 1970s, derived special strength from the zeal and skill of political activists who were determined to revive conservative ideas—and/or the GOP—in the aftermath of the drubbing they had received from the Democrats in 1964. One of these activists was Paul Weyrich, a son of German immigrants who had settled in Wisconsin. A strongly pro-life Catholic—and an admirer of former senator Joe McCarthy—Weyrich established advantageous relationships with wealthy conservatives such as Joseph Coors, of the Coors beer empire, and Richard Mellon-Scaife, heir to the Carnegie-Mellon fortune. Drawing on their funding, he established the Heritage Foundation in 1973, which became a leading conservative think tank. Other conservative think tanks—the Cato, Manhattan, and American Enterprise institutes—added intellectual firepower to the Right. In 1974, Weyrich founded the Committee for the Survival of a Free Congress, yet another conservative interest group.

An equally effective organizer was Richard Viguerie, a staunchly anti-abortion Catholic who had grown up in a working-class Louisiana family. Skilled at directing massive direct mail appeals, Viguerie attracted more than 4 million contributors to the GOP by the late 1970s. Like Weyrich, he worked hard to spread the gospel of Republican conservatism beyond the confines of country clubs and upper-middle-class suburbs and to reach

56. Lisa McGerr, *Suburban Warriors: The Origins of the New American Right* (Princeton, 2001), 6–11, 271–72.

Catholics and blue-collar workers who had previously voted Democratic. Conservatives, he declared, must adopt the values of "Main Street, not Wall Street."[57] By 1980, political operatives like Weyrich and Viguerie had given the GOP a more populist image, restored its infrastructure, and built up substantial grass-roots power. Liberals were becoming defensive. As Democratic senator Daniel Patrick Moynihan of New York warned at the time, "Of a sudden the GOP has become a party of ideas."[58]

Though some of these conservatives had doubts in 1980 about Reagan's call for tax cuts—what was "conservative" about a proposal that threatened to enlarge already sizeable federal budget deficits?—others were angry about high taxes, "bracket creep," and "waste" in government. Many of these people had already joined the drive for California's anti-tax Proposition 13, which in 1978 had unleashed a surge of tax cuts throughout the American states. Howard Jarvis, the crusty seventy-five-year-old who helped to lead the fight for Prop 13, told followers, "You are the people, and you will have to take control of the government again, or else it is going to control you." As Jarvis emphasized, the combination of federal, state, and local taxes had in fact taken a bigger bite out of personal income since the 1950s, riling not only the wealthy but also millions of relatively young people—the boomers—who by the late 1970s were getting married, buying homes, and trying to get ahead in a highly inflationary economy. To Americans such as these, and to the wealthy, crusades to slash taxes—in 1980 as in later years—had very broad appeal.[59]

MANY CONSERVATIVES IN THE 1970S did not focus their fire on foreign policies, big government, or taxes. Instead, they targeted social and cultural evils—as they perceived them—such as abortion, "women's lib," gay rights, and pornography. The *Roe v. Wade* decision of 1973 aroused special outrage among conservative Catholics, who swelled the membership of a National Right to Life Committee—and in short order, the voting power of Republican political candidates. Phyllis Schlafly, "Sweetheart of

57. Richard Viguerie, *The New Right: We're Ready to Lead* (Falls Church, Va., 1981), 27–28.

58. Robert Collins, *More: The Politics of Economic Growth in Postwar America* (New York, 2000), 189–90. Moynihan had held important posts in the Nixon administration and had been a contributor to *The Public Interest* before winning a New York Senate seat in 1976. He retired from the Senate in January 2001.

59. Steven Gillon, *Boomer Nation: The Largest and Richest Generation Ever, and How It Changed America* (New York, 2004), 220–21; and Robert Self, *American Babylon: Race and the Struggle for Postwar Oakland* (Princeton, 2003), 319–27.

the Silent Majority," was an especially effective organizer of these forces. A lawyer, two-time congressional candidate from Illinois, and Catholic mother of six, Schlafly assailed the *Roe* decision. She insisted that the Equal Rights Amendment was an "anti-family" effort that would wipe out protective legislation enacted to insulate women workers from exploitation in the workplace.

Socially conservative Protestants, though slow to cooperate with Catholics like Schlafly, further strengthened the forces of the American Right in the late 1970s. In 1979, Beverly LaHaye, a San Diego housewife and best-selling author whose husband, the Reverend Tim LaHaye, was a Baptist minister known for his writings opposing pornography and homosexuality, formed Concerned Women for America (CWA).[60] An excellent organizer and promoter, LaHaye shaped CWA into a formidable force against the ERA, abortion, and no-fault divorce laws. CWA soon had a far larger membership—estimated at 500,000 by the mid-1980s—than the much more liberal National Organization for Women.[61] Like LaHaye, most crusaders of this persuasion were traditionalists. They emphasized that they were "pro-family," by which they meant the patriarchal family of the past. They maintained that many women who left home to join the labor force upset family harmony and prevented men from finding work.[62]

Hosts of socially conservative, religiously motivated Americans began to join activists such as Schlafly and LaHaye in the late 1970s, thereby advancing what became known, variously, as the New Christian or Religious Right. Many of these religious activists backed a rapidly growing lobby, Focus on the Family, which was founded in 1977 by James Dobson, a devoutly evangelical child psychologist. Focus on the Family aired a popular radio show, which crusaded for yet another set of rights—of parents, who were urged to war against sex education in the schools. Other conservatives, relying on constitutional guarantees of free speech, began mounting lawsuits—some of them successful in the 1980s and 1990s—that asserted the right of reli-

60. Tim LaHaye also co-authored a series of dramatic novels (the Left Behind series), the first of which was titled *Left Behind: A Novel of the Earth's Last Days* (Wheaton, Ill., 1995). Deriving their inspiration from the Book of Revelation, these focused on Last Judgment themes. These novels (twelve in all) were estimated to have sold a total of 60 million copies by the end of 2004. *New York Times*, Dec. 23, 2004.

61. William Martin, *With God on Our Side: The Rise of the Religious Right in America* (New York, 1996), 164.

62. For developments in American conservatism during these years, see Godfrey Hodgson, *The World Turned Right Side Up: A History of the Conservative Ascendancy in America* (Boston, 1996). For Schlafly and LaHaye, see Susan Faludi, *Backlash: The Undeclared War Against American Women* (New York, 1991), 239–56.

gious groups to meet on school grounds and on school time, and the right of religious schools to receive public funding.[63]

The majority of these activists, like a great many Protestant believers earlier in American history, were evangelical in their approach to religion — that is, they generally claimed to be born again via some form of crisis conversion, often in enthusiastic revivals, and they were eager proselytizers. Most accepted the literal truth of the Bible, and many looked ahead to the Second Coming of Christ, which would be followed in time by a millennium and a final judgment.[64] The Reverend Billy Graham, the most acclaimed of the many revivalists who had been promoting a postwar growth of evangelicalism, had whipped up considerable popular enthusiasm for beliefs similar to these. Well before the 1970s, he had been hailed as the "most admired man in America."[65]

By 1980, members of the Religious Right were well on their way to forming what was soon to become the strongest grass-roots, community-based movement of late twentieth-century American life. Developing a growing following, especially among whites in the South, they organized a host of discussion groups, Bible study classes, Sunday schools, and self-help programs and founded a large number of conservatively oriented Christian schools, seminaries, and colleges. "Mega churches" began to spring up, especially in suburbs, where they served as vital centers of social and spiritual activity. More than most other interest groups—which had come to rely heavily on wealthy donors, computerized mailing lists, and professional managers—many of these religiously motivated people recruited relatively poor as well as middle-class Americans in order to establish organizations that featured large face-to-face gatherings of members and that cut across class lines.[66]

The rise of the Religious Right in the late 1970s came as a surprise to many people in America. Though some Protestant churchmen had strenuously opposed Kennedy, a Catholic, in 1960, most Americans who were labeled "fundamentalist" because they believed in the literal truth of the Bible had even then remained quiet politically. Many had consistently

63. Steven Brown, Trumping Religion: The New Christian Right, the Free Speech Clause, and the Courts (Tuscaloosa, 2003).
64. Martin, With God on Our Side, 4–7.
65. Garry Wills, Under God: Religion and American Politics (New York, 1990), 19 20.
66. Theda Skocpol, Diminished Democracy: From Membership to Management in American Civic Life (Norman, Okla., 2003), 167–74; Robert Wuthnow, Sharing the Journey: Support Groups and America's New Quest for Community (New York, 1994), 70–76.

refused to vote. To engage in political activity, they had believed, was to depart from the realm of the spirit and to soil themselves—and their churches—with the corruption of the secular world. Some of these devout Americans continued in the 1960s and 1970s to abjure political activity.

But a series of events brought a wave of evangelical Protestants into organizations like the CWA and into the mainstream of American political life by the late 1970s, by which time they were beginning to cross once rigid denominational lines, to form ecumenical alliances with Catholics who opposed abortion, and to brand "secular humanism" as a special evil.[67] Among their special targets was the liberal Supreme Court, which in the early 1960s had ruled on First Amendment grounds against officially sponsored prayer and Bible readings in the public schools. These decisions, which a majority of Americans opposed, deeply offended many religious people, who believed that prayers and readings of scripture were keys to the development of moral values and to the sustenance of what they emphasized was the Christian heritage of the United States. Undeterred, the Court, led by Chief Justice Earl Warren, continued to aggravate religious conservatives and others. It even charted a more liberal course concerning obscenity. In 1964, it ruled that materials that could be judged as obscene must be "utterly without redeeming social significance."[68]

Roe v. Wade especially aroused religious conservatives. The decision, some of them exclaimed, amounted to "child murder" and the "slaughter of the innocent." Others saw the ruling as a sinister step toward state control of personal beliefs. As *Christianity Today*, a leading evangelical journal, editorialized in 1973, "Christians should accustom themselves to the thought that the American state no longer supports, in any meaningful sense, the laws of God, and prepare themselves spiritually for the prospect that it [the state] may one day formally repudiate them and turn against those who seek to live by them."[69] Statements such this revealed a key fact about cultural conflict in the United States for the remainder of the century and beyond: Abortion, more irreconcilable than any other social issue, incited all manner of fears among conservatives.

In 1979, Francis Schaeffer, a leading conservative thinker, and Dr. C. Everett Koop (who later because surgeon general in the Reagan admin-

67. "A Tide of Born-Again Politics," *Newsweek*, Sept. 15, 1980, 28–29.
68. *Jacobellis v. Ohio*, 378 U.S. 184 (1964). Though the Court in the early 1970s adopted tougher standards, conservatives nonetheless railed at the permissiveness, as they called it, of this and other decisions.
69. "Abortion and the Court," *Christianity Today*, Feb. 16, 1973, 11.

istration) combined to produce a film against abortion and euthanasia. Titled *Whatever Happened to the Human Race?*, it was a $1 million, four-hour production that toured twenty American cities and that urged viewers to fight against *Roe v. Wade*. Otherwise, Americans would become desensitized to the horrors of killing, to the extent of accepting infanticide. A memorable scene depicted Koop inveighing against abortion while standing amid hundreds of abandoned dolls strewn across the banks of the Dead Sea.[70]

The liberalism of the Court, however, was but one of a number of developments that alarmed religiously devout Americans in the 1970s. Many teachers were advancing Darwinian theories of evolution—and courses of sex education—in public school classrooms. Sexually graphic material, displayed openly at magazine stands, seemed ubiquitous. Gay people were slowly mobilizing with a view to influencing politics.[71] And the Carter administration supported a decision rendered by the Internal Revenue Service in 1975 that had denied tax-exempt status to Bob Jones University, a fundamentalist Protestant institution in South Carolina that at that time banned interracial dating or marriage. In 1978, the IRS, believing Carter would support its efforts, proposed to deny tax-exempt status to private schools, including many Christian academies, which failed to meet the IRS's standards of racial integration. All these developments alarmed conservative Christians, who perceived them as driving a rise in pornography, sexual license, family tension, social unrest, and "secular humanism."

The activism of the IRS especially distressed Protestants within the newly self-conscious Religious Right of the late 1970s. Many of these Protestants had long opposed abortion. Using the language of rights, they asserted that abortion violated the constitutional rights of the fetus, which they believed was fully human. Still, they were not at first as angry about the *Roe* decision as conservative Catholics had been. The Bible, after all, offered no clear guidance on the matter. Evangelical Protestants who did not like the teaching of sex education or Darwinian evolution in public schools could send their children to Christian academies or instruct them at home. The decision of the IRS, however, struck many of these folk as a threat to their rights as parents and as a frightening extension of governmental intrusion into the private lives of people. Within a few weeks of

70. Williams, "From the Pews to the Polls," chapter 5.
71. Jonathan Zimmerman, *Whose America? Culture Wars in the Public Schools* (Cambridge, Mass., 2002), 160–85, 207–11.

the IRS's announcement that it planned to move against such Christian academies, religiously inspired opponents sent at least a half million pieces of mail to the IRS, the White House, and congressional offices.[72] Backing off, the IRS rescinded its plans in 1979.

In June of that year, many of these people joined with Tim LaHaye and with the Reverend Jerry Falwell, a deeply conservative forty-five-year-old Baptist preacher from Lynchburg, Virginia, to establish the Moral Majority. Falwell was a business-oriented promoter who normally wore a three-piece suit. He had already established a small empire around him in the Lynchburg area: a school, a home for alcoholics, a summer camp for kids, a college (Liberty Baptist College, later named Liberty University), and a church that claimed a congregation of 17,000 people. For years, his church had held multiple Sunday services in order to accommodate all the people who wished to attend. Falwell insisted on the literal truth of the Bible and opposed smoking, drinking, dancing, and rock 'n' roll. Women were expected to wear dresses with hemlines at least two inches below the knee. The Bible, he maintained, commanded women to submit to their husbands. Falwell was already well known for his daily radio broadcasts, which were carried on 280 stations, and for his Sunday television program, the *Old Time Gospel Hour*, which ran on more than 300 stations and was available to 1.5 million people.[73] Among the program's many attractions was a male/female singing group, the Sounds of Liberty. The group featured good-looking women with Charlie's Angels hairstyles whose presence was presumed to advance the show's popular appeal.[74]

Though Falwell had opposed civil rights activity in the 1960s, until the mid-1970s he had been a fundamentalist who had refused to engage in politics. In 1977–78, however, he had joined Tim LaHaye in fighting to repeal a pro-gay-rights ordinance in Miami. The battle for repeal, which had been launched by Anita Bryant, a well-known Christian singer and mother, attracted national attention and inspired rising political activism among people on the Religious Right. In the end, the conservatives won the fight. In 1978, he began to preach against *Roe v. Wade*. "Abortion," he

---

72. Martin, *With God on Our Side*, 168–73. Opponents of the IRS case against Bob Jones University contested it in the courts. The Supreme Court ruled against the university in 1983, by a vote of eight to one. *Bob Jones University v. the United States*, 461 U.S. 574 (1983).

73. Martin, *With God on Our Side*, 55–58, 68–73.

74. Frances FitzGerald, *Cities on a Hill: A Journey Through Contemporary American Culture* (New York, 1986), 125–56.

said, "is a weapon that has annihilated more children than Pharaoh murdered in Egypt, than Herod murdered when seeking the Christ child, than the Nazis slaughtered of the Jews in World War II."[75]

In forming the Moral Majority in 1979, Falwell and like-minded religious conservatives moved boldly into the partisan wars. This was a historic breakthrough that carried him beyond the single-issue battles in which he had previously participated. Falwell made it clear that the Moral Majority was a political, not a religious, organization, and that it was a broad conservative coalition open to people of all faiths. By saying that he welcomed all comers, he offended a number of fellow preachers, who could not imagine coalescing with other Protestant denominations, let alone with Catholics. For these and other reasons, most of the Moral Majority's members were Baptists.

The rise of the Moral Majority nonetheless attracted widespread public attention. Falwell, who was by far the most prominent spokesman for the organization, proved to be a popular speaker and a master at garnering publicity. The Moral Majority, he exclaimed, was "pro-life, pro-family, pro-morality, and pro-American." The ERA, he charged, would lead to "unisexual bathrooms" and to women being sent into combat.[76] The Moral Majority, though relatively quiet concerning economic issues, was cool to labor unions, environmental causes, and social welfare programs, except for those that helped people who were sick, aged, or unemployed as the result of a depression.

Falwell, opposing SALT II, called on political leaders to fight against Communism: "A political leader, as a Minister of God, is a revenger to execute war upon those who do evil. Our government has the right to use its armaments to bring wrath upon those who would do evil."[77] Though he (like many others on the Religious Right) was hardly "conservative" when he called for government to increase its role in the lives of people—as, for example, by opposing abortion—he was proud to be known as a foe of liberals. "If you would like to know where I am politically," he said, "I am to the right of wherever you are. I thought Goldwater was too liberal."[78]

The Moral Majority elicited widespread hostility and ridicule from liberals, who distributed bumper stickers reading: THE MORAL MAJORITY IS NEITHER. Still, it encouraged a surge of grass-roots religious activity that

75. Williams, "From the Pews to the Polls," chapter 5.
76. Martin, *With God on Our Side*, 196–204.
77. Sherry, *In the Name of War*, 353.
78. FitzGerald, *Cities on a Hill*, 172.

boosted socially conservative Christian ideas after 1979 and that ultimately propelled cultural issues into the center of public debate in the United States. Highly visible advocates of these goals included charismatic "televangelists," as critics called them, some of whom (not including Falwell) believed in faith-healing and tongues-talking. Among these believers was the Reverend Marion "Pat" Robertson of Virginia, a former marine who had served in the Korean War and who had earned a law degree at Yale. Founder and owner since 1960 of the immensely successful Christian Broadcasting Network (CBN), Robertson resented the term "televangelist" and insisted on being referred to as a "religious broadcaster." Another such believer and television performer was the Reverend Jim Bakker, an Assemblies of God preacher who created a Praise The Lord (PTL) ministry in South Carolina in 1974. Bakker organized an empire that ultimately included a 500-room luxury hotel, an amusement park, and an amphitheater. In 1979, conservatives gained control of the Southern Baptist Convention, which had added some 2 million members to its ranks in the 1970s. With some 13 million members in 1980, it was the largest Protestant group in America and had the potential to become more powerful than the Moral Majority.

Though some popular televangelists—Oral Roberts of Oklahoma, for example—continued to shun political activity, many of them embraced the causes of the Religious Right. They managed to garner substantial sums of money (some of which, it was later learned, ended up in their pockets). One historian has estimated that the top eight televangelists in 1980 grossed $310 million from their programs. Another has concluded that radio shows featuring socially conservative and religious messages, carried on hundreds of stations, regularly attracted 840,000 listeners, that the television programs were available to 20 million viewers, and that the Moral Majority and other groups succeeded in registering at least 2 million voters in 1980.[79] (Later, in 1997, Robertson sold his Family Channel, a satellite-delivered cable television network, to Fox Broadcasting for $1.9 billion.)[80] Many of these new voters, contemporary observers

79. Martin, *With God on Our Side*, 213, is cautious about estimating audience sizes of televangelists and others, noting that no TV preacher had an audience larger than 2.5 million in 1980. Falwell's *Old Time Gospel Hour*, Martin writes, had an audience at the time of 1.4 million.
80. Jon Butler, "Jack-in-the-Box Faith: The Religious Problem in Modern American History," *Journal of American History* 90 (March 2004), 1376–77. In 2001, Disney acquired the Fox Family Channel and renamed it ABC Family.

concluded, were relatively poor southern whites, including a consider-able number of elderly women who were attracted above all by the pro-family messages.[81]

Whether these people were prepared to vote for Reagan in 1980 was difficult to predict as the election approached. Carter, after all, was widely known as a Southern Baptist who extolled the virtues of family life and taught Sunday school. Having openly and proudly announced that he had been born again, he was expected to command some support among Protestant evangelicals. Reagan, who had signed California's liberal abor-tion law in 1967, and who had opposed an anti-gay-rights referendum in California in 1978, could hardly be sure in 1979 of great backing from socially conservative Christians.[82]

It was obvious, however, that evangelical, socially conservative religious groups were gaining considerable visibility in American culture and poli-tics during the late 1970s. Some 50 million people, more than a fourth of all American adults, claimed to be born-again Christians. One-fifth of these, or 10 million people, appeared to have theological and social views that situated them solidly on the right. And the number of all Protestant churchgoers who identified themselves as members of socially conserva-tive, evangelical churches grew considerably during this time—probably by a third between 1960 and 1985. A good deal of this growth occurred in the late 1970s.[83]

Developments such as these have led some writers to maintain that yet another "great awakening" of spirituality had surged through American

81. For the figures on money, David Frum, *How We Got Here: The '70s, the Decade that Brought You Modern Life (For Better or Worse)* (New York, 2000), 152–53. For audi-ences and new voters, Sara Diamond, *Not by Politics Alone: The Enduring Influence of the Religious Right* (New York, 1998), 63–67. For church membership and church attendance figures used in these paragraphs, see *Stat. Abst.*, 2002, 55–56; Putnam, *Bowling Alone*, 65–79; and Russell Shorto, "Belief by the Numbers," *New York Times Magazine*, Dec. 7, 1997, 60–61. These statistics depend on responses given to poll-sters and are generally thought to exaggerate (though not greatly) the numbers and percentages of church members and attendees.
82. The referendum in 1978, when Reagan was no longer governor, concerned Proposi-tion 6, which would have rescinded a 1975 law (signed by Reagan) protecting homo-sexual teachers from discrimination and would have given school districts authority to fire gay teachers who publicly endorsed homosexual practices. Voters decisively defeated the proposition.
83. FitzGerald, *Cities on a Hill*, 125; Diamond, *Not by Politics Alone*, 9–10; Putnam, *Bowling Alone*, 76.

life in the 1960s, leading to wider popular religiosity (some of it countering culturally liberal trends of the 60s) by the 1970s.[84] By some definitions
of "great awakening" this is a plausible claim, for millions of people in the
1960s had appeared to be looking earnestly for some form of spiritual guidance. As Tom Wolfe and Christopher Lasch had pointed out in the 1970s,
many young people of the boomer generation—in their twenties and thirties in the late 1970s—seemed especially eager to arrive at a therapeuti-
cally consoling "new consciousness" that would help them attain "personal
enlightenment" or find "peace of mind." Still other Americans, searching
for spiritual sustenance in a fast-paced, materialistic culture of "seekers,"
had been swelling church membership in the United States since World
War II.[85]

But these searchers hardly comprised a homogeneous group. Some conservative Protestant leaders—notably members of the Southern Baptist
Convention—were believers in the separation of church and state. Fearing
that the government would support Catholic schools, they were wary of
virtually any public intrusion into the realm of religion, and they supported
the Supreme Court's ruling against state-sponsored school prayers. Other
devout Americans were by no means conservative—socially, politically, or
theologically. Some were liberals who backed the civil rights movement,
which derived a good deal of its power from religiously rooted ideals. Many
low-income people who regularly attended church remained independent
or left of center in their politics. African Americans, generally liberal on
economic and racial issues and supporters of Democratic causes and candidates, were numerous among evangelical Christians (though not among
the followers of leaders like Falwell) in these and later years.

It is not so clear, moreover, that the United States was experiencing the
sort of religious revival in the 1970s that would swell overall membership
in churches. On the contrary, though the United States—always a highly
religious country—continued to be one of the most churchgoing nations
in the developed world, the trend toward secularization that had advanced
in the Western world since the nineteenth century still operated as a powerful countervailing force. A decline in the membership of "mainstream"

84. Hugh Heclo, "The Sixties False Dawn: Awakenings, Movements, and Post-Modern
    Policy-Making," *Journal of Policy History* 8, no. 1 (1996), 34–63; and Robert Fogel,
    The Fourth Great Awakening: The Future of Egalitarianism (Chicago, 2000), 176–81.
85. Roger Finke and Rodney Stark, *The Churching of America, 1776–1990: Winners and
    Losers in Our Religious Economy* (New Brunswick, 1992); Butler, "Jack-in-the-Box
    Faith," 1375.

Protestant congregations, whose believers were aging, offset the rise in the number of evangelical Christians during the 1970s and 1980s.[86]

Thanks in part to declines in these mainline churches, membership in American religious bodies dropped from an estimated 77 percent of the adult population in 1960 to 69 percent in 1980, remaining at approximately that level into the early 2000s. Other estimates indicated that weekly attendance at church services fell from 47 percent of adults in 1960 to 40 in 1980, and then rose, but only slightly, to around 44 percent by 2000. Though Roman Catholicism held its own—according to government estimates, roughly 28 percent of American adults (including millions of Latino immigrants) were believed to be holding to the faith throughout the years between 1975 and 2000—enrollments in Catholic schools, many of which were city-based institutions that were hard hit by suburbanization, fell dramatically during these years.[87] The Catholic Church also struggled desperately to attract young people as nuns, priests, or brothers, and to resolve internal disputes that broke out over the liberal reforms that had emanated from the Second Vatican Council between 1962 and 1965. Most American Catholics, moreover, made it clear that they did not subscribe to church teachings concerning birth control, abortion, and divorce.

86. By the early 2000s, polls suggested that more than 30 million Americans belonged to large churches that generally backed socially conservative causes: Southern Baptist (16 million), Church of God in Christ (5.5 million), Mormon (5.2 million), and Assemblies of God (2.6 million). Most mainline Protestant churches were smaller. The largest of these churches, which had a total membership of more than 20 million by the early 2000s, were United Methodist (8.3 million), Evangelical Lutheran Church in America (5.1 million), Presbyterian Church (U.S.A.) (3.5 million), Lutheran–Missouri Synod (2.6 million), and Episcopalian (2.1 million). Some of these were theologically conservative, and many of their members backed socially conservative causes. Episcopalians declined in number by 44 percent and Methodists by 38 percent between 1967 and 1997. *Stat. Abst.*, 2002, 55; Shorto, "Belief by the Numbers."

87. James Davison Hunter, *Culture Wars: The Struggle to Define America* (New York, 1991), 367. According to statistics reported by the government, people identifying themselves as Protestants in 1980 were 61 percent of the population. Those who said they were Jewish were roughly 2 percent of the population. Though the percentage self-identifying as Protestants slipped a little—to a low of 56 percent in 2000—the percentage of people self-identifying as Catholics (28) remained at the level of 1980. *Stat. Abst.*, 2002, 56. These are estimates: Statistics concerning church membership and attendance, based for the most part on polls and church-derived numbers, vary considerably. A later poll, by the Pew Research Center for the People, concurred that the percentage of Americans who said they were Catholic remained steady between 1977 and 2002, but set the number at 23, not 28. Compared to some other reports, it discovered low percentages of Americans who attended religious services once or more per week. These percentages, the poll found, were around 30 in the 1980s, after which they dipped, to around 25 by 2002. *New York Times*, April 3, 2005.

As the private behavior of Catholics (among others) indicated, Americans were not always practicing what their priests, ministers, and rabbis had told them. Many people who said they had been born again did not seem to behave very differently thereafter. Nor did most people isolate themselves in theologically pure, sectarian enclaves. On the contrary, though doctrinal issues continued to divide religious leaders, most people who regularly attended services, like those who did not, were becoming more tolerant of faiths other than their own. Pope John Paul II, while unyielding in his defense of conservative Catholic doctrines concerning sexuality and family life, also advocated interfaith cooperation and worked to heal sharp rifts with Jews. Internal divisions within denominations—mostly along class and liberal/conservative lines—were becoming more significant in the United States than the primary identifications (Protestant, Catholic, or Jew) or than the denominational loyalties that had normally characterized American religious life in the past.[88]

Still, there was no doubting that by many standards of measurement the United States remained the most religious nation in the Western world in the 1970s and thereafter. Some 50 percent of Americans in the late 1970s told pollsters that they prayed every day, and 80 percent said that they believed in an afterlife. As membership figures indicated, devout people of socially conservative bent seemed to be growing in numbers and as a proportion of religiously inclined people in the United States. More politically engaged than at any time since battles over Darwinism had flourished in the 1920s, they had ambitions to register voters, to influence partisan debates, to select candidates, to defeat liberals, and to advance "moral values."[89] In most northern areas, they were weak. Even in the South, they were only beginning in 1980 to amass considerable political power. This was greater in 1984, by which time the Southern Baptist Convention had become more politically active.[90] Even during the 1980 campaign, however, it seemed that members of the Religious Right might

---

88. Hunter, *Culture Wars*; Alan Wolfe, *One Nation, After All: What Middle-Class Americans Really Think About God, Country, Family, Racism, Welfare, Immigration, Homosexuality, Work, the Right, the Left, and Each Other* (New York, 1998).

89. Many prominent American political figures since the 1970s have been Southern Baptists: Carter, Bill Clinton, Al Gore, Richard Gephardt, Trent Lott, Newt Gingrich, and Strom Thurmond.

90. Daniel Williams, "The Cross and the Elephant: Southern White Evangelicals' Commitment to the Republican Party, 1960–1994," *Proceedings of the South Carolina Historical Association* (2005), 59–69.

President Gerald Ford and his wife, Betty, escort Richard Nixon and his wife, Pat, from the White House to a helicopter parked on the south lawn of the White House, August 9, 1974. Standing behind them are Nixon's daughters, Tricia and Julie, and their husbands. *Courtesy National Archives, NLNP-WHPO-MPF-E3398-09.*

A characteristically unromantic reflection (in 1996) on the 1970s. *"The Buckets"*: © *United Feature Syndicate, Inc.*

President Ford meets with his chief of staff, Donald Rumsfeld, and deputy chief Dick Cheney (right) in the Oval Office, April 28, 1975. *Gerald R. Ford Library.*

President Ford and Soviet president Leonid Brezhnev, Vladivostok, November 1974. *Gerald R. Ford Library.*

President Jimmy Carter with President Anwar Sadat of Egypt (left) and Prime Minister Menachem Begin of Israel, at the signing of the Camp David accords, White House, March 1979. © *Bettmann/CORBIS*.

Facing page, top An American official punches a man clinging to the door of an airplane already overloaded with refugees seeking to flee from Nha Trang, Vietnam, April 1975. © *Bettmann/CORBIS*.

Facing page, bottom "The Soiling of Old Glory": An anti-busing demonstrator in Boston tries to spear a black man, April 1976. *Stanley J. Forman*.

Jimmy Carter, Rosalynn Carter, and Leonid Brezhnev, after the signing of the SALT II Treaty in Vienna, June 1979. *Jimmy Carter Library.*

Facing page Energy crisis, California, late 1970s. *Ted Cowell/Stockphoto.com.*

Blindfolded hostages being led out of the United States embassy in Tehran on the first day of its occupation, November 4, 1979. © *Bettmann/CORBIS.*

Phyllis Schlafly, 1977. *Courtesy National Archives.*

The Rev. Jerry Falwell outside his church, August 1980. © Wally McNamee/*CORBIS*.

A Youngstown, Ohio, steel mill closes in the beleaguered "Rust Belt," April 1980. © *Bettmann/CORBIS*.

An evacuated house at Love Canal near Niagara Falls, June 1981, three years after discovery of toxic waste in the area. © *Bettmann/CORBIS.*

Students, organized by the Moral Majority, demonstrate on behalf of a school-prayer amendment. U.S. Capitol, March 1984. © *Bettmann/CORBIS.*

Bill Cosby with Malcolm Jamal Warner in a scene from *The Cosby Show*, 1985.
© *Jacques M. Chenet/CORBIS*.

Bill Gates. *Microsoft Corporation.*

Above　President Ronald Reagan and his wife, Nancy, on inauguration day, January 20, 1981. *TSGT John L. Marine/Defense Visual Information Center, Riverside California.*

Left　Reagan and Soviet leader Mikhail Gorbachev at their first summit meeting, Geneva, November 1985. *Ronald Reagan Presidential Library.*

Above   Gorbachev, Reagan, and President-elect George H. W. Bush near the Statue of Liberty, December 7, 1988. *Ronald Reagan Presidential Library.*

Left   The Rev. Jesse Jackson campaigning, June 1988. © *Jacques M. Chenet/ CORBIS.*

President Bush announces the appointment as of October 1989 of Gen. Colin Powell as Chairman of the Joint Chiefs of Staff. Defense Secretary Dick Cheney is behind them. *George Bush Presidential Library.*

Chinese students demonstrating in Tiananmen Square, Beijing, May 4, 1989. © *Peter Turnley/CORBIS.*

A crowd of West Germans gathers at a newly created opening in the Berlin Wall, November 1989. *Staff Sgt. F. Lee Corkran/Defense Visual Information Center, Riverside, California.*

Devastation in Panama during the American overthrow of Manuel Noriega, December 1989. *Spec. Morland/Defense Visual Information Center, Riverside, California.*

December 7, 1941

December 7, 1989

Renewed fears of Japan, 1989. *Mike Luckovich, Creator's Syndicate.*

Madonna, 1990. © *S.I.N./CORBIS.*

be able to deliver significant support to conservative candidates.[91] Not for the first time in American history, a politics of the pulpit was reemerging in the United States.

IN DEVELOPING HIS CAMPAIGN, Ronald Reagan made a number of appeals, some of them politically opportunistic, to religious conservatives. Republicans, he emphasized, stood firmly against crime, pornography, and immorality. Bob Jones University, he said, should have tax-exempt status. Repudiating his earlier support for a liberalization of abortion, Reagan backed the GOP platform, which called for a constitutional amendment opposing the practice. Breaking with past GOP platforms, he stood against the ERA. He said that he would back a constitutional amendment to restore prayer in the public schools and that schools should teach creationism — "the biblical story of creation" — as well as Darwinism.[92] Carter, meanwhile, refused to endorse a constitutional amendment banning abortion.

Although Reagan had fashioned a career in left-leaning Hollywood and only occasionally attended church, these aspects of his past seemed to do him little harm among religious conservatives. Some early polls suggested that he was leading Carter — who had confessed to illicit sexual urges in *Playboy* — among such voters by a two-to-one margin. Newly formed anti-gay groups, such as the Traditional Values Coalition and the Umbrella Voice, also came out against Carter. Falwell, a prodigious fund-raiser, amassed a reported $100 million for Moral Majority causes in 1979–80, an amount that was much higher than that collected by the Democratic National Committee.[93] As the campaign moved forward, Reagan had good reason to hope that white voters partial to the Religious Right, having formed common cause with southern whites who opposed civil rights activism, with conservative blue-collar workers and Catholics, and with people who rejected big government, would help him win the election.[94]

91 James Morone, *Hellfire Nation: The Politics of Sin in American History* (New Haven, 2003), 450–55.
92. Wills, *Under God*, 120–21.
93. Erling Jorstad, *The Politics of Moralism: The New Christian Right in American Life* (Minneapolis, 1981), 48.
94. Diamond, *Not by Politics Alone*, 62. Polls, however, tended to be imprecise on these matters. Some have suggested that white churchgoers in general did not turn strongly to the GOP until the 1990s. See *New York Times*, Dec. 6, 2003. In 1952 and 1956, Adlai Stevenson, who had been divorced, probably suffered as a result. In 1964, Nelson Rockefeller went from likely GOP presidential nominee to also-ran (behind Goldwater) because he divorced his wife and married a woman who divorced and left her children to marry him.

Reagan, however, was not primarily interested in waging war for social conservatism. Confident that many adherents of the Religious Right were on his side, he concentrated his fire against the many other chinks, as he saw them, in Carter's armor. One of these, Reagan exclaimed, was the president's record concerning foreign affairs. Speaking as if American foreign policies had not hardened after the invasion of Afghanistan, Reagan hammered repeatedly at Carter's rejection of the B-1 bomber and the neutron bomb. He promised to spend much more money on defense than Carter, by 1980 a hawk, was allocating. Concerning Carter's earlier backing of détente, he quipped, "Détente: isn't that what a farmer does with his turkey—until Thanksgiving Day?" Carter and his supporters in Congress, he said, "seem like Santa Claus. They have given the Panama Canal away, abandoned Taiwan to the Red Chinese, and they've negotiated a SALT II treaty that could well make this nation NUMBER TWO."[95]

In demanding that America act forcefully in the world, Reagan was determined to pull the nation out of what he charged was the pusillanimous posture that the United States had assumed since the Vietnam War. That conflict, he later said, had been a "noble cause." Again and again Reagan emphasized his vision of the United States as an exceptional nation that had historically been a force for good in the world. America, the last great hope, had a special mission to overcome Communism, which he said was a tyrannical and ultimately doomed system. Reagan promised to transform an imperiled presidency into a dynamically effective institution. He would enable the United States, humiliated by Iranian revolutionaries who still held fifty-two Americans hostage, to stand tall once more.

Appalled by rhetoric such as this, many of Reagan's opponents denounced him as a warmonger. Others dismissed him as a Neanderthal who was ignorant of or incurious about a whole host of issues. These negative impressions remained forever etched in the minds of detractors. Clark Clifford, a prominent Democrat, later and famously said that Reagan was an "amiable dunce." Edmund Morris, an unsympathetic biographer who observed him carefully during the mid- and late 1980s, later called him an "apparent airhead."[96]

In assailing Reagan as a hard-line conservative, critics were correct. Opposing affirmative action, choice, and big government, he stood stubbornly and proudly on the right wing of his party. Those who thought he was an airhead, however, underestimated him. Well before 1980, Reagan had been

95. Smith, *Morality, Reason, and Power*, 115.
96. Edmund Morris, *Dutch: A Memoir of Ronald Reagan* (New York, 1999), 4, 579.

passionate about political issues—to the extent that acquaintances who had known him during his Hollywood days thought he had both bored and neglected his first wife, the actress Jane Wyman.[97] For years he had been a diligent reader of *Human Events*, a leading journal of conservative opinion. After 1975, when he finished his second term as governor of California, he spent a good deal of time studying contemporary problems. Between 1976 and 1979, he gave hundreds of speeches, many of which he had written out longhand, mainly concerning foreign policy and defense.[98] By 1980, he scarcely paused to rethink his opinions. Knowing where he wanted to go, he steered a straight and usually predictable course, even if others, less set in their ways, perceived rocks and other hazards in his path. Reagan's stubborn certitude continued to appall his opponents, but it fortified an ideological consistency, as his supporters perceived it, which was to be a major source of his considerable political popularity.

As the campaign of 1980 progressed, it became obvious that Reagan was a formidable political figure. Despite his age, he remained a graceful, athletic, physically fit man who seemed far younger than sixty-nine. He had a marvelously soothing baritone voice and an easy platform manner, and was a captivating public presence and speaker. Americans seemed drawn to his supreme self-confidence and especially to his optimism, which led him to assert that that the United States had by no means entered an "Age of Limits." On the contrary, he said, the United States was an exceptional nation in the entire history of the world. It had the capacity—and the responsibility—to do almost anything that would advance freedom abroad. This unfailingly upbeat message contrasted sharply with the atmosphere of "malaise" that had come to surround Carter's ill-fated presidency.[99]

Put off by his cheeriness, his daughter Maureen later said, "It's enough to drive you nuts." She had a point: Reagan's "the United States can do it all" approach to domestic and international problems was as simplistic as Carter's claim had been in 1976—that he could ride into Washington as an outsider and clean up the country. But Garry Wills, a Reagan biographer, understood the key sources of his political appeal, stressing first of all that his self assurance was contagious and second that he was an oddity—a "cheerful conservative."[100]

97. Pemberton, *Exit with Honor*, 28–29.
98. For 670 of these, see Kiron Skinner et al., eds., *Reagan, in His Own Hand* (New York, 2001).
99. Edmund Morris, "The Unknowable," *New Yorker*, June 28, 2004, 40–51; Greenstein, *The Presidential Difference*, 147.
100. Wills, "Mr. Magoo Remembers," *New York Review of Books*, Dec. 20, 1990, 29; Wills, *Reagan's America* (Garden City, N.Y., 1988), 2. Maureen Reagan in Pemberton, *Exit with Honor*, 17.

Though these assets served Reagan well in 1980, the miserable state of the economy helped him most of all. In 1979, inflation had so worried Carter that he had named Paul Volcker, a conservative who was widely admired by business leaders, as chairman of the Federal Reserve Board. With the president's support, Volcker instituted tough-minded policies, including curbs on the money supply, to cut inflation. The result in the short run, however, was recession, the worst imaginable political development for an incumbent president. Unemployment, which had averaged 6 percent in 1977, climbed to 7.8 percent by May 1980. Interest rates shot through the roof, with the prime rate soaring to the scarcely believable level of 18.5 percent in April. Bad economic news persisted later in the year.[101]

Reagan, seizing on Carter's inability to cure the nation's domestic maladies, understandably highlighted the magic of his own remedies. As his demand for greater defense spending indicated, he was hardly as consistent an advocate of small government as some conservatives might have hoped. He spoke so fondly of FDR in his acceptance speech for the GOP nomination that the New York Times carried a lead editorial the next day, "Franklin Delano Reagan." In calling for tax reductions of 30 percent, he risked running up huge budget deficits. But he nonetheless directed his appeals to conservative foes of big government. He insisted that domestic spending had to be cut and that the federal bureaucracy had to be slashed. He promised to dismantle the recently created Cabinet departments of energy and education. "Government," he quipped, "is like a baby, an alimentary canal with a big appetite at one end and no sense of responsibility at the other."

As the campaign neared its end, Reagan intensified his ridicule of Carter's economic policies. By then he was regularly posing a rhetorical question to audiences: "Are you better off than you were four years ago?"[102] Republican audiences especially relished his favorite line: "A recession is when your neighbor loses his job, and a depression is when you lose your job, and"—here he paused for effect—"recovery is when Jimmy Carter loses his."[103]

Though barbs like these stung Democrats, the contest seemed close into the final week of the campaign. Democrats asserted repeatedly that Reagan was too old for the job: If elected, he would be the oldest man in American history to be voted into the presidency. Moreover, John Ander-

101. Collins, More, 158–60.
102. Cited by Douglas Brinkley, introductory comments in American History 38 (Oct. 2003), 7.
103. Boller, Presidential Campaigns, 359.

son, a fiscally conservative, socially moderate Republican congressman from Illinois who was running as an independent, seemed likely to cut into Reagan's support. More Americans still identified themselves as Democrats than as Republicans. If Carter could hang on to the remnants of the New Deal electoral coalition that had helped to him to win in 1976, he might prevail again.

Reagan, however, was impressive in a long-awaited late-October television debate with Carter. Relaxed and poised, he pretended to be saddened by the president's attacks. When Carter accused him of favoring deep cuts in Medicare, he shook his head and interjected, "There you go again." Within the next few days, Reagan forged into the lead.

Results of the election, in which Reagan easily outpolled Carter, suggested that the Democratic electoral coalition had retained some residual strength, notably among blacks, union members, and low-income people in the cities. Subsequent analyses of the voting also revealed that a "gender gap" was opening. Women, worried by Reagan's hawkish positions on foreign affairs and by his conservative approach to issues such as education and health care, supported him by only a narrow margin, of 46 percent to 45 percent. By contrast, 54 percent of men backed Reagan (as opposed to 37 percent for Carter).[104] The gender gap was to persist in later years. Reagan, moreover, did not draw masses to the polls: Turnout, at 54.7 percent of eligible voters, was a tiny bit lower than the 54.8 percent that had voted in 1976.[105] He won only 28 percent of those eligible to vote and 51 percent of those who voted, just 3 percent more than Ford had

104. *World Almanac, 2001,* 40.
105. Here and elsewhere in this book, turnout percentages cited are of the voting-*eligible* population, not of the larger voting-*age* population, which until fairly recently has been the population most often cited when pundits complain about low turnouts. America's voting-age population since 1972 has been defined as "all U.S. residents 18 years and over," but it includes many people who are ineligible to vote, notably non-citizens and (in most states) felons. Because the numbers of immigrants and felons have risen considerably since 1970, higher percentages of this "voting-age population" have become ineligible to vote. Turnouts of this population have therefore declined, especially since 1980, leading many pundits to bewail a falling-off of voting participation in the United States.

   If one uses the voting-*eligible* population as the basis for measuring turnout, a slightly happier picture emerges. In presidential elections between 1984 and 2000, the turnouts of the voting-eligible population remained fairly stable, averaging around 56 percent—or between four and five percentage points higher than the average turnouts of the voting-age population. See Michael McDonald and Samuel Popkin, "The Myth of the Vanishing Voter," *American Political Science Review* 95 (Dec. 2001), 963–74.

captured four years earlier. Democrats also retained control of the House, 243 to 192.

Still, there was no doubting that voters had repudiated Carter. Many liberals, having supported Ted Kennedy during the primary season, remained cool to him. The president received only 41 percent of the vote, 9 percent less than he had won in 1976. Anderson, cutting into the totals for both candidates, received 8 percent. Reagan was especially successful in the Sunbelt, losing only in Georgia, Carter's home state. His popularity among white voters in the South, where Carter had been strong in 1976, exposed the powerful influence of racial feelings—and to a lesser extent of the Religious Right—in American life and politics.[106] Then and for the next quarter century, Democratic presidential candidates fared poorly among white voters in Dixie and among religious conservatives. Reagan otherwise lost only Maryland, the District of Columbia, Hawaii, Rhode Island, West Virginia, and Mondale's home state of Minnesota. He scored an overwhelming victory in the electoral college, 489 to 49.

Reagan could also claim to have carried a good many Republicans into office on his coattails. Though the House remained Democratic—as it had been since the election of 1954—the GOP gained thirty-three seats in 1980. Most impressively, GOP numbers jumped from forty-one to fifty-three in the Senate, which in 1981 was to be under Republican control for the first time since January 1955. Several liberal Democratic senators, on conservative "hit lists" during the campaign, lost their seats. They included Frank Church of Idaho and George McGovern of South Dakota, the Democratic presidential nominee in 1972. In Indiana, Senator Birch Bayh fell to a Republican conservative, J. Danforth Quayle.

Explanations for the Democratic disaster understandably varied. Bill Moyers, a liberal who had been a top aide to Lyndon Johnson, observed: "We didn't elect this guy [Reagan] because he knows how many barrels of oil are in Alaska. We elected him because we want to feel good."[107] Moyers had a point: A majority of Americans were obviously tired of Carter and hoped that the ever optimistic Reagan would deliver them from the dark days of the late 1970s. In this sense, the election resembled that of 1932, when voters had chosen the jauntily optimistic FDR over the incumbent,

106. Evangelical Protestant voters appeared to split their votes between Carter and Reagan in 1980 but to come out in unusually large numbers for conservative congressional candidates, especially in the South, and therefore to be important in enabling the GOP to take control of the Senate in 1981. Butler, "Jack-in-the-Box Faith," 1372–73.

107. Michael Schaller, *Reckoning with Reagan: America and Its Presidents in the 1980s* (New York, 1992), 5.

Herbert Hoover, the dour embodiment of hard times. Carter was the first incumbent president since Hoover to lose in a bid for reelection.

Many voters in 1980 also liked the prospect of tax cuts—these appeared to be a simple (and simplistic) way to make life better—and supported Reagan's war against the cultural excesses, as he saw them, of the 1960s. Results like these were hardly consoling to Democrats, who recognized that Reagan had won a striking personal triumph and that his victory foretold an era in which political conservatives might dominate national affairs. Speaker O'Neill was grimly forthright about the outcome: "A tidal wave hit us from the Pacific, the Atlantic, the Caribbean, and the Great Lakes."[108]

108. *Newsweek*, Nov. 24, 1980, 4.

5

"Morning Again in America"

Ronald Reagan loved to spin a yarn about two young brothers, one of whom was an inveterate pessimist, the other an incurable optimist. Their parents tried to narrow these extremes by giving them very different gifts on Christmas Day. The pessimist, presented with a huge pile of toys, cried in the corner, certain that the toys would break. The optimist, staring at a pile of horse manure, dug happily into it and exclaimed, "I just know there's a pony in here somewhere."[1]

Throughout his presidency Reagan was like the optimist. As he had during his campaign, he repeatedly scoffed at the notion that the country had entered an Age of Limits or was tumbling into an Era of Decline, and he never stopped telling Americans that they had what it took to climb to unimaginable heights. The United States, he reiterated, was "as a city upon a hill," an exceptional, liberty-loving nation whose democratic institutions were destined to spread about the world.[2] In his inaugural address, he urged Americans to "believe in ourselves and to believe in our capacity to perform great deeds, to believe . . . we can and will resolve the problems which now confront us." He demanded, "Why shouldn't we believe that? We are Americans."

1. Robert Collins, *More: The Politics of Economic Growth in Postwar America* (New York, 2000), 192.
2. The phrase "as a city upon a hill" was Puritan leader John Winthrop's, delivered in 1630 on the ship *Arabella* as it sailed to what was to become the Massachusetts Bay Colony. At Reagan's funeral in June 2004, Supreme Court Justice Sandra Day O'Connor read Winthrop's words, emphasizing that Reagan often used them during his presidency.

That Reagan truly believed this optimistic message was obvious to everyone who came into contact with him or heard him speak. His faith in the capacity of the United States continued to know no bounds. And his media-wise aides made sure that the message got across. As Michael Deaver, a top aide, later put it, "We kept apple pie and the flag going the whole time." In 1984, Deaver and others made "It's Morning Again in America" the central theme of Reagan's feel-good campaign for reelection. Then as always they carefully orchestrated his public appearances, often providing television reporters with a "line-of-the-day" sound bite — almost invariably an optimistic one — for use in the evening news.

Staged this way, Reagan struck opponents as little more than a pitchman — a national master of ceremonies who was disconnected from events about him. That was often the case, especially in his second term, but some of the goals that he advanced — winning the Cold War, shoring up traditional values, embracing the American Dream of upward social mobility — resonated with millions of voters. Blaming liberals for being "soft" on Communism and "permissive" about developments at home, many Americans were receptive to his rhetoric and supportive of his policies. That is to say, they were not fools who were seduced by flash and dash. Reagan's message, as much as his manner of delivering it, helped to explain why his political appeal, though fluctuating during his eight years in office, managed to endure.

He was nonetheless a masterful television presence. When he prepared a major address, he memorized his scripts to the extent that he needed only to glance at cue cards when he spoke.[3] At his best he was a powerfully moving, inspiring orator — the Great Communicator of legend. House Speaker Tip O'Neill, listening to Reagan speak to the nation following the fiery explosion of the space shuttle *Challenger* in 1986, admitted that he wept, and added, "He [Reagan] may not be much of a debater, but with a prepared text he's the best public speaker I've ever seen. . . . I'm beginning to think that in this regard he dwarfs both Roosevelt and Kennedy."[4]

Reagan was a seasoned enough politician and administrator to recognize in January 1981 that he had to do more than talk: He had to act as quickly as possible on his electoral mandate. Whereas Carter had assumed that he and his team of young Georgians could conquer Congress, Reagan

3. Mary Ann Watson, *Defining Visions: Television and the American Experience Since 1945* (Fort Worth, 1998), 255.
4. Edmund Morris, *Dutch: A Memoir of Ronald Reagan* (New York, 1999), 586.

took no chances. Assembling a strong transition team, he selected James Baker, Bush's campaign manager in 1980, as chief of staff. Baker proved to be a politically shrewd, media-savvy, and highly efficient insider during Reagan's first term, after which he took over as treasury secretary.[5] Reagan also visited Washington before his inauguration to meet with O'Neill and other key figures in Congress. His affability and obvious desire to consult and cooperate impressed titans on the Hill. Then, as later, political opponents found him to be unfailingly civil and friendly, never demonizing them. His gifts as a raconteur stood him in especially good stead with O'Neill, who enjoyed swapping yarns with him.

Unlike Carter, Reagan knew enough not to send a pile of big programs to Capitol Hill. Instead, he concentrated on the most important issues of the campaign: increasing expenditures for the military, cutting domestic spending on social welfare, and—above all—reducing federal income taxes by 30 percent over the next three years. Reagan's zeal for lower taxes was partly grounded in his understanding of contemporary theoretical arguments for supply-side economics, as it was called, but it was primarily visceral—a result in large part of his own experience with the IRS. Donald Regan, treasury secretary in Reagan's first term, later explained why Reagan felt as he did about taxes:

> When he was in Hollywood he would make about three or four hundred thousand dollars per picture. Reagan would work for three months, and loaf for three months, so he was making between six and seven hundred thousand dollars per year. Between Uncle Sam and the state of California, over 91 percent of that was going in taxes. His question, asked rhetorically, was this: "Why should I have done a third picture, even if it was *Gone with the Wind*? What good would it have done me?"
>
> So he loafed for a part of the year. And he said the same thing was happening throughout America. People would reach a certain peak, and they weren't willing to do the extra effort that was needed to keep us a first-class nation.[6]

The fundamental concept behind supply side-economics was simple: Cutting taxes would enable Americans, notably employers and investors, to retain more income, which would give them the incentive to make even more. Greater entrepreneurial activity would spur rapid economic

5. David Halberstam, *War in a Time of Peace: Bush, Clinton, and the Generals* (New York, 2001), 62–65.
6. Deborah Hart Strober and Gerald Strober, *Reagan: The Man and the Presidency* (Baltimore, 1994), 131.

growth, which would hike personal income — and bring in greater tax revenue, even at the lower rates. Many economists ridiculed these ideas, complaining that people who supported supply-side ideas had a "have your cake and eat it, too" approach to government: They demanded benefits from Washington but refused to pay for them. There was surely truth in such complaints, but Reagan was unmoved. "You know economists," he was wont to say. "They're the sort of people who see something works in practice and wonder if it works in theory." Reagan also emphasized that the tax bite had grown sharper in recent years. For this reason, among others, tax cuts had great political appeal. And the economic stagflation of the 1970s had convinced many policy-makers that prevailing economic wisdom, notably Keynesian ideas, had not worked.

Supply-side economics had developed widespread support in the late 1970s. As early as 1977, Republican congressman Jack Kemp of New York, a presidential aspirant in 1980, had argued strongly for supply-side ideas. Democratic senator Lloyd Bentsen of Texas, chairman of the Joint Economic Committee of Congress, declared in 1980 that America had entered "the start of a new era of economic thinking. For too long we have focused on short-run policies to stimulate spending, or demand, while neglecting supply—labor, savings, investment, and production. Consequently, demand has been over-stimulated and supply has been strangled." The committee, following Bentsen's lead, recommended a "comprehensive set of policies designed to enhance the productive side, the supply side, of the economy."[7]

Bentsen's position indicated that Reagan's tax plans could expect to receive some bipartisan support. Still, most Democrats opposed him. With a majority in the House—divided government persisted throughout Reagan's presidency—they had enough votes to stop him. Tax cuts, they said, would benefit the rich more than the poor and exacerbate economic inequality. They would also expand budget deficits, the more so because the president was also calling for huge increases in defense spending. As Reagan and his aides lobbied hard for the bill in March 1981, it was by no means clear that the measure would pass.

At this point fate dealt the president a cruel but, as it happened, a politically beneficial hand. On March 30, a deeply troubled twenty-five-year-old man, John Hinckley Jr., tried to assassinate him as he left a speaking engagement at a Washington hotel. Firing six times with a .22 caliber pistol, Hinckley shot James Brady, Reagan's press secretary, in the head.

7. Collins, *More*, 189.

Severely wounded, Brady became permanently disabled. Other shots bloodied a Washington policeman and a Secret Service agent. One of Hinckley's shots ricocheted off the presidential limousine, hit Reagan under his left arm, struck a rib, and lodged in his left lung close to his heart. He was rushed to a nearby hospital, where he was bleeding heavily. Doctors operated for two hours in order to remove the bullet and to save his life. Reagan's brush with death, closer than Americans understood at the time, kept him in the hospital until April 11.

While Reagan recovered in the hospital, news releases informed a frightened American public how calm and good-humored he had been. As he was being taken into the operating room, he told his wife, Nancy, "Honey, I forgot to duck." When doctors were about to operate, he quipped, "Please tell me you're all Republicans." Polls recorded that his courage and humor were helping him to soar to new heights of popularity, with more than 70 percent of the people giving him favorable ratings. After returning to the White House, Reagan kept a fairly low profile until April 28, when he emerged to give an eagerly awaited televised speech to a joint session of Congress. Still recovering, he seized this dramatic, emotionally charged occasion to call upon the legislators to enact his tax and spending programs.

How could Congress defy such a popular man? During the next three months Reagan worked hard to get his budget and tax bills through the Congress. One historian has calculated that during the first 100 days of his term (within which time he was recovering from his wound) he met sixty-nine times with 467 members of Congress, in addition to lobbying many others over the phone.[8] In so doing he showed patience and good humor. Though Reagan rejected major changes to his plans, his actions indicated (as had been the case when he was governor of California) that he was far from the inflexible ideologue that critics had described. When he needed votes, he compromised in order to craft bipartisan coalitions of Republicans and conservative Democrats — "boll weevils," critics called them. O'Neill, who had underestimated him, complained to a constituent, "I'm getting the shit whaled out of me." James Wright of Texas, the House majority leader, wrote in his diary in June: "I stand in awe . . . of [Reagan's] political skill. I am not sure that I have seen its equal."[9]

The president's persistence paid off in July, when Congress passed slightly modified tax and budget bills. Reagan signed both into law on

8. William Pemberton, *Exit with Honor: The Life and Presidency of Ronald Reagan* (Armonk, N.Y., 1998), 101.
9. Collins, *More*, 192.

August 13. The tax law, which forty-eight Democratic House members supported on the final vote, called for a 23 percent cut in federal income taxes over the next three years. It reduced the top marginal rate on individuals from 70 percent to 50 percent, and it cut rates in lower brackets. The administration estimated that the reductions would amount to $750 billion—an enormous sum—over the next five years. The budget bill, along with new regulations that his appointees put into place, gave Reagan many of the cuts in domestic spending—in public assistance, food stamps, and other means-tested programs for the poor—for which he had campaigned. Reagan also terminated a Carter-era jobs program, the Comprehensive Employment and Training Act (CETA), which had provided work for some 300,000 people in 1980. At the same time, he approved the paring of some 500,000 names from the rolls of people covered under Social Security's disability program.[10] Reagan said that cuts in the budget bill alone would total some $130 billion over the next three years.[11]

In securing these large goals, Reagan greatly advanced the salience of conservative economic ideas, thereby driving liberals—then and thereafter—onto the defensive. His successes wowed many seasoned observers. Reporters spoke of the "Reagan Revolution" that he had wrought in fiscal policy. Hedley Donovan of *Fortune* wrote that the tax and budget acts represented the "most formidable domestic initiative any president has driven through since the Hundred Days of Franklin Roosevelt."[12] At last, it seemed, the United States had a president who could oil the gears of government and make them turn.

Just a few days after Congress passed his tax and budget bills, Reagan took a step that gave him an undying reputation for firmness under pressure. When federal employees who were members of the Professional Air Traffic Controllers' Organization (PATCO) threatened to strike for better pay and benefits, he determined to resist their demands. When they voted to strike, he gave them forty-eight hours to return to work or be fired. Many Americans were appalled, sure that air safety would collapse, but Reagan (who was the first American president in history to have served as the head of a union, and who had received the endorsement of PATCO in 1980) believed that such a strike would be illegal, and he held firm.

10. Federal courts soon restored 200,000 of these to the rolls.
11. James Patterson, "Afterword: Legacies of the Reagan Years," in W. Elliot Brownlee and Hugh Davis Graham, eds., *The Reagan Presidency: Pragmatic Conservatism and Its Legacies* (Lawrence, Kans., 2003), 355–75; Gareth Davies, "The Welfare State," ibid., 209–32.
12. Donovan, "Reagan's First Two Hundred Days," *Fortune*, Sept. 21, 1981, 63.

When the deadline passed, he announced that 38 percent of the strikers had returned to work and that military controllers would step in to help. Ten days later, having fired more than 11,000 air traffic controllers, he reassured the nation that flight schedules had returned to 80 percent normal. His action destroyed the union and sent an unmistakable message to other labor leaders that he could be a man of steel.

To liberals and labor union leaders, Reagan's behavior was anathema. An imperial presidency, they complained, had returned with a vengeance — and with long-range consequences, for Reagan's action not only broke the strike; it further demoralized organized labor. Thereafter, the number of strikes per year—which had already been declining from their highs in the early 1970s—plummeted to all-time lows.[13] Some of the most dramatic of these failed, notably a bitterly contested strike of packers at Hormel in Minnesota in 1985–86. But the president, having acted boldly in 1981, remained deaf to complaints that he had sought to crush the union movement. Perhaps no single act of his administration better demonstrated that Reagan could be, and often was, a stubborn man of conviction. Millions of conservative Americans who had admired his courage when he was shot were now more certain than ever that they had a leader who stood behind his beliefs, even if these were harsh and might seem politically perilous at the time. His image as a consistent defender of a core of ideas helped him again and again to shrug off a host of criticisms, thereby causing opponents to lament that he was a "Teflon President"—nothing stuck to him.[14]

Reagan, who was thoroughly enjoying himself, was delighted by the course of events during the first seven months of his term, but his economic policies remained extraordinarily controversial. Throughout his administration critics lamented that "Reaganomics"—tax cuts combined with increased military spending—created unprecedented budget deficits. Between the fiscal years 1980 and 1989, the national debt tripled from $914 billion to $2.7 trillion.[15] Some of this increase stemmed from congressional spending, driven by Republicans as well as Democrats who lavished federal funds on constituents and interest groups. The president and

13. There were 187 work stoppages in 1980, down from a high of 424 in 1974. The number dropped to 96 in 1982 and to a low in the 1980s of 40 in 1988. In the 1990s, the number fluctuated between 17 and 45 per year. Stoppages as enumerated here involved 1,000 or more workers and lasted a day or longer. *Stat. Abst.*, 2002, 410.

14. Pemberton, *Exit with Honor*, 107; Haynes Johnson, *Sleepwalking Through History: America in the Reagan Years* (New York, 1991), 163.

15. Collins, *More*, 203.

his advisers, failing to anticipate the power of pork barrel politics, could not stop it. Still, Reagan's administration, which never submitted a balanced budget, was far and away the major source of governmental red ink.

As critics pointed out, the deficits required the treasury to borrow heavily to service the debt, and to pay high interest rates in the process. Reaganomics, they complained, deprived the government of money that it might otherwise have had available to spend for infrastructure and social needs, and swallowed up private investment (much of which was attracted by high-interest government bonds) that might have advanced more rapid economic growth. High deficits, they added, set a poor example, encouraging people to run up debt in their own lives and promoting higher levels of stress and insecurity throughout American society.

Worst of all, Reagan's alarmingly high budget shortfalls seemed to indicate that the government itself, lacking fiscal discipline, had spun out of control. By the end of his term in office, the national debt was 53 percent of GDP, compared to 33 percent in 1981.[16] Some economists feared that disaster might loom ahead. An accomplished biographer, Lou Cannon, concluded in 1989, "The deficit is Reagan's greatest failure."[17]

Liberal critics were equally appalled by Reagan's hostility to large-scale spending for social welfare, especially when this parsimony was contrasted to the lavishness of Nancy Reagan's lifestyle and to the glitter of the celebrations that had surrounded the inaugural ceremonies—"a bacchanalia of the haves." Nancy Reagan's wardrobe for these events was said to have cost $25,000.[18] Firing the air controllers, they added, was nothing more than union busting. Cutting taxes on the wealthy while paring benefits for the poor seemed especially unfair. "When it comes to giving tax breaks to the wealthy of this country," O'Neill exclaimed, "the president has a heart of gold." A joke went around (perhaps originating from the president himself) that Reagan's right hand didn't know what his far right hand was up to.

Liberals, however, did not laugh. Senator Daniel Patrick Moynihan of New York was one of many Democrats who maintained that Reagan deliberately ran up deficits via tax cuts and military spending in order to starve social programs. This, Moynihan charged, was "Reagan's Revenge," a diabolical plot to sabotage the welfare state.[19] Moynihan could not prove

16. *Stat. Abst.*, 2002, 449.
17. *Newsweek*, Jan. 9, 1989. See also Collins, *More*, 210–13.
18. Johnson, *Sleepwalking Through History*, 20–21.
19. Moynihan, "Reagan's Bankrupt Budget," *New Republic*, Dec. 26, 1983, 15–20; Alan Brinkley, "Reagan's Revenge," *New York Times Magazine*, June 19, 1994, 37.

that this was Reagan's primary purpose, nor did the welfare state collapse, but he was correct that conservatives sought to cut social spending and that large deficits did stymie efforts for new liberal programs.

Reagan's detractors highlighted other flaws, as they saw them, in his performance. A common complaint was that he spent too much time off the job. Compared to Carter, who was a workaholic, this was true. Reagan, who turned seventy in February 1981, refused to hold early morning staff meetings, and he was normally out of the Oval Office before five. Especially after his brush with death, he needed to nap, and it was rumored that he dozed at meetings in the afternoon. During his eight years in office he spent almost a year of days at his beloved ranch in California, as well as 183 weekends at Camp David. Another joke went around: Question: "Would Reagan be a threat to blow up the world?" Answer: "Only between the hours of nine to five." Reagan did not in fact fall asleep at meetings, but he was clearly aware of the rumors. He joked that his chair in the Cabinet room should be labeled "Reagan Slept Here."[20] Humor did help disarm critics. He told reporters, "I am concerned about what is happening in government—and it's caused me many a sleepless afternoon." He quipped, "It's true hard work never killed anyone but I figure, why take the chance?"[21]

Other foes wondered if Reagan was really in control of his administration. Some thought that the power behind the throne was his wife, Nancy, who was known to consult astrologers and to hold very strong opinions about people who worked for her husband. If they knew what was good for them, they were careful not to cross her. Others considered Reagan to be putty in the hands of aides like Deaver, Baker, or Edwin Meese, his counselor, who trotted him out for grand ceremonial occasions and otherwise conspired to shelter him from the press. To many, including his own children, Reagan seemed to be oddly disconnected from people and from important events around him. White House staffers, finding him affable but elusive, liked to joke, "Who was that masked man?"[22] O'Neill observed that Reagan, an actor by profession, was "most of the time an actor reading lines, who didn't understand his own programs." The president, he cracked, "would have made a hell of a king." Baker recalled a time in 1983 when he left Reagan a thick briefing book on the eve of an

20. Edmund Morris, "The Unknowable," *New Yorker*, June 28, 2004, 40–51.
21. Pemberton, *Exit with Honor*, 112. For Reagan's humor, see Lou Cannon, *President Reagan: The Role of a Lifetime* (New York, 2000), 95–114.
22. Richard Brookhiser, "Reagan: His Place in History," *American Heritage*, Sept./Oct. 2004, 34–38.

economic summit meeting of the world's democratic leaders. The next morning Baker could see that the book lay unopened. He asked Reagan why he had not looked at it. "Well, Jim," the president replied calmly, "*The Sound of Music* was on last night."[23]

Baker was not the only member of the administration who worried at times about the president's inattentiveness. Deaf in his right ear and hard of hearing in his left, Reagan seemed passive during discussions at meetings.[24] Saying little on such occasions, he left aides wondering what he wanted them to do. As Martin Anderson, a domestic policy adviser, later observed, Reagan "made decisions like a Turkish pasha, passively letting his subjects serve him, selecting only those morsels of public policy that were especially tasty. Rarely did he ask questions and demand to know why someone had or had not done something. He just sat back in a supremely calm, relaxed manner and waited until important things were brought to him."[25]

Some people recognized that Reagan had difficulty at times separating fact from fiction. One of his favorite patriotic stories, which he told during the 1980 campaign, concerned an American bomber pilot in World War II whose plane had been hit and was going down. A badly wounded member of the crew, however, had been pinned inside the plane. As Reagan told the story, the pilot ordered the other members of the crew to bail out and then lay down beside the injured man. The pilot then said to the crewman, "Never mind, son, we'll ride it down together." The trouble with this story was that it never happened, except in a World War II movie, *A Wing and a Prayer*, starring Dana Andrews, that the president presumably had seen. Though critics complained publicly that Reagan had made it all up, he used the story again in 1982, while speaking to American soldiers in Europe. This time he contrasted the heroism of the pilot with the evil behavior of the Soviets.[26] On another occasion Reagan told of having helped to film German death camps while an officer in the army air corps during World War II. This story, too, derived from his imagination—Reagan, who was extremely nearsighted, had done his wartime military service in the United States, mostly in Culver City near his home, during which time he worked at turning out government training and propaganda films.[27]

23. Cannon, *President Reagan*, 37. *The Sound of Music* (movie version) appeared in 1965.
24. Morris, "The Unknowable."
25. Martin Anderson, *Revolution: The Reagan Legacy* (Stanford, 1990), 289–91.
26. John White, *The New Politics of Old Values* (Hanover, N.H., 1990), 12.
27. Michael Korda, "Prompting the President," *New Yorker*, Oct. 6, 1997, 87–95. Reagan later wore contact lenses to correct his eyesight.

Some of these criticisms of Reagan were close to the mark. The president, knowing how to pace himself, was not lazy, but he was a hands-off administrator who seemed oblivious to the many disagreements and feuds that divided his top advisers. Unlike Carter, he did not often bother to scribble suggestions on memoranda or position papers.[28] As Martin Anderson said, Reagan relied upon his top aides to bring things to him for decision. Passionate about a few matters—the iniquity of Communism, the need for high defense spending, the virtues of low taxes—he otherwise had narrow interests. As an advocate of smaller government, he seemed deliberately to ignore issues—housing, health care, urban problems, education, the environment—that he thought the free market ought to settle or that local officials should manage. "Government," he said again and again, "is not the solution, it's the problem." In part for this reason, he was casual in making appointments of personnel—some of them disastrous—in these departments.[29] On one public occasion he failed to recognize his only black Cabinet officer, Samuel Pierce of Housing and Urban Development.

WHETHER REAGAN'S ECONOMIC POLICIES were good for the country was—and is—hard to judge. Most historians, however, credit his efforts to reverse the inflationary spiral that had deeply frightened Americans since the late 1970s. Reagan gave strong and undeviating support to Federal Reserve Board chairman Paul Volcker, who continued to pursue the tough monetary policies that he had initiated under Carter. The recession that Volcker's stern approach had helped to create remained painful in late 1981 and 1982. Unemployment averaged 9.7 percent in 1982, the highest since the Great Depression. Republicans, blamed for widespread suffering, lost twenty-six House seats in the midterm elections. The recession helped to drive Reagan's job approval ratings below 50 percent throughout much of 1982 and 1983. Though people still gave him high personal ratings, the recession served to stem some of the political momentum that he had established in the spring and summer of 1981.

But Reagan, making "Stay the Course" his slogan during the midterm election campaigns of 1982, exhibited his characteristic self-confidence throughout these difficult times. And Volcker's medicine was curative in the long run. Inflation, which had seemed runaway in 1980, dropped to around 3.5 percent five years later and remained in this range, helped by

28. Author's conclusion, from exploring Reagan's papers at the Reagan presidential library in California.
29. Before the end of Reagan's first administration, more than a dozen of his appointees faced charges of improper financial dealings.

disarray within OPEC that drove down oil prices after 1985, for the remainder of the decade. Gasoline prices at the pump dropped from $1.38 per gallon in 1981—an all-time high when adjusted for inflation—to a low of 95 cents in 1986, and remained in that range until 1990.[30] Though unemployment was stubborn, it also declined, to around 5.5 percent by 1988.[31] The return of good times in the mid- and late 1980s was greatly reassuring.[32]

Reagan, moreover, was not so doctrinaire a conservative as liberals made out. While fond of damning big government—and of denunciations of "welfare queens"—he recognized that liberal interest groups had effective lobbies on the Hill, that major New Deal–Great Society social programs—many of them entitlements—were here to stay, and that rights-consciousness had become a powerful political force. He understood that though people said they distrusted government, they expected important services from it. So though he blundered badly in May 1981 by ineptly recommending nearly immediate cuts in Social Security benefits for early retirees (as a way of dealing with the program's looming insolvency problems), he ducked for cover when a firestorm of opposition—from Republicans as well as Democrats—overwhelmed his proposal. Attacked from all sides, he took the politically more prudent step of appointing a bipartisan commission (headed by Alan Greenspan) to recommend ways of shoring up the resources of the program.[33]

Social Security was in truth a near-untouchable "third rail" of American politics—a cherished entitlement that at the time insured 140 million people and sent benefit checks to some 36 million retirees, disabled workers and their families, and survivors of workers who had died. Benefit checks for these purposes totaled $121 billion in 1980. Young people, too, supported

30. For oil prices, Alfred Eckes Jr. and Thomas Zeiler, *Globalization in the American Century* (New York, 2003), 90–93. The high of $1.38 per gallon in 1981 was the equivalent of $2.80 in 2004 prices. *New York Times*, Sept. 29, 2004. Gasoline prices then fluctuated between $1.20 and $1.30 per gallon until 1999.

31. Michael Bernstein, "Understanding American Economic Decline: The Contours of the Late-Twentieth-Century Experience," in Bernstein and David Adler, eds., *Understanding America's Economic Decline* (New York, 1994), 3–33.

32. "Economists Assess the Presidency," in Eric Schmerz et al., eds., *Ronald Reagan's America* (Westport, Conn., 1997), 759–82.

33. For data concerning government social programs, see *Stat. Abst.*, 2002, 342–57. See also John Scholz and Kara Levine, "The Evolution of Income Support Policy in Recent Decades," *Focus* (Institute for Research on Poverty) 21, no. 2 (Fall 2000), 9–16. For Reagan and Social Security, see Martha Derthick and Steven Teles, "Riding the Third Rail: Social Security Reform," in Brownlee and Graham, *The Reagan Presidency*, 182–208; Cannon, *President Reagan*, 212–15; and Collins, *More*, 200–201.

Social Security, which promised to nurture their parents when they retired.[34] Congressional leaders on the commission, trembling before the political power of seniors, shrank from recommending changes that might cut it back. After the election of 1982, however, the commission dared to act, recommending in early 1983 a series of amendments to the program. These called for increased payroll taxes, thereby building up a trust fund that would convert Social Security from a pay-as-you-go program to one that collected large sums of money that were to be used to pay retirement and disability benefits in the future. The amendments also hiked the retirement age (sixty-five) for full benefits; this would increase over time to sixty-six in 2009 and to sixty-seven in 2027.[35]

Relieved to have in hand bipartisan recommendations, Congress quickly accepted them, and Reagan signed them into law. As it turned out, the changes did not take care of the longer-range structural problems of Social Security—notably the predictable crunch that would hit the program in the 2000s, when millions of baby boomers would retire (and, living longer than people had done in the past, would collect benefits for many more years than earlier retirees had). Still, the reforms addressed Social Security's shorter-term financing difficulties.[36] For the next twenty-five or so years, the viability of the program was assured.

Social Security payroll taxes, which were regressive, landed with special impact on low-income people. Along with the cuts in marginal tax rates for the wealthy that the Reagan administration had secured, they contributed to already rising economic inequality in the United States. As earlier, millions of Americans (33.1 million in 1985, 31.5 million in 1989) continued to live in households below the poverty line. Millions more, including hosts of low-wage workers, teetered on the brink of poverty.[37]

---

34. Lawrence Friedman, *American Law in the Twentieth Century* (New Haven, 2002), 536–37.
35. The amendments also provided for the taxation—for the first time—of the benefits of high-income retirees and delayed payment by six months of annual cost-of-living (COLA) adjustments. These important changes greatly improved the financial health of the program.
36. Payroll tax money not needed for benefits was commingled after 1983 with other federal revenues, thereby helping the government to pay for other programs but depriving Social Security of billions of dollars that it would need when the boomers retired. For later issues, highlighted in struggles over proposals to partially privatize Social Security, see *New York Times*, March 8, 2005.
37. The number of Americans officially defined as living in poverty in 1981 (a recession year) was 31.8 million. The percentage of Americans in poverty declined slightly between 1981 and 1989, from 14 to 12.8. *Stat. Abst.*, 2002, 441.

But by accepting bipartisan changes in Social Security, Reagan had avoided political catastrophe, and he made no further efforts to trim the largest entitlement programs, Social Security and Medicare. These continued to grow in later years.

Means-tested programs like SSI, Medicaid, the Earned Income Tax Credit, food stamps, and Aid to Families with Dependent Children (AFDC) also expanded incrementally after 1982, offering needy recipients slightly larger benefits in real dollars in 1990 than they had received in 1980.[38] Reagan and his conservative advisers succeeded in slowing, but by no means arresting, the rising tide of federal expenditure for entitlements and other social purposes.[39]

Concerning the impact of the income tax cuts of 1981, economists and others continued to disagree many years later. Foes of the president were correct to point out that neither he nor his advisers always knew what they were doing. Chief among these advisers was David Stockman, whom Reagan made director of the Office of Management and Budget (OMB). Stockman, only thirty-five in 1981, had been a member of the left-of-center Students for a Democratic Society (SDS) while an undergraduate at Michigan State in the late 1960s. In 1977, he had entered the House as a Republican congressman from Michigan. Energetic and hard-driving, Stockman had moved well to the right politically since his student days. In 1981, he was a zealous supply-sider determined to cut government spending. At that time he impressed Reagan and others in the White House as a genius concerning numbers and economic forecasts.

But Stockman and his team at OMB failed to achieve many of their fiscal goals. Federal spending overall—much of it owing to hikes for defense—peaked at 23.5 percent of GDP in 1983, dipping slowly thereafter to 21.2 percent in 1989. This latter percentage was still a point or so higher than those of the late 1970s—and higher by two points than those in the late 1990s, when federal spending in constant dollars at last came close to leveling off, and when deficits briefly disappeared.[40] Federal civilian employment, which had fallen slightly in the 1970s, rose during Reagan's tenure from 2.9 million to 3.1 million.[41] Reagan, like other presidents in the post-1960s era, discovered that interest groups and constituents had the power to preserve and to enlarge the size of government.

38. Davies, "The Welfare State"; R. Shep Melnick, "Governing More but Enjoying It Less," in Morton Keller and Melnick, eds., *Taking Stock: American Government in the Twentieth Century* (New York, 1999), 280–306; *Stat. Abst.*, 2002, 342.
39. Collins, *More*, 201.
40. *Stat. Abst.*, 2002, 305. For the 1990s, see chapter 11.
41. Ibid., 320. It declined in the 1990s, to 2.7 million by 2001.

The president and his advisers were also off base in believing that tax cuts, by stimulating the economy, would hike tax revenues that would thereby prevent deficits. These were gross miscalculations. Though tax revenues did increase in the 1980s, they fell far short of covering the jump in federal outlays, and gross federal debt as a percentage of the GDP skyrocketed from 33 in 1981 to a post-1960 high of 53 percent in 1989.[42] Stockman himself confessed in late 1981, "None of us really understands what's going on with all these numbers."[43]

Reagan, bending to foes who assailed the rising deficits, soon disappointed supply-siders. In 1982 (and later) he agreed to increases in excise, corporate, and income taxes. These increases, added to the hikes in Social Security taxes that he accepted in 1983, ensured that the overall tax load in America did not fall during his administration. Though a major tax law enacted in 1986 further lowered marginal income tax rates (to 28 percent for those in the top bracket), it also closed a number of loopholes that had deprived the government of revenue. For all these reasons, income from federal taxes remained steady at around 19 percent of GNP during the 1980s.[44]

Nor did supply-side practices seem to contribute to two of Reagan's major economic goals: great expansion of funds pouring into productive investment, and more rapid economic growth. Many investors took advantage of high interest rates to buy government bonds. Others, paying less in taxes, indulged in speculative endeavors, such as unproductive buyouts and "junk bonds." Thanks in part to still sluggish growth in productivity, increases in real per capita money income were modest during Reagan's presidency, averaging around 2 percent per year—below the rate of growth during the Good Old Days following World War II, and roughly the same as had occurred during the 1970s.[45]

In fact, the overall economic picture in the mid-1980s, though improved, was uneven. While many of the wealthy prospered as never before, the real wages of full-time male production workers continued to stagnate.[46]

42. Ibid., 305. This percentage continued to rise in the next few years, peaking at 67 percent between 1995 and 1997 before dipping to 57 by 2001. It rose again—boosted by tax cuts and by costs of the war against Iraq—to more than 70 in 2003.

43. William Greider, "The Education of David Stockman," *Atlantic Monthly* 248 (Dec. 1981), 27.

44. Over time, expert accountants and attorneys figured out new loopholes to help people avoid taxes, whereupon cries for tax simplification arose again.

45. *Stat. Abst.*, 2002, 440.

46. Ibid., 422; *New York Times*, Feb. 17, 2003. See also Pemberton, *Exit with Honor*, 206–8. Benefit packages for some of these workers improved, so that their total compensation, on the average, did not change much. For a grim view of family economics in the 1980s, however, see Barbara Ehrenreich, *Fear of Falling: The Inner Life of the Middle Class* (New York, 1989).

As in the 1970s, job-seekers frequently complained that the fastest-growing occupations were in low-paying parts of the service sector: waiters and waitresses, nurses, janitors, cashiers, and truck drivers.[47] Though the Sunbelt continued to grow impressively, other regions, notably the Rust Belt, still floundered. Grain farmers, who faced increases in world production that lowered prices for their goods, also suffered. The number of farm foreclosures increased. Hit by considerable competition from abroad, the United States in the mid-1980s went from being one of the world's largest creditor nations to the world's largest debtor.[48]

For these reasons, the soundness of supply-side ideas remained hotly debated. Then and later, opponents complained that tax cuts aggravated economic inequality, which (thanks also to America's comparatively porous social safety net) became sharper than anywhere else in the industrialized world. They also argued that there is no necessary connection between tax cuts and economic progress: The runaway deficits of the 1980s, these critics said, had made investors skittish and limited economic growth.

Supply-siders nonetheless kept the faith. Rejecting the argument that they had been fiscally irresponsible, they stressed that big federal deficits had come into existence in the 1970s, not in the 1980s, and that Carter, not Reagan, had initiated large hikes in military spending. Rising economic inequality, they pointed out, stemmed primarily from structural trends in the labor markets, notably expanding gaps in wages between skilled and unskilled workers. They added that relatively high earnings reaped by two-income families and by well-educated, technologically savvy people in an onrushing Information Age further accentuated inequality. These were indeed among the major reasons why income inequality increased not only in the 1980s, when tax rates on the wealthy went down, but also in the 1990s, when they inched up. Similar, though gentler, increases in inequality occurred for comparable structural reasons in other industrialized nations.[49]

Reagan's defenders further maintained that though the cuts of 1981 were especially generous to the very wealthy, people at all income levels were

47. William Strauss and Neil Howe, *Generations: The History of America's Future, 1584 to 2069* (New York, 1991), 330–33.
48. Edward Luttwak, *The Endangered American Dream: How to Stop the United States from Becoming a Third-World Country and How to Win the Geo Economic Struggle for Industrial Supremacy* (New York, 1993), 49; Bernstein, "Understanding American Economic Decline"; Eckes and Zeiler, *Globalization in the American Century*, 208–10.
49. Robert Plotnick et al., "Inequality and Poverty in the United States: The Twentieth-Century Record," *Focus* 19, no. 3 (Summer/Fall 1998), 7–14.

doing better in the 1980s. This was in fact the case: Though the wealthy advanced most rapidly, the real disposable income of every stratum of the population rose during the decade.[50] For this and other reasons—Americans tend to envy the rich, not to castigate them—class resentments did not flourish in the 1980s. Most young Americans, managing better after 1983 than they had in the 1970s, were acquiring more education than their elders had and were using it to advance in life. Advantages of birth and of religion, key determinants of social mobility in the past, seemed to be becoming a little less important.

So it was that a majority of those Americans who had struggled in low-income categories when they were young were managing by the mid- and late 1980s to rise to higher stations in life. Millions of Americans, moving into white-collar jobs, purchasing houses, and buying all manner of household goods, said that they were optimistic about their own personal lives in the 1980s—even as they grumbled loudly about trends in society at large and predicted all manner of disasters for *other* people. They did not seem to be abandoning the American Dream, which had been nourished by the great natural abundance of the United States, the political ideals of the Revolutionary era, and the faith, dreams, and entrepreneurial drive of millions of immigrants and their descendants.[51]

It is even plausible to argue that the overall effect of Reagan's fiscal policies—including the tax law of 1986, which succeeded for a time in narrowing loopholes—promoted slightly greater popular faith in the capacity of the IRS and of government in general.[52] From Reagan's anti-state perspective, this was surely an ironic development. It is also evident that the reductions in tax rates had long-range consequences. Thereafter, politicians shrank from bringing back the high marginal tax rates of the early post–World War II era. These had been as steep as 70 percent in 1981. As of 2004, the highest marginal rate stood at 35 percent.

Some of Reagan's defenders also claimed that the tax cuts of 1981 helped to sustain consumption during the recession of 1981–82, thereby quickening recovery. Reagan did not have such Keynesian effects in mind, but some experts continued to maintain that government deficits, though driving up interest rates and expenditures for debt retirement, may offer good medicine when an economy needs a shot in the arm.

50. Cannon, *President Reagan*, 746; *Stat. Abst.*, 2002, 422.
51. Daniel McMurrer and Isabel Sawhill, "The Declining Importance of Class," Urban Institute paper no. 4 (April 1997); C. Eugene Steuerle, *The Tax Decade: How Taxes Came to Dominate the Public Agenda* (Washington, 1992), 24–25.
52. Elliot Brownlee, "Taxation," in Brownlee and Graham, *The Reagan Presidency*, 155–81.

These debates aside, there was no doubting that the American economy brightened after 1982, and that real growth, though modest, continued for the rest of Reagan's tenure. As the economy improved, an ever greater variety of consumer goods—many of these, including cars, better made than in the past—came within the buying power of the American people. By the early 1990s, Americans owned nearly a billion credit cards, which they used with an abandon that ratcheted up personal debt. As in previous decades, families, though smaller in average size than in the past, bought and lived in bigger, more comfortable houses, which they were filling with VCRs, personal computers, telephone answering machines, cable TV, and remote controls—electronic items that had not existed in 1970.[53]

It was by no means obvious that all these developments promoted deep personal satisfactions: The more there was to buy, the harder the choices. The more people consumed, the more they seemed to want. This gap— between the comforts that people enjoyed and their still higher expecta- tions about the Good Life—continued to be a source of popular restlessness in late-twentieth-century America. How fulfilling was self-gratification that depended heavily on the acquisition of consumer goods? Sensing that something was missing, many Americans, while doing better, still seemed to feel worse.

By contrast to the darker days of apparently runaway inflation and "mal- aise" under Carter, however, the economy of the mid- and late 1980s was obviously ushering in a more glittering material world for a great many people.[54] Reagan basked happily in this glow, attributing it not only to his fiscal policies but also to deregulatory moves that he said had unleashed market forces spurring entrepreneurial activity and productive investment. His supporters pointed out that the number of jobs grew by some 200,000 a month—or by more than 18 million overall—between 1981 and 1989.[55]

53. Cannon, *President Reagan*, 23, writes that between 1983 and 1988 Americans bought 105 million color television sets, 88 million cars and light trucks, 63 million VCRs, 62 million microwave ovens, 57 million washers and dryers, 46 million refrigerators and freezers, 31 million cordless phones, and 30 million telephone answering machines. In 1985, there were 86.8 million households in the United States, 62.7 million of which were family households.
54. Stanley Lebergott, *Pursuing Happiness: American Consumers in the Twentieth Cen- tury* (Princeton, 1993), 26–27; Thomas McCraw, *American Business, 1920–2000: How It Worked* (Wheeling, Ill., 2000), 159.
55. A great many of these jobs, as earlier and later, were relatively low-paying positions— often filled by women—in the expanding service sector. Moreover, growth in jobs (both in absolute numbers and in rate of increase) was a little more robust in the economically troubled 1970s than in the 1980s. *Stat. Abst.*, 2002, 367.

The Dow Jones industrial average jumped from 950.88 at the time of his first inaugural to 2,239 eight years later. More than any other development of Reagan's time in the White House, the turnaround in the economy accounted for the popularity that he was to regain when unhappy memories of the recession of 1981–82 finally dissipated.

WHILE GOVERNOR OF CALIFORNIA, Reagan had enjoyed poking fun at hippies and radicals, especially those who aroused furious controversy at the Berkeley campus of the University of California. Political battles involving abortion and welfare had also engaged him. Then and later, though, the domestic concerns that most excited him involved taxes and spending. Many other issues—urban affairs, labor relations, race, women's rights, the environment—scarcely interested him at all. It is hardly surprising, therefore, that liberal foes of his administration, perceiving him as an agent of the rich, have given him low marks in these areas of policy.[56]

Among the contemporary critics were labor union leaders. Assailing his firing of the PATCO workers, they also denounced his closeness to corporate interests, which rewarded him with lavish campaign contributions, and his successful opposition to a higher federal minimum wage, which stayed at $3.15 per hour throughout his presidency.[57] Union membership continued to fall during his term, from approximately one-fourth of all employees to one-sixth by 1989. By the late 1980s, liberals were also blaming the president for the plight of homeless people, whose numbers rose from roughly 200,000 in the early 1980s to as many as 400,000 by the end of the decade.[58]

Like union leaders, advocates for African Americans and other minority groups had little use for Reagan. To be sure, as in earlier decades, they had a few things to celebrate—Reagan's policies notwithstanding—in the 1980s. In 1983, Harold Washington was elected mayor of Chicago and Wilson Goode mayor of Philadelphia. Both were African Americans. In

---

56. Many books echo these criticisms. As titles and subtitles suggest, four of these are Garry Wills, *Reagan's America: Innocents at Home* (New York, 2000); Robert Dallek, *Ronald Reagan: The Politics of Symbolism* (Cambridge, Mass., 1999); Michael Schaller, *Reckoning with Reagan: America and Its Presidents in the 1980s* (New York, 1992); and Johnson, *Sleepwalking Through History*.
57. This was the federal rate; states had varied minimums.
58. The estimate of Christopher Jencks, *The Homeless* (Cambridge, Mass., 1994). Jencks found many sources of this increase: the deinstitutionalizing of the mentally ill, demolition of "skid row" hotels that had previously housed people, the rise of crack cocaine in the inner cities, and budget cuts.

late 1983, Reagan signed a bill establishing the third Monday in January as Martin Luther King Jr. Day, a national holiday. In 1984, the Reverend Jesse Jackson became the first black American man to make a run for the presidency. In the same year, *The Cosby Show* first appeared, earning top ratings for the remainder of the decade. *The Oprah Winfrey Show* began its extraordinarily long and successful run in 1985. August Wilson, a talented dramatist, crafted a series of highly regarded plays in the mid- and late 1980s, including *Ma Rainey's Black Bottom* (1985) and *Fences* (1986). Toni Morrison, already an acclaimed writer, published *Beloved* in 1987, an imaginatively rich novel about the evils of slavery. It helped her win a Nobel Prize for literature six years later.

Reagan, meanwhile, reluctantly concluded that it would be politically dangerous to try to end affirmative action, which by the 1980s had become cherished as a right within much of the corporate and educational world and which was zealously protected by liberals in the federal government bureaucracy. Federal officials continued to oversee set-aside provisions benefiting minorities engaged in government-sponsored construction projects. The survival in the Reagan years of programs such as these revealed that blacks—like other determined interest groups—could hold their own even in politically unfriendly times.

Many minority group leaders were especially pleased by two developments on the Hill late in Reagan's second term. In an extended, vicious battle in late 1987, they coalesced with other liberals to bring about the defeat (58 to 42) in the Senate of the nomination of Robert Bork to the Supreme Court. Bork, a federal judge who had earlier been a law professor at Yale, was an outspoken conservative who had served as Nixon's compliant solicitor general. He had also opposed the Civil Rights Act of 1964, affirmative action, and *Roe v. Wade*.[59] This extraordinarily bitter confirmation struggle, which centered on Bork's political and social views, not his qualifications—those were solid—featured mudslinging from both sides. It indicated that appointments to the Court, which was then deeply divided, were becoming highly partisan. Energizing ideologues on the right as well as the left, the fight led to a sharp intensification of inter-party warfare in Congress in the 1990s.

---

59. Terry Anderson, *In Pursuit of Fairness: A History of Affirmative Action* (New York, 2004), 196–97; Hugh Davis Graham, "Civil Rights Policy," in Brownlee and Graham, *The Reagan Presidency*, 283–92; David O'Brien, "Federal Judgeships in Retrospect," ibid., 327–54; and Andrew Hacker, *Two Nations: Black and White, Separate, Hostile, Unequal* (New York, 1995), 99–114.

The second development was even more unambiguously pleasing to liberals—and to many others. In 1988, Democrats and Republicans set aside partisan battling to approve the so-called Japanese-American Redress Act (sometimes called the Civil Liberties Act). The measure offered an admission of wrongdoing to Japanese Americans for the relocation and incarceration that 120,000 of them had suffered during World War II. It also provided reparations of $20,000 to each of the 60,000 still-living Japanese Americans who had been interned, as well as to heirs of some others. When the Justice Department closed the books on this program in 1999, it reported that 82,210 payments had been made, totaling more than $1.6 billion.[60]

Notwithstanding these political victories, minority group leaders had little cause to celebrate during these years. Two highly publicized incidents of racist violence provoked especially lasting tensions. The first took place in June 1982, when Vincent Chin, a twenty-seven-year-old Chinese American draftsman, was clubbed to death in a Detroit suburb by two white autoworkers who thought he was Japanese—and therefore to blame for layoffs in the industry. The killers were convicted of second-degree manslaughter and sentenced to three years' probation. Though one of the attackers was later found guilty of violating Chin's civil rights—and sentenced to twenty-five years in prison—the verdict was thrown out on a technicality, and a later trial in 1987 resulted in his acquittal. The long-drawn-out, highly publicized litigation angered many Asian Americans, some of whom formed militant pan-Asian organizations to fight for better rights and protections.

The second act of violence aroused huge public controversy. It featured Bernhard Goetz, a slight, thirty-six-year-old electronics engineer. In December 1984, he found himself surrounded in a New York City subway car by four aggressive black youths who demanded money from him. Goetz, a white man, had earlier been robbed and injured by blacks. He pulled out a .38 caliber revolver and shot the four of them. One, wounded again as he lay on the floor of the train, became brain-damaged and paralyzed for life. At a trial in 1987, it became clear that all four of the young men had criminal records and that three of them had screwdrivers in their pockets. The jury (on which only two blacks served) accepted Goetz's plea of self-defense and acquitted him of charges of attempted murder and assault. It convicted him only on charges of illegally possessing a fire-

---

60. *New York Times*, Feb. 15, 1999. President Ford had earlier issued an official apology for the internments. Nearly 70 percent of the internees had been American citizens.

arm and sentenced him to a year in jail. A local poll indicated that 90 percent of white respondents agreed with the verdict, as opposed to 52 percent of blacks. Many white Americans, traumatized by racial polarization and by an apparent epidemic of crime and disorder in the cities, regarded Goetz, the "Subway Vigilante," as a heroic figure.[61]

African American leaders in the 1980s denounced Reagan's general approach to race relations. Vetoing economic sanctions against South Africa's apartheid regime in 1986, he conceded defeat only when Congress overruled his veto. Clarence Thomas, a conservative African American whom he appointed to head the EEOC in 1982, disappointed minorities who charged that under his leadership the agency was slow to challenge discrimination in employment. Like Reagan, Thomas opposed affirmative action. Minority group leaders especially lamented the low priority that Reagan gave to contending with problems that continued to afflict the inner cities, notably high rates of crime, poverty, and unemployment. Thanks to a spreading scourge of crack cocaine in the late 1980s, these problems may have worsened during the decade.

Despairing of progress in the North, throngs of black people had already been returning every year to the South, only to discover that Dixie, too, was not a promised land.[62] Though court decisions mandating desegregation of public schools generally remained in force, progress toward the hotly contested goal of greater racial balance in schools was far slower than it had been in the 1970s. Resources for most inner-city schools continued to be inadequate. Gaps between the test scores of black and white children, while closing a little, remained large. Linda Brown, who had been the named plaintiff in the *Brown v. Board of Education* case of 1954, declared sadly on the thirtieth anniversary of the decision, "It was not the quick fix we thought it would be."[63]

The Reagan administration's major legacy in race relations, one that minority group leaders deplored, lay in its judicial appointments. For the most part the president did not play an especially active role in the nominee-selection process, but during the 1980 campaign he had said he would

61. Malcolm Gladwell, *The Tipping Point: How Little Things Can Make a Difference* (New York, 2000), 133–38, 147–49; Hacker, *Two Nations*, 99–100. Goetz served eight months. In 1996, a jury in a civil suit awarded Darrell Cabey, the paralyzed youth, $18 million for past and future suffering and $25 million in punitive damages, but Goetz had little money, and Cabey was not expected to benefit from the verdict.

62. Nicholas Lemann, *The Promised Land: The Great Black Migration and How It Changed America* (New York, 1991).

63. *Washington Post*, May 17, 1984.

appoint to judgeships only those candidates who promoted "family values." Zealously conservative Justice Department officials who took charge
of the selection of nominees had no doubt where he stood. By the time
Reagan left office he had appointed 368 district and appeals court judges,
more than any other president. They were nearly half of all judges on
these federal courts. The vast majority were conservative white males. Of
the 368 appointees, seven were black, fifteen were Hispanic, and two were
Asian.[64]

Reagan succeeded in turning the Supreme Court toward the right.
Whereas Carter had had no opportunity to make an appointment at that
level, Reagan had three. In 1981, he named Sandra Day O'Connor, an
Arizona state judge, to be the first woman to serve on the Court. Though
many on the Religious Right were unhappy with this choice—as a state
senator in Arizona O'Connor had supported the legalization of abortion,
and she had backed the ERA—the president was determined to select a
woman, and the Senate confirmed her, 99 to 0.[65] In 1986, when Chief
Justice Burger stepped down, Reagan nominated Justice William
Rehnquist, a Nixon appointee to the Court, for the post. The Senate confirmed him, but only after a struggle, by a vote of 65 to 33. At the same
time, Reagan appointed Antonin Scalia, who was unanimously confirmed,
to fill Rehnquist's place. Scalia was America's first Italian American justice. In 1987, after failing to get Bork (and a second nominee for the va-
cancy, Douglas Ginsburg) appointed, he chose Anthony Kennedy, who
was confirmed in February 1988.[66] These three appointees remained on
the Court for many years. Though O'Connor (and to a lesser extent
Kennedy) occasionally sided with liberals, Scalia and Rehnquist stood
strongly on the right. As of 1989, the Court began to issue conservative
decisions in hotly contested cases involving minority set-asides and racial
balance in the schools.

Reagan's liberal foes also damned his regulatory policies, which they
said routinely favored corporate interests. Reagan tried to reduce appro-

64. Cannon, *President Reagan*, 721; O'Brien, "Federal Judgeships in Retrospect." Reagan
    named higher percentages of women and Hispanics to the federal bench than had
    any previous president except Carter, who nominated forty women to district and
    appeals court judgeships, compared to Reagan's twenty-nine. Reagan named fewer
    blacks to judgeships than had his four predecessors.
65. William Martin, *With God on Our Side: The Rise of the Religious Right in America*
    (New York, 1996), 227–30.
66. News that Ginsburg had smoked pot when young killed his nomination before it got
    off the ground.

priations for liberal federal agencies such as Housing and Urban Development (HUD) and Health and Human Services (HHS). He called for a "new federalism" aimed at reducing the size and scope of government in Washington and at returning regulatory authority to the states. One supporter of this new federalism exclaimed: "Thousands and thousands of white-collar workers [in Washington] . . . do nothing but shuffle paper and don't do anything that's of any value to anyone. And they get a pay increment, they get incredible benefits, for what? It's just flab, it's just waste."[67]

Reagan's often colorful denunciations of big government, like those of other conservatives since the 1960s, may have been popular with a majority of Americans. "The nearest thing to eternal life we'll ever see," he quipped in 1986, "is a government program." Liberals, however, blocked his attempt to establish a new federalism and to weaken federal bureaucracies. The Department of Energy survived. Though Reagan managed to reduce federal aid to education in 1981, he made no serious attempt to carry out his politically perilous promise to dismantle the Education Department, which grew in size and influence in the 1980s. No highly controversial government program—for instance, affirmative action—or agency was terminated.

Still, Reagan clearly encouraged advocates of deregulation. In 1982 he signed a bill, little noticed at the time, that increased the amount of federal insurance available to savings-and-loan (S&L) depositors, from $40,000 to $100,000. Congress further authorized S&Ls to engage in a wide range of loans and investments, such as junk bonds and other high-risk securities. Heads of S&Ls soon leaped into all sorts of bad deals; some stole from their institutions and stashed away millions. Though a few mid-level administration officials tried to stop these activities, Reagan and other top aides paid them no heed, thereby making a bad situation worse. In the late 1980s, many S&Ls collapsed, devastating depositors and necessitating a series of huge governmental bailouts. Estimates of the cost of these bailouts vary, but one reliable account set the amount by 1999 at $161 billion, of which $132 billion came from public funds.[68] The S&L collapse was the costliest financial scandal in United States history.

Other scandals that stemmed in part from Reagan's lax oversight of federal agencies marred his administration. Especially notable were revelations of high-level corruption in HUD, which a House investigation concluded was "enveloped by influence peddling, favoritism, abuse, greed, fraud, embezzlement, and theft." A criminal investigation by an independent counsel lasted nine years and resulted in seventeen convictions and more than $2 million in fines.[69]

Nothing better revealed Reagan's negative attitude toward governmental regulation than his approach to environmental policy. The president, who loved to tend to his ranch in California, considered himself a great friend of the outdoors, but he did not believe that the environment was seriously endangered, and he largely ignored scientific studies concerning acid rain and global warming. On one occasion Reagan blundered by saying that trees and other vegetation were a source of air pollution. Students at Claremont College greeted him with a sign tacked to a tree: CHOP ME DOWN BEFORE I KILL AGAIN.[70]

Reagan's secretary of the interior, James Watt, proved to be a special target of environmentalist opponents of the administration. A Wyoming native, Watt had been a strident supporter of a "Sagebrush Rebellion" of westerners who hotly resented federal interference in their affairs. They complained bitterly that the federal government clung to ownership of millions of acres of land in the West—some 40 percent of all acreage in California and 90 percent in Nevada. There, as in other western states, disputes over water, forests, predators, and grazing rights roiled state politics. For these reasons, the roots of western hostility to "elitist eastern bureaucrats" and governmental "meddlers" ran deep. Drawing upon these and other resentments, the GOP was to enjoy great success in western political contests from 1980 on.

Watt, however, was politically maladroit. Deeply religious, he stated publicly that protecting the environment was unimportant compared to the imminent return of Jesus Christ to the earth. He divided people into two categories, "liberals" and "Americans." When Audubon Society leaders demanded his dismissal, he called them a "chanting mob." Vowing to "mine more, drill more, cut more timber," he favored oil exploration off the California coast and a moratorium on the acquisition of land for national parks. Within a short time, Watt's extremism galvanized environmentalists: Membership in the Wilderness Society, at 48,000 in 1979, shot up to 100,000 to 1983—and to 333,000 in 1989.[71] Bumper stickers read: I KNOW WATT'S WRONG.

69. Fraser, *Every Man a Speculator*, 714–15.
70. On Reagan and environmental issues, see Cannon, *President Reagan*, 145, 463–71; and Hal Rothman, *The Greening of a Nation? Environmentalism in the United States Since 1945* (Orlando, 1995), 186–92.
71. Rothman, *Greening of a Nation*, 180.

By early 1983, it was clear to Reagan's advisers that Watt was a political liability. When he made the mistake of announcing that a departmental advisory committee consisted of "a black . . . a woman, two Jews, and a cripple," these advisers forced him out. Thereafter, contentious environmental battles over Reagan's policies quieted down, but the president continued to resist advocates of environmental protection, angering them by moving slowly to clean up toxic sites. As earlier, he called for cuts in appropriations for the EPA and the Consumer Product Safety Commission.

Reagan's narrow focus on economic and foreign policy issues led him to pay relatively little attention even to the agenda of social conservatives, including the Religious Right. Conservative Christians were stepping up efforts to censor textbooks, develop private academies, and home-school their children.[72] Though Reagan said he favored a constitutional amendment to ban abortion, he never gave a live address to an anti-abortion rally. Congress, meanwhile, predictably refused to endorse the amendment. Reagan declared May 6, 1982, a "national day of prayer," and he backed a proposed constitutional amendment to restore prayer in the public schools, but this, too, did not receive the two-thirds majorities in Congress that were necessary to send it to the states for ratification.

Frustrated by the lack of change, religious conservatives grew restive. Reagan and his political advisers responded by naming opponents of choice, such as C. Everett Koop (who became surgeon general) to federal positions, by inviting religious leaders from time to time to the White House, and by offering them other symbolic reassurances, as when they enlisted Falwell to give the final benediction at the 1984 GOP nominating convention. Reagan did little of substance, however, for he was less of a true believer than—as Garry Wills later put it—an "amiably and ecumenically pious" politician. Well aware that a small but steady majority of Americans was pro-choice, he was careful not to take steps that would hurt him badly at the polls. He knew that most adherents of the Religious Right, faced with choosing between the GOP and liberal Democrats, would ultimately have no option but to back him.[73] Failing to achieve their political goals, leaders of the Religious Right complained with increasing bitterness in the late 1980s of discrimination against them by government and the media.

This, however, did not mean that activists for choice and other women's rights were confident during the Reagan years. They were not. Though

72. Martin, *With God on Our Side*, 139–43.
73. Ibid., 221–34.

the earnings gap that separated women's wages from those of men narrowed (from 62 percent of men's wages and salaries in 1980 to 72 percent in 1990), it remained far too large to satisfy activists for equality. As earlier, many women complained about the "double shift" that kept them on the go at home as well as at work. Advocates of choice were especially worried during the Reagan years. Anti-abortion activists, employing rights-based rhetoric, continued to champion the rights of the fetus.[74] After 1987, many of them joined a militant new organization, Operation Rescue, which adopted the direct action methods, notably sit-ins, of Martin Luther King in efforts to block access to abortion clinics. Thousands were arrested and jailed in 1988–89.[75] A few, failing in their campaigns, later resorted to violence, bombing clinics and killing medical practitioners. Advocates for women, using rights talk of their own, devoted major energies to contesting these activities. Their broader agenda, in the 1980s and thereafter, also included struggles against sexual harassment and wife battering. During the Reagan years, however, advocates of women's rights often felt beleaguered.

Trends in popular culture during these years further discouraged activists for women's causes. Gone was the She Decade of the 1970s. Popular magazines featured articles cool to feminism, such as *Newsweek*'s cover story in 1984, "What Price Day Care?" that lamented the record-high rates of divorce and questioned whether career-oriented "Supermoms" were doing the right thing.[76] *Ms.* magazine abandoned its feminist stance after mid-decade and focused on stories about celebrities. In the clothing industry, suits for women fell out of fashion, replaced by "feminine" attire that featured frills and bustles. Miniskirts sold well again after 1986. "Girls want to be girls again," a designer (like most, a man) explained. By the end of the decade, Victoria's Secret stores were proliferating and promoting a so-called Intimate Apparel Explosion.[77]

---

74. Jonathan Zimmerman, *Whose America? Culture Wars in the Public Schools* (Cambridge, Mass., 2001), 179–85.
75. Garry Wills, *Under God: Religion and American Politics* (New York, 1990), 323–28.
76. *Newsweek*, Sept. 10, 1984. For women's agendas in the 1980s, see Alice Kessler-Harris, *The Pursuit of Equity: Women, Men, and the Quest for Economic Citizenship in 20th-Century America* (New York, 2001), 289–96. For cultural resistance to women's rights in the 1980s, see Susan Faludi, *Backlash: The Undeclared War Against American Women* (New York, 1991).
77. Faludi, *Backlash*, 108–11, 176–87.

LIBERALS AND OTHERS WERE ANGERED, finally, by the administration's unfeeling reaction, as they saw it, to the rise of acquired immunodeficiency syndrome, or AIDS. First noticed in 1981, AIDS was transmitted sexually and via contaminated needles, many of them shared by IV drug abusers. In 1984, by which time AIDS had begun to spread around the world, researchers managed to identify the infectious agents—human immunodeficiency viruses (HIV)—but had no way to alleviate the syndrome, let alone to cure it: A diagnosis of AIDS was a virtual death sentence. To millions of Americans who had come to question authority since the 1960s, AIDS was bitter confirmation of how little the "experts" knew about serious medical problems. Many people continued to believe that AIDS could be acquired from toilet seats, from kissing, or from the air.[78] It quickly became a scourge that wasted and killed its victims, most of whom were young males. By the beginning of 1985, AIDS had felled an estimated 5,600 Americans. By the end of December, 1988, the Centers for Disease Control (CDC) had confirmed 98,935 AIDS cases and 57,542 deaths. The CDC estimated that ten Americans were infected with the virus for every case that had been confirmed.[79]

By the mid-1980s, it was clear that AIDS was especially devastating to the gay population, but it baffled all Americans, three-quarters of whom said at the time that they did not know anyone who was gay.[80] The president, uncomprehending, was slow to confront the issue, mentioning it only once publicly before the movie actor Rock Hudson, a friend of the Reagans, died of AIDS in October 1985. At that point Reagan sought out the White House physician, who gave him a full explanation of the syndrome. Still, the president did not speak about AIDS again until February 1986, at which point he asked Koop to draw up a report on the problem. Reagan's budget at that time, however, called for a reduction in AIDS research.[81]

An evangelical Christian with a Dutch sea captain's beard, Koop was a famed pediatric surgeon. Liberals, identifying him as a foe of abortion, had opposed his appointment, but he undertook a serious study of the matter and issued a no-nonsense report on it in late 1986. It estimated that

---

78. John D'Emilio and Estelle Freedman, *Intimate Matters: A History of Sexuality in America* (Chicago, 1997), 354–67.
79. For Reagan and AIDS, see Cannon, *President Reagan*, 731–36, 815; Johnson, *Sleepwalking Through History*, 454.
80. By the early 2000s, more than half of Americans said they knew people who were gay. *New York Times*, Feb. 29, 2004.
81. Congress then and later appropriated more funds than Reagan requested.

179,000 Americans would have died of AIDS by the end of 1991.[82] The American people, he declared, must change their personal behavior. His remedy was, "one, abstinence; two, monogamy; three, condoms." Koop called for widespread sex education in the schools, even in the elementary grades.[83]

Though some conservatives supported Koop, many others, including Phyllis Schlafly and William Bennett, the president's secretary of education, hotly opposed his support of the use of condoms and of sex education. AIDS, many conservatives insisted, was a "gay plague" stemming from deviant homosexual behavior that violated biblical injunctions. Patrick Buchanan, who was Reagan's director of communications, had earlier (before signing on with the administration) exclaimed: "The poor homosexuals. They have declared war on nature and now nature is exacting an awful retribution."[84]

As Buchanan's comment indicated, the rise of AIDS exposed already widespread American hostility toward homosexuality. In 1986, the Supreme Court upheld, five to four, a Georgia law that criminalized sodomy that involved private and consensual same-sex relations between adults.[85] At the time twenty-four other states and the District of Columbia had similar measures on the books, all aimed against what some of the laws termed "deviant sexual intercourse," even in private. Many Americans, especially older people and social conservatives, refused to jettison such laws; gay rights issues, like other cultural struggles at the time, provoked sharp generational and regional divides. Americans resisted a range of public health initiatives, including needle exchanges and televised messages about safe sex. In most areas of Western Europe, where such initiatives were common, the incidence of HIV infection remained far lower than in the United States.[86]

Attitudes such as these infuriated gays and lesbians, some of whom had been organizing to promote their rights since the late 1960s. As early as 1977, gay activists had attracted nationwide attention in their efforts to

82. The actual number of AIDS cases in the United States, according to the Centers for Disease Control, was 103,000, with 60,000 deaths, as of the end of Reagan's presidency in 1989. Martin, *With God on Our Side*, 241. Between 1980 and 2001, 482,904 Americans died of AIDS. AVERT.org, "HIV and AIDS Statistics by Year."

83. For Koop and AIDS, see Martin, *With God on Our Side*, 239–43, 252–57.

84. Cannon, *President Reagan*, 773.

85. *Bowers v. Hardwick*, 478 U.S. 186 (1986).

86. James Morone, *Hellfire Nation: The Politics of Sin in American History* (New Haven, 2000), 480–81, states that HIV incidence in the United States soon became ten times as high as in Britain.

prevent the repeal of the ordinance protecting gay rights in Miami. Though they had lost this battle, the struggle accelerated the growth of an increasingly militant movement to promote equal rights. Gay rights activists were especially vocal in some big-city areas, notably the Castro section of San Francisco. By the 1980s, the Castro had become a virtually all-gay community, featuring gay bars, restaurants, stores, political organizations, and public celebrations.[87]

Once AIDS broke out, gay activists in San Francisco and elsewhere were so determined to protect their rights that they fought against efforts to ban gay bathhouses, which public health officials had identified as sites of dangerously promiscuous sexual behavior. Only in late 1984 did the activists lose this fight in San Francisco. Militant gay people also organized ACT-UP (AIDS Coalition to Unleash Power), which staged a parade of 500,000 people in New York City on Columbus Day 1987. Spokesmen for the marchers demonstrated loudly for better funding of AIDS research and laws guaranteeing equal rights. Larry Kramer, an especially vocal militant, proclaimed that "AIDS is our Holocaust and Reagan is our Hitler."[88]

The president, facing pressures such as these, went so far as to say in 1987 that AIDS was "public enemy Number One," but even then he had not yet spoken personally with Koop about his report. Ignoring the counsel of his wife, he refused to endorse the use of condoms. From a widely awaited address in May 1987 to the American Foundation for AIDS Research, he allowed his speechwriters to delete mention of Ryan White, a hemophiliac teenager who had been ostracized in his hometown of Kokomo, Indiana, after he had contracted AIDS from a blood-clotting agent. By 1987, White had become a national spokesman for AIDS victims. Reagan did not meet with White until March 1990, fourteen months after he had left office and less than a month before White died in an Indianapolis hospital at the age of eighteen. At that point Reagan wrote an op-ed piece for the *Washington Post* in which he paid tribute to White and added, "How Nancy and I wish there had been a magic wand we could have waved that would have made it [AIDS] all go away."[89]

87. For the Castro area, see Frances FitzGerald, *Cities on a Hill: A Journey Through Contemporary American Cultures* (New York, 1986), 25–119.
88. Michael Sherry, *In the Shadow of War: The United States Since the 1930s* (New Haven, 1995), 453–56; D'Emilio and Freedman, *Intimate Matters*, 366–67. For funding to fight AIDS, see Steven Gillon, *Boomer Nation: The Largest and Richest Generation Ever, and How It Changed America* (New York, 2004), 199–200.
89. Cannon, *President Reagan*, 736.

As a sharp letter to the editor made clear, this was a belated gesture. Reagan's leadership on the issue was badly flawed. Even so, his dithering while president did not seem to hurt him with the American people, many of whom singled out homosexual behavior as the source of AIDS. Attitudes such as these indicated that cultural changes can be slow to occur. In the 1980s, as in the 1970s, Americans were more ready to watch sexually titillating material on television and film (or to pay for dial-a-porn, which began to flourish on cable TV) than they were to consider frank public discussion of condoms or sexually transmitted illness.

These struggles over AIDS policies, among the bitterest battles in a host of contemporary cultural controversies involving sex and gender issues, were noteworthy as political phenomena.[90] Later, in the early 1990s, they showed what a highly determined interest group—one that demanded action, and action now!—might ultimately accomplish if it besieged government, the ultimate dispenser of rights and entitlements. By 1992, lobbies like ACT-UP managed to secure from Congress $2 billion for AIDS research, prevention, and treatment. This was more than the government spent to fight cancer, which killed twenty-two times as many people.[91] Still, popular American attitudes toward homosexuality remained predominantly cool during the early 1990s.

These attitudes did liberalize a little in the late 1990s, driven mainly by young people. Concerning homosexuality, as so many other controversies involving sex, gender, and race, the younger generations led the charges for change. The pace of movement quickened a little early in the new century. In 2003, the Supreme Court (in a six-to-three vote) reversed its decision of 1986 that had upheld the criminalizing of same-sex sodomy. In November of that year, the Massachusetts Supreme Court decided, by a vote of four to three, that it was a violation of the state constitution to deny same-sex couples access to marriage. The court set May 17, 2004—the fiftieth anniversary of *Brown v. Board of Education*—as the day when such marriages must be permitted. So it was that grass-roots activism, interest group politics, rights-consciousness, and rulings from America's ever more influential courts came together, however slowly, to advance liberal goals in the nation's sometimes tempestuous struggles over cultural issues.[92]

90. See chapter 8 for "culture wars."
91. Gillon, *Boomer Nation*, 199–200.
92. *New York Times*, March 27, 2003. At the time of the Court's decision, concerning a sodomy law in Texas, thirteen states—all in the South, West, or Plains—still had laws on the books criminalizing sodomy.

DESPITE THE RISE OF THE AIDS EPIDEMIC, a number of advances in technology, basic science, and public health in the 1980s encouraged optimistic visions in America. In April 1981, the first reusable space shuttle, using the orbiter *Columbia*, shot into space.[93] In 1988, scientists introduced genetic fingerprinting, and later improved genetic understanding of such ailments as schizophrenia and cystic fibrosis. Per capita cigarette smoking, which had declined only slightly during the 1970s, at last began to drop sharply—and continued to do so for the remainder of the century. By the late 1980s, cities and towns began banning smoking from public buildings and restaurants.[94] Other social trends that had alarmed Americans in the 1970s—record or near-record-high rates of divorce and welfare take-up—remained worrisome but stabilized during the 1980s. For these and other reasons, popular alarm that the nation was in decline, which had been pervasive in the mid- and late 1970s, weakened after the mid-1980s.

Optimists derived further satisfaction from an event in 1982 that may have helped to ease angry feelings about the Vietnam War. This was the dedication of Maya Lin's innovative, widely praised Vietnam Memorial in Washington. Many Vietnam vets marched in a cathartic "welcome home" parade on that occasion, pleased to participate in the first important public commemoration of their participation in the war. Thereafter, the "Wall," though criticized by some veterans' groups, became by far the most visited Washington site. Two years later, many Americans commemorated a very different military experience: D-Day. Led by a triumphant President Reagan in Normandy, they jubilantly celebrated the fortieth anniversary of that militarily huge event, thereby reaffirming widespread patriotic feelings.

Notwithstanding healing occasions such as these, many Americans during the Reagan years continued to bewail the sorrier sides of life in the United States. As earlier, liberals demanded reform of the nation's health insurance system. A combination of forces—the aging of the population, the spread of high-tech and often life-saving medical procedures (an area of R&D in which the United States outpaced the rest of the world), escalating paperwork expense, and rising expectations about what it meant to be "healthy"—were jacking up the cost of medical care, which rose rapidly

93. A total of 113 such shuttle launches took place between then and February 2003, when a crash killed seven. Another crash, of *Challenger*, had killed seven in 1986.
94. *New York Times Almanac*, 2003, 384. Americans over the age of eighteen smoked 4,171 cigarettes per capita in 1960, 3,985 in 1970, 3,849 in 1980, and 2,817 in 1990. The drop during the 1980s was nearly 27 percent. In 1985, 30.1 percent of American adults smoked, a percentage that fell to 25.5 in 1990 and to 23.3 in 2000. *Stat. Abst.*, 2002, 124.

from the 1970s on (from 7 percent of GNP in 1970 to 14 percent by 2000). Thanks in part to the weakening of labor unions, corporate health benefits were also in danger. Though Medicare offered partial insurance coverage for most of the elderly, and Medicaid assisted many of the poor, large holes remained in the medical safety net. In the late 1980s some 14 percent of Americans lacked health insurance. Conservative interests, however, opposed major efforts to expand governmental involvement. For this and other reasons, the United States remained the only developed nation in the West without a system of universal health insurance coverage.

As in the 1970s, many Americans also worried about moral decline. Rates of out-of-wedlock pregnancy and teenage pregnancy continued to increase. In 1981, MTV arrived on the scene, highlighting sex to capture an audience, mostly of young viewers, that was estimated in 1984 to consist of 23 million people.[95] Reagan seemed to oppose the excesses, as he saw them, of sex and violence on TV, which Americans on the average still watched for twenty-eight hours a week, but his support of deregulation extended to the policies of the Federal Communications Commission (FCC), which adopted a laissez-faire attitude toward programming in the 1980s. Taking advantage of the obvious—sex sells—TV producers and Hollywood boldly featured sex and violence. The irresponsibility of TV producers at the peak of the AIDS crisis so angered the Planned Parenthood Federation of America in 1988 that it took out full-page ads in magazines and newspapers. Characters on TV, the ad said, "did it 20,000 times on television last year, but nobody used a condom."[96]

Critics of Reagan emphasized above all that he set a poor example by delivering a crass and materialistic message to the nation. "What I want to see above all," he said in 1983, "is that this remains a country where someone can always get rich."[97] Critics who deplored this message asserted that while the culture of the 1970s, the Me Decade, had been greedy, the 1980s were worse. Thanks to Reagan's message, they grumbled, "yuppies," or young, upwardly mobile professionals, were becoming role models. Joining these supposedly avaricious college graduates, they added, were ever larger numbers of "buppies" (black urban professionals), "dinks" (dual-income couples with no kids), and "grumpies" (grim, ruthless, upwardly mobile young professionals). All these people, it seemed, could not wait to plunge their hands

95. Johnson, *Sleepwalking Through History*, 150–51.
96. Watson, *Defining Visions*, 121.
97. Bruce Schulman, *The Seventies: The Great Shift in American Culture, Society, and Politics* (New York, 2001), 249.

into the cornucopia of goods that had seduced the United States into becoming a nation of uninhibited, acquisitive consumers.[98]

A single-minded pursuit of wealth and possessions, these critics complained, was commercializing virtually all of American culture and creating a new Gilded Age. "Hanoi Jane" Fonda, who in 1972 had traveled to Vietnam to protest the war, was now making millions selling exercise videos and promoting physical fitness. (The money, she said, supported workers' rights causes advanced by her politically left-wing husband, Tom Hayden.) Rennie Davis, a prominent radical from the 1960s, was working as a stockbroker. Geraldine Ferraro, the Democratic vice-presidential nominee in 1984, signed on after the election to do a Pepsi-Cola ad. Michael Jackson did the same, earning $1.5 million (and having his hair accidentally singed) in the process.

Foes of materialism bemoaned the fact that television shows such as *Dallas* and *Dynasty*, which featured the manipulations of the rich and powerful, were among the most popular programs on the air early in the decade. Later in the 1980s, a boastful, in-your-face autobiography of the hitherto uncelebrated Donald Trump, a real estate magnate, became a best-seller.[99] Many observers were especially appalled by a widely circulated report that one-third of Yale graduates in 1985 were interviewing for jobs as financial analysts at First Boston Corporation.[100] What a change from the socially conscious '60s!

By mid-decade, the enemies of excessive materialism directed much of their firepower against large-scale corporate takeovers and mergers, which began to proliferate—as is often the case during economically prosperous periods—at the time. Conservatives tended to welcome mergers, perceiving them as helping the United States weed out its inefficient companies, invest in up-to-date technology, and outperform foreign competition. Other Americans, however, charged that the mergers were "downsizing" employment, wiping out well-managed small businesses, enriching CEOs, smashing labor unions, and hiking the cost of goods.[101] Moreover, there

98. See Fraser, *Every Man a Speculator*, 546–54, for examples of materialism in the 1980s.
99. *The Art of the Deal* (New York, 1988).
100. Schaller, *Reckoning with Reagan*, 75. Robert Putnam, *Bowling Alone: The Collapse and Revival of American Community* (New York, 2000), 260, cited polls that asked American college freshmen how much it mattered to them to be "Very Well Off Financially. Is It Essential or Very Important?" In 1970, 40 percent of these freshmen answered yes to this question. In 1975, 45 percent did, and in the mid-1980s, 75 percent did.
101. Naomi Lamoreaux et al., "Beyond Markets and Hierarchies: Toward a New Synthesis of Business History," *American Historical Review* 108 (April 2003), 404–33.

was no hiding the crassness associated with some of the by-products of mergers. Vivid phrases—"junk bonds," "leveraged buyouts," "corporate raiders," "golden parachutes," "hostile takeovers"—entered everyday language. It was estimated that the average compensation of America's highest-paid CEOs rose in constant 1980 dollars from $3 million a year in 1980 to more than $12 million in 1988. Strategically placed hustlers made a killing, sometimes illegally. One of the most flamboyant of these, Ivan Boesky, famously announced at a commencement ceremony in Berkeley in 1986, "Greed is healthy." Another insider, "junk bond king" Michael Milken, raked in $550 million in 1987. Both men were later indicted, hit with whopping fines, and sent to jail.[102]

Excesses such as these sparked considerable cultural criticism, especially in mid- and late decade. In 1985, a team of social scientists headed by Robert Bellah of the University of California, Berkeley, published the results of their well-regarded surveys of American values in the late 1970s and early 1980s. Reflecting a growing consensus among liberals—and among critics of Reagan—they concluded that during these years "American individualism may have grown cancerous" and "may be threatening the survival of freedom itself." Calling on people to develop more community spirit, the authors concluded, "The citizen has been swallowed up in economic man."[103]

Filmmakers and writers joined this attack on materialism. In 1987, Oliver Stone, the son of a broker, directed *Wall Street*, in which a speculator, played by Michael Douglas, was portrayed as greed personified. Echoing Boesky, he proclaimed "Greed is good." In the same year, Tom Wolfe's novel *The Bonfire of the Vanities* received considerable critical acclaim. Highlighting the huge gulfs that divided rich from poor, black from white, the book portrayed New York City as a violent concrete jungle and satirized amoral bond traders and corporate lawyers as self-deluded "masters of the universe." It sold millions of copies.

IF REAGAN WAS BOTHERED by laments such as these, he did not say so. He had little reason to worry, for even the staggeringly huge S&L scandal of late decade did not seem to shake the majority of Americans from

102. Johnson, *Sleepwalking Through History*, 215–19; Cannon, *President Reagan*, 747. Boesky was convicted of insider trading, fined $100 million, and sentenced to two years in prison. Milken was convicted of securities fraud, fined $600 million, and sentenced to ten years. He ultimately did twenty-two months' time.
103. Robert Bellah et al., *Habits of the Heart: Individualism and Commitment in American Life* (Berkeley, 1985), viii, 271.

their faith in traditional values, including the acquisition of wealth. Far from resenting the rich, many people in the United States continued to admire those who had achieved the American Dream, which they tended to equate with the accumulation of personal wealth and property. Reagan, of course, was the most dramatic example of a small-town boy who had risen on his own merits to adulation and fame. Another was Lee Iacocca, who was extolled for leading the Chrysler Corporation out of corporate crisis (though aided by a government bailout) in the early 1980s, and who became a minor cultural hero. His 1984 autobiography, a formulaic rags-to-riches story that traced his ascent from boyhood as a son of Italian immigrants to the heights of corporate success, celebrated traditional American values. It was a best-seller for two years.[104]

Highly popular television shows of the mid- and late 1980s reinforced other traditionally heralded values, among them the virtues of the two-parent, upwardly mobile family. One such production was *The Cosby Show*, a sitcom that featured Bill Cosby as the upper-middle-class patriarch of a two-parent family of five well-behaved children. Family concerns that were then widespread in the United States—premarital sex, drug abuse, teen rebellion—received relatively little attention in the episodes. Cosby himself, playing an obstetrician, exuded a warm and fatherly image; his character's wife was a successful lawyer. *The Cosby Show*, which first appeared in 1984, attracted some 63 million viewers a week and was the top-rated program for most of the late 1980s.

Another popular "warmedy" (warm family comedy) of the late 1980s was *Family Ties*, which starred Michael J. Fox as the eldest sibling in a close-knit family. As in *The Cosby Show*, there was little intergenerational tension in the series, save that which occasionally pitted the parents, described as "'60s Democrats," against Fox, a loyal Republican. In one episode, Fox's character carried a school lunchbox with a picture of Richard Nixon on its cover. Some critics likened the show to saccharine staples of the 1950s such as *Leave It to Beaver* and *Father Knows Best*.

Programs such as these, reflecting the more conservative culture of the 1980s, differed considerably from post–Vietnam War shows such as *All in the Family*, the top-rated TV sitcom of the early and mid-1970s. The father in that show, a working-class bigot named Archie Bunker, was a great admirer of Nixon and other anti-liberal politicians. (The show's theme song, "Those Were the Days," included the line, "Mister, we could use a

104. Lee Iacocca with William Novak, *Iacocca: An Autobiography* (New York, 1984). See also White, *New Politics of Old Values*, 23–36, 114–16.

man like Herbert Hoover again.") His bluntly disrespectful, long-haired son-in-law, by contrast, ridiculed virtually all sources of authority. Archie called him "Meathead." When Archie's wife, Edith, appeared to side with the son-in-law, Bunker called her a "dingbat." *All in the Family*, much more than highly rated sitcoms of the 1980s, sparked sharp political responses.

Even *M*A*S*H*, a hit television show that in its early years during the 1970s had derided military authority in the Korean War, softened its sting in the 1980s. By then the unit commander, Colonel Sherman Potter, was depicted as a far more competent and effective army officer than his pre-decessor, the inept and often inebriated Henry Blake. Major Margaret Houlihan, nicknamed "Hot Lips" in early installments, evolved from a highly sexed woman who drank heavily into a respected leader of the nurses under her command. The show continued to mock the idiocies of army life, but with less of the sharply anti-authoritarian and satirical bite that had launched it to commercial success in the 1970s.[105]

REAGAN, WHO HAD EARNED WIDESPREAD ADMIRATION as a figure of authority in 1981, seemed to embody many of the traditional values that were featured in sitcoms such as *Family Ties*. After the economy turned around—a wondrous, long-awaited development—his poll numbers im-proved steadily. In the election year of 1984, he enjoyed especially great popularity. American successes at the Los Angeles Olympics—boycotted that summer by the Soviets—further promoted patriotic, feel-good emo-tions that benefited the administration. Political action committees favor-able to Reagan's candidacy amassed $7.2 million, compared to $657,000 raised by groups partial to his opponent, Vice President Walter Mondale.[106] That Mondale had the early support of all ninety-nine AFL-CIO labor unions seemed likely to do him relatively little good under such circumstances.[107]

Republican leaders made especially effective use of key GOP televi-sion ads, "Morning Again in America." While never depicting Reagan, the ads highlighted the homespun, family-centered values, as if lifted from a Norman Rockwell painting, that had supposedly made the nation great and that many Americans by then were associating with the president. They featured communities of friends: a wedding party at which a bride is hugging her mother; an old man and a policeman hoisting a flag to which

105. For this and the preceding two paragraphs, see White, *New Politics of Old Values*, 117–21.
106. Congressional Quarterly, *Guide to the Presidency* (Washington, 1989), 197.
107. Matthew Crenson and Benjamin Ginsberg, *Downsizing Democracy: How America Sidelined Its Citizens and Privatized Its Public* (Baltimore, 2002), 131–33.

schoolchildren are pledging allegiance. Voice-overs intoned: "America is prouder, stronger, better. Why would we want to return to where we were less than four short years ago?" Democrats derided these lyrical commercials as hokey. But Reagan loved them. Many Americans who watched the "Morning Again in America" ads were said to be inspired by them, to be pleased that traditional values remained powerful in the United States, and to feel good that a strong leader such as Reagan was in command.

Mondale soldiered on, coping as best as he could against attitudes such as these. Pundits thought that he bested the president in the first televised debate. Democrats, sensing that the president's poor performance in the debate made him vulnerable on grounds of his age (seventy-three), took heart. But Reagan was at his best in the next debate. With mock seriousness, he said to Mondale: "I will not make age an issue in this campaign. I am not going to exploit, for political purposes, my opponent's youth and inexperience." The audience broke out in laughter.

Mondale fired away at Reagan's big deficits and said that he would raise taxes if elected. This promise, which made little political sense, delighted Republicans, who branded Mondale a "typical tax-and-spend, gloom-and-doom" Democrat. Reagan appealed to patriotic voters, proclaiming that he had vastly strengthened American defenses and had stood tall against Communism throughout the world. He reminded Americans — as if they needed reminding — that the Carter-Mondale administration had presided over the stagflation years of the late 1970s. Democrats, he added, were captives of interest groups, especially unions, and mindlessly advocated big government. Republicans also implied that Ferraro, the first woman on the presidential ticket of a major American political party, had a husband who was involved in shady financial deals in New York.

Results of the election confirmed what polls had predicted: Reagan won in a walk. He triumphed everywhere except in the District of Columbia and in Mondale's home state of Minnesota, taking the electoral college 525 to 13. He received 54.5 million votes (58.8 percent of the total) to Mondale's 37.6 million (40.6 percent). Mondale, like every Democratic presidential candidate since the 1960s, swept all but a very small minority of black voters. He fared better among labor union members and urban voters than among people who lived in the suburbs. He was more popular among women (winning 44 percent of their votes) than among men (37 percent). But it was obvious that Ferraro's presence on the ticket had not worked wonders.[108]

108. *World Almanac*, 2001, 40.

It was even more obvious that Reagan enjoyed great popularity among white southerners—especially, it seemed, among those who sympathized with the Religious Right.[109] Exit polls indicated that Mondale won only 28 percent of the southern white vote. Though southern Democrats fared respectably in state and local races—political parties at these levels were fairly competitive in the 1980s—Republicans increased their representation among southerners in the House and Senate. The election advanced the steady shift that was transforming southern—and hence national—politics.

Seeking solace from the results, Democrats insisted that Reagan's triumph was mainly personal: Americans, they said, voted for him because they liked him, not because they agreed with most of his conservative views. Liberal social policies, they maintained, remained popular. Liberals—and other analysts—also argued correctly that the election had not given Reagan a mandate to do anything very specific and that it had not realigned American politics in the dramatic way that FDR's triumphs had done in the 1930s. Though Republicans still controlled the Senate in 1985, with 53 seats to 46 for the Democrats—they had led 54 to 46 in 1984—they won only seventeen more seats in the House in 1984 and remained a minority in 1985, with 182 seats as opposed to 252 for the Democrats. In 1987, Democrats appeared to maintain a small edge in the partisan identification of voters.[110] Thanks to Democratic strength on Capitol Hill, partisan warfare continued to be a feature of divided government during Reagan's second term.

Still, the election showed that though Reagan had not devoted great attention to party building, the GOP had advanced dramatically between 1974 and 1984. His triumph also moved Democrats, shaken by their defeat, to the right. In February 1985, moderate conservatives and centrists in the party, many from the South, established the Democratic Leadership Council (DLC). Its first president was Richard Gephardt, a Missouri congressman. (Governor Bill Clinton of Arkansas was to head it in 1990–91.) Blaming liberals, including Mondale, for pandering to unions and other interest groups, these "New Democrats" embarked on a quest to broaden the appeal of the party. Many liberal Democrats, however, derided these efforts. Jesse Jackson branded the DLC as "Democrats for the

109. James Hunter, *Culture Wars: The Struggle to Define America* (New York, 1991), 280, concluded that Reagan won 79 percent of "evangelical" white voters in the South.
110. Byron Shafer, *The Two Majorities and the Puzzle of Modern American Politics* (Lawrence, Kans., 2003), 24; Robert Samuelson, *Washington Post*, Dec. 3, 2003.

Leisure Class." Battles between these two factions raged within the Democratic Party for many years thereafter.

The election of 1984 also indicated that critiques of American materialism had had little if any political effectiveness. Yuppies, to be sure, were a convenient target, but they were hardly the majority among the young. Most Americans in their twenties and thirties in the early 1980s were members of the 75-million-strong baby boom generation. While many had embraced liberal causes or hippie styles of life in the 1970s, millions by the mid-1980s had married and bought houses in the suburbs and were trying to provide for young families and keep up their mortgage payments. Having resources to lose, they were becoming a little more conservative, not only concerning economic issues but also concerning some (not all) social and cultural matters, such as the importance of "family values." "Do as I say, not as I did," they told their children. In 1984, they were nearly 40 percent of the nation's voting-age population.[111]

For these and other reasons, liberals who lamented the president's conservative views struggled against the tide during the 1980s. In fact, Reagan had proved to be a consequential president, more so perhaps than any chief executive since FDR. His policies had dramatically changed tax laws, greatly increased defense spending, and challenged liberal assumptions about the virtues of big government. His "politics of values," stressing the blessings of family togetherness, neighborhood solidarity, and hard work, appeared to have resonated favorably with the majority of the electorate. Southern whites, evangelical Christians, and many middle-class suburbanites seemed to be especially receptive to values such as these, as well as to Reagan's uncompromising opposition to Communism abroad. At least for the time being, political opinion on many issues in the United States had moved to the right.[112]

The return of good times especially benefited the president. Many Americans in 1984 continued to be uneasy about the economy, but they felt better about their prospects—a whole lot better—than they had in 1980. Reagan, his supporters believed, had also succeeded in resurrecting the majesty of the presidency, which had taken a battering under Nixon and Carter. Perhaps most important, his infectiously optimistic manner, like that of the boy who dug into a pile of manure in search of a pony, had

111. Gillon, *Boomer Nation*, 118–20.
112. For this conclusion, see Johnson, *Sleepwalking Through History*; White, *New Politics of Old Values*, 74–102; and Eric Foner, *The Story of American Freedom* (New York, 1998), 332–35.

helped him to win. This manner—and his vision of the United States as a great and exceptional nation—continued after 1984 to appeal to millions of Americans and to help him survive serious bungling in his second term. As Lou Cannon later concluded, "Because of his ability to reflect and give voice to the aspirations of his fellow citizens, Reagan succeeded in reviving national confidence at a time when there was a great need for inspiration. This was his great contribution as president."[113]

113.   Cannon, *President Reagan*, 837.

6

America and the World in the 1980s

General Alexander Haig, Reagan's first secretary of state, was never comfortable in his job. The president's people, he grumbled, were a "bunch of second-rate hambones." He added, "to me, the White House was as mysterious as a ghost ship; you heard the creak of the rigging and the groan of the timbers and sometimes even glimpsed the crew on deck. But which of the crew had the helm? Was it Meese, was it Baker, was it someone else? It was impossible to know for sure."[1]

Haig, who struck many associates as arrogant, did not last long in his post. In June 1982, Reagan replaced him with George Shultz, a calm and steady man who managed capably at the State Department for the next six and a half years. But Haig's indictment of the president's style was only a little more vehement than that of many officials who moved in and out of defense and foreign policy positions under Reagan in the 1980s. Six men served as national security adviser during those eight years, the fourth of whom, Admiral John Poindexter, was at the center of the Iran-contra scandal that threatened to ruin Reagan's presidency in late 1986. Only under Frank Carlucci, who took over from Poindexter in January 1987, and General Colin Powell, who succeeded Carlucci a year later, did the office begin to operate effectively.

Reagan's defense secretary until October 1987, Caspar Weinberger, brought a bulldog-like tenacity to the task of expanding the military budget but

---

1. Lou Cannon, *President Reagan: The Role of a Lifetime* (New York, 2000), 162.

fought almost incessantly with Shultz.[2] Reagan, ignoring their feuding, sometimes kept both of them in the dark about his intentions. In 1983, he announced a hugely ambitious space-based anti-missile plan, the Strategic Defense Initiative—critics called it "Star Wars"—without informing either of them until the last moment that he would do so. This was one of the few times that Shultz and Weinberger agreed on anything of substance. Weinberger did not like the idea. Shultz said it was "lunacy."[3] Reagan, demonstrating the preternatural self-assurance and stubbornness for which he was both beloved and reviled, brushed aside the opinions of these strong-minded men and went ahead with the plan.

Given management such as this, it is ironic that some of the most dramatic transformations of international relationships of the twentieth century took place in the 1980s—transformations that elevated the United States to an economic and military preeminence such as no nation had enjoyed since the days of the Roman Empire. Reagan, who told an audience of southern evangelicals in March 1983 that the Soviet Union was an "evil empire," was by mid-1985 embracing a useful relationship with Mikhail Gorbachev, who by then had become president of the Soviet Union. In late 1987, the two men fashioned a deal to cut back nuclear arms and—at last—to thaw the Cold War. When Reagan left office in January 1989, some of his admirers were crediting him with promoting a "Pax Reaganica" in the world. Then and for some time thereafter, the majority of American voters seemed to believe that the GOP—since the days of the war in Vietnam the more aggressive party in calling for American hegemony in the world—was the party to be trusted with the management of foreign and military affairs.

By 1989, Communism was collapsing in Eastern Europe and in the Soviet Union, which was evacuating the last of its troops from Afghanistan. The suddenness of these changes, which American intelligence agencies had failed to predict, stunned students of international affairs.[4] Other nations, long burdened with authoritarian regimes, were also developing democratic systems of governance. In the summer of 1989, Francis Fukuyama, a conservative writer, rhapsodized about these changes, especially the triumph of liberalism over Communism, in an essay that attracted widespread notice. "What we may be witnessing," he wrote, "is not just the passing of

2. Carlucci replaced Weinberger at the Pentagon, at which point Powell took Carlucci's job as national security adviser.
3. Cannon, *President Reagan*, 287.
4. One notable exception was New York's Senator Moynihan, who recognized the large internal weaknesses of the Soviet Union.

a particular period in modern history but the end of history . . . the end point of mankind's ideological evolution and the universalization of Western liberal democracy as the final form of human government."[5]

By this time, George H. W. Bush, having won the presidential election of 1988, was in the White House. During Bush's four years in office, a host of nearly unimaginable developments—most of them accomplished without significant bloodshed—revolutionized international politics. Rhapsodic crowds dismantled the Berlin Wall; Germany was reunited (remaining in NATO); the nuclear arms race slowed down; and South Africa began slowly to jettison its system of apartheid. The Soviet satellites of Eastern Europe escaped from the oppressive hold that the Soviet Union had clamped on them during and after World War II. Gorbachev, having presided over many of these dramatic changes, was forced out of office on Christmas Day, 1991, by which point the Communist Party had been banned and the once vast Soviet empire was crumbling into fifteen independent states. At the end of the year, the red flag was hauled down at the Kremlin and replaced by the Russian tricolor. Bush and Russian president Boris Yeltsin, who had taken over as the most powerful figure in a new federation of republics that aspired to democratic governance, formally declared the Cold War to be history in February 1992.[6]

The exhilarating trend toward democratization in the world that continued during Bush's tenure soon led him to proclaim the arrival of a "New World Order" under American auspices. Lebanon's long and destructive civil war, which killed more than 100,000 people, came to an end in 1990, whereupon a beleaguered democracy began to take shape there. Other nations that turned toward democracy in these years included Senegal, Mozambique, the Philippines, Nicaragua, El Salvador, Indonesia, Bangladesh, and Chile, where dictator Augusto Pinochet, in power since 1973, was forced to step down as president in 1990. Within a few years the only nations in the Western Hemisphere remaining under authoritarian rule were Cuba and Guyana. It was later estimated that thirty-two new democracies appeared between 1982 and 2002. By 2004, a majority of people in the world lived in countries regarded as democratic—the first time in history that this had been the case. Notwithstanding horrific bloodletting

5. Fukuyama, "The End of History?" *National Interest* 16 (Summer 1989), 3–28.
6. For reflections on the end of the Cold War, by Gorbachev, Bush, British prime minister Margaret Thatcher, and French president François Mitterrand, see "Defrosting the Old Order," *New Perspectives Quarterly* 13 (Winter 1996), 18–31. For the fall of the Soviet Union, see William Hitchcock, *The Struggle for Europe: The Turbulent History of a Divided Continent* (New York, 2002), 375–79.

that savaged Rwanda and other places, ethnic and civic strife also declined between 1990 and 2004.[7] Fukuyama's optimism about the future, though a little breathless, seemed to be justified.

Even as Fukuyama wrote, however, it was obvious that instability continued to threaten many parts of the world. The sudden end of the Cold War, for more than forty years the centerpiece of international relations, delighted Americans, who were correct to say that the patient and resolute foreign policies of the West had triumphed in the end. But the collapse of the Soviet Union did not signify the end of Communism. China was building a stockpile of long-range nuclear weapons. North Korea remained a remote and hostile outpost of Stalinism. Vietnam, Laos, and Cuba continued to be Communist states. Murderous fighting between Communists, other leftists, and their enemies continued to ravage Guatemala into the mid-1990s. Other problems also persisted. Syrian troops remained in Lebanon until 2005. Both Russia and the United States retained large numbers of nuclear warheads.

Though the triumph of the West in the Cold War closed what had been a frightening era in world history, many nations, freed from the pressure to side with either the Soviet or American bloc, grew increasingly nationalistic.[8] Unrest escalated among the host of ethnic groups, including Muslims, which had earlier been suppressed within the Soviet Union. In Afghanistan, which the United States largely ignored after the Soviets departed in 1989, radical, anti-Western Muslims, the Taliban, came to power and abetted the training of terrorists. Millions of people in the world's twenty-two Arab nations—all of them authoritarian states that badly oppressed women—were restless under their own rulers and angry about many economic and military policies of the richer, non-Muslim West. A host of Asian and African countries, having liberated themselves from colonialism, struggled to combat poverty, famines, AIDS, civil wars, and aggression from neighboring states. India and Pakistan (which was presumed by 1990 to possess nuclear weapons) nursed historic religious and territorial grievances and regularly threatened to attack each another. Israel, a democratic nation, had invaded Lebanon in 1982 and was constructing settlements for Jews on Arab territory in Gaza and the West Bank that it had taken following the 1967 war. It was surrounded by Muslim nations that refused to accept its legitimacy and that longed to destroy it.

7. Michael Ignatieff, "Democratic Providentialism," New York Times Magazine, Dec. 12, 2004, 29–34.
8. Tony Judt, "Why the Cold War Worked," New York Review of Books, Oct. 9, 1997, 39–44.

Meanwhile, frightening arsenals continued to develop: In 1990 it was estimated that fifteen countries had the capacity to manufacture chemical weapons.[9]

Thanks to the sudden and unexpected implosion of the Soviet Union, the United States quickly found itself to be an economic and military giant, the only superpower on the planet. An affluent, open society, America lured millions of immigrants to its shores in these and later years. Its ideals of freedom and democracy encouraged many other people in the world: Dissidents at Beijing's Tiananmen Square in 1989 erected a plastic "Goddess of Democracy" modeled on the Statue of Liberty and proudly displayed Statue of Liberty symbols on their clothing. Latin American and Eastern European nations drew inspiration from the American Constitution in crafting changes to their own governmental systems. Prestigious universities in the United States, the world's finest in many fields, attracted streams of ambitious young people, many of whom remained in the States and became productive citizens. Many others, having discovered America to be a free and welcoming place, returned to their native countries to tout its virtues.

Aspects of America's vibrant popular culture—ranging from McDonald's, Coca-Cola, and jeans to TV programs, Hollywood films, and rock 'n' roll—acted as magnets to people all over the world. Penetrating everywhere, these cultural exports irritated cosmopolitan foreigners but at times beguiled even some of the angriest and most religious of dissidents. Las Vegas, America's "last frontier," became a mecca for millions of foreign tourists. The English language, especially American English, was becoming a lingua franca. To maintain, as hostile observers often did, that American culture aroused only disgust or hatred was surely to underrate the allure of its dynamism, its non-military institutions, and its democratic ideals. Inspiring goodwill and imitation, these were formidable sources of "soft power" that bolstered America's image abroad.[10]

On the other hand, the wealth, power, and foreign policies of the United States frequently incited envy and resentment among millions of people in the world—many of them poor and without prospects for a decent life. Some people, notably in Chile and Iran, remembered bitterly that the CIA had helped to impose tyrannical regimes on their countries. For these

9. Joseph Nye, *Bound to Lead: The Changing Nature of American Power* (New York, 1990), 182–88.
10. Richard Pells, *Not Like Us: How Europeans Have Loved, Hated, and Transformed American Culture Since World War II* (New York, 1997); Joseph Nye, *Soft Power: The Means to Success in World Politics* (New York, 2004), x–xii, 127–47.

and other reasons, overseas acts of murder and terrorism aimed at Americans proliferated during the 1980s. American diplomats, military personnel, and government officials were killed in Greece, Pakistan, Lebanon, and Mexico. Violence, much of it perpetrated by Muslim extremist groups, had escalated even before the Iranian revolutionaries had seized American hostages in 1979. Islamic Jihad was formed in that year, Hamas, a militant Palestinian group, in 1987. Hezbollah, the Iran-backed, Shiite "Party of God," emerged as perhaps the most implacably anti-American and anti-Israeli organization of all. In April 1983, a delivery van filled with explosives blew up on the grounds of the United States Embassy in Beirut, killing sixty-three people, seventeen of them Americans. Six months later, Hezbollah exploded a truck bomb that killed 241 United States marines at their headquarters in Beirut, where they had been deployed since August 1982 as part of a multinational peacekeeping force. In early 1984, Hezbollah began seizing Americans as hostages in Lebanon.

Elsewhere in the 1980s, bombs and rockets exploded near American embassies or military bases in Portugal, Italy, Bolivia, Peru, Colombia, West Berlin, and Kuwait City. Iraqi aircraft accidentally hit an American frigate with a missile in the Persian Gulf in 1987 and killed thirty-seven sailors. An American warship in the Persian Gulf accidentally shot down an Iranian passenger plane in 1988, sending 290 people to their deaths. In December 1988, a terrorist connected to Libya managed to hide explosives on Pan American Airways flight 103. Flying over Lockerbie, Scotland, on its way to New York City, the plane blew up, resulting in the death of 259 passengers and eleven people on the ground.

Contradicting optimism about the eclipse of authoritarian government, a number of long-ruling dictators clung to power during the 1980s, some of them for many years thereafter: Hafez el-Assad in Syria, Saddam Hussein in Iraq, Fidel Castro in Cuba, Robert Mugabe in Zimbabwe, Muammar el-Qaddafi in Libya, Suharto in Indonesia, and Kim Il Sung in North Korea, to name only a few. The ultra-conservative royal family of Saudi Arabia, which had the world's largest known oil reserves, imperiously ruled the country. A number of other nations, including many former republics of the Soviet Union and unstable governments in Latin America, struggled as "illiberal democracies" whose legal and political institutions teetered on fragile foundations.[11] Mexico, outwardly a democratic nation, had been a one-party state since 1929. Some regimes brutally stifled dissent. In one

11. This is the theme of Fareed Zakaria, *The Future of Freedom: Illiberal Democracy at Home and Abroad* (New York, 2003).

of the most barbarous events of the era, the People's Republic of China used tanks to crush a protest of students in Beijing's Tiananmen Square in June 1989, killing hundreds, perhaps thousands, of people.

In 1993, Samuel Huntington, a prominent professor of government, published a widely noted article that reminded readers of persistent dangers in this post–Cold War world. Titled "The Clash of Civilizations," his essay identified serious "fault lines" throughout the world and argued that international relations were entering a new phase in which hatreds and rivalries among "different civilizations" would seriously threaten world peace. Huntington predicted that cultural and religious forces would prove to be especially disruptive. "Islam," he warned, "has bloody borders." The "central axis of world politics," he emphasized, would be "THE WEST VERSUS THE REST."[12]

Some reviewers wondered if Huntington had given too little attention to divisions *within* non-Western nations: between rich and poor, religious radicals and moderates, and ethnic and sectarian factions. These divisions—within Islam as well as within other religions—were complex, and they could be as fierce as the furies that incited rage and resentment against the West. In the next few years, ethnic and religious conflicts spilled blood in Chechnya, India, Sri Lanka, Iraq, Yugoslavia, Rwanda, Sudan, Congo, and many other places. Still, there was no doubting that Huntington had a point: Cultural and religious differences in the post–Cold War years posed profoundly complicated problems for American policy-makers in the 1990s.

This, then, was the unsettled world that was evolving during the time when Ronald Reagan was fashioning America's foreign and military policies. Given the historic transformations that were developing during these years, it is perhaps no surprise that he, like other Western leaders, often improvised, sometimes clumsily, as he searched for answers to the dangers that threatened American interests and peaceful international relations.

DESPITE THE INFIGHTING that disrupted Reagan's team of foreign policy advisers in the early 1980s, the direction of his administration was

12. Samuel Huntington, "The Clash of Cultures," *Foreign Affairs* 73 (Summer 1993), 22–49. His capital letters. See also his book *The Clash of Cultures: Civilizations and the Remaking of World Order* (New York, 1996). Others who warned about serious post–Cold War divisions included Bernard Lewis, an authority on the Middle East, in "The Roots of Muslim Rage," *Atlantic Monthly* 266 (Sept. 1990), 60; and Zbigniew Brzezinski, President Carter's national security adviser, in *Out of Order: Global Turmoil on the Eve of the Twenty-First Century* (New York, 1993), 187–207.

clear. This had already been the case during the 1980 campaign, when the future president had emphasized again and again his belief that the United States was an exceptional nation that was destined to outlast and ultimately to overcome tyrannical systems such as Communism and to spread its democratic virtues throughout the world. This vision, which lay at the core of Reagan's view of American history, was unwavering. It imparted a thrust to United States foreign policy that his admirers, looking for optimistic approaches that would dispel the "malaise" of the Carter years, found all but irresistible.

During the 1980 campaign, Reagan had repeatedly promised to invigorate America's national defense. This, he asserted, was not a budget line: "You spend what you need." And so he did. Reinstating development of the B-1 bomber, he secured funding for a new B-2 bomber, cruise missiles, the MX missile, and a 600-ship navy. American defense spending jumped by an estimated 34 percent in real 1982 dollars between 1981 and 1985, from $171 billion to $229 billion. Over the course of Reagan's eight years in office, military spending totaled nearly $2 trillion. His defense expenditures represented a lower percentage of the federal budget than had been the case in the Eisenhower-JFK years (when the Cold War had been at its chilliest and when funding for domestic purposes had been relatively low). But Reagan's defense spending was nonetheless huge, accounting for nearly one-quarter of federal expenditures for most of the decade.[13]

In building up America's defense, Reagan and his top advisers hoped that they would intimidate enemies abroad, thus minimizing the likelihood of war. In November 1984, Weinberger spelled out this kind of thinking, which reflected his horror at the killing of American marines in Lebanon in 1983, as well as the continuing influence of the Vietnam War on American military thinking. The United States, he argued, should send troops into combat abroad only as a last resort and only under certain special conditions: when important national interests were threatened, when it was clear that Congress and the people backed such a move, and when policy makers had "clearly defined political and military objectives," including a well-thought-out exit strategy. Above all, the United States should fight only when it had such overwhelmingly superior military force

13. Defense spending as a percentage of GDP rose from 4.9 percent to 5.2 percent between 1980 and 1990, and from 22.7 percent to 23.9 percent of total federal outlays. *Stat. Abst.*, 2002, 305–7. Also see H. W. Brands, *The Devil We Knew: Americans and the Cold War* (New York, 1993), 174; Robert Collins, *More: The Politics of Economic Growth in Postwar America* (New York, 2000), 201–2; Nye, *Bound to Lead*, 9; *Stat. Abst.*, 2002, 305.

at hand that it was sure to win without significant loss of American life.[14] Later, when Colin Powell embraced this thinking as President Bush's chair of the Joint Chiefs of Staff, it came to be known as the Powell Doctrine, which dictated American actions in the Gulf War of 1991. "War," Powell said, "should be a last resort. And when we go to war we should have a purpose that our people can understand and support; we should mobilize the country's resources to fulfill that mission and then go in to win."[15]

After 1983, a good deal of the money raised for defense went to Reagan's Strategic Defense Initiative (SDI), which personally engaged him more than any other policy of his presidency except tax-cutting. SDI was not something that he suddenly dreamed up while in the White House. It stemmed from his alarm at warnings from hawkish scientists such as Edward Teller and from his horrified surprise at learning in 1979 that the United States, having spent billions on offensive weapons, had virtually no defense against incoming missiles. Reagan had a visceral horror of nuclear war, and he thought that the existing Soviet-American standoff of mutual assured destruction (MAD) via buildup of offensive missiles might result in mutual suicide. Establishment of a defensive shield such as SDI, he believed, would convince the USSR that it was futile to build up its stockpiles of offensive weapons. Disarmament might then follow.

Ever an optimist, Reagan also had a near-mystical faith in the nation's scientific and technological ingenuity. Though he did not understand the technological aspects of SDI, he insisted that the United States should emphasize basic research on space-based defensive weapons, such as chemical lasers and particle beams, ground-based lasers, and a wide variety of kinetic-energy weapons. The essence of SDI was nuclear-powered lasers that would function in space. Not for nothing did a host of incredulous skeptics label SDI "Star Wars."[16]

Though various defense contractors jumped to Reagan's side, opponents were quick to challenge his assumptions. Some of these critics feared that SDI would militarize space, perhaps setting off explosions that would ravage it. Others asserted that Star Wars circumvented the anti-ballistic missile

14. James Mann, *Rise of the Vulcans: The History of Bush's War Cabinet* (New York, 2004), 119–20.

15. Powell and Joseph Persico, *My American Journey* (New York, 1995), 303; Robert Divine, "The Persian Gulf War Revisited: Tactical Victory, Strategic Failure?" *Diplomatic History* 24 (Winter 2000), 129–38.

16. Cannon, *President Reagan*, 275–83; Frances FitzGerald, *Way Out There in the Blue: Reagan, Star Wars, and the End of the Cold War* (New York, 2000). For the movie *Star Wars* (1977), see chapter 2.

(ABM) treaty that the Soviets and Americans had signed in 1972. Still others speculated darkly that SDI was a cover under which offensive weapons, too, might be positioned in space. They worried that the Soviet Union, fearing that SDI would enable the United States to attack with impunity, might respond to the initiative by launching a pre-emptive strike, so as to smash America before it could emplace its new system of defenses. At the very least, critics added, the Soviets would devise new and deadlier offensive weapons that could penetrate any defensive shield that American scientists might claim to erect. Most scientists stressed that no defensive system could offer full protection against enemy attacks. Some foes of SDI thought that Reagan had lost his mind and was launching the nation on a grossly expensive, half-insane adventure into the bizarre and unknown.[17]

As American spending for SDI and other defense items increased in the mid- and late 1980s, critics such as these managed to spark considerable debate. An especially visible skeptic was Paul Kennedy, a British scholar of international relations who taught at Yale. In late 1987, he published a long and learned book, *The Rise and Fall of the Great Powers*, which attracted great attention and sold more than 225,000 copies in the following year.[18] The United States, Kennedy conceded, was still a powerful nation—"in a class of its own economically and perhaps even militarily"— but it was overcommitting by intervening all over the world. For far too long it had been contributing heavily to a "spiraling cost of the arms race," thereby exciting world tensions. Heavy defense spending in the United States, he said, was distorting economic priorities, weakening domestic infrastructure, and creating a "massive long-term decline in American blue-collar employment." In short, the United States was guilty of "imperial overstretch." If it did not mend its ways, it would suffer the fate of imperial Spain in the late sixteenth century and Britain in the late nineteenth. Rephrasing a deadly serious quip about Britain by George Bernard Shaw, he wrote: "Rome fell; Babylon fell; Scarsdale's turn will come."[19]

The attention accorded Kennedy's book, which was hardly a quick read, suggested that he had touched a nerve. Within the next two years, fears about American economic and political "decline"—a decline caused in part, Kennedy and others argued, by overspending on defense—seemed to spread throughout the culture. Many Americans had already come close

17. This is a central theme in FitzGerald, *Way Out There in the Blue.*
18. (New York, 1987). Kennedy's subtitle is *Economic Change and Military Conflict from 1500 to 2000.* See especially 442–46, 514–33. For sales, see Mann, *Rise of the Vulcans,* 161.
19. Kennedy, *Rise and Fall,* 533. From Shaw's *Misalliance* (1909).

to panic following a precipitous drop in the stock market on October 19, 1987. On that day, "Black Monday," the Dow Jones industrial average dropped by 23 percent, or 508 points, closing at 1738.74. It was the largest single-day decline in United States history. The Federal Reserve—then headed by Alan Greenspan—moved quickly to avert further slippage by offering credit that shored up banks and investment houses. In doing so, Greenspan pleased corporate leaders, many of whom lionized him thereafter. But the plunge in stock values dramatically exposed the speculative excess that had overtaken Wall Street in the 1980s, and it frightened CEOs, stockholders, and many other Americans. It was not until September 1989 that the market surpassed the high that had existed before the crash of 1987.

The rise of "Asian tigers," notably Japan, whose rapid economic growth seemed to threaten American hegemony, aroused special alarm. Japanese interests between 1987 and 1989 bought a number of American properties, including CBS Records and Rockefeller Center. When it was reported in 1989 that Sony had purchased Columbia Pictures, *Newsweek* featured a cover story, "Japan Buys Hollywood." A 1992 best-seller, *Rising Sun: A Novel* by the popular writer Michael Crichton, raised the specter of the Japanese taking over the American economy. Slightly shorn of its racial coding, it was made into a popular Hollywood film of that name in 1993. One anguished scholar, upset that the United States was lagging in research and development, wrote in 1993 that the nation was in danger of becoming a "third world country" and that the American Dream itself was under siege.[20]

Given the consumerist nature of American culture—and the relatively low attention that most schools and universities paid to math, science, and foreign languages—there was cause to be concerned about the competitive capacity of the United States in the future. But many pessimists exaggerated the nation's plight at the time. To be sure, America's share of international production, at around 50 percent of world GNP in 1945, had declined since the end of World War II, but it was hardly surprising that energetic industrial nations such as Germany and Japan would advance after recovering from the devastation that had overwhelmed them. Moreover, these nations still had a long way to go to close in on the United

20. Edward Luttwak, *The Endangered American Dream: How to Stop the United States from Becoming a Third World Country and How to Win the Geo-Economic Struggle for Industrial Supremacy* (New York, 1993), esp. 251–54. For political ramifications, see Kevin Phillips, *The Politics of Rich and Poor: Wealth and the American Electorate in the Reagan Aftermath* (New York, 1990).

States, which remained an economic giant in the 1980s. With 5 percent of the planet's population, America accounted for 25 percent of world production in 1990. Knowledgeable observers, eyeing the sluggishness of the Japanese bureaucracy and the infighting that divided its potent interest groups, predicted (correctly, as it turned out) that Japan would someday lose its competitive edge and that the United States would continue to be a giant in the world economy.[21]

Reagan seemed to pay little, if any, attention to debates such as these. From 1983, when he launched SDI, to 1989, when he left office, he vigorously, even passionately, championed the plan. As the research inched ahead, many top officials still did not believe that he truly expected the "science" to pan out. They speculated that he supported SDI primarily to force the Soviets to consider developing their own defensive shields, the costs of which would bankrupt their economy, or that he was using SDI as a bargaining chip to get the USSR to enter into negotiations. Later, when the Soviets did seriously negotiate, some observers said that Reagan had succeeded in this clever purpose.[22] Reagan denied that he pushed SDI for these reasons. Certain that MAD was potentially catastrophic, he thought SDI would avert Armageddon.

He was equally certain of another thing: Communism was a corrupt and oppressive system that would die out in the end. Sure of this outcome, he took steps to hasten the process. From the start, he proclaimed what became known as the Reagan Doctrine, which provided military aid, either openly or covertly, to anti-Communist military forces in Nicaragua, El Salvador, Guatemala, Afghanistan, Cambodia, Mozambique, and Angola.[23] Some of these recipients, notably in El Salvador and Guatemala, responded to insurrections by carrying out murderous attacks on democratically inclined opponents, including unarmed peasants. Their actions, following upon those of the United States in the Vietnam War, helped to swell worldwide human rights movements in the 1980s.

Reagan, largely ignoring human rights activists, showed no inclination in the early 1980s to back away from his anti-Communist policies in the world. Working with the AFL-CIO and Pope John Paul II, a Pole, he encouraged the forces of Solidarity, workers that were leading a struggle

21. Nye, Bound to Lead, 232–33.
22. See Godfrey Hodgson, The World Turned Right Side Up: A History of the Conservative Ascendancy in America (Boston, 1996), 273–74.
23. American aid in Afghanistan went to radical Muslim nationalists who led the anti-Soviet resistance. After 1989, these radicals dominated the Taliban government that sheltered Osama bin Laden once he settled there in 1996.

against Soviet domination in Poland. In a speech at Notre Dame in May 1981 he famously branded Communism as a "sad, bizarre chapter in human history whose last pages are even now being written." Addressing the British Parliament in June 1982, he announced that the world had reached a "historic turning point" and that "communist tyranny could not stop the march of freedom." "Marxism-Leninism," he proclaimed, was facing a "great revolutionary crisis" and would end up "on the ash heap of history." In September 1983, when a Soviet fighter plane shot down a Korean Air Lines passenger jet that had wandered into Soviet airspace, he denounced the act, which killed 269 people, including sixty-one United States citizens, as a "crime against humanity."

In late 1983, Reagan also ordered deployment of Pershing II missiles, a new generation of arms, to augment NATO nuclear weapons in Western Europe, where they were expected to counter Soviet SS-20 missiles. In so doing he had to face down huge and anguished outcries, many of them from intrepid women's groups, from advocates of a "nuclear freeze" in European NATO nations. A widely publicized letter from Catholic bishops called for nuclear disarmament. *The Day After*, a television special in 1983 that vividly showed the effects of an imagined nuclear attack on the United States, attracted an estimated audience of 75 million Americans. Fears of nuclear catastrophe had seldom seemed more pervasive than they became in 1983.

Though Reagan, who foresaw Armageddon if nuclear weapons proliferated, may have sympathized with the long-range goals of activists such as these, he remained deaf to criticisms of his anti-Communist policies. When pro-Communist forces staged a bloody coup that overthrew the government of the tiny Caribbean island of Grenada in October 1983 and were discovered to be using Cuban workers to construct a 10,000-foot-long airfield runway, he concluded that the Soviets and Castro were establishing a Communist beachhead on the island. Branding the new leaders as a "brutal gang of leftist thugs," he sent some 5,000 elite troops to restore order, protect American residents (notably 800 or so medical students), and overthrow the leftists. In two days of fighting, American forces killed forty-five Grenadians and fifty-nine Cubans. A total of nineteen Americans were killed and 115 wounded. A large cache of arms—sufficient to supply 10,000 soldiers—was seized, along with coastal patrol boats and armored vehicles.[24]

Most of these moves alarmed liberal and partisan critics. Like Reagan, they opposed Communism, but unlike him, they believed that the Cold

24. Cannon, *President Reagan*, 389–95.

War had become a more or less permanent and manageable state of affairs. The president's fierce, undiplomatic rhetoric, they said, was amateurish and dangerous. His invasion of Grenada, they added, was a ploy to divert popular attention from the horrific event that had shaken the nation two days earlier: the death of 241 United States marines in Beirut when the truck bomb fashioned by terrorists had blown up their barracks.

This last accusation was hard to prove. Plans for an invasion to oust the rebel Grenadian regime and protect the medical students were under way before the disaster in Lebanon and might have been acted upon in any event. Reagan, moreover, genuinely feared the creation of a new Communist outpost in the Caribbean. Remembering the taking in 1979 of American hostages in Iran, he was determined that it not be repeated in Grenada. For these reasons, he sent in the troops—the only time during his eight years in office that he engaged American soldiers in fighting abroad. Still, it seemed to many people that Reagan's invasion of Grenada was a politically inspired overreaction.

Foes of the president also charged that his hard-line foreign and military policies were stimulating warlike fantasies at home. In 1982, *First Blood*, a violent film starring Sylvester Stallone as a vengeful Green Beret who had survived the Vietnam War, drew large and enthusiastic audiences. *Red Dawn*, released in 1984, featured Russian invaders overrunning the United States in World War III. Tom Clancy's book *The Hunt for Red October* appeared in the same year, followed in 1986 by *Red Storm Rising*. These were among Clancy's many best-selling books that highlighted the evil deviousness of Communist enemies.[25]

The president, however, adhered to his course: In his struggle against Communism, as in many other things, he was dead sure of himself. Immediately following the successful invasion of Grenada, Reagan delivered a politically well received televised address, in which he wove the downing of the Korean Air Lines jet, Beirut, and Grenada into a patriotic indictment of terrorist, Soviet, and Communist iniquity. He said nothing about the badly flawed decision-making process that in August 1982 had led him to place the marines as peacekeepers in war-torn Lebanon.

In so doing, he had hoped to succeed in resolving Arab-Israeli hostilities in the Middle East. Weinberger and the Joint Chiefs of Staff, however, had opposed such a move, warning that the ill-protected marines

25. Capitalizing on the favorable response to *First Blood*, Stallone starred in two follow-ups, *Rambo: First Blood: Part 2* (1985), and *Rambo 3* (1988). Both featured mindless action and violence. *Rambo 3*, costing an estimated $58 million to make, was then the most expensive film ever produced.

would stand precariously between Israeli troops under the direction of Defense Minister Ariel Sharon, Syrian forces, and fighters loyal to Hezbollah and the Palestine Liberation Organization (PLO). Reagan also had nothing to report about his subsequent decision not to retaliate militarily against the enemies who had pulled off the attack.[26]

It might not have mattered to his popularity if he had spoken about such matters: After Grenada, many Americans were in so euphoric a mood that they seemed unwilling to criticize Reagan, who had posed as the fearless defender of United States interests, for having exposed the marines to danger and for having done nothing of substance to punish the killers of 241 of them. Having suffered since the 1960s through a number of international humiliations, of which the bloodshed in Beirut was only the most recent, they rejoiced that the United States had triumphed in Grenada. During the 1984 presidential campaign, the invasion of that tiny island was celebrated as an example of Reagan's resoluteness against the red tide of Communism.[27]

BETWEEN 1982 AND 1984, and throughout Reagan's second term, tensions in the Middle East deeply engaged his administration. Reagan was especially anxious about the plight in Lebanon of American hostages, which Hezbollah terrorists—perhaps emboldened by the reluctance of the United States to retaliate for the bombing in Beirut—began seizing in February 1984. While Iran, still under the sway of Ayatollah Khomeini, was believed to be the major force behind Hezbollah, other nations in the area were also guilty of terrorism. One, the president concluded, was Libya. After a bombing by Libyans killed two American soldiers in a West Berlin disco in April 1986, Reagan froze Libyan assets and ordered heavy retaliatory air raids aimed at the nation's strongman, Muammar el-Qaddafi. The attacks killed scores of civilians. Among those killed was a two-year-old adopted daughter of Qaddafi.

Reagan's anguished concern for the hostages proved to be a key to what became known after November 1986 as the Iran-contra scandal, which among other things revealed the many flaws that plagued his style of management. The scandal nearly wrecked his administration.

The origins of the scandal lay in Central America. In July 1979, Nicaraguan rebels—so-called Sandinistas—forced Anastasio Somoza, the brutal, American-backed dictator of the country, into exile. During the next

26. In December 1983, Reagan did take responsibility for decisions that led to the bombing of the marine barracks in Beirut.
27. Cannon, *President Reagan*, 394–95.

eighteen months their leader, Daniel Ortega, made efforts to promote social and economic reforms. But the Sandinistas were also oppressive, hauling Somoza-era officials before kangaroo courts. Moving closer to Moscow, the Sandinistas offered military assistance to Marxist rebels fighting against the pro-American government of nearby El Salvador. In the last days of his administration, Carter sent military personnel to aid the El Salvadorean government and cut off United States assistance to Nicaragua. Beginning in 1981, Reagan dispatched further economic and military aid to the El Salvadorian government as well as CIA-arranged covert assistance to Nicaraguan forces—the contras—that were forming to fight against the Sandinistas. Then and later, the secret aid forced the Sandinistas to focus on military needs, thereby inhibiting progress toward social and economic reform.[28]

In 1982, by which time word had leaked out about Reagan's aid to the contras, the House passed an amendment, sponsored by Democratic congressman Edward Boland of Massachusetts, which prohibited the CIA and the Department of Defense from using funds to overthrow the Sandinistas. The Boland Amendment, as it was called, revealed the continuing presence of a powerful source of political division in late twentieth-century American politics: tension between Congress and the executive over presidential war-making authority. The amendment passed the House 411 to 0 and was signed by the president. The administration, however, ignored the amendment and increasingly used the National Security Council (NSC) as the conduit for deliveries of covert aid. Robert "Bud" McFarlane, NSC director, and Marine Lt. Col. Oliver "Ollie" North, a gung-ho staff assistant who worked with him, oversaw the process.

In 1984, McFarlane and North secured secret aid for the contras from the Saudi government—assistance that rose to $2 million a month in 1985. When they told the president about the Saudi assistance, he was pleased and told them to keep it quiet. The NSC also enlisted private arms brokers and Manuel Noriega, the drug-trafficking dictator of Panama, in aid of their cause. In addition, the administration secretly mined Nicaraguan harbors. Learning in 1984 of the mining, which CIA director William Casey lied about in testimony on the Hill, many in Congress were outraged. Conservative senator Barry Goldwater of Arizona whipped off a note to Casey, saying, "This is no way to run a railroad. I am pissed."[29]

28. For the history of Iran-contra, see Haynes Johnson, *Sleepwalking Through History: America in the Reagan Years* (New York, 1991), 245–371; William Pemberton, *Exit with Honor: The Life and Presidency of Ronald Reagan* (Armonk, N.Y., 1998), 172–90; and Cannon, *President Reagan*, 298–320, 580–662.
29. Hodgson, *The World Turned Right Side Up*, 266.

In an effort to stop these activities, the House passed a second Boland Amendment in October 1984. It barred even non-military American support for the contras. North and others, however, knew that Reagan was eager to do all he could to help the contras in order to avert the spread of Communism in Central America. So encouraged, McFarlane and North assured themselves that the amendment did not apply to actions of the NSC, which continued its machinations. In mid-1985, Reagan proclaimed that the contras were the "moral equivalent of the Founding Fathers," and in March 1986, he went on television to deliver what critics called his "red tide" speech. The Soviets, Cubans, and "other elements of international terrorism," he exclaimed, were directing vast Communist activities in Central America that would ultimately undermine Mexico and threaten the United States.

But Reagan could not get the American hostages in Lebanon out of his mind. Though he publicly declared that the United States would never deal with terrorists—we "make no concessions; we make no deals," he said in June 1985—he encouraged McFarlane and Admiral John Poindexter, McFarlane's successor in late 1985, to embark on secret arms sales to Iran, which was eager to secure aid in its ongoing war with Iraq. These sales were arranged by an exiled Iranian businessman and, in order to cover America's involvement, funneled through Israel. McFarlane and Poindexter hoped that the aid, which contravened an arms and trade embargo on Iran, would go to "moderates" within the country, who would tilt the nation in a more pro-Western direction, counter Soviet pressure in the Middle East, and facilitate release of American hostages held by terrorists in Lebanon. There were seven such hostages when the United States started the sales.[30]

Shultz and Weinberger, hearing of these plans, were appalled. When Powell, then a military aide to Weinberger at the Pentagon, showed his boss a top-secret NSC memo on the sales, Weinberger scribbled on it: "This is almost too absurd to comment on. . . . The assumption here is 1) that Iran is about to fall & 2) we can deal with that on a rational basis—It's like asking Quadhaffi to Washington for a cozy chat."[31] But McFarlane and Poindexter, with Reagan's approval, managed to exclude Shultz and Weinberger from the loop of policy making concerned with the issue. Meanwhile, North secretly arranged for profits from the sales of arms to Iran to go to the contras in Nicaragua. Shultz and Weinberger continued

30. Mann, *Rise of the Vulcans*, 151–53.
31. Ibid., 153. Pemberton, *Exit with Honor*, 179. "Qhadhaffi" is Weinberger's spelling.

to oppose the arms sales, which by 1986 had evolved into a direct arms-for-hostages swap, but they understood that Reagan was desperately anxious to secure release of the hostages, and they were unable to stem the momentum of the deals.

As Shultz, Weinberger, and other opponents had predicted, the arms sales did not advance the influence of "moderates" in Iran. Khomeini and his followers remained firmly in power until his death in 1989. Nor did the sales succeed in relieving Reagan's concern about the hostages. The captors, recognizing that the United States was essentially offering bribes, knew that by seizing more people they would further strengthen their bargaining power. Though a few hostages were released in 1985 and 1986, others were taken. One hostage, Beirut CIA section chief William Buckley, died of medical neglect in June 1985, whereupon his captors displayed his corpse on television. Terry Anderson, Associated Press bureau chief in Beirut, who was seized by Hezbollah in March 1985, was not released until December 1991.[32]

All these elaborate and devious arrangements literally crashed in October 1986, when an American cargo plane carrying arms to the contras was shot down over Nicaragua. The crash killed three Americans, but one was captured. By early November, newspapers and magazines in Iran and Lebanon were reporting the essence of the Iran-contra story. Shultz and Vice President Bush, remembering how Nixon's cover-up had ruined him, urged Reagan to admit that the United States had been trading arms for hostages. The president, however, insisted that his administration had dealt with Iranian middlemen, not with terrorists. In mid-November, he proclaimed that his administration "did not, repeat, did not trade arms or anything else for hostages."

Shultz then went to the White House and told the president that he, Reagan, had been misled. Reagan, however, still did not admit that there was a problem. "I didn't shake him one bit," Shultz told an aide.[33] The president, however, did ask Attorney General Ed Meese to look into the situation. Poindexter, present when Reagan issued this request, alerted North, who immediately started shredding documents. When Meese reported back to the president on November 24 that North had in fact turned over profits from arms sales to the contras, Reagan's face turned pasty white, as if this were the first time he had become fully aware of the diversion. Poindexter

32. Adam Shatz, "In Search of Hezbollah," New York Review of Books, April 29, 2004, 41–44.
33. Pemberton, Exit with Honor, 187.

confirmed that the diversions had been made and came to the Oval Office to resign. Reagan accepted his resignation and asked no questions.

Only then, on November 25, did Reagan appear again before the press. Looking old and stricken, he announced that Poindexter had resigned, that North had been relieved of his duties, that aides had not kept him properly informed, and that he was forming a special review board (to be headed by former senator John Tower of Texas) to look into the controversy. Meese then shocked the press by describing the diversion. Within a few weeks, Reagan felt obliged to ask a panel of judges to appoint an independent special prosecutor to investigate. The man they selected was Lawrence Walsh, a Republican and a former federal judge. The House and Senate pursued their own separate investigations. All these developments badly damaged the political standing of the president, whose party had already suffered losses in the off-year elections: Gaining eight seats, the Democrats had regained control of the Senate, fifty-five to forty-five. The news that the administration, which had posed as the firmest foe of terrorism, had traded arms for hostages especially stunned Americans. Reagan—of all people—had bribed terrorists! In early December a *New York Times*/CBS poll showed that the president's job approval ratings, which had been higher than 60 percent since mid-1985, had plunged from 67 percent to 46 percent.[34]

Investigators sought answers to a key question: Did the president know that North and others had been turning over profits to the contras? Reagan finally made a public stab at answering this question in a nationally televised talk in early March 1987. Lamenting "activities undertaken without my knowledge," he said that what had taken place was "a mistake." "As the Navy would say," he added, "this happened on my watch." He emphasized that he had never intended the arms sales to be connected to release of hostages. "A few months ago," he explained, "I told the American people I did not trade arms for hostages. My heart and best intentions still tell me that is true, but the facts and the evidence tell me it is not."[35]

Reagan's carefully crafted half-confession seemed to mollify many listeners, but investigators kept digging: Was it truly the case that Reagan himself had not known about the business of arms-for-hostages? Poindexter, falling on his sword, testified under oath that he had approved the diversions to the contras himself and had not told the president about them. "I

34. Cannon, *President Reagan*, 626. His ratings did not rise above 50 percent again until early 1988.
35. Ibid., 655.

made a very deliberate decision," he said, "not to ask the president so I could insulate him . . . and provide future deniability." His statement helped to shield the president, though it also exposed Reagan's abstracted, hands-off style of management. Was he or was he not informed of the activities of his aides? Did he or did he not recall what he had been told? As the final congressional report concluded, "If the President did not know what his National Security Advisers were doing, he should have."[36]

Investigators could find no "smoking gun" that directly connected Reagan to the diversions to the contras. Independent prosecutor Walsh, who spent years pursuing the evidence, reported in 1994 that Reagan had "created the conditions which made possible the crimes committed by others" and that he had "knowingly participated or acquiesced in covering up the scandal." Walsh added, however, that there was "no credible evidence" that the president "authorized or was aware of the diversion of profits from the Iran arms sale to assist the contras, or that Regan [Reagan's chief of staff], Bush, or Meese was aware of the diversion."[37]

The focus on what Reagan did or did not know about the diversions was understandable. The Watergate scandal had led people to look for a smoking gun and had intensified congressional suspiciousness about presidential excesses in the making of foreign and military policy.[38] Still, the focus on presidential actions (and inactions) tended to deflect public attention from serious discussion of the administration's fundamental policies—the badly misguided and illegal arms-for-hostages trading and the provision of covert aid to the contras in defiance of the Boland amendments. Oddly enough, Walsh seemed to sympathize with Reagan's frustrations concerning congressional opposition to aid for the contras. It may have been unfair, he later told Reagan's biographer, for Congress abruptly to have cut off such aid while the contras were active in the field. Still, in his final report, Walsh said that if Congress had had all the facts in 1987–88 that he finally put together in 1994, it should have considered impeachment of the president.

Congress never seriously considered taking such a step. Though the Iran-contra scandal damaged Reagan's presidency, the American people still showed affection for him—far more than they had ever displayed for

36. Pemberton, *Exit with Honor*, 191.
37. Ibid., 192; Cannon, *President Reagan*, 662.
38. In 1994, when Reagan disclosed that he had Alzheimer's disease, many people speculated that this illness had contributed to the mismanagement that led to Iran-contra. Those who saw Reagan regularly in those years, however, saw no evidence of impairment during his presidency. See Edmund Morris, "The Unknowable," *New Yorker*, June 28, 2004, 40–51.

Nixon in 1974. They tended to believe that Reagan, known for his inattention at meetings, truly did not know everything that his aides were doing. In this odd sense, public awareness of his poor management skills may have worked to his political advantage. Democrats also looked ahead: They realized that if Reagan were to be impeached and removed from office, Bush would become president and would thereby become more formidable as an incumbent opponent in the election of 1988.

Walsh's investigations did not have much impact. Though he secured fourteen indictments and eleven convictions, most of the convictions followed plea bargains and resulted in light fines or community service. Other convictions — of Poindexter and North — were overturned on appeals. Only one small fish went to jail, for misrepresenting his income on federal tax forms. In October 1992, Walsh managed to indict Weinberger (an opponent of arms-for-hostages) on a charge of making false statements (about what he had known at the time) to investigators. On Christmas Eve 1992, however, twelve days before Weinberger's trial was to begin, President Bush pardoned Weinberger and five others, including McFarlane.[39]

WHILE REAGAN WAS STRUGGLING TO SURVIVE the Iran-contra scandal, he was also moving ahead toward historic accommodations with the Soviet Union. These not only helped many Americans forgive him for the Iran-contra scandal; they also represented the most remarkable foreign policy achievements of his eight years as president.

Almost no one, of course, could have anticipated that Reagan, the consummate Cold Warrior, would seek such accommodations, let alone manage to make them. The Kremlin, moreover, was something of a geriatric ward between 1981 and early 1985, ruled by aging — then dying — leaders who evinced little desire for a serious softening of Soviet-American relations. But Reagan had always hoped to end the potentially catastrophic arms race. Shultz, moreover, shared these hopes and worked patiently to achieve them. Even as Reagan was denouncing the Soviet Union as an evil empire in 1983, American negotiators were holding ongoing discussions with Soviet representatives concerning arms reductions. Though the Soviets broke off these talks after the United States sent Pershing II missiles to Western Europe, Reagan still dreamed of progress in the future. In March 1985, when Mikhail Gorbachev took control in Moscow, Reagan saw a chance to reopen serious summit talks with the Soviet Union.

39. McFarlane had been convicted earlier after pleading guilty to four misdemeanor counts of withholding information from Congress. His sentence was two years probation.

There was good reason to try. Gorbachev, fifty-four years old in 1985, was a much younger man than his predecessors. Well before taking power, he recognized that the freedoms—and prosperity—of the West had a seditious appeal to the largely impoverished, oppressed people of the Communist bloc. He knew that the Soviet system was badly in need of reform. As Politburo member Aleksandr Yakovlev later wrote, the USSR at that time "was in a state of long-lasting and potentially dangerous stagnation." Only 23 percent of urban homes and 7 percent of rural homes in the USSR had telephones. Ethnic and religious divisions (Russians were only one-half of the population) fragmented the country. Spending for defense swallowed two to three times as much of GNP in the Soviet Union as in the United States. Military commitments in Afghanistan and Africa were draining the Russian economy and killing thousands of Soviet soldiers. Unrest, notably the rise of Solidarity in Poland after 1980, was spreading in the USSR's Eastern European satellites.[40] Hoping to ameliorate these difficult problems, Gorbachev pressed for *glasnost*, the opening up of Soviet society, and for *perestroika*, the restructuring of the economy.

Gorbachev was especially anxious to reduce military expenditures, which he knew were bleeding his country. It was obvious, however, that Reagan was not only building up America's conventional weaponry; he was also calling for the extraordinarily ambitious Strategic Defense Initiative. Gorbachev believed that if the Soviet Union was forced to engage in astronomically expensive spending for defensive weapons, it might never remedy its internal weaknesses. He concluded that he had to try to reach an arms reduction agreement with the United States. Nothing else would enable him to advance the *perestroika* that would rescue the Soviet economy.

The rapprochement that ensued developed with almost breathtaking speed. Beginning with a meeting in Geneva in November 1985, for which Reagan prepared meticulously (even seeking the counsel of historians of Russia), the two men held five summit conferences and forged an occasionally contentious but increasingly productive personal relationship. Their friendship aroused consternation among hard-liners in both countries: The conservative columnist George Will charged that Reagan was accelerating the "moral disarmament of the west by elevating wishful thinking to the status of political philosophy."[41] Defense Secretary Weinberger, a forceful hard-liner, was equally alarmed by Reagan's efforts, believing

---

40. Nye, *Bound to Lead*, 118–30.
41. Dinesh D'Souza, "How the East Was Won," *American History* 38 (Oct. 2003), 37–43.

that the Soviets would not negotiate in good faith. The two leaders brushed such opposition aside. Though Reagan continued to denounce Communist adventurism, as in Central America, his rhetoric softened after 1985.

Other summits followed the one at Geneva. The first of these, at Reykjavik, Iceland, in October 1986, seemed at one point close to reaching an astonishingly sweeping agreement—which Reagan suddenly proposed—that would have eliminated all American and Soviet nuclear weapons within ten years.[42] American aides at the conference were appalled by Reagan's idea, which would have given the Soviets, whose conventional weaponry was more powerful, a considerable edge.[43] But Gorbachev, alarmed by the thought of trying to match the SDI, then sought to limit research on it to the laboratory. Reagan grew angry, telling Gorbachev, "I've told you again and again that SDI wasn't a bargaining chip," thereby backing off from any sweeping agreement about strategic nuclear weapons. The two sides, having engaged in what one historian later called a "surrealistic auction," parted without concluding a deal.[44] In June 1987, Reagan expressed his continuing frustration when he stood before the Brandenburg Gate in divided Berlin and challenged the Soviets to bring on a new era of freedom in Europe. "Mr. Gorbachev," he thundered, "open this gate! Mr. Gorbachev, tear down this wall!"

Even then, however, quieter negotiations were making progress toward an agreement on arms reduction. In February 1987, Gorbachev made the key decision to separate the issue of SDI from deals that might be made on cuts in nuclear weapons. The Soviet Union, he said, would accept "without delay" the elimination within five years of Soviet and American intermediate-range missiles in Europe. This was a major breakthrough, enabling Reagan and Gorbachev to agree to an intermediate nuclear forces (INF) treaty, which the two leaders signed with great fanfare in Washington in December 1987. It committed both sides to the ultimate destruction of their intermediate- and short-range missiles, thereby reducing tensions in Europe. It included procedures for on-site monitoring, the absence of which had stymied many previous discussions between the two superpowers. It was the first time that the United States and the Soviet Union had agreed to scrap any nuclear weapons.

42. Robert Cottrell, "An Icelandic Saga," *New York Review of Books*, Nov. 4, 2004, 26–29.
43. John Gaddis, *The United States and the End of the Cold War: Implications, Reconsiderations, Provocations* (New York, 1992), 128–29; Brands, *The Devil We Knew*, 196–99.
44. Gaddis, *The United States and the End of the Cold War*, 129; Cannon, *President Reagan*, 690–92.

Reagan then had to convince Cold War hard-liners to accept the treaty. This proved to be problematic at first; some foes of the treaty likened him to Britain's Neville Chamberlain, who had appeased Hitler in the 1930s. But Gorbachev soon announced that the USSR would begin to pull its troops out of Afghanistan and complete the process by February 1989. Reagan, meanwhile, worked to bring the Senate around. All but a few holdouts started to swing over to support the treaty, which was ratified in May with an impressive margin of victory, 93 to 5. INF was a major step toward reduction of tensions between the world's two most powerful nations.

Then and later, politically engaged observers of this historic agreement argued about whether Gorbachev or Reagan deserved most of the credit for these remarkable developments—and, in time, for the ending of the Cold War. Some of these observers have emphasized Reagan's role. Prime Minister Margaret Thatcher of Britain, a strong ally, stated simply, "Reagan won the Cold War without firing a shot."[45] Other observers have properly gone beyond citing the efforts of a single man such as Reagan, crediting not only the major role of Gorbachev but also the resoluteness of a host of Western leaders and of NATO for more than forty years. They further point to pressure from dissident groups within the Soviet bloc, such as Solidarity. To identify any individual as the person who "ended the Cold War" is to oversimplify a complex combination of technological and economic forces and to ignore the courage and determination of a great many people—leaders as well as followers—who had opposed the Soviets and their Communist allies for more than a generation.

Many evaluators nonetheless correctly concede Reagan's contributions. From the beginning of his presidency, he had rejected the notion that the Cold War must be permanent or that Communism would long remain a force in world politics. In holding such beliefs, he ignored the opinions of virtually all experts, including CIA officials, most of whom had failed to predict the collapse of the Soviet Union. From 1981 on, he had favored nuclear arms reductions along the lines of the INF treaty. Though hard-liners in the Soviet Union had frustrated him before 1985, he had bided his time, meanwhile building up American defenses. Reagan's unyielding insistence on SDI, his admirers emphasize, frightened Gorbachev, who understood that the United States had far greater economic and technological capability. All these policies, they add, established Reagan as a dedicated foe of Communism, thereby enabling him to do what more liberal American leaders might not have been able to do politically: nego-

45. D'Souza, "How the East Was Won."

tiate an INF treaty, sell it to the American people, and get it through the U.S. Senate.[46]

Other observers give Gorbachev more of the credit. SDI, they agree, worried him. Moreover, the initiative was a bizarre and diplomatically destabilizing idea that impeded serious conversation with the Soviets. By arousing hard-liners in the USSR, these critics add, SDI probably made it more difficult for Gorbachev to seek accommodation with the United States. The key to success, these observers maintain, was Gorbachev's early recognition that the USSR must cut its spending for armament and strike a deal to prevent further escalations in military technology. The road to warmer relations and to the end of the Cold War, they insist, began with the economic and political crises of the Soviet Union—a vast Potemkin village that Gorbachev other reformers were determined to reshape—not in the White House. Not everything good that happens in the world, these observers remind us, emanates primarily from the United States.[47]

These debates may go on forever, or at least until many more key documents are declassified and made available to scholars. In any event, it is clear that both Gorbachev and Reagan negotiated in good faith to ameliorate tensions. A good deal of difficult diplomacy lay ahead—long after the United States and the USSR (and, later, Russia) started cutting back their arms, the two nations still possessed awesome nuclear might, notably in long-range weapons—but after 1989 the world was a safer place than it had been for decades. And SDI was never deployed. Reagan's role in helping to ease the nuclear threat enabled him to regain some of the popularity he had lost as a result of the Iran-contra scandal and to leave office with very high (68 percent) job approval ratings.[48] Facilitating the melting down of the Cold War, which almost no one had predicted in 1981, was his most important international legacy as president.

46. Gaddis, *The United States and the End of the Cold War,* 291; Hodgson, *The World Turned Right Side Up,* 268.

47. Samuel Wells, "Reagan, Euromissiles, and Europe," in Elliot Brownlee and Hugh Davis Graham, eds., *The Reagan Presidency: Pragmatic Conservatism and Its Legacies* (Lawrence, Kans., 2003), 133–52; David Allin, *Cold War Illusions: America, Europe, and Soviet Power, 1969–1989* (New York, 1998); Brands, *The Devil We Knew,* 227.

48. Mann, *Rise of the Vulcans,* 159.

7

Bush 41

Americans, who are intensely proud of their democratic institutions, have often picked patricians and multimillionaires as their presidential candidates. In the years between 1904 and 1960, these included Theodore Roosevelt, William Howard Taft, Herbert Hoover, FDR, Adlai Stevenson, and JFK.

In selecting George Herbert Walker Bush as its nominee in 1988, the Republican Party followed this tradition. Bush, who turned sixty-four in June of that year, was the son of Dorothy Walker and Prescott Bush, a stern and accomplished man who had risen to become managing partner of Brown Brothers, Harriman, a top Wall Street firm, and to serve between 1953 and 1963 as a Republican senator from Connecticut. George fashioned a record that would have made any parent proud. Sent to Phillips Academy, Andover, he flourished as a student and an athlete and was chosen president of his senior class. After graduating in 1942, he quickly joined the navy, becoming its youngest pilot. During World War II he flew fifty-eight missions in the Pacific, receiving the Distinguished Flying Cross for completing a mission in a burning plane before bailing into the sea. After the war he attended Yale, where he captained the baseball team and graduated Phi Beta Kappa in 1948. His accomplishments to that point were as substantial as any presidential candidate in modern United States history.[1]

1. For Bush, John Greene, *The Presidency of George Bush* (Lawrence, Kans., 2000); and Herbert Parmet, *George Bush: The Life of a Lone Star Yankee* (New York, 1997).

After leaving Yale, Bush set out for Texas, where family money helped him fare handsomely in the oil development business. He then turned to the world of politics, serving on Capitol Hill as a Republican representative from a suburban Houston district between 1967 and 1971. After losing to Lloyd Bentsen in a race for the Senate in 1970, he served as Nixon's ambassador to the United Nations and then as chairman of the GOP National Committee. Ford then tapped him to head the CIA. Though he failed to win the GOP presidential nomination in 1980, he became Reagan's running mate. For the next eight years he was a discreet and totally loyal vice president—so conscientiously that many people, slow to recognize that he was keenly ambitious and competitive, derided him as a "wimp" and an "errand boy" who would never be able to stand on his own. Others who knew him (including some Reagan loyalists) thought he was a political chameleon who had no strong opinions. Most people who worked with him, however, found him to be an unusually genial, courteous, and well-mannered man. He generated considerable and lasting loyalty among his inner circle of friends and advisers.[2]

Though Bush hit a few snags on the path to his nomination in 1988, he proved to be more popular in the primaries than his major foes, Kansas senator Robert Dole and Pat Robertson, who had resigned his ordination in the Southern Baptist Convention before launching his challenge.[3] By March, Bush was assured of the nomination, which—like all major party presidential nominees in late twentieth-century America—he took on the first ballot at the GOP convention in August. (By then, the political conventions had become scripted, anachronistic rituals, not decision-making events.) Bush selected Indiana senator J. Danforth Quayle as his running mate, arousing widespread complaints that he had chosen a poorly regarded senator who had used family connections to escape the draft during the Vietnam War. Though the criticism of Quayle, an often lampooned figure, was unnerving, Bush—who was distrusted by many conservatives—hoped that his running mate, a vocal supporter of "family values," would help him with white evangelical Christian voters. In accepting the presidential nomination, Bush gave a strong speech in which he pledged to hold the line on taxation. "Read my lips," he told the delegates. "No new taxes."[4]

2. David Halberstam, *War in a Time of Peace: Bush, Clinton, and the Generals* (New York, 2001), 69–73.

3. William Martin, *With God on Our Side: The Rise of the Religious Right in America* (New York, 1996), 278–82.

4. For the campaign see Greene, *The Presidency of George Bush*, 41–43; Parmet, *George Bush*, 340–48; Jules Witcover, *Party of the People: A History of the Democratic Party* (New York, 2003), 636–42; and Fred Greenstein, *The Presidential Difference: Leadership Style from FDR to Clinton* (New York, 2000), 163–64.

A herd of hopefuls left the starting gates in 1987 to run for the Democratic nomination, with Representative Richard Gephardt of Missouri, Senator Al Gore Jr. of Tennessee, and Senator Paul Simon of Illinois in the pack. Delaware senator Joseph Biden, former Colorado senator Gary Hart, and the Reverend Jesse Jackson charged ahead among the early leaders. Well before 1988, however, the suspiciousness incited by Vietnam and Watergate had become pervasive and had spurred increasingly aggressive investigative reporters to dig into the personal lives of major candidates. It was soon revealed that Biden had plagiarized speeches. In May 1987, the *Miami Herald* broke a story indicating that Hart, a married man who had dared reporters to pry into his personal life, had been having an affair with a part-time model. Newspapers and tabloids featured a photograph of Hart sitting on a yacht, *Monkey Business*, with the model, Donna Rice, perched on his knee. Both aspirants dropped out of the race.

Jackson fared well for a while, winning five southern primaries on "Super Tuesday" in early March. But he was well to the left of most people in the party. As a black man, he was thought to have no chance of winning a national election. And Jackson had his own political liabilities. Speaking in New York four years earlier, he had referred to the city with the anti-Semitic slur of "Hymietown." When Louis Farrakhan, head of the Nation of Islam, described Judaism as a "gutter religion," Jackson refused to criticize the statement.

The winner of what proved to be a contested campaign for the Democratic nomination was Massachusetts governor Michael Dukakis, who was the son of successful Greek immigrants. Winning the early primary in neighboring New Hampshire, Dukakis, a liberal on most issues, built a large lead in fund-raising. He then maintained a precarious advantage by winning key primaries over Gore and Jackson in the next few months. Like Bush, he took the nomination on the first ballot. At the convention he balanced the ticket by choosing Texas senator Lloyd Bentsen, a conservative, as his running mate. No Democratic presidential candidate had ever won the election in November without carrying the state of Texas.

When the Democratic convention came to a close in July, Dukakis enjoyed a seventeen-point lead in the polls over Bush. As a three-times elected governor, he had a reputation as an incorruptible, intelligent, and efficient administrator. In an effort to capitalize on his strengths — and to attract the broad middle of the electorate — he announced in his acceptance speech, "This election is not about ideology, it's about competence." During the campaign he sought to link Bush to the Iran-contra scandal, asking voters, "Where was George?" Other Democrats zeroed in on Quayle, ridiculing him as a draft dodger and as an intellectual "lightweight." Texas treasurer Ann Richards, a feisty campaigner, had great sport mocking Bush's efforts (which were clumsy) to adopt the folksy ways of Texans, by saying that he had been "born with a silver foot in his mouth." Democrats also ridiculed his malapropisms, or "Bush-speak." On one occasion Bush announced, "Everyone who has a job wants a job"; on another he promised to increase "experts," when he meant to say "exports."[5]

Like Jimmy Carter in 1976, however, Dukakis lost his early lead. Try as he did, he could not prove that Bush had known about the arms-for-hostages swaps. The former vice president protested that he had been "out of the loop."[6] Though voters appeared to agree that Dukakis was "competent," they also found him to be aloof, imperturbably calm, and without clearly articulated goals. The satirist Mort Sahl groused that Dukakis was "the only colorless Greek in America." Republicans made fun of an ad, intended by Democratic strategists to show that Dukakis would be a strong commander-in-chief, which showed him grinning foolishly, clad in a jumpsuit and an outsized, Snoopy-style helmet while riding a tank. Bush quipped, "He thinks a naval exercise is something you find in Jane Fonda's exercise books." Bush also seized on the fact that Dukakis (in an earlier term as governor in 1977) had vetoed a law requiring teachers to lead students in reciting the Pledge of Allegiance. Dukakis's advisers had told him, correctly, that the measure, which would have subjected non-complying teachers to criminal charges, was unconstitutional. Bush was unmoved, labeling Dukakis a "card-carrying member of the American Civil Liberties Union."[7]

While coping with symbolic and cultural matters such as these, Dukakis had trouble holding his unwieldy party together. Centrists in the Democratic Leadership Council formed in 1985 still battled liberals for supremacy Liberals also fought with one another, fragmenting the old New Deal coalition. Robert Reich, a Massachusetts liberal, complained after the election that "liberalism, and, inevitably, the Democratic Party, too, appeared less the embodiment of a shared vision and more a tangle of

5. John White, *The New Politics of Old Values* (Hanover, N.H., 1989), 149.
6. Only later, after Bush had lost the election of 1992, did he acknowledge that he had in fact been kept informed about progress in the arms-for-hostages dealings. *Lou Cannon, President Reagan: The Role of a Lifetime* (New York, 2000), 661.
7. Michael Sherry, *In the Shadow of War: The United States Since the 1930s* (New Haven, 1995), 434. For Dukakis, see Garry Wills, *Under God: Religion and American Politics* (New York, 1990), 58–60.

narrow appeals for labor unions, teachers, gays, Hispanics, blacks, Jews . . .
fractious Democratic constituencies, each promoting its own agenda."[8]

Though Republicans had to contend with internal divisions, they were
not so quarrelsome as the Democrats. For the most part they agreed on
key issues, notably the need for high defense spending, low taxes, and (at
least in theory) small government in most domestic matters. They remained
popular among politically engaged voters who supported the causes of the
Religious Right.[9] Republicans also enjoyed large advantages in fund raising. By 1988, the number of corporate political action committees, most
of which were solidly Republican, had risen to 1,806 (compared to 89 in
1974 and 1,206 in 1980). By contrast, labor had 355 PACs.[10] It was reported
later that 249 contributors, barred by campaign finance regulations from
giving more than $1,000 directly to a candidate, donated $100,000 or more
to the GOP's "Team 100," an organization of big-money donors, in 1988.
This was permitted under the law, which had gaping loopholes.[11]

Bush was a centrist Republican who had never been comfortable with
the right wing within his party. A moderate Episcopalian, he had few ties
with the evangelical Christian Right, members of which tended to regard
him as an irreligious country-club Republican. But in 1988, as during his
years as vice president, he was careful not to antagonize it. Like many
other Republicans, he demonized the *l* word, "liberal." Opposing gun
control, he supported voluntary prayers in the public schools and the death
penalty for people who committed extraordinarily violent crimes. He opposed abortion, except in cases of rape or incest, or to save the life of the
mother. Among the aides who helped him get in touch with socially conservative religious people was his eldest son, George W. Bush. Young
George had kicked a serious drinking habit two years earlier and had found
God. "It was goodbye Jack Daniels, hello Jesus," he said.

Republicans zeroed in with special zeal on what they called the "re-
volving door prison policy" of Dukakis's governorship. This was a program —
instituted by a Republican predecessor — which enabled prisoners to take
brief furloughs. Most states, including California during Reagan's tenure
as governor, had comparable programs, as did the federal prison system,
though only Massachusetts made it available to lifers.[12] One of these Mas-

---

8. Robert Reich, *The Resurgent Liberal* (New York, 1989), 69.
9. For religious issues in 1988, see Wills, *Under God*; and Martin, *With God on Our
   Side*, 263–66, 278–82, 294.
10. Congressional Quarterly, *Guide to the Presidency* (Washington, 1989), 197. There
    had been 201 labor PACs in 1974 and 297 in 1980.
11. Kevin Phillips, *Arrogant Capital: Washington, Wall Street, and the Frustration of
    American Politics* (Boston, 1994), 39.
12. Wills, *Under God*, 70–75.

sachusetts prisoners was Willie Horton, a convicted first-degree murderer, who on a weekend furlough had repeatedly beaten and stabbed a man and assaulted and raped his fiancée. Dukakis, defending the program, did not discontinue it until April 1988. Some of Bush's state party committees and independent groups circulated pictures of Horton, an ominous-looking black man, and produced TV ads that showed streams of prisoners going in and out of prison via a turnstile. Though Bush's national committee disavowed material that identified and pictured the prisoner, there was no doubting that the Bush team knew and approved of the ads.[13]

Tactics like these revealed that Bush, for all his gentility, could be ruthless in pursuit of his ambitions. They also indicated that social and cultural issues involving crime and race continued to be large and divisive in American life, and that Republicans would use these issues, as they had since 1968, in order to blunt the appeal of bread-and-butter economic platforms favoring Democrats. In 1988, these negative tactics virtually dominated Bush's campaign, making it difficult to know what he stood for. At times, he dismissed "the vision thing"—that is, the idea that he should try to sell any sweeping or inspiring message (as Reagan had tried to do) to the American people.

GOP tactics such as these relegated larger issues, such as the enormous budget deficit, to the periphery and placed Dukakis on the defensive. Until the last two weeks of the race, when he campaigned more vigorously, he seemed almost unaware of how effectively the Republicans had identified him—and the Democratic Party—as "soft" on issues that ranged from crime to foreign policy. Dukakis also seemed reluctant to take the offensive. When he was asked in a presidential debate if he would favor the death penalty for someone who raped and murdered his wife, he responded by saying that he would not and then by offering a cool, impersonal, and—it seemed to many onlookers—politically fatal defense of his opposition to capital punishment.[14] Bush referred to his opponent as the "ice man."

Dukakis labored under one final, perhaps crucial political disadvantage: In 1988, Republicans claimed credit for having lifted the spirits of Americans during the previous eight years. Though Iran-contra was fresh in voters' memories, Reagan still enjoyed widespread popularity. Senate confirmation in the spring of the INF treaty solidified a popular impression that he had been resolute in his handling of the Cold War. Perhaps

13. Parmet, *George Bush*, 335–36, 350–53.
14. White, *New Politics of Old Values*, 161; Wills, *Under God*, 59–60; Parmet, 355.

most important, the economy had been growing slowly but uninterrupt-edly since 1983. Bush, as Reagan's vice president, benefited politically from the more optimistic national mood that had developed since the Bad Old Days of the Carter years.

Results of the election in November were hardly encouraging to advo-cates of democratic government: Only 54.2 percent of eligible voters turned out, the lowest in a presidential election since 1924. Why so low? Observ-ers speculated that neither Bush nor Dukakis was an inspiring candidate, that the nasty campaign had disgusted voters, that the issues had not been especially gripping, and that a great many people (as in earlier elections) cared more about personal matters than about what their political leaders were promising. Whatever the causes, the low turnout prompted rising alarm that Americans were becoming steadily more apathetic about poli-tics and public affairs.[15]

Though Bush did not match Reagan's resounding success of 1984, he won easily, thereby becoming the nation's forty-first president. (When his son George W. Bush became the forty-third in 2001, many people labeled the father "Bush 41.") Receiving 48.9 million votes to 41.8 million for Dukakis, he captured 53.4 percent of the vote to his opponent's 45.6 per-cent. He carried forty states for a triumph in the electoral college of 426 to 111. He was especially strong in the South, which (like Reagan in 1984) he swept, and where he won an estimated 66 percent of the white vote. Ana-lysts concluded that he received 60 percent overall of middle-class votes and that he even bested Dukakis, 50 percent to 49 percent, among women voters.[16] Three straight GOP victories in presidential elections indicated that the Republican Party, which had been badly battered by Watergate, had staged a considerable comeback.

As in 1984, however, the results in 1988 did not indicate that a funda-mental political realignment had occurred.[17] Democrats maintained ma-jorities in the Senate and the House that they had held since recapturing the Senate in 1986, prompting Democratic representative Pat Schroeder of Colorado to wisecrack, "Coattails? Bush got elected in a bikini."[18] In 1989–90, Bush would have to contend with Democratic advantages of 55

15. See Michael McDonald and Samuel Popkin, "The Myth of the Vanishing Voter," *American Political Science Review* 95 (Dec. 2001), 963–74, and note 105, chapter 4, for a corrective to this pessimistic view of American political engagement.

16. John Judis and Ruy Teixeira, *The Emerging Democratic Majority* (New York, 2002), 25–6; *World Almanac, 2001*, 40.

17. Greene, *The Presidency of George Bush*, 41–43.

18. White, *New Politics of Old Values*, 168.

to 45 in the Senate and of 259 to 174 in the House. The elections of 1990 gave Democrats still more strength on the Hill. Bush, like Nixon, Ford, and Reagan before him, had to cope with divided government and with high levels of partisan antagonism.

TO MANAGE AMERICAN FOREIGN POLICY, which was his primary interest as president, Bush assembled an experienced team of advisers. James Baker, a Texan political supporter who had served Reagan as chief of staff and secretary of the treasury, became secretary of state. Richard Cheney, Ford's staff coordinator before becoming an influential congressman from Wyoming, took over defense and quickly established a high level of control over the Pentagon.[19] Brent Scowcroft, a retired air force general and professor of Russian history at West Point, was selected as national security adviser. A well-informed and efficient man, he had held this post under Ford. In October 1989, General Colin Powell became chairman of the Joint Chiefs of Staff, the first African American to occupy the position. Though tensions occasionally divided these advisers, they were a cohesive team on most issues.[20]

By the time this team left office in January 1993, a number of late-developing issues remained unresolved. One of these involved Yugoslavia, which imploded in 1991–92 amidst savage fighting between Eastern Orthodox Serbs, Roman Catholic Croats, and Bosnian Muslims. A host of outraged observers, including United Nations peacekeepers sent to the area in November 1992, reported evidence of massive "ethnic cleansing," especially by Bosnian Serbs backed by the Serbian regime in Belgrade. Throughout 1992, stories about Serbian-run death camps and "genocide" appeared in American newspapers. By the end of the year it was estimated that more than 1.7 million Muslim refugees were scattered about one-time Yugoslavia and nearby nations. The Bush administration, however, was focusing at the time on the election campaign and was seriously distracted by a severe recession. It was also hoping to maintain cordial relations with Russia, which had historically supported the Serbs. NATO allies, moreover, opposed significant military action in the region. The United

19. Bush's first choice as defense secretary was former Texas senator John Tower, but he failed to be confirmed.
20. James Mann, *Rise of the Vulcans: The History of Bush's War Cabinet* (New York, 2004), 184; Greenstein, *The Presidential Difference*, 165–67. Scowcroft added to his staff a person who was to become national security adviser and secretary of state in the administration of George W. Bush, Condoleezza Rice. An African American, Rice was a professor at Stanford University and an expert in Soviet affairs.

States and its Western allies placed an embargo on arms to the area, even though such a policy harmed the Bosnian Muslims, who had little in the way of economic or military resources, more than it did the Serbs or the Croats. Powell and high officials at the Pentagon feared that American military engagement in the region would lead to another disaster like Vietnam. For all these reasons, the Bush administration kept its distance from the Balkans.[21]

Bush left other foreign policies in an uncompleted state. In late 1992, his administration succeeded in negotiating a North American Free Trade Agreement (NAFTA), which proposed to eliminate tariffs between Canada, the United States, and Mexico. But when he left office in 1993, the pact still needed Congressional assent, which was expected to be difficult. In the last month of his administration, he sent 28,000 American troops on a humanitarian mission to help U.N. peacekeeping forces in Somalia, where famine threatened the population. Though the Americans were not expected to remain for long, they were still in the country when he departed from the White House. Dealing with the tense situation in Somalia, like gaining approval for NAFTA, fell into the lap of his successor.

In Latin America, however, the president was luckier than Reagan, who had been nearly ruined by the Iran-contra scandal. In February 1990, the Sandinistas in Nicaragua were badly defeated by a coalition of opponents in a free election. The United States then ended its trade embargo, and the contras ceased operations. By 1992, the civil war in El Salvador that had caused the death of 75,000 people in the 1980s—most of them peasants who had been fighting against their oppressive government— had finally come to an end. While savage battling continued in Guatemala, and while people throughout Central America continued to cope with widespread poverty, some of the warfare that had bloodied the region, and drawn the United States deeply into the area, had abated at last.

In late 1989, Bush acted to remove another source of turmoil in the region: Panamanian strongman Manuel Noriega. Like many anti-Communist tyrants, Noriega had received generous American support over the years. Under Reagan, the CIA had provided his regime with military and economic assistance, in return for which Noriega had aided the contras. But when the Sandinistas began to weaken in the late 1980s, his usefulness to the United States declined. Moreover, Noriega was a cruel and corrupt

---

21. For Bush and the Balkans, see Halberstam, *War in a Time of Peace*, 24–46, 86–100, 121–42; and William Hitchcock, *The Struggle for Europe: The Turbulent History of a Divided Continent, 1945–2002* (New York, 2003), 380–95.

dictator who had enriched himself through gifts from the CIA and through drug trafficking. In May 1989, he annulled a presidential election, after which his henchmen beat and badly bloodied Guillermo Endara, the legitimately elected candidate. Bush, well aware that the Panama Canal would come under Panamanian control at the end of 1999, also worried about what a criminal like Noriega might do if he were allowed to operate such a strategic asset. In mid-December 1989, when Noriega's men shot and killed an American marine lieutenant, beat a navy lieutenant, and beat and groped the naval officer's wife in Panama City, Bush, Cheney, and Powell resolved to topple him.

The intervention, which Bush named Operation Just Cause, was the largest American military move since Vietnam. It featured the dispatch of 24,000 paratroopers who made a dramatic early morning assault on December 20 at key locations in Panama. Navy SEALs landed on the coast. After bloody street fighting, American troops quickly secured the Canal Zone and Panama City, only to learn that Noriega had taken refuge in the residence of the papal nuncio in the city. To roust him, American troops and tanks surrounded the site and blared earsplitting rock music twenty-four hours a day. Military vehicles gunned their engines to add to the racket. After a show of bravado that lasted until January 3, Noriega surrendered when elite American forces threatened to attack. A day later he was in jail in Miami.

Bush's handling of the situation in Panama bothered some critics, who pointed out that civilians died in the fighting. Civil libertarians later complained that Noriega was imprisoned for more than a year while awaiting a trial in the United States that could hardly be fair. In April 1992, Noriega was convicted on eight charges, including cocaine trafficking, money laundering, and racketeering, and sentenced to forty years in federal prison.[22] But Bush's Panama operation energized his administration: With the Cold War ending, America, at last, had carried out a large-scale military operation. It was highly popular in the United States. The fighting killed 23 Americans and wounded 394. Endara was immediately sworn in as the legitimately elected president of Panama. Though he struggled during his five-year term, he and his successors managed to promote democratic institutions, including an independent press and judiciary, competitive political parties, and fair elections. Given the sad history of American military intervention in Latin America, these were heartening results.[23]

22. Later reduced to thirty years, with eligibility for parole in 2006.
23. Greene, *The Presidency of George Bush*, 100–106; Parmet, *George Bush*, 411–19.

While dealing with conflict in Latin America, Bush had to cope with events that arose from the sudden and stunning collapse of Communism in the Soviet Union and in Eastern Europe. Some conservatives, having chafed at Reagan's accommodation with the Soviets, urged him to take a harder line with Gorbachev, who, while remaining Communist, was struggling to keep several nationalistic Soviet republics from breaking free and declaring their independence. Advocates of human rights also pressed Bush to act firmly against the Chinese Communists—the "butchers of Beijing" who killed hundreds, maybe thousands, of pro-democracy protesters in Tiananmen Square in June 1989.

Bush and his advisers moved cautiously to manage problems such as these. At first he maintained a wary distance from Gorbachev, and he threatened to toughen trade policies involving the People's Republic of China unless it released dissidents and embraced more moderate policies. By 1990, however, he had forged a fairly satisfying personal relationship with Gorbachev, and the historic developments of 1990–92—the reunification of Germany within NATO, the independence of the Baltic states, the removal of Soviet troops from the satellite nations of Eastern Europe, the sovereignty of Soviet republics, the fall from power of Gorbachev and the rise to authority of President Boris Yeltsin of Russia—took place with minimal loss of blood. Bush also worked to patch up relations with China, which had become an important trading partner. After the administration worked out a deal with the Chinese that provided amnesty for several hundred Tiananmen Square protestors, Sino-American relations improved slightly.[24]

This did not mean that advocates of a tough American foreign policy disappeared from the scene. Defense Secretary Cheney, among others, believed that the United States must step vigorously into the vacuum that was developing after the disintegration of the Soviet Union. In 1992, Cheney joined Paul Wolfowitz, his deputy undersecretary for policy, in supporting staffers who had drafted an ambitious plan, the Defense Planning Guidance, concerning America's international obligations. It stated that the United States in the new post–Cold War world must "discourage [all other nations] from challenging our leadership or seeking to overturn the established political and economic order."[25] Though aimed in part at poten-

24. Parmet, *George Bush*, 398–400.
25. *New York Times*, Oct. 26, 2002. Cheney became vice president under George W. Bush ("Bush 43") in 2001, and Wolfowitz became Cheney's deputy. Both men were known to be strong advocates within this administration of war against Iraq, which was launched in early 2003.

tial competitors such as Japan and Germany, the document was more broadly a statement that the United States must maintain unrivaled superpower status as a colossus against all comers. Then, as in later years, it remained a guiding document of American foreign and military policy.[26]

In keeping with this prescription, the Bush administration maintained fairly high spending on defense—thereby angering liberals who were seeking a "peace dividend" to be used for domestic social programs. Though expenditures for defense—and for overseas intelligence—did decline a little over the four years of Bush's presidency, Cheney and other high-ranking officials continued to embrace the Powell Doctrine, which, carried over from the Reagan years, maintained that the United States must maintain a high level of military readiness so that if it ever had to fight a war, it could do so with overwhelming force, thereby protecting American soldiers from the risk of Vietnam-like casualties.[27]

For the most part, the president and his advisers acted prudently in dealing with the dissolution of the Soviet Union. In 1991, Bush concluded an agreement with Gorbachev that led to the removal of most tactical weapons from overseas positions and reduced the alert status of nuclear arsenals. In START I, negotiated in mid-1991, the two leaders agreed to cut back their nuclear weaponry—from 13,000 warheads in 1990 to 9,000 in 1992 and to 7,000 by 1995.[28] Shortly before leaving office in 1993, Bush and Yeltsin negotiated START II, which placed the top limits for each side in the future at between 3,000 and 3,500 warheads. This agreement showed that the United States and its once most powerful enemy were building on the breathtaking advances accomplished by Reagan and Gorbachev. Most observers of American foreign policy gave Bush good marks for his diplomacy with Moscow, for his role in advancing the reunification of Germany, and for his attempts to involve Western allies in efforts to assist the fragile new states that were replacing Soviet republics as well as the Soviet Union's formerly Communist satellites in Eastern Europe.[29]

26. Mann, *Rise of the Vulcans*, 209–15. The final version of this document, issued under Cheney's name in early 1993, was reworded but reiterated the central point: The United States must maintain permanent military superiority in the world.
27. United States defense spending declined from $299 billion in 1990 to $282 billion in 1994. In constant 1996 dollars this was a decrease of roughly 16 percent, from $354 billion to $298 billion. *Stat. Abst.*, 2002, 326.
28. *New York Times*, Nov. 14, 2001.
29. Frances FitzGerald, "George Bush and the World," *New York Review of Books*, Sept. 26, 2002, 80–81.

WITH ACCOMPLISHMENTS SUCH AS THESE, Bush might well have expected to go down in history as one of America's more skillful presidents in the management of foreign policy. By the time he left office, he was especially well remembered as the president who led a carefully established and formidable international alliance into a war against Iraq. Though the war did not prevent instability from returning to the deeply troubled Middle East, the coalition swept to triumph after triumph in the fighting itself.

In the eyes of Bush — and of many other heads of state — the major source of trouble in the region was President Saddam Hussein of Iraq. After taking power in 1979, Hussein had come to imagine himself as a modern Nebuchadnezzar who would lead the Arab world to magnificent heights. Among his idols were Hitler and Stalin. Over time he built a string of lavish palaces for himself and his family. Statues and portraits of him proliferated in the country. In 1980, he opened war against neighboring Iran, a far larger nation. The fighting lasted eight years, during which Hussein used chemical weapons against the Iranians, before the war sputtered to an inconclusive end in 1988. During this time Hussein supported efforts to manufacture nuclear bombs, and he murdered hundreds of thousands of his own people, most of them Kurds and Shiites who were restive under the oppressive rule of his tightly organized clique of Sunni Muslim followers.[30] In March 1988, he authorized use of chemical weapons in the Kurdish village of Halabja, killing 5,000 people in one day.

Reagan administration officials, believing Iran to be the bigger threat to stability in the Middle East, had turned a mostly blind eye to Hussein's excesses and had cautiously supported his regime between 1981 and 1988. Hussein benefited during the Iran-Iraq war from American intelligence and combat-planning assistance. As late as July 1990, America's ambassador to Iraq may have unintentionally led Hussein to think that the United States would not fight to stop him if he decided to attack oil-rich Kuwait, Iraq's neighbor to the south. But the Iraqi-American relationship had always been uneasy, and it collapsed on August 2, 1990, when Iraq launched an unprovoked and quickly successful invasion of Kuwait. Bush, sensitive to memories of the quagmire of Vietnam, and conscious of the potentially vast implications of military intervention, was taken aback by Iraq's bold aggression. Britain's "Iron Lady," Prime Minister Margaret Thatcher, was

30. Human rights groups in Iraq later placed the number of Iraqis killed, many of them thrown into mass graves, during Saddam Hussein's regime at more than 300,000 between 1979 and 2002. *New York Times*, Dec. 23, 2003.

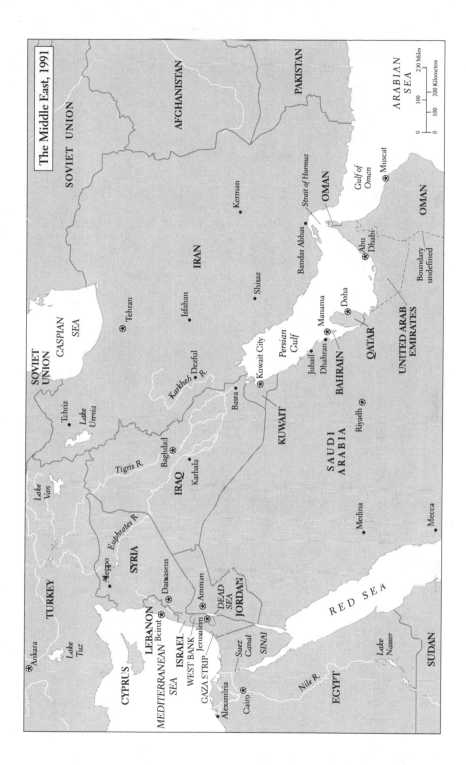

The Middle East, 1991

said to have tried to stiffen his spine. "Remember, George," she was rumored to have warned, "this is no time to go wobbly."[31]

In fact, Bush needed no stiffening. Quickly imposing economic sanctions on Iraq, he emerged as the strongest voice within the administration against Hussein's aggression. Declaring, "This will not stand," the president overrode warnings from advisers, notably Powell, that war against Iraq would be costly and dangerous. Cheney and Powell estimated at the time that as many as 30,000 American soldiers might die in such a conflict.[32] Sending Secretary of State Baker on a host of overseas missions, Bush succeeded in enlisting thirty-four countries in a multinational coalition that stood ready to contribute in some way to an American-led fight against Iraq. In late November, Bush secured passage of a U.N. Security Council resolution authorizing the use of force to drive Iraq from Kuwait if Hussein did not pull out by January 15, 1991. The resolution passed, twelve to two, with the Soviet Union among the twelve. China, one of the five nations with a veto power, abstained. Only Yemen and Cuba dissented.[33]

From the beginning, however, Bush realized that Hussein, who claimed Kuwait as Iraqi territory, had no intention of backing down. Like Carter, who had pronounced that America would go to war if necessary in order to prevent enemies from controlling the Persian Gulf, he was prepared to fight against aggressors in the region. So while the wheels of diplomacy were turning, he energized the Powell Doctrine. No longer fearful of Soviet military designs on Western Europe, he pulled a number of American troops from Germany in order to bolster what soon became a formidable coalition fighting force. The coalition, which had the nervous support of several Muslim nations (including Pakistan, Afghanistan, Egypt, Syria, and Turkey)—and which was to rely heavily on the willingness of Saudi Arabia to serve as a staging area—ultimately included troops from five Arab states. More than 460,000 American troops, 1,500 aircraft, and sixty-five warships moved to the Persian Gulf region.[34]

As Bush prepared for a conflict that he believed to be inevitable, he was reluctant to seek the approval of the heavily Democratic Congress. In

31. Parmet, *George Bush*, 453–54.
32. *U.S. News & World Report, Triumph Without Victory: The Unreported History of the Persian Gulf War* (New York, 1992), 141; Mann, *Rise of the Vulcans*, 182–97.
33. Greene, *The Presidency of George Bush*, 113–33.
34. The troops were more than twice the number that the United States and its allies dispatched in the next war against Iraq, in 2003. Congress estimated that the cost of the Gulf War of 1991 was $61 billion. Other estimates rise as high as $71 billion. Coalition partners, especially the Gulf States and Saudi Arabia, paid an estimated $42 billion of these costs. *U.S. News & World Report, Triumph Without Victory*, 413.

January 1991, however, he succumbed to political pressure urging him to do so. As he had anticipated, most Democrats opposed him. Some charged that the president, who had made millions in the oil business, was eager for war in order to protect wealthy oil interests in the United States. Others argued that Hussein should be subjected to further economic and diplomatic pressure, which, they said, would force him to come to terms. Some foes of war worried that the president might authorize an invasion and takeover of Iraq itself, thereby miring the United States in a drawn-out, potentially perilous occupation.

Bush got what he wanted from the Hill, though by narrow margins. By heavily partisan votes, Congress passed a joint resolution authorizing war pursuant to the U.N. resolution of November 1990. The vote in the House was 251 to 182, with Republicans approving, 165 to 3, and Democrats opposing, 179 to 86. In the Senate, which decided on January 11, the tally was 52 to 47, with Republicans in favor, 42 to 2, and Democrats against, 45 to 10. Among the handful of Senate Democrats who voted for the resolution was Al Gore Jr. of Tennessee. Among those opposed was John Kerry of Massachusetts.[35] This was the closest senatorial vote on war in United States history.

There was no doubting that Hussein's conquest threatened Western oil interests. It was estimated at the time that Iraq produced 11 percent, and Kuwait 9 percent, of world supplies. Neighboring Saudi Arabia, the leading producer, accounted for 26 percent. The Persian Gulf area had more than half of the world's proven reserves. The United States, having become increasingly dependent on overseas production, at that time imported a quarter of its oil from the Gulf. Fervent supporters of the war, such as Defense Secretary Cheney and Wolfowitz, were keenly aware of the large economic assets that Iraq's conquest had threatened.[36]

In defending his position, however, Bush insisted that the key issue was Iraq's naked aggression, which must not be tolerated. He also maintained that Hussein was secretly developing the capacity to make nuclear bombs.[37] He displayed special outrage at Hussein's cruel and murderous treatment of his own people. Hussein, he charged, was "worse than Hitler." When the U.N. deadline of January 15 passed, he wasted no time in going to war, which started on January 16.

35. In 2002, Kerry voted to authorize President George W. Bush to go to war against Iraq.
36. Mann, *Rise of the Vulcans*, 184–85.
37. *New York Times*, March 27, 2003.

The coalition attack featured two phases. The first entailed massive bombing of Kuwait, Baghdad, and other Iraqi cities and installations. This lasted thirty-nine days. Coalition aircraft fired off 89,000 tons of explosives, a minority of them laser-guided "smart bombs" and cruise missiles, at these targets. The bombing was frightening, causing the desertion of an estimated 100,000 or more of the 400,000 or so Iraqi troops that were believed to have been initially deployed. It was also devastating. The air offensive destroyed Iraq's power grid and sundered its military communications. A number of contemporary observers thought that the bombing created severe food shortages, damaged facilities guarding against water pollution, provoked outbreaks of cholera and typhoid, and seriously disrupted medical care.[38]

Some of this air war was featured on network television and on Cable News Network (CNN), which since its creation in 1980 had established itself as a successful network providing twenty-four-hours-a-day news of events all over the world. CNN offered mesmerizing coverage from Baghdad of streaking missiles and flashing explosions. Iraqi Scud missiles were zooming off toward targets in Israel and Saudi Arabia, and American Patriot missiles were shooting up to intercept them. Though one of the Scuds (of the eighty-six or so believed to have been fired during the war) killed twenty-eight American military personnel in Dhahran, Saudi Arabia, most of them did no serious damage. American claims to the contrary, later studies concluded that the Patriots had relatively little luck hitting the Scuds. The Scuds, however, did prompt a widely told joke: "Question: How many Iraqis does it take to fire a Scud missile at Israel? Answer: Three, one to arm, one to fire, the third to watch CNN to see where it landed." President Bush avidly followed CNN, which he said was a quicker source of news than the CIA.

With Iraqi defenses rendered virtually helpless, coalition forces undertook the second stage, Operation Desert Storm, of the Gulf War. Led by American general Norman Schwarzkopf, this was the ultimate demonstration of the Powell Doctrine, which called for the dispatch of overwhelmingly superior military power. Some of the troops used GPS gadgetry enabling them to navigate the desert. In only 100 hours between February 23 and 27, this army shattered Iraqi resistance. Tens of thousands of Iraqi troops were taken prisoner. Most of the rest fled from Kuwait into Iraq.

38. Ibid., April 20, 2003. For accounts of the fighting, see Michael Gordon and Bernard Trainor, *The Generals' War: The Inside Story of the War in the Gulf* (Boston, 1995); and Robert Divine, "The Persian Gulf War Revisited: Tactical Victory, Strategic Failure?" *Diplomatic History* 24 (Winter 2000), 129–38.

Unreliable early estimates of Iraqi soldiers killed varied wildly, ranging as high as 100,000.

The actual numbers, most later estimates concluded, had probably been far smaller. One carefully calculated count, by a former Defense Intelligence Agency military analyst, conceded that estimates varied greatly, but set the maximum number of Iraqi military casualties from the air and ground wars at 9,500 dead and 26,500 wounded. His minimum estimates were 1,500 dead and 3,000 wounded. Civilian deaths, he added, may have been fewer than 1,000. American losses may have been tiny by comparison. Most estimates agreed that the number of United States soldiers killed in action was 148 (at least 35 of them from friendly fire) and that the number who died in non-battle accidents was 145. A total of 467 American troops were wounded in battle. These same estimates concluded that a total of 65 soldiers from other coalition nations (39 from Arab nations, 24 from Britain, 2 from France) had also been killed in battle.[39]

As Iraqi soldiers fled on February 27, Bush stopped the fighting. The abrupt end allowed many of Hussein's assets, including Russian-made tanks and units of his elite Republican Guard, to escape destruction or capture. When the coalition armies ground to a halt, they left Baghdad and other important cities in the hands of their enemies. Saddam Hussein and his entourage licked their wounds but regrouped and remained in control until another American-led war toppled him from power.

Needless to say, the decision to stop the fighting aroused controversy, much of which resurfaced twelve years later when President George W. Bush (Bush 43) sent American troops into another war against Saddam Hussein's Iraq. Bush 41 called off the fighting in 1991 for several reasons. First, he and his advisers were said to have worried that coalition forces would be accused of "butchery"—a "turkey shoot"—if they slaughtered near-defenseless Iraqi soldiers in full flight on a "Highway of Death" into Iraq. He insisted, however, that his exit strategy had always been clear: to

39. For the estimates cited here of Iraqi troop sizes, desertions, and casualties, see John Heidenrich, "The Gulf War: How Many Iraqis Died?" *Foreign Policy* 90 (Spring 1993), 108–25. Heidenrich rejects a range of other early estimates, most of which were higher. Generally agreed-upon statistics concerning American and coalition casualties may be found in Rick Atkinson, *Crusade: The Untold Story of the Persian Gulf War* (Boston, 1993), 491–92; U. S. *News & World Report, Triumph Without Victory*, vii–ix, 402–13; *New York Times*, April 20, 2003; and *World Almanac, 2003*, 209. Later, 15,000 to 20,000 U. S. soldiers reported symptoms—fatigue, aches and pains, difficulty in thinking, loss of memory—that they attributed to service in the Gulf at the time of the war. These ailments were collectively given the name of Gulf War Syndrome. *New York Times*, March 25, 2003.

free Kuwait and to drive Hussein back into Iraq. This had also been the mandate of the U.N. and congressional resolutions. "I do not believe," Bush said later, "in what I call 'mission creep.'"[40]

In refusing to go after Saddam Hussein, the president was acutely aware of how difficult it had been to locate Noriega in the immediate aftermath of the American assault on Panama, a far smaller nation. Bush pointed out another important consideration: Some of America's coalition partners, such as Syria and Egypt, feared a disruption of the balance of power in the Middle East. Worried that unrest in Iraq would spread and threaten their own regimes, they opposed a wider mission that might have toppled Hussein from power.

Bush also figured that Operation Desert Storm had badly damaged Iraq's military capacity. It had in fact helped to finish off Hussein's never well managed efforts to build nuclear bombs. To ensure that Iraq would remain weak in the future, Hussein was forced to agree to a prohibition of imports of military value and to refrain from rearming or developing weapons of mass destruction. United Nations inspectors were authorized to oversee these restrictions and remained in Iraq into 1998. The U.N. also established "no-fly zones" over Shiite and Kurdish areas of Iraq, from which Hussein's aircraft were prohibited. An embargo on the export for sale of Iraqi goods, notably oil, was expected to limit Hussein's capacity to rearm. These economic sanctions (combined with Hussein's greed and callousness toward his own people) are believed to have been a cause of considerable suffering among the people of Iraq before December 1996, when Hussein finally agreed to a U.N.-managed "oil-for-food" arrangement that enabled him to buy food and medical supplies from proceeds of limited oil sales.[41]

40. Comment in 1999, reported in *Providence Journal*, Dec. 16, 2003.
41. David Rieff, "Were Sanctions Right?" *New York Review of Books*, July 27, 2003, 41–46. Though most observers believe that international sanctions against Iraq helped to prevent Hussein from developing weapons of mass destruction, it later became clear that Hussein—both before and especially after the $64 billion oil-for-food arrangements that lasted until early 2003—managed to siphon off an estimated $10.9 billion ($1.7 billion of which went into his own pockets), mainly by illegally smuggling oil to nearby countries like Jordan, Turkey, Syria, and Egypt. Illicit surcharges and kickbacks further enriched his inner circle. United Nations officials overseeing the oil-for-food program badly mismanaged it, and British and American officials charged with monitoring some of the arrangements did a poor job of preventing smuggling. Hussein also succeeded in hiding large caches of conventional arms, components, and high explosives—some of which Iraqi rebels later used with telling effect during the American-led occupation of Iraq that began in 2003. *New York Times*, Feb. 29, June 4, Nov. 16, Dec. 8, 2004, April 24, 2005.

In 1992, Defense Secretary Cheney laid out the administration's rationale for not taking Baghdad, capturing Hussein, and trying to reform the country. It was very different from the arguments that he was to make as vice president eleven years later, when he defended Bush 43's occupation of Iraq. Hussein, Cheney said in 1992, would have been very hard to find. Moreover, would the United States be able to accomplish significant reform in Iraq? Though Iraq had a sizeable middle class, and might in time establish democratic institutions, such a process might take many years. Given the fratricidal hatreds that divided Shiites, Sunnis, and Kurds (a non-Arab people) in Iraq, it was difficult to conceive of a stable alliance of factions that might arise to rule the country. How long would American and coalition forces, besieged by guerrilla fighters, have to remain before Iraq—a product of long ago boundary-making by the British—could become anything like a constitutional republic? As Cheney put it at the time, "Once we had rounded him [Saddam Hussein] up and gotten rid of his government, then the question is what do you put in his place?" It was also clear in 1992 that the Bush administration, never having intended to undertake such long-range tasks, had given little thought to an "exit strategy" involving postwar occupation and reform.[42]

The dearth of postwar planning became painfully clear in the spring of 1991 when thousands of Kurdish and Shiite people in northern and southern Iraq, having earlier been encouraged by the United States, rose in rebellion against Hussein's rule. They were crushed. The savagery of Hussein's reprisals embittered many Kurds and Shiites, who did not forget that the United States had failed to protect them. Nor did the coalition's military successes of 1991 advance warm feelings about America among other Middle Eastern people. Arab leaders—all of them authoritarian—continued to worry that the war, having battered Hussein, might stir restless democratic yearnings in their own countries. Many Muslims especially resented the expanded postwar presence of the American military—and of liberal American cultural practices—in Bahrain, Oman, and Qatar, and especially in Saudi Arabia, which was the Holy Land of Islam.[43] The close relations that the United States maintained with Israel, which Bush had persuaded to stay out of the war, remained an especially infuriating source of anti-American feeling in the area.

42. Interview with the BBC later reported in *New York Times*, Dec. 16, 2003; ibid., Sept. 30, 2004.
43. Osama bin Laden, a mastermind of Muslim terrorism in later years, repeatedly emphasized the evil of America's presence in these nations—especially in Saudi Arabia, his native land—and advocated terrorist activities as a means of driving the Americans out.

Second-guessing of Bush, however, did not harm his political prospects at the time. After all, the prewar diplomacy had been skillful, and the military triumph had been glorious. The coalition had liberated Kuwait, punished aggression, and preserved Western access to oil in the region. Bush exulted, "By God, we've kicked the Vietnam Syndrome once and for all."

This was a considerable exaggeration: Many of the administration's major decisions during the crisis—rejecting the rotation of troops, managing popular perceptions of the war by keeping the media away from the battlefield, reliance on the Powell Doctrine—were adopted in order to minimize the likelihood of another Vietnam-like experience. But there was no doubting the happy political consequences of the war for the president. Shortly after the fighting stopped, a *New York Times*/CBS poll reported that he had a popular approval rating of 89 percent. This was the highest for a president since the appearance of these polls in 1977.

IN HIS FIRST INAUGURAL ADDRESS, Bush deliberately distanced himself a little from Reaganesque foes of big government. He pledged "to make kinder the face of the nation and gentler the face of the world." But he also reiterated a campaign theme: that government alone could not guarantee a gentler domestic scene. Americans must rely on a "thousand points of light"—"all the community organizations that are spread like stars throughout the nation, doing good."

Neither then nor later did Bush imagine that government could ignore domestic policy, but international relations most engaged him. As during the campaign, when he had dismissed "the vision thing," he did not believe that it was his task to propose a large number of new domestic initiatives. A fiscal conservative, he was painfully aware of the huge deficits that had mounted during the Reagan years—deficits that crippled ambitious domestic ventures. Bush also recognized the obvious: Divided government, the result of large Democratic majorities in both houses of Congress, would stymie most plans that he might have proposed. He therefore allowed his chief of staff, former New Hampshire governor John Sununu, to oversee many domestic concerns. Sununu, a blunt and undiplomatic administrator, made few friends on the Hill before being forced by revelations about his use of perks to quit in December 1991.[44]

One policy area that Bush did bring to America's domestic agenda was education. In this regard he was reacting in part to the ferment that the

44. Parmet, *George Bush*, 492–93, 500.

much-debated condemnation of American educational practices, *A Nation at Risk*, had stirred after its release in 1983.[45] Like the commissioners who wrote that report, Bush believed that schools had to adopt higher standards in order to promote greater academic achievement. Though average SAT scores had stabilized in the 1980s, they remained below their levels of the 1960s.[46] In the fall of 1989, Bush called the nation's governors to Charlottesville, Virginia, for an "Education Summit," which he hoped would stimulate debate at the state level. The governors, notably Bill Clinton of Arkansas, seemed receptive. In April 1991, Bush called on Congress to approve his plan for America 2000. This enterprise envisaged more detailed standards in core academic subjects and encouraged states to develop rigorous testing of children in the fourth and eighth grades. Bush also backed federal demonstration grants for vouchers that would help parents to send their children to private schools.[47]

America 2000 got nowhere in Congress. Liberals opposed the idea of vouchers and worried about the possible introduction of national testing. As they had since the 1960s, they urged more federal spending for programs such as Title I of the Elementary and Secondary Education Act of 1965, so as to advance greater educational opportunity for minorities and for the poor. Bush, however, believed that spending for education was primarily a state-local concern. Like most Republicans, he thought that funding for "compensatory education" had not accomplished much. He called for less, not more, federal education money in his budget for fiscal year 1992.[48]

Still, over time Bush's emphasis on achievement and standards was significant. No president since LBJ had done more to dramatize the problems of schools. Like *A Nation at Risk*, Bush's thinking exposed the growth of two powerful trends in ideas about education. The first revealed the force of rising expectations — in this case, expectations that schools should enhance academic achievement so as to promote America's international competitiveness. A well-educated student of the 1990s, many contemporaries had come to believe, must be equipped to deal with a far more

45. See chapter 1.
46. Average SAT verbal scores were 502 in 1980, 500 in 1990. Average SAT math scores rose a little, from 492 in 1980 to 501 in 1990. Average verbal scores in 1970 had been 537, average math scores, 512. *Stat. Abst.*, 2002, 159. For school issues, including the issue of tests, see chapter 1.
47. Greene, *The Presidency of George Bush*, 69–71.
48. John Jennings, *Why National Standards and Tests? Politics and the Quest for Better Schools* (Thousand Oaks, Calif., 1998), 17–20, 25–32.

technologically complex world than his or her parents had needed to be. Higher percentages of young people had to be well prepared for serious college-level work.

The second was that what mattered in educational reform was not so much providing wider *access* to equal opportunity — the emphasis of Title I — as ensuring academic *results*. The key, reformers said, was to improve "outputs," not to focus on "inputs," such as money for compensatory education aimed at the poor. A focus on achievement — and on hard-nosed assessments via testing — developed bipartisan political support in the 1990s, leading conservatives as well as liberals to support a degree of federal oversight of public schools that Bush 41 scarcely could have imagined while he was president. In 1994, Congress passed a program, Goals 2000, which provided money to states for such purposes. A so-called No Child Left Behind Act, triumphantly signed by Bush 43 in January 2002, empowered the federal government to take an unprecedented role in public education — so much so that many people, raising the banner of states' rights, came to complain after 2002 of excessive federal intrusion. Not for the first time, "conservatives," who commonly complain of big government, had drifted from their ideological moorings.[49]

Concerning most other domestic issues during Bush's presidency, congressional Democrats took charge. During his four years in office they skirmished repeatedly with him over environmental policies. In this area of policy, Bush had a mixed record. He issued executive orders that protected or restored 1.7 million acres of wetlands and doubled funding for parks and wildlife refuges.[50] On the other hand, environmental activists lamented his refusal to sign a treaty that was aimed at preserving the biodiversity of plants. The United States was the only developed nation that did not sign. Bush demanded the watering down of another treaty, to curb the causes of global warming, before he agreed to back it.

Liberals in Congress scored victories on a few fronts. They succeeded in almost doubling appropriations for the Head Start program for children in families below the poverty line. In 1990, their most active year, they expanded federal funding for welfare recipients needing day care, approved amendments that strengthened clean air protection, passed a family and medical leave bill that authorized workers to take up to twelve weeks of unpaid leave per year in order to deal with family emergencies,

49. Liberals also complained after 2002 that Republicans appropriated insufficient funds to support the act and that the emphasis on testing was misplaced.
50. Greene, *The Presidency of George Bush*, 76–77.

and passed a Native American Graves Protection and Repatriation Act that among other things established criminal penalties for unauthorized trafficking in Native American remains and cultural artifacts.

Two of the most heralded congressional initiatives in these years also passed in 1990. The first was a civil rights bill that promised to advance the legal rights of minorities who complained of discrimination in employment. These complaints had mounted steeply in the 1980s, keeping the Equal Employment Opportunity Commission busy. Liberals hoped that the measure would counter recent Supreme Court decisions that were jeopardizing non-discrimination in the workplace and minority set-aside programs.[51] The second initiative, which Bush, too, championed, was the Americans with Disabilities Act. It countered discrimination against the disabled in employment.[52]

The Americans with Disabilities Act was a comprehensive civil rights law that prohibited private employers from discriminating against the disabled in employment, public services, public accommodations, and telecommunications. Hailed as the Emancipation Proclamation for the disabled, it significantly advanced America's late twentieth-century rights revolution. The Clean Air Act was a major accomplishment that among other things toughened enforcement of national air quality standards regarding ozone, carbon monoxide, and various pollutants. But the other measures that passed during Bush's time in the White House did not reach very far. As in the past, only a tiny minority of women workers received public aid for day care. Only 40 percent of children eligible for Head Start managed to find places in it after 1990. Many Native Americans continued to live in appalling conditions on poverty-stricken reservations, where the rate of alcohol-related deaths remained high.[53]

Bush, moreover, refused to agree to all that Democrats presented to him. He twice vetoed family and medical leave acts. He vetoed the civil rights bill, maintaining that it promoted racial quotas. The Senate failed by one vote to override this veto, whereupon Congress, slightly more Democratic in its makeup after the 1990 elections, successfully enacted a similar bill in 1991. This law aimed directly at recent Supreme Court decisions concerning discrimination in employment. It enlarged the legal rights of

51. *City of Richmond v. J. A. Croson Co.*, 488 U.S. 469 (1989), involving minority set-asides in construction contracting; and *Ward's Cove Packing Co. v. Atonio*, 490 U.S. 642 (1989), concerning racial discrimination in employment.
52. John Skrentny, *The Minority Rights Revolution* (Cambridge, Mass., 2002), 332–33.
53. In 2003, this rate was seven times as high as the rate for the population at large. *New York Times*, Jan. 18, 2004.

aggrieved workers, notably by enabling them to call for trial by jury. Though it did not end partisan and legal battling over the always contentious issues involving race and employment—the EEOC did a land-office business during the 1990s—it pleased minority group leaders.[54]

As wrangling over this law indicated, liberals worried a great deal at the time about the rising activism of the Rehnquist Court, as it was called after William Rehnquist became chief justice in 1986. From 1989 on, conservatives on the Court seemed receptive not only to challenges to affirmative action and set-asides but also to suits that jeopardized choice.[55] In a widely anticipated ruling in July 1989, the Court upheld a Missouri law that banned abortions in publicly funded hospitals and clinics.[56] Advocates of choice, who had turned out for a mammoth 500,000-person demonstration in Washington while the Court was hearing the case, were frightened and outraged by the ruling.

Reporting on the Court's activity, New York Times correspondent Linda Greenhouse dubbed 1989 "The Year the Court Turned Right." The term, she wrote, "was a watershed in the Court's modern history. For the first time in a generation, a conservative majority was in a position to control the outcome on important issues," notably those concerning the rights of minorities and of women.[57] While this majority proved in later years to be a little less audacious than Greenhouse had predicted, it was obviously feisty.[58] Bush, moreover, was advancing efforts begun by the Reagan administration to appoint conservative Republicans to the federal bench. By 1992, all thirteen federal appeals courts had Republican majorities.[59] As in Reagan's second term, appointments to the courts, which had become ever more influential in the affairs of the nation, continued to spark acrimonious political struggles.

Bush's first Supreme Court nominee, David Souter in 1990, did not arouse opposition among congressional Democrats. Though Souter did

---

54. Skrentny, The Minority Rights Revolution, 333; Terry Anderson, The Pursuit of Fairness: A History of Affirmative Action (New York, 2004), 276.

55. Anderson, The Pursuit of Fairness, 201–2.

56. Webster v. Reproductive Health Services, 492 U.S. 490 (1989).

57. New York Times, July 8, 1989; James Patterson, Brown v. Board of Education: A Civil Rights Milestone and Its Troubled Legacy (New York, 2001), 195–97.

58. Lawrence Friedman, American Law in the Twentieth Century (New Haven, 2002), 524–25.

59. After 1992, President Bill Clinton set about to reverse this process. His efforts, like those of Bush, aroused great controversy on the Hill. When he left office, eight of the thirteen courts still had GOP majorities.

not seem to be the passionate liberal that his recently retired predecessor, William Brennan, had been, he frequently sided with moderates and liberals on the Court. In an especially controversial case in 1992, Souter's vote helped to produce a last-minute, five-to-four majority in a hotly contested decision that reaffirmed the essence of *Roe v. Wade*. Three of the five justices in this majority of five were appointees of Reagan and Bush.[60] Advocates of choice, though still harassed by militants from organizations such as Operation Rescue, rejoiced that choice had survived.

On the other hand, Bush's second nomination, of Clarence Thomas in 1991, provoked one of the nastiest congressional battles in years. Thomas, only forty-three years old at that time, was a relatively rare phenomenon: a black conservative. In selecting him, Bush and his advisers expected that liberals, while disapproving of Thomas's conservative opinions, would think twice before rejecting an African American. But Thomas, as head of the EEOC and then as a federal judge, had opposed affirmative action procedures. Advocates of choice fretted that he would vote to overturn *Roe v. Wade*. The national boards of the NAACP and the Urban League opposed his nomination. They were appalled to think of such a conservative taking the "black seat" that Thurgood Marshall, "Mr. Civil Rights," had filled since 1967.

Thomas's road to confirmation in the Senate, already bumpy, became rocky when Anita Hill, a black law professor at the University of Oklahoma, charged that he had sexually harassed her when she worked for him at the EEOC. Her reluctant but startling testimony—which among other things revealed that Thomas looked at porn movies—infuriated his supporters. Thomas, denying Hill's accusations, exclaimed hotly that he was the victim of a "high-tech lynching for uppity blacks." Some Democrats, including a few liberals, worried about the wisdom of voting against a black nominee Thomas's nomination opened a rift between his supporters, most of them Republican men, and a great many women, black as well as white.

All but two of forty-six Republicans in the Senate ultimately voted for Thomas's confirmation, which was finally approved, 52 to 48, in October

---

60. *Planned Parenthood of Southeastern Pennsylvania v. Casey*, 505 U.S. 833 (1992). Justice Harry Blackmun, informed that Justice Anthony Kennedy was joining him to create a majority, was greatly relieved, scribbling, "Roe sound." *New York Times*, March 4, 2004. These three Republican-appointed justices were Sandra Day O'Connor and Kennedy, named by President Reagan, and Souter. Conservatives, greatly disappointed by Souter's liberal positions, later pleaded, "No more Souters."

1991.[61] But the partisan, often vicious fight—reminiscent in many ways of the battle against the nomination of Bork that had polarized the Senate in 1987—left bruises. Politically liberal women charged that the Senate, which was 98 percent male, had brushed aside Hill's accusations concerning sexual harassment. They resolved to fight back at the polls, where in 1992 women succeeded in winning five Senate races and increasing their numbers in the House and in state legislatures. Encouraged, they hailed 1992 as "the Year of the Woman."[62] Hill's accusations also highlighted the issue of sexual harassment. Sexual harassment lawsuits, which multiplied in number during the 1990s, further empowered the courts as arbiters of the rights revolution in American life.

While controversy over Thomas's nomination was dominating the headlines, racial tensions were mounting in the Los Angeles area. In March 1991, highway police had given chase to a speeder, Rodney King, for 7.8 miles on the Foothill Freeway near San Fernando. When King, an African American, finally stopped and got out of his car, he resisted arrest by Los Angeles police. Hearing commotion outside, a nearby resident trained his home video camera on the confrontation, filming baton-wielding white policemen who subdued King by stunning and then beating him as he lay on the ground. Thanks to the tape, four policemen were charged with the beatings. The venue for the trial was moved to nearby Simi Valley, an area that was predominantly white and whose residents were known to be strong advocates of law and order.

The televised trial, which finally took place more than a year after King's beating, captured a large audience throughout the greater Los Angeles area. Testimony revealed a number of damning facts about the LAPD—notably that it was shorthanded and that it did a poor job of training its officers—but the all-white jury from Simi County was ultimately convinced that the behavior of the LAPD was within California's legal guidelines for handling unruly suspects like King. In April 1992, the jury found three of the policemen not guilty and deadlocked in the case of the fourth.

61. A total of forty-one Republicans and eleven Democrats (seven of them from the South) backed Thomas on the final vote. Two Republicans, Robert Packwood of Oregon and James Jeffords of Vermont (who became an independent in 2001), joined forty-six Democrats in opposition. *New York Times*, Oct. 16, 1991.
62. One of the women elected to the Senate was Carol Moseley Braun of Illinois, the first black woman in Senate history. Still, in 1993 women had only six seats (6 percent) in the Senate and forty-seven seats (11 percent) in the House (as compared to twenty-eight seats [6 percent] in 1991–92), and 20 percent of those in state legislatures (as compared to 18 percent in 1991–92). Moseley Braun was defeated for reelection in 1998. *Stat. Abst.*, 2002, 247.

News of these verdicts immediately touched off rioting, looting, and burning in many parts of Los Angeles. Lasting four days, the rampaging left 55 people dead and 2,300 injured. Fires burned some 800 buildings to the ground and caused an estimated $1 billion in property damage. It was clear that a complex of class and ethnic tensions had exacerbated those that already divided blacks and whites. Minority groups in Los Angeles, like those in many urban areas, confronted serious social problems, including poverty, family breakup, and schools that had difficulty educating inner-city pupils. Violent gangs patrolled minority-dominated neighborhoods and fought over drug dealing and other matters. Unemployment was especially high in the area, in part because of post–Cold War cutbacks that depressed the region's aerospace industry. Many blacks in Los Angeles resented the rising numbers of Latinos and Asians who were competing with them for jobs. Latinos, too, felt ill treated and angry: Half of the arrestees were Latinos. Many rioters had targeted Korean American and other Asian American storekeepers, whose economic progress—and allegedly hostile treatment of non-Asians of color—infuriated many of the Latinos and blacks engaged in the disturbances.

The riot, though frightening, did not necessarily show that American race relations in general were deteriorating.[63] Still, it was evident that the expectations of many African Americans, whose hopes had greatly risen in the 1960s, continued to outpace the gains that they had made since that time. And it was indisputable that volatile relations between Los Angeles blacks and whites, notably white police, had ignited the rioting. Widely shown footage of blacks dragging a white truck driver out of his cab, beating him unconscious, and kicking him while he lay on the street appalled television viewers throughout the country. The riots, which were the worst since the draft riots of the Civil War era, were followed by interracial violence in a number of cities, including Atlanta, Birmingham, Chicago, and Seattle.[64]

THE LOS ANGELES RIOTS CLEARLY INDICATED that racial tensions, accompanied by divisions of ethnicity and class, remained strong and troubling. Bush, however, did not imagine that these troubles would greatly affect his political prospects for reelection. Having been buoyed by the

63. See chapter 9 for race relations in the 1990s.
64. Lou Cannon, "Official Negligence," PBS Online Forum, April 7, 1998; Haynes Johnson, *Divided We Fall: Gambling with History in the Nineties* (New York, 1994), 169–208. In 1993, a racially mixed federal jury in Los Angeles found two of the policemen guilty of having violated King's civil rights.

fantastic approval ratings that had lifted him after the Gulf War, he expected to soar safely into a second term. Two burdens helped to drag him down to earth: splits within his party, and a serious recession. Together, these enabled one of the most charismatic, intelligent, politically shrewd, slick, and personally reckless politicians in American history to drive him out of the White House.

The split within the GOP, which pitted conservatives against moderates such as Bush, owed some of its development to the ending of the Cold War. During that long and grim conflict, anti-communist feeling in the United States had done much to boost the political fortunes of Republicans, who posed as the firmest foes of the Soviet Union. Anti-Communism had served as a glue to hold diverse conservative Republicans together. With the threat from the Soviet Union a matter of history, domestic issues moved more to the fore, thereby offering Democrats a better shot at winning. Anti-Communist Republicans, deprived of a common bond, found it easier to squabble among themselves. In these unanticipated ways, the end of the Cold War improved Democratic political opportunities in the 1990s.

A more calamitous source of GOP divisions in 1992 dated to the summer of 1990, when Bush had decided that he had to stem the escalating federal debt. In current dollars, this had risen from $909 billion in 1980 to $3.2 trillion in 1990. Thanks in part to the enormous costs of the government bailout of savings-and-loan institutions, the federal deficit, which totaled $153 billion in fiscal 1989, leapt to $221 billion a year later.[65] Bush thereupon worked out a tax hike and deficit reduction package that promised over time to reduce the federal debt by as much as $500 billion. Marginal tax rates in the top bracket were scheduled to increase from 28 to 31.5 percent.

Many Democrats welcomed this deal, but supply-siders were outraged. Some pointed out that federal expenditures in the early 1990s, though at record highs in dollar terms, represented roughly the same percentages of GDP (21.8 percent in 1990) as had existed in the mid-1970s. Conservatives were especially outraged that Bush had gone back on his pledge in 1988: "Read my lips: No new taxes." The *New York Post* headlined, "Read My Lips: I Lied." In October, when Congress finally enacted the deal—the so-called Budget Enforcement Act—large majorities of Republicans voted against it. Following congressional elections a month later, when the GOP lost seven seats in the House and one in the Senate, these conservatives angrily blamed Bush for weakening the Republican Party.[66]

65. *Stat. Abst.*, 2002, 305. For the S&L crisis and bailout, see chapter 5.
66. Greene, *The Presidency of George Bush*, 79–88, 183–86.

Whether the deal had great economic effects is unclear. Thanks in part to inexorable increases in government entitlements, and in part to continuing costs of the S&L bailout, federal expenditures rose in the next few years, and at roughly the same rates as earlier. The annual federal deficit climbed to an all-time high of $290 billion in fiscal 1992, before descending at last in the mid-1990s. The tax increases, however, had enduring political consequences. Led by Representative Newt Gingrich, a firebrand Republican from Georgia, conservative Republicans could scarcely contain their fury at the president. The budget deal widened a rift within the party.

The recession began to emerge in 1990 and lasted until early 1992, when recovery slowly took place. As usual, explanations for the slump varied. Some blamed the end of the Cold War, which caused modest cutbacks in defense spending. Others, including Bush loyalists, criticized Federal Reserve chairman Alan Greenspan, who they said was slow to lower interest rates that would have countered or prevented the economic slowdown. Other observers pointed out that the economy had improved every year since 1982—a recession was to be expected sooner or later. Whatever the causes, the decline was severe. An estimated 4.5 million Americans lost their jobs, including many who had been members of the middle classes. Contemporaries spoke of a "white-collar recession." Unemployment jumped from 5.3 percent in 1989 to a peak of 7.5 percent in early 1992. This was the highest rate in nine years.

Bad economic news dominated many headlines in 1991 and 1992. AT&T fired 100,000 workers, GM 74,000. Pan American and Eastern Airlines went under, throwing 48,000 people out of work. Japan, though beginning to lose its competitive edge, still seemed to threaten America's economic hegemony. In 1991, Matsushita, a Japanese corporation, paid $6.4 billion to buy MCA, which owned Universal Studios and MCA Records. Former senator Paul Tsongas of Massachusetts, who was making a run for the Democratic presidential nomination, exclaimed, "The Cold War is over, and Japan won."

In early 1991, with Bush enjoying high ratings in the aftermath of the Gulf War, Tsongas was the only Democrat in the field, but as the economy wobbled, others entered the fray. They included former California governor Jerry Brown, Senator Robert Kerrey of Nebraska, who had won the Medal of Honor in Vietnam, Senator Tom Harkin of Iowa, and L. Douglas Wilder of Virginia, who in 1989 had become the first African American since Reconstruction to win a gubernatorial race. In October, Bill Clinton, who was serving his sixth two-year term as governor of Arkansas, joined these aspirants. By the end of the year, as Bush's approval ratings were plunging to below 40 percent, the Democrats were excited about the prospects of winning in 1992.

Clinton soon emerged as the strongest challenger to Tsongas. Born in Hope, Arkansas, in 1946, he was named William Jefferson Blythe III, but his father had died in an auto crash three months before he was born, and he later took his surname from his stepfather, Roger Clinton. His home life—mostly in Hot Springs west of Little Rock—was far from serene, because his stepfather was an alcoholic who abused Bill's mother.[67] But Clinton was a bright and ambitious young man. He loved politics, idolized JFK, and yearned to be at the center of political life in Washington. He left home to attend Georgetown University, later won a Rhodes scholarship to Oxford, and then went to Yale Law School, where he met the classmate he would marry, Hillary Rodham. Returning to Arkansas, he plunged quickly into politics and won election as attorney general in 1976. In 1978, he won his first term as governor. Only thirty-two at the time, he was the youngest American governor in thirty years. Though he lost in 1980, he served five more two-year terms between 1982 and 1992. Only forty-five years old in late 1991, Clinton aspired to become the first product of the post–World War II boomer generation to win the presidency. He was twenty-one years younger than President Bush.

Extraordinarily well informed about domestic issues, Clinton had impressed many party leaders when he headed the Progressive Policy Institute, a think tank that blossomed after 1989 within the ideologically centrist Democratic Leadership Council. Like a great many boomers, he took liberal positions on a range of social issues such as abortion and health care, but though he had a populist touch as a campaigner, he did not position himself on the left. A moderate as governor, he distanced himself as a presidential candidate from liberals like Mondale and Dukakis, who had been badly beaten in 1984 and 1988.

Instead, Clinton campaigned as a cautiously progressive "New Democrat" who championed centrist policies directed at bringing middle-class voters back to the party. Democrats, he said, would never win unless they avoided overidentification with interest groups such as labor unions. Though they must protect entitlements such as Social Security and Medicare, they had to cast aside their "old tax-and-spend policies." Again and again, Clinton insisted that his party must stand for "opportunity," "responsibility," and "community." Like Jimmy Carter, he said that he was a

---

67. Garry Wills, "The Tragedy of Bill Clinton," *New York Review of Books*, Aug. 12, 2004, 60–64.

born-again man of faith. During the campaign he stood behind the death penalty. He promised to reform welfare, primarily by limiting the length of time that recipients might receive cash assistance, and to push for enactment of a middle-class tax cut. Without explaining how he would do it, he said he would halve the federal deficit within four years.[68]

Clinton, however, had to overcome several political liabilities. Like many well-educated young men during the Vietnam War era, he had manipulated the Selective Service system so as to avoid military service. How could he expect to beat a war hero like Bush? Rumors circulated that he had smoked marijuana. Worst of all, persuasive evidence indicated that as a married man he had been a womanizer. During the early New Hampshire primary, the first major test, the media had a field day tracking down stories about his long-standing sexual relationship with Gennifer Flowers, a former Arkansas state employee. Clinton grumbled, "All I've been asked about by the press are a woman I didn't sleep with and a draft I didn't dodge."

But Clinton could not explain all these stories away. It was true that he had outfoxed his draft board and that—like the huge majority of young boomers in the late 1960s—he had smoked marijuana. (With a straight face Clinton said that he had tried it once, but that he didn't inhale, and never tried it again.) Appearing with his wife, Hillary, on a widely watched showing of 60 Minutes, he sought to downplay stories about his sexual escapades, admitting only that he had "caused pain in his marriage." In the end, he lost the primary to Tsongas. In the process he also acquired an enduring reputation as an adroit but glib and slippery politician—a "Slick Willie" who promised all manner of things and talked out of all sides of his mouth.[69] One Republican branded him a "pot-smoking, philandering, draft-dodger."[70]

It soon became obvious, however, that Clinton's sexual exploits were far less damaging than political pundits had been predicting during the primary. Unlike Gary Hart, whose womanizing had knocked him out of the contest for the Democratic presidential nomination of 1988, Clinton came out of New Hampshire in politically good shape. What was happening? Some observers noted that Hart had been hypocritical, posturing as Mr. Clean before being exposed, whereas Clinton made no such claims.

68. Byron Shafer, *The Two Majorities and the Puzzle of Modern American Politics* (Lawrence Kans., 2003), 59–63; Greene, *The Presidency of George Bush*, 166–75; and Witcover, *Party of the People*, 642–51.
69. For Clinton and the primary, see Halberstam, *War in a Time of Peace*, 101–20.
70. Paul Boller, *Presidential Campaigns* (New York, 1996), 391.

Others credited the artful performance that Clinton, a winsome character, had managed on television, and marveled at Hillary, who was standing by him. If Clinton's behavior was all right with her, voters seemed to say, why should they worry?

In retrospect, it also seems that two long-range developments helped to enable Clinton to survive his deserved reputation as a womanizer. The first was that the ever more inquisitive media had by then helped to accustom Americans to hearing about the sexual transgressions of their political leaders—not only Gary Hart but also FDR, Ike (maybe), JFK, and LBJ. Clinton, though a transgressor, thereby developed a sort of immunity. (A comparable immunity helped to protect later presidential candidates, such as Al Gore in 2000, from attacks concerning youthful use of marijuana.) The second development, related to the first, was one of the many signs that cultural norms had steadily been changing in the United States. Many Americans of Clinton's huge and politically influential baby boom generation, having matured in the more permissive 1960s and '70s, understood from personal experience—or from the experiences of friends and relations—that Clinton's behavior was hardly unique. They were considerably more tolerant of wayward personal behavior than were their elders. What public officials had done in the bedroom, they believed, need not affect their candidacies.

Tsongas, moreover, was not a strong opponent. A self-styled "pro-business liberal," he was stiff on the stump. Even in New Hampshire, his neighboring state, he had won only 33 percent of the votes compared to Clinton's 25 percent. Clinton, ever resilient and energetic, emerged confident after New Hampshire, calling himself the "Comeback Kid." He was comfortable on television and appeared often on talk shows. These were becoming such a key feature of American politics that Russell Baker of the *New York Times* wrote that presidential campaigns had entered the "Larry King era."[71] For all these reasons, Clinton attracted ample funding and moved aggressively ahead. On Super Tuesday in March, he won eight of eleven primaries. Tsongas quit the race soon thereafter, and though Brown stayed in the running, Clinton defeated him in key primaries that followed. Well before the Democratic convention, he had the nomination in his pocket. In a move calculated to attract southerners and young people to the Democratic fold, he then named Gore of Tennessee, a fellow baby boomer, as his running mate.

Bush, meanwhile, encountered challenges from conservatives who rallied to Patrick "Pat" Buchanan, a former speechwriter for Nixon, director

71. Ibid., 387.

of communications for Reagan, columnist, and TV talk-show host. Buchanan was a forceful, often strident speaker who enjoyed being called a "right-wing populist" and the "pit bull of the Right." A strong Catholic, he vehemently opposed abortion and directed his appeals to the Religious Right. As an isolationist in his views about foreign policy, he had argued against American military engagement in Iraq, and he called for sharp cutbacks in immigration. Though no one expected him to wrest the GOP nomination from Bush, he ran in the New Hampshire Republican primary, where he received 36 percent of the vote to the president's 53 percent. His showing fired up a flare that illuminated the rift in the party.[72]

In April another critic, H. Ross Perot, entered the campaign as an independent candidate. Perot was a billionaire businessman from Texas who paid for his own TV ads and thereby did not have to worry about campaign finance regulations. Announcing his candidacy on *Larry King Live*, he waged his campaign almost entirely on television, appearing before voters only late in the race. In the course of blasting Bush's economic policies, the folksy Perot proclaimed that the "engine is broke," and "we got to get under the hood and fix it." Concerning Bush's contributions to the rising national debt, he wisecracked, "Maybe it was voodoo economics. Whatever it is, we are in deep voodoo." The deficit, he added, was "like a crazy aunt we keep down in the basement. All the neighbors know she's there but nobody wants to talk about her."[73] In the summer, when Bush worked for the NAFTA agreement with Canada and Mexico that promised to eliminate tariffs between the three nations, Perot predicted that it would produce a "giant sucking sound" of American jobs whooshing across the border to the cheap labor markets of Mexico.

While these threats were mounting, Bush was slow to develop an organized team, and he remained strangely distracted and uninvolved.[74] Reporters wrote that he was "out of touch" with ordinary Americans. He did not seem to grasp an important fact about late twentieth-century American politics: Winning a presidential election had come to require full-time, all-absorbing attention. His disengagement proved disastrous at the GOP convention in August, which he carelessly allowed religious conservatives to dominate. They approved a strongly conservative platform that

72. Halberstam, *War in a Time of Peace*, 143–54.
73. Robert Collins, *More: The Politics of Economic Growth in Postwar America* (New York, 2000), 216.
74. In May 1991, Bush was found to have Graves' disease, a hyperthyroid condition, which some people later speculated may have sapped his energy in 1992. The evidence for such speculation was inconclusive. Greene, *The Presidency of George Bush*, 153.

focused on preserving "family values," called for the restoration of prayer in the public schools, and denounced abortion. Buchanan was given a prime-time speaking slot on the first night of the convention, where he preached a stern and religious message to a nationwide television audience. Slamming "radical feminism," "abortion on demand," and "homosexual rights," he proclaimed, "There is a religious war going on in this country. It is a cultural war as critical to the kind of nation we shall be as the Cold War itself. This war is for the soul of America."[75]

With Bush apparently unable to control his own party, Clinton had a fairly easy time of it. He promised not only a middle-class tax cut but also some form of national health insurance coverage for all Americans. Though he kept his distance from Jesse Jackson and other African Americans on the left, he was highly popular among black voters. Perhaps because of his identity as a southerner, he fared better in the South (later carrying four of eleven southern states) than any Democratic nominee since Carter in 1976.[76] For the most part he stuck to a centrist position that he had earlier held on the issue of crime, notably by leaving the campaign trail and returning to Arkansas in order to approve the execution of a mentally retarded black prisoner.

Clinton paid little attention to foreign affairs. After all, the Cold War had ended, and the nation was at peace. Bush, moreover, was a war hero and therefore a more attractive candidate to many Americans who had fought in World War II or Vietnam. Instead, Clinton led with his strength, domestic policies. Speaking as if the recession had not abated, he concentrated on hammering home a central message: The economic policies of the Reagan and Bush administrations had badly damaged the nation. Republicans, Clinton charged, had compiled "the worst economic record since the Great Depression." A prominent sign at his "war room" in Little Rock made his strategy clear: The main issue was THE ECONOMY, STUPID.

For all these reasons, Clinton triumphed easily in November. He won 44.9 million votes, 43 percent of the total, to Bush's 39.1 million, 37.4 percent. Women, ignoring Clinton's reputation as a philanderer, were stronger for him than men were.[77] In an election that brought almost 13

75. David Frum, *Dead Right* (New York, 1994), 18.
76. The four states were Arkansas, Georgia, Louisiana, and Tennessee. He also carried the border states of Kentucky, Missouri, and West Virginia.
77. Some 45 percent of women were believed to have voted for Clinton, 37 percent for Bush, and 17 percent for Perot. Men divided a little more evenly: 41 percent for Clinton, 38 percent for Bush, and 21 percent for Perot. *World Almanac, 2003*, 40.

million more voters to the polls than in 1988, Bush received 9.7 million fewer votes than he had attracted four years earlier. He was strong only in the Sunbelt, the Plains states, and the Mountain West. These areas, which Reagan had also carried and where religious conservatives had been especially active, had become fairly solid Republican country. But Bush was badly beaten in the key urban states of the Northeast, Middle West, and the West Coast. Clinton won a big victory in California, which led the nation with votes (54) in the electoral college. He took the electoral college, 370 to 168.

Most analyses of the voting suggested that Perot's candidacy had hurt Bush. Perot won 19.7 million votes, or 19 percent of the total. This was the most impressive performance by a third party candidate since Theodore Roosevelt had won 27 percent as the Progressive Party nominee in 1912. Studies estimated that as much as 70 percent of Perot's support may have come from people who said they had voted for Bush in 1988.[78] The most likely explanation for Perot's strong showing, which astonished many observers, is that a great many Americans chose to register their dissatisfaction with both parties.

Though Clinton had won handily, he knew he had little to crow about. His percentage of the vote, at 43, was the lowest for any winner since Woodrow Wilson had triumphed with 42 percent in 1912. Even Dukakis, with 45 percent in 1988, had fared a little better. Democrats gained one seat in the Senate, for a margin that would be 57 to 43 in 1993, but lost nine in the House, where they would have an advantage of 258 to 176.

Still, it was a heartening victory for the Democrats, who had been out of the White House for twelve years. Moreover, Clinton, a skilled, often charismatic campaigner, seemed to have papered over at least a few of the cracks that had weakened the Democratic Party since the 1960s. Though liberals worried that he might steer the party too far toward the right, they were delighted to have driven the GOP from power. Because Democrats had gained control of the presidency while maintaining majorities in both houses of Congress, they had good reason to hope that the plague of divided government would not afflict the new administration. With the recession becoming a thing of the past, supporters of Clinton anticipated that his "progressive centrism," as some people called it, would reinvigorate the nation.

78. Judis and Teixeira, *The Emerging Democratic Majority*, 28–29.

8

"Culture Wars" and "Decline" in the 1990s

Robert Bork, having been denied a seat on the Supreme Court by the Senate in 1987, emerged in the 1990s as a belligerent conservative in the "culture wars," as contemporary writers saw them, of that contentious decade. He opened his angry, widely noticed *Slouching Toward Gomorrah* (1996) by citing William Butler Yeats's "The Second Coming," written in 1919 in the aftermath of World War I. Among the poem's despairing lines were these: "Things fall apart; the center cannot hold; / Mere anarchy is loosed upon the world, / The blood-dimmed tide is loosed, and everywhere / The ceremony of innocence is drowned; / The best lack all conviction, while the worst / Are full of passionate intensity."[1]

The subtitle of Bork's polemical book, *Modern Liberalism and American Decline*, highlighted two main themes that many conservatives bemoaned in the 1990s: America was in "decline," and liberals were to blame for culture wars that were splintering the nation. Bork wrote, "There are aspects of almost every branch of our culture that are worse than ever before and the rot is spreading." He fired at an array of targets: America's "enfeebled, hedonistic culture," its "uninhibited display of sexuality," its "popularization of violence in . . . entertainment," and "its angry activists of feminism, homosexuality, environmentalism, animal rights—the list could be extended almost indefinitely." He closed by complaining that the United States was "now well along the road to the moral chaos that is the end of radical indi-

1. Bork, *Slouching Toward Gomorrah: Modern Liberalism and American Decline* (New York, 1996), frontispiece. Yeats closed his poem with the lines "And what rough beast, its hour come round at last, / Slouches toward Bethlehem to be born?"

vidualism and the tyranny that is the goal of radical egalitarianism. Modern liberalism has corrupted our culture across the board."[2]

Bork was by no means the only writer to lament the "decline" of America in the 1990s. Carl Rowan, an African American journalist, weighed in, also in 1996, with an irate book titled *The Coming Race War in America: A Wake-up Call.* Though his major target was the totally different one of white racism, Rowan agreed that the United States was "in decline . . . on the rocks spiritually, morally, racially, and economically." He added, "Everywhere I see signs of decadence, decay, and self-destruction." America, he said, was "sinking in greed" and in "sexual rot and gratuitous violence." Inviting readers' attention to the fates of ancient Rome and Greece, and of the British Empire, Rowan despaired, "this country . . . is in precipitous decline."[3]

Perceptive readers might have noted that Rowan's allusion to Rome, Greece, and the British Empire echoed warnings that Paul Kennedy, a liberal, had issued in his widely cited *Rise and Fall of the Great Powers*, published in 1987. They would also have known that the ideological and cultural warfare that seemed to wrack the early and mid-1990s had its origins in battles that had escalated as far back as the 1960s. These had heated up in the late 1980s, when the literary critic Allan Bloom, in his aggressively titled *The Closing of the American Mind*, had lashed out against the trivialization of American intellectual life. In the same year, E. D. Hirsch Jr., in *Cultural Literacy: What Every American Needs to Know*, more temperately complained of what he and fellow authors considered to be the bewildering and culturally divisive nature of curricula in the schools.[4]

Jeremiads about "American decline," however, seemed to hit a larger cultural nerve in the early and mid-1990s. Many of these, like Bork's, emanated from conservatives who were feeling marginalized by liberalizing cultural changes and who were outraged by what they perceived as ever expanding evils: sexual immorality, violent crime, vulgarity and sensationalism in the media, schools without standards, trash that passed as "art," and just plain bad taste.[5] As Zbigniew Brzezinski wrote in 1993, a

2. Ibid., 1–5, 331.
3. (New York, 1996), 3–5.
4. Bloom, *The Closing of the American Mind* (New York, 1987); Hirsch et al., *Cultural Literacy: What Every American Needs to Know* (Boston, 1987).
5. Some of these books, in order of publication: Bork, *The Tempting of America* (New York, 1990); Dinesh D'Souza, *Illiberal Education: The Politics of Race and Sex on Campus* (New York, 1991); William Bennett, *The De-Valuing of America: The Fight for Our Culture and Our Children (New York, 1992)*; and Bennett, *The Book of Virtues* (1993). As head of the National Endowment for the Humanities under Reagan between 1981 and 1985 and then as education secretary (1985–88), the voluble Bennett had fired some early salvos in the culture wars. A more temperate and thoughtful example of conservative unease is James Wilson, *The Moral Sense* (New York, 1993).

"massive collapse . . . of almost all established values" threatened to destroy American civilization.[6] What was one to supposed to think, other critics demanded, about a jury that awarded a woman $2.9 million because she had spilled hot coffee from McDonald's that had badly scalded her? Or about Bill Clinton, president of the United States, who responded to a questioner who asked him on MTV whether he wore boxers or briefs? Perhaps thinking of the youth vote, Clinton replied, "Usually briefs."

As earlier, many conservative writers located the source of cultural decline in the way Americans—especially boomers—had raised their children. For culture warriors such as these, old-fashioned "family values" were among the highest of virtues. Alarmed by what they perceived as the catch-as-catch-can quality of family life, they highlighted articles that reported only 30 percent of American families sitting down to eat supper together— as opposed to 50 percent that were supposed to have done so in the 1970s. As David Blankenhorn, director of the revealingly named Institute for American Values, exclaimed in 1993, America's central problem was "family decline." He added, "It's not 'the economy, stupid.' It's the culture."[7]

Religious conservatives, enlarging organizations such as the Family Research Council, swelled this chorus of laments, evoking outcries from liberals who warned that that the Religious Right was becoming ever more aggressive in waging wars against abortion, gay rights, and other matters.[8] Though Falwell, having weakened the Moral Majority by giving highly controversial speeches (in one, he defended the apartheid policies of South Africa), disbanded the organization in early 1989, a new force, the Christian Coalition, grew out of Pat Robertson's presidential campaign of 1988. Appearing on the scene in 1989, it rapidly gained visibility under the leadership of Ralph Reed, a young, boyish-faced Georgian who had earlier headed the College Republican National Committee. Reed displayed extraordinary political, organizational, and fund-raising skills and managed at the same time to earn a PhD in history from Emory University in 1991. By mid-1992, the Christian Coalition claimed to have more than 150,000 members and to control Republican parties in several southern states.[9]

6. Brzezinski, *Out of Control: Global Turmoil on the Eve of the Twenty-First Century* (New York, 1993), x.
7. Cited in Kevin Phillips, *Arrogant Capital: Washington, Wall Street, and the Frustration of American Politics* (Boston, 1994), 62.
8. See Sara Diamond, *Not by Politics Alone: The Enduring Influence of the Religious Right* (New York, 1998), 174–76.
9. William Martin, *With God on Our Side: The Rise of the Religious Right in America* (New York, 1996), 299–303, 329–32; and Daniel Williams, "From the Pews to the Polls: The Formation of a Southern Christian Right" (PhD diss., Brown University, 2005), chapter 7.

In the early 1990s, another religious group, the Promise Keepers, also came into being. Founded by Bill McCartney, football coach at the University of Colorado, this was an all-male organization of evangelical Christians who vowed to cherish their wives and children and thereby strengthen family life in America. Growing slowly at first, Promise Keepers surged forward by mid-decade. At its peak in 1997, it staged a massive meeting and rally on the mall in Washington, where an estimated 480,000 men were said to promise to be loving and supportive husbands and fathers.

Many Americans who joined groups such as these were still contesting the divisive cultural and political legacy of the 1960s—a secular legacy, as they saw it, of pot smoking, bra burning, love beads, radical feminism, black power, crime in the streets, pornography and sexual license, abortion, family decline, Darwinian ideas of evolution, and gross-out popular culture. Stung by what they considered to be the hauteur of upper-middle-class liberals, they complained that an elitist left-wing/liberal culture had captured universities, foundations, Hollywood, and the media. A "great disruption" was ravaging late twentieth-century America.[10]

Liberals rejected these laments, perceiving them as rants by the Christian Right, political Neanderthals, and hyper-patriots who were endangering civil rights and civil liberties and threatening the tolerant values of the nation. But some on the left, too, worried about social and cultural decline. In 1993, Senator Moynihan of New York, a prominent liberal, wrote an article that attracted considerable attention. It argued that America was "defining deviancy down"—that is, too calmly accepting as normal all sorts of once stigmatized and often dysfunctional behaviors, such as out-of-wedlock pregnancy.[11] Other liberals identified different signs of decline: conspicuous consumption, rising inequality, and misallocation of resources that—in the phrase of one frightened writer—threatened to turn the United States into a "third world country."[12]

Still other observers of cultural developments in the early and mid-1990s, many but not all of them centrist or slightly left of center in their

10. Francis Fukuyama, *The Great Disruption: Human Nature and the Reconstruction of Social Order* (New York, 1999). Fukuyama's book, reflecting the more optimistic mood of the late 1990s, argued that by then the worst of the disruption had passed.
11. Moynihan, "Defining Deviancy Down," *The American Scholar* 62 (Winter 1993), 17–30.
12. See, for instance, David Calleo, *The Bankrupting of America* (New York, 1992); Edward Luttwak, *The Endangered American Dream: How to Stop the United States from Becoming a Third World Country and How to Win the Geo-Economic Struggle for Industrial Supremacy* (New York, 1993); Robert Hughes, *Culture of Complaint: The Fraying of America* (1993); Brzezinski, *Out of Control*; and Phillips, *Arrogant Capital*.

politics, advanced a communitarian movement. As Robert Bellah and his co-authors had argued in *Habits of the Heart* (1985), they asserted that unbridled individualism was undermining America's long-admired capacity for cooperative community involvement.[13] Popularizing a similar view in 1995, Harvard professor Robert Putnam published a widely discussed article titled "Bowling Alone." Putnam observed that while bowling remained a popular sport, people were less likely to bowl together as teammates in leagues. Instead, they bowled alone. Americans, he said, were turning inward and looking out for themselves. Rising numbers of rich people were moving into gated enclaves. The American people, renowned for their voluntarism, were becoming more fragmented, isolated, and detached from community concerns.

To Putnam and others, the fate of league bowling was symptomatic of a larger, generational abdication from participation in the group activities that America's historically community-minded people had earlier been famous for: voting, churchgoing, home entertaining, and volunteering in beneficent organizations such as service clubs, the YMCA, the PTA, and the League of Women Voters. Critics such as these had a point: Many of the groups that in the 1980s and 1990s did report large and expanding memberships—such as the AARP and the Sierra Club—were largely top-down, professionally managed organizations that relied on foundations, mass mailings, and manipulation of the media to amass financial resources. Endangered, it seemed, were grass-roots, face-to-face meetings of concerned and unpaid local people who devoted time and effort in order to promote better communities.[14]

Putnam considered a number of possible reasons for these alleged declines in community-minded activity—people were ever more busy commuting; two-parent working schedules were cutting into time once available for volunteering (a great deal of which in the past had been carried out by women); the ever wider reach of big business and globalization were eclips-

13. See Amitai Etzioni, comp., *Rights and the Common Good: The Communitarian Perspective* (New York, 1995).
14. Putnam, "Bowling Alone: America's Declining Social Capital," *Journal of Democracy* 6 (Jan. 1995), 65–78. See also Putnam's later book, *Bowling Alone: The Collapse of American Community* (New York, 2000). Communitarian writing of the time includes Amitai Etzioni, *The Spirit of Community* (New York, 1993); and Michael Sandel, *Democracy's Discontent: America in Search of a Public Philosophy* (Cambridge, Mass., 1996). Among the many reactions to Putnam are Theda Skocpol, *Diminished Democracy: From Membership to Management in American Civic Life* (Norman, Okla., 2003); Jeffrey Berry, *The New Liberalism: The Rising Power of Citizen Groups* (Washington, 1999); and Everett Ladd, *The Ladd Report* (New York, 1999).

ing local attachments; the extension of big government was centralizing things—before concluding that the loss of community stemmed mainly from generational trends: The public-spirited generation that had grown up during the Depression and World War II was slowly dying out.

Like many Americans at the time, Putnam deplored developments in the media, especially the negative impact of television. Thanks in part to the proliferation of cable channels, many of them relying on niche marketing to attract people with special interests, Americans had become less likely than in the past to receive their information from newspapers, or even from network news. Worse, he said, Americans devoted long hours to mindless watching of the tube—an unblinking eye that was titillating the masses. To Putnam, the absorption of people in television since the 1950s was a fundamental source of the increasing isolation of Americans from one another.[15]

A host of scholars and journalists jumped into vigorous debates with communitarians and with writers such as Putnam. Laments about the baneful influence of television, some of these debaters observed, had a long history that dated at least to highly publicized congressional hearings held in 1954 by Senator Estes Kefauver of Tennessee. In 1977, a widely noted book, *The Plug-In Drug*, had bemoaned the deleterious effects of TV on children and family life.[16] Though the introduction in the 1980s of remote controls greatly advanced mindless channel surfing, it remained difficult in the 1990s, as earlier, to prove that the impact of television on community life had become much more damaging over time.

Some writers who joined these debates wondered if people like Putnam were clinging to romantic concepts of the past. The ideal of "community," they agreed, was attractive, but had it ever taken very deep hold in the United States, a dynamic land of capitalist energy and of restless geographical mobility? Others in these debates, taking a different tack, pointed out that conservative religious groups in the 1980s and 1990s were very much engaged in grass-roots community-building, though normally only among like believers. Still, concerns over decline in community, though challenged, seemed to resonate widely at the time, earning Putnam coverage in *People* magazine and an invitation to Camp David to meet President Clinton. "Americans," Putnam proclaimed, "have been dropping out in droves, not merely from political life, but from organized community life more generally."[17]

15. Putnam, *Bowling Alone*, 277–84.
16. Marie Winn, *The Plug-In Drug* (New York, 1977).
17. Putnam, *Bowling Alone*, 100.

"WARS" OVER CULTURAL PREFERENCES and standards were hardly new in the early 1990s: In a multicultural nation of diverse religious and racial groups and of immigrants such as the United States, these struggles had a long history.[18] In the early and mid-1990s, however, they coexisted with, and drew sustenance from, the often harsh partisan political struggles of the Clinton years. Though accounts in the media often exaggerated the ferocity and power of the "wars," the controversies did seem more clamorous than they had been in the past.

Why such battling over culture at this time? Responses to this question suggest that a combination of forces helped to highlight it. One answer emphasizes that the passing of the Cold War, which until the early 1990s had helped to unite Americans, enabled people to drop their fears of Communism and to focus on domestic concerns and in many situations to reaffirm ethnic and religious identities. No longer caught up in patriotic crusades against Communists abroad, they fought more passionately than earlier over social and cultural concerns. This is a plausible, though hard to prove, argument. A convincing second explanation—important in accounting for the force of cultural controversies after 1992—centers on Clinton's triumph in that year, which broke the twelve-year hold of the GOP on the White House. To deeply disappointed conservatives, who launched most of the culture wars, Clinton was the epitome of all that was wrong with his baby boom generation—and with the elitist liberals, amoral Hollywood celebrities, and left-wing academics who supported him.

Whatever the causes, the clamor of cultural conflict over social trends, coexisting with laments about national decline, seemed especially cacophonous in the early 1990s. Conservative declinists, yearning for what they recalled as the more decorous days of the 1950s, even more loudly deplored America's high rates of out-of-wedlock pregnancy, divorce, and abortion.[19] Liberals shot back at what they considered the aggressiveness and intolerance of the Religious Right.

Widely reported acts of violence further empowered a popular sense in the early 1990s that the nation was coming apart. Many people were outraged by the tactics of extremists—terrorists, in fact—within Operation Rescue, who killed seven people—doctors and people in clinics—at the

---

18. Jonathan Zimmerman, *Whose America? Cultural Wars in the Public Schools* (Cambridge, Mass., 2002).
19. See chapters 1 and 2. Divorce rates were highest in the South, in part because the average age of first marriage was lowest there. The South, of course, was also the region where the Religious Right was strongest.

time,[20] and by the militaristic activities of right-wing hate groups, such as the Freemen and the Aryan Brotherhood. In 1995, two anti-government zealots, Timothy McVeigh and Terry Nichols, succeeded in blowing up the federal building in Oklahoma City, costing the lives of 168 people. A year later a pipe bomb exploded at the Atlanta Olympics. It killed one person and injured many more. Some gay-haters, too, were vicious: In 1998, two men beat a twenty-one-year-old gay man, Matthew Shepard, and tied him to a fence outside Laramie, Wyoming. Five days after being discovered, Shepard died of his injuries in a hospital.

Highly publicized culture wars over art in the late 1980s and early 1990s, although non-violent, were especially harsh. In 1988, Martin Scorsese directed the film *The Last Temptation of Christ*, which was based on a novel of that name that had been published in 1955 by Nikos Kazantzakis. The movie portrayed Christ as an ordinary man who was tempted by many things and who fantasized about being married to and having sex with Mary Magdalene. Though a number of film critics gave the movie good reviews (Scorsese was nominated for an Oscar), many conservative Americans furiously denounced it. Falwell exclaimed that the film featured "blasphemy of the worst degree." Conservative organizations, led by Concerned Women for America, promoted letter-writing campaigns, street protests, and picketing. One demonstration, at Universal City, drew some 25,000 protestors. Leaders of the Eastern Orthodox, Roman Catholic, and many evangelical Protestant faiths called for a nationwide consumer boycott of the movie. Though this did not develop, opponents of the film scored some victories. A few of the nation's largest theater chains refused to screen it. Blockbuster Video declined to stock it on its shelves.[21]

In 1989–90, the National Endowment for the Arts (NEA), whose modest budget assisted a number of arts projects each year, indirectly funded two photographic exhibits that touched off new controversies over high culture. One of these exhibits, by the photographer Andres Serrano, featured a shot of a crucifix in a jar of his urine. It was titled "Piss Christ." The second exhibit, by Robert Mapplethorpe, included a photograph that turned an image of the Virgin Mary into a tie rack. Other offerings in his show featured homoerotic and sadomasochistic shots—one showing

20. *New York Times*, March 3, 2003. The worst year was 1994, when four people were killed in attacks on clinics or doctors. There were eight other attempted killings in that year, in addition to arson and vandalism of clinics.
21. James Davison Hunter, *Culture Wars: The Struggle to Define America* (New York, 1991), 234.

Mapplethorpe with a bullwhip implanted in his anus, another depicting a man urinating in another man's mouth.[22] As in the case of Scorsese's film, these exhibitions aroused fierce controversy. Most art critics and museum people tried to defend the exhibits, either as imaginative creations or (more commonly) as free expression that must not be censored. Many other Americans were irate. Congress, led by Senator Jesse Helms, a staunch conservative from North Carolina, reluctantly reauthorized funding for the NEA, but at reduced levels, and on the condition that it sponsor works that were "sensitive to the general standards of decency."[23]

Although these were perhaps the most visible of contemporary cultural struggles over art, two other controversies involving museums and the treatment of American history further frayed the bonds of cultural peace in the United States. Both these battles excited tempestuous public debates in which conservatives assailed "politically correct" approaches to United States history. The first swirled about an exhibit, "The West as America: Reinterpreting Images of the Frontier, 1820–1920," staged in 1991 at the Smithsonian Institution's National Museum of Art in Washington. Demythologizing American history, it highlighted the role of white exploitation of Native Americans during the exploration and settlement of the American West. A number of viewers, having read in school about the heroic struggles of white explorers and settlers who had spread democracy across the frontier, erupted in protest.[24] A few GOP senators threatened to cut the museum's budget.

The second fight erupted three years later when the National Air and Space Museum readied plans for a major exhibit that was to feature the *Enola Gay*, the B-29 from which the Bomb had fallen on Hiroshima in 1945. Conservatives, joined by veterans' groups, protested when they were permitted to see the museum's early draft of the exhibit, which seemed to question the wisdom of dropping the Bomb and which, they said, badly distorted American history. The pilot of the *Enola Gay*, Paul Tibbett, exclaimed that the proposed exhibit was a "package of insults." Forced to the defensive, the director of the museum resigned, and the draft exhibit was drastically rewritten and cut, so as to feature the plane itself without a great deal of interpretive context. Many academic historians protested against this cave-in, as they saw it, but to no avail.[25]

22. Garry Wills, *Under God: Religion and American Politics* (New York, 1990), 288–89; Hunter, *Culture Wars*, 231; Hughes, *Culture of Complaint*, 159–66.
23. Myron Marty, *Daily Life in the United States, 1960–1990: Decades of Discord* (Westport, Conn., 1997), 313.
24. Hughes, *Culture of Complaint*, 188–90.
25. Robert Newman, *Enola Gay and the Court of History* (New York, 2004).

Conservatives also mobilized to battle against liberal faculty members at universities such as Stanford, where in 1988, discussions took place that later resulted in the widely reported dropping of a required freshman core course in Western culture. It was replaced by a variety of humanities offerings that, though including many Western classics, were a little less Western-centered. Anguished defenders of the "Western canon," including Education Secretary William Bennett, explained that Stanford was "trashing Western culture." Stanford faculty members retorted by hailing the changes as enabling, at last, a "birth of multiculturalism" within the core of university courses.

A still more hotly contested fight over humanities teaching broke out in 1994 and 1995, this time over proposed national standards aimed at assisting teachers of United States history. Produced by leading scholars in the field, the standards recommended that teachers help students understand the importance in American history of such evils as slavery, the Ku Klux Klan, and McCarthyism. Conservatives, however, complained that the guidelines had not nearly enough (or nothing at all) to say about patriots such as Paul Revere, inventors such as Thomas Edison and Alexander Graham Bell, soldiers such as Ulysses S. Grant and Robert E. Lee, and the Founding Fathers.

This bitter controversy ultimately quieted down after scholars revised the standards so as to moderate a little the complaints of conservatives. Published in 1996, the standards were read by many thousands of teachers in the following years. Well before then, however, Lynne Cheney, former head of the National Endowment for the Humanities (and wife of Dick Cheney), had entered the fight against the standards. The battle had also reached the floor of the U.S. Senate, which in 1995 denounced the standards in a vote of 99 to 1. This was a procedural roll call that had no practical effect, but the testy debates on Capitol Hill vividly exposed the gulf that separated cultural conservatives—and a great many national politicians—from most academic historians. A Republican senator, Slade Gorton of Washington, exclaimed that the standards confronted Americans with a choice. He demanded to know: "George Washington or Bart Simpson"—which person represented a "more important part of our Nation's history for our children to study?"[26]

26. Peter Stearns et al., *Knowing, Teaching, and Learning History: National and International Perspectives* (New York, 2000), 1; Zimmerman, *Whose America?* 216–17. For an account by historians of the long-running struggle over history standards, see Gary Nash et al., *History on Trial: Culture Wars and the Teaching of the Past* (New York, 1997).

Conservatives such as Gorton also fumed about the proliferation of "political correctness," or "PC," as it became called, in the early 1990s. Much of this PC arose, they complained, from the zeal of liberal faculty and university administrators, who were introducing detailed codes of speech and conduct aimed at promoting tolerance on university campuses. Some of these codes took special aim at "hate speech" that students were said to be using when they targeted women, gays and lesbians, and minorities of color. Conflict over such issues roiled a number of universities, especially in the early 1990s, and prompted a host of excited exchanges among students, intellectuals, and others.[27]

Some of these fights over culture were nasty, featuring language by protagonists that was harsher and more unforgiving than in the past. Religious conservatives damned their foes as "masters of deceit," "amoral," and "arrogant and self-righteous." Liberals, they said, supported the "forces of the anti-Christ." Liberals retorted in kind: Their foes were "moral zealots," "fanatics," "latter-day Cotton Mathers," and "patriots of paranoia" who stood sanctimoniously for "God, flag, and family."[28] The rancor exposed sharp regional and class divisions. Cultural conservatism developed increasing appeal to people—notably white working-class Americans— in the South and in the Plains and Rocky Mountain states, while liberal ideas continued to appeal to well-educated academic and professional people on the east and west coasts and in the metropolitan centers of the East and Midwest. Some of these antagonists appeared to think that the enemy had to be not merely defeated but also destroyed.

At the time that these struggles were stealing headlines, a number of contemporaries thought that they would have powerful, long-range consequences. James Davison Hunter, who in 1991 published a thorough account of the controversies, concluded, "America is in the midst of a culture war that has and will continue to have reverberations not only within public policy but within the lives of ordinary Americans everywhere."[29] Eight years later, a leading conservative writer, Gertrude Himmelfarb, published a book that received considerable attention. Its title, *One Nation, Two Cultures*, revealed her central argument: Culture wars were cutting the

27. For a widely discussed critique of PC, see D'Souza, *Illiberal Education*. A vigorous response is John Wilson, *The Myth of Political Correctness: The Conservative Attack on Higher Education* (Durham, N.C., 1995).
28. Hunter, *Culture Wars*, 144–45.
29. Ibid., 34.

nation in half.[30] Assessments such as these echoed the opinions of many contemporaries. Especially in the early 1990s, talk about "culture wars," complementing complaints about "decline," attracted a good deal of impassioned coverage in the media.

From the vantage point of the early 2000s, two broad observations seem fairly clear about these assessments. The first is that many in the media, which frequently fixated on conflict, exaggerated the ferocity of the culture wars, which in any event abated a little bit (though not among politically engaged elites and partisan politicians) in the late 1990s.[31] Hunter himself observed that a "vast middle ground" (60 percent or so, by his estimate) of Americans paid little attention to such battles.[32] Even in presidential elections, nearly 50 percent of the voting-eligible population did not turn out. Of those who did, one-third or so identified themselves as independents, and many others said that they found it very difficult to decide on candidates. About many social and cultural issues, including the aesthetic and political messages of academe and of high culture, most Americans did not get terribly excited.[33]

The influence of the Religious Right, about which many liberals did get excited, was a little less potent between the late 1980s and the mid- and late 1990s than it had appeared to be in the early 1980s. In 1987, Jim Bakker, then at the peak of his fame as a television star, had been exposed as an adulterer with his church secretary, and as an embezzler of millions of dollars from his ministry. Convicted of fraud, he was fined $500,000 and sentenced in 1989 to forty-five years in prison. (He served five.) A second Assemblies of God television preacher, the piano-playing, hyper-emotional Jimmy Swaggart, was photographed taking a roadside prostitute into a motel room on the outskirts of New Orleans.[34] Swaggart appeared before his congregation of 7,000 in Baton Rouge, where he begged tearfully for

30. (New York, 1999). Himmelfarb agreed that some aspects of American culture had improved by 1999.
31. Morris Fiorina et al., *Culture War? The Myth of a Polarized America* (New York, 2004). Though the wars did seem to abate, some writers after 2000 remained convinced that cultural divisions, exacerbated by rising immigration, threatened the United States. See Samuel Huntington, *Who Are We? The Challenges to America's National Identity* (New York, 2004).
32. Hunter, *Culture Wars*, 43.
33. Alan Wolfe, *One Nation, After All: What Middle-Class Americans Really Think About God, Country, Family, Racism, Welfare, Immigration, Homosexuality, Work, the Right, the Left, and Each Other* (New York, 1998), 16.
34. Martin, *With God on Our Side*, 275, 289.

forgiveness of his sins and resigned from his ministry. Publicity surrounding the tribulations of these self-righteous crusaders tarnished some of the glitter of religious conservatism.

Though polls in the 1990s continued to indicate that virtually all Americans believed in God, they also revealed that most people—especially young people—were disposed to be tolerant of the private behavior of others and that they were uneasy about forceful religious intervention in political matters. A good deal of conservative political activism in the 1990s, moreover, arose from secular, not religious, sources. Leading conservative newspapers and magazines—the *Wall Street Journal, Human Events, The Public Interest, National Review,* and the *Weekly Standard*—focused more on economic and foreign policy issues than on moral concerns dear to deeply religious people.

To be sure, many members of the Christian Right continued to champion theological positions that differed sharply from those of more secular Americans. It was surely inaccurate to maintain that the United States had become an overwhelmingly secular nation in which religion was no longer important. While Catholic advocates of public funding for parochial schools were quieter in the 1990s than they had been in the past, they believed as strongly as ever—as did Protestant evangelicals—in the virtues of religious instruction in the schools.[35]

Religious conservatives, moreover, remained a significant cultural force in the United States. Though battles over the content of textbooks tended to abate by the mid-1990s—by then, many history texts had become multicultural, featuring not only the Founding Fathers but also Sacajawea, César Chávez, Frederick Douglass, and Malcolm X—conservatives continued to fight against sex education in schools and Darwinian messages in biology texts and courses.[36] Crusaders such as these found numerous ways of spreading their gospels. Cable TV at the time made Pat Robertson's Family Channel available to some 50 million homes. James Dobson's daily radio show, *Focus on the Family,* which was carried on 4,000 stations, attracted an estimated 5 million listeners. It was estimated that there were 399 full- or part-time Christian radio stations on the air in the late 1990s.[37]

As Pat Buchanan's visibility suggested, conservative Christians also retained political muscle in the 1990s and in 2000. They were strong enough

35. Leo Ribuffo, "If We Are All Multiculturalists Now, Then What?" *Reviews in American History* 32 (Dec. 2004), 463–70.
36. Zimmerman, *Whose America?* 1–8, 126–29.
37. Diamond, *Not by Politics Alone,* 3–9, 20–22.

to drive GOP candidates, Bush included, to the right during presidential primaries and at quadrennial party conventions. In some areas, notably in the Sunbelt, they had the numbers and the zeal to affect electoral outcomes. In the off-year congressional elections of 1994—when turnout was otherwise low—their activities, efficiently organized by the Christian Coalition, helped enable the GOP to win a number of races in the South and thereby to construct a majority in the House of Representatives for the first time since 1954. Culturally conservative Republican representatives and senators, having gained control in Congress, were thereafter in a better position to press for their goals, such as restrictions on abortion and gay rights, and the appointment of conservative federal judges. In close presidential elections (as in 2000 and 2004), they were among the many blocs that could help to make the difference between victory and defeat. In both these presidential races, a majority of white Catholic voters, too, supported the GOP.

But some worried liberals overreacted. As earlier, people associated with the Religious Right disagreed among themselves. The Christian Coalition, having revealed itself in 1994 to be a politically savvy religious lobby, ran up $3 million in debt and fell into disarray. Shortly after Reed left it in 1997, it virtually imploded. So within a year did the Promise Keepers, which also suffered from poor financial management. Other major organizations representing the Christian Right, notably the Family Research Council and Concerned Women for America, continued to thrive, but they faced determined counter-organization, especially from liberals in urban areas and on the east and west coasts. Later, in the presidential elections of 2000 and 2004, it was clear that these and other groups within the Religious Right had become vital assets to the GOP, mainly in the South. But in the late 1990s, with Clinton still in the White House, the full political power of Christian conservatism remained to be demonstrated.[38]

Sensing their political limitations, a number of religious conservatives in the late 1990s grew pessimistic. Neither Reagan nor Bush, they recognized, had truly advanced their agendas. None of their major goals—regarding abortion, prayer in the public schools, or pornography—had been met. Liberals remained powerful in universities and in the media. Discouraged, some advocates on the right wondered if their causes, struggling against the ongoing secularization and commercialization of American culture, might be declining. Himmelfarb, writing in 1999, observed glumly that the United

---

38. Steven Gillon, *Boomer Nation: The Largest and Richest Generation Ever, and How It Changed America* (New York, 2004), 305–7.

States had become less religious than it had been in the 1950s and 1960s. Only 58 percent of Americans, she noted, told pollsters in 1998 that religion was important in their lives—compared to 75 percent who had said so in 1952.

The sociologist Alan Wolfe (not a religious conservative) had reached similar conclusions in 1998. Most middle-class Americans, he wrote, distrusted televangelists and other proselytizing religious leaders who tried to impose their ideas on people. Americans, he said, practiced "Quiet Faith." They were "free-agent churchgoers" who signed on for "short-term contracts" with a series of congregations. David Frum, a conservative journalist, agreed, writing in 1994 that the number of white Southern Baptists, Pentecostals, and charismatics was "not large"—perhaps 15 million people (of a total population at that time of 276 million) spread over thirty states. They were a "dispersed, poor, relatively uneducated group." Refuting liberal fears about the power of the Religious Right, Frum concluded that there was "no vast theocratic menace out there."[39]

Some of the social problems that had especially alarmed conservative Americans, though remaining more serious than they had been in the 1960s, also seemed to become a little less fearsome later in the decade. Rates of teenage pregnancy and births, and of abortion, which had soared in the 1980s, decreased after 1991—the result, it was believed, of AIDS prevention programs, increased use of condoms, and new methods of birth control.[40] Crime rates dropped at last. The murder rate, having peaked in 1980 at 10.2 per 100,000 of population, declined dramatically, to 6 per 100,000 by 2000. By then, American rates of property crime, notably larceny and theft, had fallen below those in Sweden, Canada, New Zealand, and Britain.[41] Thanks in part to rising prosperity in the late 1990s, and in part to a major overhaul of welfare policies after 1996, welfare rolls plummeted.[42] The incidence of cigarette smoking, though high among teens, continued to fall. Drug and substance abuse appeared to be a little less serious in the late 1990s than it had been during the 1970s and during the crack cocaine epidemic that had peaked in the 1980s. For all these reasons, the cultural despair that had afflicted many urban areas, such as New York City after the blackout of 1977, began to abate. (In New York City, even the subways had become

39. Himmelfarb, One Nation, Two Cultures, 96–99, 108–14; Wolfe, One Nation, After All, 40–72, 83–84; David Frum, Dead Right (New York, 1994), 168–70.
40. Pregnancy rates for Americans aged fifteen through nineteen decreased by 28 percent between 1990 and 2000. New York Times, Feb. 20, March 7, 2004.
41. Between 2000 and 2003, homicide rates inched upward, but other violent crimes (rape, aggravated assault, and robbery) continued to decrease a little. Rates of property crime (burglary, larceny, auto theft) were stable. New York Times, May 25, 2004.
42. See chapter 10 for discussion of welfare policies in the 1990s.

clean.) All these changes slightly allayed the fears of conservatives who had waged culture wars earlier in the decade.

It also seemed that many among the youngest generation of Americans — so-called Millennials born after 1982 — were rejecting in the late 1990s the behavioral excesses, as these young people saw them, of the boomers and of their children, the so-called Generation X. While these young Millennials were hardly enrolling in large numbers behind conservative crusades against sex education, abortion, or gay rights — like their parents, they grew up in the more liberal, permissive culture of the era — they seemed to be acting more responsibly in sexual matters, drinking less, and avoiding drugs. Most of these Millennials said that they believed in God and loved their country.[43]

Whether such generational generalizations held water was hard to say: Diversity within age cohorts remained enormous in America's multicultural population. Were "generations" easily definable? But broad and deeply pessimistic assertions about national decline in the 1990s did seem misconceived. It also remained debatable whether community involvement — grass-roots organizing, volunteering, philanthropic spirit — was truly in decline in the 1990s or whether, instead, it just seemed that way to nostalgic Americans who cherished rose-colored memories of neighborhood cohesiveness in the past.[44]

THE SECOND OBSERVATION TO BE MADE about late twentieth-century social and culture wars is that liberals were winning a great many of them. As in the 1970s and 1980s, more and more Americans in the 1990s, especially younger Americans, were demonstrating by their beliefs and their behavior that they were tolerant of liberal mores. Defying their elders, the young persisted in dressing, wearing their hair, and — by late in the decade — piercing and tattooing their bodies as they pleased. Regarding a range of more important personal matters — sexual practices, marriage and divorce, and family life — Americans were becoming less censorious about the behavior of other people. By the 1990s, the rising cultural permissiveness that had shaken traditionalists in the 1960s and that had spread over the years seemed virtually unstoppable.

43. Neil Howe and William Strauss, *Millennials Rising: The Next Great Generation* (New York, 2000), 209–14. Electoral turnouts of young people, however, were lower than those of older people.

44. Robert Samuelson, "We Are Not Really 'Bowling Alone,'" *Providence Journal*, April 16, 1996. Fukuyama, *Great Disruption* (1999), 92–95, agrees, seeing the late 1990s as ushering in a "great reconstruction" in many ways. For reflections on communitarian thinking, see also Skocpol, *Diminished Democracy*, 175–200, 221–30.

A number of behaviors that had become more common since the 1960s, notably cohabitation and out-of-wedlock pregnancy, continued in the 1990s to be widespread and to arouse conservative complaints. During the presidential campaign of 1992, Vice President Dan Quayle touched off a headline-stealing row when he criticized the TV character Murphy Brown (played by Candice Bergen in a popular sitcom of that name) for bearing a baby without getting married and for indicating calmly that the father's identity did not matter. Quayle, slamming the show as well as the liberalism of the medium that aired it, exclaimed that Murphy Brown's behavior could not be defended as "just another lifestyle choice." Critics of Quayle leapt happily into the fray, ridiculing him as a prig and branding him an enemy of free expression. Writers for *Murphy Brown* responded cheekily by including his criticisms in later episodes, whereupon the show's ratings increased.

Advocates of traditional family patterns such as Quayle did manage to hold their own in a few of the culture wars of the 1990s, notably those concerning abortion. Though the Court did not overturn *Roe v. Wade*, many states enacted laws calling for parental notification or consent before minors might get one. Between 1988 and the early 2000s, twenty-one states approved legislation that mandated waiting periods before abortions. Another twenty-eight states limited or cut off public financing for abortion. By 2000, NARAL Pro-Choice America (the new name for the National Abortion Rights Action League) grudgingly recognized that laws such as these were likely to remain on the books.[45]

As the enhanced popularity of *Murphy Brown* suggested, however, conservatives otherwise had little success in their efforts to reverse long-range cultural trends in America. By 2000, 69 percent of all black babies and 27 percent of all white babies were being born out of wedlock. Thanks mainly to increases in out-of-wedlock births among whites during the 1990s, the overall percentage of such births in 2000 was a record high of 33, up from 27 in 1990.[46] Though abortion rates declined a little in the 1990s, these, too, remained far too high to placate conservatives—at a ratio of roughly

45. William Saletan, *Bearing Right: How Conservatives Won the Abortion War* (Berkeley, 2003); Diamond, *Not by Politics Alone*, 140–41; *New York Times*, Jan. 15, 2003.

46. *Stat. Abst.*, 2002, 59. An increase in the percentage of babies born out of wedlock to whites accounted for most of this increase in the 1990s. The rise in such births was the result primarily of the fact that *married* women were having fewer children, compared to non-married women, than earlier—not that the *number* of out-of-wedlock babies was rapidly rising. (It was rising, but slowly.) Awareness of this complicated chain of causation, however, was not widespread, nor did such awareness change the fact that the *percentage* of such births had become extraordinarily high over time.

one for every three live births in 2000. A majority of Americans at the time, as earlier, said either that they approved of *Roe v. Wade* or that they favored the protection of choice with modest limits.[47] Roughly 40 percent of marriages still ended in divorce. Attitudes toward gays and lesbians were slowly liberalizing. And nothing that traditionalists could say or do prevented steadily higher percentages of women from working away from the home. The comic strip character Blondie, who had long been a housewife, started a catering business in 1991, as if to keep pace with the many millions of women who had joined the civilian labor force by that time. As earlier, the percentage of such women kept increasing, to 60 among women sixteen and over by 2001.[48]

Ongoing trends in family patterns also continued in the 1990s. By then it was becoming obvious that high divorce rates, later-age marriages, greater sexual freedom, cohabitation, and rising female employment had combined to make the traditional family—married couples with children—just one of a variety of family styles. There was no longer an obvious cultural norm. The census of 2000 reported that 23.9 percent of America's adult population (over eighteen) had never been married. This compared to 20.3 percent that had never been married in 1980. The census further indicated that married couples headed only 53 percent of American households (55.3 million of the total of 104.7 million). Female householders living without spouses but with their own children under eighteen years of age numbered 7.6 million in 2000—22 percent of all families with children of that age. Only 60 percent of American children in 1995 lived in the same residence with their two biological parents.[49]

As earlier, mothers who worked outside the home struggled to resolve varied goals: a wish for satisfaction from home management and child-rearing on the one hand, and the desire (and often the need) to earn a living or fashion a career apart from the home on the other. They still had to contend with the double shift, to scramble for affordable day care, and to cope on occasion with sexual harassment on the job. The average earnings of women who had full-time, year-round employment were only 77.5 percent of those of similarly employed men in 2002. Sexual segregation and discrimination in hiring and promotion, though considerably less

47. *New York Times*, Nov. 23, 2004.
48. Andrew Hacker, "How Are Women Doing?" *New York Review of Books*, April 11, 2002, 63–66; *Stat. Abst.*, 2002, 368, 370. For earlier figures, see 54–55.
49. *Stat. Abst.*, 2002, 47–49; Diamond, *Not by Politics Alone*, 115; Andrew Hacker, "Gore Family Values," *New York Review of Books*, Dec. 5, 2002, 20–26; Hacker, "How Are Women Doing?"; *New York Times*, March 11, 2003.

widespread than in the past, still confronted women in various occupations. In 2000, women held only 136 of 655 federal district court judgeships and only 20 percent of law professorships.[50] Feminism, in eclipse since the 1970s, was hardly vibrant.

In a number of ways, however, many career-oriented and wage-earning women in the late 1990s had reason to be pleased by the continuation of earlier improvements in their relative position. By 2000, women were nearly 50 percent of entering classes at American law, medical, and graduate schools. They were more than 55 percent of college undergraduates. Federal laws such as Title IX were being enforced, though not always vigorously, to advance equal rights for women in sports and other activities at schools and colleges. The average wages of full-time women workers, though still lower than men's, were closer to parity than in 1979, when they had been 62.5 percent of those of men. The earnings of childless young women in 2000—those aged between twenty-seven and thirty-five—were virtually the same as those of employed men of the same age.

By the 1990s, many employers of women were a little more likely than in the past to understand the necessity for flex-time scheduling and leave time, especially after the signing by Clinton in 1993 of the Family and Medical Leave Act, which called upon businesses with more than fifty employees to provide up to twelve weeks of unpaid leave for workers, including fathers or mothers with new babies, who needed time off. Thanks to the spread of personal computers and the Internet, slightly higher percentages of employed women were able to work at least part-time at home.[51] These and other trends, adding to earlier advances since the 1960s, amounted to significant gains for American women. On the average, women workers were faring considerably better economically than they had done in earlier decades. They also made slow but heartening advances politically: The number of women holding seats in the House rose from twenty-eight in 1991 to sixty-two in 2001; the number in the Senate increased in the same years from three to thirteen.[52]

These and other developments, reflecting the receptivity to progressive change that had often been a feature of American culture, represented forward strides away from many social and cultural patterns of the supposedly Good Old Days. Though conservatives in the 1990s had successes in *political* battles against Clinton's public policies, such as health care reform, they continued to struggle when resisting the tides of *cultural* change. They were surely not winning all the culture wars.

50. *New York Times*, March 26, 2001.
51. Ibid., Jan. 31, 2003.
52. *Stat. Abst.*, 2002, 247.

IT WAS EVIDENT that some of these social and cultural developments of the 1990s came at a price. Many liberals warned that this was especially the case concerning the most celebrated of these changes: declining crime rates. Though there was no clear consensus about the sources of this widely welcomed improvement, experts enumerated several likely causes, including a decline since the 1970s in the percentage of young people in the population, improving economic conditions, and much better community policing, which featured quicker public attention to signs of neighborhood deterioration, such as graffiti and broken windows.[53]

Worried observers, however, pointed to related trends, notably the impact of harsher sentencing procedures, such as California's "three strikes and you're out" law of 1994. This act, harsher than a federal measure and than twenty-four similar laws that state legislatures enacted in the next few years, hit three-time felony offenders, including those whose third conviction had been for small-time shoplifting or for possession of drugs, with mandatory prison sentences ranging from twenty-five years to life.[54] National crackdowns, especially in "wars" against drugs, also became tougher in the 1990s than earlier, resulting in a considerable rise in convictions and in a 13 percent increase in the average length of sentences during the decade. Between 1970 and 2000, America's jail and prison population increased fivefold, jumping (especially during the 1990s), to approximately 2.1 million.[55] More than 50 percent of all federal prisoners and 22 percent of state and local prisoners during these thirty years were incarcerated as a result of drug-related convictions.

Many conservatives rejoiced over the crackdowns, believing that by removing criminals from the streets they did a great deal to deter serious crime. But the rates of many varieties of serious crime, though lower than they had been in the 1980s, were still considerably higher than they had been in the 1950s and early 1960s. Harsher laws and sentencing, notably of non-violent offenders, did little to inhibit the still flourishing drug trade. The laws led especially to a surge in jail and prison building, which drained public funds from other uses, such as schools, roads, and health care.[56] The rise in the

53. Gregg Easterbrook, *The Progress Paradox: How Life Gets Better While People Feel Worse* (New York, 2003), 74–76; James Q. Wilson and George Kelling, "Broken Windows: The Police and Neighborhood Safety," *Atlantic Monthly* 249 (1982), 29–38. A widely read endorsement of this "broken windows" argument is Malcolm Gladwell, *The Tipping Point: How Little Things Can Make a Difference* (New York, 2000), 133–51.

54. Though controversial, California's law remained on the books. In 2004, a proposition aimed at moderating it failed to pass.

55. And to 2,212,475 million by the end of 2003. *New York Times*, Nov. 8, 2004.

56. Ibid., Nov. 18, 2004.

number of prisoners was staggeringly high. By 2003, nearly 8 Americans per 1,000 of population were behind bars. This was a far higher rate than in Britain, the nation whose numbers were second highest in this respect.

Statistics on crime in relation to race, as earlier, remained especially unnerving. In the early 2000s, it was officially reported that 12 percent of black males aged twenty to thirty-four and 4 percent of Hispanics of these ages were in jail or prison. By contrast, only 1.2 percent of similarly aged white men were incarcerated. In 2003, African Americans, who were 12.3 percent of the population, were 46 percent of all prisoners in the United States (as opposed to 36 percent who were white and 17.6 percent who were Hispanic). Roughly one-fourth of all federal prisoners were not citizens of the United States. In the same year, the Justice Department estimated that 28 percent of black men would serve time in jail or prison at some point in their lifetimes.[57]

Statistics like these inevitably aggravated culture wars over race. While minority group leaders, backed by white liberals, saw the numbers in part as proof of the oppression, especially by police, that continued to afflict people of color, many other Americans found the statistics to be confirmation of their belief that blacks and (to a lesser extent) Hispanics were prone to lawlessness and deserved whatever punishments they got.

MANY OTHER CULTURAL AND SOCIAL TRENDS of the 1990s continued to alarm contemporary Americans, both on the right and on the left, and to suggest to worried people that the nation was in decline and at war over culture.

One of these trends—long a bane to conservatives as well as to many communitarians—was what they thought was an overheated rights-consciousness. Rising expectations, they complained, were continuing to strengthen "selfish" interest groups whose sense of entitlement knew no bounds. *Rights Talk*, a sober assessment of such expectations by Harvard law professor Mary Ann Glendon that appeared in 1991, helped to spur growing attention to this development. Rights talk, she wrote, "promotes unrealistic expectations, heightens social conflict, and inhibits dialogue that might lead toward consensus."[58]

---

57. For these and other statistics in these paragraphs, see "Do Not Pass Go," *New York Review of Books*, Sept. 25, 2003, 44–46; Fukuyama, *Great Disruption*, 71; *New York Times*, April 7, July 28, 2003, Jan. 6, Oct. 26, Nov. 8, 2004; *Providence Journal*, May 7, 2002, April 7, 2003. For similarly graphic statistics concerning 2004, see *New York Times*, April 25, 2005.

58. Glendon, *Rights Talk: The Impoverishment of Political Discourse* (New York, 1991), 9–14.

Others who fretted about the rise of rights-consciousness pointed to trends in the legal profession, which seemed to become steadily more powerful in the United States. It was estimated in 1993 that America had more than 800,000 lawyers, or 307 for every 100,000 of population—as opposed to 103 per 100,000 in Britain and only 21 per 100,000 in Japan. A decade later the number of lawyers in America had leapt to more than a million.[59] Though the largest growth in the profession took place in the fields of business and corporate law, many of these attorneys specialized in sexual harassment or personal injury cases, such as the one that hit McDonald's for $2.9 million, and created what one scholar called a "litigation explosion." A few of these cases, especially those involving medical malpractice, resulted in damage awards for "pain and suffering" that soared into the nine-figure range. Trial lawyers who were skilled before juries, such as John Edwards, a North Carolina attorney who won election to the United States Senate in 1998 (and ran as the Democratic vice-presidential nominee in 2004), earned fees—normally around one-third or more of awards—that catapulted them into the ranks of multimillionaires.

Lawyers for plaintiffs in these cases predictably spoke as champions of the rights of underdogs. Their opponents, denounced as faceless corporations with deep pockets, were depicted as hard-hearted villains whose blunders or deceptions had helped to harm or kill people. To the extent that juries sided with plaintiffs, they exposed what some observers regarded as rising class resentments in America. This was a doubtful generalization, but confrontations such as these did exacerbate already sharp cultural conflicts between liberals and conservatives. Personal injury lawyers, conservatives exclaimed, were members of the "only true parasitical class" in the nation. Backed by manufacturers, insurers, and many physicians, these conservatives demanded tort reform, especially to deter a few "hellhole" states and county court districts where "jackpot juries" were known to render lavishly anti-corporate verdicts. The Association of Trial Lawyers of America, which had become an increasingly active interest group, fired back angrily and effectively at charges such as these.

Whether the surging of rights-consciousness—and the "scourge" of litigation—was good or bad obviously depended on one's point of view. Liberals contended persuasively that these developments were long overdue, that marginalized people who had been abused or oppressed were finally receiving justice.[60] They rejoiced that the American Civil Liberties

---

59. Luttwak, *The Endangered American Dream*, 215; Lawrence Friedman, *American Law in the Twentieth Century* (New Haven, 2002), 8–9.
60. Samuel Walker, *The Rights Revolution: Rights and Community in Modern America* (New York, 1998).

Union was becoming a considerably more influential organization than it had been in the Bad Old Days of McCarthyism, at which time it had been smeared as a "pinko" front. It was also true that in some ways the litigiousness of the United States was a healthy development—a sign not only of the diversity and dynamism of American society and politics but also of the trust that people were placing in the courts and in the ultimate fairness of the justice system.

Other Americans, especially but not only conservatives, emphatically disagreed, and they fought back vigorously in lawsuits of their own. By turning so often to the courts, they charged, litigants abandoned efforts at negotiation and compromise and ratcheted up societal ill will. Critics such as these further complained that litigation of this sort drove up the price of goods and services, such as medical malpractice insurance. Physicians, they said, were being forced out of business. Advocates of tort reform insisted that recourse to litigation bypassed and weakened democratic institutions, notably legislatures. The result, as Glendon put it, was the "impoverishment of political discourse."[61]

A related manifestation of litigiousness did seem fairly clear in the 1990s: the durable power of conspiratorial thinking. Popular suspicions of authority figures were hardly new at the time; these had spread at least since the assassination of JFK and had swelled as a result of the deceptions that government leaders had practiced during the Vietnam War and the drawn-out crisis of Watergate. Some conspiracies—like the one that destroyed the federal building in Oklahoma City in 1995—surely existed in the 1990s. Other supposed conspirators, however, lived only in the fevered imaginations of racists and self-promoters: Louis Farrakhan, head of the Nation of Islam, was among the small but sometimes noisy group of bigots who circulated rumors through the media during the 1990s about a vast conspiracy of Jews. Popular notions of conspiracy—and resentments aimed at people of power—nonetheless attracted considerable public attention.

As earlier, distrust of authority spurred conspiratorial thinking, especially among hustlers looking for a buck. In 1991, the filmmaker Oliver Stone brought out *JFK*, which implied that all manner of authority figures, including LBJ and members of the "military-industrial complex," had plotted Kennedy's assassination. Stone's irresponsible film was a success at the box office and sparked congressional efforts to reexamine the conclusions of the Warren Commission Report, which in 1964 had identified Lee Harvey

61. The subtitle of her book.

Oswald as the lone killer of Kennedy. A majority of Americans, attracted by conspiratorial notions, still rejected these conclusions.[62]

Dark rumors never stopped swirling in the 1990s about other conspiracies, such as those that had supposedly brought about the deaths of Elvis Presley and Princess Diana and the assassination of Martin Luther King. Some rumormongers identified a "satanic underground" that abducted young girls and abused them in demonic rituals. Conspiratorially minded Americans especially targeted members of the government, which had always been the most distrusted authority of all. When Vincent Foster, a top aide of President Clinton, was found dead of apparent suicide in 1993, rumors (never in any way substantiated) abounded that the president had had a hand in having him killed. As earlier, the Pentagon was blamed for withholding the truth about UFOs, for concealing evidence about MIAs in Vietnam—would the scars of that awful conflict ever heal?—and for downplaying the extent of the Gulf War Syndrome, the illnesses that were thought to afflict American soldiers who had taken part in the recent war against Iraq.[63]

It is impossible to gauge the size or influence of the many groups of people who bought into these and other conspiracy theories in late twentieth-century America. Thinking of this sort had a long history, not only in the United States but also throughout the world. There is little doubt, however, that media reports helped, as earlier, to sustain popular American suspicions about all manner of people and things. As one critic of the media put it, "We have a system of news that tells people constantly that the world is out of control, that they will always be governed by crooks, that their fellow citizens are about to kill them."[64] The prevalence in the 1990s, as earlier, of such reports may have helped to contribute to a popular sense, though inchoate and inaccurate, that the nation was not only in decline but also in danger.

YET ANOTHER SIGN OF DECLINE, as pessimists saw it in the 1990s, was of a very different sort: the continuing spread of hyper-commercialization, consumerism, and materialism. Advertising, relying ever more heavily on sophisticated forms of niche marketing, had long since become virtually omnipresent. Ads were said to affect—and to afflict—Americans when

62. Jonathan Raban, *Bad Land* (New York, 1996), 309.
63. Robert Goldberg, *Enemies Within: The Cult of Conspiracy in Modern America* (New Haven, 2001), 232–60.
64. James Fallows, *Breaking the News: How the Media Undermine American Democracy* (New York, 1996), 142.

they were very young. By the age of nine, children were estimated to have seen some 20,000 TV commercials a year. By then the children had become "brand-washed." Large corporations paid millions for "naming rights" that enabled them to plant their logos and names on stadiums and buildings. Children were seduced by ads and persuaded their parents to buy sneakers costing more than $100 a pair. Logos—Nike, Adidas, Reebok—were ubiquitous on sportswear.

Some aspects of this commercial culture were potentially corrupting. Pharmaceutical companies poured money into medical schools and gifts into physicians' offices, hoping to influence scientific research and to promote sales of their high-priced products. Some critics believed that pressure from drug companies hastened decisions of the Food and Drug Administration concerning approval of new medicines. Supposedly disinterested academic and government scientists earned large sums as consultants to corporations. Schools and universities struck deals that gave soft-drink- and snack-producing corporations monopolies on sales, notably from vending machines, of company brands. In return for video equipment, an estimated 12,000 public schools (including 40 percent of high schools in the country) provided Channel One to a captive audience of 8 million pupils. This was an MTV-style commercial channel that delivered two minutes of ads for every ten minutes of "news."

Major universities spent huge sums of money on quasi-professional athletic teams, hoping that gate receipts and broadcasting contracts would cover their enormous budgets for varsity sports. Requiring their athletes to display commercial logos on their uniforms, they received considerable payments from sportswear and equipment companies. By the early 2000s, several university football coaches earned salaries and perquisites (including commercial endorsements) that totaled more than $2 million per year. In most cases, however, revenue from university sports events did not meet costs, thereby threatening academic programs. Even where the money did cover expenses—at perhaps a dozen universities—the victory-obsessed culture created by the emphasis on big-time athletics obscured the educational mission of campus life.[65]

Before the 1992 Olympics in Barcelona, the United States Olympic Committee (USOC) signed a contract calling for Reebok to provide the

---

65. Derek Bok, *Universities in the Marketplace: The Commercialization of Higher Education* (Princeton, 2003); and Benjamin DeMott, "Jocks and the Academy," *New York Review of Books*, May 12, 2005, 29–32. For estimates of the economic costs and benefits of big-time college football, see *New York Times*, Jan. 2, 2005.

warm-up suits that American athletes were to wear at the games. The Reebok logo appeared prominently on the jackets. But several Americans on the "Dream Team" basketball squad that won the gold medal had lucrative endorsement deals with Nike and balked at wearing the Reebok jackets when they stood on the stand to receive their awards. Michael Jordan, a Nike endorser, explained that it was a matter of loyalty, whereupon critics wondered, loyalty to whom: Nike or country? After tense negotiations, the athletes agreed to appear on the stand with American flags draped over their shoulders, covering the logos. Though the use of the flags—"for pride and to hide"—quieted the big-stakes bickering, the controversy exposed the considerable reach of commercial interests, not only in the United States but also in sports throughout the world.

Especially in the mid- and late 1990s, when prosperity advanced, materialistic values seemed to surge ahead. More than ever, it appeared, wants were becoming needs. Credit card debt, driven by fantastic consumer spending, reached new heights.[66] Casino gambling and mega lotteries proliferated, filling the often poorly fixed coffers of state governments with millions of dollars in tax revenue while emptying the pockets of hosts of suckers. Las Vegas, where billion-dollar hotels were springing up, boomed as never before. Attracted by ads, image-conscious Americans bought name-brand bottled water costing $5, Italian biscuits priced at $1.50 apiece, and coffee at $3.50 or more per cup. SUVs, Jacuzzis, and other high-end products captured growing markets. Wealthy people laid out colossal sums for powerboats, cosmetic surgery, and "McMansions" erected in styles that ranged from Colonial Williamsburg to Godfather Mediterranean. The average floor area of new houses reached 2,310 square feet in 2000, as compared to 1,595 square feet in 1970 and 1,905 square feet in 1990.[67] The author/columnist David Brooks satirized the tastelessness of "Bobos," materialistic Americans who were at once *bohemian* and *bourgeois*. He gaped in awe at a kitchen "so large it puts you in mind of an aircraft hangar with plumbing." Kitchens today, he wrote, "have lunch counters and stools and built-in televisions and bookshelves and computer areas and probably 'You Are Here' maps for guests who get lost on their way to the drink station."[68]

Polls suggested that the rush to get rich especially overwhelmed young people. A poll in 1999 asked teenagers, "By the time you're 30, what do

66. Easterbrook, *The Progress Paradox*, 136–38.
67. Gillon, *Boomer Nation*, 162.
68. Brooks, *Bobos in Paradise: The New Upper Class and How They Got There* (New York, 2000), 87.

you expect to earn?" The median answer was $75,000, which was almost three times as high as the actual median income ($27,000) of thirty-year-olds at the time.[69] In the same year the British television show *Who Wants to Be a Millionaire?* was revised (and dumbed down) for showing in the United States and became a top-rated program. Attitudes and preferences such as these indicated that materialistic expectations, always strong in America's abundant society, were if anything more powerful then ever. Bill Bryson, a smart and witty explorer of life in the United States, wrote in 1998 that Americans have the "intoxicating notion that almost any desire or whim can be simply and instantly gratified."[70]

PUNDITS WHO SURVEYED TRENDS in popular culture perceived especially precipitous declines in taste during these years. They had a point. A dwelling on sex, always good for sales, seemed to be even more gratuitous and graphic. In 1991, Michael Jackson produced a video, "Black or White," in which he grabbed his crotch, unzipped and zipped his fly, and appeared to masturbate. The sitcom star Roseanne clutched her crotch and spat on the ground after singing the national anthem (deliberately off-key) at a San Diego Padres baseball game. In 1992, Madonna published *Sex*, a coffee table book of photographs of herself, some of which displayed her hitchhiking and hang-gliding in the nude. Others showed her with naked celebrities—men as well as women—and engaging in graphic sexual encounters with men. *Sex*, which sold for $49.95, grossed an estimated $25 million during its first week in the stores.[71]

Raunchiness such as this would have boggled the imagination of Americans in the 1950s, but by the 1990s it seemed difficult to shock people, most of whom had already been desensitized. One episode of *Seinfeld*, a well crafted, enormously successful sitcom, revolved around the question of which character could hold off the longest from masturbating. A survey in 2003 found that two-thirds of all television shows available during the prime-time hours between 7:00 and 11:00 P.M. had some sexual content, including simulated depictions of sexual acts. The commercialization of hard-core sex became very big business. By the early 2000s, the "adult entertainment industry" grossed an estimated $8 to $10 billion per year from live shows, magazines, home videos, and pornography available on

69. Howe and Strauss, *Millennials Rising*, 280–82, 318.
70. Bryson, *Notes from a Big Country* (London, 1998), 397.
71. Madonna's excesses seemed to enhance her popular appeal. Roseanne's did not.

the Internet or by pay-per-view on cable television.[72] Major hotel chains such as Marriott, Hilton, Sheraton, and Holiday Inn, which profited handsomely from pay-per-view "adult" TV, reported that 50 percent or more of their guests demanded to have access to such channels in their rooms.

The "gross-out" nature of popular culture in the 1990s was indeed impressive. Profane radio "shock-jocks" like Howard Stern, who had risen to fame in the 1980s, employed bathroom humor and attracted large and devoted followings.[73] By then it was common to hear words and phrases on radio and TV such as "kiss my a——," "bitch," "pi——ed off," and the ubiquitous "this sucks." Some rap groups reveled in the use of offensive language and misogyny. 2 Live Crew's "As Nasty as They Wanna Be," released in 1989, used the *f* word more than 200 times, offered more than eighty descriptions of oral sex, and shouted the word "bitch" more than 150 times.[74]

Long gone, for sure, were the days when Clark Gable (in *Gone with the Wind*, 1939) was supposed to have shocked movie audiences by saying to the character Scarlett O'Hara, "Frankly, my dear, I don't give a damn." Or the 1950s, when producers of the immensely popular *I Love Lucy* television show did not dare to use the word "pregnant."[75] That word, like "virgin," had long been banned on the air. By contrast, in the 1990s it was estimated that profanity occurred once every six minutes on over-air TV, and once every two minutes on cable.[76] Because virtually all households had at least one TV set, and Americans still watched television for an average of four hours a day, the boob tube had considerable potential as a vocabulary builder.[77]

The *Jerry Springer Show*, an over-the-air afternoon television talk show whose popularity rivaled *The Oprah Winfrey Show*, featured guests who humiliated themselves, thereby mesmerizing audiences in millions of

72. Eric Schlosser, "Empire of the Obscene," *New Yorker*, March 10, 2003, 61ff. John D'Emilio and Estelle Freedman, *Intimate Matters: A History of Sexuality in America* (Chicago, 1997), 373.

73. In 2004, Viacom, the parent company of CBS, settled complaints of indecency lodged with the FCC against Stern and others by paying a fine of $3.5 million. *New York Times*, Nov. 24, 2004.

74. Hunter, *Culture Wars*, 232.

75. Lucille Ball, the star of *I Love Lucy*, was pregnant during the 1952–53 season of the series and was shown wearing a maternity clothes. This was a bold step for television.

76. Haynes Johnson, *The Best of Times: America in the Clinton Years* (New York, 2001), 206.

77. Margaret Talbot, "Turned On, Tuned Out," *New York Times Magazine*, Feb. 16, 2003, 9–10.

American homes. One guest described her five-year marriage to a horse; another told of his romance with his dog. Fights between enraged guests—maybe staged, maybe not—enlivened the action on the show. When Madonna appeared on David Letterman's late-night show in 1994, she used the *f* word thirteen times in twenty minutes. Though the word was bleeped out—network TV, after all, is "family entertainment," even late at night—there was no doubting what she was saying. Madonna told Letterman that there was a pair of her panties in his desk drawer. "Aren't you going to smell them?" she asked. Later in the interview she recommended peeing in the shower. "It fights athlete's foot," she said. "I'm serious. Urine is an antiseptic."[78]

Violence of various sorts seemed bloodier than ever in lyrics, videos, television, and movies of the late 1980s and 1990s. A few up-and-coming stars of "gangsta rap" reveled in the shouting of misogynistic and other hateful messages. One rap song, Ice-T's "Cop-Killer," released in the aftermath of the Los Angeles riots, urged audiences to kill the police. Then as since the early days of TV, some of the most popular television shows starred professional wrestlers, among them women who (like many other female performers by that time) wore leather bras. The circus-like world of televised wrestling was so obviously unreal, featuring fake blood, vicious-looking body slams, and screamed obscenities, that its nearly nonstop mayhem was mainly amusing. *Cops*, a long-running, popular program, captivated viewers by showing real chases, fights, and arrests. Local news broadcasts, which in many areas of the nation preceded the national news, spent much of their time zeroing in on bloody car wrecks, shootings, knifings, and other scenes of violence.

Local television station managers thought nothing of firing experienced, middle-aged reporters in order to replace them with supposedly more attractive-looking (and lower-paid) neophytes. A few stations dumped personnel so as to free up money to buy helicopters that whisked excited reporters to crime scenes, fires, and other catastrophes. On-the-spot coverage of action scenes such as these—delivered in rapid-fire, sound-bite fashion—was believed to be the key to retaining the all-important loyalty of the so-called young adult audience. "If it bleeds, it leads," station managers ordered. They insisted that the vast majority of viewers, having literally grown up before the tube, had little patience with slow-moving or time-consuming presentations of current events. Television, after all, was

---

78. Mary Ann Watson, *Defining Visions: Television and the American Experience Since 1945* (Fort Worth, 1998), 201–3.

a visual medium that was most gripping when dramatic and confrontational. It aimed to offer immediacy and black-versus-white dialogues, leaving complexity for newspapers and magazines to provide.

Local news programs were tame compared with the sex-saturated soap operas that dominated TV during the day and with the violence-filled dramas that appeared later in the evening. Prime-time network programs of this kind showed an average of five violent acts per hour. Between 10:00 P.M. and 6:00 A.M., when standards applied to the networks were more relaxed, the sexual and violent content of television shows expanded. The emphasis on sex and violence increased over the course of the 1990s, especially on cable TV, which was not subject to the relatively strict (though still permissive) guidelines that the FCC expected radio and over-the-air television stations to follow. In 1997, Comedy Central initiated its weekly cartoon series *South Park*, which featured foul language and racially offensive jokes. It was a hit, bringing millions of dollars in salaries to its stars. In 1998, *Sex and the City* appeared, highlighting swinging young people who slept around. That millions of Americans paid for cable TV to bring such programs into their homes indicated the ongoing drift of the culture. That violent shows were readily accessible to children understandably outraged critics.

Hollywood, too, offered a great deal of sex and violence. Releasing films almost every week, movie producers competed frantically in efforts to fill the seats, five times a day, of the 4,000-odd multiplex theaters that had sprung into being during the 1970s and 1980s. In their quest for profits, they relied especially on "blockbusters," some of which cost more than $100 million to make and tens of millions more to market. Most of the blockbusters aimed to attract adolescents and other young people; older Americans were far less likely to go to the movies. That effort meant featuring what the young had already come to expect from their vast experience with television and video and computer games: near non-stop noise, movement, and action. Spectacular special effects, bloodshed, profanity, nudity, and gross-out humor added to the mix. A dream of many young people under seventeen was to see R-rated (Restricted) movies. Even movies rated PG-13 (Parental Guidance for children under thirteen) contained strong stuff. Ads for PG-13 films made that clear, noting that the films included "sex, profanity, adult themes," "violence, some disturbing images," "crude and sexual humor," "scenes of violence and mild gore," "intense terror sequences." In these and many other films, sex and violence drove the action; subtlety and characterization lost out.

Some widely watched movies of the late 1980s and 1990s offered viewers virtually all they might desire in the way of gore and ghoulishness: *RoboCop* (1987), its shoddier sequels, *RoboCop 2* (1990) and *RoboCop 3* (1991), *Goodfellas* (1990), *Silence of the Lambs* (1991), *Natural Born Killers* (1994), and *Pulp Fiction* (1994). All these films, save *RoboCop 3* (PG-13), were R-rated. A few, notably *Goodfellas*, were well crafted and received favorable reviews. More commonly, however, macabre and violence-filled movies relied on ear-shattering, eye-catching, and blood-spattering sequences to engage their viewers.

Naked or near-naked bodies seemed to be almost required in R-rated films. *Basic Instinct* (1992) included highly erotic sexual activity. *Body of Evidence* (1992), starring Madonna, featured S&M sex, some of it involving hot wax and broken glass. *Titanic* (1997), though a far tamer movie that received a PG-13 rating, threw in what critics perceived to be obligatory sex scenes. The film showed the actress Kate Winslet in full frontal nudity, as well as a sequence that made it obvious that she was having sexual intercourse in the backseat of an automobile. The hot and heavy sex steamed up the car's windows. Thanks in part to the enthusiasm (for the love story) of a great many teenaged girls, who paid to see the movie five and six times, *Titanic* was the highest-grossing movie of all time. It won an Academy Award for Best Picture.

Many magazines, emulating the glitz of TV, continued to focus on America's celebrity culture, thereby slighting hard news in favor of exciting envious and materialistic urges among viewers. *People* often led the way, as it had since first appearing in 1974. Its commercially successful obsession with coverage of the rich and beautiful—especially of their troubled private lives—spread to other magazines as well. *Newsweek*, which had earlier featured political and world leaders on one-third of its covers, seemed eager to keep pace. By 1997, one-third of its covers depicted celebrities, compared to only one-tenth that showed world leaders.[79] Most newspapers and magazines, like television, gave breathless and extended coverage to sensational stories with some sort of sexual angle. When an angry abused wife, Lorena Bobbitt, cut off her husband's penis in 1993, television stations and tabloids seemed unable to report anything else. Well before the end of the decade it became a virtual cliché that there was little if any difference in the commercial media between news and entertainment.

Thanks to the power of celebrity culture, a number of performers raked in enormous sums in the 1990s. Among them were "personalities" mas-

79. Johnson, *The Best of Times*, 184.

querading as newsmen, notably Larry King, who signed a contract with CNN for $7 million a year, and Geraldo Rivera, who contracted with CNBC for $30 million over six years. Jerry Seinfeld, producer and lead character of *Seinfeld*, was reported to have earned $66 million in the 1996–97 season. Tim Allen, star of *Home Improvement*, agreed to a contract in 1997 that paid him $1.25 million per show. Given the money expended at the time by televisions advertisers (estimated to be as much as $500,000 per thirty seconds for the Thursday evening line-up that included *Seinfeld*), the enormous sums earned by stars such as these were expected to more than pay for themselves. At its peak between 1996 and May 1998, *Seinfeld* drew viewing audiences of 76 million per episode.

Other celebrities fared as well or better in the 1990s. Arnold Schwarzenegger, one of Hollywood's highest-paid stars, received an estimated $12 to $15 million for his performance in *Terminator 2: Judgment Day* (1991), $20 million for *Jingle All the Way* (1996), and $25 million for *Batman and Robin* (1997). Michael Jordan in his most enriching years received $70 million, most of it from endorsements. So long as celebrities avoided scandals, corporate sponsors competed vigorously for their presence in commercials.

Still other celebrities who prospered in the 1990s included Steven Spielberg, who earned a reported $175 million per year at his peak, and Harrison Ford, who took in $53 million. (Both Spielberg and Ford agreed to divorce settlements that paid their former spouses more than $100 million.) In 2000, the baseball star Alex Rodriguez signed a ten-year contract that promised him $252 million.[80] At that time the nation's economy was strong, but news stories regularly reported the rise of income inequality, and poverty afflicted 31 million Americans, 11.3 percent of the population.[81] In a commercialized world such as this, contemporary observers could be excused for believing that materialistic values had triumphed and that the nation was in decline.

Ownership and control of the media, moreover, became ever more concentrated, notably in huge multimedia corporations such as Walt Disney Company, Time Warner, and Capital Cities. By the end of the decade, General Electric owned NBC; Viacom, CBS; the Walt Disney Company, ABC; and Time Warner, CNN. Rupert Murdoch's News Corporation, a sprawling international business, was busily buying radio and television outlets, sports teams, newspapers, magazines (including *TV Guide*), and film companies (among them Twentieth Century Fox). The

---

80. "What People Earn," *Parade*, Feb. 14, 1999.
81. *Stat. Abst.*, 2002, 863 (figures for 1999).

politically conservative slant of Murdoch's far-flung empire, notably the FOX News Channel, increasingly enraged liberals and partisan Democrats in the United States.

There were, of course, potent reasons for the frequently frenetic races to the bottom (races that were replicated in most free-market countries around the world) that television producers resorted to. Competition among the networks—faced also with the proliferation of cable channels—was intense, leading producers to look anxiously at the all-important audience ratings that they needed in order to secure the advertisements (these, too, sex-laden) that paid for time.[82] In their quest for audience-share, and therefore for larger profits, television stations ran eye-catching specials about Great Problems and Crises, and talk shows that pitted advocates of polar positions shouting at one another.[83] During "sweeps weeks," when the number of viewers was counted, channels highlighted whatever might glue people to the tube. Producers and managers defended themselves against charges of presenting low levels of entertainment by explaining that they were giving the people what they wanted—if popular taste was degraded, that was not their fault.

Defenders of television, including many civil libertarians, added that no one commanded viewers to immerse themselves in the sludge that critics said was befouling the screen. In the late 1980s and 1990s, as earlier, millions of consumers exercised their judgment and declined to do so, watching instead smoothly crafted shows such as *Cheers, The Cosby Show, ER, NYPD Blue,* and *Frasier.* Televised sports programs, notably the NCAA college basketball tournament ("March Madness"), the World Series, and the Super Bowl, attracted huge audiences and normally generated enormous advertising revenue. Quiz shows, holiday-time specials, oft-seen film classics, and happy-ending reruns continued to appeal to millions of viewers.

It was also a fact, then as always, that in America's diverse and competitive culture, there was no such single thing as *the* media. Television viewers looking for serious approaches to the news could tune in to ABC's *Nightline* with Ted Koppel, or to the *MacNeil/Lehrer News Hour* on the Public Broadcasting Service (PBS). C-SPAN, expanding since its creation in 1979, provided live coverage of Congress and of many significant speeches, hearings, and panel discussions. Its *Booknotes* program, which

82. David Halberstam, *War in a Time of Peace: Bush, Clinton, and the Generals* (New York, 2001), 161–66.
83. Easterbrook, *The Progress Paradox,* 188–212.

started in 1989, enabled viewers to watch wide-ranging conversations about important books, most of which concerned history, politics, and public policy. National Public Radio, when not pleading for contributions, featured commercial-free programs dealing with a host of national issues, as well as shows such as Garrison Keillor's *A Prairie Home Companion*, which enjoyed considerable popularity for many years.[84]

Filmmakers, too, churned out a great deal of inoffensive stuff: chase and spy dramas, historical epics, comedies, movies for children, and boy-meets-girl romances with happy endings.[85] Innovative computer-generated and animated films, such as *Jurassic Park* (1993), *The Lion King* (1994), and *Toy Story* (1995), entranced millions of viewers. So did sports movies, such as *Field of Dreams* (1989), *A League of Their Own* (1992), and *Rudy* (1993). In the 1980s and early 1990s, a number of critically well regarded films concerned with serious subjects, some of them imported from Britain—*Gandhi* (1982) (voted Best Picture), *A Passage to India* (1984), *Rain Man* (1988), *Glory* (1989), *My Left Foot* (1989), *Schindler's List* (1993), *Apollo 13* (1995)—enjoyed respectable runs at American box offices. The angst-ridden Woody Allen, a prolific playwright and filmmaker, continued to please many of his fans. Art cinemas, surviving in major cities, specialized in showing films that appealed to sophisticated audiences.

Parents with young children, like other concerned moviegoers and VCR users, could consult the movie industry's rating system—television developed guidelines in 1996, but they were feeble and complicated—if they wished to watch films without a great deal of violence or sex. They had a considerable variety of inoffensive shows from which to choose. Music lovers, too, had ample choice. Those who disliked heavy metal, rap, or pop gyrators like Madonna could buy CDs, attend a great many performances of country, folk, or religious music, or enjoy hit musicals staged by touring companies. Long-popular singers such as Reba McEntire, Cher, Willie Nelson, Ray Charles, and Tony Bennett continued to attract enthusiastic crowds.

---

84. *A Prairie Home Companion* first aired in July 1974.
85. Among relatively non-sex-saturated and non-violent movies that enjoyed box office (and in most cases, critical) success in the 1990s were *Home Alone* (1990), *A River Runs Through It* (1992), *Sleepless in Seattle* (1993), *Forrest Gump* (1994), *The Bridges of Madison County* (1995), *Twister* (1996), *As Good as It Gets* (1997), and *You've Got Mail* (1998). *Jurassic Park* broke box-office records. Some films of the 1990s that included a good deal of explicit sex or violence, such as *The Piano* (1993), *Fargo* (1996), and *A Simple Plan* (1998), received favorable reviews from critics.

It also remained the case in the 1980s and 1990s that many institutions of high culture—museums, art galleries, repertory theaters, symphony orchestras, and chamber music groups—were managing to stay afloat, despite receiving far less generous public support than had long been available in nations like France or Germany. The plays and music of Stephen Sondheim, Sam Shepard, and David Mamet earned critical acclaim and box-office success. Tony Kushner's two-part, seven-hour epic concerning homosexuality, AIDS, and political conservatism, *Angels in America* (1992), won a host of awards. Public-spirited citizens' groups and philanthropists raised their support of university endowments and of cultural institutions, helping thousands of artists and musicians to carry on with their creative work. Though many publishers and bookshops struggled to break even, fiction by highly talented authors—Toni Morrison, Alice Munro, Anne Tyler, Richard Ford, John Updike, and others with smaller name recognition—sold well. So did excellently researched works of non-fiction. James McPherson's prize-winning *Battle Cry of Freedom* (1988), a history of the Civil War era, enjoyed huge sales. A considerable variety of serious magazines and journals (many of them subsidized by wealthy publishers or universities) awaited buyers at bookstores and magazine counters.[86] Americans looking for cultural edification, including a larger number of people with higher education, had wider choice than in the past.

Were gruesome scenes on TV and film provoking a rise of violent behavior in the United States? This was surely difficult to prove. Blood-filled classics of stage, screen, and high school English courses—*Macbeth*, for example—had had no such effect in the past. Violent crime, moreover, sharply declined in America, the spread of mayhem on TV and film notwithstanding, during the 1990s.[87] The very gratuitousness of violence in most productions of popular culture, like the staginess of TV wrestling, may have lessened its capacity to affect real-life behavior. At any rate, it remains doubtful that the proliferation of blood and gore in America's visual popular culture, though distressing when available to children, incited greater violence among the general population.

It was equally debatable whether television had "declined" all that much over time: Since the 1950s it had hardly been a significant source of cultural uplift. Consumers of high culture recalled nostalgically that CBS had earlier set aside television time for Sunday afternoon concerts featur-

---

86. In 2004, it was estimated that Americans supported approximately 1,000 literary magazines, a record number. *New York Times*, Dec. 27, 2004.

87. See chapter 2 for discussion of similar debates in the 1970s.

ing Leonard Bernstein and the New York Philharmonic. Those days, to be sure, had passed, overtaken by professional football and other offerings on Sunday afternoons. But Americans who imagined that television and film had been much more edifying in the past might have done well to remember that shots of thigh and cleavage had always enjoyed great popular appeal: A common motto of television producers in the 1960s, when shows such as *The Beverly Hillbillies* had earned top ratings, had been "bosoms, broads, and fun."[88] Movies in the 1970s, some observers argued, had been at least as graphic sexually as those in the 1990s.

Still, the crassness of TV and of other manifestations of American popular culture in the 1990s understandably distressed many people, who blamed it for a further commercialization and degradation of American civilization. Despite rising levels of educational experience, the percentage of American adults in the 1990s who were reading literary works — poems, plays, or fiction — may have been smaller than it had been in years past. So may have been the percentage of people, especially young people, who read any books at all. Competition from movies, and especially from television, was said to be a primary cause of this decline.[89]

Finally, there was no doubting that the display of sex in popular culture in the 1990s had become pervasive and graphic, and that young children were often exposed to it, especially on television. Whether such presentations profoundly affected behavior was regularly disputed — after all, teenage pregnancy declined in the 1990s. Moreover, the sexual focus of many sitcoms — such as the *Seinfeld* episode featuring masturbation — was hardly subversive. Still, sex did seem to be virtually ever-present on the tube. Robert Lichter, director of the Center for Media and Public Affairs, a non-profit research group, expressed a historically accurate judgment in 1998: "People used to think that television was aimed at the mind of a 12-year-old. Now it seems aimed at the hormones of a 14-year-old."[90]

88. Frank Rich, "What the Tube Is For," *New York Times Magazine*, Sept. 20, 1998, 53–56
89. According to a study in 2002 of American reading habits, the percentage of adults who read literary works declined from 57 in 1982 to 54 in 1992 and to 47 in 2002. The percentage of young adults (aged eighteen to twenty-four) who read such books dropped especially rapidly, from 60 in 1982 to 43 in 2002. The percentage of adults that read any book declined from 61 to 57 between 1992 and 2002. The study, which claimed to rely on U.S. Census data, was released by the National Endowment of the Arts. It did not report whether Americans read more non-fiction, such as history, or whether they read a good deal of serious writing — whether fiction or non-fiction — in magazines. It blamed the Internet for the decline that continued after 2000. *New York Times*, July 8, 11, 2004.
90. Ibid., April 6, 1998.

POLLS IN THE MID-1990S suggested that most Americans considered themselves fortunate to live in the United States, which they perceived as a dynamic, forward-looking, and efficient society. In 1994, a poll asked: "Earlier in American history, many people thought the U.S. was the best place in the world to live. Do you still think it is, or not?" Eighty percent of respondents—including nearly identical percentages of college graduates, high school graduates, and those who had not finished high school—answered yes. Alan Wolfe, a careful scholar who employed both polls and interviews to assess American attitudes, reported similar findings in 1998. For the middle classes, he wrote, "the idea of living in any other nation of the world is barely conceivable."[91]

On the other hand, polls at the time also exposed an underlying popular edginess that may have helped in the early and mid-1990s to make many Americans perceive both "decline" and the intensification of "culture wars." Notable was a Gallup survey in 1995 that indicated bits of good news: As earlier, most people were content in their personal lives. This was hardly surprising, for the United States, having helped to win the Cold War, was a giant on the world stage. More important, the economy was rapidly improving. But the poll also revealed an interesting pattern— one that in fact had often seemed to characterize popular attitudes throughout the expectant, restless, rights-conscious years since the 1960s: Americans continued to desire more in the way of entitlements and protections, and they wondered uneasily whether the world would get better, or worse, in the future.

It is obviously risky to conclude that polls or interviews such as these represented a last word. Still, the attitudes revealed by such surveys suggested a trend that, while visible in the 1980s, seemed fairly strong by the mid-1990s: In many ways the majority of Americans were doing better— in terms of real incomes, possessions, health, and comforts—and they were pleased about that. They were not so confident, however, about what lay ahead for the culture at large. A perceptive writer had a label for these feelings: "I'm OK—They're Not."[92] Only 35 percent of Americans in the 1995 Gallup poll believed that the world had become better than it had been in their parents' time. (Three percent had no opinion, and 52 per-

91. Robert Samuelson, *The Good Life and Its Discontents: The American Dream in the Age of Entitlement, 1945–1995* (New York, 1995), 214; Wolfe, *One Nation, After All*, 176.

92. David Whitman, *The Optimism Gap: The I'm OK—They're Not Syndrome and the Myth of American Decline* (New York, 1998). For a similar view, see Easterbrook, *The Progress Paradox*.

cent thought it was worse.) Only 23 percent believed that the "next generation of children" would live in a better world."[93]

Polls such as this suggested that "decline" was less a reality of American
life in the 1990s than a perception among people, especially among the
mostly middle-class white populace that was generally living more comfortably than in the past but that had developed large expectations about
rights and gratifications and that was living in a society that in some ways —
witness the shoddier manifestations of popular culture — seemed to be in
decline. In a manner that they found difficult to define, these Americans
were restless, both because they wanted more for themselves and because,
still cherishing ideals, they hoped to make their nation a better place.

In retrospect, however, it also seems accurate to conclude that the much-
discussed culture wars of the decade were a little less divisive than they
appeared to be, especially to polemicists like Bork, to political partisans,
and to conspiracy-minded, sensation-seeking, and crisis-raising profit-
seekers in the media. Perceptions of course matter in a society — culture
wars did worry politically engaged Americans, especially at their peak
during the early and mid-1990s. *Political* polarization remained sharp thereafter. Still, the United States maintained a large *cultural* center that was
both more broad-minded and more easygoing than one might have imagined from focusing on the extremes that dominated headlines and that
led off local newscasts on television.

93. Samuelson, *The Good Life and Its Discontents*, 261.

9

Immigration, Multiculturalism, Race

In challenging George H. W. Bush for the GOP presidential nomination in 1992, Patrick Buchanan proclaimed that rising immigration was threatening to tear the United States apart. "Our own country," he said, "is undergoing the greatest invasion in its history, a migration of millions of illegal aliens yearly from Mexico. . . . A nation that cannot control its own borders can scarcely call itself a state any longer."[1]

Though Buchanan was an especially vocal opponent of large-scale immigration, he was by no means the only American to fret about the "Balkanization" of the nation, or about the surge of "multiculturalism," as rising rights-consciousness by various minorities was dubbed at the time. Six years earlier, 73 percent of voters in California had approved Proposition 63, which amended the state constitution so as to establish English as the state's "official language." Seventeen other states followed California's example in the late 1980s.[2] Though Proposition 63 was not implemented in California, its symbolic thrust—aimed in part against bilingual education programs—was clear. In California, as in Texas and other states where high numbers of immigrants had been arriving since the 1970s, ethnic tensions were rising.

1. David Frum, *How We Got Here: The '70s, the Decade That Brought You Modern Life (For Better or Worse)* (New York, 2000), 144. For earlier developments of many of the social issues described in this chapter, see chapters 1 and 2.
2. Steven Gillon, *"That's Not What We Meant to Do": Reform and Its Unintended Consequences in Twentieth-Century America* (New York, 2000), 192–94.

The rush of immigration, however, was but one of a number of social and economic developments that seemed to be intensifying conflict in the United States at the time. As the Los Angeles riots demonstrated, racial confrontations seemed to be especially dangerous. Popular reactions to the sensationalized, long-drawn-out arrest and murder trial in 1994–95 of the black football hero O. J. Simpson, who had been arrested on charges of killing his former wife and a male friend of hers — both white — revealed extraordinary polarization by race. In 1998, three white racists in Jasper, Texas, tied James Byrd, a black man, to the back of a truck and dragged him to his death.

Class divisions, though less dramatic than these, also continued to trouble American society. As earlier, many blue-collar workers and labor union leaders protested against rising income inequality and against what they said was outrageous corporate arrogance and selfishness. The liberal economist and columnist Paul Krugman, a forceful critic of the rich and powerful, wrote that average salaries of corporate CEOs had risen from $1.3 million in 1970 to $37.5 million in 1998 — or from thirty-nine times to more than a thousand times the average earnings of their workers. He was convinced that the United States had entered a "New Gilded Age."[3]

Like Americans who were then insisting that the nation was in "decline" and beset by "culture wars," people who endorsed the arguments of partisans like Buchanan on the right and Krugman on the left maintained that a wide range of fights over rights and social justice was polarizing the United States. Media reports intensified such feelings. Politicians — more fiercely partisan and unforgiving in the Clinton years than at any other time since Watergate — added to a popular sense that Americans were at one another's throats in the 1990s.

Given the rapidly rising numbers of immigrants to America since the 1970s, it was hardly surprising that alarmists such as Buchanan captured attention in the late 1980s and 1990s. These numbers were striking compared to those of the recent past. Between the early 1920s, when restrictive and racially discriminatory immigration laws had been enacted, and the late 1960s, when new, more liberal legislation of 1965 began to take effect, immigration to the United States had remained low. In the thirty-four years between 1931 and 1965, the total number of legal immigrants had averaged around 150,000 per year, or around 5 million in all. Thereafter, the numbers exploded in size, to 4.5 million during the 1970s, 7.3 million during the

3. Krugman, "For Richer," *New York Times Magazine*, Oct. 20, 2002, 62ff.

1980s, and 9.1 million during the 1990s. Many millions more—guesses placed these numbers at between 250,000 and 350,000 per year in the 1980s and 1990s—entered illegally.[4] The total number of immigrants who came to the United States between 1970 and 2000 was therefore estimated to be slightly more than 28 million. Their arrival raised the percentage of Americans who were foreign-born from 4.7 in 1970 (an all-time twentieth-century low) to 10.4 in 2000, or 29.3 million people in a total population that had risen from 203.3 million in 1970 to 281.4 million thirty years later.[5]

People who welcomed this influx urged activists like Buchanan to relax. They emphasized that high rates of immigration had once before, in the early years of the twentieth century, dramatically altered the ethnic mix of America without harming the nation. Between 1900 and 1910, immigration had accounted for nearly 40 percent of overall population growth in the United States—the largest percentage in the nation's history.[6] The percentage of foreign-born in the population in 1910 had been 14.7—or more than 4 percent higher than it had become by 2000. Opponents of Buchanan in the 1990s insisted that the United States, a nation of immigrants, could comfortably accommodate its surge of newcomers.

Still, the influx of immigrants between 1970 and 2000 was large.[7] The *number* of Americans in 2000 who were foreign-born was roughly twice as

4. By early 2005, following several years of very high migrations, it was estimated that there were 11 million illegal immigrants in the United States. *New York Times*, March 14, May 20, 2005.
5. For statistics, *Stat. Abst.*, 2002, 10–11; and *New York Times Almanac*, 2003, 291–98. The percentage of the population that was foreign-born kept increasing in the early 2000s, to an estimated 11.5 by 2003 and to 35.7 million in number by 2004. *USA Today*, March 22, 2005. Key sources on American immigration include Hugh Davis Graham, *Collision Course: The Strange Convergence of Affirmative Action and Immigration Policy in America* (New York, 2002); John Skrentny, *The Minority Rights Revolution* (Cambridge, Mass., 2002); Tamar Jacoby, "Too Many Immigrants?" *Commentary* 113 (April 2002), 37–44; David Hollinger, "Amalgamation and Hypodescent: The Question of Ethnoracial Mixture in the History of the United States," *American Historical Review* 108 (Dec. 2003), 1363–90; Reed Ueda, "Historical Patterns of Immigrant Status and Incorporation in the United States," in Gary Gerstle and John Mollenkopf, eds., *E Pluribus Unum: Contemporary and Historical Perspectives on Immigrant Political Incorporation* (New York, 2001), 293–327; and Gillon, "That's Not What We Meant to Do," 163–99.
6. Immigration accounted for 19.4 percent of American population growth in the 1970s, 32.8 percent in the 1980s, and 27.8 percent in the 1990s.
7. *New York Times*, June 19, 2003. According to the census, America's population grew from 203.3 million in 1970 to 281.4 million in 2000, or by a little more than 38 percent over these thirty years. Between 2000 and mid-2003, it grew by another 9.4 million, to 290.8 million. During these three years the Hispanic population increased by 13 percent, the Asian population by 12.8 percent, and the white population by 1 percent. Ibid., June 15, 2004.

large as the previous all-time high (14.2 million in 1930) in modern United States history. The total number of people (56 million) who were foreign-born or who had one foreign-born parent reached 20 percent of the population by 2000. Moreover, growth in immigration was concentrated in a relatively few states, such as California, Texas, Florida, New Jersey, Illinois, and New York. By 2000, California's population had become 27 percent foreign-born. Though 800,000 residents, mostly whites, left the state between 1995 and 2000—many of them for the Mountain West—its population, driven upward by immigration, increased by 1.5 million during these five years.

The primary origins of these new arrivals—Latin America and East Asia—were strikingly different from those early in the century, when most immigrants had come from Eastern and Southern Europe. Between 1980 and 2000, only two million people arrived from Europe, most of them from Eastern Europe or from the Soviet Union and its successor states. Considerably more people, 5.7 million, came from Asia, and 6.8 million were natives of Mexico, Central America, and the Caribbean. An additional million hailed from South America. Smaller numbers migrated from Africa (around 600,000) and from Canada (250,000). Some 4 million legal immigrants—nearly a fourth of the total of legal arrivals from all countries during these twenty years—came from Mexico alone.

If migrants from Asia and from south of the border were identified as "people of color"—as many were—the United States was experiencing something of a "complexion revolution" in these years. Nearly three-fourths of the newcomers were either Asian (26 percent of the total) or Latino (46 percent) by background. By 2002, the number of American people (immigrants and others) identified as Latinos (38.8 million, or 13.5 percent of the population) had surpassed the number who were African American (36.7 million, or 12.7 percent of the population). The number of Asian Americans, which had been tiny in 1970, had also become impressive: 13 million, or 4 percent of the population by 2002. As of 2000, more than half of California's population was Asian, Latino, or black.[8]

In 1965, when Congress passed its major reform of immigration law, it had almost no idea that the measure would have consequences such as these. Caught up in the civil rights revolution of the time, reformers on the Hill were focused on ending the racially discriminatory national origins quota system that for many decades had dominated American immigration

---

8. Ibid., June 6, June 16, 2003. By that time the number of foreign-born had swelled from 28 million to 32 million.

procedures and that had damaged the country's international image. That new law included provisions establishing a limit on immigration of 290,000 per year. Of this total, 120,000 might come from places in the western hemisphere, and 170,000 from the rest of the world. No nation from the Old World would be permitted to send more than 20,000 per year.[9]

The legislation, however, included provisions that favored "family re-unification" over skills. Especially preferred were parents, spouses, and unmarried minor children of immigrants who had become United States citizens: All these relatives—"non-quota" immigrants—could come to America outside the overall numerical limits. Lesser preferences, in or-der, favored unmarried adult children of citizens, spouses and unmarried adult children of permanent resident aliens, and married children of United States citizens. Inasmuch as it continued to be relatively uncom-plicated for legal immigrants to become naturalized American citizens—after five or more years of residence—millions of people did so in order to enable their family members to join them. When these relatives became citizens, many of *their* relatives could gain admittance. The numbers ad-mitted via family unification thus exploded in ways that few legislators had anticipated in 1965. More than two-thirds of legal immigrants by the 1990s were entering the United States in this way.[10]

In the early 1980s, by which time the rising tide of newcomers was prompting nervous debate over these policies, pressure arose for Congress to narrow the gates. Advocates of restriction advanced an array of argu-ments: Immigrants (who were entitled to education in the public schools and if necessary to free emergency health care) crowded America's class-rooms and hospitals and burdened state and local governments; many immigrants, working off the books, paid no taxes; some immigrants landed on the welfare rolls; illegal immigration, uncontrolled by understaffed federal officials, was way out of hand. African American advocates of re-striction complained that low-wage immigrants were displacing them from the work force.[11] Labor leaders charged that employers were exploiting the newcomers, driving down overall wage rates and exacerbating poverty and income inequality in the United States.[12]

9. For details of this important legislation, see Roger Daniels, *Coming to America: A History of Immigration and Ethnicity in American Life* (New York, 2002), 338–44.
10. Gillon, *"That's Not What We Meant to Do,"* 163–99.
11. Orlando Patterson, *The Ordeal of Integration: Progress and Resentment in America's "Racial" Crisis* (Washington, 1997), 155–56.
12. For debates over affirmation action and immigration, see chapter 1.

Advocates of restriction included environmentalists and others who worried about population growth. The Federation of American Immigration Reform (FAIR), founded in 1978, took the lead in advancing this argument.[13] The rising tide of newcomers, they exclaimed, was mainly responsible for a swelling of America's population, which in the 1990s expanded by 32.7 million people—the largest number for any decade in the history of the country.[14] Other advocates of immigration restriction insisted that the crush from newcomers ratcheted up the costs of bilingual education programs, which in turn (they charged) impeded the process of acculturation.

The surge from Mexico, Central America, and the Caribbean especially aroused advocates of greater restriction. Thanks in part to the ease of air travel, they complained, these and other "birds of passage" frequently returned to their homelands, thereby acculturating to American ways more slowly than immigrants had done in the past. Advances in global communication, notably satellite television and cell phones, further helped immigrants to maintain close ties—and loyalties—to their home countries. Moreover, many immigrants in the 1980s and 1990s, like newcomers throughout American history, congregated in neighborhood enclaves. For all these reasons, worried Americans feared that the United States would soon find itself confronted with a large underclass of resentful, poorly assimilated people—like Turkish "guest workers" in Germany—who would undermine national harmony.

When substantial numbers of Latinos joined the rioters in Los Angeles in 1992, proponents of immigration restriction became especially clamorous. Calls for curbs intensified. Other voices, echoing the cries of restrictionists early in the century, called for stronger programs of "Americanization" in the schools and for the abolition of bilingual education programs. Still others filled the media with essentially racist scenarios that foresaw the

13. For opposition to high levels of immigration, see Peter Brimelow, *Alien Nation: Common Sense About America's Immigration Disaster* (New York, 1995); and Ronald Steel, "The Bad News," *New Republic*, Feb. 10, 1997, 27. Arguments pro and con are well presented in Roger Daniels and Otis Graham, *Debating American Immigration, 1882–Present* (Lanham, Md., 2001).

14. America's population grew from 248.7 million in 1990 to 281.4 million in 2000. The *rate* of population growth in the 1990s was 13.1 percent, higher than in the 1970s (11.4 percent) or 1980s (9.8 percent), but below the rate of 18.5 percent in the 1960s, when population had grown by 28 million (the second highest number, next to the 1990s, for any decade in American history). Most of the growth in the 1960s had come from natural increase of the resident population—not from immigration. *Stat. Abst.*, 2002, 8.

United States becoming less than half "white" within four or five decades.

Americans alarmed by the influx from abroad soon took action to cut the costs of immigration. In 1994, 60 percent of voters in California approved Proposition 187, which aimed to deny illegal immigrants access to public schools and various social services, including health care. When a federal judge ruled the measure unconstitutional, agitation for restriction increased in the state. In 1996, Congress approved a highly controversial welfare bill that denied to most *legal* immigrants federal money for a variety of social services—SSI, food stamps, and Medicaid—during their first five years in the country.[15]

People who opposed greater restrictions fired back point-for-point at these arguments.[16] Many immigrants, they said, took jobs—as busboys, dishwashers, yard workers, day laborers, maids, child-care workers—that had become vital to the functioning of the nation's service-based economy and that many other Americans, demanding higher wages, refused to accept. Supporters of immigration pointed out that though the use of public services by immigrants exacerbated budgetary problems in selected cities and states such as California, newcomers paid considerably more in sales and Social Security taxes (for retirement benefits that many of them would not be likely to receive) than they received from these services. They added that the contributions of immigrants—most of them young—to Social Security helped considerably to augment the funding of that all-important social entitlement. The majority of immigrants, they emphasized, were beyond school age, hardworking, and productive. The federal government, they said, should relieve overburdened local areas from some of their costs.

Most proponents of liberal immigration policy conceded that the influx of foreigners depressed wage rates in selected local labor markets, and that the tide of impoverished newcomers added to poverty and inequality in the United States. They asserted, however, that after twenty years in America, immigrants were no poorer on the average than was the population at large. The hard work of young and ambitious immigrants, they emphasized, further energized America's economy and promoted growth that eluded other nations with relatively low levels of in-migration. The real goal of immigration "reform," many observers said, should not be to establish low ceilings on the number of people annually admitted to the United States but to amend the laws so that preference would go to skilled

15. For discussion of this law, see chapter 11. In 1997, some of these provisions were softened.
16. Jacoby, "Too Many Immigrants?"

and productive people (as opposed to migrants, many of them elderly, who made use of the family reunification provisions).

Opponents of greater restriction also sought to refute the claim that immigrants were slow to acculturate. On the contrary, they maintained, most newcomers were as eager as earlier generations of immigrants had been to embrace American ways, including mastery of the English language. One estimate of the pace of acculturation concluded in 2004 that 60 percent of third-generation Mexican American children spoke only English at home.[17] Supporters of liberal immigration policy added that many Latinos and Asians (and Native Americans) were quick to out-marry. In 1990, the census reported that of those getting married, one-third of native-born Latinos and 50 percent of native-born Asian Americans were choosing spouses from outside their own ethnic groups.[18] Percentages such as these indicated that considerable numbers of newcomers to America, most of them young people, were taking steps that moved them beyond their ethnic enclaves.

Thanks to an odd coalition of interests with influence in Congress, the liberal immigration policies that had flourished since 1965 managed to survive. This coalition united legislators (many of them conservative on other issues) who heeded the interests of employers in their constituencies — cash crop farmers, retail chain managers, hotel and restaurant owners, parents looking for housekeepers or babysitters — with liberals and others who sympathized with the plight of would-be immigrants (many of them refugees from oppression) and who proclaimed the virtues of cultural pluralism and ethnic diversity. Allying with the employer interests that clamored for low-wage workers, Americans with multicultural views such as these — including increasing numbers of newly naturalized voters — were more successful politically in the 1990s than they had been earlier in the century, when Congress had enacted tough, racially discriminatory immigration laws and when highly ethnocentric Americanization programs had proliferated in school districts.[19] The political influence of pro-immigration views such as these was one of many indications that the United States in the 1980s and 1990s, a more welcoming nation than many other Western countries, was more receptive to ethnic diversity — more tolerant — than it had been in the past.

17. David Brooks, Op-Ed, *New York Times*, Feb. 24, 2004.
18. Hollinger, "Amalgamation and Hypodescent"; Christopher Jencks, "Who Should Get In?" *New York Review of Books*, Dec. 20, 2001, 94–102.
19. For these laws, see John Higham, *Strangers in the Land: Patterns of American Nativism, 1865–1925* (New York, 1963), 264–330.

In 1986, when Congress made a major stab at revising immigration policy, lawmakers behind this coalition succeeded in passing a measure that offered amnesty to illegal immigrants who had been continuously in the country since 1982. President Reagan signed it, and an estimated 1.7 million immigrants, nearly 70 percent of whom hailed from Mexico, took advantage of this offer.[20] The law included provisions aimed at requiring employers to verify the eligibility of newly hired employees to work in the United States. Employers who hired illegal immigrants faced seemingly tough sanctions, including prison terms. But Congress, bowing to the wishes of employers and many civil libertarians, did not really expect these sanctions to be widely observed. The act set up no reliable system of personal documentation (for instance, a computerized registry of Social Security numbers, or identity cards—widespread in other nations—featuring photographs, bar codes, and fingerprints) that might have enabled enforcement of these provisions.[21]

Non-enforcement of the law thereby sent a message that subsequent waves of illegal immigrants came to understand: The pro-immigration coalition of employers, liberals, and legislators with significant numbers of newly naturalized voters in their constituencies had no stomach for rigorous enforcement of sanctions. Nor did presidential candidates seeking Latino and Asian votes. Moreover, it continued to be extraordinarily difficult to track down the whereabouts of large numbers of people who overstayed tourist visas, to police the long Mexican-American border, or to stop the throngs of very poor and often desperate people in nearby nations from seeking a better life. The Border Patrol was hopelessly outnumbered, and the Bureau of Immigration and Naturalization was underfunded and inefficient.

In 2000 and later, immigration remained a fairly contentious issue in the United States. Most people favored reductions in the size of it, as well as tougher measures against illegal entrants, but political leaders still tried to craft compromises that would enable undocumented but needed agricultural workers to earn temporary (or, in time permanent) residency. Benefiting from the low-wage labor of immigrants, most Americans—also enjoying Chinese takeout or salsa and chips—seemed cautiously accepting of the more ethnically diverse world that large-scale immigration had helped to create since the 1970s.

---

20. A separate amnesty, for farm workers, aided another 1.3 million. See Daniels, *Coming to America*, 391–97.
21. Otis Graham, "The Unfinished Reform: Regulating Immigration in the National Interest," in Daniels and Graham, *Debating American Immigration*, 152–57.

A cartoon in 2003 captured the political power of pro-immigrant interests in the United States—interests that helped to sustain one of the greatest social and cultural changes of late twentieth-century American history. It depicted a cluster of reporters with microphones surrounding a United States senator. A newsman asked him, "So you endorse the idea of sending all illegal immigrants back where they came from, Senator?" He replied, "Right! As soon as the grass trimming, cleanup, farm picking, and fast food work is done."[22]

MANY OTHER AMERICANS, however, complained in the late 1980s and '90s of what they saw as a surge of contentious and separatist "multiculturalism," driven in large part by the rights-conscious efforts of second-generation immigrants, especially middle-class Asians and Hispanics (and by certain liberal intellectuals). Like blacks, many of whom as of the early 1990s began to identify themselves as "African Americans," increasing numbers of Hispanic Americans, Asian Americans, and other ethnic groups organized in order to protest against what they perceived as their marginalization in American life and against the negative stereotyping of their cultures that they saw in films, television, advertisements, and textbooks.

American Indians were among the groups that proudly began to assert ethnic identifications that they had not emphasized in the recent past. Prior to 1970, most Native Americans had not identified themselves as such to census enumerators. Thereafter, they seemed increasingly eager to do so. Though natural population increase among Indians was low, the number of Americans who proclaimed their Indian-ness thereby ballooned. In 1970, the census had reported a Native American population of approximately 800,000, or roughly four-tenths of 1 percent of total population. By 1980, this number had jumped to 1.4 million, and by 2000 it had risen to 2.5 million—or nearly 1 percent of total population. This was an increase in numbers that may have been bolstered here and there in very small ways by the eagerness of people to claim Native American ancestry in order to share in astonishingly high profits from Indian-run casinos, but it was driven far more powerfully by the rise in self-identification that many American Indians, joining the culture-wide surge of ethnic and racial pride, had come to feel.[23]

22. *Chicago Tribune* cartoon, syndicated in *Providence Journal*, June 1, 2003.
23. *Stat. Abst.*, 2002, 13, 41; Andrew Hacker, ed., *U/S: A Statistical Portrait of the American People* (New York, 1983), 35–36; Hollinger, "Amalgamation and Hypodescent."

Multiculturalist activism of this sort was entirely understandable, for Anglocentrism had long dominated American popular culture and fostered unflattering stereotypes and discriminatory treatment of outsiders. Recognizing the power of white oppression in the past—Indians, for example, had suffered extraordinarily at the hands of whites—many Americans came to agree that change was long overdue. Hailing the spread of ethnic and cultural diversity, they began to challenge the Anglocentric curricula that had long predominated at schools and universities.[24] When famous people proudly proclaimed their multiethnic heritages, many people smiled. The golf star Tiger Woods, for instance, told Oprah Winfrey in 1997 that he wished to be called "Cablinasian"—that is, a blend of Caucasian, black, Indian, and Asian. Though his statement irritated a number of African American leaders who wondered why he did not celebrate his blackness, "liberal multiculturalism" of this sort had an appeal to the millions of Americans who were recognizing the desirability—or the inevitability—of greater cultural diversity.[25] Business leaders, perceiving such a future, began to mount aggressive campaigns of niche marketing in order to target the many consumers who asserted ethnic identifications.

Other Americans, however, resisted what they regarded as the exaggerated claims to entitlements by minority groups. The United States, they thought, was becoming a crazy quilt—a ragged one—of aggressive ethnic interests that were playing a selfish and therefore divisive game of identity politics. They objected especially to the extension of preferences such as affirmative action to people other than blacks and Native Americans, groups that had experienced uniquely brutal discrimination throughout the American past. Why, they asked, should Mexican Americans, most of whom fared far better in the United States than they had in their home country, enjoy rights and entitlements that other ethnic groups had not been offered in the past? Why should Asian Americans from upper-middle-class backgrounds expect to benefit from admissions procedures at universities? Why were schools required to spend large sums of money on bilingual education? As the Los Angeles riots had demonstrated, some African Americans and Latinos seconded popular resentments about Asians—aggressive newcomers, they complained, who displaced them from their jobs and/or looked down on them.

24. See Lawrence Levine, *The Opening of the American Mind: Canons, Culture, and History* (Boston, 1996).
25. Nathan Glazer, *We Are All Multiculturalists Now* (Cambridge, Mass., 1997); Glazer, "Multiculturalism and a New America," in John Higham, ed., *Civil Rights and Social Wrongs: Black-White Relations Since World War II* (University Park, Pa., 1997), 120–33; Anthony Appiah, "The Multicultural Misunderstanding," *New York Review of Books*, Oct. 9, 1997, 30–36.

Complex and often resentful feelings such as these mounted in California, where voters approved Proposition 209 in 1996. This prohibited the state and local governments from giving preferences in hiring, university admissions, or contracting on the basis of "race, sex, color, ethnicity, or national origin." In 1997, California voters approved Proposition 227, which was aimed at ending bilingual education programs in the state. Analyses of this vote exposed the gulf that divided Latinos from non-Latinos. Though the referendum passed easily, 61 to 39 percent, Latinos opposed it, 63 to 37 percent.[26]

Many Americans bridled at what they regarded as expressions by immigrants and others of "excessive self-esteem" or "romantic ethnicity." Some of these expressions, they complained, encouraged ethnic or racial separatism — that is, "illiberal multiculturalism." The eminent historian Arthur Schlesinger Jr., a liberal in his politics, published a widely noticed book on the subject in 1991. Its title, *The Disuniting of America: Reflections on a Multicultural Society*, revealed the extent of his concern. Schlesinger was caustic about the spread on college campuses of detailed and politically correct speech codes that sought to protect minorities but that in some cases threatened rights guaranteed by the First Amendment. Highly Afrocentric versions of history appalled him. One racist version, taught by a provocative professor at the City College of New York, described whites as materialistic and aggressive "ice people" who brought the three "D's," "domination, destruction, and death," to the world. Africans, having been raised in sunlight, were warm, humanistic, and communitarian "sun people." Rich Jews, this teacher told his classes, financed the slave trade.[27]

Ethnic chauvinism especially worried Schlesinger, who believed that it was severing bonds that had held the United States together. "A cult of ethnicity," he wrote, "has arisen both among non-Anglo whites and among nonwhite minorities to denounce the idea of a melting pot, to challenge the concept of 'one people,' and to protect, promote, and perpetuate separate ethnic and racial communities." This "multiethnic dogma," he emphasized, "abandons historic purposes, replacing assimilation by fragmentation, integration by separation. It belittles *unum* and glorifies *pluribus*."[28]

26. Skrentny, *Minority Rights Revolution*, 337–39. In 1998, the state of Washington approved its own version of California's Proposition 209. A referendum in Arizona also abolished bilingual education there.

27. (New York, 1993), 115, 66–67. Some other contemporary writers went well beyond Schlesinger and predicted dire consequences if high immigration continued in the future. See Brimelow, *Alien Nation*.

28. Schlesinger, *The Disuniting of America*, 15–17.

Outside of a few hotbeds of continuing conflict, such as California, battles over multiculturalism, like many other struggles over cultural change in the United States, seemed to ebb a bit in the late 1990s. Indeed, in most parts of America these controversies had been far less heated that they were in many other countries at the time. In the 1990s, as earlier, violence flared in Sri Lanka, Spain, Northern Ireland, and the Balkans, to name but a few of the spots on the globe where angry activists and separatists stoked the flames of rebellion. By contrast, surveys of attitudes in the United States revealed that large majorities of middle-class Americans, regardless of race or ethnicity, continued to subscribe to common values— notably democracy and the importance of hard work and achievement— and that they mostly accepted the diversity that multiculturalism was promoting. Weathering extremes, this center normally held.[29]

For the most part, the legacy of multiculturalist activism that had risen in the early 1990s seemed as of the early 2000s to be fairly benign. By then, it had succeeded to an extent in challenging the Anglocentrism that had been common in American textbooks, museums, films, and the media. Fights over political correctness on college campuses had subsided. In their reaction to rising immigration and multiculturalism, as to many other trends that arose in the United States during the late twentieth century, most American people exhibited higher degrees of acceptance and adaptability than had been the case in earlier years of the century.

Even so, the social and economic deprivations affecting many people of color, including immigrants, remained serious. To the extent that advocates of multiculturalism focused on campus speech codes, textbooks, and course offerings, as many did, they may have helped to divert public attention from these larger issues of social and economic justice. Some ethnic leaders continued to believe that this was the case. As one advocate for immigrants exclaimed, multicultural agitation was often "a pacifier, an antidote to the anger and outrage that we bitterly repress."[30]

29. David Hollinger, *Postethnic America: Beyond Multiculturalism* (New York, 1995), 137–42; Alan Wolfe, *One Nation, After All: What Middle-Class Americans Really Think About God, Country, Family, Racism, Welfare, Immigration, Homosexuality, Work, the Right, the Left, and Each Other* (New York, 1998).

30. Hazel Carby, "Can the Tactics of Cultural Integration Counter the Persistence of Political Apartheid? Or, the Multicultural Wars, Part Two," in Austin Sarat, ed., *Race, Law, and Culture: Reflections on Brown v. Board of Education* (New York, 1997), 221–28.

Gen. Colin Powell in desert gear, Saudi Arabia, September 1990. *SRA Rodney Kerns/ Defense Visual Information Center, Riverside, California.*

President Bush and his wife, Barbara, Saudi Arabia, November 1990. General Norman Schwarzkopf is at Bush's left. *George Bush Presidential Library.*

Condoleezza Rice, a specialist concerning Soviet and East European affairs on the National Security Council, with President Bush, Secretary of State James Baker (on Bush's left), and senior staff, Helsinki, September 1990. *George Bush Presidential Library.*

Clarence Thomas.
© *Reuters/CORBIS.*

Anita Hill.
© *Bettmann/CORBIS.*

Supreme Court nominee Clarence Thomas and University of Oklahoma law professor Anita Hill testify at Thomas's highly publicized confirmation hearings, held by the Senate Judiciary Committee in 1991.

H. Ross Perot, a presidential candidate, 1992. © *Reuters/ CORBIS.*

Facing page, top   Riots in Los Angeles: a police officer holding a gun on two suspected looters, May 1, 1992. *AP/Wide World.*

Facing page, bottom   Patrick Buchanan, seeking the GOP nomination, March 1992. © *Robert Maass/CORBIS.*

Above President Bill Clinton and his wife, Hillary. © *Jeffrey Markowitz/CORBIS SYGMA.*

Left Clinton with Senate GOP leader Robert Dole (left) and Rep. Newt Gingrich, 1993. *Clinton Presidential Library.*

Demonstrations concerning abortion, outside the Supreme Court, December 1993.
AP/Wide World.

Somalis drag a dead American soldier on a street in Mogadishu, Somalia, October 1993. © *Watson/CORBIS SYGMA*.

Oprah Winfrey holding a town meeting, November 1994. © *Najlah Feanny/ CORBIS SABA*.

The Supreme Court, November 1994. Back row, left to right: Ruth Bader Ginsburg, David H. Souter, Clarence Thomas, Stephen G. Breyer. Front Row, left to right: Antonin Scalia, John Paul Stevens, William H. Rehnquist, Sandra Day O'Connor, Anthony Kennedy. *Richard Strauss Collection, The Supreme Court Historical Society.*

Newt Gingrich holding the Republicans' "Contract with America," 1994. © *Reuters/ CORBIS.*

A T-shirt vendor outside the courthouse during the O.J. Simpson trial in Los Angeles, July 1994. © *Ted Soqui/CORBIS SYGMA.*

The shattered Oklahoma City federal building, bombed April 19, 1995. *Staff Sgt. Dean W. Wagner/Defense Visual Information Center, Riverside, California.*

Independent counsel Kenneth Starr reading from
the U.S. Constitution during the impeachment
inquiry of the House Judiciary Committee, November 19, 1998. © *Reuters/CORBIS.*

Facing page, top Cartoonist Mike Peters on affirmative action, *Dayton Daily
News,* December 1997. *King Features Syndicate.*

Facing page, bottom A nation of immigrants. © *The New Yorker Collection
2004 Mick Stevens from cartoonbank.com. All Rights Reserved.*

President-elect George W. Bush and Federal Reserve
Chairman Alan Greenspan, Washington, D.C., December
2000. *AP/Wide World.*

Facing page, top   Damage to the U.S.S. *Cole,* following its bombing at Aden
on October 12, 2000. © *Reuters/CORBIS.*

Facing page, bottom   Bill Clinton with Democratic presidential candidate Al
Gore, August 2000. © *Reuters/CORBIS.*

"Everything was better back when everything was worse."

A reflection, 2003, on America's past and present. © The New Yorker Collection
2003 David Sipress from cartoonbank.com. All Rights Reserved.

CHIEF AMONG THESE more serious social and economic problems, as ever in American history, were divisions between blacks and whites. Were these divisions narrowing or widening? One prominent scholar of race relations, Harvard sociology professor Orlando Patterson, was guardedly optimistic, writing in 1997, "Relations between ordinary Afro-Americans and Euro-Americans are, in fact, the best they have ever been, although still far from ideal."[31] Many other writers, especially in the early and mid-1990s, were if anything more pessimistic than in the past. Their books flung apocalyptic-sounding titles at readers: *American Apartheid, Tragic Failure, The Coming Race War in America*. Andrew Hacker, author of one such book (revealingly titled *Two Nations*), concluded in 1992, "A huge racial chasm remains, and there are few signs that the coming century will see it closed."[32]

Patterson and others of his persuasion pointed to several encouraging developments. These included the rise of steadily more liberal racial attitudes among whites, at least as measured by polls; continuing support by a majority of blacks for integration, not separatism; the successful integration of the nation's armed services; and less stereotypical representation of blacks in film, television, and ads. Blacks, they added, were gaining representation in government bureaucracies, police and fire departments, and labor unions.[33] African Americans were pleased in 1994 when Byron De La Beckwith, long suspected of having murdered civil rights hero Medgar Evers in 1963, was finally convicted and sentenced to life in prison for the killing.

Most black leaders were also happy that affirmative action procedures—by then solidly entrenched in major corporations as well as universities—had

31. Patterson, *The Ordeal of Integration*, 2. Other cautiously optimistic accounts of race relations in the 1990s are Paul Sniderman and Thomas Piazza, *The Scar of Race* (Cambridge, Mass., 1993); Stephan Thernstrom and Abigail Thernstrom, *America in Black and White: One Nation, Indivisible* (New York, 1997); and Howard Schulman et al., *Racial Attitudes in America: Trends and Interpretations* (Cambridge, Mass., 1997).

32. Andrew Hacker, *Two Nations: Black and White, Separate, Hostile, Unequal* (New York, 1995), 245. See also Derrick Bell, *Faces at the Bottom of the Well* (New York, 1992); Douglas Massey and Nancy Denton, *American Apartheid: Segregation and the Making of the Underclass* (Cambridge, Mass., 1993); Tom Wicker, *Tragic Failure: Racial Integration in America* (New York, 1996); and Carl Rowan, *The Coming Race War in America: A Wake-up Call* (Boston, 1996).

33. Terry Anderson, *In Pursuit of Fairness: A History of Affirmative Action* (New York, 2004), 277–79.

survived, and they were pleased by the integration that had developed in the military. They also welcomed advances that they were making in local politics. Though blacks still had little chance of being elected to the Senate—Carol Moseley Braun of Illinois became only the second African American to succeed in doing so (in 1992)—they scored victories elsewhere.[34] During the late 1980s and 1990s, African American candidates won mayoralties in the predominantly non-black cities of New York, Seattle, Denver, and Minneapolis.[35]

Relative to whites, blacks also made encouraging economic gains in the 1990s. Thanks to rapid economic progress late in the decade, the median household income for blacks increased considerably—from roughly $24,000 (in constant 2000 dollars) in 1990 to $30,400 in 2000, or by 27 percent. In the same period, median household income for whites rose more slowly, from $40,100 in 1990 to $44,200 in 2000, or by 10 percent.[36] The median money income of black households in 2000 was nearly 69 percent of white households in 2000, compared to 60 percent ten years earlier. The income of African American married couples, which had been 67 percent of the income of white couples in 1967, had risen to 87 percent by 1995.[37] College-educated black women fared very well in the workforce.

Black poverty declined during the decade from 9.8 million in 1990, affecting 31.9 percent of all blacks, to 7.9 million in 2000, or 22 percent. This was a stunning decrease, at last knocking down percentages of black poverty that had hovered between 30.7 and 35.7 between 1970 and 1990. All of this improvement occurred after 1993, following recovery from the

34. The other black senator was Edward Brooke of Massachusetts, who served two terms between 1967 and 1979. In 2004, Barack Obama of Illinois, the son of a black Kenyan father and a white American mother, became the third black person to be elected to the Senate. During Reconstruction in the 1870s, two African American men had been appointed to the Senate.

35. Blacks, however, still held a smaller percentage of elective offices in America than their numbers in the population would otherwise have suggested. For the armed services, see David King and Zachary Karabell, *The Generation of Trust: Public Confidence in the U.S. Military Since Vietnam* (Washington, 2003), 46–48.

36. Median household income for people classified by the census as Hispanics rose in constant 2000 dollars during the 1990s from $28,700 to $33,400, or by 17 percent. For Asian Americans it increased from $49,400 to $55,500. Overall, household income rose in constant 2000 dollars during the 1990s from $38,400 to $42,200. *Stat. Abst.*, 2002, 433.

37. James Wilson, review of Orlando Patterson, *The Ordeal of Integration*, in *New York Review of Books*, Nov. 16, 1997, 10.

recession of the early 1990s.[38] The number of blacks who lived in crowded, poverty-stricken central cities declined during the decade, from an estimated 4.8 million people in 1990 to 3.1 million in 2000. This was 9 percent of overall black population in 2000.[39] A considerable number of African Americans were residing in racially mixed areas: In the mid-1990s, one-half of all black people lived in neighborhoods that were 50 percent or more white. Greater racial integration was developing in workplaces.[40]

Optimists, finally, derived satisfaction from signs that the sharp and historically powerful dualism of black versus white was at last becoming a little more blurred. Virtually all scientists by then agreed that the concept of "race" was a "social construct" that had no significant meaning as a genetic matter, and that the old "one drop rule" that had hardened racial categories was inane.[41] Perhaps more important in changing (though slowly) the ways that people identified "race" was the greatly increased number of other "people of color," notably Latinos. Almost half of Americans who told census takers in 2000 that they were Latinos did not identify themselves as either "white" or "black." They replied instead that they were of "some other race" or of "two or more races." The *New York Times*, noting in 2003 the apparent weakening of once sharply defined racial categories, reported happily, "Simply put, most Latinos do not see themselves playing in the colored jerseys that are provided."[42]

38. *Stat. Abst.*, 2002, 441. Poverty among people classified as Hispanics decreased during the 1990s from 28.1 percent to 21.2 percent. Poverty among whites, already far lower, fell more slowly, from 10.7 percent to 9.4 percent. Poverty among Asian Americans decreased from 12.2 percent to 10.7 percent. The overall poverty rate was 13.5 percent in 1990 and 11.3 in 2000, which was the lowest recorded rate since such statistics had first been gathered in the early 1960s.

39. Estimates of William Julius Wilson, *New York Times*, June 16, 2003. Total black population in 2000 was 34.7 million, or 12.3 percent of overall population. *Stat. Abst.*, 2002, 41. Wilson used a common definition of such areas: census tracts in which at least 40 percent of residents were poor. Some other estimates of the black "underclasses" were considerably lower. James Wilson, *New York Review of Books*, Nov. 16, 1997, 10, placed the numbers at only 900,000.

40. Patterson, *The Ordeal of Integration*, 42–45.

41. *New York Times*, March 14, 2005. A notable exception, from social scientists, was a highly controversial book that highlighted the importance of hereditary factors in the development of human intelligence: Richard Herrnstein and Charles Murray, *The Bell Curve: Intelligence and Class Structure in American Life* (New York, 1994). Widely denounced as racist, the book received a dismal reception from reviewers.

42. The census reported that 48 percent of Hispanics described themselves as white, 2 percent as black, 6 percent as two or more races, and 42 percent as "some other race." *New York Times*, June 20, Nov. 19, 2003; Hollinger, "Amalgamation and Hypodescent." By mid-2003, 4.3 million Americans identified themselves as being of more than one race. This was an increase of 10.5 percent over the number that had so self-identified in 2000. *New York Times*, June 15, 2004.

IN 2004, HOWEVER, the black scholar Henry Louis Gates was among the many worried Americans who looked back on recent trends and surveyed some roads not yet taken. The 1990s, Gates concluded, were "the best of times, the worst of times."[43] As he pointed out, black-white relations continued to be the nation's number one socio-economic problem.

Central to this problem was the enduring power of social class—a power nearly as great, many observers maintained, as that of race.[44] Though middle-class blacks gained economically in the late 1990s, the median money income of African American households in 2000 was still only 69 percent as high as that of white households. Statistics measuring personal resources that include not only income but also inheritance, possessions, and investments revealed that the average net worth of African Americans may actually have declined relative to that of whites, from one-eighth of white net worth in the 1970s to one-fourteenth by 2004.[45]

Though poverty rates among blacks were declining, millions of African Americans remained in need. Their poverty rate in 2000 was still 2.5 times that of whites. The unemployment rate for blacks (7.6 percent in 2000) remained more than twice what it was for whites (3.5). A third or more of black people who were eligible for means-tested programs like food stamps or Medicaid were unaware of their eligibility.[46] African Americans were far more likely than whites to lack health insurance. For these and other reasons, the life expectancy of blacks continued to lag behind that of whites: In 2000, it was 71.2, compared to 77.4 for whites.[47]

The "underclass" problem, while slightly less severe during the more prosperous late 1990s, had surely not gone away. The grim statistics on black crime and imprisonment were vivid, shaming reminders of that fact.[48]

43. *Providence Journal*, Feb. 2, 2004.
44. Orlando Patterson, "Racism Is Not the Issue," Op-Ed, *New York Times*, Nov. 16, 1997.
45. *New York Times*, Feb. 15, 2003. A study published by the Pew Hispanic Center in the economically unsettled year of 2004 used census data to conclude that the median net worth of black households, at $6,000, was less than one-fourteenth of that of white households ($88,000) and slightly less than that of Hispanic households ($7,900). Inequality of wealth worsened during the late 1990s. Ibid., Oct. 18, 2004. For earlier figures for the 1970s, see note 14, chapter 1.
46. For unemployment rates, see *Stat. Abst*, 2002, 36. In the early 2000s, it was estimated that more than 30 percent of eligible Americans were not receiving benefits from food stamps or from Medicaid. *New York Times*, Feb. 21, 2004.
47. Compared to life expectancy at birth in 1975 of 66.8 for blacks and 73.4 for whites. The racial gap, changing little in twenty-five years, was 6.6 years in 1975 and 6.2 in 2000. *Stat. Abst.*, 2002, 71.
48. See chapter 8 for discussion of blacks, crime, and imprisonment.

Dramatizing these problems, Louis Farrakhan, head of the Nation of Islam, organized a widely publicized Million Man March of black men in Washington in 1995. Black men, he said, were going to "clean up their lives and rebuild their neighborhoods."[49]

Equally worrisome were numbers regarding poverty among black children. By 2000, these numbers looked better than they had between 1970 and 1995, when more than 40 percent of black children under the age of eighteen had been so classified. But in large part because of the still high percentages of female-headed black families, 30.4 percent of African Americans under the age of eighteen lived in poverty in 2000.[50] Many of these children had serious health problems: Like millions of children in low-income white families, they suffered from high rates of asthma, mental retardation, lead poisoning, diabetes, and learning disabilities.

It was also obvious that residential segregation remained widespread in the 1990s. Though it was true that one-half of African Americans resided in neighborhoods that were at least 50 percent non-black, an additional 40 percent lived within almost wholly black enclaves. In a great many parts of the country, America remained a nation of vanilla suburbs and chocolate cities. Some suburbs, too—such as Prince George County, Maryland—had become heavily African American in composition. Many blacks, of course, preferred to reside in predominantly black areas; living close to whites had little appeal to them. It was also clear that significant cultural preferences continued to hinder relaxed interracial socialization: African Americans and whites had distinctly different tastes in music, film, and television shows. In any event, truly mixed-race neighborhoods and social groups remained very much the exception rather than the rule in the United States.

Studies of marriage further exposed continuing racial divisions. Concerning this ever sensitive issue, some statistics suggested that increasing numbers of black-white marriages might be launching a trend toward interracial amalgamation. In 2000, for instance, there were an estimated 363,000 black-white married couples in the United States, a 70 percent increase over the number (211,000) in 1990. This signified a rise in the percentage of married African Americans with non-black spouses from 6 to 10 within only ten years. The percentage in 2000, moreover, was higher

---

49. The National Park Service estimated that the number of men who marched was 400,000. The event had no clearly beneficial results.
50. *Stat. Abst.*, 2002, 441. Poverty among white children in 2000 was 12.3 percent, and among Hispanics, 27.3 percent.

than the percentage of Jewish-gentile marriages had been in 1940—a rate that escalated to 50 percent during the ensuing sixty years. In time, some people speculated, comparably rapid increases in black-white marriages might develop. Moreover, percentages of white-black cohabitation in the 1990s were thought to be higher than those of white-black marriage.[51]

Statistics such as these made it obvious that America had moved substantially beyond the situation in 1967, when the Supreme Court, in *Loving v. Virginia*, had finally ruled that laws against interracial marriage were unconstitutional.[52] As of the early 2000s, however, the percentage of blacks and whites who were intermarrying was still small—far smaller than the percentages of American-born Latinos, American-born Asians, or Native Americans who were doing so.[53] And neither TV nor Hollywood appeared eager in the early 2000s to depict romance across the color line. In the new century, it was premature to predict large increases in the number of black-white marriages in the future.

THEN THERE WAS THE EXTRAORDINARY CONTENTIOUSNESS and publicity surrounding the O. J. Simpson case in 1994–95. Not even the Los Angeles riots, horrifying though they had been, seemed as discouraging to people who hoped for a closing of the racial divide in America.

The "Juice," a black man, was a celebrity: a Hall of Fame football star, a movie actor, a TV sports announcer, and a dashing, bounding presence in television ads for Hertz rental cars. In June 1994, he was arrested on charges of having stabbed to death his divorced wife, Nicole Brown Simpson, a white woman, and a white friend of hers, Ron Goldman. The two bloody bodies were found outside the front door of her condominium in the upscale Brentwood section of Los Angeles. This was not far from Simpson's own substantial residence.

Five days after the bodies were discovered, police issued warrants for Simpson's arrest on charges of murder. When he failed to turn himself in as he had promised, they launched an all-out hunt for his car, a white Ford Bronco. By early evening they had located it, whereupon television reporters, learning of its whereabouts, entered the act. Following the Bronco

---

51. Statistics from Hollinger, "Amalgamation and Hypodescent," 1385–86. See also Jencks, "Who Should Get In?" 94–112. Other reports, using 2000 census data, concluded that the percentage of married black men with white spouses was 6, and the percentage of married black women with white spouses was 3. See *New York Times*, March 11, 2001, April 24, 2005.

52. *Loving v. Virginia*, 388 U.S. 1 (1967).

53. See sources cited in note 51 for these numbers.

from helicopters, TV cameras captured the car moving at moderate speed along the Artesia Freeway in Los Angeles. A friend, Al Cowlings, was driving it, with Simpson said to be armed and suicidal in the backseat. Police helicopters and a phalanx of cruisers, red lights flashing in the gathering darkness, accompanied the Bronco for more than fifty miles in a stately procession that lasted for nearly two hours.

By the time the procession ended, it had preempted programming on a vast number of stations. It was estimated that 100 million Americans saw parts of the pursuit. Only a few national events—Kennedy's assassination, the moonwalk of 1969—had ever attracted such an audience. Rapt viewers wondered what would happen. Would the Bronco crash? Would Simpson kill himself? Would there be a shootout? None of the above, as it turned out. After the car reached Simpson's home, the troubled celebrity eventually emerged from it. Though he was carrying a handgun, he did not shoot anybody. After more suspense, police made the arrest. It was nearly 9:00 P.M. Pacific time, and midnight on the East Coast, when the televised drama finally ended.[54]

From then on, and throughout a nationally televised trial that lasted for nine months in 1995 (jurors were locked in hotel rooms for 265 nights), millions of Americans fixated on the many sordid details of the murders. In doing so they followed a drama that exposed many unflattering aspects of American society and culture: the powerful role of money in the criminal justice system, the extraordinary allure of celebrity culture, the seductive appeal to Americans of stories featuring sex and violence, and the saturation coverage by TV of sensational events. Television lavished greater attention on the trial than it did, combined, on the contemporaneous bloodletting in Bosnia, the forthcoming presidential election, and the terrorist bombing that killed 168 people in Oklahoma City. As much as any event of the 1990s, the Simpson trial spurred the development on television, especially on cable news stations, of "infotainment"—wherein "reality shows" featuring day-by-day, week-by-week, month-by-month updates of sensational crimes involving sex and violence dominated the screen.

Simpson, a wealthy man, hired a battery of prominent lawyers and DNA analysts to defend him against charges that most white Americans considered to be manifestly true. Within a month of his arrest, 77 percent of white Americans said that the case against him was either "very strong" or "fairly strong." By contrast, only 45 percent of blacks saw the case that way.

54. For an extensive exploration of this case, see Haynes Johnson, *The Best of Times: America in the Clinton Years* (New York, 2001), 107–64. Also Hacker, *Two Nations*, 207–22.

People who believed that Simpson was guilty emphasized that he had seemed to be avoiding arrest and that he had a history of battering his former wife, who had often called police. After one such complaint, Simpson had pleaded no contest to a misdemeanor charge of abusing her and was fined, sentenced to 120 hours of community service, and placed on two years' probation.

Without his attorneys, whom few Americans—black or white—could have afforded, Simpson might have had no chance in court. But he was a celebrity, and his lawyers were smart and determined. Leading them was Johnnie Cochran, a shrewd and experienced African American trial lawyer. Cochran and his assistants introduced carefully analyzed DNA evidence and picked damaging holes in the actions and testimony of a white policeman who had conducted the murder investigations. Cochran emphasized to the jury—made up of nine blacks, two whites, and one Latino—that racial prejudice in the criminal justice system had inspired the charges against his client. Prosecutors, including a leading African American attorney, angrily retorted that Cochran was brandishing the "race card."

The case vividly exposed the commercialization that often accompanied sensational events involving sex, violence, and celebrities in America. It was later estimated that the total in commercial spin-offs from the case approximated $200 million. A slew of books on the case soon appeared. Even while the trial was taking place, some of the jurors sold their stories for later use by tabloids. Purchases of Broncos (and of other SUVs) boomed as never before. The *National Enquirer* paid Nicole Brown Simpson's father $100,000 for her diary and featured the case on its cover in twenty-one of twenty-seven issues in late 1994. Her father also received $162,000 from a syndicated tabloid TV show for selling and narrating a home video of her wedding to Simpson. A girlfriend of Simpson's pocketed an advance of $3 million for a book on the case, and posed for *Playboy* as the trial opened. It was reported that Cochran and Marcia Clark, the lead prosecutor, between them received some $7 million in advances for their books on the case.[55]

Especially disheartening to many Americans was the polarization along racial lines that the case continued to reveal about attitudes toward the criminal justice system. It replicated the divide that had been exposed over reactions to police actions in the arrest of Rodney King in 1991. Not long after Simpson was arrested, 63 percent of whites opined that he would get a fair trial. Sixty-nine percent of blacks disagreed. When he was ac-

55. This and other information in the above paragraphs is from Johnson, *Best of Times*.

quitted of first-degree murder charges in October—after the jurors had deliberated for only three hours—polls revealed similarly sharp divisions along racial lines. Jubilant celebrations erupted in black sections of L.A. "The Juice is loose," blacks rejoiced. African American law students at Howard University, having anxiously awaited the verdict, broke out in prolonged cheering. White law students—like virtually all whites in America—were stunned and disbelieving. As since the beginning of the Simpson case dramatics, racial polarization remained strong.[56]

WAS THERE HOPE THAT RACE RELATIONS in the United States might improve in the future? The answer depended partly on America's public schools, where it was hoped that subsequent generations of minority students might do better.

Formidable racial problems, however, continued to plague the public schools, especially in inner-city areas. Stubbornly persistent residential segregation, along with conservative Supreme Court decisions that terminated a number of school desegregation orders, combined to promote resegregation of public education in the 1990s.[57] In 1988, when the long and arduous drive to desegregate public schools had peaked, 43 percent of black students in the South had attended public schools that were 50 percent or more white. Thirteen years later the percentage of southern blacks in such schools had skidded to 30—roughly the same as it had been in the early 1970s. "Tracking"—the placement of white students in college-bound classes and of blacks in less demanding courses—increased in many of these schools. Thanks to very high concentrations of African Americans in many large cities of the North and Midwest, segregated schools were more common there than they were in the South. Similar trends pushing greater school segregation separated Latinos from whites.[58]

The quality of a large number of predominantly black and Latino inner-city schools at the end of the twentieth century was scandalously poor.

---

56. In February 1997, an all-white jury in Orange County, California, found Simpson guilty of the wrongful deaths of Nicole Brown Simpson and Ron Goldman in a civil suit. Simpson was ordered to pay $33.5 million to the Goldman family, but most of his money could not be taken.
57. The first two of these decisions were *Board of Education of Oklahoma City v. Dowell*, 489 U.S. 237 (1991), and *Freeman v. Pitts*, 503 U.S. 467 (1992). See James Patterson, *Brown v. Board of Education: A Civil Rights Milestone and Its Troubled Legacy* (New York, 2001), 195–99.
58. Data from Harvard University Civil Rights Project, reported in *Providence Journal*, Jan. 19, 2004. Other data in this report revealed increases in segregation of Hispanics in schools during these years.

Why was this so? After all, real per pupil spending for American schools, including most schools with high percentages of minority students, had increased over time, and student-teacher ratios had improved. Average SAT test scores crept upward in the 1990s.[59] Thus it was at best an oversimplification to say—as many Americans did—that public schools in general were a great deal "worse" than they had been in the Good Old Days.[60]

Most black students by the 1990s had access to considerably better educational resources than they had had in the days of Jim Crow, or in the 1970s, when desegregation had finally begun to take place. In the 1990s, as earlier, American schools steered steadily higher percentages of their pupils, including blacks, through to graduation, and then to colleges and universities.[61] The percentage of American white people twenty-five years of age or older who had graduated from four-year colleges or universities increased from 11.3 in 1970 to 26.1 in 2000. The percentage of similarly educated blacks who were twenty-five years of age or older rose during the same thirty years from 4.4 to 16.5.[62] If anything comparable to the encouragingly high rate of these increases for African Americans—nearly 400 percent over the previous thirty years—were to persist in the near future, historically large gaps in educational attainment could narrow.[63]

As in the past, however, more than 90 percent of money for public schools came from state and local coffers. A substantial amount of this money continued to nourish urgently demanded but expensive programs such as special and bilingual education. These were among the many rights that had been mandated by the federal government since the 1970s and that had therefore become available to millions of students. In 2004, 6.5 million public school students were in special education classes, but

---

59. Average math SAT scores increased from 501 in 1990 to 514 in 2001; average verbal SATs increased in the same years from 500 to 506. *Stat. Abst.*, 2002, 159.

60. A point stressed by David Tyack and Larry Cuban, *Tinkering Toward Utopia: A Century of Public School Reform* (Cambridge, Mass., 1995), 36; and by Neil Howe and William Strauss, *Millennials Rising: The Next Great Generation* (New York, 2000), 167–68.

61. According to official statistics, 85 percent of white Americans aged twenty-five and over in 2000 had graduated from high school, compared to 79 percent in 1990 and 55 in 1970. Estimated percentages for similarly aged blacks who graduated from high school indicated a closing of this racial gap; these were 79 in 2000, as opposed to 66 in 1990 and 31 in 1970. *Stat. Abst.*, 2002, 139.

62. Ibid.

63. In 1960, 7.7 percent of Americans over the age of twenty-five had college bachelor's degrees; by 1998, 24 percent did. Daniel McMurrer and Isabel Sawhill, "The Declining Importance of Class," *Urban Institute* no. 4 (April 1997).

these were not mainstreaming programs, and for the most part they did not feature academic work aimed at college placement. Despite the inching ahead of average test scores, it was also obvious that millions of American children, especially minority children, graduated from high school unprepared for challenging college-level work. Some 75 percent of American universities at the turn of the century felt obliged to offer an array of remedial academic services.

Large inequities in per pupil spending—across states, across districts, across schools within districts—continued to characterize America's public education system. Per student spending for predominantly black and Latino schools in many central-city areas lagged behind spending for largely white schools in the suburbs. "Back of the classroom" disorder disrupted learning in many of these inner-city schools, some of which relied on poorly trained teachers. Substantial black-white gaps in a number of standardized test scores, having narrowed slightly in the 1970s and early 1980s, increased in the 1990s. These gaps were a little larger than those separating Latino and white students. Studies of these and other test results confirmed two long-standing facts about America's public education: The lower the social class of the student, the lower the scores; and blacks and Latinos had considerably lower scores on the average than whites at every level of social class.[64]

The educational difficulties of black and (to a lesser extent) Latino pupils in America in the 1990s were profoundly demoralizing. Reformers called for a variety of changes: eliminating racially biased questions from standardized tests, spending more money per pupil on classroom education and tutoring for minority children, strengthening the hand of principals and superintendents, improving the training of teachers, lowering class sizes, raising expectations about what students could accomplish, and—above all—raising academic standards, as measured by rigorous testing.[65] By the late 1990s, demands for "standards-based" public education that had spread since publication in 1983 of *A Nation at Risk* grew more insistent.[66]

64. Michael Berube, "Testing Handicaps," *New York Times Magazine*, Sept. 21, 2003, 18.
65. For a review of debates over education of minorities, see Richard Rothstein, "Must Schools Fail?" *New York Review of Books*, Dec. 2, 2004, 29–37. See also John Chubb and Tom Loveless, eds., *Bridging the Achievement Gap* (Washington, 2002); Abigail Thernstrom, *No Excuses: Closing the Racial Gap in Learning* (New York, 2003); and Christopher Jencks and Meredith Phillips, eds., *The Black-White Test Score Gap* (Washington, 1998).
66. For *A Nation at Risk*, see chapter 1. It was this drive for higher educational standards that led to passage in 2001 of the No Child Left Behind Act. See chapter 7.

Losing faith in the public education system, many black parents by the late 1990s were joining white parents in pressing for voucher programs that would offer them money for tuition at private schools. Other parents swelled a chorus of voices calling for charter schools. Some minority leaders stopped struggling for integration of public education, preferring instead to agitate for well-supported neighborhood schools with properly trained black or Latino teachers. There, they thought, their children might learn better—or at least experience less racial tension than they had had to confront in the "educational dead zones" of their inner-city schools.[67]

Because the socio-economic problems facing many minority children continued to be formidable, though, little seemed to change for the better in their schools, which should not have been expected to compensate for these large and fundamental handicaps. A characteristically discouraged assessment of the situation, focusing on the still substantial racial gaps in academic achievement, concluded in 2001: "W.E.B. Du Bois correctly predicted that the problem of the twentieth century would be the color line. The problem of the twenty-first century might be the color line in academic achievement."[68]

FOR ALL THESE REASONS, the 1990s were truly the best of times and the worst of times for black Americans. Not surprisingly, therefore, African Americans conveyed mixed opinions and feelings to the many pollsters who asked them about their lives. These opinions, like those of whites at the time, indicated that most blacks (like most recent immigrants) subscribed to a core set of beliefs: that hard work, if combined with equal opportunity, would lead to social and economic advancement in America. Three-quarters of blacks in the economically prosperous late 1990s professed to be satisfied with their standard of living. Some 60 percent said that they had not personally experienced discrimination. A majority anticipated good futures for their children. Only a small percentage told pollsters that they were bitter or alienated. Responses such as these sug-

67. See, for example, Derrick Bell, *Silent Covenants: Brown v. Board of Education and the Unfulfilled Hopes for Racial Reform* (New York, 2004); and Patterson, *Brown v. Board of Education*, 191–223. Other books on the legacy of the *Brown* case, fifty years old in 2004, include Michael Klarman, *From Jim Crow to Civil Rights: The Supreme Court and the Struggle for Racial Equality* (New York, 2004); and Charles Ogletree, *All Deliberate Speed: Reflections on the First Half-Century of Brown v. Board of Education* (New York, 2004).
68. Alan Krueger and Diane Whitmore, "Would Smaller Classes Help Close the Achievement Gap?" in Chubb and Loveless, *Bridging the Achievement Gap*, 11.

gested that a great many blacks—like other minorities—probably continued to embrace some versions of the American Dream.[69]

But the polls also exposed negative responses. While most African Americans said that they had not personally suffered from racial discrimination, they did believe that racism—in general—was alive and well in the United States. Harassment and discrimination, they said, were afflicting *other* black people, notably in "racial profiling" by white police. This sort of response—one of "I'm OK—They're Not"—echoed those of other Americans in the 1990s. People repeatedly said, for instance, that their congressional representatives were doing a good job (in part because of that belief—and because of gerrymandered districts—incumbents were very hard to beat) but that Congress as a body lay prostrate under the heel of special interests. Most Americans also reported that their own children attended good schools but that public education in general was poor. Critical but often conflicted responses about these and many other American institutions made it a relatively simple (but often distorted) matter for Jeremiahs to conclude that the nation was deeply divided and declining.

The poll responses of minorities, notably African Americans, were revealing in another way. Though blacks advanced faster economically during the 1990s than in any other decade in United States history, many remained restless, often dissatisfied. As one careful scholar concluded, blacks were "succeeding more and enjoying it less."[70] Feelings such as these indicated that the majority of African Americans, like most whites, continued to have high expectations. The more rights and comforts that they gained, the more they desired. Moreover, most black Americans (and Latinos) knew that they had a long road to travel before they might catch up with whites. Acutely aware of their relative deprivation, they understood all too well that an arduous trek lay ahead.

69. Jennifer Hochschild, *Facing Up to the American Dream: Race, Class, and the Soul of the Nation* (Princeton, 1995), 56–57; Paul Sniderman and Thomas Piazza, *Black Pride and Black Prejudice* (Princeton, 2002), 110–12; David Whitman, *The Optimism Gap: The I'm OK—They're Not Syndrome and the Myth of American Decline* (New York, 1998), 102.
70. Hochschild, *Facing Up to the American Dream*, 214.

10

Political Wars of the
Early Clinton Years

William Jefferson Clinton, an admirer of FDR and JFK, often thought about his place in American history. Remarkably self-absorbed, he yearned to be remembered as a great president. Throughout his frequently troubled time in office he continued to hope that he could reverse the anti-government tide with which his Republican predecessors had ridden to power. In his first inaugural address he proclaimed: "Let us resolve to make our government a place for what Franklin Roosevelt called 'bold, persistent experimentation,' a government of our tomorrows, not our yesterdays. Let us give this capital back to the people to whom it belongs."[1]

He cared above all about domestic policies. Having worked on these matters for twelve years as governor of Arkansas, he was knowledgeable about even the smallest details of many of them. He had a quick intelligence and a capacious memory. Whatever the subject—Social Security, health care, the minimum wage, taxes, trade, welfare, education, obscure social programs—Clinton appeared to have an amazing command of information. He loved to talk, sometimes in college-like bull sessions with staffers that ran far into the night, about the intricacies of government policies and about ways that government—his government—might improve the lot of Americans in need.

The new president possessed extraordinary political skills. Wherever he went, he seemed totally at ease, eager to shake hands and exchange a few words with anyone within reach. Having grown up around black people

1. *New York Times*, Jan. 21, 1993.

in Arkansas, he was especially comfortable among African Americans. The novelist Toni Morrison, impressed, said he was the nation's first black president. Like JFK, his idol, he radiated a personal magnetism that drew people to him, and he possessed a physical presence that enabled him to dominate almost any room he entered. Clinton also had seemingly inexhaustible energy. He was constantly on the move, and he gave hundreds of speeches. Though he could be long-winded, he was normally an articulate and compelling extemporaneous speaker. Like Reagan, he projected great enthusiasm and optimism. As a discerning biographer emphasized, Clinton as campaigner and politician was a "Natural."[2]

Clinton was almost desperately eager to please. In the manner of many fellow boomers who were comfortable with open displays of emotion, he was quick to touch, hug, and reassure his fellow Americans. "I feel your pain," he told anguished people. His yearning to be liked struck some contemporary observers as neurotic—a compulsion so powerful that it led him to say nearly all things to all people and to dither before making decisions that might offend anyone. Clinton fretted over matters small and large, garrulously rehashing pros and cons in drawn-out meetings, and sometimes reversing himself. Partly for these reasons, he was habitually late for appearances, and he was a careless administrator who greatly distressed his aides. As Michiko Kakutani of the *New York Times* noted in 1998, Clinton was "emotionally needy, indecisive, and undisciplined."[3]

His need to please, however, seemed over time to become a political asset. Slowly but increasingly, millions of Americans appeared to identify with him, regarding him—warts and all—as an unusually caring and sympathetic man. As Kakutani wrote in 2001, Clinton was America's "first user-friendly president. . . .The president as the guy next door—an Oprah guest who feels our pain because he struggles like the rest of us with his weight, his marriage, and his golf game." She added, "In his adolescent craving to be liked . . . and the tacky spectacle of his womanizing, Mr. Clinton gave us a presidency that straddled the news pages and the tabloid gossip columns."[4]

2. For Clinton's style and politics, see Joe Klein, *The Natural: The Misunderstood Presidency of Bill Clinton* (New York, 2002), 194–95; Fred Greenstein, *The Presidential Difference: Leadership Style from FDR to Clinton* (New York, 2000), 195–98; Lewis Gould, *The Modern American Presidency* (Lawrence, Kans., 2003), 218; and William Berman, *From the Center to the Edge: The Politics and Policies of the Clinton Presidency* (Lanham, Md., 2001), 5–17.
3. *New York Times*, Sept. 13, 1998.
4. Ibid., Jan. 19, 2001. See also Klein, *The Natural*, 206.

Though many of these characteristics helped him politically, they did not endear him to people who had to work under him. Aides who marveled at Clinton's political skill or who approved of his policies nonetheless resented not only his indecisiveness and sloppiness but also his unpredictability and hot temper. They came to believe that he was unusually self-indulgent, inconsiderate, self-pitying, and narcissistic. If it suited his purposes, he might lie to them. If things went wrong, he might fly into a temper tantrum and blame long-suffering people around him.[5] While he was skilled at "feeling the pain" of voters, he was often a poor listener who dominated conversations. What mattered above all to Clinton, these aides concluded, was advancing his own political standing.

Like Nixon, who was in most ways a very different man, Clinton was a permanent campaigner who never stopped thinking about reelection and about the polls. Especially after 1994, he relied heavily on the advice of Dick Morris, a politically opportunistic guru and student of polls who periodically helped him refashion his ideas so as to move with the ever shifting currents of popular opinion.[6] The president spent great amounts of time fund-raising, at which his skills were outstanding, and trying to manipulate the reporters who covered his activities. "Slick Willie," as many people called him, was a master of "spin"—an art that earlier presidents had practiced but that he often elevated to new heights. Most reporters recognized that Clinton, even more than most politicians, was using them, and they never warmed up to him. Members of Congress, too, resented his politically driven self-absorption. An aide to House Democratic leader Richard Gephardt observed—without revealing his own name—that "the thing that drives Dick [Gephardt] absolutely crazy is that every time they have a conversation, Clinton spends all his time talking about polling numbers."[7]

Though reporters exposed Clinton's personal flaws, they did not break the political hold that he managed to gain on voters over time. This was a distinctively personal hold: Clinton did not succeed in building up his party. Democrats lost ground to the GOP in the 1990s. Weaving his way through dangerously partisan minefields, he nevertheless survived a great many missteps and left the White House in January 2001 with unusually

5. For an example of Clinton's self–pity and hot temper, see David Halberstam, War in a Time of Peace: Bush, Clinton, and the Generals (New York, 2001), 316–17.

6. Morris kept a low profile after 1996, when the media exposed his involvement with a prostitute. News accounts stated that she was with Morris on an occasion when he was talking on the phone with Clinton.

7. New York Times, Sept. 27, 1998.

favorable job performance ratings. After he had departed from the White House, many Americans said that they missed his colorful and highly entertaining presence.[8]

WHEN CLINTON TOOK OFFICE in January 1993, he had reason to hope that he might expand liberal social policies. To help him do so, he could call on a host of aides: Thanks to the growth of government since the 1960s, the presidential and vice-presidential staffs included more than 800 people.[9] Clinton might also expect to enjoy a reasonably friendly relationship with Congress, where Democratic majorities of 258 to 176 in the House and 57 to 43 in the Senate seemed reliable.

The president recognized that most Americans, notwithstanding their grousing about politicians, continued to expect Washington to *do* things for them. And over time government, containing conservative resistance, had slowly responded. In 1970, non-discretionary entitlements of various sorts (notably the largest, Social Security, Medicare, and Medicaid) had amounted to 30 percent of the federal budget; by 1995, they accounted for 60 percent.[10] While a leveling off of defense spending after the end of the Cold War helped boost the percentages allotted for domestic programs such as these, the main source of change came from slow but real increases in spending for social purposes. The total expended (in constant 1999 dollars) for the most important programs such as Social Security and Medicare had tripled between 1970 and 1999.[11] The value of income-tested benefits (in constant 2000 dollars) nearly doubled in these years.[12]

Clinton had cause to anticipate popular support for expansion of such programs. As in 1977, when liberals had cheered the end of eight years of Republican control of the White House, they had high expectations that the new administration might reverse the conservative initiatives set forth during the twelve previous years of GOP rule. In particular, they hoped to stem the tide of income inequality, which had been rising since the 1970s. An important cause of this inequality was the increase in the numbers of

8. Haynes Johnson, *The Best of Times: America in the Clinton Years* (New York, 2001), 451.
9. Gould, *The Modern American Presidency*, 218.
10. R. Shep Melnick, "Governing More but Enjoying It Less," in Morton Keller and Melnick, eds., *Taking Stock: American Government in the Twentieth Century* (New York, 1999), 280–306; Joseph Nye, "The Decline of Confidence in Government," in Nye et al., *Why People Don't Trust Government* (Cambridge, Mass., 1997), 6.
11. John Scholz and Kara Levine, "The Evolution of Income Support Policy in Recent Decades," Institute for Research on Poverty, *Focus* 21, no. 2 (Fall 2000), 9–16. See also *Stat. Abst.*, 2002, 340–47.
12. *Stat. Abst.*, 2002, 343.

immigrants, but liberals correctly maintained that some of it emanated from other sources, notably Reagan's tax cuts.

Liberals had other expectations from the new administration. Popular complaints concerning whopping corporate salaries, the woes of the Rust Belt, neglect of infrastructure, and the spread of low-paying, "dead-end" service sector jobs, encouraged reformers to argue that more generous social policies, notably some form of national health insurance, would secure considerable popular support.[13] Two widely held beliefs underpinned these familiar arguments and assumptions. One was the conviction that the federal government had a responsibility to advance the rights and entitlements of deserving people. The other was the sense that the government had the capacity to do so.

Clinton was too shrewd a political navigator to think that he would enjoy clear sailing. After all, having received only 43 percent of the vote in 1992, he lacked a popular mandate to chart a bold new course, and a host of obstacles—the same that had frequently frustrated liberals since the late 1960s—loomed in his way. Though the once powerful Democratic electoral coalition forged by FDR still showed some signs of life, notably in urban areas inhabited by substantial percentages of unionized workers, minorities, and low-income people, a number of economic and demographic trends continued to favor Republicans and conservative Democrats. By the early 1990s, a majority of Americans lived in suburban areas—more than double the percentage in the early 1950s. Rising numbers of people, including a great many white families with young children, were moving to developments in exurbs, once rural areas that were being bulldozed into sites for shopping centers and subdivisions. Having escaped the cities, exurbanites were more likely to identify with the haves than with the have-nots. Many, voicing a faith in self-reliance, opposed expansion of means-tested social programs.[14]

13. Jeffrey Madrick, *The End of Affluence: The Causes and Consequences of America's Economic Decline* (New York, 1995); Edward Luttwak, *The Endangered American Dream: How to Stop the United States from Becoming a Third World Country and How to Win the Geo-Economic Struggle for Industrial Supremacy* (New York, 1993).

14. Generalizations in this and following paragraphs derive from the following revealingly titled books about American politics in the 1980s and 1990s. Jonathan Rauch, *Demosclerosis: The Silent Killer of American Government* (New York, 1994); Matthew Crenson and Benjamin Ginsberg, *Downsizing Democracy: How America Sidelined Its Citizens and Privatized Its Public* (Baltimore, 2002); Byron Shafer, *The Two Majorities and the Puzzle of Modern American Politics* (Lawrence, Kans., 2003); and Benjamin Ginsberg and Martin Shefter, *Politics by Other Means: Politicians, Prosecutors, and the Press from Watergate to Whitewater* (New York, 2002).

It was also questionable whether the class resentments that had helped to create the New Deal coalition were as sharp as they had been in the past. While most labor union leaders continued to support liberal programs, their clout had been weakening since the 1950s. By 2001, only 13.5 percent of American workers (and but 9 percent of those in the private sector) belonged to unions.[15] The level of personal and family income in America, moreover, was no longer as reliable a predictor of partisan preference as it had been. As early as the late 1960s, when Nixon had highlighted social and cultural issues—many of them involving race—rising numbers of white working-class people had begun to turn to the GOP. In the 1980s, many of these people had proudly called themselves Reagan Democrats. By contrast, increasing numbers of middle- and upper-middle-class professionals—teachers, professors in law and the humanities and social sciences, people engaged in the creative arts, journalists, public interest and personal injury lawyers—had come to favor liberal policies and to vote Democratic in national elections. In 1996, Clinton carried thirteen of the seventeen most affluent congressional districts in America.[16]

Regional animosities, stoutly persisting amid the supposedly all-centralizing tendencies of modern life, further threatened the aspirations of Democratic liberals. Progressive Democrats were strong in urban areas of the Northeast and the Pacific Coast, and in many industrial regions of the Midwest, but they had become increasingly vulnerable in most parts of the still rapidly growing and more politically conservative Sunbelt, where Republicans continued to gain during Clinton's tenure in the White House. A majority of Americans living in the Plains states and in the Mountain West, though benefiting from a range of government programs—notably irrigation and power projects and farm subsidies—continued to complain about the influence, as they saw it, of "elitist" eastern liberals, environmentalists, and regulatory bureaucrats who told them how to run their lives. Many other westerners hotly opposed the surge of illegal immigration from Mexico. In Colorado some motorists proudly displayed bumper stickers: DON'T CALIFORNICATE COLORADO.

15. *Stat. Abst.*, 2002, 412. Compared to approximately 35 percent of all workers in the mid-1950s and 20 percent in 1983. Union leaders, however, continued to be effective at getting people to the polls. In the presidential election of 2000, it was estimated that 26 percent of all votes came from members of union households, 63 percent of which went to Al Gore, the Democratic candidate. *New York Times*, March 11, 2004.
16. David Brooks, *Bobos in Paradise: The New Upper Class and How They Got There* (New York, 2000), 258–59.

Partisan warfare, already intense during the culture wars of the late 1980s and early 1990s, frequently seemed out of control during the Clinton years. As earlier, these partisan battles were not so deep-rooted in popular feelings as media accounts—ever highlighting conflict, scandal, and controversy—implied. On the contrary, the major parties had weakened over time, casualties of the rise of independent and split-ticket voting and of the entrepreneurial, candidate-centered, television-driven style of politics that had ascended since the 1960s. This "de-alignment" of parties, as political scientists tended to call it, revealed that the American people were less partisan than most of their elected representatives.

Still, there was no doubting that partisan rancor soured the political scene. Many conservatives developed a special loathing for Clinton—and for his wife, Hillary, a liberal lawyer and career woman who emerged as a highly visible adviser. They fumed at Clinton's closeness—a pandering closeness, they thought—to the glitterati of Hollywood, many of whom contributed lavishly to the Democratic Party and gave highly enthusiastic backing to left-wing causes. Among these angry conservatives were radio talk-show hosts whose listeners numbered in the millions. By far the best known of these was Rush Limbaugh, who attracted an avid following estimated at 20 million people by the mid-1990s. Limbaugh reveled in ridiculing "feminazis" and "environmentalist wackos."[17]

Many liberals further bewailed what they considered to be the baneful consequences of the scrubbing in 1987 of the so-called Fairness Doctrine by the then GOP-dominated Federal Communications Commission. Under this doctrine, radio and over-the-air TV stations had been expected to offer "reasonable opportunity" on the air "for the discussion of conflicting views on issues of public importance." After the FCC put an end to the doctrine, liberals charged, conservative radio and television announcers felt ever more free to abet what Hillary Clinton later denounced as a "vast right-wing conspiracy" in America.

Liberals especially detested House Republican whip Newt Gingrich of Georgia, an avid partisan who led the assault against Clinton from Capitol Hill. Gingrich was a hyper-energetic, irrepressible firebrand who brimmed with ideas and who had no interest in compromising with liberals. Unlike Robert Dole of Kansas, the GOP leader in the Senate, he was an ideologue and a warrior, not a deal maker. As if to demonstrate his toughness, Gingrich decorated his office with the skull of a *Tyrannosaurus rex*. Bellicose in his rhetoric, he proclaimed that liberals were "pathetic," "sick," "corrupt," "left-

17. Gould, *The Modern American Presidency*, 216–17.

wing elitists," and "counter-cultural McGoverniks." Aided by a corps of mostly southern Republicans, such as Tom DeLay of Texas, Gingrich brought a new level of intensity to partisan battling in the House. These ideological wars, in turn, soured many Americans on politics in general.[18]

Although Clinton compromised on occasion, he frequently gave as good as he got, thereby further infuriating conservatives on Capitol Hill. Unsatisfied with blocking presidential initiatives, they continued to practice a politics of "R.I.P."—Revelation, Investigation, Prosecution.[19] Within the next few years they made special use of the Ethics in Government Act of 1978, which had authorized the appointment of independent counsels.[20] Five of these investigated members of Clinton's Cabinet, two of whom were forced to resign. A sixth independent counsel, Kenneth Starr, devoted more than four years to an investigation of Clinton, ultimately seeking the president's impeachment.[21]

Two additional features of American politics, both familiar, further affected some of Clinton's efforts in the 1990s. The first was the predictably weighty influence of interest groups. Some of these groups—those representing the elderly, for instance—helped him to ward off conservative threats in the 1990s to politically powerful entitlements such as Social Security and Medicare. "Public interest" lobbies such as Common Cause further bolstered liberal efforts. As Clinton was to discover, however, conservative interests were strong enough to wage war on new social programs, such as his quest for universal health insurance coverage.[22] Opponents of federal gun control, led by the National Rifle Association, had considerable influence on Capitol Hill.

The second feature was equally familiar and dated to the late 1960s: widespread popular disgruntlement with politicians.[23] This did not mean

---

18. For Gingrich, Jonathan Franzen, "The Listener," *New Yorker*, Oct. 6, 2003, 85–99; John Taylor, "Thinking of NEWT," *Esquire*, Nov. 1995, 64–79; Joe Klein, "Whither Liberalism?" *Time*, Nov. 21, 1994, 56. For the legacy of ideologues such as Gingrich, see Peter Keating, "Wake-up Call," *AARP: The Magazine*, Sept./Oct. 2004, 55.

19. The acronym used by Ginsberg and Shefter, in *Politics by Other Means*, 37–45.

20. See chapter 3 for this act and for other information about politics in the 1970s, when partisanship had also been especially corrosive.

21. See the following chapter.

22. Ted Halstead and Michael Lind, *The Radical Center: The Future of American Politics* (New York, 2001), 15; Crenson and Ginsberg, *Downsizing Democracy*, 16–19; Rauch, *Demosclerosis*. For the influence of corporate interests, see Kevin Phillips, *Arrogant Capital: Washington, Wall Street, and the Frustration of American Politics* (Boston, 1994).

23. E. J. Dionne, *Why Americans Hate Politics* (New York, 1991); Alan Wolfe, *One Nation, After All: What Middle-Class Americans Really Think About God, Country, Family, Racism, Welfare, Immigration, Homosexuality, Work, the Right, the Left, and Each Other* (New York, 1998), 286–93.

that a majority of people yearned to overhaul their political system. Polls showed that Americans continued to be immensely proud of their democratic institutions, which remained among the most stable in the world. Even while grumbling about the burden of taxes, most people took care to pay them. Able and idealistic citizens continued to enter public service.[24] But many popular feelings that had been powerful since the 1970s—resistance to federal regulation, distrust of authority, resentment of special interests, and suspicion about conspiracies, especially governmental conspiracies—persisted in the 1990s. H. Ross Perot's strikingly strong showing in the election of 1992, rooted as it was in denunciations of leaders of both major parties, had amply demonstrated the strength of such attitudes.

The media, moreover, continued to play up partisan disagreements and ideological confrontations, further exciting sound and fury that discouraged citizens from undertaking sustained political involvement.[25] Within the next few years, twenty-five states approved term limits for selected officeholders. In the 1990s, as in the 1970s and 1980s, distrust of politicians made it hard for people with large ambitions to accomplish great things.

Clinton was such a politician. As he began his term, he was determined to overcome these and other obstacles—including persistent divisions within his own party—and to achieve a transcendent position in United States history.

EARLY IN HIS ADMINISTRATION Clinton managed to win a few minor victories. Pleasing advocates of liberal abortion policies, he revoked a "gag rule" that his predecessors had enforced against abortion counseling in federally funded clinics, and he issued an executive order authorizing the use of fetal tissue for medical research. When Congress passed a Family and Medical Leave Act that guaranteed many workers up to twelve weeks a year of unpaid leave for medical emergencies—a measure that Bush had twice vetoed—he was quick to sign it.[26]

Like Jimmy Carter, however, Clinton quickly discovered how harsh the Washington political environment could be. Slow to find his way, often indecisive, he and his advisers—some of them old friends from Arkansas—frequently seemed to be out of their depth. Having proclaimed that he would have a Cabinet that "looked like America," he was determined to

24. Nye, "The Decline of Confidence in Government," 1–18.
25. Theda Skocpol, *Diminished Democracy: From Membership to Management in American Civic Life* (Norman, Okla., 2003), 232–36.
26. The measure exempted employers with fewer than fifty workers.

appoint a woman as attorney general. His first nominee for that post, Zoe Baird, had to withdraw her name when it was revealed that she had hired an illegal immigrant as nanny for her children and had not paid Social Security taxes relating to her employment. A second choice, also a woman, proved unacceptable for similar reasons. It was not until early March that Janet Reno, a Florida prosecutor, was confirmed in the position. She was America's first female attorney general. "Nannygate," as the media termed this messy business, indicated the heightened investigatory zeal of the media when it came to high-level government appointments. It also caused people to ask if Clinton and his staff knew what they were doing.

Reno had barely settled in when she had to deal with David Koresh, head of a cult of Seventh-Day Adventists called the Branch Davidians that was suspected of illegally amassing automatic weapons at their compound in Waco, Texas. Following a gun battle on February 28 with agents of the Bureau of Alcohol, Tobacco, and Firearms that had killed four agents and two members of the cult, Koresh and many of his heavily armed followers holed up at their compound. FBI agents, supervised by Reno, maintained a siege there for seven weeks. On April 19—the Patriots Day anniversary of the battles of Lexington and Concord in 1775—the agents battered the walls of the compound with tanks and fired tear gas inside, whereupon Koresh ordered his followers to pour gasoline around the compound and to burn it down.

The explosive blaze that broke out killed more than seventy members of the cult, including Koresh and twenty-one children, several of whom he had fathered with some of his many wives. Only nine followers survived. Reno justified the assault by explaining that she had received reports of children being beaten inside the compound, and Clinton backed her up. Many Americans wondered, however, how carefully Clinton himself had followed the situation, and whether he—or was it Reno?—had acted precipitously.[27]

Meanwhile, Clinton found himself tangled in protracted struggles over his early announcement—the initial act of his administration—that he would end a ban against homosexuals in the military. From the start, a wide range of opponents, including General Colin Powell, chairman of

---

27. Two years later to the day, April 19, 1995, two anti-government zealots, Timothy McVeigh and Terry Nichols, exacted revenge for the deaths at Waco, blowing up the federal building in Oklahoma City. The blast killed 168 people. Many conspiratorially oriented Americans believed that McVeigh and Nichols were part of a wider plot involving white supremacist groups, but as of mid-2005 no smoking gun establishing such links had yet been found.

the Joint Chiefs, demurred. Following protracted acrimony, which dragged on into July, foes of change succeeded in forcing Clinton to accept a compromise: Military personnel were not to reveal their sexual orientation, and their superiors were not to ask them about it. "Don't ask, don't tell," as this policy was called, pleased no one. Over the course of the next ten years it resulted in the discharge of some 10,000 service men and women who revealed their homosexuality.[28]

Clinton blundered again when he tried to fire the White House travel staff. They were to be replaced by political supporters and friends of his wife. Though the president claimed that the employees had mismanaged their tasks, it became clear that this explanation was a cover for a partisan housecleaning of experienced workers who had served his predecessors. When critics counter-attacked, Clinton felt obliged to restore most of those whom he had fired. "Travelgate," as the media named this imbroglio, further advertised his political clumsiness during the early months of 1993.

By then many observers were ridiculing the president, whose poll numbers were dropping steadily. The cartoonist Garry Trudeau depicted him as a waffle. A cover story in *Time* featured him as architect of the "Incredible Shrinking Presidency." A biographer, Joe Klein, later dismissed Clinton's performance during these early months as "amateur hour."[29]

Though jolted by these controversies, Clinton consoled himself with the hope that he would succeed in achieving his major goal of 1993: securing legislation reforming America's jerry-built system of health insurance coverage. "If I don't get health care," he said, "I'll wish I didn't run for President." As he emphasized in calling for reform, private expenditures for health purposes were continuing to skyrocket—from $246 billion in 1980 to $880 billion in 1993.[30] Yet more than 35 million Americans—around 14 percent of the population—had no medical insurance, either private or governmental, and another 20 million were said to lack adequate coverage. Most of these people were poor or unemployed. Their plight graphically exposed the persistence of poverty and inequality in the world's richest nation.

In selecting health insurance reform as his major objective, Clinton surprised many solons on the Hill, who had expected him instead to overhaul the welfare system. After all, he had pledged during the campaign to

28. *New York Times*, March 25, 2004.
29. Jules Witcover, *Party of the People: A History of the Democrats* (New York, 2003), 666–72; Greenstein, *Presidential Difference*, 178–82; Klein, *The Natural*, 44.
30. *Stat. Abst.*, 2002, 91.

reform public assistance, proclaiming that the United States must "put an end to welfare as we know it," so that it will "cease to be a way of life." New York senator Daniel Moynihan, a liberal, was eager to manage revision of welfare and denied that the country faced a "health care crisis." Most Americans, he said, had fairly decent coverage. The president ignored Moynihan's appeals. In choosing the health issue, Clinton was sailing on a more liberal tack than he had seemed to steer in 1992, when he had campaigned as a centrist "New Democrat."[31] Reform of health care insurance, moreover, was a daunting project that had frustrated previous presidents dating back to Harry Truman. Still, he pressed ahead, entrusting development of a plan to a team headed by his wife and an old friend, Ira Magaziner.

Unfortunately for advocates of reform, Magaziner and Mrs. Clinton enshrouded their activities in secrecy. They virtually ignored Congress, including moderate Republicans, as well as the Department of Health and Human Services, where such a proposal might otherwise have gestated. They listened instead to a host of academics and other "experts," sometimes in gatherings of 100 or more people who wrangled far into the night. When a plan finally emerged from this laborious process in September, it was bulky beyond belief—1,342 pages long.[32] Liberals were upset that Clinton, perhaps fearing political repercussions in 1996 if he called for tax increases to support a governmentally financed plan, did not recommend a "single-payer" system such as the one in Canada. Rather, the plan required most employers to pay for 80 percent of their workers' health benefits. The key to this system would be regional insurance-purchasing alliances that were expected to promote "managed competition" among private health insurers, thereby lowering premiums. The government was to pay for the uninsured, ensuring universal coverage.[33]

Most liberals agreed that the plan, though complicated, promised to reduce economic inequality in the United States. Some large employers, too, backed it, in the hope that it would reduce the cost of their health care benefits for their workers. From the start, however, the proposal ran into sharp opposition from interest groups, notably from small insurers, who feared that larger companies would squeeze them out of the action, and from many small employers, who bridled at being told to pay for 80 percent of their workers' health premiums. Aroused, they spent millions

31. Shafer, The Two Majorities, 39–41.
32. Skocpol, Diminished Democracy, 242–44.
33. Klein, The Natural, 118–25.

of dollars on television ads denouncing the plan. On Capitol Hill, Gingrich aroused his forces to fight the effort. The Clintons, he said, "were going against the entire tide of Western history. I mean central-ized, command bureaucracies are dying. This is the end of that era, not the beginning of it."[34]

Foes such as these seriously damaged chances for reform, as did Clinton when he refused to consider compromises that would have settled for less than universal coverage. In 1994, when congressional committees began to consider his plans, the opposing interest groups mobilized effectively. As Moynihan had warned, moreover, it was not only "selfish interest groups" that were cool to Clinton's plans: The majority of Americans (those with health insurance) seemed mostly content with their fee-for-service arrangements and exerted little pressure for the erection of a new and com-plicated system. So it was that Clinton's most ambitious dream never even reached a vote on the floor of the Democratic Congress. It finally collapsed in August 1994. Badly beaten, the president was forced to drop the issue, leaving millions of Americans without coverage and millions more depen-dent on the will or the capacity of employers to provide for them.

Amid disappointments such as these, Clinton still managed to secure some of his lesser goals in 1993–94. Thanks in part to Democratic majori-ties, Congress approved his two nominees for positions on the Supreme Court, Ruth Bader Ginsburg in 1993 and Stephen Breyer in 1994. Be-cause these new justices replaced a liberal (Harry Blackmun) and a mod-erate (Byron White), Clinton's appointments did not greatly change the ideological balance of the Court: Conservatives still maintained a tenu-ous majority in many of the hotly contested cases that arose over the next ten years, during which time the membership of the Court did not change. But the presence of Ginsburg and Breyer seemed to ensure a pro-choice majority on the Court, thereby moderating the culture wars over abortion that had prompted massive Washington rallies in earlier years. For the next decade, political conflicts over abortion abated a little.[35]

The president prevailed in a few other struggles in his first two years in office. In 1994, he signed into law a measure banning the sale of nineteen

---

34. James Patterson, *America Since 1941: A History* (Fort Worth, 2000), 265–67; Berman, *From the Center to the Edge*, 26–28.

35. White, a Kennedy appointee, had dissented (as had Rehnquist) in *Roe v. Wade* in 1973. Blackmun, who had been named by Nixon, had written the majority decision in that case and joined liberals on the Court in many cases thereafter. See chapter 11 for Court decisions in 1995.

kinds of semi-automatic assault weapons. Lawmakers approved a "motor-voter" law enabling citizens to register to vote while applying for drivers' licenses; a modestly funded national service program that offered federal aid for college costs to young people who performed community service; an education law titled Goals 2000, which authorized $2 billion to help states advance educational standards; and a Freedom of Access to Clinic Entrances Act.

Except for the Clinic Entrances Act, which made obstruction of clinics or places of worship a federal crime, these measures did not accomplish a great deal. Huge loopholes limited the reach of the gun control measure, which in any event did not affect some 25 millions guns, including an estimated 1.5 million semi-automatic assault weapons, already in private hands. After the passage of the law in 1994, gun manufacturers, slightly adapting assault weapons, continued to make and sell such guns.[36] Motor-voter registration did not advance voter participation. The modestly funded Goals 2000 encouraged education officials to develop statewide achievement tests but had little impact on school practices, which (as always in American educational history) continued to be dictated by local officials.[37] Even so, these laws revealed a significant aspect of Clinton's performance as president: Though failing to achieve a major goal such as health care reform, he remained a persistent advocate of federal social programs. Willing to use the veto, he staved off conservative efforts to cut back the welfare state.

Well before these minor victories, Clinton had concluded that he had to bolster his credentials as a moderate. Otherwise, he believed, he faced defeat in 1996. For this reason, and because he was a prudent fiscal manager, he decided early in his term to concentrate on reducing annual federal deficits, which, though finally showing a modest decline in fiscal 1993, still amounted to $255 billion.[38] In doing so he was especially mindful of

36. *New York Times*, April 24, 2005. In 2004, Congress refused to renew the gun control law, which the National Rifle Association strongly opposed.
37. Robert Schwartz and Marion Robinson, "Goals 2000 and the Standards Movement," *Brookings Papers on Education Policy* 7 (2000), 173–214; and John Jennings, *Why National Standards and Tests? Politics and the Quest for Better Schools* (Thousand Oaks, Calif., 1998).
38. Between fiscal years 1987 and 1992 the annual federal deficit had risen (in current dollars) from $150 billion to $290 billion, an all-time high. The budget shortfall of $255 billion in fiscal 1993, though large, was the first significant decline in the deficit in many years and was attributed in part to delayed effects of the budget deal that Bush and Congress had struck in 1990. *Stat. Abst.*, 2002, 305. Fiscal years end in the year indicated.

advice from Treasury Secretary Lloyd Bentsen and Federal Reserve Board chairman Alan Greenspan, who had emerged as a widely admired and vocal advocate of deficit reduction. If that could be achieved, Greenspan told him, major players in the important "bond market"—bankers, lenders, money-market managers, other investors—would be reassured, thereby encouraging the Fed to call for lower long-term interest rates. These, in turn, would promote greater investment and economic growth.[39]

In siding with Greenspan, Clinton faced down angry liberals among his own advisers and among congressional advocates of greater government spending for infrastructure and social programs. Positioning himself as a New Democrat against "tax-and-spend" liberals, he recognized ruefully that he was appealing more to business leaders and conservatives than to his own party's traditional base. "I hope you're all aware we're the Eisenhower Republicans," he remarked sarcastically to his advisers. "We stand for lower deficits and free trade and the bond market. Isn't that great?" Still, he felt driven to lower the deficit. The government's lack of fiscal discipline, he said, was "like a bone in the throat."[40]

Clinton, displaying unaccustomed decisiveness, thereupon worked hard to secure a budget package in 1993 that would reduce federal debt by $500 billion over the next five years. In doing so he dropped his pledge, highlighted during his campaign for election, to press for a middle-class tax cut. Conservatives in Congress, meanwhile, rejected his quest for an emergency stimulus package that would have authorized $16 billion for job creation in the summer of 1993. Liberals, still demanding high levels of social spending, fumed at this course of events.

The partisan struggle that followed resembled the battle that Bush had faced when he, too, had sought to curb the deficit, thereby breaking his famous pledge, "Read my lips: No new taxes." In 1993, as in 1990, most Republicans—conservatives who said they believed in balanced budgets— hotly opposed efforts to raise taxes, especially on the wealthy, even though such increases would presumably have lowered the deficit. But Clinton stayed the course, hoping that most Democrats would stick with him. When the battle ended in August 1993, he secured a good deal of what he had requested, including a 1 percent hike in the highest corporate tax rate and a higher (39.6 percent) marginal tax on incomes of $250,000 or more. Modest spending cuts, some in defense and overseas intelligence, some

39. Halberstam, War in a Time of Peace, 212–13.
40. Robert Collins, More: The Politics of Economic Growth in Postwar America (New York, 2000), 217–19.

in social programs, accompanied these tax increases. The package also authorized expansion of the Earned Income Tax Credit to low-income working families with children. This became a little-discussed but important social benefit during the course of the decade. The package was expected to achieve the president's goal of cutting the deficit by nearly $500 billion within five years. Clinton won without getting a single Republican vote in the House. His margin of victory there was 218 to 216. Vice President Gore had to break a fifty-to-fifty tie in the Senate.[41]

Passage of the budget package made a difference over time. During the next six years, federal outlays in current dollars—many of them for entitlements tied in part of cost-of-living increases—continued to rise, from $1.41 trillion in 1993 to $1.65 trillion in 1998. But they decreased as a percentage of GDP, from 21.5 in 1993 to 19.1 in 1998. This was the lowest percentage since the late 1960s. Government receipts increased during the same period, from $1.15 trillion in 1993 to $1.72 trillion in 1998. In that fiscal year the federal budget showed a surplus of almost $70 billion, the first since fiscal 1969. Even higher surpluses followed, averaging $156 billion a year between fiscal 1999 and 2001.[42]

The main reason for this astounding turnabout was the strong performance of the economy, especially after 1995, which brought in higher tax revenues. Lower interest rates, which Greenspan helped to promote after 1994, further advanced this surge. Clinton was fortunate to be president while changes such as these softened memories of the recession of the early 1990s. Still, enactment of the budget package of 1993 was widely credited with contributing to the turnabout. It sent a message to skittish American investors that the federal government was finally serious about reforming its fiscal affairs. One of the most impressive accomplishments of Clinton's presidency, the budget deal of 1993 enhanced his reputation as an economic manager.

Having secured the budget package, Clinton concentrated on another domestic goal that he favored on its merits and that he hoped would further establish his credentials as a moderate. This was congressional approval of the North American Free Trade Agreement that Bush had negotiated with Canada and Mexico in December 1992. The agreement proposed to create a free-market trading zone involving the three nations. Clinton, a strong advocate of more open trade, allied himself with leading corporate figures and with Republicans in Congress, including Gingrich.

41. Berman, *From the Center to the Edge*, 23–26.
42. *Stat. Abst.*, 2002, 305.

In the process he encountered heated opposition from labor union leaders and from many Democrats, including House majority leader Gephardt, who feared that American corporations would move their operations to cheap-labor Mexico, thereby harming American workers. Opponents of NAFTA also demanded better safeguards against environmental pollution that they expected would spread in Mexico and across its border into the United States. Clinton, however, refused to compromise, and NAFTA, approved in late 1993, went into effect in January 1994.

NAFTA did not seem to greatly benefit Mexico, which suffered, as earlier, from widespread poverty and unemployment. Struggling peasants raising maize, hit hard by competition from the United States, were devastated. These and other desperately poor people continued to stream into the United States, provoking rising tensions in many parts of the Southwest. Meanwhile, soil and air pollution, already heavy in many areas of Mexico, increased. Whether NAFTA was good or bad for the economy of the United States continued to be hotly debated during the 1990s and later.[43] Clinton and a great many economists maintained that breaking down trade barriers forced American exporters to become more efficient, thereby advancing their competitiveness and market share. American workers, therefore, would benefit, at least in the long run. The flight of American jobs to Mexico, moreover, turned out to be smaller than many NAFTA opponents had predicted, and thanks to America's strong economy in the late 1990s, most people who were displaced from their jobs in the United States seemed to find other work. America's unemployment rate decreased from 6.1 percent in 1994 to a low of 4 percent in 2000.[44]

But some corporations did move operations to Mexico, and pollution did plague some areas near the Mexican-American border. Labor leaders, complaining of the persisting stagnation of manufacturing wages in the United States, continued to charge that American corporations were not only "outsourcing" jobs to Mexico (and to other cheap-labor nations) but were also managing to depress payrolls by threatening to move. When the American economy soured in 2001, foes of NAFTA stepped up their opposition to it.

CLINTON NEVER CLAIMED TO CARE DEEPLY about international politics. "Foreign policy is not what I came here to do," he exclaimed unhappily when he found himself embroiled in it.[45]

43. Alfred Eckes Jr. and Thomas Zeiler, *Globalization and the American Century* (New York, 2003), 252–53.
44. *Stat. Abst.*, 2002, 562.
45. Berman, *From the Center to the Edge*, 35.

As his comment indicated, a host of problems dogged his foreign policy advisers, the first Democratic team to deal with the new and uncharted post–Cold War era of international relations. Heading this team was Warren Christopher, a hardworking, cautious, and undemonstrative attorney whom Clinton named as secretary of state. Christopher had been Secretary of State Cyrus Vance's deputy in the Carter years. Bland and uninspiring, he struck some observers as being "Dean Rusk without the charisma." Neither Christopher nor other top advisers to Clinton, such as Defense Secretary Les Aspin, a former Democratic congressman from Wisconsin, articulated grand strategic ideas.[46] Aspin's casual and unstructured style made him unpopular with many Defense Department personnel and frustrated General Powell, an orderly administrator who stayed on as chairman of the Joint Chiefs of Staff for part of Clinton's first year in office.[47]

Nor did there seem to be a compelling reason in 1993 why Clinton should have revamped the nation's military and foreign policies. With the Cold War over, no overarching threat seemed to endanger the United States or the peace of the world. Clinton, freed from worrying about the Soviets, became an enthusiastic and consistent supporter of economic globalization — opening markets via NAFTA and other agreements—to the extent that some people thought that the doings of the International Monetary Fund and the Treasury Department, which were active in promoting international financial stability, mattered more to him than the National Security Council.[48]

Still, Clinton was as eager as his predecessors had been to maintain America's preeminence in the world. He also made a special effort to promote better relations between Israel, then headed by Prime Minister Yitzhak Rabin, and the Palestine Liberation Organization, led by Yasser Arafat. In September 1993, following secret negotiations that had been facilitated by the government of Norway, Rabin and Arafat shook hands in a highly publicized show of harmony orchestrated by Clinton on the White House lawn. The once bitter enemies also signed the so-called Oslo Accords, which temporarily brought to a close a Palestinian intifada, or armed uprising, that had broken out in 1987. The accords featured a Declaration of Principles, which outlined a transition to control by a Palestinian Authority of parts of

46. Halberstam, War in a Time of Peace, 190–91, 244–47.
47. James Mann, Rise of the Vulcans: The History of Bush's War Cabinet (New York, 2004), 178.
48. Ibid., xvi.

the West Bank and the Gaza Strip. The PLO recognized the right of the state of Israel to exist, renounced terrorism, and agreed to establish interim government in these areas.

After the assassination of Rabin by an angry Jewish man, however, the Oslo Accords fell victim to the hatreds that had long divided these implacable foes in the Middle East. By 1996, it was clear that Clinton's efforts to establish lasting peace had failed. Moreover, like most Americans in the 1990s, the president did not propose to use the nation's awesome military preeminence to press for major changes in international relationships, either in the Middle East or elsewhere in the world. His more prudent foreign policies tended instead to respond to problems and crises as they developed.

A rising concern for the administration, though not a new one, was foreign-inspired terrorism, which took the lives of fifty-four Americans between 1993 and the end of 1997. Another thirty-six were killed between 1998 and the end of 2000.[49] In February 1993, Muslim terrorists set off a bomb at the World Trade Center in New York City, killing six, injuring 1,000, and forcing 5,000 people to evacuate the building. After the CIA concluded that extremists connected to Saddam Hussein had tried to assassinate former president Bush in Kuwait in early 1993, Clinton ordered a strike of cruise missiles on Baghdad in June. It destroyed Saddam Hussein's intelligence headquarters. The president also had to worry about nuclear proliferation. Including the United States, eight nations possessed nuclear weapons in 1993, and others, among them the despotic governments of Iran and North Korea, were clearly anxious to join the club.[50] Russia, troubled with domestic instability, still possessed large stockpiles of carelessly stored nuclear weapons.

Moving cautiously in this uncertain post–Cold War world, the president continued the economic sanctions, U.N. weapons inspections, and no-fly zones that had been fastened on Iraq after the Gulf War. He authorized production of B-2 (Stealth) bombers and only marginally reduced defense expenditures, which still helped to employ an estimated two million Americans. In 1997, the United States spent $271 billion on defense, a sum that was only a little lower than the $290 billion expended in 1993.

49. Melvyn Leffler, "9/11 and the Past and Future of American Foreign Policy," *International Affairs* 79 (Oct. 2003), 1045–63.
50. These eight nations were the United States, Britain, Russia, France, China, India, Israel, and (it was generally believed) Pakistan.

Sums such as these were nearly 100 times the amount appropriated for Goals 2000, Clinton's education initiative.[51]

While maintaining these policies, the Clinton administration necessarily had to worry about a host of troubles around the globe. Civil wars and separatist movements in 1993 continued to shed blood in many areas, including the Balkans, Indonesia, Sri Lanka, and Spain. Though South Africa finally ended apartheid in early 1994, civil wars and AIDS still ravaged many other African countries. Religious confrontations—Muslims against Jews, Sunnis against Shiites, radical Islamists against moderates—threatened mayhem in parts of the Middle East and Central Asia. Many millions of impoverished and oppressed people in the world continued to rage against the economic and military policies of the far richer nations of the West—and especially against those of the United States, whose seductive consumer goods and television programs penetrated virtually every culture in the world. Perplexed, some Americans seemed to be almost nostalgic for the Cold War era, when a simpler bipolar world had confronted them.

How should the United States, the dominant power in the world, respond to these matters? Should America engage in activities, including "nation-building," aimed at bringing democracy and economic development to other countries? Then and later, a wide range of Americans argued vociferously over these difficult questions. "Realists," many of whom were conservative in their politics, insisted that the United States should not become seriously involved in foreign conflicts unless the nation's important security interests were at stake. A number of liberals, remembering the horrors of Vietnam, agreed with them. The prevalence of cautious views such as these indicated that Bush may have been wrong in declaring after the Gulf War that the United States had "kicked the Vietnam Syndrome once and for all." Other Americans, however, were prepared to pursue more activist foreign policies. They included hard-liners who favored defense buildups that would intimidate potential troublemakers, evangelicals who hoped to

51. An estimated 3.6 million Americans had been engaged in defense work during the mid- and late 1980s. Defense spending had ranged between 23 and 27 percent of federal outlays between 1975 and 1990, peaking during the mid-1980s before dropping slowly to between 21 and 22 percent between 1991 and 1993. This percentage slipped further after 1993, ranging between 16 and 18 percent between 1994 and 2001. The sums for defense during the mid-1990s also decreased as a percentage of GDP, from 4.4 in 1993 to 3.1 in 1998. *Stat. Abst.*, 2002, 326. See also William Greider, *Fortress America: The American Military and the Consequences of Peace* (New York, 1998); and Eliot Cohen, "Calling Mr. X," *New Republic*, Jan. 19, 1999, 17–19.

save souls, and liberals who believed that carefully considered American interventions might advance human rights.

Until October 1993, no single crisis made Clinton devote great attention to international affairs. What then happened in Somalia forced his hand and had long-range repercussions for the foreign policies of the United States. Some 440 elite American troops in that poverty-stricken, politically chaotic country, having been dispatched by Clinton himself in August, were seeking to capture a powerful warlord—one of many in Somalia—whose followers had killed and mutilated twenty-four Pakistani U.N. peacekeepers in June. In October, rebels using hand-fired, rocket-propelled grenades shot down two Black Hawk helicopters carrying American soldiers. In fierce fighting that lasted off and on for seventeen hours, Somalis killed eighteen and wounded eighty-four Americans, all of them cut down in the capital city of Mogadishu.[52]

Americans ultimately "won" this battle, killing hundreds of Somalis, including many civilians, and wounding hundreds more. Meanwhile, however, television viewers in the United States and elsewhere were horrified by footage that showed jubilant Somalis dragging a dead American soldier through the streets of Mogadishu. Many outraged Americans, with agonizing memories of Vietnam revived, demanded to know what the United States was doing in such a God-forsaken place as Somalia, and why Clinton had allowed "mission creep" to endanger American lives. Other critics blasted the administration for apparently having failed to provide sufficient military backup for the troops.

Clinton, furiously denouncing aides for his own inattention to Somalia, sent in reinforcements but also announced that American troops would ultimately be withdrawn. Defense Secretary Aspin, who in late September had declined to supply armored reinforcements, was blamed for the American losses and replaced. When Somali factions signed a precarious peace agreement in March 1994, an obviously relieved president pulled United States combat forces from the country. United Nations peacekeepers, including some Americans, stayed on. But anarchy continued to prevail in Somalia, and the images of a dead American soldier being dragged through the streets remained powerful, promoting in the United States what some observers called a new syndrome, that of "Vietmalia." A vivid film, *Black Hawk Down* (2001), later revived these awful memories.[53]

---

52. For Clinton and Somalia, see Halberstam, *War in a Time of Peace*, 248–66.
53. Based on the widely read book by Mark Bowden, *Black Hawk Down: A Story of Modern War* (New York, 1999). See also James Chace, "War Without Risk," *New York Review of Books*, March 28, 2003, 31–33.

Only ten days after the bloodshed in Mogadishu, events in Haiti seemed further to humiliate the world's most powerful nation. Some 100 armed and angry Haitians, shouting "Somalia, Somalia," blocked the disembarkation at Port-au-Prince of 200 American non-combat soldiers who had been dispatched in order to train Haitian police as part of a "nation-building" mission there. This effort was expected in time to restore to the presidency the legitimately elected Jean-Bertrand Aristide, a defrocked radical priest who had been driven into exile by a coup in 1991. The ship carrying the soldiers, *Harlan County*, was forced by the protestors to turn away, thereby leading the president to launch another tirade at his aides. As he recognized, the event bared an obvious fact: He had no backup plan to cope with the resistance.

The debacles, as many Americans saw them, of Mogadishu and Port-au-Prince clearly unnerved Clinton and his advisers, who hoped to promote order and democracy abroad but who also greatly feared endangering the lives of American soldiers. The near-mesmerizing power of memories of Mogadishu became especially clear during one of the greatest horrors of modern times: genocide ravaging Rwanda that broke out in April 1994 and lasted for 100 days. When the vicious, often hand-to-hand fighting and butchering involving Hutu and Tutsi people finally subsided, at least 800,000 people lay dead, most of them Tutsis and moderate Hutus slashed to death by extremist Hutus brandishing machetes. The Tutsis, a minority in Rwanda, lost an estimated 70 percent of their people. (Later, establishing a despotic government in the country, they exacted revenge by killing untold thousands of Hutus both in Rwanda and in neighboring Congo.)[54] What the U.N. or the United States should have done in order to avert or significantly limit this slaughter was unclear in 1994. What America did do after ten U.N. peacekeepers were butchered in April was to take the lead in discouraging Western intervention and to call for the departure from Rwanda of the peacekeepers, thereby giving the killers carte blanche. The United States, like other Western nations, had no important economic or strategic interests in Rwanda, and it showed little desire to protect black people in the region. With most of the U.N. peacekeepers gone from Rwanda, America stood aside while the carnage mounted.

During Clinton's first two years in office, he seemed to have no good answers about how to calm intensifying savagery that was devastating fratricidal contenders—Croats, Serbs, and Muslims—in Croatia and Bosnia.

54. Philip Gourevitch, *We Wish to Inform You That We Will Be Killed with Our Families: Stories from Rwanda* (New York, 1998), 219; *New York Times*, July 10, 2004.

Between April 1992 and October 1995, more than 200,000 people were killed in these regions, most of them Muslims slaughtered by Bosnian Serbs who had initially been egged on by the nationalistic leader of Serbia, Slobodan Milosevic.[55] The majority of the dead were civilians who were murdered in surgical-style "ethnic cleansing" operations that also raped thousands of women and drove masses of people from their homes. During the 1992 campaign, Clinton had criticized Bush for standing aside while such carnage was taking place, but he, too, refrained from bold steps that might lead to the death of American soldiers. Maintaining the arms embargo that continued to hurt the underequipped Muslims, neither the United States nor NATO intervened. Some 6,000 overmatched U.N. peacekeepers, stationed in Bosnia since November 1992, were virtual hostages to the bloodthirsty contenders on the ground.[56]

In late 1994, Clinton slightly toughened America's stance concerning trouble spots in the world. In September, having threatened an armed invasion of Haiti, he managed to restore Aristide to power and to send in forces to help train a local police constabulary. In October he concluded an "agreed framework" with North Korea, whose leaders promised to freeze the nation's nuclear program and open its borders to international inspection. In return, the United States committed to supply North Korea, where millions of people were thought to be starving, with food, medical supplies, and heavy fuel oil. But Americans still showed little stomach for long-range nation-building in Haiti, from which Clinton withdrew American forces within two years. Aristide then conscripted the police as his personal army. Violence and political corruption soon returned to plague the people of that strife-ridden country.[57] Events in North Korea were equally discouraging. Critics of Clinton asserted that the secretive North Korean government, having bamboozled the United States, would renege on its agreement.[58]

---

55. *New York Times*, Nov. 9, 2004. Another 20,000 were missing, and presumed dead.
56. For Clinton and the Balkans, see Halberstam, *War in a Time of Peace*, 195–204, 283–351; and William Hitchcock, *The Struggle for Europe: The Turbulent History of a Divided Continent, 1945–2000* (New York, 2003), 390–403.
57. James Traub, "Making Sense of the Mission," *New York Times Magazine*, April 11, 2004, 32. Aristide, returning to power as president in 2001 after a disputed election in 2000, encountered violent unrest early in 2004, at which point American and French forces arrived in an effort to restore order. Aristide fled the country, accusing the United States of kidnapping him and driving him away. Starting in June 2004, U.N. peacekeepers policed the still distressed country.
58. Later revelations in 2002, indicating that North Korea had embarked on a clandestine uranium enrichment program, suggested to some analysts that these critics might have been correct. In early 2005, North Korea announced that it possessed nuclear weapons. *New York Times*, Feb. 11, 2005.

Given these frustrations, it was no wonder that Clinton lamented the intrusion of foreign policy on his plans for domestic reform. In part, he had himself to blame, for he spent relatively little time in 1993–94 on international matters. Aspin, moreover, had proved to be inept at developing defense policies. The president was especially disengaged from intelligence matters, virtually ignoring his CIA chief, James Woolsey. When a deranged pilot crashed a plane into the White House in 1993, the joke went around that the aviator was Woolsey, trying desperately to engage Clinton's attention.[59]

It is evident in retrospect that no Western leaders at that time had sure solutions for coping with the unfamiliar international scene that had so quickly replaced the bipolar world of the Cold War years. There were no obvious answers—only hard choices. Should Clinton have sent American forces to Somalia in 1993, or kept them there after the battle of Mogadishu? Should he have intervened more quickly or forcefully in Haiti? Could he have found a way to deter the remote and apparently fanatical leaders of North Korea? Mobilized the West in time to stop genocide in Rwanda? Sent American troops to stop ethnic cleansing in the Balkans? In considering these problems, Clinton was acutely aware of polls in 1993–94 revealing that the American people were skittish about undertaking moves such as these.

Still, few Americans in late 1994 gave Clinton high marks for foreign policy. In dealing with the international scene, as in handling health care reform, he was still feeling his way.

CLINTON WAS EVER AWARE of political considerations and rarely stopped thinking in 1993–94 about the upcoming off-year elections, or about his own campaign for reelection in 1996. Especially concerned about the power of conservative voters, he sought during mid- and late 1994 to distance himself from liberals in the Democratic Party. Thus he backed a welfare bill that would have cut the length of time during which people might stay on the welfare rolls. As Clinton anticipated, the bill, which he introduced late in the congressional session, did not pass, but he had let conservative voters know that he still had welfare reform in mind. He was more successful with Congress in September 1994, when he secured passage of a $30 billion crime bill. Stealing the thunder of conservatives, the law provided money for 100,000 new policemen in communities around

59. Halberstam, *War in a Time of Peace*, 244.

the nation and for construction of prisons. It also included a "three strikes and you're out" penalty for federal crimes.[60]

Unimpressed by Clinton's moves to the center, partisan foes of the president hammered at his liberal initiatives of 1993–94: health care reform, admitting gays to the military, gun control. They seized especially on media accounts that appeared to implicate the Clintons in financial and political improprieties surrounding earlier land development deals along the Whitewater River in Arkansas. Bowing to political pressure, Clinton agreed in 1993 to the appointment of an independent counsel to investigate these and other financial and legal activities of his wife and himself. Attorney General Janet Reno, overseeing the issue at a time when the statute of 1978 setting up the mechanisms for appointment of such counsels had temporarily been allowed to lapse, then selected Robert Fiske, a former federal prosecutor (and a Republican), to conduct the investigations.

In the summer of 1994, however, Congress renewed the statute, whereupon a three-person panel of federal judges charged by the law with the authority to appoint such counsel intervened. The panel, named by Chief Justice Rehnquist, determined that an independent prosecutor (that is, Fiske) ought not to be named by an executive official such as Reno, a presidential appointee. The judges replaced Fiske with Kenneth Starr, who had been solicitor general of the United States during the Bush administration.

This proved to be a major step toward the widening of probes into the doings of the Clintons. Fiske had investigated impartially and had not discovered evidence incriminating the Clintons. Starr, however, proved to be a zealously partisan prosecutor. Given wider authority over time, his investigations into the Clintons' involvement in the complicated Whitewater matter, which dated to the 1970s, soon broadened to include the president's handling of "Travelgate," the flap in early 1993 over his firing of White House travel office employees, and of "Filegate," a controversy that had surfaced in December 1993 over the mysterious disappearance from the White House of files relating to Whitewater and other matters.

By the time of Starr's appointment, the president had already been confronting accusations of sexual harassment brought against him by Paula Corbin Jones, a former Arkansas state employee who claimed that Clinton, while governor (and therefore her boss), had exposed himself to her in a Little Rock hotel room in 1991. Because Jones named a state trooper whom

---

60. Berman, *From the Center to the Edge*, 38–40.

she accused of bringing her to the hotel room for a sexual liaison with Clinton, the media labeled this story, too, as a "-gate"—this time, "Troopergate." In May 1994, she filed suit in an Arkansas federal court seeking $700,000 in damages.[61]

While in private practice between May and August 1994, Starr served as an adviser to Jones's legal team. When his name surfaced as a possible successor to Fiske, critics cried angrily but to no avail that he had a conflict of interest and should not accept such an appointment. Later, when Starr's investigations widened to focus on the president's sexual activities, furious defenders of the president, notably Mrs. Clinton, insisted that his appointment had been a partisan move that had launched a vast right-wing conspiracy.

These legal battles received extraordinarily extensive exposure in the media. In one week during mid-March, when they became front-page news, the three TV networks carried 126 stories about Clinton's alleged involvement in Whitewater and other matters, compared to 107 during the first three months of 1994 concerning bloodshed in Bosnia, 56 concerning tensions in the Middle East, and 42 concerning the ongoing struggle for health care reform.[62] Amid sensationalism of this sort, it was hardly surprising that many Americans wondered if "Slick Willie," already known as a philanderer, might be guilty as charged. Jay Leno, host of *The Tonight Show*, quipped that Clinton had complained about "powerful forces threatening to bring down his administration. I think that they are called hormones."[63]

Gingrich then acted boldly to promote GOP success in the 1994 elections. In an unprecedented move, he drew up a so-called Contract with America and in late September succeeded in getting 367 Republican House candidates to endorse it. Its preamble proclaimed that the election "offers the chance, after four decades of one-party control, to bring the House a new majority that will transform the way Congress works. That historic change would be the end of government that is too big, too intrusive, and too easy with the public's money. It can be the beginning of a Congress that respects the values and shares the faith of the American family."[64]

61. See chapter 12 for the outcome of these legal matters.
62. Johnson, *Best of Times*, 227–39; Joseph Lelyveld, "In Clinton's Court," *New York Review of Books*, May 29, 2003, 11–15.
63. Berman, *From the Center to the Edge*, 40.
64. For the text of the Contract, see *New York Times*, Sept. 28, 1994.

The Contract wisely skirted divisive cultural issues such as abortion or school prayer. Otherwise, however, it was a concise summation of long-cherished conservative positions concerning economic, foreign, and military policies. It opened by calling for a series of measures that promised to reform procedures in the House, including the establishment of limits on the terms of committee chairs. It then highlighted ten broader goals. These included approval of a constitutional "balanced budget/tax limitation amendment" and of a "legislative line-item veto"; tougher action against welfare programs and crime, including "effective death penalty provisions"; "tax incentives for private long-term care insurance to let Older Americans keep more of what they have earned over the years"; a "Common Sense Legal Reform Act" that would set "reasonable limits on punitive damages and reform product liability laws to stem the endless tide of litigation"; cuts in capital gains taxes; a $500-per-child tax credit; a prohibition against American troops being placed under U.N. command; stronger defense efforts that would "maintain our credibility around the world"; and a "first-ever vote on term limits to replace career politicians with citizen legislators."

By moving toward the center in 1994, Clinton had already tried to narrow the distance between his own policies and conservative goals such as these. A budget balancer, free trader, welfare reform advocate, and self-described crime fighter, he was by no means the ardent liberal that Gingrich portrayed him to be. It is therefore hard to say whether the Contract greatly influenced voters, most of whom had only a dim idea of what it said. But as the off-year elections approached it was obvious that Republicans, aided by religious voters who had mobilized behind the Christian Coalition, had managed to turn the upcoming elections into a referendum on Clinton himself. Well-organized foes of gun control, directed by the National Rifle Association, were especially active in denouncing the administration. All these groups did their best to paint the president as a knee-jerk liberal. Moreover, polls indicated that voters had a low opinion of him. Many Democratic congressional candidates avoided being closely associated with him.

The results in November were devastating to Democrats. Republicans scored the most impressive off-year comeback in modern times, adding nine members in the Senate, where they recaptured a majority (of 52 to 48) for the first time since 1986. They gained fifty-two seats in the House, taking command there, 230 to 204, for the first time since 1954. In 1995, the House was to include seventy-three freshman Republicans, many of them southerners who were ideologically to the right of Gingrich. Harvey

Mansfield, a conservative professor of government at Harvard, said that the election meant the "end of the New Deal" and the "completion of what Ronald Reagan began."[65]

To a degree, that was wishful thinking on his part. The major programs of the New Deal and the Great Society survived. Still, it was obvious after 1994 that politicians on the right were high in the saddle and that the familiar phenomenon of divided government—Congress vs. the White House—had returned with a vengeance. The GOP, having wrested control of the House, maintained it for the next decade and more. During the remainder of Clinton's time in the White House, it did its best to dash his high hopes of being remembered as a great American president.

65. Berman, *From the Center to the Edge*, 42.

11

Prosperity, Partisanship, Terrorism

Of the many developments highlighting the last years of the twentieth century in the United States, two stood out. The first was a surge in the economy. As rising prosperity promoted good feelings, it stimulated still higher expectations, which in turn continued to produce many of the anxieties that had troubled Americans since the 1960s. The second was a heating up of the partisan warfare that had already beset the first two years of Clinton's presidency. Intensifying to unprecedented levels, this warfare polarized the politics of his second term, relegating even concerns about terrorism to the background.

IN 1993–94, WHEN THE UNITED STATES was still recovering from recession, some analysts of economic trends continued to emphasize the theme of decline. One historian noted a widespread belief that "the American economy is weak and failing, destined to be a second echelon participant in a new twenty-first-century world economic order." Another writer, Edward Luttwak, lamented the "spent power of Calvinism" in the United States and complained that Americans, refusing to save or invest in infrastructure, were piling up huge amounts of personal debt. The major question to be asked about the economy, he concluded, was not *if* the United States would become a "third world country," but *when*. He speculated, "The date might be as close as the year 2020." He concluded, "If present trends continue, all but a small minority of Americans will be impoverished soon enough, left to yearn hopelessly for the last golden age of American prosperity."[1]

Declinists such as these ticked off a number of familiar trends to bolster their case. Economic growth, they said, remained sluggish; productivity, though showing signs of resurgence, was still smaller than it had been in the 1960s; inequality of wealth and income, ascendant since the 1970s, was sharpening; poverty (in 1994) still afflicted 14.5 percent of the population, or 38 million people, including 21 percent of children under 18; public schools, especially in the inner cities, continued to falter; the downtown areas of many large cities, though glitzier here and there, were still languishing; jobs were still disappearing in the Rust Belt and other centers of American manufacturing; and the United States, facing strong competition from abroad, was running up large trade and payments deficits. Knowledgeable observers wrote that America's economy was becoming dangerously dependent on overseas investors, notably central banks that bought Treasury securities.

The laments went on: The real wages of production and non-supervisory workers in manufacturing, having slipped slowly since the 1970s, were showing no signs of improvement; "outsourcing" of jobs to cheap-labor nations was throwing Americans, including white-collar employees, out of work; apparently insatiable consumerism was ratcheting up credit card debt and diverting money from productive investment; ever greater corporate centralization was fattening the salaries and perks of CEOs and swallowing small businesses; the rise of huge, anti-union retail chains such as Wal-Mart was accelerating the growth of low-wage service sector work; and "downsizing" was threatening middle managers as well as blue-collar workers, thereby fostering what some pessimists were calling the "democratization of insecurity."[2]

---

1. Michael Bernstein, "Understanding American Economic Decline: The Contours of the Late-Twentieth-Century Experience," in Bernstein and David Adler, eds., *Understanding American Economic Decline* (New York, 1994), 3; Edward Luttwak, *The Endangered American Dream: How to Stop the United States from Becoming a Third World Country and How to Win the Geo-Economic Struggle for Industrial Supremacy* (New York, 1993), 118.

2. For a critique of such complaints, see Joseph Nye, "Introduction: The Decline of Confidence in Government," in Nye et al., *Why People Don't Trust Government* (Cambridge, Mass., 1997), 1–18. This is the source of the phrase "democratization of insecurity." Indictments of American consumerism include John de Graaf et al., *Affluenza: The All-Consuming Epidemic* (San Francisco, 2001); and Thomas Frank, *One Market Under God: Extreme Capitalism, Market Populism, and the End of Economic Democracy* (New York, 2000). For trends in business and trade, see Thomas McCraw, *American Business, 1920–2000: How It Worked* (Wheeling, Ill., 2000); and Maury Klein, "Coming Full Circle: The Study of Big Business Since 1950," *Enterprise and Society* 2, no. 3 (Sept. 2001), 425–60. For Wal-Mart, see Simon Head, "Inside the Leviathan," *New York Review of Books*, Dec. 16, 2004, 80–89.

Contemporary critics especially deplored the persistence of social and environmental problems, caused by what they perceived as the scandalously excessive wastefulness and materialism of life in the United States, the world's leading "throw-away society." The old adage "Waste not, want not," they complained, had gone the way of the horse and buggy. Echoing earlier pessimists, they railed at the political influence of growth-at-all-costs developers and at the rapid expansion of "exurban sprawl," where office parks, malls, fast-food outlets, and ticky-tacky subdivisions were said to be blighting the countryside.[3]

In their familiarly grim descriptions of suburban and exurban life as "cultural wastelands," many of these critics continued to be elitist and patronizing: Contrary to the message of movies such as *American Beauty* (1999), it was surely not the case that the majority of suburbanites were bored, tasteless, or neurotic. Most city-dwelling Americans who moved to suburbs and exurbs—which varied considerably in size and levels of personal income—hoped to find better schools and safer neighborhoods. They yearned for more space. Those who settled in "ticky-tacky" housing tracts were not tasteless; they were relatively poor. Struggling to get ahead, they moved to places that they could afford. They shopped at stores such as Wal-Mart because that was where goods were cheapest. Still, critics continued to bewail the mores and tastes of suburban and exurban folk: Like far too many other Americans, they asserted, many exurbanites were mindless, acquisitive consumers.

Critics of American society in the 1990s further maintained that the popular obsession with automobiles had roared out of control, creating mammoth traffic jams and leaving the nation ever more reliant on foreign production of oil. Increases in the number of gas-guzzling SUVs, pickups, and other high-powered motor vehicles, they added, were endangering people and befouling air that was dirtied already by emissions from carelessly regulated power plants, refineries, and manufacturing industries.[4] Many of these facilities loomed over low-income and predominantly minority neighborhoods, subjecting children in such areas to asthma

---

3. Andres Duany et al., *Suburban Nation: The Rise of Sprawl and the Decline of the American Dream* (New York, 2000). For commentary on exurban sprawl see David Brooks, *On Paradise Drive: How We Live Now (and Always Have) in the Future Tense* (New York, 2004).

4. The number of motor vehicle registrations in the United States increased from 156 million in 1980, when the population was 226.5 million, to 189 million in 1990, when the population was 249 million, and to 221 million in 2000, when the population was 281 million. *Stat. Abst.*, 2002, 675.

attacks and raising the risk of chronic bronchitis among adults. Green-house gases, environmentalists insisted, were seriously exacerbating global warming. Al Gore declared in 1992 that environmental degradation was threatening the "very survival of the civilized world."[5]

Other commentators focused grimly on the stressful culture of work in the United States. Americans, they pointed out, toiled for far more hours per week than did people in most other industrialized nations. Workers, stressed out, had little time to spend with their families or to volunteer for community activities. Wages and salaries, though rising for many people in the late 1990s, never seemed sufficient. As one unhappy Chicagoan, managing director of a company, despaired in 1997, "I earn more in a month than my dad did in a year, but I feel my life is more difficult." He added, "I don't gamble, I don't have season tickets to the Bulls. How can I earn this much but not have anything left over?"[6]

SOME OF THESE MANY COMPLAINTS about American economic, environmental, and social conditions in the mid- and late 1990s were on target. Until very late in the decade, poverty remained stubborn, reflecting not only the large number of low-income female-headed families—and racial inequalities—but also the persistence of holes in the nation's safety net, which was still more porous than those of most industrialized countries. Thanks to poverty, drug abuse, and lack of adequate prenatal services in low-income areas, infant mortality rates in the United States, though roughly half of what they had been in the 1970s, continued to be higher than they were in many industrialized nations.[7] The "underclasses"

---

5. Al Gore, *Earth in the Balance: Ecology and the Human Spirit* (Boston, 1992), 92. Widely noted books of the time concerned with environmental damage also include John McPhee, *The Control of Nature* (New York, 1989); and Bill McKibben, *The End of Nature* (New York, 1989).

6 *Time*, issue of Dec. 29, 1997–Jan. 5, 1998, 92. Books of the early 1990s that discuss the effects of work in America include Juliet Schor, *The Overworked American: The Unexpected Decline of Leisure* (New York, 1991); Arlene Skolnick, *Embattled Paradise: The American Family in an Age of Uncertainty* (New York, 1994); and Jeremy Rifkin, *The End of Work: The Decline of the Labor Force and the Dawn of the Post-Market Era* (New York, 1995). For problems of labor unions, see Nelson Lichtenstein, *State of the Union: A Century of American Labor* (Princeton, 2002), 218–25; and Andrew Hacker, "Who's Sticking with the Union?" *New York Review of Books*, Feb. 13, 1999, 45–48.

7. Tony Judt, "Europe vs. America," *New York Review of Books*, Feb. 10, 2005, 37–41. The rate of such mortality in the United States had been 12.6 per 1,000 live births in 1980. In 1999 it was 7.1. At that time the rate for blacks was 14.6, compared to 5.8 for whites. *Stat. Abst.*, 2002, 78.

in America's urban ghettos, Native Americans on reservations, and migrant workers and other low-income people in depressed rural areas still struggled to stay afloat. As in the 1970s and 1980s, long-range structural trends advancing the spread of relatively low-wage service work, as well as competition from abroad, threatened American manufacturing jobs.[8] The wages of production and non-supervisory workers continued to stagnate. Though Congress raised the minimum wage in 1996 (from $4.25 to $5.15 an hour), its real buying power, having fallen since the 1970s, continued to decline.[9]

Americans with full-time employment (still reckoned, as it long had been, at forty hours per week) did in fact work considerably longer hours on the average—perhaps 350 to 400 more a year—than did Western Europeans, who enjoyed shorter workdays and more holidays.[10] Many Europeans (living in the cradle of Calvinism) were stunned by the strength of the work ethic in the United States and deplored the stress that they said it created. Critics were also correct to point out that American energy use remained enormous: With approximately 6 percent of the world's population, the United States in the late 1990s was annually responsible for a quarter of the planet's total energy consumption and emitted a quarter of the world's greenhouse gases. By 2002, the United States had to import 54 percent of its crude oil, compared to less than 40 percent during the frightening energy crises of the late 1970s.[11]

It was also true that America's eager consumers and investors were continuing to amass levels of personal debt that were far higher than those in other nations. People were also gambling more than ever, and speculating eagerly in the stock market, sometimes as day traders and as members of proliferating investment clubs. Given the listed value of stocks, this activity was hardly surprising: Between January 1991, when the Dow Jones industrial average hit a low of 2,588, and January 2000, by which time it had soared to a high of 11,722, stock prices more than quadrupled.[12] In the same month of 2000, starry-eyed (though, as it later turned out, badly

---

8. The number of manufacturing jobs declined from 21.9 million in 1980 to 19.9 million in 2000. *Stat. Abst.*, 2002, 385.
9. The value of the minimum wage in constant 2000 dollars was $6.72 in 1975, $5.36 in 1985, $4.80 in 1995, and, of course, $5.15 in 2000. Ibid., 405.
10. *New York Times*, June 8, Nov. 25, 2002.
11. Ibid., Jan. 16, Feb. 18, 2002. By mid-2004, it was estimated that 60 percent of American oil consumption was from imports. Ibid., June 20, 2004.
12. Steven Fraser, *Every Man a Speculator: A History of Wall Street in American Life* (New York, 2004), 600; *Stat. Abst.*, 2002, 735.

blurred) visions of the future led AOL to acquire Time Warner for $180 billion in stock and debt. This, the largest corporate merger in United States history, was but the most spectacular instance of a merger mania that dwarfed that of the Reagan years. Successful investors such as Warren Buffett (the "oracle of Omaha") of Berkshire Hathaway and Peter Lynch, who managed the Magellan Fund of Fidelity Investments, received adulatory attention in the media, in a culture that seemed more mesmerized than ever by dreams of moneymaking. By 2001, 51 percent of American families had some investments in stock, compared to 32 percent in 1989 and 13 percent in 1980.[13]

Trouble lay ahead, especially for tech-obsessed buyers who were plunging their money into increasingly overpriced "dot-com" stocks. Federal Reserve chairman Alan Greenspan, who most of the time intoned that the United States was entering a "new age" economy of huge potential, paused in December 1996 to warn against America's "irrational exuberance."[14] Greenspan did not want to stick a pin in the bubble, however, and stock prices continued to increase greatly until early 2000. By that time, enthusiastic onlookers were declaring that the United States had become a "shareholder nation." The boom in stocks, part of the larger advance of prosperity in the late 1990s, did much to give Americans—already feeling good about the end of the Cold War—a triumphant but illusory sense of empowerment.[15]

Most economists agreed that inequality of income, as measured by shares of national earnings held by various levels of the income pyramid, was not only continuing to rise in the United States but also that it was sharper than in other industrial nations. The share of aggregate income held by the poorest one-fifth of American households declined from 4.4 percent of total income in 1975 to 3.7 percent in 1995, or by almost one-sixth. The share held by the richest fifth increased in the same years from 43.2 percent to 48.7 percent, a rise of more than 12 percent. The IRS reported in 1999

13. Robert Samuelson, "The Age of Inflation," New Republic, May 13, 2002, 32–41. Most of these holdings were in mutual funds, retirement accounts, and other managed assets, all of which expanded greatly in the 1990s. By 2000, 34 million Americans had 401(k) pension plans, with assets totaling $1.7 trillion (compared to 7.5 million people who had had these in 1985). Fraser, Every Man a Speculator, 582–83. Ownership of stocks, as of other sources of wealth in America, was hardly democratic in nature. It was estimated that the wealthiest 1 percent of Americans in the mid-1990s owned almost 50 percent of all stocks. Godfrey Hodgson, More Equal than Others: America from Nixon to the New Century (Princeton, 2004), 92.
14. Fraser, Every Man a Speculator, 590.
15. Ibid., 579.

that 205,000 American households had incomes of more than $1 million.[16] The very wealthy, including many CEOs, were enjoying salaries, perks, and comforts on an unprecedented scale. By 1998, the average income of the 13,000 wealthiest families in the United States was 300 times that of average families. These families earned as much income as the poorest 20 million families.[17]

Why this inequality continued to mount remained disputed. Some writers emphasized that top corporate leaders had become greedier and less paternalistic and that tax cuts favoring the very wealthy were to blame.[18] Others stressed that racial discrimination still played a key role, and that female-headed families, which were disproportionately African American, and steadily larger numbers of relatively poor immigrants weighted the bottom of the income pyramid. The increase in immigration was surely an important source of ascending inequality. Virtually all analysts agreed that another major cause of inequality was lack of growth in relatively well paid manufacturing employment and the ongoing rise in the number of low-wage service-sector jobs. Many of these openings were taken out of necessity by women, recent immigrants, and other people with low levels of education and skill.

All these factors helped account for the worsening of economic inequality. So did the actions of some large corporations. The inflated sense of monetary entitlement expressed by a large number of corporate executives — "we made big profits for the company, and we deserve big rewards," they insisted — exposed in an especially crass and magnified fashion the entitlement mentality of much of the culture at large.[19] Some major corporations, anxious to lessen huge obligations, began cutting back or discontinuing

16. Gregg Easterbrook, *The Progress Paradox: How Life Gets Better While People Feel Worse* (New York, 2003), 127. It was later reported that the number of "millionaire households" in the United States in 2003 was 3.8 million (3.4 percent of 111 million households in all at that time). These were households with $1 million or more in investible assets (not including primary residences, 401 (k) plan assets, stock options, investments in real estate, and annuities). *New York Times*, May 24, 2004.

17. Timothy Smeeding, "Changing Income Inequality in OECD Countries," in Richard Hauser and Irene Becker, eds., *The Personal Distribution of Income in an International Perspective* (New York, 2000), 205–24; Paul Krugman, "For Richer," *New York Times Magazine*, Oct. 20, 2002, 62ff. American inequality since the 1970s is the central theme of Hodgson, *More Equal than Others*.

18. Hodgson, *More Equal Than Others*, 87–111, stresses the greed of rich people and of corporate leaders.

19. For an account emphasizing the greed and sense of entitlement of corporate leaders, see John Cassidy, "The Greed Cycle," *New Yorker*, Sept. 23, 2002, 64–77.

long-promised defined-benefit pension and medical plans. Many employers continued to take a hard line with trade unions, whose losses of members badly sapped the bargaining power of organized labor.[20] Lobbying effectively in Washington and in state capitals, representatives of big business, including titans of agribusiness, demanded—and often received—generous subsidies, protections, and tax breaks from legislators. Not without cause, liberals (and others) concluded that the harshly dog-eat-dog approach of many American business leaders in the 1990s was creating a new, often nastier "corporate culture."

Trends in education further threatened equality of opportunity in America. In the "knowledge economy" of globalization and computerization that spread in the 1990s, specialized expertise became particularly important in the professions, the sciences, and the business world, yet the cost of tuition and fees at most colleges and universities increased at a considerably more rapid rate than wages and salaries. Although a handful of wealthy private universities managed to offer substantial financial aid to students, very few could afford to establish "need-blind" admissions programs or to set aside the large sums necessary to support graduate students. The sons and daughters of wealthy parents, enabled to attend expensive private schools and elite universities, were gaining an increasingly enviable edge over their economically less fortunate competitors. By 2000, many critics, including university presidents, worried that an intergenerational educational elite was taking shape, which in the future would dangerously expand the power of class privilege in the United States.

NOTWITHSTANDING THE POSSIBLE consequences of these alarming long-range trends, most middle-class Americans in the mid- and late 1990s did not seem to be terribly exercised. As earlier, they did not worry much about inequality of income: As at most times in the history of the United States, class resentments continued to be muted. Instead, most people focused on their own situations, and those of their friends and families. In so doing, they had reason to be pleased with a great many developments at the time. Take, for instance, the environment. Serious concerns, to be sure, persisted. The surge of immigration, which more than any other development caused America's population to rise (from 203.3 million in 1970 to 281.4 million in 2000, or by 38 percent) continued to alarm a number of environmentalists who lamented the impact of population increase

20. For statistics on unions, see *Stat. Abst.*, 2002, 412, and note 15, chapter 10.

on resources and on the quality of American life.[21] Thanks in part to population growth, battles over access to water and land still provoked bitter controversy in the West. Fights over commercial and residential development polarized communities all about the country. Most scientists agreed that global warming presented serious problems. Chemical runoff from agricultural fertilizers and pesticides polluted a number of lakes, rivers, and bays, such as Chesapeake Bay.[22] Hundreds of toxic sites remained to be cleaned up. Millions of Americans lived in areas where soot and smog threatened air standards established by the Environmental Protection Agency.[23]

In a great many ways, though, the environmental movement that had surged ahead in the 1970s had become a mainstream phenomenon by the 1990s.[24] By then, pressure from activists, including "eco-feminists," had prompted increasing public awareness about the dangers from toxic chemicals and lead poisoning. Other activists had stopped the authorization of environmentally controversial dams.[25] Recycling became the norm in most communities. Acid rain decreased by one-half between 1970 and 2000.[26] The ongoing development of high-yield agriculture led to the reforestation of a great deal of once cultivated land. Though runoff from agricultural chemicals was damaging, tougher controls on the dumping of sewage and industrial waste enabled many streams and lakes—including Lake Erie, where pollution had been near catastrophic—to regenerate.

Curbs on emissions from cars and smokestacks had helped clean the air. Despite population growth and a doubling of car miles traveled between 1970 and 2000, smog declined by one-third over those thirty years. The spread of energy-efficient household appliances, significant since the

21. Otis Graham, "The Unfinished Reform: Regulating Immigration in the National Interest," in Roger Daniels and Graham, *Debating American Immigration, 1882–Present* (Lanham, Md., 2001), 89–185. Thanks mainly to immigration, America's population continued to climb after 2000, to 290.8 million in mid-2003.

22. Easterbrook, *The Progress Paradox*, 86.

23. Barbara Freese, *Coal: A Human History* (Cambridge, Mass., 2003), 167–72, where she estimated that the number of Americans so threatened was 81 million.

24. This is the central message of Gregg Easterbrook, *A Moment on the Earth: The Coming Age of Environmental Optimism* (New York, 1995), and of Easterbrook, *The Progress Paradox*, 41–45.

25. Marc Reisner, *Cadillac Desert: The American West and Its Disappearing Water* (New York, 1993), 512–14; Robert Gottlieb, *Forcing the Spring: The Transformation of the American Environmental Movement* (Washington, 1993), 222–26.

26. David Whitman, *The Optimism Gap: The I'm OK—They're Not Syndrome and the Myth of American Decline* (New York, 1998), 110.

1970s, slowed the rise in use of electricity. SUVs aside, most automobiles were more fuel-efficient than they had been in the 1970s. Thanks to improvements such as these, and to lower oil prices, energy costs, which had peaked at 13 percent of GDP during the oil crisis of 1979, declined to between 6 and 7 percent between 1995 and 1999.[27] Per capita consumption of energy in America, though increasing since the mid-1980s, rose more gradually than did population, or than economic output per capita. The Very Bad Old Days of the 1970s, when extraordinarily wasteful uses of energy had helped to provoke national crises, appeared by 2000 to have ended.[28]

In other ways, too, the quality of life in the late 1990s was better for most people than it had been in the 1970s and 1980s. One such change involved food. Though the massive consumption of junk food (and the sedentary life of riding around in cars and watching television) helped to drive a rise in obesity, the majority of Americans were also enjoying considerably greater choice in deciding what and where to eat.[29] In supermarkets as well as in urban and suburban restaurants, which proliferated greatly during the late 1990s, a wide variety of fresh, local, and seasonal foods, as well as ethnic and organic foods, was becoming more readily available. Television chefs—Julia Child had been a pioneer in the field—captured growing audiences. Wealthy patrons of restaurants in major cities such as New York could feast on all manner of imaginative appetizers, salads, entrées, and desserts. Consumption of fine wines rose enormously. No longer could it dismissively be said, as it often had been, that most American people soldiered on in a bland and unimaginative gastronomic culture of casseroles, turkey and stuffing, and (for those who could afford it) Sunday dinners of roast beef, potatoes, and apple pie.

Another improvement for most people was more basic: in health. Though 14 percent of Americans—roughly 40 million—still suffered from a lack of health insurance at the turn of the century, a host of technological advances

27. *New York Times*, March 1, 2003. The cost of a barrel of imported oil (in constant 2002 dollars) hit a low of $12 per barrel in 1999, compared to a high in 1979–80 of $88 per barrel.

28. Theodore Caplow et al., eds., *The First Measured Century: An Illustrated Guide to Trends in America, 1900–2000* (Washington, 2001), 256–57; *Stat. Abst., 2002, 563.

29. According to the Centers for Disease Control and Prevention, American adults, though only an inch or so taller on the average in 2002 than they had been in 1960, had become nearly twenty-five pounds heavier on the average. Children, too, had become notably heavier than in the past. The percentage of Americans who were overweight or obese (by the CDC definitions) had increased from 56 in the early 1990s to 65 in 2002. *New York Times*, Oct. 28, 2004.

in medicine continued to better the quality of life for the majority of people who had adequate coverage.[30] The introduction of more effective anti-retroviral drugs was at last moderating the epidemic of AIDS in the United States. Preventive measures were becoming effective in improving personal health: Per capita smoking continued to decline, lessening mortality from tobacco, and bans on smoking began to cleanse the air in public places.[31] Rates of infant mortality slowly decreased. Thanks especially to improvements in dealing with cardiovascular disease, life expectancy at birth, which had averaged 70.8 years in 1970, rose to 76.9 by 2000.[32] Better roads (and seat belt laws and tougher penalties for drunk driving) made it safer to drive: Though the number of miles driven greatly increased, fatalities from motor vehicle accidents declined absolutely, from 51,090 in 1980 to 41,820 in 2000.[33]

Insofar as household possessions were concerned, Americans had never had it so good. In 2001, a record-high percentage of houses—68 percent—were owner-occupied, up from 64 percent in 1990.[34] The living spaces of the housing units built in the 1990s were even larger on the average than earlier (and households were smaller in size), thereby offering more personal comfort and privacy and making room for a wide variety of goods and gadgets. Many other goods, such as automobiles, were of higher quality than in earlier years and cost less in inflation-adjusted dollars. The Web site eBay was becoming an extraordinarily popular destination for bargain hunters. Wal-Mart was a special boon to low- and middle-income shoppers. It was estimated that sales at Wal-Mart stores helped to lower the rate of inflation nationally by as much as 1 percent per year.[35]

---

30. The number of Americans without health insurance continued to increase after 2000—to 45 million in 2003.

31. The decline in smoking probably helped to cause the rise in obesity, but in most instances the physical consequences of being a little overweight were not so serious as those caused by smoking.

32. *Stat. Abst.*, 2002, 71. The gap (of roughly six years) between the life expectancy at birth of blacks and whites had hardly changed during these thirty years. In 2000, black life expectancy at birth was 71.7 years, compared to 77.4 for whites.

33. Edward Tenner, *Why Things Bite Back: Technology and the Revenge of Unintended Consequences* (New York, 1996), 261–68; *Stat. Abst.*, 2002, 661, 678. Better-constructed cars (excepting many SUVs) also helped reduce the number of fatalities on American roads and highways.

34. *Stat. Abst.*, 2002, 600. This statistic, like many that follow, conceals significant differences stemming from racial inequalities. In 2001, whites owned 73 percent of housing units in which they lived, whereas blacks owned 48 percent. Ibid., 599.

35. *New York Times*, April 17, 2004.

At the turn of the century, the United States was truly a utopia of consumer goods, conveniences, and personal comforts. Of the 107 million households in the country in 2001, 106 million had color television (76 million had two or more sets); 96 million, VCR and/or DVD players; 92 million, microwave ovens; 84 million, electric clothes washers; 82 million, cable TV; 81 million, either room or central air-conditioning; 79 million, electric or gas clothes dryers; 60 million, personal computers; and 51 million, access to the Internet. More than 85 million households had one or more cars or trucks.[36] Americans had the means to enjoy travel as never before—for a total of 1,602 billion miles in 2000, as compared to 1,418 billion miles in 1990 and 1,126 billion miles in 1980.[37] Consumer choice was even more dazzling than earlier, to the point of prompting shoppers to complain of "catalog-induced anxiety." Comforts and possessions once only dreamed of—two or three cars, sail and power boats, frequent and faraway travel, second homes—were becoming affordable for steadily higher numbers of people who had ascended to the ranks of the upper-middle and upper classes.

A key force behind these developments was the rapidly improving economy of the late 1990s, which enabled the United States to emerge from the decade as even more incontestably the wealthiest nation in the history of the world. In 2001, the United States produced 22 percent of the world's output, a considerably higher percentage than Britain had managed (8 percent) at the peak of its empire in 1913.[38] America's per capita GDP in constant dollars increased at an average rate of more than 3 percent per year between 1996 and 2000.[39] By 2000, charitable giving (via individuals, bequests, foundations, and corporations) reached an all-time high as a percentage of GDP, 2.3 percent.[40] Unemployment declined, bottoming out at 4 percent in 2000, the lowest in many years. Notwithstanding complaints about outsourcing, joblessness was considerably lower in the United States than in the more troubled economics of most other western nations at the time.[41] Defenders of outsourcing maintained—probably accurately—that

36. *Stat. Abst.*, 2002, 604, 605. In 1995, Americans for the first time bought more trucks than cars. In 2001, 33 million of the nation's 107 million households had two or more cars or trucks.
37. Ibid., 677.
38. Niall Ferguson, "2011," *New York Times Magazine*, Dec. 2, 2001, 76–79.
39. *Stat. Abst.*, 2002, 422.
40. *Providence Journal*, June 21. 2004. In 2001–2, as the economy faltered, this percentage slipped a little, before inching up again in 2003 to 2.2.
41. Ibid., 367. Critics of official statistics concerning unemployment emphasize that these do not include a great many "discouraged workers." Michael Katz, *The Price of Citizenship: Redefining the American Welfare State* (New York, 2001), 349–51.

the practice, though devastating to those who were fired, improved the long-run competitiveness of many American producers, thereby protecting or enhancing employment over time. The cost of living in the United States, meanwhile, increased only a little during these bountiful years.

Though the very wealthy reaped the greatest benefits from these changes, the majority of other Americans had more to spend in real dollars in 2000 than they had in the mid-1990s. Much of the rise in income inequality in the 1990s seems to have reflected the very large gains that were enjoyed by a relatively small number of hyper-rich people at the top of the income pyramid; shares of total income changed modestly in the vastly more populous middle and lower levels.[42] Per capita disposable income (in constant 1996 dollars), which had risen only slowly between 1991 and 1995, increased from $20,795 in 1995 to $23,687 in 2001.[43] Median household money income (in constant 2000 dollars) rose from $38,262 in 1995 to $42,151 in 2000.[44] As in previous decades, dual-income households fared especially well economically.[45]

Poverty began to plummet—down to 11.3 percent of the population in 2000. That meant that 31.1 million people, 7 million fewer than in 1994, lived in households below the government's official poverty line.[46] The real per capita income of Native Americans, though still only one-half of the national average in 2000, improved by roughly one-third during the decade.[47] Americans still enjoyed the highest per capita incomes in real buying power of any people on the planet.[48] Contemporaries marveled

42. Daniel McMurrer and Isabel Sawhill, "The Declining Importance of Class," Urban Institute Report no. 4 (April 1997); New York Times, June 5, 2005.
43. Stat. Abst., 2002, 422. In 1996 dollars, it had been $12,823 in 1970, $14,393 in 1975, and $18,229 in 1985.
44. Ibid., 433. In 1980, median money household income in 2000 dollars had been $35,238.
45. New York Times, Nov. 1, 2004.
46. Stat. Abst., 2002, 441. In 2000, the poverty rate for whites was 9.4 percent, down from 11.7 in 1994; for blacks it was 22 percent, down from 30.6 in 1994. The official poverty line in 2000 was $8,794 for an individual, $13,738 for three persons, and $17,603 for four persons. Ibid., 442.
47. Based on census data. The incomes of Native American groups that were not engaged in the gaming industry seemed to improve at the same rate as those that were. Providence Journal, Jan., 6, 2005.
48. Robert Samuelson, "The Grand Illusion," Newsweek, special issue, Dec. 1999–Feb. 2000, 48–49. Samuelson estimated that per capita income in the United States was then 33 percent higher than in Germany and 26 percent higher than in Japan. Hodgson, More Equal Than Others, 94–99, agrees that per capita purchasing power of consumer goods continued in the 1990s to be higher in the United States than in other nations, but that the "monetary value of [public] services"—notably medical care—was higher in the socially democratic countries of Scandinavia and in Luxembourg and Switzerland, thereby enabling people in these nations to have a higher standard of living as measured by this different standard.

that America's low inflation and low unemployment could coexist. This was a "Goldilocks economy"—hot enough to advance prosperity yet cool enough to prevent inflation.

Pro-American observers from Europe swelled the chorus of hosannas about economic life in the United States in the late 1990s, stressing what they correctly perceived as the positive openness, creativity, and risk-taking dynamism of American culture. Small wonder, they said, that millions of people around the world continued to flock to the New World's land of opportunity. In the United States, they emphasized, abundant resources stimulated large visions of possibility: People who scrambled and gambled still had a good chance of advancing in life. Josef Joffe, a conservative German commentator, remarked of the American scene in 1997, "Traditions are being cracked right and left. The trend is toward individualization, nonhierarchical cooperation and breathless innovation. Creativity rather than order rules. These values have always defined American culture, but today they are shaping Europe and Asia willy-nilly because otherwise they could not keep up." Jonathan Freedland, a British writer, added in 1998, "On a bad day Britain can feel so fixed in the past, change seems all but impossible." He added, "Put crudely, the ambitious Brit hopes to find his place in a system that already exists and seems to have existed for ever, while the ambitious American hopes to change it—or even to build a new one."[49]

Why such prosperity in the United States in the late 1990s? Answers to this question pointed first of all to a number of historically important forces, notably America's huge domestic market, its great natural resources, the strong work ethic of its people, the revitalizing infusion of energetic immigrants, and the openness of its democratic and entrepreneurial culture. Downsizing in the 1980s, business leaders added, had helped to streamline major corporations so that they could compete in international markets. Other beneficial forces were more specific to the 1990s: the government's newfound fiscal discipline that was ending budgetary deficits; low interest rates, which the Federal Reserve maintained after mid-1995; strong consumer confidence and spending; low oil prices; and a weaker dollar (allowed to drop against other currencies by Clinton and his advisers) that benefited a number of American exporters.[50]

49. Josef Joffe, "America the Inescapable," *New York Times Magazine*, June 8, 1997, 38–43; Jonathan Freedland, *Bring Home the Revolution: The Case for a British Republic* (London, 1998), 161.
50. A useful summary of the reasons for late-1990s prosperity in the United States is William Nordhaus, "The Story of a Bubble," *New York Review of Books*, Jan. 15, 2004, 28–31. See also Joseph Stiglitz, *The Roaring Nineties: A New History of the World's Most Prosperous Decade* (New York, 2003).

Many analysts of economic trends also emphasized the virtues of America's embrace of free trade policies, which, they said, helped to promote a more open and connected world of international trade and finance.[51] This was hardly an entirely new embrace: Especially since World War II, when the United States had taken the lead in establishing the International Monetary Fund and the World Bank, American business and political leaders had vigorously pursued policies that aimed at lowering trade barriers.[52] This effort had greatly helped American producers gain access to overseas markets and served to bolster the already gigantic economic power of the United States. With the passing of the Cold War, the goal of expanding America's international economic power rose even more to the forefront of foreign policy concerns, and by the late 1990s "globalization" had become a buzzword among many politicians and businessmen in the United States. The size of American exports and imports increased in these years as a percentage of GNP, from around 17 percent in 1978 to 25 by 2000.[53]

American champions of globalization—that is, market-friendly expansion of free and easy flows of money, goods, communications, and people across international borders—hailed it as a boon for exporters and consumers and as forwarding the "knowledge economy." They asserted that it also benefited people in poor nations, lifting millions of peasants out of misery by enabling them to advance to a better world of wage labor. Change of this sort appeared to be taking place during the 1990s in various parts of the world, notably in rapidly growing areas of India and China. President Clinton, a fervent advocate of such freer trade, urged Americans to accept the "ultimate logic of globalization, that everything, from the strengths of our economy to the health of our people, depends on events not only within our borders but half a world away."[54]

A related source of America's economic progress in the late 1990s, many analysts maintained, was computerization, which expanded dramatically

---

51. See, for example, Thomas Friedman, *The Lexus and the Olive Tree* (New York, 1999).
52. David Kennedy, *The American People in World War II* (New York, 1999), 430.
53. McCraw, *American Business*, 160–61; *Time*, issue of Dec. 29, 1997–Jan. 5, 1998, 91; *Stat. Abst.*, 2002, 417, 793.
54. Alfred Eckes Jr. and Thomas Zeiler, *Globalization and the American Century* (New York, 2003), 238. Clinton's successor, George W. Bush, agreed, proclaiming in 2001 that globalization was "the triumph of human liberty stretching across borders . . . it holds the promise of delivering billions of the world's citizens from disease and hunger and want" (ibid.). Later, however, Bush raised American tariffs on foreign steel, so as to protect domestic economic interests (and his electoral prospects) in politically competitive states such as Ohio and West Virginia.

during these years. The spread of computers and of the Internet was said to be creating what one enthusiastic writer called a "third industrial revolution of communications and technology."[55] The Internet, advancing rapidly after 1991, seemed to become an almost irresistible force, at least to investors. When stock in Netscape, which created a popular Web browser, was initially offered to the public in August 1995, its price per share zoomed upward from $14 to $71 in one hour.[56] Within four months its capitalization exceeded that of Apple Computer, Marriott International, United Airlines, and Tyson Foods. A dot-com mania obsessed investors in the next few years, driving the NASDAQ index, which featured technology stocks, up by 86 percent in 1999 alone. By 1999, the stock of Microsoft, the leading producer of software, had a listed value of more than $500 billion. Its rapid growth enabled its widely photographed chairman, Bill Gates, with a net worth of more than $50 billion, to become by far the richest person in the United States.

The explosive expansion of the software industry, and the spread of computer ownership and Internet connection, prompted a spate of rosy predictions in the late 1990s. Excited promoters of the expanding cyber world proclaimed that the World Wide Web, unlike TV, which tended to isolate its passive viewers, would bring people together. Because the Internet enabled users to seek their own sources of information, optimists added, it was a powerfully liberating, egalitarian force that would break down corporate hierarchies and revive community participation. Some enthusiasts, hailing the speed with which information traveled on the Web, anticipated that the Internet would ultimately become more important than television or newspapers as a source of news. The editors of *Time* magazine, enthralled, selected Andrew Grove, chairman of Intel, the computer chip maker, as their Man of the Year in 1997. The microprocessor, *Time* proclaimed, was a "force for democracy and individual empowerment."[57] Jack Welch, CEO of General Electric, hyped his company's successes by declaring in 1999 that advances in electronic communication were "clearly the biggest revolution in business in our lifetimes."[58]

55. Joseph Nye, *Bound to Lead: The Changing Nature of American Power* (New York, 1990), 223–26.
56. Haynes Johnson, *The Best of Times: America in the Clinton Years* (New York, 2001), 17–21.
57. *Time*, issue of Dec. 29, 1997–Jan, 5, 1998, 49–51.
58. McCraw, *American Business*, 206. See also Friedman, *The Lexus and the Olive Tree*, in which the Internet is repeatedly lauded as paving the way for the "democratization of finance."

Not everyone, of course, heartily applauded the surge of globalization and computerization. Skeptics of globalization pointed out that it created losers as well as winners. They added the obvious: It could not and would not benefit millions of people in the world, such as most of those who lived in sub-Saharan Africa and other very poor and troubled places lacking in electricity, medical services, and decent sanitation. Skeptics added that globalization did not seriously threaten many long-standing sources of economic injustice and political oppression in the world. The Chinese, for instance, embraced freer trade when it benefited their rich and well-connected business interests while their Communist bosses maintained a corrupt and despotic hold on the country. China's booming factories, relying on low-wage labor, dirtied the environment and flooded other nations with cheap exports. Overmatched textile plants in the United States, threatened with bankruptcy, lowered wages and dismissed thousands of workers in desperate but sometimes losing efforts to stay afloat.

Echoing foes of NAFTA, opponents of globalization reiterated that it accelerated outsourcing of workers from companies in the United States and elsewhere. By championing market forces, critics added, governments in developed nations such as the United States were surrendering their supervision of trade policies to large-scale business interests. These interests, allied with the World Bank and the International Monetary Fund, were said to be enriching themselves in an increasingly unregulated economic world. Moreover, it was evident that developed nations were hardly consistent devotees of free trade. The United States, for instance, was one of many countries that continued to subsidize wealthy agribusiness interests, therefore sponsoring what some critics called "farm socialism" that undercut the prices of foreign providers and that aroused widespread anger among farmers in developing nations. Policies such as these spurred some 35,000 people to protest angrily against the World Trade Organization, an enabler of globalization, in Seattle in December 1999.

Skeptics about computerization and the World Wide Web were equally outspoken. Robert Putnam, observing that relatively few blacks could afford personal computers, wrote of a "digital divide" and of "cyber-apartheid."[59] The *Washington Post* grumbled that the Internet was "digital Ritalin for the attention-deficit generation."[60] Other writers, questioning the potential of the Internet as an egalitarian or community-enhancing force, argued that

59. Robert Putnam, *Bowling Alone: The Collapse and Revival of American Community* (New York, 2000), 173.
60. Neil Howe and William Strauss, *Millennials Rising: The Next Great Generation* (New York, 2000), 274.

it spit out a glut of scarcely digestible information that glued people to their computers: Like television, it was a "weapon of mass distraction." Still other people disturbed by the spread of the Internet perceived it as primarily a marketing tool that was accelerating the commercialization of the country, as well as a dangerous threat to privacy.[61]

It remained to be seen, doubters emphasized, whether computerization and the Internet would have anything like the revolutionary impact on productivity and economic growth that the greatest of earlier technological advances—the steam engine, the electric motor, and the gasoline engine—had had. To be sure, these skeptics conceded, the Internet was an amazing source of information. E-mail became a virtual necessity for millions of people. Computers revolutionized workplaces, virtually eliminating typewriters and steno pools and vastly speeding up the exchange of information. High-powered computers were vital to the work of researchers, physicians, economists and financial analysts, bankers and businessmen, the military, and many other people. They transformed the production and design of a host of products, including automobiles. Skeptics nonetheless argued that computers had not done a great deal—at least not yet—to advance productivity or to enhance creative thinking or better writing. They also worried that the boom in dot-com stocks, which took off in the late 1990s, was a speculative orgy. Sooner or later, they predicted, the enormous bubble would burst and gullible investors would be blasted to the ground.[62]

DOUBTS SUCH AS THESE exposed broader unease even amid the good times of the late 1990s. Many Americans remained restless and unsatisfied. Novelists such as Richard Ford, John Updike, and Philip Roth captured some of these emotions, describing Americans as hyper-competitive and materialistic people who often compensated for feelings of spiritual emptiness by lusting after possessions, drinking excessively, and engaging in promiscuous sex. In these and in other ways, it seemed that many people were following in the footsteps of their forebears. As Alexis de Tocqueville had observed a century and a half earlier, Americans, more nearly enjoying social equality than the citizens of other nations, appeared to suffer from "that strange melancholy which oftentimes will haunt the inhabitants of

61. Timothy May, "Culture, Technology, and the Cult of Tech in the 1970s," in Beth Bailey and David Farber, eds., *America in the Seventies* (Lawrence, Kans., 2004), 208–27.
62. Tenner, *Why Things Bite Back*, 184–209; Hodgson, *More Equal than Others*, 73–86, 103–8.

democratic countries in the midst of their abundance, and [from] that disgust at life which sometimes seizes upon them in the midst of calm and easy circumstances."[63]

Reflecting restlessness of this sort, polls in the mid-1990s suggested that while most Americans were very satisfied with their personal lives, they also believed (as they had since the early 1970s) that their parents had lived in a better world.[64] In 1998, the newscaster Tom Brokaw seemed to capture nostalgic sentiments such as these in his popular book *The Greatest Generation*, which hailed as "greatest" those Americans who had coped bravely with the Great Depression of the 1930s, fought and won World War II, and later stood firm during the Cold War.[65] A film about American heroes of the Normandy invasion of 1944, *Saving Private Ryan*, presented a similar (though gorier) message in the same year.

Other polls at the time indicated that most Americans expected their children's world to be worse than theirs. Responding to attitudes such as these, James Wilson, a thoughtful social scientist, observed in 1995: "Today most of us have not merely the hope but enjoy the reality of a degree of comfort, freedom, and peace unparalleled in human history. And we can't stop complaining about it."[66] His reflection, which echoed Tocqueville's, underlined two key points about American attitudes, then as in the 1970s and 1980s: Americans had grown hypersensitive to national flaws; and expectations about life had grown steadily during these years, to the point where they often exceeded the possibility of realization. Though the majority of Americans were more comfortable, wealthier, healthier, and assured of more rights than ever before, many longed for the past, complained of stress, and worried about the future.[67]

Anxieties such as these, however, did not overwhelm an important reality of life in the United States during the mid- and late 1990s: In part because many troubling problems of the not-so-distant past (the Vietnam War, Watergate, the stagflation of the 1970s, the Iran-contra crisis, the Cold War, the recession of the early 1990s) had passed, a lot of people were better able to concentrate their efforts toward enlarging the satisfactions

63. Alexis de Tocqueville, *Democracy in America* (New York, 1841), book 2, 147.
64. For many such polls, see Robert Samuelson, *The Good Life and Its Discontents: The American Dream in the Age of Entitlement, 1945–1995* (New York, 1995), 257–65.
65. Tom Brokaw, *The Greatest Generation* (New York, 1998).
66. Whitman, *The Optimism Gap*, 34.
67. Stanley Lebergott, *Pursuing Happiness: American Consumers in the Twentieth Century* (Princeton, 1993), 69–71; Easterbrook, *The Progress Paradox*, 160–81.

and rewards of their own lives—and of others. The culture of the United States, though crass in many respects, also continued to be dynamic, forward-looking, and supportive of the rights that millions of people had won in earlier years.

Confirming realities such as these, a good many aspects of American society did improve at the time. Rates of teenage pregnancy, motherhood, and abortion continued to drop. So did rates of violent crime. Welfare dependency and homelessness declined. Liberals were pleased that the number of death sentences, and of executions, began to fall.[68] Above all, the economy was booming, in what was to become a ten-year stretch of uninterrupted economic growth that extended from 1991 to March 2001. This was the longest continuous expansion in modern American history. Clinton, addressing the Democratic national convention in 2000, proudly recited developments such as these and maintained, for the most part plausibly, that the United States was not only a richer nation—it had also become a better, more decent, more caring place.

By then, more and more Americans seemed to share this positive view. While worrying that their children would be worse off than they were, they told pollsters that they were content with their personal lives in the present.[69] Michigan's Survey Research Center reported in 1998 that Americans had more confidence in the economy than at any time since 1952. Greenspan added a few months later that the combination of strong economic growth, low unemployment, and price stability was "as impressive [a performance] as any I have witnessed in my near half-century of daily observation of the American economy."[70]

68. *Providence Journal*, Dec. 14, 2004; *Christian Science Monitor*, Nov. 22, 2004. The number of death sentences fell from a high of 320 in 1996 to 144 in 2003. This was a thirty-year low. The number of executions fell by 40 percent between 1999 and the end of 2004, to a total of fifty-nine in 2004. Explanations for the decline in executions varied: among them, the rising role of DNA evidence, and the increase in number of state laws authorizing life-without-parole sentences. Some states, however, continued to house large numbers of prisoners on death rows. In December 2004, California (which had executed only ten people since 1976) had 641 on its death row at San Quentin prison. Texas (which consistently led the nation in executions, with a total of 336 between 1976 and 2004) then had 444 on its death row. Many other prisoners on death row had died of AIDS or suicide in earlier years. In 2004, more than 60 percent of Americans still said that they approved of the death penalty, and thirty-eight American states still authorized it. *New York Times*, Dec. 18, 2004.
69. Samuelson, *The Good Life and Its Discontents*, 257–59.
70. Robert Collins, *More: The Politics of Economic Growth in Postwar America* (New York, 2000), 222–23.

THE SURGING ECONOMY had significant political ramifications. Until 1998, when scandal imperiled his presidency, it helped Clinton, a charmer, to lead a happier political life. Blessed with the good fortune to preside over an era of rising prosperity, he was able to climb out of the political hole into which he had fallen in late 1994.

Having suffered large losses to Republicans in the elections of that year, however, the president had to remain cautiously on the defensive in early 1995. Some of his troubles at the time emanated from the Supreme Court, which under Chief Justice Rehnquist started to take bolder conservative positions. Three five-to-four decisions in 1995 especially worried liberals. One, *Missouri v. Jenkins*, was the latest of several High Court rulings in the 1990s that placed the future of school desegregation plans in serious doubt.[71] A second, *Adarand Constructors Inc. v. Pena*, called for state and federal courts to give "strict scrutiny" to "all racial classifications," such as those that facilitated set-asides for minority contractors.[72]

The third decision, *United States v. Lopez*, overturned a congressional statute, the Gun-Free School Zones Act of 1990, that had made it a federal offense to bring guns into a school zone. Rehnquist ruled that gun controls of this sort were matters for the states, not the federal government, to determine. The decision, limiting the reach of the commerce clause of the Constitution, suggested that conservatives on the Court were deadly serious about shoring up federalism—states' rights—in the United States.[73] For the remainder of his term in office, Clinton waited in vain for one or more of the more conservative justices—Rehnquist, Clarence Thomas, Sandra Day O'Connor, Antonin Scalia, Anthony Kennedy— to retire from the bench.

Clinton had to worry most urgently in early 1995 about conservatives on the Hill. Gingrich, ascending to the post of Speaker of the House, ignored seniority rules so as to engineer the selection of key committee chairmen who were loyal to him. He forced through changes in party rules that concentrated power in his circle of leaders.[74] So fortified, he led

71. James Patterson, *Brown v. Board of Education: A Civil Rights Milestone and Its Troubled Legacy* (New York, 2001), 197–201. The decision was 515 U.S. 1139 (1995).
72. Terry Anderson, *In Pursuit of Fairness: A History of Affirmative Action* (New York, 2004), 241–42. The case was 515 U.S. 200 (1995).
73. Lawrence Friedman, *American Law in the Twentieth Century* (New Haven, 2002), 597–98. The decision was 514 U.S. 549 (1995).
74. David Price, "House Democrats Under Republican Rule: Reflections on the Limits of Bipartisanship," *Miller Center Report* (University of Virginia) 20 (Spring/Summer 2004), 21–28.

Republicans to minor victories in the lower chamber, which quickly approved a few of the goals enumerated in the Contract with America. (Not surprisingly, his colleagues rejected term limits.) Though the more moderate Republican majority in the Senate did not follow Gingrich's lead, it was clear that conservatives were eager to approve cuts in taxes and social programs. Republican senators were also refusing to bring to the floor many of Clinton's judicial nominees.[75] Congressional Democrats, whose political center of gravity had shifted to the left following the defeat of a number of moderate and conservative party members in 1994, angrily resisted. On the Hill, the two parties had never been farther apart. With partisanship deadlocking Congress, Clinton seemed to be losing his way. In April 1995, his job performance rating slipped to a low of 39 percent. Attempting to refute a popular sense that what he did no longer made much difference, Clinton declared plaintively on April 18 that he was not superfluous, because "the Constitution makes me relevant."[76]

The next day, April 19, a truck bomb fashioned by Timothy McVeigh and Terry Nichols succeeded in blowing up the federal building in Oklahoma City and in killing 168 people. Clinton flew to Oklahoma and delivered a moving address at a memorial service, thereby boosting his political standing. He then staged a political comeback, masterminded by Dick Morris, based on "triangulation." This was a strategy—dictated by careful attention to public opinion polls—that enabled him to position himself as a sensible, moderate alternative at the apex of a triangle whose other two bases were liberal and conservative. In June, Clinton surprised (and distressed) many liberal Democrats in Congress by calling for a middle-class tax cut and a balanced budget within ten years.

Clinton paid special attention to issues involving cultural values. Appealing to the broad middle of American opinion, he lamented the escalation of violence on television shows (without seeking greater regulation that might have antagonized liberal Hollywood friends). In calling for a study of the role of religion in the schools, he headed off Republican moves for a constitutional amendment permitting prayer in the public schools. He reiterated his support of tough police responses against crime and of campaigns to reduce smoking among teenagers. In July, he strengthened his standing among liberals and minority groups—notably among potential political challengers such as Jesse Jackson—by speaking of his

75. During the eight years of Clinton's presidency Congress refused by various procedures to approve 114 such nominees. *New York Times*, Jan. 17, 2004.

76. Fred Greenstein, *The Presidential Difference: Leadership Style from FDR to Clinton* (New York, 2000), 180–81.

continuing determination to combat racial discrimination in employment. At the same time, however, Clinton reassured foes on the right by opposing racial quotas. "Mend it," he said of affirmative action, "but don't end it." Polls showed that his position satisfied a majority of whites as well as blacks. For the time being, angry debates over affirmative action subsided a little.[77]

DURING THESE POLITICALLY TENSE SUMMER MONTHS of 1995, Clinton tried to reestablish diplomatic relations with Vietnam. Though his initiative aroused heated controversy, it succeeded in July after senatorial veterans of the war—John Kerry of Massachusetts, John McCain of Arizona, Robert Kerrey of Nebraska—aided him politically by stating that Vietnam was not hiding POWs.

Debates over the recognition of Vietnam, however, paled in seriousness compared to political controversies over the fighting and ethnic cleansing, ferociously conducted by Bosnian Serbs, that continued in 1994 and 1995 to ravage Croatia and Bosnia. Clinton, carefully studying public opinion polls, still recognized that most Americans (like NATO allies) remained nervous indeed about being swept into the carnage. The United Nations, equally cautious, had agreed only to keep their weakly supported force of 6,000 peacekeepers in Bosnia and (as of late 1994) to authorize minor air strikes by NATO planes. These were pinpricks that in no way deterred the Bosnian Serbs. In July 1995, the Serbs forced some 25,000 women and children to flee chaotically from the town of Srebrenica, a "safe area" in eastern Bosnia that sheltered 40,000 Muslim refugees who were supposedly being protected by the U.N. peacekeepers. The Bosnian Serbs then murdered between 7,000 and 7,500 Muslim men and boys.

This barbaric act coincided with major developments on the military front. A Croatian army, having been trained in part by the United States, joined uneasily with Muslim military forces and waged a devastating offensive that soon drove the Bosnian Serbs out of Croatia and northwestern Bosnia. President Milosevic of Serbia, who once had dreamed of controlling sizeable chunks of Croatia and Bosnia, watched glumly as thousands of Serbs fled toward Belgrade.[78]

77. For political battles in 1995–96, see William Berman, *From the Center to the Edge: The Politics and Policies of the Clinton Presidency* (Lanham, Md., 2001), 45–72; and Joe Klein, *The Natural: The Misunderstood Presidency of Bill Clinton* (New York, 2002), 142–49. For affirmative action, see Anderson, *In Pursuit of Fairness*, 243–44.

78. For these and later developments in the Balkans, see David Halberstam, *War in a Time of Peace: Bush, Clinton, and the Generals* (New York, 2001), 283–359; and William Hitchcock, *The Struggle for Europe: The Turbulent History of a Divided Continent, 1945–2002* (New York, 2003), 392–403.

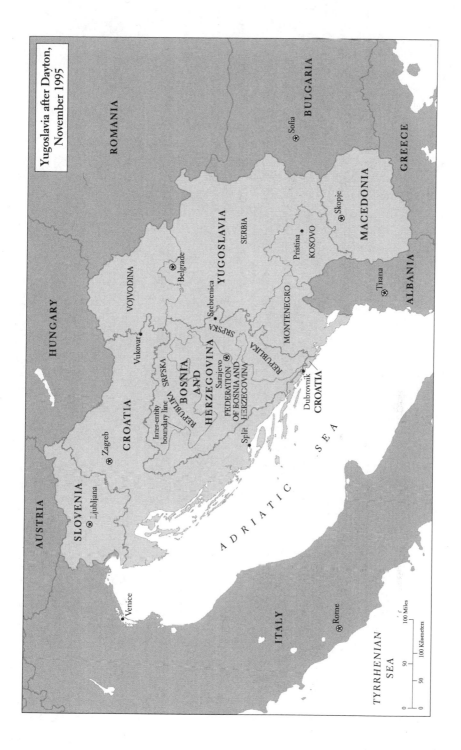

Yugoslavia after Dayton, November 1995

AUSTRIA

HUNGARY

ROMANIA

SLOVENIA
⊗ Ljubljana

CROATIA
⊗ Zagreb

Venice •

VOJVODINA

Vukovar •

• Belgrade ⊗

BULGARIA
⊗ Sofia

REPUBLIKA SRPSKA

Inter-entity
boundary line

BOSNIA
AND
HERZEGOVINA

Srebrenica •

REPUBLIKA SRPSKA

YUGOSLAVIA

SERBIA

Pristina •
KOSOVO

MACEDONIA
⊗ Skopje

Sarajevo ⊗
FEDERATION
OF BOSNIA AND
HERZEGOVINA

Split •

MONTENEGRO

Tirana ⊗
ALBANIA

Dubrovnik •
CROATIA

A D R I A T I C   S E A

ITALY

⊗ Rome

TYRRHENIAN
SEA

GREECE

0   50   100 Miles

0   50   100 Kilometers

These dramatic events spurred new approaches to the situation in the region. The massacre at Srebrenica appalled many Americans, including members of Congress who had long urged the United States to take a tougher stance against the Serbs. The impressive Croat-Muslim offensive, they insisted, indicated that forceful NATO engagement would finally win the war. Dick Morris, appearing again as a guru at the White House, warned the president that continued bloodletting such as that at Srebrenica might soon create irresistible popular pressure for American military intervention. As Clinton pondered his options, the Serbs shelled the marketplace of Sarajevo, killing thirty-eight civilians. This attack on August 28 induced the president to act. Two days later he authorized American participation in massive NATO air strikes against Bosnian Serb positions around Sarajevo.

Many Americans opposed this move, perceiving it as meddling in a faraway civil war. But seventeen days of more extensive bombing smashed Serbian positions. Together with the continuation of aggressive fighting by Croatian and Muslim ground forces, the bombing forced Milosevic to negotiate. In November, he met for three weeks with European and American representatives and with Croatian and Bosnian Muslim leaders for talks at an American airbase in Dayton, Ohio. These discussions confirmed an uneasy cease-fire and produced a settlement. Under the Dayton Peace Accords, brokered by Assistant Secretary of State Richard Holbrooke, a single state, the Federation of Bosnia and Herzegovina, was created. It was to have a "dual government" in which Muslims and Croats were to share power. Displaced persons were to return to their homes, and an international tribunal was to try alleged war criminals. An international authority was to oversee the area. The United States agreed to send 20,000 troops to the region as part of a force of 60,000 NATO soldiers who would uphold the accords.

Because these troops, heavily armed, were expected to succeed in maintaining order, and because Clinton indicated that the American soldiers would leave within a year, most Americans seemed to acquiesce in this considerable expansion of United States military presence abroad. As Morris and others had hoped, savage fighting in Bosnia largely ceased, and the issue of American engagement did not play an important role in the forthcoming presidential election. More important, the forceful military intervention of the United States, aided by its NATO allies, was a turning point of sorts in the post–Cold War history of American foreign policies. It signified that when the world's number one military power decided to use its awesome might as part of efforts to stamp out killing in Europe, fighting was likely to stop. It also suggested that the end of the Cold War would not enable the United States to retreat back across the Atlantic: Its international responsibilities as a military giant might be difficult in the future to limit.

Still, it had taken the United States and NATO four years to stop the murder and ethnic cleansing that had torn up the region. Until August 1995, Milosevic and his Bosnian Serb allies had been permitted to wage genocidal war on his enemies. The Dayton Accords, moreover, allowed the Bosnian Serbs to have their own state, Republika Srpska, in northern and eastern Bosnia. Their aggression had paid dividends. Muslims, disillusioned, nursed grievances against the United States and its European allies, and longed for revenge against the Serbs. As of 2005, European troops were still on the ground in Bosnia, where they were likely to remain for the foreseeable future.[79]

RELIEVED, THE PRESIDENT THEN FOCUSED on reaching agreement over a very contentious domestic issue: the budget for 1996. Congressional Republicans, however, refused to compromise. When they presented him in mid-November with two resolutions that among other things eliminated a scheduled drop in Medicare premiums, Clinton boldly vetoed the resolutions. At that time, the fiscal year having ended on October 1, an earlier continuing resolution was all that was enabling the government temporarily to meet a number of obligations for the new fiscal year. Clinton's vetoes thereby forced a partial shutdown of the government. Acrimonious negotiations ended the shutdown after six days, but the GOP then approved a conservative budget that proposed generous tax cuts for the wealthy and that called for reduced spending on social programs such as food stamps and Medicare. Its budget also sought to move welfare and Medicaid to state control. Gingrich proclaimed: "This is the largest domestic decision we

79. Richard Holbrooke, "Why Are We in Bosnia?" *New Yorker*, May 18, 1998, 39–45; Klein, *The Natural*, 73–74. The terms of the Dayton Accords were similar to those in a brokered peace plan that Clinton had disdained in early 1993, after which two and a half more years of ethnic blood-letting had taken place. The Dayton Accords did not resolve tensions in Bosnia. Although a million refugees were enabled to return to their homes over the next nine years, hundreds of thousands more dared not go back. Key Serbian leaders who were widely believed to be war criminals remained at large as of 2005. In December 2004, forces from nations of the European Union took the place of the 7,000 NATO peacekeepers (including 900 Americans) that had still been there. *New York Times*, Dec. 2, 2004.

have made since 1933. . . . This is a fundamental change in the direction of government."[80]

Clinton, assured by Morris that the American people opposed cuts in social programs, vetoed the GOP's budget on December 6, and on December 16, the government partially shut down again, this time for twenty-one days. Some 800,000 federal employees went without scheduled paychecks; national parks closed. Finally, the Republicans blinked, agreeing in January 1996 to fund departments and agencies that lacked money for the current fiscal year. They accepted Clinton's budgetary calculations, which proposed to end deficits in seven years. The partisan battle— one of the fiercest in memory—finally abated, and normal government operations resumed.[81]

When this warfare stopped, reporters noted that the president had edged toward the political center in order to accommodate Republican demands. Then, as earlier, he pursued policies aimed at balancing the federal budget. But having branded Republicans as foes of Social Security and Medicare, Clinton had outmaneuvered them politically. Polls at the time indicated that the majority of Americans had come to regard Gingrich and other conservative Republicans as hard-hearted and extreme. In 1995–96, as on many other occasions since the 1960s, a great many Americans who denounced big government also resisted attempts to cut back middle-class entitlements.[82]

With this victory in hand, Clinton charged ahead into the 1996 presidential campaign. From the beginning, his journey was smooth. The GOP chose Dole as its presidential nominee. A World War II veteran who had earned two Purple Hearts and a Bronze Star, Dole had lost use of an arm while fighting in Italy. Long a senator from Kansas, he had been Gerald Ford's running mate in 1976. Though acerbic, he was a witty man who had many friends in Congress, where as a moderately conservative Republican he tried to cool the ardor of firebrands such as Gingrich. But Dole, like Bush in 1992, felt obliged to placate Pat Buchanan, who had surprisingly beaten him in the New Hampshire primary, and to appease Buchanan's strong allies on the Republican right. He therefore accepted an anti-abortion plank in the party platform. Dole also agreed to name former New York congressman Jack Kemp, a moderate on most matters

80. Berman, *From the Center to the Edge*, 54–55.
81. Jules Witcover, *Party of the People: A History of the Democrats* (New York, 2003), 676–80.
82. Berman, *From the Center to the Edge*, 47.

who was also a strong pro-life advocate, as his running mate. As if emulating Reagan's campaign in 1980, Dole called for an across-the-board tax cut of 15 percent. At the same time, however, he demanded movement toward a balanced budget. These stances seemed contrived at best, and surely hard to accomplish, especially since he also urged increases in defense spending.

Dole was an uninspiring campaigner. At age seventy-three, he was the oldest major party nominee ever to seek the presidency for the first time, and he was neither an energetic nor compelling speaker. Democrats denounced him as an old-timer who had been Gerald Ford's "hatchet man" in 1976. Especially toward the end of the campaign, Dole appeared to be bored and distracted. Increasingly stiff, he seemed to lapse into a stream-of-consciousness style of discourse on the stump. Some associates believed he had become bitter because he had felt obliged to give up his powerful place in the Senate in order to run for the presidency.[83]

Though Clinton expected to win, he was never one to take political chances. Looking for support from labor interests, he sought and received from the Republican Congress—which during the campaign in mid-1996 was anxious to soften its politically damaging right-wing image—passage of an increase in the minimum wage. A bipartisan majority also approved the so-called Kassebaum-Kennedy bill, which protected workers from losing their health insurance when they changed jobs. Clinton focused especially on positioning himself as a centrist. This posture had already been obvious in his 1996 State of the Union address, when he staggered liberals by intoning, "The era of Big Government is over." The conservative tone of this message could hardly have contrasted more sharply with the call for governmental activism that he had sounded in his first inaugural.

This speech highlighted a main theme of his campaign: the preservation and expansion of "family values." Parents, Clinton said, should work to curb youth gangs, reduce teen pregnancy and smoking, and help with community policing. Later in the campaign he emphasized his support of school uniforms and of television "V-chips" that would enable parents to block unwanted television programming.[84] He also championed a Defense of Marriage Act in 1996 that defined marriage as a union between a man and a woman. The law added that no state was obliged to recognize same-sex marriage from another state. The Defense of Marriage Act was a

83. Witcover, *Party of the People*, 678–80.
84. In 2000, the Federal Communications Commission required all new television sets thirteen inches or larger to contain V-chips.

symbolic move that reaffirmed prevailing understandings of marriage as well as laws that already existed in most states, but the measure was therefore hard for politicians to oppose, and it pleased foes of gay rights. Clinton's campaign paid for seventy-odd spots that emphasized his administration's support of the law.[85]

Clinton's most controversial move in 1996 was to honor his pledge to "put an end to welfare as we know it," by which he mainly meant establishing limits on the length of time that recipients might get cash assistance. This he accomplished in August, after vetoing two earlier, more conservative versions, by signing the revealingly titled Personal Responsibility and Work Opportunity Reconciliation Act. This fiercely contested measure terminated the Aid to Families with Dependent Children program, a federal-state entitlement that since 1935 had offered cash assistance to low-income families—most of them headed by single mothers with children under the age of eighteen.[86] In 1995, federal-state appropriations for AFDC had given a total of $22.6 billion in aid to 4.8 million families—or to 13.4 million people.

At the time that the new law passed in August 1996, thereby establishing a program titled Temporary Assistance to Needy Families (TANF), economic recovery had begun to kick in, lowering the number of people receiving aid to 12.2 million and the total in aid to $20.3 billion.[87] This was not a huge outlay: Social Security, America's biggest social program, offered $365 billion in old age, survivors, and disability insurance to 43.8 million beneficiaries in 1996. Medicare paid $196 billion more.[88] Nor were AFDC benefits large—life on welfare was often miserable. But while many Americans had come to believe, as Clinton did, that welfare dependency needed to be challenged, most liberals had long defended AFDC, which had been a key source of support for poor families headed by women. These liberals almost unanimously opposed the changes.

TANF, they complained, shifted responsibility for such families from the federal government to the states, which were to receive federal block grants that administrators would have wide discretion in allocating. Before long, foes of TANF predicted, welfare provisions would differ dra-

---

85. Berman, *From the Center to the Edge*, 60. The law was in response to a decision by the Hawaii Supreme Court in 1993 that seemed to require that same-sex couples be allowed to marry. One senator who voted against the bill was John Kerry of Massachusetts.

86. The program was initially titled Aid to Dependent Children (ADC) but was later expanded to provide additional aid and renamed AFDC.

87. *Stat. Abst.*, 2002, 340, 354.

88. Ibid., 340, 345, 346.

matically across the fifty states. Conservatives shot back that the new law distributed $16.5 billion a year—a generous sum that the states were expected to supplement. It was assumed that state officials would set up better programs of job training and education and improve support for child care. TANF, they said, would finally break the dependence of "welfare mothers" on cash assistance and ease them into the labor market. But liberals wondered: Would states be liberal in determining eligibility or in providing aid, especially if a recession were to descend? In case of hard times, they prophesied, states would join a "race to the bottom" that would devastate the welfare poor.

The new law included other features that outraged liberals. It stipulated that able-bodied heads of welfare families must find work within two years or face the loss of federal aid, and established a five-year lifetime limit on the length of time that most recipients might receive federal money. The law also restricted the eligibility of legal, non-citizen immigrants for a range of social programs, including food stamps and Medicaid. Senator Moynihan of New York called the law the "most brutal act of social policy since Reconstruction." E. J. Dionne, a syndicated columnist, branded the act "a horror." He added: "The bill's premise is that if we kick poor people and their kids around a little more, maybe they'll go to work. Then again, maybe they won't. We have no idea. But, hey, maybe the savings from this bill can pay for a little election-year tax cut."[89]

Long after passage of this landmark law, many liberals continued to rage at it. The historian Michael Katz wrote in 2001 that it revealed a "mean-spirited and truncated conception of obligation and citizenship."[90] The new system, these critics said, was all but forcing women off welfare, generally into low-paying, "dead-end" jobs. The costs of child care, transportation, and clothing, they added, often canceled out earnings from these jobs. Conservatives, however, retorted that AFDC for far too many years had subsidized out-of-wedlock pregnancies and trapped recipients in "welfare as a way of life." In the late 1990s and early 2000s, they cited statistics showing that TANF, aided substantially by the vibrant economy, and supplemented by increased funding for the working poor that Congress had approved in 1993 for the Earned Income Tax Credit, was rapidly moving onetime welfare recipients into jobs.[91] The higher minimum wage further benefited some of these workers.

89. James Patterson, *America's Struggle Against Poverty in the Twentieth Century* (Cambridge, Mass., 2000), 234–39.
90. Katz, *The Price of Citizenship*, 359.
91. Gertrude Himmelfarb, *One Nation, Two Cultures* (New York, 1999), 71–73.

By 2001, the number of Americans on cash public assistance had dropped considerably—from 12.2 million in 1996 to 5.3 million. Even between 2001 and 2003, years of economic sluggishness, the rolls continued to decline. In 2003, TANF supported only 2 million families, less than half the number (4.8 million) that had received AFDC in 1995. By then, welfare—long a highly divisive program—was fading as a campaign issue in America. A conservative government official went so far as to exclaim delightedly in early 2004 that onetime welfare recipients, having gained experience at job-seeking and working, had become relatively "recession-proof."[92]

Dramatic numbers such as these suggested that the welfare law of 1996, bolstered by other social policies, was probably less horrible in its consequences than many liberals had predicted. These numbers, however, would have seemed unimaginable to most people in 1996. What was clear at that time was that "ending welfare as we know it" strengthened Clinton's political appeal to centrists—many of whom shared his sense that America's system of public assistance needed reforming—and to voters further on the right. Polls after passage of the bill showed him widening his margin over Dole.

Still, Clinton took no chances. Energetically crisscrossing the country, he claimed credit for the surging economy: In 1996, as in 1992, this was the key issue of the campaign. He made sure to remind people of the help that he had directed their way in the previous three years. As earlier, television cameras featured him hugging and consoling people who had endured one calamity or another. In that election year he issued a record-high seventy-five orders designating communities as deserving of emergency federal aid. The TV correspondent Brit Hume concluded at the time that Clinton had become "almost the national chaplain to those in distress."[93]

Clinton proved a wonder at raising money. As one historian later pointed out, he turned the Lincoln bedroom at the White House, where big spenders might stay for a night or two, into a "combination casino and tourist attraction for well-heeled donors."[94] Democrats also succeeded in acquiring donations of questionable legality from people close to foreign governments, notably Indonesia and China. Morris and others were especially adept at taking advantage of loopholes in campaign finance regulations

---

92. *New York Times*, March 22, 2004. For a guardedly favorable assessment of TANF eight years after passage, see Jason DeParle, *American Dream: Three Women, Ten Kids, and a Nation's Drive to End Welfare* (New York, 2004).

93. *New York Times*, Nov. 2, 2003.

94. Ibid., March 1, 1998; Lewis Gould, *The Modern American Presidency* (Lawrence, Kans., 2003), 223–24.

that opened the way for use of "soft money." Though these contributions were supposedly earmarked for party-building activities, not for direct assignment to the Clinton-Gore ticket, they were controlled by the White House and found their way into the president's reelection campaign.

Clinton complained sometimes about all the hustling for money that he had to undertake. He told Morris: "I can't think. I can't act. . . . I can't focus on a thing but the next fund raiser. Hillary can't. Al [Gore] can't— we're all getting sick and crazy because of it."[95] Worse, he had to confront scathing criticism of his money-raising activities, especially from Perot, who once again ran as a third-party candidate, this time as leader of the Reform Party. But the president knew that he had to hustle, for the GOP was equally clever at collecting soft money for Dole. He was truly skillful: Thanks to his tireless efforts, the Democrats raised nearly as much cash as the Republicans in 1996, greatly lessening the huge advantage that the GOP had enjoyed in fund-raising during the 1980s.[96]

Though Clinton's lead narrowed a little toward the end of the campaign, he continued to benefit from the health of the economy and perhaps from his appeals to centrist and conservative voters. In November, he won with ease in a contest that featured the lowest turnout since 1948. He captured 49.2 percent of the vote—6.2 percent more than he had in 1992. Dole received only 40.7 percent. Perot, whose luster had dimmed since 1992, took 9 percent, considerably less than the 19 percent that he had won four years earlier. The president triumphed in the electoral college, 379 to 159. (In 1992 he had beaten Bush by 370 to 168.) Women, many of whom apparently backed Clinton's stands in favor of choice, gun control, safe neighborhoods, and federal educational and social programs, voted overwhelmingly for him, 54 percent to 38 percent. So did voters in most areas of the urban Northeast and Midwest. Dole failed to carry a single congressional district in New England or New York. Not for the first time, the election demonstrated the president's extraordinary agility as a political fighter. It was a highly satisfying comeback for a man who had reeled on the ropes after the near-knockout Republican victories of 1994.

Republicans, though downcast in defeat, did not despair. They noted that among men voters, Dole fared slightly better than Clinton, winning

95. Berman, *From the Center to the Edge*, 67–70.
96. In 1996, as in earlier campaigns, the money raised by the major candidates was penny ante compared to the amounts that corporations regularly spent for advertising. It was estimated that Clinton spent $169 million in 1996. In the same year, Procter & Gamble spent $8 billion marketing shampoos and other products. Gil Troy, "Money and Politics: The Oldest Connection," *Wilson Quarterly* (Summer 1997), 14–32.

by a margin of 44 percent to 43 percent.[97] Carrying forward GOP gains in the South, he took seven of eleven southern states. Dole fared even better in Rocky Mountain and Plains areas, losing only Nevada and New Mexico among the thirteen states in these regions. Even more than in previous contests, the contest exposed the sharp regional cleavages that were becoming predictable features of America's electoral maps.

Dole's poor showing, moreover, did not greatly harm Republican candidates for Congress. Clinton had campaigned mainly for himself and had devoted little attention to the exertions of other Democrats. Overall, the election revealed that the two parties continued to be very competitive. The GOP lost four seats in the House but retained control there, 226 to 207. It gained three seats in the Senate, thereby fashioning a margin of 55 to 45 in the upper chamber. Though Republicans were a little less feisty after the election than they had been following their extraordinary sweep in 1994, they were surely angry about losing to Slick Willie. In January 1997, they returned to the Hill ready and eager to engage in four more years of partisan combat.

FOR THE MOST PART, conservative Republicans dominated Congress after 1996. Recognizing the odds, Clinton refrained from calling for large initiatives. In 1997, he nonetheless managed to get modest proposals enacted. Congress restored to legal, non-citizen immigrants some of the benefits they had lost in the welfare act of 1996, and it maintained support of the EITC program, which helped many among the working poor. It approved measures to help the health care of poor children and to provide tax credits for higher education. The latter was welcomed by middle-class families beset by escalating tuition costs.

Congress also readily enacted the president's proposal to lower the capital gains tax rate from 25 to 20 percent. Business leaders and investors hailed this reduction, which they said contributed to the ongoing economic boom. The arrival, at last, in fiscal 1998 of federal government budget surpluses stimulated especially enthusiastic applause. Clinton, admirers said, continued to be politically adept at sustaining domestic social programs, and at economic management in general. The surge since 1994 of the economy especially helped to elevate his job approval ratings, which soared above 70 percent in early 1998. These ratings remained high—generally over 60 percent—for the remainder of his term in office.[98]

97. World Almanac, 2001, 40.
98. Klein, The Natural, 158–60; Berman, From the Center to the Edge, 81, 85–86.

The president made a concerted effort to reinforce his credentials as an advocate of environmentalism—a domain of policy that Gore, his vice president, had staked out as a special concern. During his presidency he placed more land in the lower forty-eight states under federal protection than had any other twentieth-century president.[99] In 1997, he signed the so-called Kyoto Protocol, which called on the United States and other developed countries collectively by 2012 to reduce emissions of carbon dioxide and other heat-trapping greenhouse gases to 5.2 percent under 1990 levels. A total of 141 nations agreed to it by 2005. Because the protocol exempted developing nations like China from cuts in emissions, the measure had almost no appeal in Congress, and Clinton never submitted it to Capitol Hill for approval. The protocol, lacking ratification from the United States (which was responsible for 36 percent of the world's greenhouse-type emissions) and from Russia (17 percent), was not implemented at the time. Still, many liberals were pleased that Clinton had joined in the effort.[100]

LOOMING IN THE POLITICAL BACKGROUND in 1997—and for the remainder of Clinton's term—was a far more consequential matter: mounting threats of terrorism. While some of these threats emanated from North Korea, whose government was suspected of violating its agreement with the United States in 1994 to stop work on nuclear weapons, the groups that appeared to pose the greatest immediate danger were militantly anti-western Muslims, especially from the Middle East.[101] A good deal of this danger, American intelligence agents believed, emanated from Iraq, which remained under the brutal rule of Saddam Hussein, and from Iran.

Increasingly worrisome to Clinton were terrorists loyal to Osama bin Laden, a well-educated, wealthy native of Saudi Arabia who was expelled from Sudan in 1996 after possibly having been involved in an unsuccessful plot to assassinate Egyptian president Hosni Mubarak. Bin Laden took refuge in Afghanistan in May 1996, where he allied with the zealously anti-Western regime of the Taliban that had established control over much of the country following the withdrawal of Russian troops in 1989. Bin Laden and his followers, like the Taliban, embraced the teachings of

99. Berman, *From the Center to the Edge*, 106.
100. Eckes and Zeiler, *Globalization and the American Century*, 213–14. In late 2004, Russia agreed to the protocol, enabling it to take effect in February 2005. At that time, the United States and Australia were the only major industrialized nations that had not agreed to it. *New York Times*, Dec. 28, 2004.
101. Concerning the so-called Agreed Framework with North Korea, see Joel Wit et al., *Going Critical: The First North Korean Nuclear Crisis* (Washington, 2004).

Muslim clerics whose ideological message was profoundly hostile to virtually everything about Western civilization: its cosmopolitanism, secularism, materialism, sensuality, arrogance, support of women's rights, and obsession with technology.[102] Bin Laden especially hated the United States, whose soldiers in Saudi Arabia, he believed, were corrupting the culture of his native land—the holy land of Islam—and whose military power was shoring up the despised Jewish state of Israel.

Bin Laden, aided by wealthy donors from throughout the Persian Gulf region, organized a terrorist network, Al Qaeda, which stepped up recruitment and training of radical Muslim operatives at bases in Afghanistan. Though it was difficult to secure solid information about this secretive and ever evolving organization, rough estimates later concluded that the numbers so trained in the late 1990s exceeded 15,000.[103] In February 1998, bin Laden issued a public call for holy war—a *"Jihad* Against Jews and Crusaders"—in which he said that it was the duty of every Muslim to kill Americans and their allies anywhere. In August 1998, truck bombs fashioned by Al Qaeda operatives simultaneously blew up United States embassies in Kenya and Tanzania. The explosions killed more than 300 people, most of them Africans, and wounded more than 4,500. Among the dead were twelve Americans. In October 2000, two Al Qaeda suicide bombers maneuvered an explosives-laden inflatable boat next to an American warship, the U.S.S. *Cole*, which was at anchor at the port of Aden in Yemen. Ramming their boat into the *Cole*, they set off a blast that blew a hole in the side of the warship. The explosion killed seventeen American sailors and wounded thirty-five.

Violent acts such as these indicated that the radical ideas motivating Muslim militants such as bin Laden endangered people in Western nations, including the United States. It was equally obvious that many people loyal to Al Qaeda, to local terrorist cells scattered throughout the world, and to anti-Jewish groups such as Hamas and Hezbollah were fanatics. Unlike commando-style assassins or bomb-planters—as, for instance, many of those who plagued Spain and Northern Ireland—some of these killers were suicide bombers who believed that murder and suicide were holy duties. A few, including teenagers, seemed almost eager to blow them-

102. Ian Buruma and Avishai Margalit, *Occidentalism: The West in the Eyes of Its Enemies* (New York, 2004).
103. Melvyn Leffler, "9/11 and the Past and the Future of American Foreign Policy," *International Affairs* 79, no. 8 (Oct. 2003), 1045–63. For Al Qaeda and other terrorist groups, see Jonathan Raban, "The Truth About Terrorism," *New York Review of Books*, Jan. 15, 2005, 22–26.

selves up, along with children and others who happened to be in the way, in order to follow the orders of zealous superiors, to be remembered as martyrs, or to consummate their visions of a glorious afterlife.

American intelligence personnel in the late 1990s realized that the World Trade Center in New York City, having been blasted in 1993, was one of a number of possible targets that terrorists might try to hit in the United States. By late 1998, they also knew that radical Muslim terrorists were considering—among a great many other ideas—hijacking of commercial planes and crashing them into buildings.[104] As of early 1997, the CIA considered various schemes to capture or kill bin Laden. Clinton mounted diplomatic initiatives—with Saudi Arabia, Pakistan, and the Taliban—aimed at persuading the Taliban to evict bin Laden so that he might be captured and put on trial.[105] In early 1998, after Saddam Hussein had begun to expel U.N. arms inspectors, Clinton stepped up America's military presence in the Persian Gulf region for possible war with Iraq. The president, widely criticized abroad as a war-monger, relented only when Hussein finally permitted U.N. arms inspectors to go through his palaces.

After the bombings in Kenya and Tanzania in 1998, Clinton authorized retaliatory cruise missile attacks on a suspected Al Qaeda guerrilla site in Afghanistan and on a pharmaceuticals plant in Sudan that was believed to be manufacturing chemical weapons. In December 1998, by which time Hussein had totally stopped U.N. arms inspections, Clinton asserted that Iraq was developing weapons of mass destruction. Starting on December 16, American and British planes launched Operation Desert Fox, which featured four days of around-the-clock air attacks on Iraqi sites. Anglo-American raids resumed in January 1999 and continued, off and on, until the United States invaded Iraq in 2003.

Some of these raids were part of a broader counter-terrorism effort during Clinton's second term, when Congress and executive officials slowly began to build up resources that they had allowed to dwindle following the end of the Cold War. Though it remained a source of energetic partisan dispute in later years whether funding for counter-terrorism rose or fell during the late 1990s, one apparently reliable estimate concluded that appropriations increased considerably—by 50 percent (to $9.7 billion) between fiscal 1998 and fiscal 2001.[106] Some terrorist plans, such as so-called

104. *New York Times*, March 29, 2003, Sept. 14, 2005.
105. Ibid., July 26, 2004.
106. Ibid., April 4, Aug. 3, 2004. Estimates of federal spending for American intelligence in the 1990s—normally classified—vary widely. For later debates about the size of funding in the late 1990s, see ibid., Jan. 7, 2005.

millennium plots to bomb Los Angeles Airport and American and Israeli tourists in Jordan in January 2000, were foiled. But an alert Border Patrol guard, not intelligence tips emanating from Washington, was the key to uncovering the plot in Los Angeles: In general, neither Clinton nor the intelligence bureaucracy succeeded in advancing national security.

Reluctant to risk American or Afghan operatives in efforts to kidnap bin Laden, Clinton was also nervous about being branded a "mad bomber."[107] Because he was acutely aware of a selective ban that Ford had ordered on governmentally backed assassinations in peacetime, he apparently refused to approve of such an effort against bin Laden.[108] He was also unwilling to damage relations with the oil-rich Saudi regime, an important ally in the Middle East, and did not demand that the Saudis clamp down on terrorist groups believed to be operating in that hotbed of radical, anti-Western resentments.

Legal restrictions, as well as bureaucratic rivalries and miscommunication within the many American government agencies and departments concerned with intelligence, impeded well-coordinated policy formation against terrorism. The FBI, facing restrictions since 1976 on proactive investigations into the activities of domestic extremist groups, was ill informed about terrorist doings in America.[109] Computers and other communications equipment at the FBI, which was supposed to foil domestic threats, were antiquated—to the extent that the agency had difficulty circulating information within its own offices, let alone sharing it with the CIA. Moreover, a little-noticed Foreign Intelligence Surveillance Act (FISA), passed in 1978, had appeared to establish a "wall" of sorts against sharing of certain kinds of information between the CIA, which gathered and interpreted overseas intelligence for foreign policy purposes, and the FBI, a criminal investigation bureau. Relations between the two turf-conscious bureaucracies, never warm, remained cool in the 1990s. So did rivalries between the CIA and fourteen other federal intelligence offices, many of which were managed within the Defense Department. These Pentagon offices, employing more than 30,000 people, were estimated to control 80 percent of the American intelligence effort.[110]

107. Brian Urquhart, "A Matter of Truth," New York Review of Books, May 13, 2004, 8–12; Michael Ignatieff, "Lesser Evils," New York Times Magazine, May 2, 2004, 46–51, 86–88.

108. This ban dated to the 1970s, following revelations at the time of CIA efforts to assassinate Castro and others. See chapter 3. The late 1990s were "peacetime" years, though Osama bin Laden called for killings of Americans in 1998.

109. Richard Powers, "A Bomb with a Long Fuse: 9/11 and the FBI 'Reforms' of the 1970s," American History 39 (Dec. 2004), 43–47.

110. New York Times, Aug. 3, 2004.

In part because of blunders in the past—dating at least to the Bay of Pigs disaster—American intelligence agencies, notably the CIA, had allowed their use of covert activity to decline. They relied instead on high-tech methods, such as surveillance by satellites, for collecting information. For this reason, and because the United States trained relatively few operatives who were fluent in the languages of hostile nations, intelligence picked up on the ground was weak.[111] Moreover, CIA intelligence-gatherers were often the agency's chief analysts—a practice that impeded fresh evaluation of data. In 1998, the CIA did not discover that India was about to test nuclear bombs; when India did so, Pakistan followed, intensifying tensions between the two nations. America's intelligence agencies failed to recognize until later that A. G. Khan, Pakistan's leading nuclear scientist, was shipping centrifuges and nuclear goods to Iran, North Korea, and Libya.[112]

In any event, the Taliban had no desire to turn over bin Laden, whose training of terrorists and issuance of blood-curdling proclamations continued. The Clinton administration's attacks on Sudan and Afghanistan in 1998, provoking greater rage from bin Laden and his fellow radicals, were of dubious utility.[113] With hindsight, it is arguable that the United States might have done well to develop well-financed social and economic policies aimed at improving the lot of oppressed people in the Middle East (and elsewhere)—policies that in the long run might have helped to diminish the fermentation of anti-Western rage in the Arab and Muslim worlds. The United States might also have engaged more aggressively in a war of ideas, as it had during the Cold War era, so as to encourage democratic yearnings among the people of authoritarian nations. It is especially

---

111. For a best-selling and highly critical account of American efforts against terrorism in the Clinton and George W. Bush administrations, see Richard Clarke, *Against All Enemies: Inside America's War on Terror* (New York, 2004). Clarke had been head of counter-terrorism at the National Security Council in both administrations. Ignatieff, in "Lesser Evils," was one of a number of Americans, including some liberals, who later called for the United States to develop some sort of national ID card using the latest biometric identifiers. At least seven of the nineteen hijackers who succeeded in taking over planes and blowing up the World Trade Center and the Pentagon on September 11, 2001, used Virginia ID cards or drivers' licenses that enabled them to board the planes.

112. *New York Times*, June 4, 2004. Later, in 2001, the CIA concluded—apparently wrongly—that Iraq then possessed weapons of mass destruction.

113. Critics of Clinton charged that he authorized these raids in order to distract attention from mounting scandals that were then threatening his presidency. For these scandals, see the next chapter.

clear in retrospect that the president (and Congress) could have done more to reform the substantial flaws in America's intelligence gathering. Later events made it obvious that Clinton, who had poor working relationships with top military leaders (and with FBI director Louis Freeh), failed to lessen the likelihood of successful terrorist acts in the United States.

This is not to say, however, that the Clinton administration deserves especially harsh censure for its policies regarding terrorism. The sources of radical Muslim ideas, some of which emanated from fury against earlier American foreign policies in the Middle East—support of the shah of Iran, the Gulf War, backing of Israel—were deep, and surely not easy to counter in the short run. The threat of terrorism from groups such as Al Qaeda, while worrisome to government officials after 1996, was but one of many absorbing foreign policy and military concerns—anti-missile defense, Kosovo, Bosnia, North Korea, Iraq, Iran, Hamas, Hezbollah, and the Palestine Liberation Organization—that devoured the administration's time and energy. Subsequent probes into American intelligence identified memoranda that between the late 1990s and September 2001 had urgently warned top officials about bin Laden and Al Qaeda: One warning titled "Bin Laden Determined to Strike in the U.S." was delivered to President George W. Bush in an intelligence briefing on August 6, 2001.[114] But these warnings were among an avalanche of information about terrorism that tumbled into the in-boxes of officials who had to evaluate cyber-age data of all sorts.

It is always easier to assign blame after a disaster, such as the extraordinarily well executed hijackings that stunned the world on September 11, 2001, than it is to appreciate the complexities and uncertainties that face officials beforehand. Notwithstanding the tragedies that befell the embassies in Kenya and Tanzania, and the bombing of the U.S.S. *Cole*, the fact of the matter is that in the late 1990s, Americans, including most media sources, did not pay great attention to terrorist activities. Neither immigration officials nor the Federal Aviation Administration (FAA) bolstered security in ways that were likely to succeed in detecting terrorists, or weapons in carry-on baggage. (In September 2001, only twelve suspected terrorists, of thousands so identified by the CIA and FBI, were on the FAA's "no-fly" list.)[115] Dramatic preemptive

114. This briefing included the warning that Al Qaeda members had recently been engaged in surveillance of federal buildings in New York City. Bush administration spokespeople maintained, however, that it was not specific enough to have enabled them to expect the terrorist attacks of 9/11. Most top officials in the Bush administration, like those in the Clinton administration, could not imagine attacks such as these.

115. *Boston Globe*, July 23, 2004. Many civil libertarians, among others, questioned the accuracy of the no-fly list.

moves by the United States would likely have had little popular support during the late 1990s or 2000. Prior to 9/11/2001, neither Clinton nor Bush, his successor, dared to mount serious attacks against the Taliban, to order the assassination of bin Laden, or to impose truly tough measures at home concerning travel, immigration, or civil liberties.

The largest obstacle to dealing with threats from terrorism stemmed from what the 9/11 Commission emphasized in its final report of July 2004: a failure of imagination. It was difficult prior to 9/11 for Americans, including most high government officials, to imagine that terrorists had the courage or capacity to mount bold and coordinated attacks in the United States. No suicidal hijacking, for instance, had been carried out anywhere in the world for more than thirty 30 years, and none had ever occurred in the United States. As in 1941, when the Japanese managed a surprise attack on Pearl Harbor, most Americans in the late 1990s (and until September 2001) had a false sense of security.

Nor did there seem to be any foolproof way to prevent terrorist activity. Afghanistan, for instance, had proved too confounding a place in the past for either the British or the Soviets to monitor, let alone to control. Some 8,000 miles distant from the United States, it was a landlocked nation where xenophobic jihadism had escalated during the struggles against the Soviet Union in the 1980s, and where bitterly turf-conscious warlords controlled substantial areas of the countryside. Nearby countries, such as Pakistan, refused to confront the Taliban or to help in the capture of bin Laden. In that area of the world, as in many others, the sources of anti-western feeling remained almost unfathomably deep—and impossible to combat in the short run.

The advance of globalization, which required relatively open borders, made it tough to keep track of terrorists who jetted freely about and who would stop at nothing to achieve their goals. Technological developments, such as cell phones and the Internet, further facilitated terrorist communications. So did lax immigration procedures in the United States, which prided itself on being an open society, and where tourist visas and false identities were easy to acquire. America's lengthy borders continued to be thinly policed and porous. Tourists from many countries needed no visas at all: They could enter the United States and stay for ninety days, after which they could disappear. It was simple for immigrants to blend illegally into the background, like the nineteen determined Muslim hijackers, fifteen of them of Saudi extraction, who wreaked such havoc in the United States on 9/11/2001. Most of these radicals had entered the United

States with fraudulent passports; one had left and reentered the United States six times in 2000 and 2001.[116]

Unlike overseas dangers during the Cold War, when the primary sources of international violence—state-sponsored—had been relatively easy to identify, terrorist threats in the post-Cold War era sprang not only from secretive and authoritarian regimes but also from a host of semi-autonomous, stateless groups that were very hard to locate. By 2000, it was believed that agents connected in one way or another with Al Qaeda were operating in as many as sixty nations. Other terrorists seemed to move in and out of a wide range of secretive cells and anti-American groups. It was widely understood that bin Laden's suicidal terrorists, not the Taliban, called the shots in many areas of Afghanistan.

For all these reasons, the United States remained vulnerable to terrorism when the Clinton administration left office in January 2001. Three additional reasons—beyond those cited above—help account for popular and official neglect that worsened this vulnerability. The first was the surging economy, which had helped to promote pride in American accomplishments and to spread widespread popular complacency about the future course of international developments, terrorism included. In those prosperous, self-indulgent times, neither the Congress nor the administration faced significant popular pressure to stiffen American defenses against violence from overseas.

The second was Clinton's irresponsible and scandalous personal behavior, news of which burst into the public arena with headline-grabbing momentum in January 1998. The third was the partisan zeal with which the president's Republican enemies, especially in Congress, thereafter tried to drive him from office.

The political recriminations that ensued riveted millions of Americans, often wrenching their attention from more serious matters, including terrorism. The partisan hassling and its aftermath unavoidably distracted the Congress as well as the president and his top advisers. When the political warfare abated a little after February 1999, at which point the embattled president finally outlasted his many foes, it left his administration in a wounded state. Though with the passage of time Clinton's personal excesses may occupy a relatively small place in American textbooks, historians and others will necessarily wonder how much better the United States might have prepared against terrorism if the eyes of its political leaders— and of the media—had not been clouded by steamier concerns.

116. *New York Times*, July 25, 2004.

12

Impeachment and Electoral Crisis, 1998–2000

Thanks in large part to the influence of a family friend, who contributed generously to the Democratic Party, Monica Lewinsky secured an internship at the White House in July 1995. Raised in Brentwood—O. J. Simpson's Los Angeles neighborhood—and a recent graduate of Lewis and Clark College in Oregon, she was then twenty-one years old. Once in the nation's capital, she lived at the Watergate apartment complex. Four months later, on November 15, she and Bill Clinton had a tryst in the White House, the home, of course, of the president and his wife. This was the second day of the partial shutdown of the federal government that had stemmed from partisan battling over the budget that summer and fall, and the White House staff of 430 had temporarily shrunk to 90.

Their tryst was the first of ten meetings, nine of them involving Lewinsky performing oral sex, that the furtive couple arranged over the next sixteen months, most of them between November 15, 1995, and April 7, 1996, by which point Lewinsky, who had by then become a government employee, had been transferred to the Pentagon. Most of these rendezvous took place either in a small private study just off the Oval Office or in a windowless hallway outside the study. According to Lewinsky, the president telephoned her frequently, fifteen times to engage in phone sex. The couple also exchanged gifts. The last of their serious assignations took place on March 29, 1997, after which they had two meetings at the Oval Office, in August and December 1997, involving kissing.[1]

---

1. See *Clinton: The Starr Report* (London, 1998), 204–13. Hereafter cited as *Starr Report*. For a lengthy narrative placing Clinton's troubles within the larger political struggles of the era, see Haynes Johnson, *The Best of Times: America in the Clinton Years* (New York, 2001), 227–439.

There the matter might have rested. Though Lewinsky was a bold and brazen young woman who flirted with the president, lifting up her skirt before him and flashing her thong underwear, and though Clinton was known for his roving eye, no one on the scene imagined that the president was engaging in oral sex next to the Oval Office. Until January 1998, the American public had no idea that such meetings might be taking place. If Clinton's near-legendary luck had held out—as it might have done if he had been chief executive during pre-Watergate days when reporters had turned a relatively blind eye to the promiscuity of politicians—he would have joined a number of other American presidents who had engaged in extramarital relations without being publicly exposed while in office.

A complex set of developments deprived Clinton of such good fortune. One of these was the partisan zeal of conservative political enemies, who had long regarded him as a schemer and a womanizer. Well before January 1998, when the Lewinsky affair hit the headlines, the president had been forced to hire attorneys to contest two investigations into his conduct. Both had landed him in the glare of often sensational news coverage. One of these was the probe by Kenneth Starr, the independent counsel who in mid-1994 had begun to dig into the Clintons' involvement in a range of matters, notably the Whitewater River land development project in Arkansas. The other was the civil suit that Paula Corbin Jones had filed in May 1994, alleging that as governor of Arkansas in 1991 he had sexually harassed her in a Little Rock hotel room.[2]

Though Clinton's lawyers had fought these probes every step of the way, they had not been able to quash them. In May 1997, the Supreme Court unanimously rejected Clinton's claim that the Constitution immunized him while in office from civil suits such as the one that Jones had initiated. It ruled that the case must go forward.[3] Many legal analysts criticized this decision, arguing that it placed all future chief executives at risk of having to contend with time-consuming, potentially frivolous litigation alleging misbehavior that might have taken place before a president took office. The Court's decision nonetheless stood, forcing Clinton and a battery of high-priced legal help to cope with the suit thereafter.[4]

Still, neither Starr nor the lawyers helping Jones began to learn much about Clinton's involvement with Lewinsky until the fall of 1997. At that point Linda Tripp, a co-worker of Lewinsky's at the Pentagon, became a

2. For the origins of these actions, see chapter 10.
3. 520 U.S. 681 (1997).
4. See Ronald Dworkin, "The Wounded Constitution," *New York Review of Books*, March 18, 1999, 8–9.

· major actor in the drama that was soon to unfold. Tripp, nearly fifty years old when she met Lewinsky in 1996, nursed a number of grudges, especially against Clinton and his aides, who had earlier moved her out of her secretarial position at the White House and sent her to the Pentagon. When she came across Lewinsky, a fellow exile at the Pentagon, she realized that her young colleague was infatuated with Clinton. Pretending to befriend her, she learned that Lewinsky had enjoyed a sexual relationship with the president.

Starting in September 1997, Tripp secretly recorded a number of conversations in which Lewinsky revealed intimate details of her trysts. Tripp then began sharing the tapes with Paula Jones's legal team, which had been searching for evidence concerning extramarital affairs that Clinton might have engaged in over the years. When Lewinsky submitted an affidavit in January 1998 in the Jones case, Starr (who had talked to Jones's attorneys before becoming independent counsel and who had closely monitored developments in that case) saw a chance to broaden his probe.

This complicated chain of circumstances and personal connections indicated several facts. First, Lewinsky, like many people having affairs, could not keep a secret. Second, Tripp was a friend from hell. Armed with apparently damning information from Tripp, Starr sought authority from Attorney General Janet Reno to broaden his office's inquiries. In particular, he hoped to prove that Clinton had engaged in a conspiracy to obstruct justice by getting Lewinsky a new job in New York and by encouraging her to commit perjury in her affidavit in the Jones case, and that he had violated federal law in his dealings with witnesses, potential witnesses, or others concerned with that case.

Reno, confronted with developments such as these, recommended to the three-judge federal panel empowered to oversee the activities of independent counsels that Starr receive authority to widen his investigation, and the panel quickly gave it. For Starr, who been unable to gather evidence that implicated the president in improprieties surrounding the Whitewater deals, this authority was wonderful. It was the key decision that enabled him to dig deeper and deeper and that led to one astonishing news story after another—and eventually to the impeachment of the president.[5]

At the same time, moreover, word leaked out, via the Drudge Report, an Internet site, that Clinton had been involved in an ongoing sexual

5. William Berman, *From the Center to the Edge: The Politics and Policies of the Clinton Presidency* (Lanham, Md., 2001), 79–81; Joe Klein, *The Natural: The Misunderstood Presidency of Bill Clinton* (New York, 2002), 177–81, 199–201; Johnson, *The Best of Times*, 265–77.

relationship with a White House intern. The next day the Report updated the information, naming Lewinsky. Newspapers, distrusting the source, were at first reluctant to print such a sensational story, but the facts seemed to check out. When the *Washington Post* published the Drudge Report's information on January 21, its revelations rocked the nation. On and off for the next thirteen months, "Monicagate" dominated the front pages.[6]

Clinton, who was a dogged fighter, refused to give ground. When the *Post* account appeared, he contacted Dick Morris, who agreed to conduct an instant poll to find out how Americans might be reacting to Clinton's behavior. When they talked again late that evening, Morris said that the American people would tolerate a presidential affair, but not perjury or obstruction of justice. He also advised the president not to make a public confession. Voters, he said, were "just not ready for it." "Well," Clinton replied, "we'll just have to win, then."[7]

Pursuing this bold strategy, Clinton denied everything in the first few days after the news broke out—to his wife, Cabinet members, friends, aides, and interviewers. On January 26, in the presence of his wife and Cabinet officers in the Roosevelt Room of the White House he faced a battery of television cameras and vigorously proclaimed his innocence. Wagging his finger forcefully at the cameras, he exclaimed: "I want to say one thing to the American people. I want you to listen to me. I'm going to say this again. I did *not* [here he slashed his finger downward] have sexual relations with that woman, Ms. Lewinsky. I never told anybody to lie, not a single time, *never*. These allegations are *false* [more vigorous gestures here] and I need to go back to work for the American people."[8]

His wife, Hillary, accepting her husband's statement, forcefully backed him up the next day, telling a huge television audience watching the *Today* show that his administration was being victimized by a "vast right-wing conspiracy." Denouncing Starr, she added: "We get a politically motivated prosecutor who . . . has literally spent four years looking at every telephone . . . call we've made, every check we've ever written, scratching for dirt, intimidating witnesses, doing everything possible to try to make some accusation against my husband. . . . It's not just one person, it's an entire operation."[9]

---

6. Johnson, *The Best of Times*, 292–95; Berman, *From the Center to the Edge*, 79–81, 84–86.
7. Johnson, *The Best of Times*, 239–40. Johnson adds that Morris then said, "You bet your ass."
8. Ibid., 233.
9. Ibid., 245.

Having constructed this stonewall of a defense, the president said nothing in public about the matter for the next seven months, during which time he six times declined invitations by a federal grand jury to testify about his actions. It was during these months that Starr, avidly pursued by television crews, became a highly visible figure. Only four weeks older than the president, he had grown up in East Texas near the Oklahoma border, not far from where Bill Clinton had been born. His father was a barber and minister in the conservative Church of Christ denomination. Starr at first went to Harding College in Searcy, Arkansas, an institution affiliated with his church. During summers he sold Bibles door-to-door. Starr's religiously oriented, conservative upbringing contrasted sharply with that of Clinton, a young man of the 1960s who was leading a considerably more adventuresome social life at the same time.[10]

Like Clinton, Starr left his geographical roots to strike out for the East, transferring from Harding College after a year and a half to complete his college education at George Washington University. He then received a master's degree in history at Brown University and graduated from Duke Law School. He rose rapidly in the legal world, clerking for Chief Justice Warren Burger at the Supreme Court, serving as a judge on the prestigious federal court of appeals for the District of Columbia circuit, and then becoming solicitor general in the Bush administration. Political insiders predicted that he would some day sit on the Supreme Court. A conservative Republican, he had worked methodically since taking over the task of investigating the Whitewater tangle in 1994, and he was eager to pursue evidence of wrongdoing that might incriminate the president.

Having talked to Jones's lawyers in 1994, Starr was sure that Clinton was an adulterer, and the tapes that Tripp had recorded seemed almost heaven-sent. A churchgoing man who prided himself on his moral rectitude, he found the details of Clinton's affair repellent. Subsequent testimony by various of Lewinsky's friends, in whom she had also confided her relationship, further steeled Starr's resolve to expand his investigation in the hope that he might find the president guilty of perjury and obstruction of justice. That summer he gave Lewinsky immunity from prosecution (among other things for perjury arising from her affidavit in the Jones case), whereupon she told a federal grand jury about her sexual adventures with the president. She also produced a semen-stained navy blue dress that she said she had worn at a tryst with the president. In August, DNA tests required of the president revealed that the semen was Clinton's.

10. Ibid., 319–32.

With the evidence building up against him, Clinton himself gave sworn testimony to Starr's aides in a four-hour interrogation at the White House on August 17—and via televised hookup to a federal grand jury. He admitted that he had engaged in an "inappropriate" relationship with Lewinsky that involved "intimate contact," but he denied having explicitly lied about his behavior in his deposition concerning the Jones case, and he refused to answer a number of questions. That evening he defended himself via television to the American people. In a four-minute address he conceded at last: "I did have a relationship with Ms. Lewinsky that was not appropriate. . . . It constituted a critical lapse in judgment and a personal failure on my part for which I am solely and completely responsible." He admitted that he had "misled people, including even my wife." Still, the president remained self-pitying and defiant. Lashing out at Starr's investigation, he complained that it had "gone on too long, cost too much, and hurt too many innocent people." He ended by proclaiming that it was time to move on and "repair the fabric of our national discourse."[11]

Many editorial reactions to Clinton's address were scathing. One paper commented: "In a ghastly four-minute session, the President told the nation no more than he had to. It was a calculated, carefully calibrated effort at damage control. It was a hell of a comedown from a fireside chat with F.D.R." Another wrote that Clinton's "mantra of taking personal responsibility rings hollow. He has let the whole country down."[12]

Then and later, commentators lamented that the drawn-out Clinton-Lewinsky matter was virtually paralyzing consideration of other important issues, including the future financial viability of Social Security and Medicare, regulation of managed health care plans, and campaign finance reform.[13] About the only presidential accomplishment of note in early 1998 was his success in securing Senate approval, 80 to 19, of an expansion of NATO to include Poland, Hungary, and the Czech Republic.[14]

Foes of the president further complained that he was so absorbed in protecting his hide that he was endangering national security. On August 7, Al Qaeda terrorists blew up the American embassies in Kenya and Tan-

11. Berman, *From the Center to the Edge*, 84–85.
12. Ibid.
13. For instance, Garry Wills, "The Tragedy of Bill Clinton," *New York Review of Books*, Aug. 12, 2004, 60–64.
14. In early 2004, seven additional nations in Eastern Europe joined NATO. They were Latvia, Lithuania, Estonia, Slovakia, Slovenia, Bulgaria, and Romania. Then, as in 1998, Russia worried that the expansion of NATO forces to its borders threatened its security. *New York Times*, April 3, 2004.

zania. On August 20, three days after his televised address, Clinton authorized retaliatory missile strikes in Sudan and Afghanistan, leading critics to charge that he was cynically using military firepower in order to divert attention from his personal excesses. Whether this was so was impossible to prove—Clinton said he acted to thwart terrorism—but there was no doubting that his personal problems were consuming much of his time and that partisan battling over sex was hijacking the attention of Washington and the country.[15]

Starr wasted no time before moving ahead for impeachment. In a sexually graphic, 445-page report (along with more than 3,000 pages of documents) that he sent to the House on September 9—and that the House released to the public on September 11—Starr had nothing critical to say about the Clintons' involvement in Whitewater or about their role in other matters that he had explored during his four-year investigation. But he had plenty to divulge about Clinton's sexual proclivities. His report, which spared no details, charged that the president had committed perjury, a felony, by denying under oath that he had ever had "sexual relations" with Lewinsky, and that he had obstructed justice, also a felony—in many ways. Among these ways were the following: encouraging her to submit a false affidavit denying that she had engaged in sex with him; concealing that he had exchanged gifts with her; helping her to get a job in New York so that she might avoid giving testimony concerning him in the Jones case; and lying to friends so that they would give untruthful stories to the grand jury.[16]

Though the report was voyeuristic, many editorialists found its conclusions to be damning. Jokes circulated that America had a "priapic president" who had an "Achilles tendon in his groin." The New York Times called Starr's report "devastating" and predicted that Clinton would be remembered for the "tawdriness of his tastes and conduct and for the disrespect with which he treated a dwelling that is a revered symbol of Presidential dignity." Andrew Sullivan, former editor of the New Republic, penned an essay, "Lies That Matter," in which he said, "Clinton is a cancer on the culture, a cancer of cynicism, narcissism, and deceit. At some point, not even the most stellar of economic and social records is worth the price of such a cancer metastasizing even further. He should go."[17]

Unfortunately for anti-Clinton editorialists such as these, most Americans seemed to be far less censorious. To be sure, polls at the time showed

15. Johnson, The Best of Times, 338–49.
16. Starr Report, 199–201.
17. New York Times, Sept. 12, 1998; Andrew Sullivan, "Lies That Matter," New Republic, Sept. 14, 21, 1998, 22.

that roughly 60 percent of Americans disapproved of his personal conduct, but his job approval ratings dipped only slightly in late August 1998. Throughout the highly partisan warfare that dominated the headlines until early 1999, polls consistently gave Clinton job performance ratings of more than 60 percent. At times in early 1999, they exceeded 70 percent, an amazingly positive standing for a president. Similarly high job ratings persisted for the rest of his presidency.[18]

Given Clinton's personal behavior, his high job approval ratings seemed puzzling, but there were good reasons why these held up. One—relatively inconsequential—dated to the dismissal in April 1998 of the civil suit in which Jones had charged Clinton with sexual harassment. In dismissing her case, the judge made it clear that the evidence produced by her attorneys was too slight to merit trial.[19] Public awareness of this dismissal may have helped, at least a little, to make people think that he had been the target of excessive partisan zeal. A second and much more important reason for Clinton's high ratings was the economy, which along with the stock market was booming in 1998 as never before. It is a truism of American politics—of all politics—that a thriving economy is one of the best things that can happen to a chief executive, even if he or she is not mainly responsible for it.

A third reason focused on Starr. Even before he produced his report, he had struck many Americans as prudish, sanctimonious, and vindictive. Critics thought that he had allowed personal animus against Clinton—and prissy concerns about sex—to cloud his judgment, thereby turning a sex scandal into a constitutional crisis. Many Americans—urged on by unflattering portrayals of Starr in the media, which reveled in personalizing political struggles—seemed inclined to blame the prosecutor for the president's predicament. Polls in late August indicated that only 19 percent of Americans viewed the increasingly embattled prosecutor favorably, while 43 percent did not.[20] As the *Washington Post*'s Haynes Johnson later observed, Starr was likely to go down in American history as the "relentless, self-righteous Inspector Javert [of *Les Misérables*] whose dogged

18. Berman, *From the Center to the Edge*, 86, 107.
19. Jones, however, appealed this decision, and Clinton decided in November 1998 to settle rather than risk a trial. The settlement cost him $850,000, which he agreed to pay to Jones, and stipulated that he would not have to apologize or to admit guilt. Had he agreed to settle earlier, Jones's litigation would have ended, and Lewinsky's name would not have later come to the attention of Jones's attorneys, and through them to Starr. Ibid., 90.
20. Ibid., 86.

pursuit of Bill Clinton year after year results in the second impeachment of a president of the United States. . . . Ken Starr emerges in this public picture as a humorless moralist, a Puritan in Babylon, out of touch with contemporary attitudes. A zealous ideologue."[21]

The tendency of people to distinguish between Clinton's personal behavior and performance on the job suggested that Americans, especially younger Americans, were by no means so puritanical about sex as some contemporary commentators thought they were, or as many cosmopolitan Europeans had long and superciliously maintained. In 1998, even a majority of women, especially those who were liberal in their politics, appeared to rally behind the president. Though they disapproved of his relationship with Lewinsky, they did not believe that he should be judged on his moral character alone. After all, his wife had stuck with him.

Their attitudes, like those of a great many men, indicated that by the late 1990s Americans had become considerably more willing than in the past to take a live-and-let-live view of the sexual behavior of people, including public officials. Their readiness to do so was yet another sign of the long-range liberalization of American cultural attitudes that had advanced, especially since the 1960s.[22] Clinton, a freewheeling symbol of the more permissive boomer generation, was a person they could relate to and understand.[23]

CONGRESSIONAL REPUBLICANS, HOWEVER, were far less tolerant of Clinton's behavior than were the majority of the American people. Many of them hoped to advance partisan interests and raise campaign funds from their conservative base. On October 8, a month after they had received Starr's report, House Republicans voted to proceed with an impeachment inquiry. In speeches on and off the floor they excoriated the president. With the off-year elections less than a month away, they hoped for a GOP triumph and then for impeachment, which, as prescribed by the Constitution, would enable the Senate to put the president on trial. A vote of two-thirds of the senators would remove the president from office.

21. Johnson, *The Best of Times*, 320–21.
22. See Alan Wolfe, *One Nation, After All: What Middle-Class Americans Really Think About God, Country, Family, Racism, Welfare, Immigration, Homosexuality, Work, the Right, the Left, and Each Other* (New York, 1998). Wolfe noted that popular attitudes about homosexuality, still predominantly negative in 1998, were the slowest to change. But these, too, haltingly liberalized in subsequent years.
23. Steven Gillon, *Boomer Nation: The Largest and Richest Generation Ever, and How It Changed America* (New York, 2004), 306–8.

These Republicans were following the action from way out in right field, unable to see how out of touch they were with the major players— or with public opinion. This became especially clear in the election results that November. In some gubernatorial races, notably in Texas, where George W. Bush scored a resounding victory, the GOP had cause for celebration. But the voting produced no changes in the partisan lineup of the Senate, which remained in the control of the GOP, 55 to 45. In the House, Democrats gained five seats, slightly reducing the Republican majority to 222 to 212.

This was the first off-year election since 1934 in which the party holding the White House had actually enlarged its numbers in the House of Representatives. Gingrich, who had led the charge against Clinton, felt humiliated. Three days later he resigned as Speaker and announced that he would leave the House at the end of his term in January 1999. It also became known that he had been having an affair with a congressional aide young enough to be his daughter. When his designated replacement as Speaker, Robert Livingston of Louisiana, was revealed as an adulterer in December, he, too, announced that he would leave Congress in January. He proclaimed, "I must set the example that I hope President Clinton will follow." Not all the impeachers, it seemed, were of unimpeachable moral character.

Undeterred by setbacks such as these, the Republican majority in the House pressed ahead to impeach the president. On December 19, a day on which Clinton had authorized massive American air strikes on Iraq, they achieved their aims. On largely party-line votes, Republicans prevailed on two of four counts recommended by the House Judiciary Committee. One charge, which stated that the president had committed perjury before a federal grand jury, passed, 228 to 206. The other, which asserted that he had obstructed justice in the Jones case, was approved by a vote of 221 to 212. Clinton was the first duly elected president in United States history to be impeached.[24]

Because conviction in the Senate required a two-thirds vote of sixty-seven, the outcome of the trial in the upper chamber, where Republicans had only fifty-five seats, was never in doubt. The proceedings nevertheless lasted for thirty-seven days. House Republicans presenting their case to the Senate asserted that Clinton's perjury and obstruction of justice met the constitutional definition of "high crimes and misdemeanors" and justified his re-

---

24. President Andrew Johnson, impeached (but not convicted) in 1868, had been elected as Lincoln's vice president in 1864.

moval. Clinton's lawyers retorted that while he had acted badly, his misbehavior hardly justified the extreme step of ejecting him from office. On February 12, 1999, the Senate rejected the perjury charge, 55 to 45, with ten Republicans joining all forty-five Democrats in the majority. The vote on the obstruction of justice charge was closer, 50 to 50, with five Republicans joining forty-five Democrats in opposition. Clinton had won.

Though the biggest battles were over, several legal issues explored by Starr remained to be settled. By June 30, 1999 (at which point authorization for independent prosecutors was allowed to lapse), his investigations into Whitewater and other matters had succeeded in generating twenty indictments, fourteen of which resulted in pleas of guilty or convictions. Among those jailed were Webster Hubbell, a former law partner of Hillary Clinton and a deputy attorney general under Clinton, and Arkansas governor Jim Guy Tucker. Hubbell was guilty of fraud and tax evasion, Tucker of fraud. A month later Judge Susan Webber Wright, who had dismissed the Jones case in 1998, ruled that Clinton had given under oath "false, misleading, and evasive answers that were designed to obstruct the judicial process." Holding him in contempt, she ordered him to pay Jones's lawyers $90,000.

On Clinton's last day in office, he admitted giving false testimony regarding his relations with Lewinsky and was fined $25,000, to be paid to the Arkansas Bar Association. His law license was suspended for five years. In return he received immunity as a private citizen from prosecution for perjury or obstruction of justice. Finally, in March 2002, prosecutor Robert Ray, who had succeeded Starr in late 1999, delivered the concluding report of the investigation. It occupied five volumes and ran for 2,090 pages. It concluded that there was insufficient evidence that Bill or Hillary Clinton had been guilty of any crimes relating to Whitewater. It was estimated at that time that the investigation had cost American taxpayers a total of $60 million.[25]

Then and later, pundits sought to assess the legacy of this extended, nasty, and frequently sleazy struggle. Many of these assessments reflected political positions; these died hard, if at all, in an atmosphere of unrelenting partisan vituperation. House Republicans remained highly confrontational in subsequent years. Democrats complained bitterly that Republicans, having seized on sexual misbehavior to impeach a president, had tortured the constitutional meaning of "high crimes and misdemeanors" and had set a dangerous precedent that partisan members of Congress in the future might invoke in order to unseat someone whom they did not like.

25. *New York Times*, March 21, 2002.

The prolonged partisan wrangling prompted some contemporary observers to point to the cumbersomeness of America's political institutions. Had a prime minister been accused of scandalous behavior, they said, his or her party might well have been able to settle the matter quickly, either by affirming support for its leader or by picking a new one. In extreme cases, the governing party might feel pressure to call for a new election, which would be held in short order. Quick solutions were not available in the United States, whose eighteenth-century Constitution had shown admirable durability but also prescribed a system of separation of powers that encouraged adversarial relations between the executive and legislative branches of government. A host of checks and balances, notably the provision for a Congress of two equally powerful houses, further complicated American procedures. The Constitution, moreover, set four-year terms for elected presidents: Unless Clinton resigned, or was impeached and convicted, he could expect to remain in office until January 2001. When he refused to quit, Republicans determined to remove him. The complex process of investigation, impeachment, and trial that ensued not only lasted for more than a year; it also provoked a constitutional crisis. When the fighting finally ended, many people worried that it had sorely damaged the institution of the presidency.

Other observers disagreed with these dour reflections. They retorted that politicians in the future, acutely aware of the failure of partisan warriors to remove Clinton, would think twice before wielding the blunt weapon of impeachment. Some editorialists nonetheless agreed that the president had been reckless. His perjury and obstruction of justice, they said, met the constitutional definition of "high crimes and misdemeanors." As A. M. Rosenthal, a well-known *New York Times* columnist, had exclaimed in December: "Mr. Clinton did not lie simply to cover up his affair with Monica Lewinsky. He lied and lied, under oath and directly to the people, and lied to aides who became a chain letter of lies, to build a wall around the White House."[26]

Several less heated conclusions about Monicagate seem irrefutable. First, though the partisan confrontation had been extraordinary, it was but the most sensational episode in a series of highly politicized conflicts over cultural issues that had arisen in the 1960s, that had divided American society in the 1970s and 1980s, and that had exploded in the culture wars of the early 1990s. Those struggles, like Monicagate, had revealed ideological polarization over standards of sexual behavior, as well as sharp

26. Ibid., Dec. 11, 1998.

differences over religion and a range of other socially divisive matters. The impeachment and trial of the president was the latest (though it was not to be the last) of these politicized struggles, most of which liberal Americans, backed especially by younger people, had won.

A second conclusion is that the sorry business dashed Clinton's high hopes of going down in history as a great president. He had acted irresponsibly and had irreparably damaged his reputation. He destroyed whatever opportunity he might have had after 1997 of advancing desired liberal goals — or even of enhancing serious and productive discussion of public issues, terrorism included. As the historian Joseph Ellis put it, Monica Lewinsky had become a "tin can that's tied to Clinton's tail that will rattle through the ages and through the pages of history books."[27]

In the immediate aftermath of the trial, it also became evident that the nation's capacity for commercialization of sensational news events remained apparently inexhaustible. In March 1999, Lewinsky appeared on television's 20/20 to be interviewed by Barbara Walters. An estimated 70 million Americans watched her appearance. No single network "news" program had ever been seen by so many people. ABC demanded and received record payments from advertisers for commercials. And what commercials! These included Victoria's Secret lingerie, the Oral-B Deluxe toothbrush, and a promo for the movie *Cleopatra* that included the voice-over: "When she was twenty, she seduced the most powerful leader in the world." A Maytag ad boasted of its product, "It actually has the power to remove stains."[28]

Lewinsky then toured Europe to promote *Monica's Story*, a hastily put together book about her life. It rose briefly to the best-seller lists. Marketers estimated that she would pocket $600,000 from royalties on the book, as well as another $600,000 for an interview on European TV. These efforts would help to defray her legal bills, which were huge (as were Clinton's). Hustles of this sort indicated how easy it continued to be for scandals involving sex and celebrity, a potent combination, to dominate the media and to entrance people both at home and abroad.[29]

FREE AFTER FEBRUARY 1999 TO CONCENTRATE on the business of government, Clinton soon found that foreign policy concerns, as during his first term, continued to pose dilemmas. This was notably the case regarding

27. Berman, *From the Center to the Edge*, 94.
28. Johnson, *The Best of Times*, 453.
29. James Patterson, *America Since 1945: A History* (Fort Worth, 2000), 278.

the Serbian province of Kosovo, where Albanian Muslims, who comprised some 90 percent of the population there, had been intensifying their efforts for independence. Serbian president Milosevic, however, regarded Kosovo as a sacred part of Serbian soil. Seeking to stamp out armed resistance, his forces resorted to brutally efficient ethnic cleansing in an effort to drive Muslims from the province. Later estimates placed the number of Albanian Muslims who were displaced by the summer of 1999 at 863,000 and the number killed at up to 10,000. By early 1999, the savagery in Kosovo was commanding world attention.[30]

At first Clinton, backed by the Joint Chiefs and by Defense Secretary William Cohen, refused to get seriously involved—in part because he did not believe that giving military support to insurgents in Kosovo was in the strategic interest of the United States, in part because he vividly remembered what had happened at Mogadishu, in part because there seemed to be little popular support within the United States for such a move, and in part because the so-called Kosovo Liberation Army of Muslim revolutionaries, which had been staging ferocious guerrilla attacks on the Serbs, struck some knowledgeable people as ultra-nationalistic thugs and terrorists.[31]

In considering military action to manage this mounting crisis, Clinton recognized that he could not count on international backing. It seemed highly likely that U.N. opponents of armed intervention, led by Russia, would oppose such a move. Fearing a veto from Russia or China in the Security Council, Clinton bypassed the U.N.[32] As in the earlier troubles involving Bosnia, NATO nations, notably France, were also reluctant to intervene.

Hesitation of this sort irritated General Wesley Clark, an American who was then serving as supreme allied commander of NATO forces in Europe. Backed by Madeleine Albright, whom Clinton had appointed as America's first female secretary of state in 1996, Clark pressed hard for the dispatch of NATO troops, including Americans. Clinton put him off. Recalling his frustration, Clark later complained about the continuing hold of memories concerning the Vietnam War on American military and political leaders: "The attitude [of Clinton and the Joint Chiefs] was,

---

30. For the struggles over policy regarding Kosovo, see Berman, *From the Center to the Edge*, 96–100; and William Hitchcock, *The Struggle for Europe: The Turbulent History of a Continent, 1945–2002* (New York, 2003), 402–9.

31. David Halberstam, *War in a Time of Peace: Bush, Clinton, and the Generals* (New York, 2001), 422–53.

32. A fact that the administration of George W. Bush, which failed to secure U.N. sanction in 2003 for an invasion of Iraq, was later to point out.

"If you take losses, you're a loser. Your career is over. It was assured that politicians wouldn't support you, that they'd run away as soon as there were body bags. That became an article of faith."[33]

When frantic multi-nation attempts at negotiation failed in March 1999, setting off a wave of new atrocities in the province, Clinton still refused to commit American troops, but he supported NATO bombing of Serbian positions. The pilots were instructed to fly high—at 15,000 feet—to avoid getting hit. Clark complained that the bombing, which he called "tank plinking," was accomplishing very little. Because observers on the ground (placed there as a result of negotiations in October 1998) had been instructed to leave before the bombing, Milosevic used the occasion to intensify his ethnic cleansing. After forty-five days of high-level attacks, Clinton agreed to escalate the action and to authorize strikes on the Serbian capital of Belgrade. One such raid (by a B-2 Stealth bomber that flew 10,750 miles from Missouri and back to complete its thirty-hour mission) hit the Chinese Embassy there in mid-May, killing several embassy staffers and exacerbating Sino-America relations. (The United States said that the hit was accidental.) The raids by NATO planes, along with the withdrawal of Russian diplomatic support of the Serbs, finally forced Milosevic to accept a settlement in June. The overall bombing effort, lasting seventy-eight days, tore up Kosovo and was estimated to have taken the lives of some 5,000 Serbian forces, hundreds of civilians, and 500 Kosovar rebels. No pilot was killed during the campaign.[34]

The longer-range results of this intervention were hard to judge. On the one hand, Clinton had succeeded in winning the support of NATO nations. Kosovar refugees began to return to their villages and towns. The U.N., charged with oversight of the province, supervised peacekeeping by NATO forces, which included American soldiers. Milosevic was voted out of office in 2000 and later prosecuted as a war criminal. Clinton, having pursued a course that did not endanger the lives of American soldiers, managed to steer clear of political disaster.

But the settlement called for the disarming of the Kosovo Liberation Army and said nothing about conducting an election that might offer independence for Kosovo. In the next few years, unemployment ravaged the area. Vengeful Albanian Muslims, furious that the province remained part of Serbia and Montenegro, periodically killed Serbs who had not fled the region. Five years after the end of the bombing, approximately 18,000

33. Joe Klein, "Closework," New Yorker, Oct. 1, 2001, 44–49.
34. Two Americans died in a helicopter crash.

troops—the largest peacekeeping force in the world—still participated in an uphill struggle to police the area. Some 1,800 were Americans. Other American forces stayed in Bosnia, long after Clinton had indicated that they would be withdrawn. In the maelstrom of hatreds that had long roiled the Balkans and where internationally imposed protectorates remained necessary to minimize bloodletting, even a military giant such as the United States could not impose its will.[35]

IN 1999 AND 2000, CLINTON MANAGED TO DEFEND a number of liberal policies against determined conservative opposition. As earlier, this defensive stand was a major legacy of his time in office. Having learned a hard lesson from the health care fight in 1993–94, however, he knew that the Republican-dominated Congress would not enact liberal legislation concerning Social Security, health, or education. Licking their wounds from the impeachment battle, Republicans refused to agree to another hike of the minimum wage, to approve a so-called patient's bill of rights, or to pass legislation providing prescription drugs for seniors. In October 1999, the Senate dealt Clinton a sharp blow by rejecting a treaty that aimed to place restrictions on nuclear testing. It was clear that Republicans in Congress, having earlier made it possible for Clinton to secure two of the most significant legislative developments of his presidency—NAFTA and welfare reform—continued to wield the whip hand on Capitol Hill.

The president also had to contend with ongoing squabbling that afflicted his own party. These, as throughout his two terms, featured conflict between centrists and advocates of globalization, such as himself, and more liberal Democrats, many of whom were close to labor interests. Exports from China's cheap-labor industries, these liberals continued to complain, were undercutting manufacturing in the United States and throwing Americans out of work. Even as trade deficits mounted, however, Clinton resisted protectionist policies.[36] These struggles over trade, which enlisted many Republicans on the president's side, revealed the

---

35. *New York Times*, March 25, 2004, May 21, 2005. Another legacy of Kosovo was the replacement in July 1999 of Clark. Defense Secretary William Cohen and the Joint Chiefs resented what they considered Clark's headstrong attitude during the struggles over American policy in the area. Clinton signed the order removing Clark from his post. Clark retired from the army in 2000 and ran unsuccessfully for the Democratic nomination for the presidency in 2004.

36. For numbers concerning America's annual trade deficits (which rose from $67 billion in 1991 to $463 billion in 2000, see *Stat. Abst.*, 2002, 793.

persistence of Democratic divisions. They further indicated that simplistic labels typing all Democrats as "liberals" and all Republicans as "conservatives" continued to obscure the ideological complexity of some of America's political battles.

Despite these difficulties, Clinton had reason to be optimistic about the prospects for Democratic victory in 2000. A number of politically engaged groups continued to stand strongly behind him, among them African Americans. Henry Louis Gates, a leading black intellectual, proclaimed: "We are going to the wall with this President."[37] As in earlier battles, Democrats could also expect considerable support from women. Most labor union leaders, however miffed they might be about NAFTA and other trade issues, nursed grievances against corporate bosses and were all but certain to remain reliable foes of the GOP.

Clinton also sought to protect his party against charges that it might be weak on issues of national defense. In 1999, he earmarked spending of $10.5 billion over the next six years for development of a National Missile Defense (NMD) program. This proposed to rely primarily on land-based rockets that would hit incoming warheads, not on the lasers in space that Reagan's Star Wars had envisioned. Though Clinton deferred action in October 2000 on development of the program, his move indicated that he hoped to improve America's military defenses. The next administration, of George W. Bush, picked up where Clinton had left off, making anti-missile defense a higher budgetary priority in early 2001 than measures against terrorism.[38]

Clinton's greatest political asset in 1999–2000 continued to be the state of the economy. Danger signs persisted, to be sure, notably in the nation's unfavorable balance of trade, which was huge and growing, and in the mountain of personal indebtedness that consumers were building up.[39] What would happen to the economy, editorialists asked, if foreign central banks (especially from Asia) that were investing heavily in American government securities pulled back? Other experts warned prophetically about the overpricing of stocks, especially in dot-com companies. Many of these companies collapsed in 2000. They asked how America, a consumption-addicted society where expectations were high and savings were low, could sustain key entitlements in the future, notably Social Security and Medicare, benefits from which millions of retiring boomers would

37. Berman, *From the Center to the Edge*, 106.
38. Tests of anti–missile missiles, however, encountered embarrassing failures in the early 2000s. *New York Times*, Dec. 16, 2004.
39. Berman, *From the Center to the Edge*, 115.

begin to demand in a few years.[40] Both the stock market and economic growth began to taper off in 2000, prompting alarm that the nation might be headed for recession.[41]

Even so, the mood of most people remained upbeat. The percentage of Americans who were poor or unemployed had reached new lows by that time. The welfare law of 1996, though still excoriated by a number of liberals, seemed to be working—at least to the extent of cutting back the welfare rolls and placing many former recipients in jobs. Female-headed households, though poor on the average, appeared to be a little better off than they had been in 1996.[42] Most encouraging, rates of violent and property crimes continued to fall.

While many liberals complained that Clinton was not fighting very hard for larger social expenditures, they conceded that mounting federal budget surpluses (which the administration used to pay down the national debt) were popular with the American public. Clinton rarely missed opportunities to claim that his expert fiscal management had brought unparalleled prosperity to the United States. In his State of the Union message in January 2000, he bolstered a mood of optimism—indeed smugness—that was palpable in the country. "Never before," he proclaimed, "has our nation enjoyed, at once, so much prosperity and social progress with so little internal crisis and so few external threats."[43]

AND SO THE FATEFUL PRESIDENTIAL CAMPAIGN of 2000 gathered momentum. At the start, the leading contenders, Vice President Gore and Texas governor Bush, faced opponents in the primaries. Gore, however, beat Bill Bradley, a former senator from New Jersey, in early contests and wrapped up the nomination by Super Tuesday (a date when a host of primaries took place) in March. Later, he chose Senator Joseph Lieberman

---

40. Peter Peterson, *Running on Empty: How the Democratic and Republican Parties Are Bankrupting Our Future and What Americans Can Do About It* (New York, 2004).

41. Recession did arrive in early 2001. The Dow, which had peaked at 11,723 in January 2000, plunged to 7,197 by October 2002. The NASDAQ fell by 39 percent in 2000, its worst decline ever in a given year.

42. A mostly favorable assessment of the 1996 welfare law, by scholars with no conservative axes to grind, concluded in 2004 that female-headed families—benefiting not only from welfare reform but also from minimum wage laws and from the Earned Income Tax Credit—were "significantly better off" than they had been before 1996. Scott Winship and Christopher Jencks, "Welfare Reform Worked," *Christian Science Monitor*, July 21, 2004. Many liberals, however, still opposed the changes.

43. *Public Papers of the Presidents, 2000–2001*, vol. 1 (Washington, 2002), 129–40.

of Connecticut to be his running mate. Lieberman was the first Jew in American history to be honored with such a major party nomination. Bush lost the early New Hampshire primary to John McCain, a maverick Republican senator from Arizona who had spent five years as a POW in North Vietnam. But Bush rallied, buoyed by rough campaign tactics and by a war chest so enormous that he rejected federal funding for the primary season.[44] After Super Tuesday, he, too, had sewn up the nomination. He later selected Dick Cheney, his father's tough-minded, conservative defense secretary, to run with him.

Other candidates—notably Ralph Nader for the Green Party and Patrick Buchanan, this time for the Reform Party—also entered the presidential race. Nader, disdaining the policies of both major parties, directed much of his fire at the power and greed of multinational corporations. Buchanan, an isolationist, demanded a cutback of immigration and a nationalistic foreign policy. It was evident from the start of the campaign, however, that while Nader and Buchanan might be spoilers, they had no chance to win.[45]

It was equally clear that the major party candidates in 2000—as had often been the case in the recent past—enjoyed the blessings of privileged and politically well-connected backgrounds. Gore, the son and namesake of a United States senator from Tennessee, had grown up in the nation's capital, where he had gone to private school before attending Harvard University. From his earliest years, he was groomed by his father to run for the presidency.[46] In 1988, at the age of thirty-nine, he had made an ambitious but abortive run for the office. Bush, like his father, had attended private school and graduated from Yale. He also received an MBA degree from the Harvard Business School. Moving to west Texas, he later became owner of the Texas Rangers baseball team, which he sold in 1998 for $15 million. The vice-presidential nominees, Lieberman and Cheney, had

44. Campaign finance regulations stipulated that candidates who expected to receive federal funding during the pre–nomination period must adhere to spending limits (including $19 million in federal money) of $45 million. The Bush organization, having collected considerably more, rejected the federal money, thereby freeing itself from spending caps. He was the first major-party nominee in American history to be able to do that. In 2004, both Bush and his Democratic opponent, Senator John Kerry of Massachusetts, rejected federal funding during the pre–nomination phase of their presidential campaigns.

45. For accounts of the campaign and election, see Jules Witcover, *Party of the People. A History of the Democrats* (New York, 2003), 699–724; Berman, *From the Center to the Edge*, 109–11, 114–16, 118–20; Johnson, *The Best of Times*, 519–34.

46. For Gore, see David Remnick, "The Wilderness Campaign," *New Yorker*, Sept. 13, 2004, 56–71.

also attended Yale (though Cheney eventually graduated from the University of Wyoming, in his home state).

From the outset, the contest between Gore and Bush seemed too close to call, but though the race was tight, it was otherwise unexciting until the election itself. Bush, pointing to optimistic budget projections that anticipated a multi-trillion-dollar federal surplus by 2010, called for huge tax cuts. The surplus, he said, was "not the government's money" but "the people's money." In asserting the virtues of tax cuts, he was following in the footsteps of many GOP candidates, notably Reagan in 1980 and Dole in 1996. Bush proposed to allow younger workers voluntarily to divert some of their Social Security payroll taxes to personal retirement accounts. He favored drilling for oil in the Arctic National Wildlife Refuge, discounted prescription drugs for senior citizens through private insurance, a larger federal commitment to public education, and tax-supported vouchers so that parents could pay tuition at parochial and other private schools. The United States, he said, must discard its "soft bigotry of low expectations" about poorly performing students and improve its educational standards.

America, Bush emphasized, should become an "ownership society" in which enterprising people, not the federal government, played the dominant role. More of a social conservative than his father, he identified himself as a born-again, evangelical Christian, and he opposed abortion save in cases of rape or incest or when a woman's life was endangered. He repeatedly criticized the Clinton administration for risking the lives of American soldiers in places such as Haiti and for "nation-building" in foreign policy. "I would be very careful about using our troops as nation-builders," he said in a debate with Gore on October 11. "I believe the role of the military is to fight and win war. . . . I don't want to try to put our troops in all places at all times. I don't want to be the world's policeman."[47]

Like Gore, Bush called for higher defense spending, but neither candidate said much about nuclear proliferation or terrorism. The subject of terrorism did not figure in the three presidential debates, where the focus—as in most elections since the Vietnam era—was on the economy.

Predictably, Gore opposed Bush's stands on abortion and vouchers. Unlike his adversary, he favored stronger gun control. Bush's tax-cutting plan, he charged, was a huge and irresponsible handout to the wealthy. Gore proclaimed that he would put the budgetary surplus in a "lock box" so as to preserve the money for retirement benefits. The focus of both

47. James Mann, *Rise of the Vulcans: The History of Bush's War Cabinet* (New York, 2004), 256.

candidates on managing what was expected to be a rapidly mounting federal surplus reflected the high expectations in 2000 that Americans cherished about the future of government finances. Three years later, when red ink swamped the federal till, one sardonic observer noted that arguments in 2000 over what to do with the surplus sounded in retrospect "like a debate between pre-Copernican astronomers."[48]

Many political pundits predicted that Gore would beat Bush. After all, he was an experienced national politician who had served as a representative and senator from Tennessee before becoming an active, influential vice president. He had solid credentials as a supporter of environmental protection, a record that pleased liberals. His repeated defense of Social Security was expected to appeal to elderly Americans, who comprised an ever higher percentage of the population (12.4 percent, or 35 million of the nation's 281 million people, were sixty-five years old or more in 2000), and to millions of boomers who were soon to retire. Most important, Gore could claim that he had helped to promote the peace and prosperity that had flourished during Clinton's presidency.

"Dubya," as many people called Bush (after his middle initial), seemed in contrast to be unsophisticated and inexperienced. Though he had swept to victory in his races to be governor of Texas, thereby demonstrating surprisingly strong skills as a campaigner, he appeared to have no special qualifications to be president of the United States—save perhaps that the GOP had no one else who seemed likely to win the election and that he was George H. W. Bush's son.

Gore, however, squandered his advantages. In the first debate, which he had been expected to win easily, he was overconfident and condescending—smirking, sighing audibly, rolling his eyes, and raising his eyebrows when Bush was speaking. Though it was hard to say who "won" the debate, most observers, having expected Bush to be outclassed, agreed that the outsider from Texas had performed far better than had been anticipated. Moreover, Gore never seemed comfortable as a campaigner. Many of his aides found him to be demanding and brusque. Critics observed that he was "stiff," "wooden," pompous, and inconsistent, seeming to flip-flop in order to cater to critics of his earlier statements and to please whatever constituency he was trying to impress. After supporting the mostly

48. John Cassidy, "Goodbye to All That," *New Yorker*, Sept. 15, 2003, 92–95. In January 2001, the Congressional Budget Office predicted a cumulative federal budget surplus by 2011 of more than $5 trillion. In September 2004, anticipating continuing federal deficits, the same office predicted a cumulative shortfall between 2005 and 2014 of $2.3 trillion. *New Yorker*, Nov. 1, 2004, 38.

centrist policies of Clinton for much of the campaign, he lurched into a more populist mode toward the end. Many reporters wondered what he really stood for.

Some Democrats complained especially of two tactical decisions that seemed to be damaging Gore's chances. The first was his failure, as they saw it, to highlight often enough the contributions of the Clinton administration to the economic gains of the late 1990s. Though the economy was sputtering by mid-2000, there was no doubting the high gear into which it had shifted in the past few years. The second was his personal coolness toward the president. Gore, who had two daughters, had been appalled by the Lewinsky affair. So had Lieberman, who in the Senate had denounced Clinton's behavior as "disgraceful" and "immoral." Gore seems to have suspected, perhaps wrongly, that Clinton was a political liability. He was therefore reluctant to have him play a major speaking role during the campaign. The two men seldom appeared together on the stump.

Though eager to help, the president agreed to keep a low profile, even in his home state of Arkansas. For the most part, he spoke in African American churches in an effort to get out the vote. Analyses of the election were understandably inconclusive as to whether a larger role for Clinton would have turned the tide for the Democratic ticket. Most people, after all, still disapproved of his personal behavior, and in some swing states Clinton seemed to be unpopular with independent voters. But Clinton's job approval ratings still exceeded 60 percent. In the aftermath of the election, a number of pundits thought that the president, who was an outstanding campaigner, might at least have swung his home state for Gore. If Arkansas had gone Democratic (and no other states had switched), Gore would have won the election.

Bush, meanwhile, continued to surprise people. To be sure, he was far from articulate, once proclaiming, "Our priorities is our faith." On another occasion, he exclaimed, "Families is where our nation finds hope, where wings take dreams." Democrats mocked him as Governor Malaprop. Bush nonetheless came across as a folksy, energetic, physically expressive, and well-organized campaigner. Notwithstanding accusations that he was a threat to the Social Security program, he hoped to win substantial support from the elderly, who tended to be more conservative on a range of social, economic, and foreign policy issues than younger voters. Though Bush (like Gore) did not arouse great popular enthusiasm, many voters believed that he was a straight shooter who meant what he said.

Bush, promising to restore "honor and dignity" to the presidency, made sure that people did not forget Clinton's sexual wanderings. But he was careful not to repeat the mistake of his father, who in 1992 had allowed the right wing of the party to play a highly visible role in his campaign, or of Dole, who in 1996 had come across as sourly partisan on the stump. Instead, Bush proclaimed at virtually every opportunity that he stood for "compassionate conservatism" and that he would be "a uniter, not a divider," as president. If elected, he said, he would work cooperatively with Democrats in Congress, thereby breaking the partisan gridlock that had tied up the nation during the Clinton years. Bush's apparently moderate stance, like Clinton's appeal to the center in 1992 and 1996, was later said to be his greatest political asset in 2000.[49]

The contest did not greatly animate eligible voters, only 55.6 percent of whom turned out on election day. Many people who cast their ballots told pollsters, as they had done in earlier elections, that they did not much admire either candidate and that they were disgusted with the partisan behavior of politicians in general. The race, they said, pitted "Gush versus Bore." Others, including liberals who saw little difference between the largely centrist stance of Gore and that of Bush, derided the contest as a "Seinfeld election"—it was about nothing, and it didn't matter.

When the polls closed, it was apparent that Gore had edged Bush in the popular vote. That he had: Official tallies later showed that he had captured 50,992,335 votes (48.4 percent of the total) to Bush's 50,455,156 (47.9 percent). This was a margin of 537,179. Nader won 2,882,897, or 2.7 percent of the total, and Buchanan received 448,895, or 0.42 percent.[50] The combined vote for Gore and Nader—51.1 percent—was the best showing for the center-left since Lyndon Johnson had overwhelmed Barry Goldwater in 1964. As in 1992 and 1996, however, neither major candidate had managed to win 50 percent of the vote.

The election revealed that social and cultural divisions had persisted. Like previous Democratic candidates, Gore scored impressively among low-income and new immigrant voters, city dwellers, supporters of gun control, members of labor union households, and blacks, winning an estimated 90 percent of African American votes.[51] He was more popular among

---

49. Byron Shafer, *The Two Majorities and the Puzzle of Modern American Politics* (Lawrence, Kans., 2003), 26–51.

50. *New York Times*, April 20, 2004; *Stat. Abst.*, 2002, 235. The presidential candidate of the Libertarian Party, Harry Browne, won 348,431 votes, or 0.36 percent of the total.

51. It was later estimated that Gore won 63 percent of votes from people who lived in union households. Bush carried only 32 percent of these voters. The AFL-CIO, anxious to beat Bush, contributed $41 million to Gore's campaign in 2000. *New York Times*, March 9, 2004.

women than among men and among singles than married people, who were older on the average and (especially in the millions of dual-income families) wealthier.[52] Bush, however, fared better among low-income and lower-middle-class voters in rural and suburban areas than Dole had done in 1996. He was the choice of 54 percent of white voters, of 51 percent of white Catholic voters, and of 59 percent of people who said they attended church at least once a week.[53]

Regional divisions, which had sharpened steadily since Nixon had fashioned a Southern Strategy in 1968, were especially visible. Bush scored impressively among white southerners, carrying (like Reagan in 1984 and his father in 1988) every southern state, including Gore's Tennessee. He won every Plains and Mountain state except New Mexico. He beat Gore in the border states of Missouri, Kentucky, and West Virginia. But except for New Hampshire, which he won by a very narrow margin, Bush lost every state in the Northeast and Middle Atlantic regions. He trailed Gore in the West Coast states of California, Oregon, and Washington, and in the Midwestern states of Minnesota, Iowa, Wisconsin, Illinois, and Michigan. Though Gore won only twenty states (and the District of Columbia), most of these were in heavily populated, industrialized areas that had been the heart of Democratic strength since the New Deal years.

But these were later, certified results. On election night many states were too close to call. It was impossible to predict with certainty which candidate would win a required majority (270) of the 538 electoral college votes. At 7:49 P.M. the major networks, badly served by interpreters of exit polls, said that Gore had won the state of Florida. More than six hours later, at 2:16 A.M., FOX News, a conservative channel, announced that Bush had taken the state—and the election—whereupon ABC, CBS, ABC, and CNN followed suit within the next four minutes. Still later in the morning, the networks admitted that the outcome remained uncertain. In the next few days, when battles over Florida began to mesmerize the

52. Polling later indicated that Gore won 54 percent of votes from women, to 43 percent for Bush. Gore captured 63 percent of the votes of single women, compared to 32 percent for married women (to 49 percent for Bush). Among married men voters, Gore trailed Bush by 58 percent to 38 percent. See Louis Menand, "Permanent Fatal Errors: Did the Voters Send a Message?" *New Yorker*, Dec. 6, 2004, 54–60; Peter Keating, "Wake–up Call," *AARP: The Magazine*, Sept./Oct. 2004, 60; *New York Times*, Sept. 22, 2004.

53. *New York Times*, Feb. 29, 2004. Gore carried 39 percent of these churchgoers. But Bush advisers, including Karl Rove, who was regarded as an unusually shrewd political operator, were unhappy with the turnout of evangelical Christian voters in 2000 and resolved to raise it by 4 million votes in 2004.

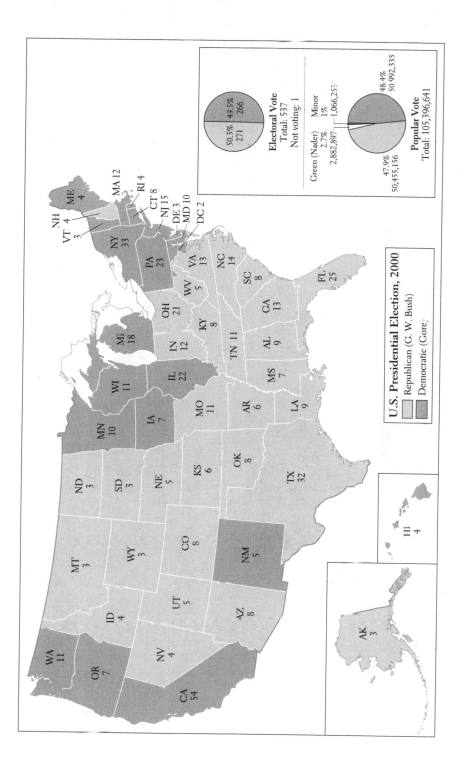

U.S. Presidential Election, 2000

Republican (G. W. Bush)
Democratic (Gore)

Electoral Vote
Total: 537
Not voting: 1

50.5% 271
49.5% 266

Popular Vote
Total: 105,396,641

Green (Nader)
2.7%
2,882,897

Minor
1%
1,066,255

48.4%
50,992,335

47.9%
50,455,156

WA 11
OR 7
CA 54
NV 4
ID 4
UT 5
AZ 8
MT 3
WY 3
CO 8
NM 5
ND 3
SD 3
NE 5
KS 6
OK 8
TX 32
MN 10
IA 7
MO 11
AR 6
LA 9
WI 11
IL 22
MI 18
IN 12
OH 21
KY 8
TN 11
MS 7
AL 9
GA 13
SC 8
NC 14
VA 13
WV 5
PA 23
NY 33
VT 3
NH 4
MA 12
RI 4
CT 8
NJ 15
DE 3
MD 10
DC 2
ME 4
FL 25

HI 4

AK 3

media, Bush supporters reminded Americans that all the important news anchors had proclaimed him the victor.

When Gore heard the networks announce for Bush, he rang him up to offer congratulations, only to be alerted by aides that he still had a good chance in Florida. So he phoned Bush back, saying: "Circumstances have changed dramatically since I first called you. The state of Florida is too close to call." Bush responded that the networks had confirmed the result and that his brother, Jeb, who was Florida's Republican governor, had told him that the numbers in Florida were correct. "Your little brother," Gore is said to have replied, "is not the ultimate authority on this."[54]

Americans, having gone to bed not knowing which candidate had won, awoke the next day to learn that the outcome was still uncertain. Within a few days, however, it seemed that Gore was assured of 267 electoral college votes, three short of the number needed to win the election. Bush then appeared to have 246. The eyes of politically engaged Americans quickly shifted to Florida, where twenty-five electoral votes remained at stake. If Bush could win there, where the first "final count" gave him a margin of 1,784 votes (out of more than 5.9 million cast in the state), he would have at least 271 electoral votes. Whoever won Florida would become the next president.

There followed thirty-six days of frenetic political and legal maneuvering, which all but eclipsed media attention to last-ditch efforts—in the end unsuccessful—that the Clinton administration was undertaking at the time to fashion an agreement between Israel and the Palestine Liberation Organization.[55] Much of the electoral maneuvering during these five weeks featured partisan disputes over poorly constructed ballots used in various Florida counties. Flaws such as these, which had long existed throughout the United States, reflected the idiosyncratic and error-prone quality of America's voting procedures, which state and local authorities

54. David Margolick et al., "The Path to Florida," *Vanity Fair*, Oct. 2004, 310–22, 355–69.
55. Most Americans blamed the inflexibility of Yasser Arafat, head of the PLO, for the failure of these efforts, which had seemed somewhat promising during a summit at Camp David in July but had virtually collapsed by late September. A second, more violent Palestinian intifada, this one aided by terrorist organizations and featuring suicide bombers, had then broken out. See Dennis Ross, *The Missing Peace: The Inside Story of the Fight for Middle East Peace* (New York, 2004). After witnessing Arafat's performance, George W. Bush decided to have nothing to do with him. Instead, he offered strong support to the policies of Ariel Sharon, Israel's hawkish new prime minister. By September 2004, four years after the start of the intifada, some 4,000 people (three-fourths of them Palestinians, of whom more than half were civilians) had been killed in the fighting. *New York Times*, Oct. 3, 2004.

determined, but they fell under an especially harsh glare of public scrutiny only in 2000. In predominantly Democratic Palm Beach County, for instance, more than 3,000 voters — many of them elderly Jews — were apparently confused by so-called butterfly ballots and mistakenly voted for Buchanan, the Reform Party nominee, instead of for Gore. Some voters there, bewildered by the ballots, punched more than one hole; these "overvotes," like thousands of overvotes on variously constructed ballots in other counties, were not validated at the time.

Elsewhere, partially punched ballots emerged from voting machines, leaving "hanging," "dimpled," "pregnant," or other kinds of "chads." In the parlance of the time, these were "undervotes" — that is, ballots that voters may well have tried to have punched but that voting machines did not record as valid at the time.[56] It was estimated that the total of disputed undervotes (61,000) and overvotes (113,000) in Florida was in the range of 175,000. Irate Democrats further charged that officials at the polls unfairly invalidated the registrations of thousands of African American and Latino voters and tossed out a great many ballots in predominantly black neighborhoods. Police, they claimed, intimidated blacks who therefore backed away from voting in some northern Florida counties. Gore's supporters further alleged that thousands of Floridians, many of whom were African American, were inaccurately included on long lists of felons and therefore denied the franchise under Florida law.[57] Angry controversies over issues such as these heated up partisan warfare that raged throughout the nation.[58]

From the beginning, Bush backers, led by former secretary of state James Baker, worked as a disciplined team in the post-election struggles involving

56. Chads were tiny pieces of ballots that were supposed to fall off when punched ballots went through voting machines, thereby leaving holes in the ballots that would reveal the preferences of voters. Many Florida ballots had chads that had not fallen off. Others had "dimpled" or "pregnant" chads that did not dangle from ballots but that might indicate voter intent. For accounts of these battles, see Jack Rakove, ed., *The Unfinished Election of 2000* (New York, 2001); Jeffrey Toobin, *Too Close to Call: The Thirty-Six-Day Battle to Decide the 2000 Election* (New York, 2001); and *Newsweek*, Nov. 20, 27, Dec. 4, 11, 18, 2000, Jan. 1, 2001.

57. It was also true, however, that the turnout of black voters was higher than it had been in earlier elections. *New York Times*, May 24, 2004. Florida was one of nine states in 2000 that permanently disfranchised felons, a third of whom were African American men. This prohibition, affecting an estimated 600,000 Floridian felons who had done their time, presumably disadvantaged Democrats. Later estimates concluded that various state laws prevented approximately 3.9 million felons from voting in 2000. Ibid., Oct. 27, Nov. 9, 2004.

58. Margolick et al., "The Path to Florida."

Florida. By contrast, the Democrats, headed by former secretary of state Warren Christopher, were cautious, even defeatist at times.[59] Baker's team relied especially on the efforts of Bush's brother, Jeb, and on the Republican-controlled Florida legislature, which stood ready to certify GOP electors. Federal law, Republicans maintained, set December 12 (six days before America's electors were to vote on December 18) as a deadline after which Congress was not supposed to challenge previously certified electors. If Gore called for a manual recount of ballots, Republicans clearly planned to turn for help to the courts in an effort to stop such a process or to tie it up in litigation so that no resolution of the controversy could be achieved by December 12.

Two days after the election, by which time late-arriving overseas ballots and machine recounts (required by Florida law in a close election such as this) had managed to cut Bush's lead, Gore's team acted, seeking hand recounts in four predominantly Democratic counties where punch-card ballots had failed to register the clear intent of many voters. In limiting their focus to four counties, Gore's advocates maintained that Florida law did not permit them to call at that time for a statewide recount. Such a statewide process, they said, could then be legally undertaken only in counties where substantial errors were perceived to have occurred. Still, Gore's move seemed to be politically opportunistic. Seizing the high ground, Bush defenders accused him of cherry-picking Democratic strongholds.

On November 21, the Florida Supreme Court intervened on behalf of Gore, unanimously approving manual recounts in the four counties and extending to November 26 (or November 27, if so authorized by Florida's secretary of state, Katherine Harris) the deadline for these to be completed. Furious Bush supporters immediately responded by charging that Florida's Democratic judges, apparently a majority on the court, were trying to "steal" the election. Manual recounts of this sort, the GOP insisted, would be "arbitrary, standardless, and selective." With tempestuous disputes flaring between hosts of lawyers and party leaders who were hovering over exhausted recount officials, Republicans on November 22 submitted a brief along these lines asking the United States Supreme Court to review the issue. The Court quickly agreed to do so and set December 1 as the date for oral argument.

As Democrats complained, the Bush team's appeal to the Supreme Court was ideologically inconsistent, inasmuch as Republicans, professing to be advocates of states' rights, normally argued that state courts should

59. Toobin, *Too Close to Call*, 210, 233.

be the interpreters of state laws, including election laws. So had the conservative Republicans on the U.S. Supreme Court. The GOP, Democrats charged, was jettisoning its ideological position and relying on crass and cynical political tactics aimed at subverting the will of Florida voters.

Republicans also insisted in their brief that the Florida court had changed the rules after the election and that it had violated Article II of the United States Constitution, which said that state legislatures, not state courts, were authorized to determine the manner in which electors were named.[60] Their brief further maintained, though at less length than in its reliance on Article II, that recount officials in the selected counties would treat ballots differently and therefore violate voters' "equal protection" under the law, as guaranteed by the Fourteenth Amendment to the United States Constitution. Republicans also continued to rely on Secretary of State Harris, who had been a co-chair of the Bush campaign in the state. As Harris had said she would do, she stopped the manual recounts on November 26 and certified that Bush had taken Florida, by the then narrow margin of 537 votes. Because Miami-Dade and Palm Beach County officials had not completed their recounts, many disputed ballots in those populous areas were not included in the final tallies that she had certified.

Though Bush hailed this certification, proclaiming that it gave him victory, Gore's lawyers predictably and furiously contested it. Attacking the GOP brief that was before the U.S. Supreme Court, they also insisted that the Florida legislature (which the Bush team, relying on Article II of the U.S. Constitution, was counting upon if necessary) did not have the authority to override Florida state law and the state constitution, which provided for judicial review of the issue by the state courts.

During the oral presentations on December 1 of arguments such as these, it was obvious that the High Court was deeply divided. It responded on December 4 by sending the case back to the Florida Supreme Court and asking it to explain whether it had "considered the relevant portions of the federal Constitution and law."[61] The justices said nothing at the time concerning the Bush team's assertion that the equal protection clause of the Fourteenth Amendment was relevant to the case. Nor did the Court indicate that it might regard establishment of specific and uniform recounting standards as the key matters in its decision.

60. Article II stated, in part, "Each State shall appoint, in such Manner as the Legislature thereof may direct, a Number of Electors, equal to the whole Number of Senators and Representatives to which the State may be entitled in the Congress." For analysis of constitutional issues, see Larry Kramer, "The Supreme Court in Politics," in Rakove, *The Unfinished Election of 2000*, 105–57.
61. Toobin, *Too Close to Call*, 227.

The Florida court, essentially ignoring the High Court's directive, replied on December 8 by ordering, on a vote of four to three, that a statewide hand recount be undertaken of the 61,000 or so undervotes that were contested. The four-judge majority did not outline specific standards that would indicate which ballots should be accepted. In deciding which ballots were acceptable, the judges said, recount officials should take into account the "clear indication of the intent of the voter."[62]

Republicans wasted no time urging the U.S. Supreme Court to stay such a recount. This time, the Court acted immediately, voting five to four on the afternoon of December 9 to grant a stay and setting the morning of Monday, December 11, as a time for oral arguments on the issues. All five votes in the majority came from justices named by Reagan or Bush.[63] This was staggeringly bad news for Gore's already discouraged supporters: There now appeared to be no way that manual recounts of undervotes, even if approved by the Court on December 11, could be completed by December 12, the date on which Florida's certified Republican electors would be safe from congressional challenges.

One day after hearing the oral arguments, at 10:00 P.M. on the deadline date of December 12 itself, the U.S. Supreme Court delivered the predictable final blow, dispatching Court employees to deliver texts of its opinions to crowds of reporters, many of whom had been waiting in the cold on the steps of the Supreme Court building. In all, there were six separate opinions totaling sixty-five pages. To the surprise of many observers, the justices did not maintain, as many of Bush's lawyers had expected they would, that the Florida court had overstepped its bounds by ignoring Article II of the Constitution. In the key decision, *Bush v. Gore*, the five conservative justices for the first time focused instead on the question of equal protection.[64] They stated that the recounts authorized by the Florida court violated the right of voters to have their ballots evaluated consistently and fairly, and that the recounts therefore ran afoul of the equal protection clause.

Their decision ended the fight. Bush, having been certified as the winner in Florida by 537 votes, had officially taken the state. With Florida's 25 electoral votes, he had a total of 271 in the electoral college, one more than he needed. He was to become the forty-third president of the United States.

62. Ibid., 241.
63. The five conservatives in the case were Chief Justice William Rehnquist, Antonin Scalia, Sandra Day O'Connor, Anthony Kennedy, and Clarence Thomas. The others were Stephen Breyer, Ruth Bader Ginsburg, John Paul Stephens, and David Souter.
64. The decision was *per curiam*, with no author named. It was generally believed, however, that the key author was Justice Kennedy and that he had received strong backing from Justice O'Connor. Margolick et al., "The Path to Florida."

The next night, Gore graciously accepted the Court's decision and conceded. But the arguments of the Supreme Court's majority unleashed a torrent of protests, not only from Democratic loyalists but also from a great many legal analysts and law professors (most of them liberals). The conservative majority of five, they complained, had violated the basic democratic principle of one person, one vote. To achieve their ends—the election of Bush—they had uncharacteristically—and, they said, desperately—turned to the equal protection clause (normally invoked by liberals to protect the rights of minorities and other out-groups) and had ignored the Court's own recently asserted rulings in favor of federalism and states' rights. The majority decision had also stated, "Our consideration is limited to the present circumstances, for the problem of equal protection in election processes generally presents many complexities." This statement meant that *Bush v. Gore*, while delivering a victory to the GOP in 2000, had no standing as precedent.

The arguments of the five conservative justices especially distressed the Court's dissenting minority of four.[65] Justices Stephen Breyer and David Souter, while conceding that the recounting as ordered by the Florida Supreme Court presented "constitutional problems" of equal protection, said that the U.S. Supreme Court should have remanded the case to the Florida court, which could have established fair and uniform procedures for recounting. That process, they added, could be extended to December 18, the date that the electors were due to meet. The Florida court should decide whether the recounting could be completed by that time. Breyer, charging that the majority decision of his colleagues had damaged the reputation of the Court itself, wrote: "We do risk a self-inflicted wound, a wound that may harm not just the court but the nation." Eighty-year-old Justice John Paul Stevens, who had been appointed to the Court by President Ford, added: "Although we may never know with complete certainty the identity of the winner of this year's Presidential election, the identity of the loser is perfectly clear. It is the Nation's confidence in the judge as an impartial guardian of the rule of law."[66]

65. Two of the dissenting justices, Stevens and Ginsburg, believed that the lack of a uniform standard for manual vote counting did not present constitutional problems. In Florida as in other states, Ginsburg pointed out, counties had long used various kinds of ballots and had decided in differing ways whether or not to accept votes, without constitutional questions being raised about equal protection. Toobin, *Too Close to Call*, 264–67; Margolick et al., "The Path to Florida"; *New York Times*, Dec. 13, 2000.

66. For much that follows, see *Newsweek*, Dec. 18, 2000, 28–42, and Dec. 25, 2000, 46–50; and *Time*, Dec. 25, 2000, 76–79.

Many Bush supporters, delighted with the Court's position, denounced the Florida Supreme Court, which they blasted as a partisan agent of Gore. "Not in living memory," New York Times columnist William Safire exclaimed, "have Americans seen such judicial chutzpah. Our political process was almost subverted by a runaway court." Like many other conservatives, Safire emphasized that Article II of the Constitution gave state legislatures the authority to appoint presidential electors. If the U.S. Supreme Court had not been willing to "take the case and take the heat," he added, the "internecine mud-wrestling would have gone on for at least another month."

Safire also pointed out that Republicans in the incoming House of Representatives would enjoy an edge in a majority of the state delegations (twenty-nine of fifty), which were the groups that the Constitution charged with resolving disputes of this sort. If legal battling persisted, causing two slates of Florida electors to be considered when Congress met in early January, the Republican-dominated House would choose Bush. The Court, Safire concluded, took a bullet in order to stop a further ratcheting up of ill feeling that would have served no useful purpose.[67]

Gore supporters, however, rejected this interpretation of Article II, which they said did not give state legislatures such sweeping authority over state laws and constitutional directives. They also deplored the Court's reliance on the equal protection clause. They were especially outraged by what they charged was the strategy of delay that Baker had masterminded. They saw nothing but partisan motives behind the Court's intervention, which they said had opportunistically relied on a December 12 deadline that neither Florida law nor the Florida court had called for. The Court's conservatives, they charged, had short-circuited the legal process in order to give Bush, for whom a minority of Americans had voted, an undemocratic victory. A prominent Los Angeles prosecutor and deputy district attorney, Vincent Bugliosi, erupted: "The stark reality . . . is that the institution Americans trust the most to protect its freedoms and principles committed one of the biggest and most serious crimes this nation has ever seen—pure and simple, the theft of the presidency. And by definition, the perpetrators of this crime *have* to be denominated criminals."[68]

Whether Gore had actually taken Florida remains uncertain, especially because hundreds of ballots disappeared between election day in 2000 and reviews of the voting that attempted in 2001 to answer this question. A

---

67. New York Times, Dec. 11, 2000. See also Safire, ibid., Dec. 11, 14, 2000.
68. Johnson, The Best of Times, 529. See also Hendrick Hertzberg, "Counted Out," New Yorker, Dec. 24, 2000, 41–42.

consortium of major news organizations that undertook a comprehensive review in 2001 of the Florida battle reached varying conclusions depending on which ballots were recounted and on which standards were used to evaluate them. They did not resolve the controversy.[69] One thing, however, did seem fairly clear: More Floridians, including most of those who had been confused by the butterfly ballot in Palm Beach County, had *intended* to vote for Gore than for Bush.[70] Another fact was obvious: No matter the exact tallies in Florida, Gore had triumphed nationally in the popular vote—by a margin (537,179) that was more than four times as large as Kennedy's (118,574) had been in 1960.

Subsequent analyses of the voting in 2000 suggested that if Ralph Nader had not been in the race, Gore would have won the election, and without any legal hassles. In Florida, Nader received 97,488 votes, far more than Bush's certified margin of 537. Later reviews concluded that if Nader's name had not been on the ballot in Florida, 45 percent of people who voted for him there would have opted for Gore, as opposed to only 27 percent who would have chosen Bush. (The remaining 28 percent would not have voted.) Studies of the election added that if Nader had not run, Gore would very likely have taken New Hampshire's four electoral votes—and therefore the election, no matter what happened in Florida. Gore had assumed that he could not win New Hampshire and slighted it, especially toward the end of the campaign. In November, Nader received 22,138 of the 569,081 votes cast in the Granite State, considerably more than Bush's narrow margin of 7,211.[71]

69. The consortium concluded that Bush would have won a popular-vote majority in Florida if the Supreme Court had approved the Florida court's order for a manual recount of the roughly 61,000 undervotes, but that Gore would have won if the state's approximately 113,000 overvotes had also been recounted manually. Margolick et al., "The Path to Florida."

70. *New York Times*, Nov. 12, 2001; Witcover, *Party of the People*, 723. Toobin, *Too Close to Call*, emphasized that more Floridians (among them the voters who mistakenly voted for Buchanan in Palm Beach County) intended to vote for Gore than for Bush and that the victory of Bush, sanctioned by the Supreme Court, was therefore a "crime against democracy."

71. *New York Times*, Feb. 24, 2004. Bush supporters, however, presented "what ifs" of their own. In each of four states that Bush lost by very narrow margins—Iowa, Wisconsin, Oregon, and New Mexico—the number of votes for Buchanan exceeded the margins of victory. Assuming that most of those voters would have opted for Bush in a straight-up contest between Bush and Gore, Bush would have taken those states, thereby gaining 30 electoral votes. He would thus have taken the electoral college even without winning Florida. Harry Browne, the Libertarian candidate, also received votes that might otherwise have gone to Bush. In Florida, Browne won 16,415 votes. The bottom line: In an election as close as this one, the "what ifs" are virtually endless.

Other observers deplored the numerous flaws in America's electoral procedures. Many of these criticisms, of course, targeted the anachronism of the electoral college, which not for the first time in United States history had played a key role in depriving the top vote-getter of victory.[72] A related focus of complaint was the winner-take-all system that states employed to determine their allocations of electoral votes.[73] In part for this reason, candidates who expected to win or lose in relatively non-competitive states (that is, most states) scarcely bothered to campaign in them. Bush, for instance, virtually ignored California (fifty-four electoral votes) and New York (thirty-three electoral votes), which Gore was certain to carry, and Texas (thirty-two electoral votes), where he was sure to win. It was equally obvious that registration and voting procedures, which were established by state and local officials, varied widely throughout the country and that in many states, including of course Florida, they were sadly deficient.

After the election, however, little changed. Many people agitated for reform or abolition of the electoral college, but opponents of change claimed that the college safeguarded states' rights and the principle of federalism. Political leaders in small states, as at most times in the past, jealously protected what they perceived as their advantages in the college, thereby rendering unattainable efforts for approval of a constitutional amendment to abolish or reform it. Defenders of the electoral college also asserted that if it were scrapped, minor-party candidates would be more likely to jump

72. The top vote-getter had previously failed to become president three times: in 1824, when a post-election ballot of the House of Representatives chose John Quincy Adams over Andrew Jackson; in 1876 when a specially created electoral commission gave Rutherford Hayes, the Republican nominee, an electoral college margin of one over Samuel Tilden; and in 1888, when Benjamin Harrison, also a Republican, won more electoral college votes than did Grover Cleveland. See Jack Rakove, "The E-College in the E-Age," in Rakove, *The Unfinished Election of 2000*, 201–34; and Alexander Keyssar, "The Electoral College Flunks," *New York Review of Books*, March 24, 2005, 16–18.

73. Maine and Nebraska authorized some of their electoral votes to be apportioned according to popular majorities in congressional districts, but that had never happened, and in 2000, Maine's four votes went to Gore and Nebraska's five went to Bush. According to a later estimate, if all states in 2000 had apportioned electoral votes according to popular votes, the final count in the electoral college would have been 269 for Gore, 263 for Bush, and 6 for Nader. Because a majority in the College of 270 is required for election, a vote of state delegations in the House of Representatives would then have had to settle the issue—presumably for Bush. *New York Times*, Sept. 19, 2004. The final electoral college tally in 2000 was 271 for Bush and 266 for Gore. One Democratic elector from the District of Columbia cast a blank ballot in protest against the denial of rights of self-government in the district.

into a presidential race. Popular candidates of this sort would surely pick up a substantial number of votes, perhaps leaving the top vote-getter with only a small plurality of the overall turnout. Such a "winner" would therefore become president without anything like a popular mandate. Other observers maintained that the electoral college, by discouraging post-election disputes in all but very closely contested states—few in number—had helped in the past to minimize litigation. Absent the college, they said, a national election featuring a close popular vote might prompt an eruption of legal battles wherever it seemed that litigation might help one candidate or another to pick up a few extra votes. Worst-case scenarios, emphasizing the nation's widely varying and careless electoral procedures, imagined thousands of lawsuits that would drag on for months or more.

Overhauling winner-take-all allocations of electoral votes did not require a constitutional amendment, but political leaders in the states, eager to deliver 100 percent of their electoral votes to the candidate of their own party, showed little disposition to change their ways. In the presidential election of 2004, as in 2000, the presidential candidates—Bush and Senator John Kerry of Massachusetts—therefore focused their attention on a small number (no more than eighteen in all) of so-called swing or battleground states where the results were expected to be close, and virtually ignored the rest.

Satisfactory repair of flawed electoral procedures and machinery was technologically complicated and expensive. Wide variations persisted after 2000, preventing anything close to national uniformity. Despite halfhearted congressional efforts that resulted in a Help America Vote Act in 2002, reforms remained to be accomplished. During and after the hotly contested election of 2004, a host of headlines highlighted electoral problems and irregularities.

As Bush prepared to take office in January 2001, three political consequences of the election were clear. The first was that Republicans had sailed out of the doldrums that had stranded them after Watergate in 1974. At that time only 18 percent of American voters had identified as Republican. In 1975, a low point for the GOP, Democrats controlled thirty-six state houses and thirty-seven state legislatures.[74] Thanks to the political skills of Ronald Reagan, to the rise of the Religious Right, and to defections of

---

74. There were only thirteen Republican governors in 1975, and only five states in which the GOP had full control of the legislature. At that time eight states had legislatures in which Democrats ran one chamber and Republicans the other.

white working-class and Catholic voters to the GOP, conservatives gradually forced liberals to the defensive. Republicans, though losing their majority in the Senate in 1987 and the presidency in 1993, swept to victory in 1994 and to control in 1995 of both houses of Congress for the first time since 1955. By 2001, the GOP enjoyed dominance in a majority of states.[75] It had control of the White House as well as of both houses of Congress—again for the first time since 1955. Democrats, meanwhile, continued to fight among themselves. Many were furious at Gore, blasting him as a bungler whose terrible campaign opened the door for Bush.

The second consequence of the election, however, was that Republicans still did not command the political power that Democrats had enjoyed for much of the time between 1933 and 1968 and that they had clung to in Congress during most years before 1995. By 2000, roughly as many Americans called themselves Democrats as Republicans.[76] And Democrats were hardly feeble on Capitol Hill in 2001. In the 2000 election, they had held their own in races for the House, leaving the GOP with a precarious ten-person edge, 221 to 211. Democrats gained five seats in the Senate, tying Republicans, 50 to 50. In case of a deadlock, Vice President Cheney would have to intervene.[77]

Finally, little about the mood of party activists in January 2001 promised political harmony in the near future. The majority of people, to be sure, continued to cluster near the political center. Americans abided by the rule of law, even when it was delivered by a five-to-four majority of a politically divided Supreme Court.[78] Polls suggested in early 2001 that public esteem for the Court, which had normally been high in American history, remained strong.[79] But the election had inflamed the passions of partisans. Politically engaged Democrats were angry to discover that the incoming president, loading his Cabinet with Republicans, seemed to have

---

75. In 2001, there were twenty-seven Republican and twenty-one Democratic governors. (The other two were independent.) The GOP then controlled sixteen state legislatures, to seventeen for Democrats. The other legislatures (bicameral) were split or (as in the case of unicameral Nebraska) officially non-partisan.

76. Though published estimates of party identifications vary, all conclude that Republicans gained over the years, as did the percentages of people who normally called themselves independents.

77. In May 2001, Senator James Jeffords of Vermont broke with the Republican Party and became an independent, thereby enabling the Democrats to take control of the Senate for the next nineteen months.

78. Morris Fiorina et al., *Culture Wars? The Myth of a Polarized America* (New York, 2004); Louis Menand, "The Unpolitical Animal," *New Yorker*, Aug. 30, 2004, 92–96.

79. Toobin, *Too Close to Call*, 275.

jettisoned his campaign pledges about cooperating with the opposition. Was he going to become a "divider," not a "uniter"? Many Democratic senators and representatives, perceiving Bush to be an illegitimate, "unelected president," returned for his inaugural on January 20, 2001, in a surly and uncompromising mood.

So, too, did a group of demonstrators on inauguration day. Almost twenty-seven years earlier, when Nixon had finally fallen on his sword, signs across the street from the White House had borne messages of relief: DING DONG, THE WITCH IS DEAD; SEE DICK RUN; RUN, DICK, RUN.[80] On January 20, 2001, a cold and rainy day, some of the placards that greeted the new Republican president were as harsh as the weather: HAIL TO THE THIEF; ELECTION FOR SALE; THE PEOPLE HAVE SPOKEN — ALL FIVE OF THEM.

CLEVER SIGNS. It was nonetheless a fact that on that damp and chilly occasion in January 2001, as had generally been the case in the years since 1974, the majority of the American people were less partisan — less attentive to political fighting — than were the protestors, the politicians, or the interest groups with causes to defend. Or than the media, which then, as so often since Watergate, focused avidly on cultural and political controversies. Conflicts such as these, inevitable in a dynamic and diverse society such as the United States, surely persisted — and continued to thrive thereafter, especially after Bush took the nation to war in Iraq in 2003. But most Americans, including the nearly 45 percent of eligible voters who had not turned out in 2000, were not greatly wrapped up in political partisanship in 2001, great though this had been immediately after the election. The nation's durable political and legal institutions — the presidency, Congress, the courts, the Bill of Rights — also continued to command widespread popular allegiance, thereby keeping partisan warfare within manageable bounds.

Like most people most of the time, the majority of Americans tended to concern themselves in early 2001 mainly with personal matters: their families, friends, neighborhoods, and jobs. Many of these matters inevitably produced anxieties: A predominant mood of Americans, to the extent that it could be briefly described, continued to be restless. In a culture where most citizens still imagined the possibility of the American Dream of upward social mobility, many people continued to have high expectations, some of which were as elusive as ever.

---

80. Johnson, *The Best of Times*, 520. See the start of my prologue for the mood surrounding Nixon's resignation.

But palpable complacency and self-congratulation helped to moderate popular restlessness in early 2001. Cautiously optimistic feelings of this sort were understandable, for a number of encouraging developments since the 1970s had helped to lift them. While many older Americans still hankered for the Good Old Days, significant features of those supposedly halcyon times—the 1940s, 1950s, and early 1960s—had been harsh, especially for racial and ethnic minorities, Catholics and Jews, the handicapped, senior citizens, the majority of women, and gay people. Owing to the spread of tolerance and rights-consciousness since the 1960s, these and other Americans in 2001 enjoyed greater civil rights, civil liberties, entitlements, protections, and freedoms—including expanded choice and privacy—than they had in the past. Because younger generations of Americans since the 1960s had most often led the forward movement for rights and tolerance, it seemed likely that the changes wrought by the rights revolution of late twentieth-century America would endure.

Poverty, racial discrimination, and inequality continued to blight American society, but economic gains, having been particularly impressive since 1995, had helped to soothe tensions and antagonisms. Though consumers were still running up levels of personal debt that astonished older generations and that alarmed analysts of economic trends, a pleasurable reality tended to elevate spirits in early 2001: Most citizens of the United States had conveniences, comforts, and real incomes that would have been hard to imagine in 1974, or even in 1994.

The Cold War had been laid to rest in 1990, ending with hardly a shot being fired in anger by contending armed forces and (after Vietnam) with scarcely any loss of American life. An international coalition, led by the United States, had stayed the course to win this long and arduous struggle, helping to deliver greater political freedom and economic opportunity to hundreds of millions of previously oppressed people. So it was that in early 2001, as since 1990, the United States towered as a military giant like no other nation in recent history. Pride in this power further advanced complacency. Though concerns about nuclear proliferation continued to beset policy-makers in 2001, popular fears of catastrophe from such weaponry were less acute than they had been during the Cold War years. Threats from terrorists troubled thoughtful Americans in early 2001, but few people imagined that these might produce carnage at home.

With changes such as these in mind, it was hardly surprising that most people of the United States, having forged ahead since the early 1970s, seemed prepared early in 2001 to put the political fighting of 2000 behind them and to anticipate peace and prosperity in the future. Almost no

Americans at that time could foresee the terrible attacks that were soon to come. These assaults, indicating that there were no safe havens in the world, helped to transform the nation's foreign and military policies, to endanger optimistic expectations, and in a host of other ways to complicate the lives of the American people.

Bibliographical Essay

As footnotes in the text suggest, the literature concerning United States history, 1974–2001, is vast. This essay mentions only those books that proved especially useful to me. It begins by identifying general interpretations of the era and follows by describing sources concerned with various themes and topics: politics, the economy, social trends, religion, race relations, and so on. The bibliography then identifies books (for other sources, see footnotes) that deal with particular time periods, beginning with the 1970s and concluding with the Clinton years through the election of 2000, with a final paragraph concerning statistical sources. Dates of publication ordinarily refer to the most recent printing.

General Interpretations: An excellent overview of this era is William Chafe, *The Unfinished Journey: America Since World War II* (New York, 2003). Godfrey Hodgson, *More Equal Than Others: America from Nixon to the New Century* (Princeton, 2004), makes rising inequality the central theme of his critical account of these years. Michael Sherry, *In the Shadow of War: The United States Since the 1930s* (New Haven, 1995) focuses mainly on foreign and military issues. My earlier book, *Grand Expectations: The United States, 1945–1974* (New York, 1996), is the chronologically previous volume in the Oxford History of the United States; many of its central themes find amplification in this volume.

A number of general books were especially useful in helping me to think about the main themes of American history between the 1970s and the early 2000s. As their titles suggest, three of these offer interpretations similar to mine: Gregg Easterbrook, *The Progress Paradox: How Life Gets Better While People Feel Worse* (New York, 2003); David Whitman, *The Optimism Gap: The I'm OK—They're Not Syndrome and the Myth of American Decline* (New York, 1998); and Robert Samuelson, *The Good Life and Its Discontents: The American Dream in the Age of Entitlement, 1945–1995* (New York, 1995). Three books that highlight the powerful role of rights-consciousness—a major theme of my volume—are Samuel Walker, *The Rights Revolution: Rights and Community in Modern America* (New York, 1998); Lawrence Friedman, *American Law in the Twentieth Century* (New Haven, 2002); and John Skrentny, *The Minority Rights Revolution* (Cambridge, Mass.,

2002). Other books that look at major trends from a broad historical perspective include Arthur Herman, *The Idea of Decline in Western History* (New York, 1997), and Daniel Bell, *The Cultural Contradictions of Capitalism* (New York, 1976). See also Robert Goldberg, *Enemies Within: The Cult of Conspiracy in Modern America* (New Haven, 2001).

Four books that challenge a gloom-and-doom approach often found in the American media are: Alan Wolfe, *One Nation, After All: What Middle-Class Americans Really Think About God, Country, Family, Racism, Welfare, Immigration, Homosexuality, Work, the Right, the Left, and Each Other* (New York, 1998); Wolfe, *Moral Freedom: The Impossible Idea That Defines the Way We Live Now* (New York, 2001); Neil Howe and William Strauss, *Millennials Rising: The Next Great Generation* (New York, 2000); and Strauss and Howe, *Generations: The History of America's Future, 1584 to 2069* (New York, 1991). Bill Bryson, *Notes from a Big Country* (New York, 1998), and Jonathan Freedland, *Bring Home the Revolution: The Case for a British Republic* (London, 1998), look at the United States from a comparative perspective (mainly with Britain) and offer acute (as well as entertaining) comments along the way.

Thematic Books: A host of books center on politics during these years. Among histories, most of them biographically oriented, that highlight presidential politics over time are William Berman, *America's Right Turn: From Nixon to Bush* (Baltimore, 1994); Alonzo Hamby, *Liberalism and Its Challengers: From F.D.R. to Bush* (New York, 1992); William Leuchtenburg, *In the Shadow of FDR: From Harry Truman to Bill Clinton* (Ithaca, 1993); Lewis Gould, *The Modern American Presidency* (Lawrence, Kans., 2003); Fred Greenstein, *The Presidential Difference: Leadership Style from FDR to Clinton* (New York, 2000); Julian Zelizer, *On Capitol Hill: The Struggle to Reform Congress and Its Consequences, 1948-2000* (New York, 2004); and Sidney Milkis, *The President and the Parties: The Transformation of the American Party System Since the New Deal* (New York, 1993).

As titles indicate, many other books lament American **political trends**, especially the role of money and interest groups. For examples, see Matthew Crenson and Benjamin Ginsberg, *Downsizing Democracy: How America Sidelined Its Citizens and Privatized Its Public* (Baltimore, 2002); E. J. Dionne, *Why Americans Hate Politics* (New York, 1991); Benjamin Ginsberg and Martin Shefter, *Politics by Other Means: Politicians, Prosecutors, and the Press from Watergate to Whitewater* (New York, 2002); Kevin Phillips, *Arrogant Capital: Washington, Wall Street, and the Frustration of American Politics* (Boston, 1994); and Steven Schier, *By Invitation Only: The Rise of Exclusive Politics in the United States* (Pittsburgh, 2000).

Other helpful books concerned with politics include Ted Halstead and Michael Lind, *The Radical Center: The Future of American Politics* (New York, 2001); Byron Shafer, *The Two Majorities and the Puzzle of Modern American Politics* (Lawrence, Kans., 2003); Joseph Nye et al., *Why People Don't Trust Government* (Cambridge, Mass., 1997); and Jules Witcover, *Party of the People: A History of the Democrats* (New York, 2003). Mary Ann Glendon, *Rights Talk: The Impoverishment of Political Discourse* (New York, 1991), is a strongly argued critique. Steven Gillon, *"That's Not What We Meant to Do": Reform and Its Unintended Consequences in Twentieth Century America* (New York, 2001), is a sprightly book that emphasizes the legacies of various "reforms," including immigration, civil rights, and campaign finance reform.

The role of **regions in American politics** (and in other matters) has engaged several authors. Books on the South and the Sunbelt, which rose in importance during these years, include Bruce Schulman, *From Cotton Belt to Sun Belt: Federal Policy, Economic Develop-*

ment, and the Transformation of the South, 1938–1980 (New York, 1991); Peter Applebome, *Dixie Rising: How the South Is Shaping American Values, Politics, and Culture* (San Diego, 1996); Numan Bartley, *The New South, 1945–1980* (Baton Rouge, 1995); and Earl Black and Merle Black, *Politics and Society in the South* (Cambridge, Mass., 1987).

The rise of **conservatism in politics** has also attracted able writers. They include Dan Carter, *The Politics of Rage: George Wallace, The Origins of the New Conservatism, and The Transformation of American Politics* (New York, 1995); David Frum, *Dead Right* (New York, 1994); Godfrey Hodgson, *The World Turned Right Side Up: A History of the Conservative Ascendancy in America* (Boston, 1996); and Lisa McGerr, *Suburban Warriors: The Origins of the New American Right* (Princeton, 2001).

Books on trends in **American law**, including actions of the **Supreme Court**, include Howard Ball, *The Bakke Case: Race, Education, and Affirmative Action* (Lawrence, Kans., 2002); Laura Kalman, *The Strange Career of Legal Liberalism* (New Haven, 1996); Michael Klarman, *From Jim Crow to Civil Rights: The Supreme Court and the Struggle for Racial Equality* (New York, 2004); my book, *Brown v. Board of Education: A Civil Rights Milestone and Its Troubled Legacy* (New York, 2001); Gerald Rosenberg, *The Hollow Hope: Can Courts Bring About Social Change?* (Chicago, 1991); J. Harvie Wilkinson, *From Brown to Bakke: The Supreme Court and School Integration, 1954–1978* (New York, 1979); Jack Greenberg, *Crusaders in the Courts: How a Dedicated Band of Lawyers Fought for the Civil Rights Revolution* (New York, 1994), and the volumes by Friedman, Skrentny, and Walker mentioned above.

Broad treatments of **foreign and military ideas and policies** provided needed perspectives. For books concerning the Cold War, I relied on H. W. Brands, *The Devil We Knew: Americans and the Cold War* (New York, 1993); Raymond Garthoff, *The Great Transition: American-Soviet Relations and the End of the Cold War* (Washington, 1994); and John Gaddis, *We Now Know: Rethinking Cold War History* (New York, 1997). American attitudes are the focus of Tom Engelhardt, *The End of Victory Culture: Cold War America and the Disillusioning of a Generation* (New York, 1995), and David King and Zachary Karabell, *The Generation of Trust: Public Confidence in the U. S. Military Since Vietnam* (Washington, 2003). A fine history of European developments is William Hitchcock, *The Struggle for Europe: The Turbulent History of a Divided Continent, 1945–2002* (New York, 2003).

Sweeping interpretations of foreign relations and recommendations for the future include Zbigniew Brzezinski, *Out of Control: Global Turmoil on the Eve of the Twenty-First Century* (New York, 1993); Francis Fukuyama, *The End of History and the Last Man* (New York, 1992); Samuel Huntington, *The Clash of Civilizations and the Remaking of World Order* (New York, 1996); Joseph Nye, *Bound to Lead: The Changing Nature of American Power* (New York, 1990); Nye, *Soft Power: The Means to Success in World Politics* (New York, 2004); and Paul Kennedy, *The Rise and Fall of the Great Powers: Economic Change and Military Conflict from 1500 to 2000* (New York, 1987).

Economic trends are closely followed in this book. Among the many helpful studies of economic developments are Richard Easterlin, *Growth Triumphant: The Twenty-first Century in Historical Perspective* (Ann Arbor, 1996); Leonard Levy, *The New Dollars and Dreams: American Incomes and Economic Change* (New York, 1998); Robert Collins, *More: The Politics of Economic Growth in Postwar America* (New York, 2000); and Thomas McCraw, *American Business, 1920–2000: How It Worked* (Wheeling, Ill., 2000). For the role of consumption, see Lizabeth Cohen, *A Consumers' Republic: The Politics of*

Mass Consumption in Postwar America (New York, 2002), and Stanley Lebergott, *Pursuing Happiness: American Consumers in the Twentieth Century* (Princeton, 1993). Steven Fraser, *Every Man a Speculator: A History of Wall Street in American Life* (New York, 2004), is a lively economic and cultural history.

For trends in **technology**, see Howard Segal, *Future Imperfect: The Mixed Blessings of Technology in America* (Amherst, Mass., 1994), and Edward Tenner, *Why Things Bite Back: Technology and the Revenge of Unintended Consequences* (New York, 1996). **Labor issues** receive scholarly treatment in Nelson Lichtenstein, *State of the Union: A Century of American Labor* (Princeton, 2002). For critical accounts of work and labor relations, see Naomi Schor, *The Overworked American* (New York, 1991), and Jeremy Rifkin, *The End of Work: The Decline of the Labor Force and the Dawn of the Post-Market Era* (New York, 1995).

Studies of **poverty and social welfare** are numerous, among them the following: Ken Auletta, *The Underclass* (New York, 1982); Edward Berkowitz, *America's Welfare State: From Roosevelt to Reagan* (Baltimore, 1991); Gareth Davies, *From Opportunity to Entitlement: The Transformation and Decline of Great Society Liberalism* (Lawrence, KS, 1996); Christopher Jencks, *The Homeless* (Cambridge, Mass., 1994); Jencks, *Rethinking Social Policy* (Cambridge, Mass., 1992); Michael Katz, ed., *The "Underclass" Debate: Views from History* (Princeton, 1993); Katz, *The Price of Citizenship: Redefining the Welfare State* (New York, 2001); William Julius Wilson, *When Work Disappears: The World of the New Urban Poor* (New York, 1996); and my book *America's Struggle Against Poverty in the Twentieth Century* (Cambridge, Mass., 2001).

For other aspects of economic life I relied on Otis Graham, *Losing Time: The Industrial Policy Debate* (Cambridge, Mass., 1992), and Alfred Eckes Jr. and Thomas Zeilin, *Globalization and the American Century* (New York, 2003). Edwin Luttwak, *The Endangered American Dream: How to Stop the United States from Becoming a Third World Country and How to Win the Geo-Economic Struggle for Industrial Supremacy* (New York, 1993), is a strongly argued account. See also the previously mentioned books by Samuelson and Kennedy.

Concerning broad **social trends**, the following books are thought provoking: David Brooks, *Bobos in Paradise: The New Upper Class and How They Got There* (New York, 2000); Barbara Ehrenreich, *Fear of Falling: The Inner Life of the Middle Class* (New York, 1989); Francis Fukuyama, *The Great Disruption: Human Nature and the Reconstruction of Social Order* (New York, 1999); and Steven Gillon, *Boomer Nation: The Largest and Richest Generation Ever, and How It Changed America* (New York, 2004). Two widely noted books lamenting social privatization are Amitai Etzioni, comp., *Rights and the Common Good: The Communitarian Perspective* (New York, 1995), and Robert Putnam, *Bowling Alone: The Collapse and Revival of American Community* (New York, 2000). See also Theda Skocpol, *Diminished Democracy: From Membership to Management in American Civic Life* (Norman, Okla., 2003). For social trends, see also the books by Wolfe and by Howe and Strauss, mentioned above.

Urban and suburban life are covered by Thomas Sugrue, *The Origins of the Urban Crisis: Race and Inequality in Postwar Detroit* (Princeton, 1996); James Goodman, *Blackout* (New York, 2003); Robert Self, *American Babylon: Race and the Struggle for Postwar Oakland* (Princeton, 2003); Robert Fishman, *Bourgeois Utopias: The Rise and Fall of Suburbia* (New York, 1987); Andres Duany et al., *Suburban Nation: The Rise of Sprawl and the Decline of the American Dream* (New York, 2000); Kenneth Jackson, *Crabgrass*

Frontier: The Suburbanization of the United States (New York, 1985); Jane Holtz Kay, *Asphalt Nation: How the Automobile Took Over America, and How We Can Take It Back* (New York, 1997); and Malcolm Gladwell, *The Tipping Point: How Little Things Make a Big Difference* (New York, 2002). For **small town and rural life** see especially Peter Davis, *Hometown* (New York, 1982); and Richard Davies, *Main Street Blues: The Decline of Small-Town America* (Columbus, Ohio, 1998).

Family patterns have changed greatly during these years. Among the many books that have looked at these changes are Arlie Hochschild, with Anne Machung, *The Second Shift: Working Parents and the Revolution at Home* (New York, 1989); Stephanie Coontz, *The Way We Never Were: American Families and the Nostalgia Trap* (New York, 1992); Arlene Skolnick, *Embattled Paradise: The American Family in an Age of Uncertainty* (New York, 1994); and James Wilson, *The Marriage Problem: How Our Country Has Weakened Families* (New York, 2002). Some of these subtitles make it obvious that writers about American families reach very different conclusions about the legacy of these changes.

Important books about **women** — and about **gender relations** — include Susan Faludi, *Backlash: The Undeclared War Against American Women* (New York, 1991); Faludi, *Stiffed: The Betrayal of the American Man* (New York, 1999); Andrew Hacker, *Mismatch: The Growing Gulf Between Women and Men* (New York, 2003); Alice Kessler-Harris, *In Pursuit of Equity: Women, Men, and the Quest for Economic Citizenship in 20th-Century America* (New York, 2001); Jane Mansbridge, *Why We Lost the ERA* (Chicago, 1986); Victor Fuchs, *Women's Quest for Economic Equality* (Cambridge, Mass., 1988); and William Saletan, *Bearing Right: How Conservatives Won the Abortion War* (Berkeley, 2003).

Studies of **sexual trends** have proliferated in recent years. For a widely cited survey, see John D'Emilio and Estelle Freedman, *Intimate Matters: A History of Sexuality in America* (Chicago, 1997). Another scholarly study is David Allyn, *Make Love, Not War: The Sexual Revolution: An Unfettered History* (Boston, 2000). See also Mirko Grmek, *History of AIDS: Emergence and Origin of a Modern Pandemic* (Princeton, 1990); Randy Shilts, *And the Band Played On: Politics, People, and the AIDS Epidemic* (New York, 1988); and Susan Sontag, *AIDS and Its Metaphors* (New York, 1989). The books by Fukuyama (*The Great Disruption*, cited above) and by Gertrude Himmelfarb, cited below, have much to say about sexual trends.

Religious developments, notably the ascendance of the Religious Right, have generated a lively literature. An excellent overview of political aspects is William Martin, *With God on Our Side: The Rise of the Religious Right in America* (New York, 1996). Other useful books are Garry Wills, *Under God: Religion and American Politics* (New York, 1990); Sara Diamond, *Not by Politics Alone: The Enduring Influence of the Religious Right* (New York, 1998); Robert Wuthnow, *The Crisis in the Churches: Spiritual Malaise, Fiscal Woe* (New York, 1997); and Robert Fogel, *The Fourth Great Awakening and the Future of Egalitarianism* (Chicago, 2000). Frances FitzGerald, *Cities on a Hill: A Journey Through American Cultures* (New York, 1986), includes material on the Reverend Jerry Falwell and the Moral Majority. For a historical approach to religion in American life, see James Morone, *Hellfire Nation: The Politics of Sin in American History* (New Haven, 2002). Wolfe, *Moral Freedom*, mentioned earlier, is relevant and useful.

Environment: Writing in this field has blossomed. An upbeat survey of developments is Gregg Easterbrook, *A Moment on the Earth: The Coming Age of Environmental Optimism* (New York, 1995). A pessimistic account is Al Gore, *Earth in the Balance: Ecology and the Human Spirit* (Boston, 1992). For a historical survey, see Ted Steinberg, *Down to*

Earth: Nature's Role in American History (New York, 2002). See also Barbara Freese, *Coal: A Human History* (Cambridge, Mass., 2003); Robert Gottlieb, *Forcing the Spring: The Transformation of the American Environmental Movement* (Washington, 1993); Samuel Hays, *Beauty, Health, and Permanence: Environmental Politics in the United States, 1955–1985* (New York, 1987); Marc Reisner, *Cadillac Desert: The American West and Its Disappearing Water* (New York, 1993); Adam Rose, *The Bulldozer in the Countryside: Suburban Sprawl and the Rise of American Environmentalism* (New York, 2001); and Hal Rothman, *The Greening of a Nation: Environmentalism in the United States Since 1945* (Orlando, 1998). Two widely read books by leading environmentalists are Bill McKibben, *The End of Nature* (New York, 1989), and John McPhee, *The Control of Nature* (New York, 1989).

Education: A helpful survey is David Tyack and Larry Cuban, *Tinkering Toward Utopia: A Century of Public School Reform* (Cambridge, Mass., 1995). See also two books by Diane Ravitch: *Left Back: A Century of Failed School Reforms* (New York, 2000) and The *Troubled Crusade: American Education, 1945–1980* (New York, 1983). John Jennings, *Why National Standards and Tests? Politics and the Quest for Better Schools* (Thousand Oaks, Calif., 1998) focuses on debates in the 1990s. Other useful books include Nicholas Lemann, *The Big Test: The Secret History of the American Meritocracy* (New York, 1999); and Christopher Jencks and Meredith Phillips, eds., *The Black-White Test Score Gap* (Washington, 1998). Advocates of school reform in the new century include Abigail Thernstrom, *No Excuses: Closing the Racial Gap in Learning* (New York, 2003), and John Chubb and Tom Loveless, eds., *Bridging the Achievement Gap* (Washington, 2002). See also the book by Zimmerman, listed below.

Cultural trends/values: Robert Bellah et al., *Habits of the Heart: Individualism and Commitment in American Life* (Berkeley, 1985) is a critical evaluation of American values in the early 1980s. John de Graaf et al., *Affluenza: The All-Consuming Epidemic* (San Francisco, 2001) raps American materialism in the 1990s. For more on consumerism, see the books by Brooks and Cohen, mentioned above. Robert Hughes, *Culture of Complaint: The Fraying of America* (New York, 1993) deplores many aspects of American culture. See also Eric Schlosser, *Fast Food Nation: The Dark Side of the All-American Meal* (Boston, 2001). Other broadly conceived books concerned with trends in American culture include Fukuyama, *The Great Disruption*, and the volumes by Brooks, Putnam, and Wolfe, all mentioned earlier.

Books concerned with the **media and film** include Mary Ann Watson, *Defining Visions: Television and the American Experience Since 1945* (Fort Worth, 1998), a fine survey; James Fallows, *Breaking the News: How the Media Undermine American Democracy* (New York, 1996); Robert Downie and Robert Kaiser, *The News about the News: American Journalism in Peril* (New York, 2002); and Ronald Davis, *Celluloid Mirrors: Hollywood and American Society Since 1945* (Fort Worth, 1997).

Among the books concerned with the **"culture wars"** of the late 1980s and 1990s are: James Hunter, *Culture Wars: The Struggle to Define America* (New York, 1991); Gertrude Himmelfarb, *One Nation, Two Cultures* (New York, 1999); Arthur Schlesinger Jr., *The Disuniting of America: Reflections on a Multicultural Society* (New York, 1991); John Wilson, *The Myth of Political Correctness: The Conservative Attack on Higher Education* (Durham, N.C., 1995); Jonathan Zimmerman, *Whose America? Culture Wars in the Public Schools* (Cambridge, Mass., 2002); Gary Nash et al., *History on Trial: Culture Wars and the Teaching of the Past* (New York, 1997); Robert Bork, *Slouching Toward Gomorrah:*

Modern Liberalism and American Decline (New York, 1996); and Fukuyama, *The Great Disruption*, listed above.

Civil Rights and Race Relations: There is an especially voluminous literature concerned with these subjects. Overviews include Gary Gerstle, *American Crucible: Race and Nation in the Twentieth Century* (Princeton, 2001); Andrew Hacker, *Two Nations: Black and White, Separate, Hostile, Unequal* (New York, 1995); Stephan Thernstrom and Abigail Thernstrom, *America in Black and White: One Nation, Indivisible* (New York, 1997); Orlando Patterson, *The Ordeal of Integration: Progress and Resentment in America's "Racial" Crisis* (Washington, 1997); Jennifer Hochschild, *Facing Up to the American Dream: Race, Class, and the Soul of America* (Princeton, 1996); and John Higham, ed., *Civil Rights and Social Wrongs: Black-White Relations Since World War II* (University Park, Pa., 1997).

For affirmative action, see Terry Anderson, *The Pursuit of Fairness: A History of Affirmative Action* (New York, 2004); William Bowen and Derek Bok, *The Shape of the River: Long-Term Consequences of Considering Race in College and University Admissions* (Princeton, 1998); Hugh Davis Graham, *Collision Course: The Strange Convergence of Affirmative Action and Immigration Policy in America* (New York, 2002); and Ball, listed above. Other books concerning developments in race relations include Nicholas Lemann, *The Promised Land: The Great Black Migration and How It Changed America* (New York, 1991); Derrick Bell, *Silent Covenants: Brown v. Board of Education and the Unfilled Hopes for Racial Reform* (New York, 2004); Gary Orfield, *Dismantling Desegregation: The Quiet Reversal of Brown v. Board of Education* (New York, 1996); and Paul Sniderman and Thomas Piazza, *Black Pride and Black Prejudice* (Princeton, 2002), a survey of attitudes about race. See also the previously mentioned books by Gillon, Gladwell, Katz, Klarman, Skrentny, Sugrue, Self, and William Julius Wilson.

Immigration/Ethnicity: Relevant books include David Hollinger, *Postethnic America: Beyond Multiculturalism* (New York, 1995); Roger Daniels and Otis Graham, *Debating Immigration, 1882–Present* (Lanham, Md., 2001); Daniels, *Coming to America: A History of Immigration and Ethnicity in American Life* (New York, 2002); and Gary Gerstle and John Mollenkopf, eds., *E Pluribus Unum: Contemporary and Historical Perspectives on Immigrant Political Incorporation* (New York, 2001). Among the books featuring worries about the size of immigration to America are George Borjas, *Heaven's Door: Immigration and the American Economy* (Princeton, 1999); Peter Brimelow, *Alien Nation: Common Sense About America's Immigration Disaster* (New York, 1995); and Samuel Huntington, *Who Are We?: The Challenges to America's National Identity* (New York, 2004). For other perspectives see Nathan Glazer, *We Are All Multiculturalists Now* (New Haven, 1997), and the books by Schlesinger and Hugh Davis Graham, cited above. A fine local study of ethnic conflict is Jonathan Rieder, *Canarsie: The Jews and Italians of Brooklyn* (Cambridge, Mass., 1985).

The 1970s/Ford and Carter Presidencies: Interpretive surveys of the 1970s include Bruce Schulman, *The Seventies: The Great Shift in American Culture, Society, and Politics* (New York, 2001); David Frum, *How We Got Here: The '70s, the Decade That Brought You Modern Life (For Better or Worse)* (New York, 2000); Peter Carroll, *It Seemed Like Nothing Happened: The Tragedy and Promise of the 1970s* (New York, 1982); and Beth Bailey and David Farber, eds., *America in the Seventies* (Lawrence, Kans., 2004). Critiques of American life in the 1970s include Christopher Lasch, *The Culture of Narcissism: American Life in an Age of Diminishing Expectations* (New York, 1978); and two collections of essays by Tom Wolfe, *Mauve Gloves and Madmen, Clutter, and Vine* (New York, 1976) and *In Our Time* (New York, 1980). Battles in Boston over busing to accomplish racial balance receive excellent treatment in Ronald Formisano, *Boston Against Busing: Race, Class, and Ethnicity in the 1960s and 1970s* (Chapel Hill, 1991), and J. Anthony Lukas, *Common Ground: A Turbulent Decade in the Lives of Three American Families* (New York, 1986).

For the Ford administration, see John Greene, *The Presidency of Gerald R. Ford* (Lawrence, Kans., 1995); A. James Reichley, *Conservatives in an Age of Change: The Nixon and Ford Administrations* (Washington, 1981); and James Mann, *Rise of the Vulcans: The History of Bush's War Cabinet* (New York, 2004). As its title indicates, Mann's book is also informative about later decades. For the Carter years, see Gary Fink and Hugh Davis Graham, eds., *The Carter Presidency: Policy Choices in the Post-New Deal Era* (Lawrence, Kans., 1998); Burton Kaufman, *The Presidency of James Earl Carter, Jr.* (Lawrence, Kans., 1993); Gaddis Smith, *Morality, Reason, and Power: American Diplomacy in the Carter Years* (New York, 1986); and Jimmy Carter, *Keeping Faith: Memoirs of a President* (New York, 1982).

The 1980s/Reagan and Bush Presidencies: General books concerned with the 1980s include Haynes Johnson, *Sleepwalking Through History: America in the Reagan Years* (New York, 1991); John White, *The New Politics of Old Values* (Hanover, N.H., 1989); and Bellah et al., listed above. Lou Cannon, *President Reagan: The Role of a Lifetime* (New York, 2000) is a balanced, comprehensive study of the Great Communicator's time in the White House. For Reagan, see also William Pemberton, *Exit with Honor: The Life and Presidency of Ronald Reagan* (New York, 1998); W. Elliot Brownlee and Hugh Davis Graham, eds., *The Reagan Presidency: Pragmatic Conservatism and Its Legacies* (Lawrence, Kans., 2003); Kiron Skinner et al., eds., *Reagan, in His Own Hand* (New York, 2001); Garry Wills, *Reagan's America: Innocents at Home* (New York, 2000); and Robert Dallek, *Ronald Reagan: The Politics of Symbolism* (Cambridge, Mass., 1999). See also Frances FitzGerald, *Way Out There in the Blue: Reagan, Star Wars, and the End of the Cold War* (New York, 2000).

John Greene, *The Presidency of George Bush* (Lawrence, Kans., 2000), and Herbert Parmet, *George Bush: The Life of a Lone Star Yankee* (New York, 1997) cover the presidency of George H. W. Bush. More focused studies include Michael Gordon and Bernard Trainor, *The Generals' War: The Inside Story of the Conflict in the Gulf* (Boston, 1995); George Bush and Brent Scowcroft, *A World Transformed* (New York, 1995); and David Halberstam, *War in a Time of Peace: Bush, Clinton, and the Generals* (New York, 2001).

The 1990s/Clinton Presidency: For aspects of the 1990s, see Haynes Johnson, *The Best of Times: America in the Clinton Years* (New York, 1991); Benjamin Barber, *Jihad vs. McWorld: Terrorism's Challenge to Democracy* (New York, 2001); and Thomas Friedman, *The Lexus and the Olive Tree* (New York, 1999), on globalization. For Clinton, consult William Berman, *From the Center to the Edge: The Politics and Policies of the Clinton Presidency* (Lanham, Md., 2001); and Joe Klein, *The Natural: The Misunderstood Presidency of Bill Clinton* (New York, 2002). For foreign policy matters, see Richard Clarke, *Against All Enemies: Inside America's War on Terror* (New York, 2004) and Halberstam, listed above. Three books that focus on the election of 2000 are E. J. Dionne and William Kristol, eds., *Bush v. Gore: The Court Cases and the Commentary* (Washington, 2001); Jeffrey Toobin, *Too Close to Call: The Thirty-Six Day Battle to Decide the*

2000 Election (New York, 2001); and Jack Rakove, ed., *The Unfinished Election of 2000* (New York, 2001).

Statistics/Trends: As footnotes indicate, I have relied heavily for statistics on various editions of the Census Bureau's *Statistical Abstract of the United States*, especially the edition of 2002. In places where the *Statistical Almanac* did not seem to provide necessary information, I have cited editions of the *World Almanac* and of the *New York Times Almanac*. Three additional books include charts, graphs, and statistics concerning important trends. They are Andrew Hacker, ed., *U/S: A Statistical Portrait of the American People* (New York, 1983); Stephen Moore and Julian Simon, eds., *It's Getting Better All the Time: 100 Greatest Trends of the Last 100 Years* (Washington, 2000); and Theodore Caplow et al., *The First Measured Century: An Illustrated Guide to Trends in America, 1900–2000* (Washington, 2001).

Index